COMPSTAT 1978

Proceedings in Computational Statistics

3rd Symposium held in Leiden 1978

Edited by
L.C.A. Corsten
J. Hermans

Physica-Verlag · Wien 1978
ISBN 3 7908 0196 8

CIP-Kurztitelaufnahme der Deutschen Bibliothek

COMPSTAT ⟨03, 1978, Leiden⟩:
COMPSTAT : 1978: proceedings in computational statistics; 3. symposium held in Leiden 1978/ ed. by L.C.A. Corsten; J. Hermans. - Wien: Physica-Verlag, 1978.
ISBN 3-7908-0196-8

NE: Corsten, Leo C.A. [Hrsg.]

Printed in Germany by repro-druck „Journalfranz" Arnulf Liebing GmbH + Co., Würzburg
ISBN 3 7908 0196 8

PREFACE.

After the Compstat Symposium 1974 in Vienna and the Compstat Symposium 1976 in Berlin the present Compstat Symposium 1978 in Leiden, Netherlands may be considered as the continuation of a tradition.

This symposium is devoted to discussions and exchange of thoughts about numerical and algorithmic aspects of statistical methods and about new techniques in computer science in relation to statistical analysis as well as to the presentation and evaluation of statistical software packages. It shows the great interest in effective statistical computing and its indispensability.

Today's position of the interface between statistics and computing is also reflected by the recent formation of the International Association for Statistical Computing as a section of the International Statistical Institute.

The Program Committee consisting of

- L.C.A. Corsten (Agricultural University, Wageningen), chairman
- I. Francis (Cornell University)
- J. Hermans (Leiden University), secretary
- R.J. Mokken (University of Amsterdam)
- W. Molenaar (Groningen University)
- J.A. Nelder (Rothamsted Experimental Station)
- N. Victor (Giessen University)

found themselves in the fortunate situation of identifying about 65 authors from over 15 countries willing to present a suitable contribution.Several participants offered explanation of their views in software packages and comments on questions from users. Two invited lectures were included in the opening session.

The symposium was organized by the Vereniging voor Statistiek(Netherlands Society for Statistics, Biometrics, Econometrics and Operational Research) in cooperation with the Compstat Society, Vienna. It was sponsored by the I.S.I. International Association for Statistical Computing. It was supported by the Computer Centre (C.R.I.) and the Department of Medical Statistics, both of Leiden University.

This symposium had the generous help of an effective Organizing Committee consisting of A.P.J. Abrahamse, H.J. Blanksma(chairman), P.J.S. Boon (treasurer), E. Köllner and F. van Nes.
We sincerely hope that the joint efforts of all concerned may be beneficial to a proper advance in statistical computing.

L.C.A. Corsten

J. Hermans.

Wageningen)
Leiden) June 1978
)

Contents

5. Contingency Tables

6. Cluster Analysis

7. Exploratory Techniques

11. Miscellaneous

1. Invited Lectures

The Future of Statistical Software

J.A. Nelder, Harpenden

Summary

Statistical software, among software in general, is characterised by having a large I/O component, complex data structures, an exploratory mode of use, and wide ranges of user interests and competence. The present state is assessed in relation to source language, the language presented to the user, and mode of use. Future developments are discussed in relation to hardware, operating systems, and languages. A plea is made for collaboration between computer scientists and statisticians developing packages, particularly in language design.

KEYWORDS: statistical software, data structures, operating systems, hardware, language design, parameter-passing.

1. Introduction

In the last decade statistical software has proliferated enormously, and the prospective user is often faced with daunting problems in choice of program (Nelder (1974)). The software produced has been constrained on the computing side by the general-purpose languages, the hardware configurations, and the operating systems available and on the statistical side by the types of statistical procedure deemed important by the writers. This paper attempts to characterise statistical software in its computing aspects, to look in general at its present state, and to forecast future developments.

2. What distinguishes statistical software?

In several areas of computing, such as optimization or the numerical solution of partial differential equations, the sub-routine library (e.g. those of NAG and IMSL) has proved a valuable software tool. In order to make effective use of such a library, the central algorithm (supplied by the library) must be 'topped and tailed' by adding one section of program that obtains the input data and another that displays (or passes on) the results. The implication is that such topping and tailing, which is the I/O component of the program, is simple and easily constructible compared to the central algorithm. The relative ineffectiveness of subroutine libraries in the statistical field arises, I believe, from the fact that the I/O component is as important as the algorithm. A simple example is given by the analysis of balanced cross-classified data using a factorial model. The algorithm is quite short, but is of little use without the substantial output procedures necessary for producing tables of means, with margins, lists of standard errors, the analysis of variance, vectors of fitted values and residuals, all of these suitably labelled with headings, the names of the classifying factors, their level names etc.

The input to the above example is not so complex, but nonetheless the algorithm alone makes a relatively modest contribution to the complete program required.

2.2 Complex data structures

The data structures needed for, say, the input to a crystallographic program are relatively simple compared to many found in survey analysis. Here the simple data matrix (a two-dimensional structure indexed by units and variates) may be extended hierarchically, e.g. to one set of records on farms and another set on fields within farms, and the number of subrecords may be variable. More generally the data may refer to a network whose structure must be defined and stored. Operations on such structures, such as tabulation, are arithmetically trivial, but they are not algorithmically trivial, because of the large component of data access and storage. Statistical software has suffered greatly from the quite absurd idea that scientific and commercial work need quite different kinds of computing, and so need quite different kinds of languages in which to express their needs. Fortunately this meaningless split shows signs of coming to an end.

2.3 Exploratory nature of statistical analysis

Many statistical procedures, e.g. principal-components analysis, can be defined in a simple closed form, and so incorporated in a program of the kind

```
get data
do algorithm
put results
stop
```

Indeed many magical black boxes have been provided, and are used daily, chiefly by unsophisticated users, to produce the analysis for their data. It may happen, of course, that data are collected over a considerable period, so that their characteristics become known; then fixed procedures for analysis may be justified. However, it is surely usually characteristic of statistical analysis (often, I think unfortunately, called 'data analysis') that the details of the procedure to be followed, or even the selection of the procedure itself, is uncertain when the analysis begins. Thus the black boxes in a statistical package or system must, if the system is to be flexible and useful, be connectable in many different ways. This has implications for language structure which will be discussed later.

2.4 Range of user interests and competence

While it is unlikely that a crystallographic package will be used by someone who does not understand what a Fourier transform does, it is not at all uncommon to find statistical packages being used by people with very little understanding of statistics. At the same time many statistical packages can be used profitably by statisticians of considerable expertise. The users also show a very wide range of competence or experience in computing. This range of user experience probably explains the effort which has gone into devising problem-oriented languages for statistical packages, and also the origin of large exhaustive manuals which attempt to cater for all types of user.

3. The present position of statistical software

Before looking at the future it is worth spending a little time trying to assess the position we have reached at present.

Most packages have developed in an environment of medium-to-large machines running programs primarily in batch. The hardware has been unpaged, and the packages have been overlaid to fit into the partition sizes available. Manufacturers have provided sub-routine libraries of statistical (or, more generally, scientific) procedures, but these have not been widely used, probably because of the difficulties described in section 2.1. Part I of the Rothamsted General Survey Program is an example of a subroutine library which requires to be driven by a main program written in the same language (Fortran) as the library itself. On the whole, however, this method of using a package requires too much knowledge of computing to be attractive to the inexperienced user, though it can be very valuable to the more experienced because the full flexibility of the general purpose language (GPL) is available. Most packages define their own language which the user must learn. Implementation can then be either via a translator into a GPL, or by an interpreter. Translators seem to have been little used, and interpretive languages have been the rule. A further possibility, using a compiler-compiler will be discussed in section 3.3.

3.1 Interpretive languages

The sophistication of the interpretive languages in statistical packages has grown steadily, though critics might say that the designers have yet to keep pace with modern knowledge of language design. In the early days the user punched a 1 in column 46 of his card if he wanted the residuals printed. Fixed format has increasingly given way to free format; naming of instances of data structures has become almost universal, and an increasing variety of data structures has been supported. However, the gaps in all these aspects are still considerable. Unpleasant mixtures of fixed and free format still occur, there exist packages without the simple scalar as a data structure (Nelder & Payne (1977)), and the control language is often primitive, having, for instance, no branching or looping facility.

A serious defect of many interpretive languages in statistical packages is that they do not allow the components of the output of a statistical procedure (e.g. the vectors of residuals and fitted values, or the (co)variance matrix in regression analysis) to be named by the user as instances of data structures supported by the package. Such a lack is a serious obstacle to multi-stage analysis, and is particularly likely to occur in packages whose basic input structure is the data matrix, and only the data matrix. A typical example is the operation of tabulation in SPSS (Nie, et al. (1975)); a table can be formed, and printed, but because the multi-way table is not a basic data structure in the system, this table cannot be named and so stored and manipulated.

3.2 Source language

Most packages have been written in Fortran (SAS, which is written in PL/1, being an exception), usually with a small nucleus of assembler routines to deal with such things as character handling. Now Fortran is by no means ideal as a language for writing packages, but it has the great advantage of being by far the most widely available, an important point if transportability is required. Algol 60 has two important disadvantages as a language for writing transportable packages: (i) its I/O procedures are not standardised and (ii) its lack of the Fortran EQUIVALENCE makes impossible the simulation of heap storage as defined in Algol 68 - in general stack storage is not enough for statistical work. The implications of the newer languages for package design will be discussed in section 4.3.

3.3 Recent developments

The increasing availability of the interactive mode of computer use has promoted statistical packages designed to be used interactively. One should distinguish simply interactive from conversational programs. The former supply nothing but a simple prompt to which the user responds with his instructions, while the latter interrogates the user with questions designed to elicit his requirements. Conversational mode is valuable to the beginner, simple interactive working to the experienced user. Of course a program may be designed to have more than one level of prompting (e.g. Package X used by the Central Statistical Office of the United Kingdom government has three). It is worth noting that a well-designed batch program can be converted to simple interactive mode quite easily, simply by allowing a recovery from error, which in batch mode would end a run. Interactive working is particularly valuable in learning how to use a package and in exploratory analysis of small data sets. For larger problems it may be less important, because the response time of the user to his intermediate results becomes the limiting factor in the analytical process.

Among the newer languages APL has become quite widely used for statistical work, where its ability to handle multi-dimensional arrays has been particularly convenient. Though sub-program libraries have been constructed in APL, it is not a suitable language for writing large programs, partly because its control structures are inadequate and partly because it is interpreted at a uniformly low level, which can lead to inefficiency.

The S language, developed by Chambers at Bell Telephone Laboratories, uses the compiler-compiler technique whereby the formal syntactic and semantic specifications of the language are used by the compiler-compiler to generate an appropriate compiler for that language. The advantages of this approach include the replacement of interpretation by compilation, coupled with the ability to extend the language rather simply. Of course the algorithms required in a statistical system still have to be provided, and a convenient form of linkage devised. The compiler-compiler technique deserves close study, particularly in relation to transportability (Johnson (1976)).

4. Forecasting the future

The rate of development in computing, both of hardware and software, shows little sign of slowing down. The world of computing is as unstable as it was 10 years ago, and forecasting is hazardous. Nevertheless, we need to look at what is appearing, or seems likely to appear, and try to gauge what effect it will have on the world of statistical computing, both as regards users and creators of packages. I shall consider three aspects, hardware, operating systems, and languages.

4.1 Hardware

The full impact of micro-electronics is probably still to come, though it has already revolutionised the pocket calculator and the small computer. Two aspects are important, the general reduction in cost of hardware, and the shift of the hardware/software boundary. A third aspect, the increasing speed of hardware, is less important in most applications of statistics, where jobs are much more likely to be I/O-bound than CPU-bound.

The reduction in cost - 64k bytes of store, with floppy discs, printer, and VDU can now be bought for £7000 in England - means that substantial programs will become available on many more machines. This will be to the advantage of established packages, provided that they have been designed to be transportable. The linkage of computers into networks will also make programs more widely available, and should improve effective use by sending jobs to environments which can run them efficiently. There remains, however, much to be done in the organising of such networks. Little is known at present about the behaviour of large programs, originally designed to run (perhaps overlaid) in fixed partitions, when transferred to paged machines, which are becoming increasingly common. There are rumours of a degradation in speed by factors of 5 or more, and work is urgently needed on the interaction between program size, data size, and the paging algorithm of paged machines. Package writers also need to know how programming strategies should be adopted for paged machines; so far they have had little or no help.

Another feature of new hardware, the arrival of vector processors, such as the Cray 1, has implications for statistics. The effective exploitation of such machines may turn out to require new features in languages, if algorithms are to be implemented most effectively.

The shift in the hardware/software boundary has already led to machines in which a high-level language has been realised in hardware, though so far this has been restricted to fairly small stand-alone machines. This is potentially a restricting development because the machine architecture will inevitably be adapted specifically to the language concerned, and this is likely to restrict programs to those written in that language. (No one is likely to take on the task of writing a Fortran compiler in Basic!). Of greater interest is the possibility of complex functions, such as the Fourier transform, becoming available as micro-circuits, and the likely impact of this on statistical computing. Such function chips may well become optional extras, producing a problem-oriented hardware. The immediate effect on the user may well be small, because he will access the special hardware by subprogram calls in the usual way; however, speed may be appreciably greater, and in the long run, the particular functions supplied by the manufacturer may well influence the way in which statistical analysis is done.

4.2 Operating systems

Until recently operating systems were written in machine code, and had various undesirable properties. They were large, not very well constructed, with redundant code, difficult to maintain, and often inefficient, in that the machine spent too much of its time deciding what to do next, and too little time in doing it. The language (JCL) for the user was often primitive and its implementors seemed to have learnt little from the experts in language design. The difficulties facing the writers of operating systems, however, should not be underestimated; they have often been frustrated by faults in the design stage, both in the general architecture of the machine and in details of the instruction code. They have to design for an enormous range of operating environments, many of which have been difficult or impossible to foresee.

The most common characteristic of an operating system that frustrates the package writer is its opaqueness. He knows it to contain many algorithms that he could usefully use, such as table look-up, sorting, encode/decode for numbers, character handling etc., yet they are not accessible to the ordinary programmer, so he is forced to write them all over again, and probably less efficiently, for his own needs. The prime need in future operating systems, both for the package writer and the user is for a transparent, flexible, operating system, with a simple but powerful JCL. The Unix system, developed at Bell Telephone Laboratories for the PDP-11, may well be the forerunner of such systems. The properties required of a link-editor illustrate well the flexibility required in a good operating system. It should be possible, with minimum work by the machine, to replace one or more subprograms in a link-edited program. Similarly the user should be able to reinvoke a compiler in the middle of a job, without losing control of his current job. The JCL should allow loops to be written over files for such tasks as editing, and the basic algorithms of the operating system should be available to the user.

4.3 Languages

Important as developments in hardware and operating systems are and will be, those in languages may well prove to be the most important of all. Great strides have been made in language design in the last 10 years; we now strive for orthogonality, whereby basic facilities correspond to independent concepts, combinable in many ways. Such orthogonality reduces both the size of compilers and the length of documentation. Transportability is being increased by the development of self-compiling compilers (Lecarme and Peyrolle-Thomas (1978)), which allow languages to be carried across machines in a systematic way. A property of the new languages, such as Simula, Pascal, and Algol 68, particularl relevant to statistical computing is their facility of structure definition. They allow the user to define new structures and to name instances of them, usin as components in the definition basic building blocks such as arrays and lists of items of modo real, integer, or logical. They also allow the user to refer to components of the structure and sometimes to extend the definition of operators in operations with those structures as operands.

Clearly the general availability of structure definition in languages will have a profound influence on statistical computing, but it has only just begun to have such an influence. The principal obstacle is still the lack of general availability of such languages, with the consequent fear that work done on developing programs for one machine may be wasted if the developer is forced to move to another where the language is not available. It is still far from clear how programs developed in one of these new languages should be presented to the general user; for example, will the subprogram package, which must be driven by a main program written in the same language, be adequate for the unsophisticated user? I was delighted to find that one could indeed define a lower triangle in Algol 68 to hold a symmetric matrix, but less delighted to find that in order to declare that A, B and C were instances of that structure of size n one had to include an obscure statement whose point was to obtain space for the values of those structures.

We may find that it is still necessary to provide users with an interface in the form of an interpretive language, even though the package itself is written in a structure-defining language. I suggest that a particular area in which even the new languages are defective in convenience relates to the passing of parameters between procedures.

4.4 Parameter-passing - room for improvement

All general purpose languages with which I am familiar require, when invoking procedures, that the programmer

(1) lists all the actual parameters at the time when the procedure is invoked

(2) lists all the actual parameters every time and

(3) lists them in the defined order

I suggest that all these requirements are unnecessarily restrictive, and may represent an unnecessary burden on the programmer. Let us look at them in turn.

The first requirement fuses two quite distinct operations, the assignment of actual parameters to the procedure and its invocation. Consider a user working interactively at a terminal, who repeatedly wishes to invoke the same procedure with the same parameters. Why should he have to repeat the parameter list, which may be lengthy? If the operations of parameter assignment and procedure invocation are separated this awkwardness disappears. Such a separation occurs in Release 3 of GLIM (Baker and Nelder (1978)) where the assignment of arguments to macros is dealt with by the directive

$ARG macro arguments

and the invocation by

$USE macro

Once the arguments can be declared separately, the way is open to declaring a subset only of them, so that if, for instance, a procedure has 10 parameters, and in two successive calls 9 remain the same and only the 10th changes, then the second argument statement need only declare the 10th. We have also found in using GLIM that it frequently makes sense to declare a subset of arguments in one place and the remainder in a second place, and this can be easily done by using an asterisk as the unset symbol. Thus

```
$ARG  M   A * C
$ARG  M   * B
```

together have the same effect as

```
$ARG  M   A B C
```

A common feature of the output parameters of statistical procedures is that the user may not wish to set them at all. Thus though the user may have the option to save the fitted values or residuals from a regression he may not wish to do so. He should therefore be allowed not to declare them; such a facility is common in the interpretive languages of statistical systems, but is not allowed in general-purpose languages.

Finally it is useful to be able to label parameters, so that the order in defining them becomes arbitrary. Thus in Genstat (Alvey et al (1977)), the

FIT directive has 9 output parameters of which the fitted-value vector (labelled FVAL) and the residual vector (labelled RES) are the 4th and 5th. If the remaining output parameters are left unset then the full form of the directive might read

```
'FIT'  X1,X2;;;;F;R;;;;
```

By naming the parameters we can replace this cumbersome list by the more immediately understandable

```
'FIT'  X1,X2 ; FVAL=F ; RES=R
```

or

```
'FIT'  X1,X2 ; RES=R ; FVAL=F
```

4.5 Future developments in language design

I have dealt with parameter-passing mechanisms at some length because it illustrates an aspect of language design which has not had the attention it deserves. In particular it shows, I believe, how little contact there has been between the people who design languages and those who develop packages, particularly statistical packages. I owe to Professor Ian Pyle of the University of York the remark that so far the language designer has thought of himself in relation to an undifferentiated population of users, which includes of course the novice (who must be protected from his own errors), and that we would do better to think in terms of a three-cornered relationship between the language designer, the package-writer, and the user. In this context the language would have to satisfy the needs of the package-writer, who often needs great flexibility and does not need to be protected from himself; such protection for the novice user can be provided at the package level by the package-writer. I am sure that thinking of languages in such a framework would change their specification, and lead to improvements for both classes of user. At present statisticians have made forays into language design in the course of writing statistical packages; they could have done better, but they need the co-operation of computer scientists who are above all interested in the application of languages to particular areas and classes of user. So far that co-operation has not occurred, and I will be content if this paper leads to a single instance of a joint programme in which statisticians interested in computing and computer scientists pool their complementary skills.

REFERENCES

Alvey N.G., et al. GENSTAT, a general statistical program, Rothamsted Experimental Station, Harpenden, Hertfordshire, U.K., 1977.

Baker R.J., and Nelder J.A., The GLIM System, Release 3, Numerical Algorithms Group, Oxford, 1978.

Johnson S.C., Compiler-compilers: where have we been and where are we going? Proceedings of the Ninth Interface Symposium on Computer Science and Statistics, Prindle, Weber, and Schmidt, Boston, 1976.

Lecarme O, and Peyrolle-Thomas M.C., Self-compiling compilers: an appraisal of their implementation and portability, Software - Practice and Experience, 8, 149-170, 1978.

Nelder J.A., A user's guide to the evaluation of statistical packages and systems, International Statistical Review, 42, 291-198, 1974.

Nelder J.A., and Payne R.W., Data structures in statistical computing, Proceedings of the Ninth International Biometric Conference, II, 191-207, 1977.

Nie N.H., Hull C.H., Jenkins J.G., Steinbrenner K, and Bent D.H. Statistical package for the social sciences, 2nd Edition. McGraw-Hill, New York, 1975.

Effects of the Computerization of Research

J. Tinbergen, The Hague

Summary

The net effect of computerization on scientific research is positive. It enables us to explore a model's sensitivity by a number of additional runs; to multiply the number of simulations with a priori values given to some coefficients; to work with much larger, including multi-disciplinary models; it invites to quantification of phenomena so far considered qualitative and to the collection of many more statistical data. These advantages overcompensate some disadvantages which moreover can be avoided by not wasting any of the components of true research, which, by the way, also implies qualitative and intuitive elements.

In an attempt to evaluate the broader social impact of computerization we may ask the most general question, how to use human efforts in order to attain an optimum of development of human happiness. A way must then be found to reduce the frightening volume of work done in military research. Precondition here is to institutionalize humankind's common interest in avoiding war and other wholesale violence. This problem has not so far been solved.

1. Introductory

The reason why I accepted to start the discussion of this Symposium is my age; I have been lucky enough to be permitted to concentrate on a number of research activities ever since I got my MA degree in physics at this very university in 1925. My only piece of empirical research in physics was unsuccessful; but with the aid of my superviser Paul Ehrenfest I shifted to economics, and received my PhD on a dissertation "Minimum Problems in Physics and Economics" in 1929. From 1926 on under Dutch law I was permitted to opt for non-military service and part of this at the Central Bureau of Statistics, where my task was to assist Dr. J.M. de Bosch Kemper in building up a research unit on business cycle analysis and forecasting. For quite some time in turn I was assisted by my colleague conscientious objector B.G.F. Buys, not only during our official working hours, but also on evenings and in weekends. It was at that time that a group of science-educated alumni of Dutch universities, including J.B.D. Derksen, P. de Wolff and Tj. Koopmans, occupied the empty territory between mathematics, mathematical statistics and economics, later to become the republic of econometrics. The republic's production function was, especially for Buys and myself, of the handicraft type, the heaviest equipment being a slide rule. The input of paper per standard output of regression equations was clearly less than in to-day's computerized process; the input of time was immensely higher; but our hourly salaries also were correspondingly lower. From 1929 to 1933 my annual income before tax amounted to hfl 2000 (or, in 1978 guilders, about 20 000, that is to-day's legal minimum wage. The latter figure was calculated on Texas Instruments SR-51A, but it could have been done by hand, of course.

Why all these details? Mainly in order to make you understand that what I propose to say about the subject announced is impressionistic rather than the result of a systematic and thorough analysis. Thus, I must disappoint those of my audience who might have thought that I used the fifty-odd years elapsed since to study the subject of this symposium. Suffice it to add that I am unable to write a computer programme.

The way I propose to deal with the subject is that I make a few remarks on, first, the scientific and, next the social effects of the computerization process. Both aspects will be discussed under the headings of positive and negative effects (or, advantages and disadvantages) and this implies a number of value judgements, but not a large number. The main value judgement I am going to apply is my dislike of totalitarian régimes; but some others will creep in. So you are warned.

2. Scientific Advantages of Computerization

As announced I am turning first to a number of advantages to scientific work arising from the emergence of the computer as of to-day. (I wonder what it will be next year). In order to facilitate discussion I will list some of the advantages and briefly illustrate them.

(a) As a matter of course the steep increase in the number of computations that can be made and the size of the statistical material that can be handled does constitute an advantage. To-day one can explore the behaviour of a model by a large number of sensitivity runs, all shown not only with such statistics as the regression coefficients, but including automatically their standard deviations or, of course, *t*-values, $\bar{R}^2$ and D.W. and so on. Changing roles of variables from dependent to independent, or from exogenous to endogenous, can be studied almost without effort, at least if the size of the model is not limited by the computer's storing capacity. As an illustration of the handicraft stage in which Buys and I established the models for the Netherlands 1923-1933 and for the United Kingdom 1870-1910 let me tell about our trick to estimate the regression coefficients and the R^2 (no more). We changed the units of our variables so as to let the deviations from average range roughly between + 10 and - 10, which implied that all moments could be calculated by heart and additions and cross checking as well. The solution of the normal equations was done by slide-rule. In order to judge beforehand whether a multiple regression equation was worth while the effort, we never made calculations before having a graphical reconnaissance in order to see whether the result looked promising. In order to judge the "reliability" of regression coefficients we used Frisch's bunch map analysis (Frisch, 1934), much easier to handle than the classical formulae for the standard deviations of regression coefficients. We used ordinary least squares for the structural equations instead of for the reduced-form equations, since Haavelmo had not yet spoken (Haavelmo, 1944). Almost simultaneously with our work Koopmans (1936) in his dissertation penetrated much more profoundly into the question of the various types of error terms than we did. In order to avoid some of the difficulties he brought to the fore, our attitude was to improve R^2 by the inclusion of "appropriate" variables. The phrase appropriate covered theoretical plausibility as well as the improvement of R^2. In a few cases a priori values for some regression coefficients could help to avoid multicollinearity. Checking for non-linearity of some of the relations was done by drawing partial scatter diagrams. All this illustrates that saving on computation work had a high priority and this priority has been eliminated almost completely by computers, once they became available.

(b) Computers also introduced the possibility to experiment with wide ranges of a priori values given to some of the regression coefficients. This operation was often indicated as "simulation", but contains less of a methodological innovation than some of our colleagues seemed to think. Even so it could be helpful, especially as a form of empirical sensitivity analysis.

(c) As a consequence of the enormous increases in the number of variables and of equations that could be introduced into a model or a "system", computerization has contributed considerably to inter- or multi-disciplinary research. Recent examples are the family of models introduced by Forrester (1971) and known all over the world is the first report to the Club of Rome by the Meadows couple and collaborators (D.H. and D.L. Meadows, Jørgen Randers and William W. Behrens III, 1972). In principle such models are a joint effort of economists, geologists, agronomists and engineers. As a favourable by-product they require team-work, as in any larger project in business or government. Another recent example of increased interdisciplinary co-operation can be found in research on education, where education sociologists, education economists and labour psychologists have discovered each other's work (cf. Psacharopoulos and Tinbergen, forthcoming). Whereas sociologists tended to use explanatory variables for schooling attained such as role of parents, of teachers and of classmates, economists tended to specify the variables as those used in job evaluation or function analysis, which may be called labour market variables. The two approaches no doubt admit integration.

(d) Another advantage of computerization seems to me to be that the tendency to quantify variables so far called qualitative. This assists us in reformulating working hypotheses into refutable assumptions and hecen enables us to further specify theories.

(e) The tendency just mentioned stimulates the collection of more statistical material. Recent examples include the information collected by Van Praag and collaborators on the welfare function of income (cf. Van Praag, 1973 and earlier work).

3. Scientific Disadvantages of Computerization

It is only natural that an innovation also entails some disadvantages, often the other side of the medals of advantage. In this section a brief list will be offered.

(a) The reduction in time and effort needed to make complicated computations automatically implies new forms of wastage of effort. One is that computations are made where previously theoretical analysis and empirical reconnaissance were used to restrict the number of computations. Trial and error has become cheap and is done more often now, implying an amount of mental laziness. Examples cannot be quoted easily from published research, since clearly superfluous computations will not, as a rule, be published. So let me only admit that a number of computations I asked some collaborators to carry out for me were indeed waste of our time.

(b) The well-known tendency to force a model into a form that is convenient from the computational aspect rather than natural from the theoretical aspect, known from mathematical economics, tends to be replaced. In many cases linearization of essentially curvilinear relations is an example, not restricted, of course, to computerized models.

(c) Not uncommon, as a consequence of computerization, is a waste of printing costs and a reduction of clarity to the reader of publications in which too large a number of decimal places is automatically taken over from the computer.

(d) Large models often prevent an author from intuitive checks on the plausibility of the results obtained. Again this can be seen as a repetition, at a larger scale, of our experience with macromodels as compared to micromodels.

(e) The quantification tendency, welcomed in Section 2 sub (d), is criticized by others. A recent example is the comment given by De Seynes in Cole's study of world models (Cole, 1977). The world models so far constructed do not pay much attention to the institutions existing in today's or an alternative world. This is correct, but there is no difficulty to introduce such institutions or, rather, their behaviour and hence their impact on the world economy or society. The estimation of such impact is another quantitative problem and hence this shortcoming of existing models can be avoided by a more intensive use of computers rather than less use.

4. A Positive Balance for Scientific Use of Computers

Inspection of the list of advantages and disadvantages seems to me to lead to a positive overall evaluation of what the computer brought us. The scope of scientific activity, in particular interdisciplinary activity, has been widened in an unprecedented way and already opened up unknown areas of information and understanding. The disadvantages are of a nature enabling us to avoid them and replace them by a number of recommendations how to behave accordingly. As a matter of fact this "code of good conduct" is even hardly new; it is old wine in new bags, for instance:

(i) let some thinking precede your using the computer;
(ii) do not force your theory too much into the straight jacket of easy algorithms;
(iii) avoid unnecessary computations;
(iv) have a good look at the nature and reliability of the inputs used;
(v) try to understand the main findings intuitively;
(vi) don't publish too many decimal places.

5. Social Advantages of Computerization

Turning now to the broader social impact of the computer, we must start by an evaluation of the advantages of scientific progress to society, that is, to mankind. It is commonplace, in the last quarter of the twentieth century, to recall that so-called scientific progress is not necessarily improvement of human welfare: it can even be maintained that on some counts we can observe decreases in welfare as a consequence of scientific development. Methodologically, however, it is also commonplace to remind us of the different meanings that can be attached to the concept of cause. The allocation to a number of causes of an observed deterioration in welfare constitutes itself a problem. In the answer to that problem we sometimes come across the word "critical cause". Let me illustrate this point by a very simple example. Increased poverty by unemployment in developing countries can be said to have been caused by the eradication of some diseases with the aid of scientific (medical) knowledge, applied by the World Health Organization in the last decades. If, however, that application had been accompanied by the transfer of another piece of scientific knowledge, namely birth control, its effect could have been quite different. My conclusion from the preceding remarks is that the best formulation of our problem is to find the optimum mix of scientific development, subject to the restrictions on manpower and other means available for that development.

In an attempt to apply this method of posing the problem to the question, what part computers have played and can play in the science mix of the recent past and the near future, I will again try to sum up some advantages and disadvantages the computer is able to bring.

On a host of details of human life scientific progress has worked out favourably. Many of the mew materials and products which have become available as a consequence of scientific development have contributed to a better satisfaction of the needs of many people in the world, including those who are in critical conditions - the poor in the developing world. Even the green revolution has, notwithstanding its unfavourable social by-products, prevented famines that otherwise already could have taken place. We did purchase time to complement the green revolution by social reform. Recent research of a multidisciplinary character has added to our knowledge of what international social reforms should be in the policy mix needed and a package of scientific research for the coming decades needed as part of such policy is widely discussed. The scientists involved will no doubt plan to make use of computers in a large number of research projects. They also have their programmes for data collection in a large variety of areas; the sort of data used in an attempt to solve the most pressing problems. Among these the improvement of food production and distribution, together with the maintenance of ecological equilibrium, rank high. So does the shift of energy sources from exhaustible to non-exhaustible ones, with a minimum of risk of nuclear pollution.

Social advantages of the development of science and technology are partly due to the help of computers, present and future generations. The way we have to pose the problem before us is, to conclude, to plan for the optimal mix. Without such a plan the world will tend to take another course, sometimes characterized as a large-scale struggle for technological knowledge.

6. Social Dangers of Computerization

In an attempt to formulate such an optimal mix we must be aware of some social dangers that may be implied. Let us mention a few of a rather different type.

(a) We must not forget that the development of computers has been pushed mainly by military research during and after the Second World War. The larger part of research and development (R and D) is being undertaken as part of the armament race between the US and the SU. Highest priority has to be given to the avoidance of a large-scale was and not even the principle of a solution has so far been found. Scientific activity of whatever type, if only promising, directed at giving institutional shape to this common interest of mankind is by far the most useful activity conceivable. Among the weak attempts to contribute to this first priority is a computerized model of the armaments race and its outcome constructed at the Canadian Peace Research Institute by Norman Alcock et al (Alcock, 1978). In a foreword to the publication I propose that IIASA at Laxenburg, Austria, take up the model for scrutiny and possible elaboration.

(b) Some concern has been expressed by a number of persons and organizations, that the data banks needed for the information processing done by computers might threaten privacy and even personal security or interests. One example is the use made in the past by the population administration of territories occupied by the Nazi regime in the early 'forties. Data which may do harm are (in this case) addresses, affiliations with certain organizations, and so on. The answer I am inclined to give to this concern is that the avoidance of an authoritarian régime is the best goal to pursue in order to avoid the risks described. This requires the education to independent thinking of as many people as possible; the rejection of doctrinaire thinking or propaganda and the active furtherance of tolerance as an important human value.

In both cases (a) and (b) we are confronted with the profound imbalance between human development of intellect and the development of morals. This imbalance partly expresses itself in the enormous and almost blind development of science and technology, including the computer and its applications, regardless of the question whether the uses made of it are ethically important. Perhaps this is human imperfection and fate and unavoidably will destroy humanity. Perhaps we can still hope for a moral revolution. You will understand that here we are faced with the most fundamental questions of life and of our lifes.

(c) It is somewhat of an anticlimax to add to my list one more danger of data banks that has been already the subject of American legislation, namely the Fair Credit Reporting Act, which tries to protect individuals against incorrect information about their creditworthiness. This must be evaluated positively and may illustrate that this sort of concern can be dealt with, without stopping computerization.

(d) Just in order to bring in an element of relaxation let me report to you an experience I had of how you can be hunted by a computer if you don't dare to face it. By some error I was booked in some computerized system connected with a publishing firm as having ordered a publication, although I had not actually. I received a computerized bill, which I didn't pay, of course, and as a consequence had to receive at regular intervals reminders whose language was increasingly menacing. Several telephone calls appeared to be unable to stop the escalation. In the end I understand some brave secretary succeeded in killing the monster.

7. Concluding Remarks

Starting out with the dezcription of my peaceful handicraft as a builder of primitive econometric models in the 'thirties, I first had to admit that the computer has contributed in an unprecedented way to widen the scope of model building. We can work with larger models, estimate as many relationships as we want, with such useful statistics as the t-values, $\bar{R}^2$, DW etc. We can perform sensitivity analyses, experiment with wide ranges of a priori values for some regression coefficients, build interdisciplinary models, and so on. The collection of quantitative information has been stimulated. All this is to the good especially if we stick to some type of economics of research, by sticking to the logical order of thinking first, testing secondly, avoid making unpromising computations, keep awake our critical intuition and don't have too many decimals printed in our articles.

In order to judge the social effects of computerization we should perhaps formulate the problem that is - or has to be - behind all our activities; this means an inversion of our usual analytical attitude and rather pose the policy problem. Moreover, we should aim at posing the widest policy problem we are faced with: how to find and then to maintain a better equilibrium between a searching and an ethical or moral attitude vis-à-vis to'day's world.

Humanity has badly neglected moral issues and used its intellectual power in a completely wrong and frightening direction of bi- or tripolar intolerance; by far the largest part of computerization has been used to create weaponry over which we may loose moral control. Each individual scientist should be aware of what has top priority today: finding a stable system of managing the earth.

References

Alcock, N. et al 1982, CPRI Press, Oakville, Ont., 1978

Cole, Sam, Global Models and the International Economic Order, UNITAR, New York, 1977

Forrester, J., World Dynamics, Cambridge, Mass., 1971

Frisch, R., Confluence Analysis, Oslo, 1934

Haavelmo, T., "The Statistical Implications of a System of Simultaneous Equations", Econometrica 11 (1943), p. 1-12

Koopmans, T., Linear Regression Analysis of Economic Time Series, Haarlem, 1936

Meadows, D.H. and D.L., J. Randers and W.W. Behrens III, The Limits to Growth, New York, 1972

Van Praag, B.M.S. and A. Kapteyn, "Further Evidence on the Individual Welfare Function of Income: An Empirical Investigation in the Netherlands," European Economic Review 5 (1973), p. 33-62.

2. Linear and Nonlinear Regression

Fitting Generalised Linear Models with the GLIM System

R.J. Baker and **P.W. Lane**, Harpenden

Summary

The GLIM system is introduced with reference to the types of statistical model it can handle. Four examples are presented. Attention is drawn to the achieved unification of several commonly-used families of models.

KEYWORDS: GLIM, generalised linear models, ANOCOVA, contingency tables, probit analysis, interactive programming.

1. Introduction

Generalised linear models as described by Nelder and Wedderburn (1972), form a class of statistical models to which a single estimation and goodness-of-fit procedure can be applied. The class includes such models as are found in the analysis of variance, regression, probit and logit analysis, and also log-linear models for contingency tables, and models with gamma distributions (including the chi-squared and exponential distributions) such as the analysis of variance components.

The computer program GLIM (Baker & Nelder (1978)) was originally developed to perform the numerical computation involved in fitting models from this class, though its uses are now considerably wider than this. Similar facilities for fitting these models have also been incorporated into the general statistical system Genstat (Alvey et al. (1977)). Both programs can handle the analyses described below, though each uses its own syntax.

A generalised linear model (GLM) is defined by specifying:

(a) the probability distribution of the observations (which must be a member of the exponential family); the observations are taken to be independent;

(b) the linear predictor, that is a linear combination of systematic effects; these can be quantitative covariates, or sets of qualitative effects, the latter being termed factors;

(c) the link function that connects the expected value of an observation to its linear predictor.

A single algorithm can be used to evaluate the maximum likelihood estimates of the parameters, the method being a form of iterative weighted least-squares. Goodness-of-fit may be assessed through the usual log likelihood ratio (or deviance) statistic.

Both programs provide a command language for specifying and fitting any particular model. For example, a log-linear model for contingency table data can be set up by declaring (a) that the data have a Poisson distribution (b) the factors which classify the table and (c) that the log function is to be used to link the linear parameters, representing factor effects, to the expected values of the observations. The specification of the actual terms that are to be estimated causes the model to be fitted and the values of the deviance and its degrees of freedom under the model to be printed. This deviance (multiplied, if necessary, by a scale parameter) may be directly compared to the corresponding chi-square distribution. Alternatively, when comparing two models, one being a sub-model of the other, the difference between the deviances under the two models provides a test for the extra parameters.

Besides the specification and fitting of generalised linear models, there are extensive facilities for the manipulation and display of data and for the storing and printing of the results of analyses. Instructions in GLIM are in the form of directives - each consisting of a directive-word, made up of the $ sign and up to three significant letters specifying the type of operation required, followed by any other items required for the instruction. For example the directives

    $ERROR POISSON $LINK LOG

declare that the observations have a Poisson error distribution with a logarithmic link function - i.e. the familiar log-linear model, as in the example of Section 3.

Sets of observations corresponding to the units of an experiment are stored by the program in data structures. If the observations are quantitative, then variate structures are used, if qualitative then factors. The structures are referred to in directives by means of identifiers consisting of a letter followed by up to three significant letters or digits. In addition, single values can be stored in scalar structures with identifiers %A, %B up to %Z and there are several system identifiers, also beginning with the % character, referring to structures set up during model calculations (these are illustrated in Section 5). GLIM also contains directives enabling data to be read in free format, calculations to be performed upon scalars and vectors, scatterplots to be drawn and macros to be stored for use in program control instructions.

An important feature of the GLIM system is that it may be used interactively so that results are obtained immediately and model-fitting can be made dependent on the interpretation of previous results.

We now give four examples of the types of model that the program can handle.

2. An analysis of covariance

The data concern weight gains of animals on two diets.

ANIMAL	1	2	3	4	5
DIET	1	1	1	2	2
IW	1	2	1	3	2
WG	8	3	7	5	4

The dependent variate (assumed to be normal) is the weight gain (WG) while the initial weight (IW) is used as a covariate to eliminate bias. DIET is a factor with 2 levels, i.e. has values of either 1 or 2 indicating whether an animal is on the first or second diet. The analysis of such data can be seen in terms of fitting two regression lines with or without common intercepts or common slopes.

Having declared the number of units (or observations) and declared and read the data in we specify the y-variate, Normal error distribution and, because the means are expressed as simple sums of the linear parameters, the identity link function. Finally, by specifying the effects in the linear predictor, we fit the model.

```
$UNITS  5        $FACTOR  DIET 2

$DATA  DIET IW WG        $READ

1  1  8    1  2  3    2  3  5    1  1  7    2  2  4

$YVARIATE  WG      $ERROR  NORMAL         $LINK  IDENTITY

$FIT  DIET + DIET.IW
```

The terms DIET and DIET.IW represent respectively the intercepts and the slopes for the two fitted regression lines (one for each level of DIET). A simpler model is obtained if "DIET + IW" is fitted, when a common slope and separate intercepts are estimated.

Fitting each model produces a deviance statistic, which for the Normal distribution is simply the residual sum of squares, so that the sum of squares for the effect of adding a term can be obtained by subtraction.

Analysis of these quantities for this example indicates that no more than a single slope and single intercept is required. This model is fitted by the directive

```
$FIT  IW
```

and the parameter estimates, given by the directive

```
$DISPLAY  E
```

are 8.4 and -1.6 for the intercept and slope respectively.

3. Analysis of a contingency table

Multiway contingency tables are often analysed using a log-linear model, under which systematic effects on the observed counts in the cells of the table are assumed to be additive on a log scale. The counts themselves are assumed to be independently distributed as Poisson variables, though there are often constraints on the margins of the table, arising from whatever sampling method is used to collect the observations. This model is therefore a GLM with a logarithmic link function.

Plackett (1974) considers the analysis of a three-way contingency table, presented originally by Ashford and Sowden (1970), derived from a survey of some 18,000 coalminers. Nine age-groups were defined, and the miners within each group were classified according to presence or absence of two respiratory systems: 'breathlesness' and 'wheeze'. Plackett investigates in particular how the association between these two respiratory symptoms varied with age.

Using GLIM, we can read the observed cell counts into a variate structure, COUNT say, and set up factor structures which classify the observations: AGE, BREATH and WHEEZE, these having 9, 2 and 2 levels respectively. The model can then be declared by the directives

```
$ERROR POISSON      $LINK LOG      $YVARIATE COUNT
```

The initial hypothesis tested is that there is no variation in the association between the two symptoms with age. This is equivalent to a hypothesis of zero three-factor interaction, which can be tested by examining the residual deviance produced by the directive

```
$FIT AGE*BREATH*WHEEZE - AGE.BREATH.WHEEZE
```

The deviance for this fit is 26.7 on 8 degrees of freedom; treating this as a chi-squared statistic leads to rejection of the hypothesis.

To explain the variation of the data, Plackett fits a component of the three-factor interaction, corresponding to the hypothesis that the log cross-product ratios of the counts decrease linearly with increasing age. This complex hypothesis can be simply tested in GLIM by setting up a variate structure, VAGE say, to represent the desired component

```
$CALC   VAGE = (AGE-1)*(BREATH-1)*(WHEEZE-1)
```

This variate has zero values for all cells in the table except those corresponding to miners who show neither respiratory symptom, where the variate is assigned one of the numbers 0,1...8 according to the age group. This linear component is added to the model using the directive

```
$FIT   + VAGE
```

and this gives a value of 6.8 for the residual deviance on 7 degrees of freedom, which indicates a satisfactory fit of the model corresponding to the hypothesis tested.

4. A more complex model

Kastenbaum and Lamphiear (1959) give data on the number of depletions in litters of mice for given treatment combinations. Koch, Tolley and Freeman (1976) present the data as a two-way table in which rows (i=1,...,10) index treatment combinations, columns (j=0,1,2+) index numbers of depletions per litter, and the cell entry r_{ij} is the observed number of litters in that class. They treat the entries as multinomially distributed on the row margin totals (n_i) with expected values related to an underlying binomial distribution -

$$E(r_{ij}) = n_i \left[\binom{m_i}{j} \theta_i^j (1-\theta_i)^{m_i - j}\right] \qquad j = 0,1$$

$$E(r_{i2}) = n_i - E(r_{i0}) - E(r_{i1})$$

where m_i is the litter size for entries in row i. Thus θ_i is the probability of death for a mouse under treatment combination i, and it is of interest to investigate how this varies with i.

By allowing for the conditioning on the row margins the data can be treated as independent Poisson. Since the expected values are functions of the θ_i (though they are more complex functions than usual) the θ_i are the linear predictors, and can be expressed as linear sums of treatment effects. (It might be desirable to define $\eta_i = \log\{\theta_i/(1-\theta_i)\}$ as the linear predictors, since the θ_i will then always lie withing range.) This is thus an example of a generalised linear model.

The model can be fitted through the OWN directive of GLIM, which permits the user to define his own error distribution and link function whilst retaining the fitting and display facilities used for standard models. The exact maximum likelihood estimates of the treatment parameters together with standard errors may then be obtained as for other models.

5. Probit analysis with control mortality

The classical model of probit analysis is an important example of a GLM. We will illustrate this model with the analysis of data arising from an experiment designed to test the effect of a pyrethroid insecticide, applied as a foliar spray at several different rates.

After spraying, leaves were sampled from the plots and enclosed in the laboratory with a number of caterpillars of the Egyptian cotton leaf worm. After 48 hours, the numbers of caterpillars remaining alive on each sample were counted. One model suggested for these observations was as follows:

$$\text{count}_i \text{ has a binomial distribution } B(\text{total}_i, p_i) \qquad (1)$$

$$E(\text{count}_i) = \text{total}_i \times p_i = \text{total}_i \times \Phi(a + b \times \log(\text{mass}_i)) \qquad (2)$$

where mass_i was the rate of insecticide used on the plot from which sample was taken, and total_i was the number of caterpillars tested for the sample. (Φ is the cumulative normal distribution function.) This model is thus a GLM; the link function is usually called the 'probit function'.

A parameter of interest in experiments of this kind is often the LD50 (median effective log dose), which is the ratio -a/b from (2). When such a model is fitted using GLIM, this ratio can be derived using a CALCULATE directive after the FIT directive. The standard error of the ratio can also be found by applying the theorem of Fieller, and as the calculations are not trivial it is an advantage to store this as a macro, which can be invoked each time an estimate is derived.

A complication in the experiment described above was that there were significant mortality among caterpillars enclosed with control samples. This required a reformulation of (2) above,

$$E(\text{count}_i) = \text{total}_i \times (c + (1-c) \times \Phi(a + b \times \log(\text{mass}_i)))$$

where c is the control mortality expressed as a percentage.

Using GLIM, the parameter c cannot be estimated in the same way as a and b, since it cannot be included as a linear term of the predictor. It is possible to carry out a sequence of FIT directives for trial values of c, and optimise the residual deviance with respect to variation in c. However, in this example it was found sufficient to estimate c separately from the replicated control samples, and to use this estimate as a fixed constant in the model. The link function in this case is not a standard one in GLIM, and so the model is fitted using the directive $OWN. This requires macros to be set up that store the calculations required in the model fitting procedure. For example, a macro is needed to calculate the variate of fitted values (referred to by the special system identifier %FV) from the linear predictor (%LP).

```
$MACRO  M1     $CALC   %FV = TOTAL * (%C + (1-%C) * %NP(%LP)     $END
```

%C is a scalar holding the estimate of control mortality and %NP is the function name for Φ. The model can then be fitted using the directives

```
$OWN   M1 M2 M3 M4      $YVARIATE  COUNT      $FIT  LOGMASS
```

where M2, M3 and M4 are three other macros storing similar required calculations.

6. Conclusions

An indication has been given of the simplicity and economy with which many of the simpler statistical models can be specified and fitted using the GLIM system. Furthermore, example 4 showed that the facilities of the system may also be applied to more complex models. Recent analyses that have been programmed in the GLIM system include models using inverse polynomials, hierarchical components of variance, orthogonal polynomials, non-linear regression for a pharmacological study, models for incidence data with the complementary log-log transformation, certain robust regression procedures, models for survival data and models with Weibull and inverse Gaussian errors. Further applications are currently being investigated, including the analyses of life-tables and retrospective case-control studies.

REFERENCES

Alvey, N.G., et al. GENSTAT, a general statistical program. Rothamsted Experimental Station, Harpenden, Hertfordshire, U.K., 1977.

Ashford, J.R. and Sowden; R.R. Multivariate probit analysis. Biometrics, 26, 535-546, 1970.

Baker, R.J. and Nelder, J.A. The GLIM System, Release 3. Oxford: Numerical Algorithms Group, 1978.

Kastenbaum, M.A. and Lamphiear, D.E. Calculation of chi-square to calculate the no three-factor interaction hypothesis. Biometrics, 15, 197-15, 1959.

Koch, G.G., Tolley, H.D. and Freeman, J.L. An application of the clumped binomial model to the analysis of clustered attribute data. Biometrics, 32, 337-354, 1976.

Nelder, J.A. and Wedderburn, R.W.M. Generalised linear models. J.R.Statist. Soc., A, 135, 370-84, 1972.

Plackett, R.L. The analysis of categorical data. London: Griffin, 1974.

Solution of Nonlinear Least Squares Problems: Numerical Results with Marquardt-Type Algorithms

A. J. Barhorst and J.P. Roos, Arnhem

Summary

The numerical aspects of (damped) Gauss-Newton and Marquardt-type algorithms for the least squares estimation of unconstrained parameters in a nonlinear model, such as nonlinear regression analysis, are considered. The main difficulty in using a (damped) Gauss-Newton algorithm is due to the possibly singular behaviour of the Jacobian matrix of the partial derivatives of the response function which respect to the parameters. A class of Marquardt-type algorithms not suffering from this disadvantage is considered. Most existing algorithms for solving the remaining problem of determining the Marquardt parameter are essentially heuristic.

The authors present a theoretical basis for these algorithms, give a geometrical interpretation, and develop a practical criterion for selecting the Marquardt parameter. Their findings have been implemented in a nonlinear regression algorithm with excellent convergence properties: under some smoothness conditions it is globally convergent.

Practical experiences, e.g. in the separation of overlapping peaks in lab-scale measuring techniques (Infrared analysis, X-ray diffraction), are discussed. The reliability of the Marquardt modification and its superiority in the case of difficult problems are shown.

Keywords

Nonlinear least squares; nonlinear regression; parameter estimation; Gauss-Newton algorithms; Marquardt algorithms; computer programs; practical experience.

Statement of the problem

The basic question we are concerned with is that of the numerical solution of nonlinear least squares problems. This means the minimization of a real valued function $F(x)$, being the sum of squared nonlinear functions $f_i(x)$ $(i = 1,2,\ldots,m)$ of the parameters x_j $(j = 1, 2, \ldots, n)$:

$$F(x) = f^T(x)f(x) = //f(x)//^2 = \sum_{i=1}^{m} f_i^2(x) \qquad (1)$$

$$x = (x_1, \ldots, x_n) \varepsilon \mathbb{R}^n \text{ and } f(x) = (f_1(x), \ldots, f_m(x)),\ m > n$$

We assume that a unique minimizer $\hat{x}$ exists. In our treatment only unconstrained minimization is considered, although in our computer programs the technique for handling general constraints as described by Schweigman (1974) has been implemented, cf. Van Houwelingen et al. (1973).
We do not intend to give theorems on convergence and convergence rates; they can be obtained by following the lines of Ortega and Rheinboldt (1970).
A separate paper on this topic is planned.

Note: By //.// the Euclidean vector norm is meant throughout. For an iterative process generating a (finite or infinite) sequence $\{x^k\}$ we define the steps $h^k = x^{k+1} - x^k$ $(k = 0, 1, \ldots)$. Furthermore we define $g(x) = \text{grad } F(x) = 2J^T(x)f(x)$, where $J(x)$ is the Jacobian matrix of f: $J_{ij} = \partial f_i/\partial x_j$. When no confusion is possible the argument x and the iteration superscript k are dropped.

Gauss-Newton algorithms

In a (damped) Gauss-Newton method the step h satisfies:

$$h = -\gamma (J^TJ)^{-1}J^Tf \qquad (2)$$

where γ is the step-length or damping factor $(0 < \gamma \leqslant 1)$. It has been assumed that J^TJ is non-singular.
This technique is usually motivated as follows. The nonlinear function f in (1) is linearized, giving the quadratic form in h

$$\psi(h) = //f(x) + J(x)h//^2 \qquad (3)$$

as an approximation of $F(x + h)$. A candidate for the minimizer of F is obtained by minimizing ψ, which is a linear least squares problem in h.

This gives the undamped Gauss-Newton step, i.e. (2) with $\gamma = 1$. The damping factor γ is computed by means of some step-length algorithm (e.g."step halving") in order to satisfy the descent condition $F(x + \gamma h) < F(x)$.

Stronger conditions are needed to guarantee convergence of a damped Gauss-Newton method, but this question will not be considered here; see Powell (1970) for an example and our Example 3.

Interpretation of Marquardt's method

We give one possible interpretation of the method of Marquardt (1963) and a new algorithm based on this interpretation. Instead of (3) we consider a family of approximating paraboloids

$$\psi_\mu(h) = //f(x) + J(x)h//^2 + \mu//Dh//^2 \quad (4)$$

where $\mu \geqslant 0$ and D is any non-singular n x n-matrix. Usually, D is a diagonal matrix taking into account the scaling of the problem.
The original Gauss-Newton paraboloid is contained in (4): $\psi = \psi_0$. The term $\mu//Dh//^2$ may be regarded as a crude estimate of the part U of the Hessian H of F that is missing in (3): $H = 2J^TJ + U$ with $H_{ij} = \partial^2F/\partial x_i \partial x_j$ and

$$U_{ij} = 2\sum_k f_k \, \partial^2 f_k/\partial x_i \partial x_j$$

For $\mu > 0$, the minimizer of ψ_μ is the Marquardt step h_μ:

$$h_\mu = -(J^TJ + \mu D^TD)^{-1}J^Tf \quad (5)$$

Note that D^TD is symmetric and positive definite. For $\mu = 0$ we define h_0 by

$$h_0 = \lim_{\mu \to 0+} h_\mu = -D^{-1}(JD^{-1})^+f \quad (6)$$

where the superscript + denotes the pseudo-inverse (or generalized inverse). So, for rank-deficient J, h_0 is the minimizer of (3) with minimum scaled length $//Dh_0//$. Furthermore, we have $\lim_{\mu \to \infty} \mu h_\mu = -(D^TD)^{-1}J^Tf$, cf.

Marquardt (1963).

Step determination

Now the problem is how to find a "good" value for μ. We could compute μ on the basis of one additional function evaluation (say, in the point $x + h_0$) by assuming $\psi_\mu(h_0) = F(x + h_0)$. As this does not lead to a practical algorithm, we proceed as follows.

The minimizers $h_\mu (\mu \geq 0)$ lie on a smooth curve defined by (5) and (6); the decrease of F as predicted by ψ_μ is

$$\Theta(\mu) = \psi_\mu(h_\mu) - \psi_\mu(0) = \tfrac{1}{2}\, g^T h_\mu$$

$\Theta(\mu)$ is negative for all $\mu \geq 0$ as long as $g \neq 0$. Our criterion is that the predicted decrease equals the actual decrease, see Fig. 1.

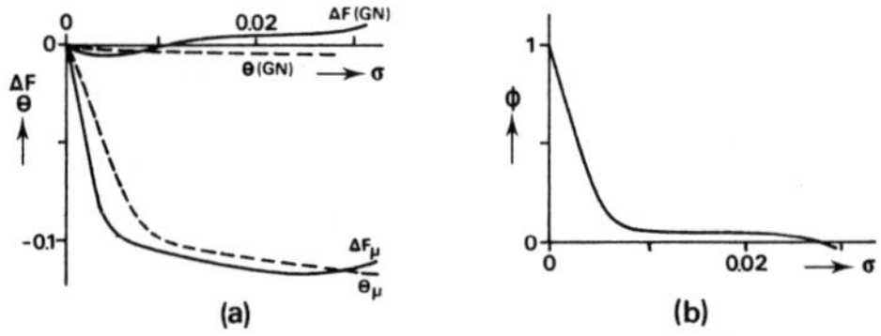

FIG.1: SOME INTERMEDIATE RESULTS TAKEN FROM EXAMPLE 2

$\sigma = \|h_\mu\| / \|h_0\|$; $\Delta F_\mu = F(x+h_\mu) - F(x)$

The optimum value $\hat{\mu}$ satisfies $F(x + h_{\hat{\mu}}) - F(x) = \Theta(\hat{\mu})$. (7)

Consider the function $\phi(\mu) = \dfrac{F(x + h_\mu) - F(x) - \Theta(\mu)}{\Theta(\mu)}$

for $\mu \geq 0$. We observe that for $\mu \to \infty$, $\phi(\mu) \to 1$. Moreover, when $F(x + h_0) > F(x) + (1 - \delta_1)\,\Theta(0)$, with $0 < \delta_1 < 1$, it follows that $\phi(0) < -\delta_1 < 0$ so that $\phi(\mu)$ has at least one zero for $\mu > 0$. We compute this zero by bisection after an interval containing the zero has been established.

The criterion (7) combines a reasonably large step with a sufficient decrease of F. In actual applications it is only approximately solved, cf. (8) and (9) below.

Existing alternatives

Most existing alternatives are essentially heuristic. Marquardt (1963) suggested to take the initial value of $\mu = 0.01$ and to modify it by a factor of 10, if necessary. This factor has been found to be too large in general, see Fig. 1 and the examples. This conclusion is substantiated by Osborne (1976) who applied Marquardt's strategy using several initial values of μ and several values of the modifying factors. In the strategy developed by Pitha and Jones (1966) three different values of μ are evaluated, followed by a cubic interpolation and a fourth evaluation. Smith and Shanno (1971) aim at minimizing $F(x + h_\mu)$ along the Marquardt curve (5). In general, this is less efficient than our procedure of solving an equation but the optimum values for μ are nearly the same.

Scaling

For the scaling matrix D we use a diagonal matrix with $D_{ii} = //\partial f/\partial x_i//$, the length of the i - th column of J. When $//\partial f/\partial x_i// = 0$, or numerically zero, we set $D_{ii} = 10^{10}$ (arbitrarily) in order to avoid singularity of D. Note that a zero column in J means that the corresponding parameter does not locally influence the sum of squares.

Proposed Marquardt algorithm

Step (I) δ_1, δ_2 are fixed numbers ε (0,1); x^0 is given; set $k := 0$, $\mu^0 := 0$ and $\mu^* := 1$

comment: we use $\delta_1 = 0.75$ and $\delta_2 = 0.25$

Step (II) comment: steps (II) - (V) are outer iterations;

set $x := x^k$ and select the scaling matrix D.

Step (III) comment: step determination;

a. Compute the basic step h_0; if J^TJ is singular, compute h_0 using (5) with $\mu = 10^{-6}$

b. if $F(x + h_0) \leq F(x) + (1 - \delta_1)\, \Theta(0)$ (8)

then $\hat{\mu} := 0$

else comment inner iterations;

evaluate $\phi(\mu)$ for $\mu := \mu^*, 10\,\mu^*, \ldots$ until $\phi(\mu) > 0$;

apply bisection until a value $\hat{\mu}$ is found satisfying

$$(1 + \delta_2)\Theta(\hat{\mu}) \leq F(x + h_{\hat{\mu}}) - F(x) \leq (1 - \delta_1)\Theta(\hat{\mu}) \quad (9)$$

and set $\mu^* := \hat{\mu}$

comment: the very first time the Marquardt parameter $\hat{\mu}$ is computed we use $\delta_1 = 0.075$ and $\delta_2 = 0.025$ in order to be certain that $\hat{\mu}$ is a good estimate of the optimum value.

Step (IV) set $\mu^k := \hat{\mu}$ and $x^{k+1} := x^k + h_{\mu^k}$

Step (V) set $k := k + 1$ and repeat from (II)

Remarks: Inequality (9) is equivalent to Goldstein's step-length criterion, cf. Ortega and Rheinboldt (1970), or Goldstein and Price (1967).
Global convergence of our proposed algorithm can be proved when F has a unique stationary point $\hat{x}$ and satisfies certain smoothness conditions. Osborne (1976) also proved global convergence for his algorithm.

Numerical Results

Some results of four examples are given and our algorithm is compared with the damped Gauss-Newton algorithm in BMDX85, Dixon (1973), and the Marquardt algorithms according to Pitha and Jones (1966), and Osborne (1972).
Note that the Pitha and Jones algorithm has been reported to be efficient, especially in the field of fitting Infrared spectra (Example 2).

Example 1: Box' example, cf. Box (1966), Brown and Dennis (1972).
Fit the model $y(p) = e^{-x_1 p} - e^{-x_2 p}$ with the parameters x_1, x_2 to the exact data generated by $p_i = i/10$ $(i = 1, 2, \ldots, 10)$ and $(\hat{x}_1, \hat{x}_2) = (1, 10)$. Take $(x_1^0, x_2^0) = (5, 0)$ as the starting point (other starting points yield similar results). This problem appears to be relatively easy and can also be solved efficiently by a damped Gauss-Newton algorithm. The results of our new algorithm are at least as good as the best results reported by Brown and Dennis (1972). In Table I some results of the Pitha and Jones algorithm are compared with those of our algorithm.

Table I Comparison of two Marquardt type algorithms (Example 1). n_k = number of funtion evaluations in each outer iteration (excluding the evaluation of the gradient, being the same for both methods).

Outer iteration number k	Our algorithm $F(x^k)$	Our algorithm μ^k	Our algorithm n_k	Pitha and Jones (1966) $F(x^k)$	Pitha and Jones (1966) μ^k	Pitha and Jones (1966) n_k
0	19.59	2.62	11	19.59	500	4
1	12.63	0	1	19.47	5	4
2	1.383	0	1	6.421	2.5	4
3	0.136	0	1	0.942	1250	4
4	0.0252	0	1	0.941	6.25	4
5	0.00020	0	1	0.927	0.0312	4
6	$7.5\ 10^{-6}$	convergence		0.533	0.0714	4
7				0.365	0.0357	4
8				0.00477	$1.8\ 10^{-4}$	4
9				0.00176	$\sim 10^{-6}$	4
10				$4.2\ 10^{-5}$	convergence	

Note that the convergence rate of our algorithm is quadratic. The unfavourable values of μ selected by the Pitha and Jones algorithm are due to the heuristic character and the fixed multiplication factors (initial value μ = 1; down = 0.01; up = 1000; change = 0.5, cf. Pitha and Jones (1966)).

Example 2: Synthesized IR diffraction pattern.

Fit the model $y(\lambda) = 10^{-z_1(\lambda)-z_2(\lambda)-z_3(\lambda)-z_4(\lambda)} - 0.05$

with $$z_i(\lambda) = \frac{A_i}{\left[1 + (2^{1/m_i} - 1)\left(\frac{\lambda - b_i}{H_i}\right)^2\right]^{m_i}} \qquad i = 1, 2, 3, 4$$

and $$m_i = \frac{1}{2 - q_i}$$

to the data generated by the parameters:

i	A_i	b_i	H_i	q_i
1	0.300	970	10	1
2	0.450	955	20/3	1
3	1.200	950	5	1
4	0.400	920	10	1

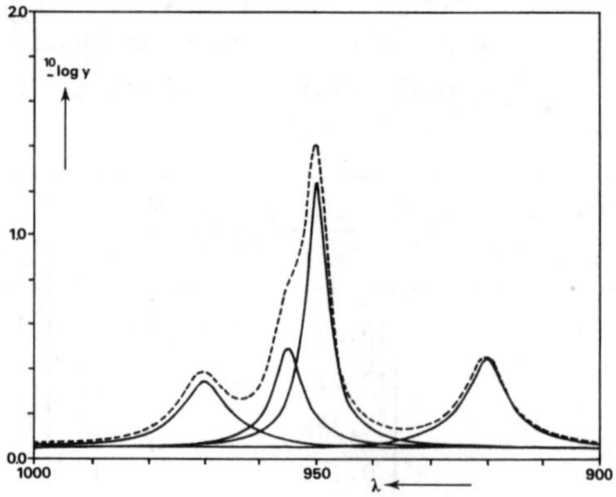

FIG.2: SYNTHESIZED DIFFRACTION PATTERN

for the wavelengths $\lambda_j = 900 + 0.5\,j$ ($j = 1, 2, \ldots, 200$) and rounded off to 3 digits (the minimum value of F is 0.000032).

Use the constraints $0.05 \leqslant A_i \leqslant 1.5$, $900 \leqslant b_i \leqslant 999$, $1 \leqslant H_i \leqslant 50$, $0{,}25 \leqslant q_i \leqslant 1.95$ for all i and the starting point:

i	A_i	b_i	H_i	q_i
1	0.268	969	11.7	0.88
2	0.283	952	13.9	0.89
3	0.589	951	8.3	1.93
4	0.381	920	10.1	1.06

(F = 0.1497)

Remarks: This starting point was generated by a damped Gauss-Newton with very slowly converging iterations: in 9 outer iterations with 21 bisections the sum of squares decreases by a factor of 10. Cf. Fig.1, where ΔF and Θ along the Gauss-Newton vector are shown, and Table II.
For this problem the constraints are redundant.

The problem of separating overlapping peaks is a difficult one, but has great practical importance, see e.g. Pitha and Jones (1966), and Heuvel et al. (1974).

Some results are shown in Table II.

Table II Comparison of two Marquardt algorithms (Example 2); cf. Table I.

Outer iteration number k	Our algorithm			Pitha and Jones (1966)		
	$F(x^k)$	μ^k	n_k	$F(x^k)$	μ^k	n_k
0	0.1497	0.0156	8	0.1497	0.0236	4
1	0.0280	0.0156	2	0.0260	0.0118	4
2	0.0182	0.0049	6	0.0179	0.0059	4
3	0.0161	0.0063	8	0.0130	2.955	4
4	0.00460	0	1	0.0123	0.0148	4
5	0.00111	0	1	0.00333	0.0325	4
6	0.000059	0	1	0.00217	0.00016	4
7	0.000032	convergence		0.00053	0.0813	4
8				0.00037	0.0019	4
9				0.00019	0.0019	4
10				0.00008	0.0045	4
11				0.00006	0.0045	4
12				0.000032	convergence	

Example 3: Our counter example against damped Gauss-Newton.

Minimize $F(x) = \left[(x_1 + x_2)^2 + x_1 - x_2\right]^2 + \left[x_2 - x_1 + 1\right]^2$

The unique minimizer $\hat{x} = (0.25, - 0.25)$ with $F(\hat{x}) = 0.5$. Along the line $x_1 + x_2 = 0$ which contains the minimizer, J^TJ is singular.
It can be proved that any damped Gauss-Newton method may diverge even when the starting point lies in an arbitrarily small neighbourhood of $\hat{x}$. Our algorithm solves this problem, which agrees with the theoretical prediction of global convergence.

Example 4: Osborne's examples.
Osborne (1972, 1976) discusses two problems and the results of his algorithm. A damped Gauss-Newton with step halving, e.g. Dixon (1973), solves both problems much more efficiently than Osborne's and our algorithms (which are competitive, although in these cases Osborne's algorithm is faster than our).

Conclusions

The proposed Marquardt algorithm is reliable and efficient, especially in the case of difficult problems. It has a theoretically sound basis, is globally convergent and is not affected by the singularity of J^TJ. We expect it to be suitable for solving general nonlinear least square problems.
For many simple problems a damped Gauss-Newton algorithm may prove more efficient, although it is generally less reliable.

References

Box M.J.; A comparison of several current optimization methods and the use of transformations in constrained problems; Computer J. 9,67-77, 1966.

Brown K.M.; Dennis Jr. J.E., Derivative free analogues of the Levenberg - Marquardt and Gauss algorithms for nonlinear least squares approximation; Numer. Math. 18, 289-297, 1972.

Dixon W.J.(ed.); BMD Biomedical Computer Programs, University of California Press; Berkely - Los Angeles - London, 1973.

Goldstein A, Price J.; An effective algorithm for minimization; Numer. Math. 10, 184-189, 1967.

Heuvel H.M., Huisman R., Lind K.C.J.B.; Quantitative information from X-ray diffraction of nylon-6 yarns I; J. Polym. Sci, Polym. Phys. Ed. 14, 921-940, 1976.

Marquardt D.W.; An algorithm for least squares estimation of nonlinear parameters; J. SIAM 11, 431-441, 1963.

Ortega J.M., Rheinboldt W.C.; Iterative Solutions of Nonlinear Equations in Several Variables; Academic Press, New York - London, 1970.

Osborne M.R.; Some aspects of nonlinear least squares calculations, in Numerical Methods for Nonlinear Optimization (ed. Lootsma F.A.), Academic Press, 1972.

Osborne M.R.; Nonlinear least squares - the Levenberg Algorithm revisited; J. Austral. Math. Soc. 19 (Series B), 343-357, 1976.

Pitha J., Jones R.N.; A comparison of optimization methods for fitting curves to Infrared band envelopes; Can. J. Chem.44, 3031-3050, 1966.

Powell M.J.D.; A hybrid method for nonlinear equations, in Numerical Methods for Nonlinear Algebraic Equations (ed. Rabinowitz P.), Gordon and Breach, London, 1970.

Schweigman C.; Constrained Minimization: Handling of Linear and Nonlinear Constraints; Thesis Technological University Delft (Netherlands), 1974.

Smith F.B., Shanno D.F.; An improved Marquardt procedure for nonlinear regression; Technometrics 13, 63-74, 1971.

Van Houwelingen H., Petiet J., Schweigman C.; Least squares estimation of restricted parameters in physical and chemical models, in Identification and Systems Parameter Estimation (ed. Eykhoff P.), North-Holland Publ. Co., Amsterdam-London, 1973.

Inequality Constraints in Regression Analysis

J.S. Baron and **S.A. Conrad**, Manchester

Summary

Judge and Takayama (1966) have provided a procedure for estimating regression coefficients subject to inequality constraints. This paper examines two areas of application of the procedure and draws attention to the problems facing the potential user.

Keywords

regression analysis; inequality constraints; quadratic programming; prior information.

BACKGROUND

In the field of econometrics, it is rare indeed for a researcher to conduct an empirical investigation, using multiple linear regression methods, without having some prior knowledge regarding the sign (and, perhaps, the approximate magnitude) of some, if not all, of the regression coefficients. In other situations where, for example, the regression coefficients represent transition probabilities, the values of the estimated coefficients must, by definition, fall within the prescribed limits of zero and one. In order to compute the estimated regression coefficients, whilst at the same time taking account of the available prior information, it is mathematically convenient to represent the prior information as a set of linear inequality constraints on the values the estimated coefficients may take.

When the constraints on the coefficients of a linear regression model are of a linear inequality form, Judge and Takayama (1966) have suggested that the estimation of these coefficients can be achieved using quadratic programming. They provide a systematic way of reformulating the standard multiple regression problem in such a way that the Simplex version of the quadratic programming algorithm by Wolfe (1959) can be employed.

The standard multiple regression model can conveniently be written as

$$\underline{y} = \underline{X\beta} + \underline{u} \tag{1.1}$$

The familiar ordinary least squares (OLS) estimator $\underline{\hat{\beta}}$ of $\underline{\beta}$ is derived for the standard model by solving the problem:

$$\text{minimise} \quad (\underline{y} - \underline{X\hat{\beta}})'(\underline{y} - \underline{X\hat{\beta}}) = \underline{y}'\underline{y} - 2\underline{\hat{\beta}}'\underline{X}'\underline{y} + \underline{\hat{\beta}}'\underline{X}'\underline{X\hat{\beta}}$$

$$\text{with respect to} \quad \underline{\hat{\beta}} \tag{1.2}$$

THE JUDGE-TAKAYAMA FORMULATION

In order to incorporate the linear inequality constraints on the regression coefficients, and, at the same time preserve the non-negativity conditions which are necessary in a quadratic programming formulation, Judge and Takayama split the 'coefficients vector' of (1.1) into convenient subsets as follows:

(i) The set of coefficients which are to be non-negative. This set is denoted by $\underline{\beta_1}$.

(ii) The set of coefficients which are to be non-positive. This set is denoted by $\underline{\beta_2}$.

(iii) The set of coefficients for which no sign restrictions are necessary. This set is denoted by $\underline{\beta_3}$.

The method of handling the non-positive sign specification of $\underline{\beta_2}$ and the unrestricted sign specification of $\underline{\beta_3}$, which is described in detail in Judge and Takayama (1966), results in replacing $\underline{\hat{\beta}}$ of (1.2) by an enlarged vector $\underline{\tilde{\beta}}$ which has the required property $\underline{\tilde{\beta}} \geq \underline{0}$.

Thus, with the desired set of linear inequality constraints represented as $\underline{A}\,\underline{\tilde{\beta}} \leq \underline{r}$, the re-formulation of (1.2) becomes:

$$\begin{aligned} &\text{minimise} \quad \underline{\tilde{\beta}}'\,\underline{\tilde{X}}'\,\underline{\tilde{X}}'\,\underline{\tilde{\beta}} - 2\underline{\tilde{\beta}}'\,\underline{\tilde{X}}'\,\underline{y} \\ &\text{subject to} \quad \underline{A}\,\underline{\tilde{\beta}} \leq \underline{r} \\ &\qquad\qquad\quad \underline{\tilde{\beta}} \geq \underline{o} \end{aligned} \tag{2.1}$$

where $\underline{\tilde{X}}$ is the expanded $\underline{X}$ matrix associated with $\underline{\tilde{\beta}}$.

As $\underline{\tilde{X}}'\,\underline{\tilde{X}}$ is positive semi-definite and the constraint set is linear, problem (2.1) can be solved, using Wolfe's quadratic programming algorithm to provide the vector of inequality constrained estimates, $\underline{\tilde{\beta}}$. On a practical level, the user must convert the regression observations matrices $\underline{X}$ and $\underline{y}$ into the quadratic programming input matrices $\underline{\tilde{X}}'\,\underline{\tilde{X}}$ and $\underline{\tilde{X}}'\underline{y}$. A FORTRAN subroutine JTDATA has been written specifically for this purpose for any combination of non-positive, non-negative and sign-unrestricted β_i coefficients.

Two specific applications of the Judge - Takayama procedure are now described. Later, the appropriateness of the procedure is discussed.

EXAMPLE 1: ESTIMATION OF PRICE AND INCOME ELASTICITIES OF DEMAND

Court (1967) provided a model for estimating the demand elasticities for different types of New Zealand meats. Linear logarithmic demand functions of New Zealand beef, mutton and pigmeat were specified as follows:

$$\log \frac{x_i}{N} = e_{io} + \sum_{j=1}^{3} e_{ij} \log \frac{p_j}{p} + e_{iM} \log \frac{M}{Np} + u_i \tag{3.1}$$

where subscripts 1,2,3 refer to beef, mutton and pigmeat, respectively,

x_i represents total consumption of the ith meat,

p_i is the retail price of the ith meat,

N is the number of consumers,

p is the retail price index,

M is total expenditure on consumer goods and services,

u_i is a disturbance term for the ith equation.

As all the variables are transformed to logarithms, the price elasticities

$$e_{ij} = \frac{p_i}{x_i} \frac{\partial x_i}{\partial p_j} \qquad (i,j = 1,2,3)$$

and income elasticities $e_{iM} = \frac{M}{x_i} \frac{\partial x_i}{\partial M}$ $\qquad (i = 1,2,3)$

appear directly as coefficients in (3.1).
The intercept for each equation is denoted by e_{io} $(i = 1,2,3)$.

Using annual data from 1950-1960, Court calculated the following OLS estimates of the elasticities.

Beef equation	Mutton equation	Pigmeat equation
$e_{11} = -0.780$	$e_{21} = 0.785$	$e_{31} = 0.547$
$e_{12} = 0.606$	$e_{22} = -0.342$	$e_{32} = 0.792$
$e_{13} = 0.047$	$e_{23} = -0.302$	$e_{33} = -1.251$
$e_{1M} = -0.231$	$e_{2M} = 0.424$	$e_{3M} = 0.968.$

(3.2)

Contrary to prior expectations, the income elasticity, e_{1M}, in the beef equation is negative and, in the mutton equation, the cross-price elasticity with pigmeat, e_{23}, is negative.

As meat is thought to be a normal, non-Giffen good with a high degree of substitutability between the different types of meat, the prior information regarding the signs of the elasticities would produce the following set of constraints.

Beef equation	Mutton equation	Pigmeat equation
$e_{11} \leq 0$	$e_{21} \geq 0$	$e_{31} \geq 0$
$e_{12} \geq 0$	$e_{22} \leq 0$	$e_{32} \geq 0$
$e_{13} \geq 0$	$e_{23} \geq 0$	$e_{33} \leq 0$
$e_{1M} \geq 0$	$e_{2M} \geq 0$	$e_{3M} \geq 0$

(3.3)

By forming the vector $\underset{\sim}{\beta}$ for each equation and using the Judge - Takayama procedure, the following estimates of the elasticities were produced.

Beef equation	Mutton equation	Pigmeat equation
$e_{11} = -0.780$	$e_{21} = 0.650$	$e_{31} = 0.547$
$e_{12} = 0.505$	$e_{22} = -0.546$	$e_{32} = 0.792$
$e_{13} = 0.098$	$e_{23} = 0.000$	$e_{33} = -1.251$
$e_{14} = 0.000$	$e_{24} = 0.515$	$e_{3M} = 0.968$

(3.4)

Predictions of the demand for New Zealand meat were made for the years 1961-1963 using the estimated elasticities from (3.2) and from (3.4). The predictions were compared to the actual demand for these years. The sum of squared deviations between actual and predicted values was 30.1 for (3.4) and 41.1 for (3.2). (It should be noted here that Court, himself, re-formulated the model to take account of an equality constraint stemming from the utility maximisation theory. The estimated elasticities from this formulation still had some 'wrong signs' but the predictions were closer to the actual demands than even (3.4)).

However, the fundamental question as to whether the results (3.4) have truly reflected the prior information is at issue. In principal, the Judge - Takayama method was used on this data because, for instance, the income elasticity of beef is generally taken for granted as being positive whereas the unconstrained procedure produced a negative estimate. In practice the Judge - Takayama method made this estimate zero.

It is suggested here that no more economists would be happy with a zero income elasticity than would be happy with a negative income elasticity. In other words, the method has not really reflected the true 'a priori' feelings about the value of this coefficient. The method has simply moved the violating coefficients to their corresponding constraint boundaries.

In general, when a subjective constraint of the form

$$a \leq \beta_i \leq b$$

is imposed, it usually means that β_i has a value "somewhere between a and b" and could often mean, in fact, that β_i is unlikely to have the value a or b.

It would seem inevitable that, if only one or two constraints are initially violated then a quadratic programming algorithm will naturally tend to the constraint limit(s). For there to be any place for the Judge - Takayama method it must be in an example with a large number of initial constraint violations and one for which the constraint boundaries are 'reasonable' values for the coefficients to take.

EXAMPLE 2: ESTIMATION OF TRANSITION PROBABILITIES

This example was inspired by Horowitz (1972) and is an analysis of changes in the U.K. Income Distribution using a first-order Markov process as the underlying model. The purpose of the study is to estimate the probability that, starting from income class i at t, a family will enter income class j at t+1. The first-order Markov process is represented as

$$\Pi_{j,t+1} = \sum_{j=1}^{n} P_{ij}\Pi_{it} + U_{j,t+1} \; ; \; j = 1,2,\ldots,n \qquad (4.1)$$

where n is the number of income groups,

$\Pi_{j,t+1}$ denotes the probability of being in income class j at time t+1,

P_{ij} denotes the probability that, starting from income class i at time t, a family will enter income class j at time t+1,

$U_{j,t+1}$ us a stochastic disturbance term.

The transition probabilities $P_{ij}(i,j = 1,2,\ldots,n)$ are the coefficients to be estimated. Regression procedures can be used to provide the estimates because a feature of Markov processes is that each P_{ij} is assumed fixed over time.

As the P_{ij}'s are transition probabilities, the following constraints are automatic.

$$0 \leq P_{ij} \leq 1 \quad \text{for all i and j} \qquad (4.2)$$

$$\sum_{j=1}^{n} P_{ij} = 1 \qquad (4.3)$$

Two regression analyses were performed. Transition probabilities were estimated

(a) subject only to constraint (4.3). The restricted least squares procedure for dealing with equality constraints (described, for instance, in Johnston (1972, p.157)) was employed.

(b) subject to both constraints (4.3) and (4.2). The Judge - Takayama procedure was employed.

U.K. Income Distribution data for the years 1964-73 were taken from the Family Expenditure Surveys and deflated, using the Index of Retail Prices, to 1962 prices. The number, n, of income groups was then reduced to four - (1) under £1000, (2) £1000-1499, (3) £1500-£1999 and (4) £2000 or more - and the proportions in each group were taken as the values of the Π_{it}'s.
The estimated transition probabilities were:

Regression (a)

$$
\begin{array}{llll}
P_{11} = .55 & P_{12} = .24 & P_{13} = .02 & P_{14} = .19 \\
P_{21} = .53 & P_{22} = .68 & P_{23} = .10 & P_{24} = -.31 \\
P_{31} = .61 & P_{32} = .09 & P_{33} = .36 & P_{34} = -.06 \\
P_{41} = -.27 & P_{42} = -.35 & P_{43} = .50 & P_{44} = 1.12
\end{array}
\qquad (4.4)
$$

Regression (b)

$$
\begin{array}{llll}
P_{11} = .81 & P_{12} = .19 & P_{13} = 0 & P_{14} = 0 \\
P_{21} = 0 & P_{22} = .66 & P_{23} = .34 & P_{24} = 0 \\
P_{31} = .52 & P_{32} = 0 & P_{33} = 0 & P_{34} = .48 \\
P_{41} = 0 & P_{42} = 0 & P_{43} = .47 & P_{44} = .53
\end{array}
\qquad (4.5)
$$

CONCLUSIONS

In this paper a procedure for estimating regression coefficients subject to linear inequality constraints is outlined. Two examples of the application of the procedure have been described with a view to assessing its practical use.

Example 1 brings to light some of the potential problems of using a quadratic programming based method when only sign constraints exist. Examination of (3.4) shows that the coefficients e_{1M} and e_{23}, which initially violated (3.3), have simply been pushed to their constraint limit of zero. The results (3.4) could have been achieved more quickly by eliminating the variables whose coefficients violated (3.3) and using OLS on the remaining variables. An added advantage of the latter method is that the standard errors can be estimated. Also, there is the question as to whether the prior information regarding, say, e_{1M} has been adequately reflected in the solutions (3.4). The problem arises because no attempt has been made to incorporate any prior knowledge regarding the magnitude of e_{1M}. The mixed estimation procedure advocated by Theil and

Goldberger (1961) or the Bayesian approach, a good example of which is given in Zellner and Richard (1973), each allow the prior information regarding the magnitude of a coefficient to be incorporated into a computational procedure.

Example 2 provides a better model for the use of the Judge - Takayama procedure. Regression (a) results contain nonsense values for some probabilities whereas Regression (b) produces a believable set of probabilities (with the possible exception of those in row 3).

It is thought that the estimation of transition probabilities, using aggregate data, may provide the greatest potential application of the Judge - Takayama procedure. Interested readers are referred to McCarthy and Ryan (1977) for a further example of its use in this field.

REFERENCES

Court R.H., Utility Maximisation and the demand for New Zealand meats, Econometrica, 35, 424-446, 1967

Horowitz A.R., Estimating racial differences in income dynamics from aggregate data, Applied Economics, 4,221-234, 1972

Johnston J., Econometric Methods, McGraw-Hill, 1972

Judge G.G., and Takayama T., Inequality restrictions in regression analysis, J. Am. Statist. Ass., 61, 166-181, 1966

McCarthy C. and Ryan T.M., Estimates of voter transition probabilities from the British General Elections of 1974, J. Roy. Statist. Soc. (A), 140, 78-85, 1977

Theil H. and Goldberger A.S., On pure and mixed statistical estimation in Econometrics, Int. Econ. Rev., 2, 65-77, 1961

Wolfe P., The Simplex method for quadratic programming, Econometrica, 27, 382-398, 1959

Zellner A. and Richard J.F., Use of prior information in the analysis and estimation of Cobb-Douglas production function models, Int. Econ. Rev., 14, 107-119, 1973

Mean Squares and Expected Mean Squares from Full Rank Reparametrizations of Random Models

G.R. Bryce, D.T. Scott and M.V. Carter, Provo

It is demonstrated that a full rank reparameterization of a random model is equivalent to a sequence of reparameterizations of the cell means model. A sequential orthogonalization operation on the matrix of independent and dependent variables is introduced and the associated distribution theory is reviewed. General rules for obtaining expected mean squares from any crossed model whether mixed or random are given.

KEYWORDS: Expected Mean Squares, Random Models, Cell Means Model

1. INTRODUCTION

The relationship between analysis of variance (Anova) and regression analysis is well known. However it is not necessary to use this relationship explicitly in balanced designs since simple rules for calculating sums of squares have been developed. These simple formulas can be derived directly from the regression approach and are a direct results of the orthogonality of the factors in a balanced design. When this orthogonality is lost however, such formulas are invalidated. Before the advent of the large scale electronic computer Yates (1934) developed several methods for handling the non-orthogonal case using "desk calculator" methods. Since his exact methods can be obtained using the regression approach, regression type analysis has become standard for the analysis of unbalanced designs.

No method was suggested by Yates for calculating expected mean square coefficients since he was dealing strictly with the fixed model. Although Yates' methods were applied to random models there was a delay of some 30 years before efficient general methods were developed for finding expected mean squares. These methods have generally required the use of the zero-one design matrix associated with the usual overparameterized model.

Applying the regression approach directly to the design matrix of the overparameterized model is not completely straight forward however. Among the problems created are the unavailability of certain sums of squares, excessive computer storage, and the use of nonunique solutions to the normal equations. These problems can be eliminated by the use of a full rank reparameterization of the random model.

In this paper we will present methodology for analyzing unbalanced designs where a random model is appropriate. We will deal primarily with models which contain only crossed factors although extensions to nested factors as well as mixed models will be suggested. In the section which follows we shall briefly lay the foundation for a general approach through the cell means model.

2. LINEAR MODELS

The cell means model is the most basic of all linear models. It has been advocated by many authors (Urqunart et. al., 1973; Kutner, 1974; Hocking and Speed, 1975; Searle, 1977) for the fixed effects case. However, we feel that it is an appropriate starting point for any model, since by a linear transformation of the cell means model the usual overparameterized model as well as any other model presently recommended for use, is obtained. This approach provides greater insight into the nature of the usual overparameterized model as well as transformations thereof.

2.1 A Recursive Direct Product Operator

In order to consider a general r factor model it will be useful to define the following matrix operator. Let

$$E_i = [\underline{e}_i | F_i],\ i = 1, 2, \ldots, r$$

be partitioned matrices with $\underline{e}_i$, being column vectors and F_i matrices. We define

$$E = G_r = \underset{i=1}{\overset{r}{Ⓡ}} E_i$$

recursively as

$$G_1 = E_1$$
$$G_2 = [G_1 \otimes \underline{e}_2 | G_1 \otimes F_2]$$
$$\vdots$$
$$G_r = [G_{r-1} \otimes \underline{e}_r | G_{r-1} \otimes F_r]$$

where the direct or Kronecker product is defined as $C \otimes B = (c_{ij}B)$. The objective of this definition is to achieve an ordering of the partitions of E which we will relate directly to factors in the model. Note that

$$E' = \underset{i=1}{\overset{r}{Ⓡ}} E_i'.$$

2.2 The Cell Means Model

We define the cell means model as

$$\underline{y} = W\underline{\mu} + \underline{\varepsilon} \tag{1}$$

where $\underline{y}$ is an n x 1 vector of responses, W an n x s matrix of zero's and ones such that a single one appears in each row, $\underline{\mu}$ is a s x 1 vector of population means sampled by the experimenter and $\underline{\varepsilon}$ is an n x 1 vector of iid error components. We will assume that there are r factors in the model with s_i levels each and that

$$s = \prod_{i=1}^{r} s_i$$

In its most general formulation we would also allow for the constraints

$$G\underline{\mu} = \underline{g} \tag{2}$$

on the cell means. Such constraints will generally relate to the nonexistance of some interactions in the model although other constraints are possible.

If observations are obtained on each cell mean then (1) will be a full rank model and each of the cell means will be estimable. However, in most analyses the objective is consideration of certain linear combinations of the cell means. Whether interest lies in estimating these linear combinations or their variances a reparameterization of (1) which will provide information relative to the factors inherent in the experimental design would seem to be useful.

2.3 Nonsingular and Singular-Nonsingular Reparameterizations

The simplest reparameterization of (1) is given by

$$\begin{aligned} \underline{y} &= WA^{-1}A\underline{\mu} + \underline{\varepsilon} \\ &= Z \quad \underline{\delta} + \underline{\varepsilon} \end{aligned} \tag{3}$$

where $\underline{\delta} = A\underline{\mu}$ and A is nonsingular i.e., we have a nonsingular reparameterization of (1). We will want to define A to reflect the various main effects and their interactions. To reduce the tedium inherent in this effort, we define C_i as an s_i-1 by s_i matrix of contrasts of levels of the ith main effect i.e., $C_i\underline{j}_i = 0$ where $\underline{j}_i$ is an s_i vector of ones. Now, letting $\underline{m}_i = 1/s_i\underline{j}_i$ we define $A_i = [\underline{m}_i | C_i']$ and note that $A_i^{-1} = [\underline{j}_i | \underline{C}_i'(C_iC_i')^{-1}]$ from which we obtain

$$A = \underset{i=1}{\overset{r}{\circledR}} A_i \text{ and } A^{-1} = \underset{i=1}{\overset{r}{\circledR}} A_i^{-1}. \tag{4}$$

Using (4) the various partitions of $\underline{\delta}$ are linear combinations of $\underline{\mu}$ corresponding to the main effects and interactions of a full model. If some interactions are known *a priori* to be null i.e., in (2) $G\underline{\mu} = \underline{0}$ for an appropriate choice of G, inclusion of the constraint is equivalent to dropping the appropriate columns of Z.

The usual overparameterized model is also a reparameterization of (1). However, in this case the transformation is accomplished through a singular matrix i.e.,

$$\begin{aligned} \underline{y} &= WBB^g\underline{\mu} + \underline{\varepsilon} \\ &= X \quad \underline{\theta} + \underline{\varepsilon} \end{aligned} \tag{5}$$

where $\underline{\theta} = B^g\underline{\mu}$ and where B^g is a generalized inverse of B such that $BB^g = I$. If

$$B_i = [\underline{j}_i | I_i], \; i = 1, 2, \ldots, r$$

where I_i is an identity matrix of order s_i then we can define

$$B = \underset{i=1}{\overset{r}{\circledR}} B_i \tag{6}$$

and X = WB is the usual design matrix of zeros and ones. We note that B is an s x p matrix, where

$$p = \prod_{i=1}^{r} (s_i + 1)$$

and thus we have performed a singular transformation of (1).

Since $\underline{\theta} = B^g \underline{\mu}$ involves a generalized inverse of B there is an infinite variety of definitions for it (see Bryce et. al., 1976 for some examples). This indeterminancy in the definition of $\underline{\theta}$ has been the source of much confusion and has led to considerable debate in the statistical world. (See e.g. Speed et. al., 1978 and their references).

The overparameterized model (5) is generally considered the starting point in the consideration of Anova models. However it is often thought useful to reparameterize it to a model of full rank. This can be accomplished by considering

$$\underline{y} = WCC^g \underline{\theta} + \underline{\varepsilon} \tag{7}$$

where C is p x s, XC is full rank and C^g is a generalized inverse of C such that $XCC^g = X$. Since XC is full rank it follows from XC = WBC that BC is also full rank and therefore from $C^g \underline{\theta} = C^g B^g \underline{\mu}$ that $C^g B^g = (BC)^{-1}$ irrespective of the choices of g-inverse for C and B. Thus we have followed our singular transformation (5) with a nonsingular transformation (7) but the end result is that we have returned to our original nonsingular transformation and (3) and (7) are equivalent.

The choice of C is somewhat arbitrary since we require only that XC be of full rank. However, it is convenient to choose C such that

$$BC = A^{-1} \tag{8}$$

and thus $A = (BC)^{-1} = C^g B^g$ and (3) and (7) will be identical i.e.,

$$\underline{\delta} = A\underline{\mu} = C^g \underline{\theta}. \tag{9}$$

C^g is easily obtained from the condition $XCC^g = X$ by premultiplying by $(C'X'XC)^{-1}C'X'$ which with (8) yields

$$C^g = AB. \tag{10}$$

2.4 The Random Model

If the populations whose means are represented in (1) are a random sample of possible populations then our interest will generally be in components of random variation rather than in fixed relations among the selected population means. In this case $\underline{\mu}$ of (1) becomes a vector of random variables with

$$E(\underline{\mu}) = \bar{\mu}\underline{j}$$

where $\bar{\mu}$ is the overall or general mean. The variance-covariance structure of $\underline{\mu}$ will depend upon the structure of the experiment and assumptions about the underlying variability of the experimental material. Our model is not complete until such assumptions are made.

If we assume variability due to main factors and their interactions, e.g., due to rows, columns and row-column interaction in a two-way layout, then the structure and assumptions given in Eisenharts (1947) model II are appropriate. In this case we are essentially defining

$$\underline{\mu} = B\underline{\theta}$$

where

$$\underline{\theta} = B^{-}\underline{\mu} \tag{11}$$

and

$$(B^{-})' = \underset{i=1}{\overset{r}{Ⓡ}} [\underline{m}_i | I_i - \underline{m}_i \underline{j}_i']$$

is a g-inverse of B. With this definition $\underline{\theta}$ will consist of the usual effects i.e., deviations of marginal means from overall means etc. Using Eisenharts definition of effects (11) and his assumptions concerning the variance of the effects along with $E(\underline{\mu})$ we have

$$E(\underline{\theta}) = \begin{bmatrix} \bar{\mu} \\ \underline{0} \end{bmatrix} \quad \text{and} \quad V(\underline{\theta}) = \begin{bmatrix} 0 & \underline{0}' \\ \underline{0} & D \end{bmatrix} \tag{12}$$

where D is a diagonal matrix consisting of the variances of the effects. Applying (12) to model (5) we have

$$E(\underline{y}) = \bar{\mu}\underline{j} \quad \text{and} \quad V(\underline{y}) = XV(\underline{\theta})X' + \sigma^2 I. \tag{13}$$

The definition (11) and assumption (12) when appended to (5) constitute a complete definition for our random model.

We note that if some of the variance components are known *a priori* to be null i.e., (2) is satisfied for some G, the corresponding elements of $\underline{\theta}$ will be identically zero and the corresponding columns of X can be omitted.

3. ANALYSIS OF UNBALANCED DESIGNS

Much of the literature on the analysis of unbalanced designs in random models deals with the application of the methods of Yates (1934). On a more practical level however, regression methods are commonly used to obtain approximate solutions for the Anova in variance component models. The major problem, irrespective of the technique used, has been in finding the expected values of the mean squares so that tests and estimation can be carried out.

Hartley (1967) presents the first general technique for finding expected mean square coefficients. It has been shown (Bryce and Carter, 1970; Gaylor et. al. 1970) that the Doolittle and Cholesky (square root) methods of factoring the normal equations are Anova algorithms to which Hartley's approach is applicable.

Of course it is not always necessary to form the normal equations. Formally we consider the system

$$[X|\underline{y}]$$

where X is an n x p design matrix and $\underline{y}$ a vector (or matrix in the case of multivariate problems) of response variables, which is operated on by an operator Q yielding

$$Q[X|\underline{y}] \Rightarrow [T|\underline{t}] \tag{14}$$

where T is p x p and upper triangular. Q can be any one of the least three basic algorithms --Cholesky (square root), Householder, or Givens (plane rotations)-- each with several variations. (For computational details see Stewart (1073) pages 131, 231, and 351, respectively).

It is important to note that all of the information carried in $[X|\underline{y}]$ is now carried in $[T|\underline{t}]$ thus greatly reducing our storage requirements. As a consequence we can center our attention on the distribution of $\underline{t}$ and realize considerable economy in computations. Bryce and Carter (1974) derive the distribution of $\underline{t}$ in the context of a general mixed model. For the random model (5) with condition (13) we would have

$$\underline{t} \sim (TE(\underline{\theta}),\ TV(\underline{\theta})T' + \sigma^2 H) \tag{15}$$

where H is essentially an identity matrix with some null diagonal elements. It is well known that a sequential analysis of variance is obtained by summing the squares of certain subsets of $\underline{t}$. Assuming that the elements of $\underline{\theta}$ are independent

$$E(\underline{t}_i{}'\underline{t}_i) = df_i\sigma^2 + \sum_{j\leq i} \sigma_j{}^2 tr(T_{ij}{}'T_{ij}) \tag{16}$$

where $\underline{t}_i$ is a partition of $\underline{t}$ corresponding to a particular factor in the model and T_{ij} is an analogous partition of T by both rows and columns (for details see Bryce and Carter; 1974).

Unfortunately, the use of the design matrix in (14) is not without problems. Since the Q operator represents a class of sequential orthogonalization procedures, the sums of squares obtained from $\underline{t}$ will be sequentially adjusted. Thus various reorderings of the factors in the model will be necessary to obtain sums of squares equivalent to those of the balanced model i.e., having the same components in their expectations. However, since X and thus T is rank deficient certain orderings of the model will yield sums of squares which are identically zero. For example, sums of squares analogous to Yates' (1934) method of weighted squares of means can not be calculated using this approach. Speed and Hocking (1974) overcome this problem by using the general linear hypothesis. Although they provide methodology for obtaining expected mean squares their approach seems unduly complicated.

Another serious problem associated with the use of the overparameterized model is the inflation of computer storage requirements. For any crossed model thre are p/s times as many columns in X as are needed to carry the necessary information. Thus when storing T we will need p(p+1)/s(s+1) times as many storage locations using the less than full rank matrix as will be necessary for the equivalent full rank matrix. For example a 3 factor design with each factor at 4 levels will require 3.8 times as many storage locations.

Methods developed for finding expected mean square coefficients in general crossed models have depended upon the use of the less than full rank design matrix. However, Paik and Federer (1974) have suggested a method for obtaining these coefficients from (7). In the following section we shall formulate this approach in matrix notation and provide simple rules for applying the method to a general r-way model.

4. FULL RANK REPARAMETERIZATION IN THE RANDOM MODEL

The choice of the matrices C_i used in defining A (4) will depend upon the emphasis we wish to place on the linear combinations $\underline{\delta}$. If $\underline{\mu}$ is a fixed vector then the C_i will be chosen to reflect any individual degree of freedom contrasts of particular interest. When A is defined through (4) the model (3) will yield direct estimates and hypotheses tests on the main effects and interactions of the fixed model as well as the individual contrasts. On the otherhand if $\underline{\mu}$ is a random vector as defined in section 2.4 our interest will be primarily in the economy of storage and broadened utility of the full rank model (3). In this case the matrices C_i need only span a space of the appropriate dimension. Therefore, to simplify the presentation let us now assume that the contrasts in C_i are orthogonal and normalized i.e.,

$$C_i C_i' = I_i^*, \; i = 1, 2, \ldots, r \qquad (17)$$

Where I_i^* is an identity matrix of order $s_i - 1$.

4.1 A General Two-way Random Model

Having laid the foundation in terms of a general r-way model let us now consider the simpler two-way model to illustrate the subsequent results. Simple rules for application to general r-way models will be given. Using the definitions of section 2.4 we note that

$$E(\underline{\delta}) = \bar{\mu}A\underline{j} = \begin{bmatrix} \bar{\mu} \\ \underline{0} \end{bmatrix} \qquad (18)$$

since by definition (4), each row of A after the first will be a linear comparison. Using (11) and (12) we have

$$V(\underline{\theta}) = \text{diag}\,(0, \sigma_1^2 I_1, \sigma_2^2 I_2, \sigma_{12}^2 I_1 \otimes I_2) \qquad (19)$$

where σ_1^2, σ_2^2 and σ_{12}^2 are main factor and interaction variance components respectively. Now using (17) and (19) we have

$$\begin{aligned} V(\underline{\delta}) &= AV(\underline{\mu})A' = ABV(\underline{\theta})B'A' \\ &= \text{diag}(\sigma_0^2, \sigma_1'^2 I_1^*, \sigma_2'^2 I_2^*, \sigma_{12}^2 I_1^* \otimes I_1^*) \end{aligned} \qquad (20)$$

where

$$\sigma_0^2 = (s_2\sigma_1^2 + s_1\sigma_2^2 + \sigma_{12}^2)/s, \; \sigma_1'^2 = \sigma_1^2 + \sigma_{12}^2/s_2, \text{ and}$$

$$\sigma_2'^2 = \sigma_2 + \sigma_{12}^2/s_1. \qquad (21)$$

Using (18) and (20) we now complete the specification of our full rank random model as (3) with

$$E(\underline{y}) = \bar{\mu}\underline{j} \text{ and } V(\underline{y}) = ZV(\underline{\delta})Z' + \sigma^2 I.$$

Computationally we now wish to apply the Q operator to the system $[Z|\underline{y}]$ i.e.,

$$Q[Z|\underline{y}] \Longrightarrow [T|\underline{t}]. \qquad (22)$$

Now $[T|\underline{t}]$ of (22) carries all of the information formerly contained in (14) at a much reduced storage cost. The distribution of $\underline{t}$ of (22) can be shown to be

$$\underline{t} \sim (TE(\underline{\delta}), TV(\underline{\delta})T' + \sigma^2 I) \qquad (23)$$

which is clearly analogous to (15). Note that (14) requires $p(p+3)/2$ storage locations while (22) requires only $s(s+3)/2$.

The calculation of expected mean square coefficients for a given ordering of the model and a given term in the model is a straightforward application of (16) with the variances σ_i^2 being replaced by the "primed" variances given in (21). Thus if the model is ordered as indicated by (19) and (20) is partitioned as

$$[T|\underline{t}] = \left[\begin{array}{cccc|c} T_{00} & T_{01} & T_{02} & T_{03} & t_0 \\ 0 & T_{11} & T_{12} & T_{13} & \underline{t}_1 \\ 0 & 0 & T_{22} & T_{23} & \underline{t}_2 \\ 0 & 0 & 0 & T_{33} & \underline{t}_3 \end{array}\right] \qquad (24)$$

the sum of the squares due to the second main effect $\underline{t}_2'\underline{t}_2$ has

$$E(\underline{t}_2'\underline{t}_2) = (s_2-1)\sigma^2 + k_{22}\sigma_2'^2 + k_{23}\sigma_{12}^2$$
$$= (s_2-1)\sigma^2 + k_{22}\sigma_2^2 + (k_{23} + k_{22}/s_1)\sigma_{12}^2$$

where $k_{ij} = tr(T_{ij}T_{ij}')$.

As we have indicated previously the sums of squares obtained from (22) will correspond to a sequential fit of the model. One could use general linear hypothesis theory and the so called "backward solution" of (24) to obtain other sum's of squares. However, the Q operator and a reordering of the columns of T can be used to obtain any sum of squares of interest with fewer computations. Let T^* be a reordering of the factor associated partitions of T. Then

$$Q[T^*|\underline{t}] \Rightarrow [T_r|\underline{t}_r] \qquad (25)$$

and $\underline{t}_r$ will contain information on the new sequential fit of the model and T_r contains information on the corresponding expected mean squares. The reader will note that we need not go to $[Z|\underline{y}]$ to obtain information on our reordered model. Rather we may work directly with permutations of T and obtain all necessary information. It is also important to note that even though we can reorder a main effect after an interaction, the interaction variance component is still present in the expected sum of squares.

When each term in a model is ordered last the resulting sums of squares correspond to those obtained by applying Yates (1934) method of weighted squares of means. If one wishes to obtain these sums of squares we need not use (25), but rather the Q operator and $R' = T^{-1}$. First partition R' by columns corresponding to the terms of the model e.g.,

$$R' = [R_0, R_1, R_2, R_3]$$

then operate on the systems $[R_i|\underline{t}]$ i.e.,

$$Q[R_i|\underline{t}] \Rightarrow [R_i^*|\underline{r}_i] \qquad (26)$$

Then $\underline{r}_i'\underline{r}_i$, i = 1, 2 will be the sums of squares for each main effect ordered last in the model with expectation

$$E(\underline{r}_i'\underline{r}_i) = (s_i-1)\sigma^2 + \sigma_i'^2 tr(R_i^{*\prime}R_i^*)$$

In practice the choice of algorithms for (22) will depend upon the amount of computer storage available. If $[Z|\underline{y}]$ cannot be contained entirely in the available memory then either the Cholesky or Givens algorithm would be recommended. While the Cholesky procedure requires the use of the normal equations and thus potentially may be somewhat less accurate the Givens algorithm generally requires more computations. For the subsequent calculations (25) and (27) either the Householder or Givens may be used with equal success. Although the Householder transformations will require less computations, operating on rows with the Givens may be more convenient than the column operations of the Householder.

4.2 Generalizations to Higher-way Models

We now state general rules for finding the "primed" variance omponents such as (21). Let M be an upper triangular matrix of expected mean square coefficients obtained by the procedures of section 4.2 and let $\underline{\sigma}$ be a vector of the variance components for the model. The set of expected mean squares can be written as $ML\underline{\sigma} = M\underline{\sigma}^*$, where $\underline{\sigma}^*$ is the vector of "primed" variance component: i.e., $\underline{\sigma}^* = L\underline{\sigma}$. We wish to find ML and therefore we need L. Let the r main effect variance components be labeled with a unique subscript and let the interaction variance components be labeled with the subscripts of the interacting main effects. If ϕ' is any "primed" variance component then the following rules will yield the appropriate linear combination of the true variance components.

1) Any variance component whose subscripts include all of the subscripts of ϕ' is a candidate for inclusion in the linear combination.
2) The coefficient for any included variance component in the linear combination will be the reciprocal of the product of the number of levels of each main effect represented in the subscripts of the included variance component after omitting all of the subscripts of ϕ'.

As an example of the rules suppose we have a model with four main effects and we seek the linear combination represented by $\phi' = \sigma'^2_{12}$. In this case σ^2_{12}, σ^2_{123}, σ^2_{124} and σ^2_{1234} would all be candidate terms by rule 1. By rule 2 the linear combination is

$$\sigma'^2_{12} \doteq \sigma^2_{12} + \frac{1}{s_3}\sigma^2_{123} + \frac{1}{s_4}\sigma^2_{124} + \frac{1}{s_3 s_4}\sigma^2_{1234} . \qquad (27)$$

It should be noted that these rules are also applicable in the special case of balanced designs.

5. EXTENSIONS - MIXED AND NESTED MODELS

If some of the main effects in our general model (1) are considered fixed we will continue to use (3) or equivalently (7). Computationally the procedures of Section 4 will remain the same except we will add a rule which has the effect of eliminating fixed terms from the linear combination of variance components. Thus we state rule

1') Eliminate the subscript of ϕ' from the subscripts of each candidate variance component. If any of the remaining subscripts are associated with fixed factors omit the variance component from consideration.

Applying the modified rules to $\phi' = \sigma'^2_{12}$ where we assume main effect 3 to be fixed we would omit σ^2_{123} and σ^2_{1234} from (27). The expected mean squares thus obtained will correspond to model I of Hocking (1973).

Although a general approach to nested models is not fully developed one may consider them as a special case of the general crossed model in which a nested term is equivalent to pooling a main effect and an interaction. For example, for a two factor model with the second main effect being nested in the first we would replace the relations (20) with

$$\sigma'^2_1 = \sigma^2_1 + \frac{\sigma^2_2}{s_2}, \quad \sigma'^2_2 = \frac{\sigma^2_2}{s_1}, \text{ and } \sigma^2_{12} = \sigma^2_2 . \tag{28}$$

The correct Anova table would be obtained by pooling the sums of squares and their expectations for the second main effect and the interaction effect and using the relations (28).

6. CONCLUSION

Using the basic cell means model as a starting point we have demonstrated that a full rank reparameterization of a random model is equivalent to performing a sequence of reparameterizations on the cell means model. With this foundation properly laid, a sequential orthogonalization operation on the matrix of independent and dependent variables was introduced. Distribution theory relating to such operations was reviewed and expected values of sums of squares were given. Finally, general rules were given for obtaining expected mean squares from any completely crossed model whether mixed or random.

We emphasize that the advantage in the full rank reparameterization is primarily computational. It is obvious that the savings in computer storage will be a function of the design but only in rare cases will the savings be less than half the core storage required for the design matrix. Savings will also be realized because of the increased accuracy and decreased number of computations realized by judicious choice of the suggested algorithms.

The methods presented in this paper are not available in any computer program. However, since the Rummage program (see Bryce 1975) uses (3) for fixed models and (5) for random models M of section 4.2 is obtained automatically by calling each main effect in the model fixed. The definition of the variance components are then easily obtained using the general rules of sections 4.2 and 5. For further information on the Rummage program contact the authors at Department of Statistics, Brigham Young University, Provo, Utah 84602.

7. REFERENCES

Bryce, G.R. and M.W. Carter (1970). "A Unified Method for the Analysis of of Unbalanced Designs." Paper presented at the Wester Region Meeting of Am. Stat. Assoc., 5 June 1970.

Bryce, G.R. (1974). "MAD--The Analysis of Variance in Unbalanced Designs-- A Software Package." Compstat 1974 Proc. on Computational Stat. Ed. G. Bruckmann, F. Ferschl, and L. Schmitterer. Vienna, Austria: Physica--Verlag.

Bryce, G.R. (1975). MAD: An analysis of variance program for unbalanced designs. JRSS, Series C 24:350-352.

Bryce, G.R., M.W. Carter and M.W. Reeder (1976), "Nonsingular and Singular - Nonsingular Transformations in the Fixed Effects Model" presented at 9th Inter. Biometric Conf., Boston, Mass., August 1976.

Eisenhart, C. (1947). The Assumptions Underlying the Analysis of Variance. Biometrics Vol 3:1-21.

Gaylor, D.W., H.L. Lucas and R.L. Anderson (1970). "Calculation of Expected Mean Squares by the Abbreviated Doolittle and Square Root Methods." Biometrics 26:641-655.

Hartley, H.O. (1967). Expectations, Variances and Covariances of Anova Mean Squares by 'Synthesis'. Biometrics 18:148-159.

Hocking, R.R. (1973). A discussion of the two-way mixed model, The American Statistician 211:148-152.

Hocking, R.R. and F.M. Speed (1975). "A Full Rank Analysis of Some Linear Model Problems." J. Am. Stat. Assoc., 70:706-712.

Kutner, M.H. (1974). Hypothesis Testing in Linear Models. The American Statistician 28:98-100.

Paik, U.B. and W.T. Federer (1974). "Analysis of Nonorthogonal n-Way Classifications". The Annals of Statistics 2:1000-1021.

Searle, S.R. (1977). Analysis of Variance of Unbalanced Data from 3-way and Higher-Order Classifications." Biometrics Unit, Cornell University, No. BU-606-M. Ithaca, New York.

Speed, F.M. and R.R. Hocking (1974). Computation of Expectations, Variances and Covariances of Anova Mean Squares. Biometrics 30:157-169.

Stewart, G.W. (1973). Introduction to Matrix Computations. New York:Academic Press, Inc.

Urquhart, N.S., D.L. Weeks and C.R. Henderson (1973). Estimation Associated with Linear Models; A Revisitation. Communications in Statistics 1:303-330.

Yates, F. (1934). The Analysis of Multiple Classifications with Unequal Numbers in the Difference Classes. J. Am. Stat. Assoc. 29:51-66.

The Efficient Estimation of a Constrained Variable Regression Model

S.A. Conrad, Manchester

Summary

Sum-constrained dependent variable regression models have been found useful in many diverse fields of economics and business. This paper describes how the parameters of such models may be readily estimated, and discusses briefly their use in representing marketing competition.

Keywords

regression analysis; generalised least-squares; sum-constrained models; model optimisation; marketing competition.

Introduction

There exist a number of situations where dependent variables in regression models should be sum-constrained. For example, household consumption expenditures for different categories of goods should sum to household total consumption expenditure, individual company sales should sum to industry sales, and market shares should sum to one.

In this paper we consider the estimation of the parameters of a model where this sum-constraint is automatically satisfied. Such a model is the multiplicative "attraction" model, discussed in detail by Bell et al (1975). Nakanishi (1972) has shown that this model is not intrinsically nonlinear, but can in fact be linearised for regression purposes. Bultez and Naert (1975) have considered the problems raised by the estimation of this model. Since there is contemporaneous correlation of the disturbances (e.g. the market share of one brand depends upon the levels of the attribute variables of the other brands), an iterative generalised least-squares (GLS) procedure is appropriate, with the variance-covariance matrix being estimated by the residuals at each iteration.

The paper shows how such a procedure may be readily implemented on a computer. It makes use of the fact that the procedure can be shown to reduce to a sequence of matrix operations on the original data block. These matrix operations are ones that are available in the software of most computer systems. The paper then discusses the use of such models in representing marketing competition.

The Model

More formally, the model construction is as follows:

$$s_{it} = \frac{a_i \prod_{j=1}^{k} Z_{ijt}^{\beta_j} e^{U_{it}}}{\sum_i a_i \prod_{j=1}^{k} Z_{ijt}^{\beta_j} e^{U_{it}}} \qquad \begin{pmatrix} i = 1,2,\ldots\ldots\ldots, n; \\ t = 1,2,\ldots\ldots\ldots, T \end{pmatrix}$$

where (within a marketing context)

s_{it} = market share of brand i at time t

Z_{ijt} = attribute j of brand i at time t

a_i, β_j = parameters (to be estimated)

U_{it} = a normally distributed random variable with mean zero and variance σ_i^2.

If we define

$$\bar{s}_{.t} = \sum_i \log_e s_{it}/n, \quad \bar{a}_{.} = \sum_i \log_e a_i/n, \quad \bar{Z}_{.jt} = \sum_i \log_e Z_{ijt}/n, \quad \bar{U}_{.t} = \sum_i U_{it}/n$$

then [see Nakanishi (1972)]

$$\log_e s_{it} - \bar{s}_{.t} = \log_e a_i - \bar{a}_{.} + \sum_j \beta_j(\log_e Z_{ijt} - \bar{Z}_{.jt}) + U_{it} - \bar{U}_{.t} \tag{1}$$

Writing $\bar{\alpha}_i = \log_e a_i - \bar{a}_{.}$, we note that $\bar{\alpha}_n = -(\bar{\alpha}_1 + \bar{\alpha}_2 + \ldots + \bar{\alpha}_{n-1})$

and therefore (1) becomes

$$\log_e s_{it} - \bar{s}_{.t} = \sum_{I=1}^{n-1} \bar{\alpha}_I \, DUM_{It} + \sum_{j=1}^{k} \beta_j(\log_e Z_{ijt} - \bar{Z}_{.jt}) + U_{it} - \bar{U}_{.t} \tag{2}$$

where

$$DUM_{It} = \begin{cases} 1 & I=i,\ i\neq n \\ 0 & I\neq i,\ i\neq n \\ -1 & i=n \end{cases}$$

In an OLS sense, there are then nT observations on k+n-1 explanatory variables (of which n-1 are dummy variables).

However in this particular case we need to examine the disturbance term $U_{it} - \bar{U}_{.t}$ in (2) rather more closely. We have so far made the assumption that U_{it} is $N(0,\sigma_i^2)$. Therefore $U_{it} - \bar{U}_{.t}$ must also be normally distributed with mean zero, and with variance depending on i. In other words the OLS assumption, usually written as $E(\underset{\sim}{U}\underset{\sim}{U}') = \sigma^2 \underset{\sim}{I}$, no longer holds.

Suppose we rewrite (2) as

$$Y_{it} = \underset{\sim}{X}_{it}\underset{\sim}{\beta} + V_{it}$$

and define $\underset{\sim}{Y}_t' = [Y_{1t}\ Y_{2t}\ \cdots\ Y_{nt}]$, $\underset{\sim}{V}_t' = [V_{1t}\ V_{2t}\ \cdots\ V_{nt}]$, and

$$\underset{\sim}{X}_t = \begin{bmatrix} \underset{\sim}{X}_{1t}' \\ \underset{\sim}{X}_{2t}' \\ \vdots \\ \underset{\sim}{X}_{nt}' \end{bmatrix} = \begin{bmatrix} X_{11t} & X_{12t} & \cdots & X_{1,k+n-1,t} \\ X_{21t} & X_{22t} & \cdots & X_{2,k+n-1,t} \\ \vdots & \vdots & & \vdots \\ X_{n1t} & X_{n2t} & \cdots & X_{n,k+n-1,t} \end{bmatrix}$$

It is assumed the $\underset{\sim}{V}_t$ are independently and identically distributed random vectors with $E[\underset{\sim}{V}_t] = \underset{\sim}{0}$, and variance-covariance matrix $E[\underset{\sim}{V}_t\underset{\sim}{V}_t'] = \underset{\sim}{W}$. It can be shown that $\underset{\sim}{W}$ is a nxn symmetric positive semi-definite matrix with rank $(\underset{\sim}{W}) = n-1$. If $\underset{\sim}{W}$ is known, the usual approach to estimating $\underset{\sim}{\beta}$ is to transform the model into one with a diagonal variance-covariance matrix. However this GLS approach requires that $\underset{\sim}{W}^{-1}$ exists, a condition which violates rank $(\underset{\sim}{W}) = n-1$. McGuire et al (1968) have shown that we may delete the $i^{\underline{th}}$ component of $\underset{\sim}{Y}_t$, $\underset{\sim}{X}_t$ and estimate $\underset{\sim}{\beta}$ from T(n-1) observations. McGuire et al have also shown that the variance-covariance matrix of the reduced sample will have full rank, regardless of the choice of observations deleted, and that the GLS estimates will be invariant with respect to the choice of observations deleted.

We are therefore in a position to state that, without loss of generality, the $n^{\underline{th}}$ observation for each t can be deleted: let $\underset{\sim}{X}_t^{(n)}$ be the $(n-1) \times (k+n-1)$ matrix, and $\underset{\sim}{Y}_t^{(n)}$, $\underset{\sim}{V}_t^{(n)}$ the (n-1)-vectors obtained by deleting the $n^{\underline{th}}$ row of $\underset{\sim}{X}_t$, $\underset{\sim}{Y}_t$, $\underset{\sim}{V}_t$ respectively. The model becomes

$$\begin{bmatrix} Y_1^{(n)} \\ Y_2^{(n)} \\ \cdot \\ \cdot \\ \cdot \\ Y_T^{(n)} \end{bmatrix} \begin{bmatrix} X_1^{(n)} \\ X_2^{(n)} \\ \cdot \\ \cdot \\ \cdot \\ X_T^{(n)} \end{bmatrix} \beta + \begin{bmatrix} V_1^{(n)} \\ V_2^{(n)} \\ \cdot \\ \cdot \\ \cdot \\ V_T^{(n)} \end{bmatrix} \tag{3}$$

or

$$Y^{(n)} = X^{(n)} \beta + V^{(n)} \tag{4}$$

If we write

$$E[V_t^{(n)} V_t^{(n)'}] = W^{(n)}$$

then $W^{(n)}$ has full rank (i.e. rank n-1). Also

$$E[V^{(n)} V^{(n)'}] = I_T \otimes W^{(n)} = W_*^{(n)}$$

[In effect it is assumed $W_*^{(n)}$ is a T(n-1)-square block-diagonal matrix, with T diagonal blocks equal to $W^{(n)}$ and off-diagonal blocks equal to 0_{n-1}.]
To estimate β in (4), we find a matrix P_* (triangular) such that $P_* P_*' = W_*^{(n)}$, and then premultiply (4) by P_*^{-1}. The resulting model can easily be shown to satisfy the usual OLS assumptions [see Johnston (1972)].

Now because of the block diagonal form of $W_*^{(n)}$, we are able to apply Choleski decomposition to the individual $W^{(n)}$ matrices. For suppose we find the (n-1)-square matrix P such that $PP' = W^{(n)}$. It is then easy to show that if we define $P_* = I_T \otimes P$, then $P_* P_*' = W_*^{(n)}$. Moreover, to invert the T(n-1)-square matrix P_*, it is only necessary to invert P since $P_*^{-1} = I_T \times P^{-1}$. In practical terms this means that (4) is to be premultiplied by

$$P_*^{-1} \quad \begin{bmatrix} P^{-1} & & 0 \\ & \ddots & \\ 0 & & P^{-1} \end{bmatrix}$$

to obtain

$$\begin{bmatrix} P^{-1} Y_1^{(n)} \\ P^{-1} Y_2^{(n)} \\ \cdot \\ \cdot \\ \cdot \\ P^{-1} Y_T^{(n)} \end{bmatrix} = \begin{bmatrix} P^{-1} X_1^{(n)} \\ P^{-1} X_2^{(n)} \\ \cdot \\ \cdot \\ \cdot \\ P^{-1} X_T^{(n)} \end{bmatrix} \beta + \begin{bmatrix} P^{-1} V^{(n)} \\ P^{-1} V_2^{(n)} \\ \cdot \\ \cdot \\ \cdot \\ P^{-1} V_T^{(n)} \end{bmatrix}$$

which satisfies the usual OLS assumptions. In other words, all that is necessary is the transformation of the re-arranged and tightened data block by the (n-1)-square matrix P^{-1}, and the use of a standard OLS package.

Since $W^{(n)}$ and $W_*^{(n)}$ are unknown, we shall first perform an OLS regression on (2): the residuals $\hat{V}_t$ will then be used to estimate the elements of a matrix W by writing

$$\hat{W} = \frac{1}{T} \sum_{t=1}^{T} \hat{V}_t \hat{V}_t'$$

We then delete the nth component of $\hat{W}$, leaving the $(n-1)\times(n-1)$ matrix $\hat{W}^{(n)}$ as the estimate of $W^{(n)}$, and $\hat{W}_*^{(n)} = I_T \otimes \hat{W}^{(n)}$ as the estimate of $W_*^{(n)}$.

The estimate of β thus obtained will be a GLS estimate. However there is no reason why we should not use the residuals from this first GLS regression to compute a new $\hat{W}_{(n)}$, and perform a second GLS regression, and so on. Estimates of β obtained in this way may be called iterative GLS (or IGLS) estimates.

Marketing Competition

Dorfman and Steiner (1954) postulated that the demand for a product is dependent on the product's price, quality, and advertising, and derived a profit-maximising rule for the optimal level of the dependent variables. The principal limitations of the D-S theorem are its static nature and its confinement to monopolistic markets. Theoretical extensions to the D-S theorem (while remaining confined to a monopoly) are due to Nerlove and Arrow (1962), to allow for current advertising expenditures affecting future demand. More recently Sethi (1977) has considered the optimal control problem of determining the rate of advertising expenditure, subject to a budget constraint, required to maximise the NPV of profit flows over a finite horizon. Extensions such as these are dynamic.

Competitive extensions, on the other hand, are many and varied. Basically this is due to the different ways in which competition can be introduced into the model. As Lambin (1970) stated (within an advertising context):

> "Three approaches are applicable in studying competitive interaction. The simplest one consists of including competitive advertising variables in the demand function to see whether increased competitive advertising reduces sales of that brand. In the second approach, one estimates directly the relation between market share, relative advertising, relative price, etc... The third approach consists of constructing simultaneous equation models of sales and advertising."

The second approach

$$\text{i.e.} \quad s_{it} = \prod_{j=1}^{k} \left(\frac{Z_{ijt}}{\sum_i Z_{ijt}} \right)^{\beta_j}$$

has been favoured by some authors because the model is immediately linearisable (by taking logarithms) and comes closest to the "attractiveness" model at that time not known to be linearisable [see Nakanishi (1972)]. Lambin, Naert and Bultez (1975) used this approach to generalise the D-S theorem to an oligopolistic market. They remained within the confines of a static analysis and derived profit-maximisation conditions for an oligopoly with "multiple competitive reactions" and expansible industry demand. Little research has as yet been carried out on the optimisation of the "attractiveness" model: Gupta and Krishman (1967) came closest with the profit-maximisation of an oligopolistic model, each competitor having two control variables, price and promotional effort. However although the contribution of promotional effort to market share was of the marketing attractiveness type, the contribution of price was assumed to be $k_j(\bar{p}_j - p_j)$ where p_j is the price of competitor j and $\bar{p}_j$ is the average price of all other competitors.

References

Bell D.E., Keeney R.L. and Little J.D.C., A market share theorem, Jnl. Mktg. Res., XII (May), 136-141, 1975

Bultez A.V. and Naert P.A., Consistent sum-constrained models, J.Am.Statist. Ass., 70, 529-535, 1975

Dorfman R. and Steiner P.O., Optimal advertising and optimal quality, Am.Econ. Rev., 44, 826-836, 1954
Gupta S.M. and Krishnan K.S., Mathematical models in marketing, Ops.Res., 15, 1040-1050, 1967
Johnston J., Econometric Methods, McGraw-Hill, 1972
Lambin J.J., Naert P.A. and Bultez A., Optimal marketing behaviour in oligopoly, Eur.Econ.Rev., 6, 105-128, 1975
Lambin J.J., Advertising and competitive behaviour: a case study, App.Econ., 2, 231-251, 1970
McGuire T.W., Farley J.U., Lucas R.E. and Ring L.W., Estimation and inference for linear models in which subsets of the dependent variable are constrained, J.Am.Statist.Ass., 63, 1201-1213, 1968
Nakanishi M., Measurement of sales promotion effect at the retail level - a new approach, Combined Proceedings of the American Marketing Association, Spring and Fall Conferences, 338-343, 1972
Nerlove M. and Arrow K.J., Optimal advertising policy under dynamic conditions, Economica, 2, 129-142, 1962
Sethi S.P., Optimal advertising for the Nerlove-Arrow model under a budget constraint, Op.Res.Q., 28(ii), 683-693, 1977

Robust Regression: LINWDR and NLWDR

R. Dutter, Graz

0. Summary

Robust regression receives more and more attention and its importance is obvious. Well-working algorithms have been developed in recent years. In this article, the implementation of well-tested algorithms in user-oriented programs is presented and their applicability in statistical problems is shown.

Keywords: Robust regression, multiple linear regression, nonlinear regression.

1. Introduction

The program package to be described consists of two main programs, one (LINWDR) designed for linear regression considering the many advantages of linearity, and the other one (NLWDR) for nonlinear regression where any user-defined model may be entered. Both programs are compatible in input and output, and produce same kinds of fits. The least-squares fit as well as the use of three different robust loss functions with robustness constants to be specified by the user, may be requested. When coding the programs we started off with the well-tested and approved regression programs LINWOOD and NLWOOD (VIM-library) (see also Daniel and Wood (1971)), revised and extended them for robust fitting.

Doing classical least-squares estimation for fitting models to data has the advantage that the estimates are (at least in the linear case) easily calculated and one can use many statistics and tests for the analysis. Unfortunately, one has to assume that the random errors are normally distributed and indeed, the method is unduly sensitive to occasional gross errors and to departures from the assumed model. Therefore it is extremely useful to have both least-squares and robust methods in a program which enables the analysis in a neighborhood of the assumed model.

In the next section we give a short introduction to the robust methods used in the regression programs, Sections 3 and 4 give a summary of the two programs LINWDR and NLWDR, and Section 5 should illustrate the use of the programs. The programs as well as user manuals are available on request from the author.

2. Robust Regression

Suppose that n observations y_i, $i = 1,\dots,n$, and the model $f_i(\underset{\sim}{\theta})$ with the unknown parameter vector $\underset{\sim}{\theta} = (\theta_1,\theta_2,\dots,\theta_p)^T$ are given. Then $\underset{\sim}{\theta}$ is calculated by essentially minimizing the function

$$g(\underset{\sim}{\theta},\sigma) = \sum_{i=1}^{n} \rho\left(\sqrt{w_i}\,\frac{y_i-f_i(\underset{\sim}{\theta})}{\sigma}\right)\sigma$$

or by equating to zero its derivative

$$g'(\underset{\sim}{\theta},\sigma) = -\sum_{i=1}^{n}\sqrt{w_i}\;\psi\left(\sqrt{w_i}\,\frac{y_i-f_i(\underset{\sim}{\theta})}{\sigma}\right)\frac{\partial f_i(\underset{\sim}{\theta})}{\partial\underset{\sim}{\theta}}$$

where ρ is an even function, $\rho(0) = 0$, $\rho(t) > 0$ for $t > 0$, with its derivative ψ, w_i are optional weights on the observations (to be specified), and σ is a scaling factor which is estimated from the data.

For $\rho(t) = \frac{1}{2}t^2$, respectively $\psi(t) = t$, we obtain the classical (weighted) least-squares estimate. Because of the quadratic influence of the residuals it is clear that this procedure is highly sensitive to occasional gross errors (large residuals). On the other hand, the most "robust" method is obtained by putting $\psi(t) = \text{sign}\,(t)$ which gives the L_1-estimate (the sum of absolute values of the residuals is minimized, and only the sign and not the size of each residual is of influence). Unfortunately this estimate is numerically difficult to handle.

Three approved functions ψ which are -- besides the least-squares algorithm -- included in the program package being described, are as follows:

a. "ψ bends at c" (Huber)

$$\psi(t) = \begin{cases} -c & \text{if} \quad t < -c \\ t & \text{if} \quad |t| \le c \\ c & \text{if} \quad t > c \end{cases}$$

for some $c > 0$ to be specified.

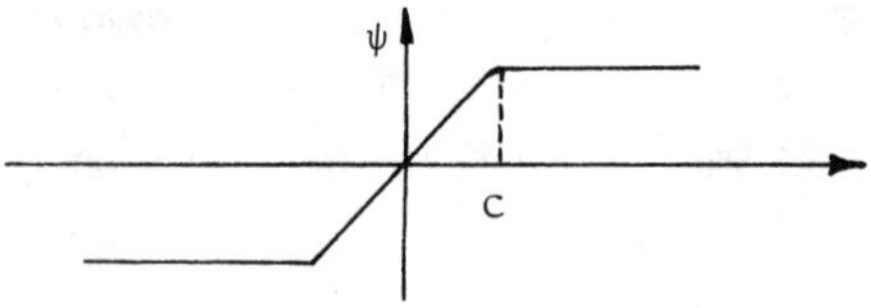

σ is simultaneously estimated by putting the side condition

$$\frac{1}{n-p}\sum_{i=1}^{n}\psi\left(\sqrt{w_i}\,\frac{y_i-f_i(\underset{\sim}{\theta})}{\sigma}\right)^2 = \mathcal{E}_\Phi(\psi(u))^2$$

(the expected value when the residuals are normally distributed).

b. "ψ bends at a, b and d" (Hampel)

$$\psi(t) = \begin{cases} t & |t| \le a \\ a\cdot\text{sign}(t) & a < |t| \le b \\ \frac{d-|t|}{d-b}\, a\cdot\text{sign}(t) & b < |t| \le d \\ 0 & |t| > d \end{cases}$$

for $0 < a < b < d$.

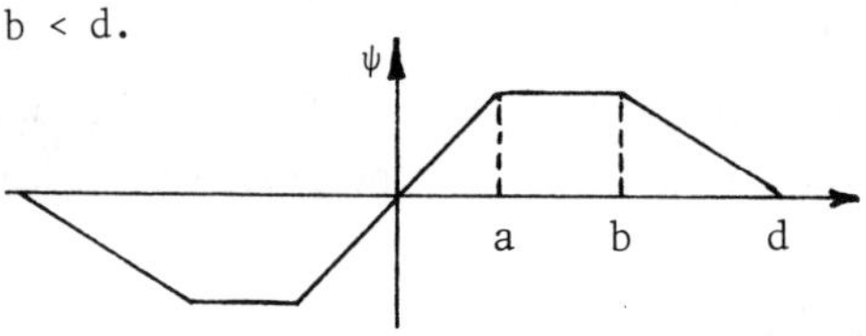

σ is estimated by a robust fit using the monotone function "ψ bends at a".

c. "ψ has the form of sine" (Andrews)

$$\psi(t) = \begin{cases} \alpha\cdot\sin(t/\alpha) & |t| < \alpha\pi \\ 0 & \text{otherwise} \end{cases}$$

for some $\alpha > 0$.

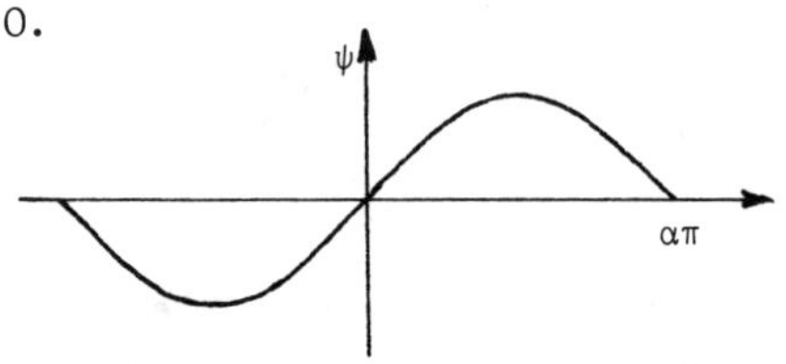

σ is estimated by "ψ bends at α". For properties of the different functions see Andrews et al. (1972).

The function "ψ bends at c" clearly gives a limitation to the influence of residuals. Moreover, it is monotone and hence, the minimization procedure -- at least in the linear model case -- is a convex problem. The function "ψ bends at a, b and d" eliminates completely the influence of large residuals

($\geq d\cdot\sigma$) which is very reasonable when "outliers" are present. Because of the nonconvexity of the problem one should be careful with finding the "right" solution (e.g. find first the solution with "ψ bends at a" and then use this as starting point for the iterative procedure). The function "ψ has the form of sine" is not essentially different from "ψ bends at $\alpha\pi/3$, $2\alpha\pi/3$ and $\alpha\pi$".

3. Program LINWDR

This program considers models of the form

$$f(\underset{\sim}{\theta}) = \theta_o+\theta_1 x_1+\theta_2 x_2+\ldots+\theta_k x_k, \quad k+1 = p$$

where the x_j's must be given, that is, the model is linear in the coefficients. The data has to be entered rowwise, that is, for each observation y_i of y (dependent variable) the values x_{ij} of the set (x_j) (independent variables) and eventually a weight w_i should be entered. If a different model with this data set is wished, variables (independent and/or dependent) may be transformed such as $x_3 \leftarrow x_1\cdot x_2$ or $x_4 \leftarrow 1/x_4$, omitted or even newly generated such as $x_5 \leftarrow x_4^2$. The transformations are requested by simple transformation cards (2o different operations possible).

Several problems can be treated in one computer run. The data set for the first problem must be entered by punched cards or by another storage medium. Further problems may reuse the same data set (but probably differently transformed) or other sets must be entered. A transformed data set (omitted variables, etc.) may still contain several dependent variables which will be sequentially treated (no multivariate structure). For each dependent variable in turn, different fits can be requested, e.g. a least-squares fit and several robust fits. Thus, a requested statistic will be calculated for each fit and for each dependent variable.

Options to direct the run stream and to be specified on a control card include

- different forms of data input (format, storage facility)
- transformation of data
- weighting of the observations
- $\theta_o = 0$ fixed
- listing of input data, transformations, sum of variables, cross products, means and standard deviations of each variable, matrix of simple correl-

ation coefficients between the variables, its inverse

- information cards for display in the printout
- names of variables to be read
- specifications about the sort of fits
- figures for cross validation (saving and reuse of the computed coefficients).

The program calculates in any case and displays maximum, minimum and range of each variable, their relative influence, the estimated coefficients with standard deviation and t-values. The residual degrees of freedom and the F-value are printed, the residual mean square, the total sum of squares and the multiple correlation coefficient squared. In case of robust fit, a "robustified" residual mean square and other "robustified" statistics are computed which are essentially based on modified observations (with the aid of the function ψ, see Dutter (1976) for details). Comparison of the residual mean square with the robustified one usually reveals whether one deals with "long-tailed" or "short-tailed" distributions of the residuals.

Tables of the observations, fitted values, residuals and distances in the factor space are supplied. Large residuals are marked. Outliers in the factor space may be spotted from a listing of the diagonal elements of the projection matrix (in the least-squares case). The variances of the errors may be checked by a calculation of the "standard deviation estimated from residuals of neighboring observations". Plots of the residuals can be requested (a) on a normal grid, (b) versus the fitted values and (c) versus each independent variable. A table as well as plots of component effects of each variable on each observation may be provided. The search for smaller sets of influencial variables is supported by the calculation of C_p-values which are preselected, tabulated and plotted.

The numerical procedure for the robust fits used in the program is essentially the H-algorithm described in Huber and Dutter (1974), that is, as starting value for the iterations the least-squares solution is taken but the user should provide the desired precision which is taken for the stopping criterion. For inverting matrices the numerically stable housholder transformations are employed.

4. Program NLWDR

This program allows the user to fit the general model $f(\theta)$ which involves the unknown parameters θ in a nonlinear way, such as e.g. $f(\theta) = \theta_1+\theta_2 e^{\theta_3 x}+\theta_4 e^{\theta_5 x}$, $f(\theta) = \theta_1/(x-\theta_2)^2$. To have an applicability of the program as general as possible, the user has to specify his model by providing a FORTRAN subroutine which calculates the value of $f(\theta)$ for given θ. Besides the form of the model, the observations and values of the dependent variables have to be entered similarly to the input of LINWDR. Most of the options to be specified, and provided tables and plots are conformable to those of LINWDR.

The iterative procedure which has been incorporated in the program for finding the coefficients of the model, goes back to an algorithm of Nagel and Wolff (1974) which is some compromise between the Gauss-Newton and the steepest descent method. It was combined with the W-algorithm (Dutter (1975)) and tested by the author on some hundred examples. The program provides a short summary of the iterations in order to give the possibility of checking the convergence behavior.

5. Illustrations

The method of least-squares estimation tends to smooth out large residuals, and spotting strange observations (outliers) may become very difficult or even impossible. The program package has options for the least-squares and robust fits as listed in Section 2, and different fits may be computed in the same computer run. This is illustrated in the following simple examples.

(a) The user believes that his data are "well-behaved", that is, the observations are independently and normally distributed and the model (the equation) is correct. He wants to estimate the coefficients of the equation but is still afraid that the data may contain some outliers. He decides to compute a robust fit "ψ bends at c" with $c = 1.5$. In case of "good" data, the obtained fit is approximately the same as a least-squares fit (about 87% of the observations are considered as in the least-squares case and the others with large residuals obtain less weight), but the procedure guards well against large outliers.

(b) The user knows little about his data. He wants to try a least-squares fit and a robust fit "ψ bends at c" with $c = 1.5$. In case other robust fits are needed to be calculated later, he would like to have retained (on punched cards or another storage medium) the estimated coefficients and the scale, and specifies this on the control card.

Suppose that the least-squares fit on the output tells nothing about an inadequacy of the model or about nonnormality of the errors. The robust fit is similar but there is an indication of two possible strange observations which could be suspected by the plot of residuals on a normal grid. To look after these possible outliers, the user will request some other fits. First, he wants to have the same kind of fit as before but with smaller $c = 1.0$ and $c = .7$. In expectation that there will be the two outliers clearly detected, he also requests the robust fit "ψ bends at a, b and d" with $a = .7$, $b = 1.4$ and $d = 2.0$, which will reject completely observations with standardized residuals absolutely greater than 2. To save computer time, use of the previously calculated coefficients and scale is specified.

(c) Daniel and Wood (1971, Chapter 5) discuss an already classical example (Stack Loss data, linear model, 3 independent variables, 21 observations) and detect after a long and tedious discussion four outliers in the data set through different trials of least-squares fits. We computed the robust fit "ψ bends at c" with $c = .4$ and display the residuals on a normal grid plot in Figure 1 (for better printing quality the output has been redrawn). The four outliers are clearly separated. Andrews (1974) published a similar result with "ψ has the form of sine" which we reproduced by LINWDR and display in Figure 2. (It should be remarked that the monotone and numerically more stable function "ψ bends at c" can often suffice for analyzing the data.)

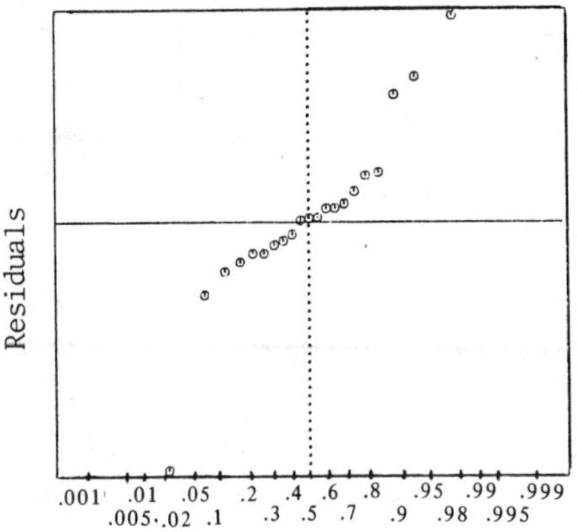

Figure 1.

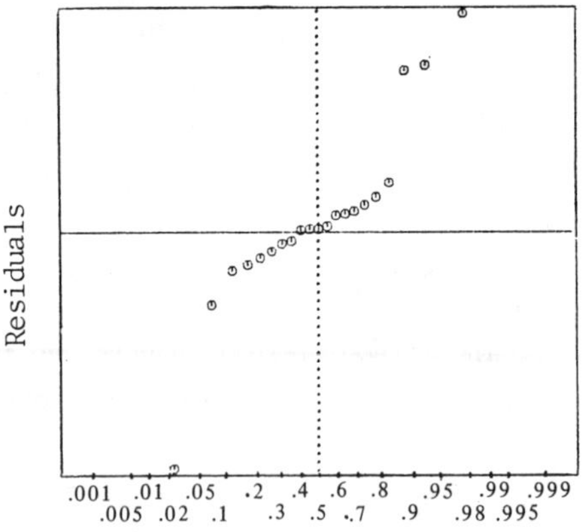

Figure 2.

References

Andrews, D.F., A Robust Method for Multiple Linear Regression. Technometrics 16, 523-531, 1974.

Andrews, D.F., P.J. Bickel, F.R. Hampel, P.J. Huber, W.H. Rogers and J.W. Tukey, Robust Estimates of Location: Survey and Advances. Princeton University Press, New Jersey, 1972.

Daniel, C., and F. Wood, Fitting Equations to Data. Wiley, New York, 1971.

Dutter, R., Robust Regression: Different Approaches to Numerical Solutions and Algorithms. Res. Rep. No. 6, Fachgruppe für Statistik, ETH, Zürich, 1975.

Dutter, R., Computer Linear Robust Curve Fitting Program LINWDR. Res. Rep. No. 10, Fachgruppe für Statistik, ETH, Zürich, 1976.

Huber, P.J., and R. Dutter, Numerical Solution of Robust Regression Problems. COMPSTAT 1974, ed. G. Bruckmann, Physica Verlag, Vienna, 1974.

Nagel, G., and W. Wolff, Ein Verfahren zur Minimierung einer Quadratsumme nichtlinearer Funktionen. Biometrische Zeitschrift, Band 16, H. 6, p. 431-439, 1974 (in German).

A Computer Program for the Construction of Experimental Plans

M.F. Franklin and **H.D. Patterson**, Edinburgh

Summary

This paper identifies the various stages in the routine computer construction of experimental plans and describes one particular program DSIGNX that has been developed for this purpose.

KEYWORDS: EXPERIMENTAL DESIGNS, EXPERIMENTAL PLANS, RANDOMIZATION, GENERATORS, BLOCK STRUCTURE, TREATMENT STRUCTURE.

1. Introduction

Much attention has been given to developing computer programs for the analysis of data from designed experiments but little to programs for the routine construction of experimental plans. The need for such a program is clear: most of the operations in the construction of a plan are laborious and mechanical but require a high degree of accuracy.

In this paper we attempt to identify the processes in the construction of experimental plans. We describe briefly a program which may be used in the construction of a range of experimental plans and which is based on many of the ideas expressed in this paper.

2. Constructing an experimental plan

We start by considering as an example the construction of an experimental plan for six treatments in a 6×6 Latin square using the method recommended by Fisher and Yates (1963, Table XV). This involves selecting a square at random from all possible 6×6 Latin squares. There are 17 distinct transformation sets (i.e. sets of squares generated by one member by permutation of rows, columns and letters). Fisher and Yates present a square from each set together with the number of standard squares in the set. First one of these 17 Latin squares is selected at random. The square to be used for the experimental plan is then derived by random permutation of rows, columns and letters.

The following stages in the construction of the above experimental plan may be recognised:

Stage 1. The set of treatments to be compared and the type of experimental plan to be used are chosen. The choice of experimental design is dependent on the structure of the treatments and units.

Stage 2. A basic Latin square is selected at random from the tables. We call this the *design* to distinguish it from squares which are derived from it. The term design is also used in this way by Clatworthy (1973) and John *et al* (1972).

The design in Figure 1(a) is the standard Latin square for transformation set III presented by Fisher and Yates (1963, Table XV).

Stage 3. The rows and the columns of the square are permuted. The choice of permutation identifies the rows and columns of the design with the rows and columns of the experimental plan. For example the first row and first column of the design (Fig. 1(a)) have become the third row and fourth column respectively of the experimental plan (Fig. 1(b)). In a 6×6 Latin square there are 36 locations defined by the intersection of rows and columns. The permutation allocates each location in the design to a location in the experimental plan.

The locations of the design may be regarded as labels and we call them unit labels. The locations of the experimental plan are the units (or more accurately, the unit identifiers). This stage thus corresponds to the allocation of a set of unit labels to the units.

Stage 4. The letters are assigned to the treatments. The letters also may be regarded as labels which we call treatment labels and this stage corresponds to the allocation of treatment labels to the treatments. An example is given in Figure 1(c) for six treatments with identifiers V1, V2, V3, V4, V5 and V6.

The stages outlined above do not form a complete breakdown of the construction of an experimental design and the methods used at the various stages in the example are not the only ones. These stages are described in more detail in §§3-6.

Mappings The experimental plan can be regarded as a list of the units together with the treatments allocated to them. We assume that each unit has one treatment allocated to it, and consider the experimental plan as defining a function or mapping from units to treatments. Stages 2, 3 and 4 can also be regarded as mappings. The design defines a mapping from unit labels to treatment labels, i.e. for any unit label the treatment label is determined by the design. The random permutations of stages 2 and 3 are mappings from units to unit labels and from treatment labels to treatments respectively. The complete mapping, F , from units to treatments can therefore be regarded as a composition of three mappings F_1, F_2 and F_3

$$\text{units} \xrightarrow{F_1} \text{unit labels} \xrightarrow{F_2} \text{treatment labels} \xrightarrow{F_3} \text{treatments} .$$

3. The structure of units and treatments

In this section we present a brief description of the structure of units and treatments based on a more extensive description by Nelder (1965). Consider an experiment for which the experimental units are 36 pigs, six pigs from each of 6 litters. There are two different sorts of unit, litters and pigs within litters. Each pig can be given unique identifier ij where i denotes the litter and j denotes the pig within the litter. Pigs with the same values of i belong to the same litter but there is no connection between pigs with the same value of j . The labels i and j can be regarded as the levels of two factors, defining litters and pigs respectively and we say the units have a nested structure with the factor for pigs nested within the factor for litters.

In the Latin square example of §2 each unit is uniquely defined by a row and a column. If we have a factor for rows with levels i and a factor for columns with levels j then each unit may be uniquely determined by an identifier ij. Units ij and ij' belong to the same row j units ij and $i'j$ belong to the same column. We say that a Latin square has a crossed structure with the factors for rows and columns crossed. The treatments are formed from the combinations of the various levels of two or more treatment factors. They may have a nested or crossed structure.

In Nelder's (1965) notation a nesting operator is denoted by / and the crossing operator by * . For two factors I and J the two structures are represented by I/J and I*J . There are five distinct structures for three factors and these may be represented by

I/J/K; I/(J*K); I*(J/K) = (J/K)*I; (I*J)/K; I*J*K .

Pseudofactors It is sometimes useful to consider a factor with $m_1 m_2 \ldots m_s$ levels to be the product of s pseudo factors with $m_1, m_2, \ldots m_s$ levels respectively. Similarly a factor with n levels can be considered as the union of two pseudo factors with m and $n-m$ levels respectively, $(m < n)$.

4. Allocating unit labels to units

Before discussing the allocation of unit labels to units we observe that in some experiments the units are selected from a population of units. The selection of units is part of the construction of an experimental plan but it will not be discussed here.

The structure of the units is the block structure and the factors defining the physical divisions among the units are the block factors. Any mapping from the units to the unit labels must be compatible with the block structure. Indeed for a wide class of block structures which Nelder (1965) called simple, the set of possible mappings may be determined directly from the block structure. The possible mappings for simple block structures with two block factors I and J are

i) I*J : permute the levels of I and the levels of J

ii) I/J : permute the levels of I and the levels of J for each level of I .

For non-simple block structures these rules are inadequate. When the number of units is not the same at all levels of any block factor the set of possible mappings is constrained not only by the block structure but also by the need to map subsets of units onto subsets of unit labels of the same size. For some designs, permutation of the levels of certain factors in the construction of the plan may destroy an essential feature of the design, e.g. in changeover designs balanced for residual effects permutation of the periods may destroy the balance.

Nelder (1965) showed that every simple block structure has a complete randomization theory which ensures validity of analysis. Whilst accepting that randomization is essential in the construction of field plans we believe that a program should not impose a rigid randomization scheme on every occasion. The changeover design mentioned above is one example where conventional randomization is harmful.

5. Allocation of treatment labels

Now consider the mapping in which one treatment label is allocated to each unit label. Labelling is standardised by the use of natural sequences of numbers or letters with specified starting points. In its most elementary form the mapping is determined by lists of treatment and unit levels, one of each for each unit. Economy is possible when the treatment or unit labels or both are in standard order. The unit labels are nearly always in standard order and can be omitted. Most of the designs presented in textbooks can be regarded as lists of treatment labels - the rows, columns, blocks etc. are implied by the order. Sometimes the treatment labels also are in standard order. This happens in, for example, designs with complete blocks or several replicates per block.

In more complicated designs the list of treatment labels cannot be omitted altogether but can often be presented in compact form using one or more design generators. For example, Fisher and Yates (1963, Table XVII) give cyclic solutions for some of their balanced incomplete block designs. The blocks fall into f families of v, where v is the number of varieties or treatments. Only one block (the initial block) is specified for each family: the remaining $v-1$ blocks are obtained by cyclic substitution. Fisher and Yates (1963, Table XVII) also give examples of dicyclic solutions in which each treatment is represented by a combination of levels of two pseudo-factors.

The cyclic method of construction is not, of course, restricted to balanced designs. John, Wolock and David (1972) give an extensive catalogue of cyclic incomplete block designs. Some of these use fractional families or sets requiring only a fraction of t blocks. Special provisions must be made for identifying such fractional sets in a computer program.

Cyclic row-and-column designs can be generated in much the same way as incomplete block designs. Initial columns are used instead of initial blocks. Davis and Hall (1969) developed methods for constructing changeover designs cyclically. The order of treatments in the initial column is important and must not be changed.

John and Dean (1975) and Dean and John (1975) extended the cyclic methods used in the construction of incomplete block designs to single-replicate factorial designs arranged in blocks. Each treatment is represented by an element of an Abelian group G. Construction starts with one or more specified elements of this group. These are used to generate a cyclic group G_*, a subgroup of G. Then the elements of G_* define the treatments of one block of the design; the other blocks are given by cosets.

Patterson (1976) described the use of design keys in the construction of factorial designs. Design keys provide a set of rules under which levels of treatment factors are derived arithmetically from levels of unit factors. They are available for any of Nelder's (1965) simple block structures in single, multiple or fractional replication.

Cyclic construction methods do not, of course, in themselves guarantee that the resulting designs are sound statistically. It is necessary, therefore, either to provide a means of checking the efficiency or other properties of the designs at the time of construction or to keep a file of designs that have been approved in advance.

Sometimes it is worth writing a design-generating program specially for a particular field of application. In the United Kingdom, for example, all designs for statutory field trials of new crop varieties are produced centrally by computer. Resolvable incomplete block designs are required for any number of varieties up to 100 in two, three or four replicates. The algorithm described by Patterson and Williams (1976) is used. This starts with generators specifying the variety on one plot in each block; the remaining varieties are obtained by cyclic substitution. The generators and information on the designs are stored within the computer.

So far the actual choice of design has been left to the user. Sometimes, however, the choice can be shared between user and computer. The user provides a partial specification of the required design and the computer examines the combinatorial arrangements meeting this specification. For example, Franklin and Bailey (1977) have given an algorithm for constructing factorial designs. The user specifies effects that must not be confounded or aliased; the computer identifies the available designs meeting the user's requirements. Jones (1976) has tackled the more difficult and general problem of constructing block designs with variance matrix as near as possible to a user's specification.

6. Allocation of treatment labels to treatments

Provision must be made for different types of allocation of treatment labels to treatments. An example of random allocation was given in §2. Sometimes randomization is not essential to be validity of analysis but is required for some other purpose. Consider, for example, the design of a large series of variety trials all testing exactly the same varieties. Equal accuracy in all comparisons is considered desirable but a balanced design cannot be used. In any one trial therefore some comparisons are less accurately estimated than others but these inaccuracies can be evened out by reallocating variety labels (possibly at random) in every trial.

Constrained random allocation of treatment labels is also needed. For example, Patterson, Williams and Hunter (1978) deliberately choose designs so as to estimate specified comparisons with the least accuracy. They also require roughly equal accuracy over a whole series on other comparisons. They therefore recommend a constrained randomization of treatment labels that does not affect the allocation of controls.

7. The DSIGNX program

Many of the ideas expressed in this paper have been included in a computer program, DSIGNX, for the automatic construction of a range of experimental plans. Currently the program is most useful in the generation of factorial designs but it is being extended to include other designs. The program is written in Fortran IV and may be used in batch or interactive mode.

Although some of the distinctions made in this paper, such as that between units and plots, are implicit in the construction of the program they have been hidden from the user so that he may use ideas with which he is familiar. Block and treatment factors may be declared; Nelder's (1965) notation for block and treatment structures is used. If randomization is requested the default randomization is controlled by the block structure. Options include restricted randomization and suppression of randomization for some block factors. Treatments also may be randomized.

The principal generator is that for the design key method, Patterson (1976), though a simpler generator for randomized complete block and split plot designs is also available. A library of useful design key generators is maintained and the user may obtain his desired generator by stating the reference number. The user may also input the design in tabular form - but at present there is no library of designs in this form. Attention may be restricted to subsets of units and treatments or, alternatively, two or more designs can be combined thus enabling a design to be formed from a mixture of methods.

The program may be annotated by descriptive captions and headings and there are several forms of output. Alternative forms of output include a listing of the plan or subsets of the plan, and a two-dimensional field plan which indicates the boundaries of the various blocks. The levels of the treatments may be numeric or descriptive. In cases where the user wishes to do more with his output, such as generate detailed field plans, this program may be readily interfaced with other programs.

Of particular interest is the program GENSTAT developed by Nelder et al (1977). The two programs share a common notation for block and treatment structures. GENSTAT is important when the designs are constructed for determining efficiency factors and later for analysing the data.

Fig. 1 Stages in the construction of an experimental plan. 1(a) the basic Latin square or design; 1(b) the square after permutation of rows and columns, 1(c) the experimental plan.

A	B	C	D	E	F	A	F	B	E	C	D	V4	V3	V6	V2	V1	V5
B	A	F	E	C	D	F	E	C	B	D	A	V3	V2	V1	V6	V5	V4
C	F	B	A	D	E	C	D	E	A	F	B	V1	V5	V2	V4	V3	V6
D	C	E	B	F	A	E	B	F	D	A	C	V2	V6	V3	V5	V4	V1
E	D	A	F	B	C	D	C	A	F	B	E	V5	V1	V4	V3	V6	V2
F	E	D	C	A	B	B	A	D	C	E	F	V6	V4	V5	V1	V2	V3

1(a) 1(b) 1(c)

References

Clatworthy W.H., Tables of two-associate-class partially balanced designs, Nat. Bur.Stand.(U.S.)Appl.Math. Ser. 63, Washington, 1973

Cox D.R., A note on weighted randomization, Ann.Math.Statist., 27, 1144-1150, 1956

Davis A.W. and Hall W.B., Cyclic change-over designs, Biometrika, 56, 283-293, 1969

Dean A.M. and John J.A., Single replicate factorial experiments in generalized cyclic designs. II asymmetrical arrangements, J.R.Statist.Soc., B, 37, 72-76, 1975

Fisher R.A. and Yates F., Statistical tables for biological, agricultural and medical research, Oliver and Boyd, Edinburgh, 1963

Franklin M.F. and Bailey R.A., Selection of defining contrasts and confounded effects in two-level experiments. Applied Statistics, 26, 321-326, 1977

Grundy P.M. and Healy M.J.R., Restricted randomization and quasi-Latin squares, J.R.Statist.Soc., B, 12, 286-291, 1950

John J.A. and Dean A.M., Single replicate factorial experiments in generalized cyclic designs. I Symmetrical arrangements, J.R.Statist.Soc., B, 37, 63-71, 1975

John J.A., Wolock F.W. and David H.A., Cyclic designs, Nat.Bur.Stand. (U.S.) Appl.Math.Ser. 62, Washington, 1972

Jones B., An algorithm for deriving optimal block designs, Technometrics, 18, 451-458, 1976

Nelder J.A., The analysis of randomized experiments with orthogonal block structure. I Block structure and the null analysis of variance, Proc.Roy. Soc. A, 283, 147-162, 1965

Nelder J.A. et al, GENSTAT manual, The Statistics Department, Rothamsted Experimental Station, Harpenden, England, 1977

Patterson H.D., Generation of factorial designs, J.R.Statist.Soc., B, 38, 175-179, 1976

Patterson H.D. and Williams E.R., A new class of resolvable incomplete block designs, Biometrika, 63, 83-92, 1976

Patterson H.D., Williams E.R. and Hunter E.A., Block designs for variety trials, J.Agric.Sci., Camb., 90, 395-400, 1978

Sample Indicators of Perturbation for Missing Value Regression Techniques

R.M. Heiberger, Philadelphia

Summary

The problem of regression analysis with missing observations on the independent variables is a frequent occurrence. This paper investigates the statistical and numerical properties of regression analyses based on the perturbed covariance matrices computed by several missing-value techniques. Sample indicators which estimate the increase in the sampling errors of the regression coefficients attributable to missingness are developed. The first and second moments of the sample indicators are derived under the simple assumption that data are randomly missing. Simulation results, based on imposing a set of independent random missingness patterns on a complete data set, suggest that the criteria provide accurate measures of the effects of missing data. In addition, the simulation suggests that one popular missing-value procedure, regression using the pairwise-present covariance matrix, is less efficient than another popular method, regression using the complete-observations-only covariance matrix.

Keywords: Missing Values, Perturbation Analysis, Regression

1. Introduction

The regression coefficients β in the model $Y=X\beta+\varepsilon$ are estimated by

(1.1) $$b = (X'X)^{-1}(X'Y) = S_{XX}^{-1} S_{XY}$$

where

(1.2) $$S = \begin{bmatrix} S_{YY} & S_{YX} \\ S_{XY} & S_{XX} \end{bmatrix} = \frac{1}{n} \begin{bmatrix} Y'Y & Y'X \\ X'Y & X'X \end{bmatrix}$$

The residual sum of squares is computed by

(1.3) $$S_{YY.X} = n\ (S_{YY} - S_{YX}S_{XX}^{-1}S_{XY})$$

or

(1.4) $$S_b = (Y-Xb)'(Y-Xb) = S_{YY.X}$$

Under the assumption of multivariate normality both b and S are unbiased estimators and (letting $X_0 = Y$)

(1.5) $$\mathrm{Cov}(S_{ij}, S_{kl}) = V_{ijkl}/n = (\sigma_{ik}\sigma_{jl} + \sigma_{il}\sigma_{jk})/n$$

When not all subjects have been measured on all variables (1.1) to (1.4) must be modified. The data actually observed are

(1.6) $$\left[Y_m, X_m\right] = (X_{mri}) = (X_{ri}P_{ri}) \text{ for } 1 \le r \le n;\ 0 \le i \le p$$

where $P = (P_{ri})$ is a presence/absence matrix of ones and zeros.

One commonly used technique computes the pairwise-present covariance matrix S_m from all observations for which both variables i and j are observed by the sample analog of (1.2)

(1.7) $$S_m = (S_{mij}) = \left(\sum_{r=1}^{n}(P_{ri}X_{ri}P_{rj}X_{rj})/n_{ij}\right)$$

where

(1.8) $$N_m = (n_{ij}) = P'P = \left(\sum_{r=1}^{n} P_{ri}P_{rj}\right)$$

Sample estimates b_m, $S_{mYY.X}$, S_{bm} are computed by analogs of (1.1) (1.3), and (1.4) respectively. The estimate S_{b_m} (1.4) is computed from the entire data set. In general it is not equal to $S_{mY.XX}$ and is unobservable except in simulation studies. Although all observed data is used, S_m is not necessarily positive semi-definite. Least squares regression may break down, giving no answer, or worse result in an incorrect answer.

Another commonly used technique computes the complete-observation only covariance matrix S_c from the subset of n_c observations for which all variables have been observed. S_c can be treated as the special case of S_m with P restricted to constant rows of all zeros or all ones. The estimates from the analogs of (1.1) to (1.4) are labeled b_c, S_c, $S_{cYY.X}$, S_{b_c}. This method loses all information contained in the observed variables of deleted observations but poses no numerical difficulties.

Additional methods for regression with missing values have been referenced in Hamilton's (1975) survey. More recent methods include BMDP8D and BMDPAM (Dixon and Brown, 1977), Beale and Little (1975), and Dempster, Laird, and Rubin (1977).

2. Perturbations Attributable to Missing Data

The differences between regression estimators based on the complete data covariance matrix S and the missing-data covariance matrices S_m and S_c are perturbations attributable to the pattern of missing data. Their moments are calculated here under the assumptions of random missingness, fixed X, and fixed $N_m = P'P$ but with exchangeable rows of P. Fixing X gives the behavior around the maximum information values for any realization X. The moments displayed here are proved in Heiberger (1977, 1978).

2.1 Perturbations in the Covariance Matrix

Define the perturbations in the sample covariance by

(2.1) $$\Delta = S - S_m = (\delta_{ij})$$

The moments of the distribution of the perturbations Δ are

(2.2) $$E(\delta_{ij}|N_m,X) = 0$$

(2.3) $$\hat{\sigma}^2_\Delta = \text{Var}(\delta_{ij}|N_m,X) = \frac{k_{ij}}{n_{ij}} \frac{\hat{V}_{ijij}}{n}$$

(2.4) $$\text{Cov}(\delta_{ij},\delta_{kl}|N_m,X) \doteq \left(\frac{nn_{ijkl}}{n_{ij}n_{kl}} -1\right) \frac{\hat{V}_{ijkl}}{n}$$

where

(2.5) $$n_{ijkl} = \sum_{r=1}^{n} P_{ri}P_{rj}P_{rk}P_{rl} \quad \text{and} \quad k_{ij} = n-n_{ij}$$

(2.6) $$V_{ijkl} = \sum_{r=1}^{n} \frac{(X_{ri}X_{rj}-S_{ij})(X_{rk}X_{rl}-S_{kl})}{n-1}$$

Under the assumption of multivariate normality $\hat{V}_{ijkl}$ can be estimated by the missing value sample analog of (1.5)

(2.7) $$\hat{V}_{ijkl} = S_{mik}S_{mjl} + S_{mil}S_{mjk}$$

The first sample indicator is the constant in (2.3) and (2.4) which can be interpreted on the additional fraction of variance in the estimate of the elements of S_{ij} attributable to missingness. This interpretation is most easily seen by assuming that δ_{ij} is independent of S_{ij} to get

(2.8) $$\text{Var}(S_{mij}) = \frac{V_{ijij}}{n}\left(1 + \frac{k_{ij}}{n_{ij}}\right) = \frac{V_{ijij}}{n} \frac{n}{n_{ij}} = \frac{V_{ijij}}{n_{ij}}$$

Neither the ratio k_{ij}/n_{ij}, nor the equivalent ratio n_{ij}/n which gives the efficiency of the technique relative to full data, depends on the number of variables or the number of observations.

2.2 Perturbations in Regression Coefficients

The moments of the perturbations in the regression coefficients b_m are

$$(2.9)\qquad E(b_m|N_m,X) = b + 0(\Delta^2)$$

$$(2.10)\qquad Cov(b_m,b_m|N_m,X) = E((b_m-b)(b_m-b)'|N_m,X) = S_{XX}^{-1}\, TS_{XX}^{-1} + 0(\Delta^3)$$

where

$$(2.11)\qquad T=(T_{ij})=(\sum_{k=0}^{p}\sum_{l=0}^{p} b_k b_l Cov(\delta_{ki},\delta_{jl}|N_m,X)) \text{ with } b_0 = -1$$

Equation (2.10) depends on the number of observations and the missingness pattern N_m only through the covariance of the δ_{ij} terms. However, it also depends on the square of the number of variables in the regression. The non-negligible part of (2.0) can be bounded.

$$(2.12)\qquad ||Cov(b_m,b_m|N_m,X)|| < ||S_{XX}^{-1}||^2||T||$$

The norm $||T||$ can in turn be bounded.

$$(2.13)\qquad ||T|| \le p^2 \max (b_i^2) \max |Cov(\delta_{ki},\delta_{jl}|N_m,X)|$$

The second sample indicator comes from (2.10). The diagonals of $Cov(b_m,b_m|N_m,X) = \hat{\sigma}^2_{b_m}$ are the estimates of the variance in the regression coefficients attributable to missingness. A sample analog of equation (2.10) using S_{mXX}, b_m, and (2.4) can be compared to the sampling error in the regression coefficients estimated from the diagonals s_b^2 of the $(X'X)^{-1} s^2$ matrix based on S_m.

2.3 Perturbations on the Residual Sum of Squares

The variance of the unobservable, biased estimator of the residual sum of squares computed by the analog of (1.4) is given by

$$(2.14)\qquad Var(S_{b_m}|N_m,X) = Var((Y-Xb_m)'(Y-Xb_m)|N_m,X) = n^2 Var((b_m-b)'S_{XX}(b_m-b)|N_m,X)$$

Equation (2.14) could be expanded to one with 12 summation signs which depends on the eighth moments of the data array. A third sample indicator could then be defined by the sample analog of that formula. Its properties have not been determined. Instead the efficiency ratio

$$(2.15)\qquad e(S_{b_m}) = S_b \div S_{b_m}$$

has been computed for each simulated realization of a random missingness pattern and its empirical distribution displayed.

2.4 Perturbations in the Principal Coordinate System

The eigenvalue decompositions of S_{XX} and S_{mXX} are given by

(2.16) $L = \text{Diag}(\ell_i) = V'S_{XX}V$

(2.17) $L_m = \text{Diag}(\ell_{mi}) = M'S_{mXX}M$

with the diagonals of both L and L_m ordered from largest to smallest. The related singular value decomposition of X is

(2.18) $X = U\ \text{Diag}(\sqrt{n\ell_i})V' = UDV'$

The eigenvectors and eigenvalues of S_{mXX} are consistent and unbiased estimators of those of S_{XX}.

The fourth sample indicator is a sample estimate of V'M based on the sample analog $\text{Cov}(\ell_{mi}, \ell_{mj} | N_m, X)$. Its formula shows that for perturbations Δ of the same magnitude the error in the eigenvectors M grows as a linear function of P, the number of variables.

When V_m is close to the identity S_m should be close to S. But closeness is hard to define since a diagonal element of .99 and a single off-diagonal of .14 are possible values. That is, an observed eigenvector could be contaminated by one seventh of another eigenvector and still be correlated .99 with the unperturbed eigenvector.

Comparison of the predicted value of Y from S in singular value decomposition form with the analog from S_m

$$\hat{Y} = XB = U(U'Y) \qquad Y_m = Xb_m = U(DV'ML_m^{-1}M'S_{mXY})$$

shows that Y_m is the wrong linear combination of the columns of U primarily because V'M is not the identity.

A related estimate of the ratio S_{mij}/S_{ij} is

(2.19) $$\text{est}(S_{mj}/S_{ij}) = 1 + \left(\frac{k_{ij}}{n_{ij}}\frac{1}{n}(1 + \rho_{ij}^{-2})\right)^{\frac{1}{2}}$$

The sample analog of 2.19 uses the correlation matrix based on S_m. Examination of 2.19 shows that the off-diagonals of S_{mij} are inflated more than diagonal elements, thus showing that S_{mij} is less well conditioned than S. Simulated values of S_{mij}/S_{ij} show the same behavior.

3. Simulation Tests

A data array X, consisting of twenty observations from the zero-centered, 4-variate normal was generated from a full-rank 4×4 covariance matrix Σ. Twenty independent random 10% missingness patterns (each a 20×4 matrix P of zeros and ones with $P(P_{ij}=0) = 1-q=.1$) were generated. For each missingness pattern the pairwise-present covariance matrix S_m and the complete-observations-only covariance matrix S_c were computed.

Comparison of the population and observed covariance matrices shows that the sample estimates of the standard deviation of Δ from equation (2.3) are of the same order of magnitude as the non-observable empirical estimates.

The ratios $s_{mij} \div s_{ij}$ indicate that the non-positive definite perturbation $\Delta = S - S_m$ stretches S away from positive definiteness. The observed missingness fractions k_{ij}/n_{ij} show that the variance in the s_{ij} due to missingness is 10 to 25% of that due to random sampling with the higher percentage on the off-diagonals.

Regression coefficients and residual sums of squares were computed for S, and each of the twenty S_m and S_c. The first column of X was used as the dependent variable, the remaining 3 columns are the independent variables. Figure A illustrates the empirical distribution of the values of b_1 computed from the twenty missingness patterns. Table 1 presents the statistics on all three b.

The observable estimate of the asymptotic standard deviation agrees in magnitude with the non-observable estimate and both are 3 to 4 times larger than the sampling error. Table 2 presents statics on the residual sums of squares calculated from the sample analogs of both (1.3) and (1.4). Efficiencies are computed by (2.15) The empirical distribution of the efficiencies in Figure B shows that S_c is more likely than S_m to give an efficiency close to one.

In this example the diagonal elements of the S_m are based on an average of 90% of the observations and the off-diagonals are based on an average of 87%. All elements of S_c are based on an average of 66% of the observations, yet the mean efficiencies are $e(S_{b_m}) = .43$ and $e(S_{b_c}) = .89$, showing the complete-observations-only technique to be twice as efficient with 25% fewer effective observations. An earlier simulation study (Haitovsky, 1968) showed similar relative efficiencies.

Comparison of the eigenvectors V of S and the eigenvectors M of S_m show major dislocations in orientation.

REFERENCES

1. Beale, E.M.L., and R.J.A. Little, "Missing Values in Multivariate Analysis". Journal of the Royal Statistical Society, Series B (Methodological) 37, pp. 129-145, 1975.

2. Dempster, Arthur P., Nan M. Laird, and Donald B. Rubin. "Maximum Likelihood from Incomplete Data Via the EM Algorithm (with Discussion)", Journal of the Royal Statistical Society, Series B (Methodological), 39, 1.pp. 1-38, 1977.

3. Dixon, W.J., and M.B. Brown, editors, BMDP-77: Biomedical Computer Programs--P-series.

4. Haitovsky, Yoel, "Missing Data in Regression Analysis", Journal of the Royal Statistical Society, Series B, p.30, 1.pp. 67-82, 1968.

5. Hamilton, Martin A. "Regression Analysis When There Are Missing Observations: Survey and Bibliography", Report No.1-3-75, Statistical Center, Montana State University, March 1975.

6. Heiberger, Richard M. "Regression with the Pairwise-Present Covariance Matrix: A Dangerous Practice", Proceedings of the Statistical Computing Section, pp. 38-47, American Statistical Association, Washington D.C., 1977.

7. Heiberger, Richard M. "Perturbation Analysis of Missing Value Regression Techniques", Technical Report No. 27, Department of Statistics, The Wharton School, University of Pennsylvania, March 1978

ACKNOWLEDGMENT: Support has been provided by the National Science Foundation through grant DCR-75-13994

1. REGRESSION COEFFICIENTS

Statistics	b_1	b_2	b_3
b	1.00	.96	1.01
b_m	.88	1.02	1.03
$\bar{b}_m$	.98	.92	1.10
s_{b_m}	.18	.26	.22
σ_{b_m}	.17	.20	.26
$\hat{\sigma}_{b_m}$	.15	.13	.24
s_b	.04	.05	.07
b_c	1.08	1.00	0.96
$\bar{b}_c$	0.99	0.95	1.01
s_{b_c}	0.06	0.04	0.04

2. RESIDUAL SUMS OF SQUARES AND EFFICIENCIES

	Residual Sums of Squares				Efficiencies	
	$S_{mYY.X}$	$S_{cYY.X}$	S_{b_m}	S_{b_c}	$e(S_{b_m})$	$e(S_{b_c})$
S	5.72	5.72	5.72	5.72	1.00	1.00
S_m or S_c	-27.19	3.71	8.73	6.83	.66	.84
Mean	-0.37	5.10	20.89	6.57	.43	.89
Std. Dev.	47.50	1.38	15.20	1.31	.28	.12

A. STEM AND LEAF DISPLAY OF FIRST REGRESSION COEFFICIENT UNDER 20 MISSINGNESS PATTERNS

b_{m1}			b_{c1}		
1.	.5	5			
3	.6	89			
4	.7	8			
6	.8	28	2	.8	17
7	.9	7	8)	.9	15567899
7)	1.0	0334899	10	1.0	0011333477
6	1.1	013468			

B. STEM AND LEAF DISPLAY OF EFFICIENCIES OF SUMS OF SQUARES $e(S_b)$ UNDER 20 MISSINGNESS PATTERNS

$e(S_{b_m})$			$e(S_{b_c})$		
1	.0	9			
4	.1	068			
6)	.2	246778			
10	.3	1			
9	.4	056	1	.4	9
6	.5		1	.5	
6	.6	57	2	.6	9
4	.7	9	3	.7	3
3	.8	4	6	.8	344
2	.9	19	14)	.9	13334566778899

Digression Analysis: Fitting Alternative Regression Models to Heterogeneous Data

S. Mustonen, Helsinki

SUMMARY

A selective least squares method for parameter estimation of alternative regression models in heterogeneous data is introduced. A test for heterogeneity of the sample is described. Computational aspects of the method are discussed and some test results are presented.
KEYWORDS switching regression, cluster analysis, least squares, heterogeneous data.

1. Introduction

Heterogeneous data appearing in a statistical investigation is seldom a pleasant surprise when a neat unimodal sample was expected. Heterogeneity proves that the observations have been affected by some unrecorded factors. If these disturbances cannot be measured afterwards heterogeneity is bound to remain in the data and it may hamper all the statistical analyses.

In this paper the problem of heterogeneity will be considered in connection with linear and nonlinear regression analysis. A method will be proposed which allows dealing with regression models despite heterogeneous data.

As an illustrative simple example, let us imagine an ambiguous situation in the ordinary linear model $y=\alpha x+\beta+\varepsilon$ where α,β are unknown parameters and ε is the error term. Assume that our data to be used for parameter estimation contains a considerable portion of exceptional observations having a different β parameter, say γ. Thus the important trend parameter α is supposed to be the same for all observations. In Fig.1 such a heterogeneous sample with $\alpha=1$, $\beta=-0.6$, $\gamma=1$ and $\varepsilon\sim N(0,0.5^2)$ is displayed. 50 observations of each kind have been generated. All the simulations, computations and graphic presentations in this paper have been carried out with the statistical data processing system SURVO 76 (Mustonen,1977).

It is disastrous to fit an ordinary linear model to this data. Although α is same for the both species of observations the common least squares estimate of this trend parameter is 0.736.

The method to be considered in this paper, digression analysis, will give without any prior information on the origin of each observation the estimates $\alpha=0.981$, $\beta=-0.632$ and $\gamma=0.968$. Simultaneously with the estimation the observations will also be classified into two groups which in this case agree well with the original partition.

Fig.1a A heterogeneous sample

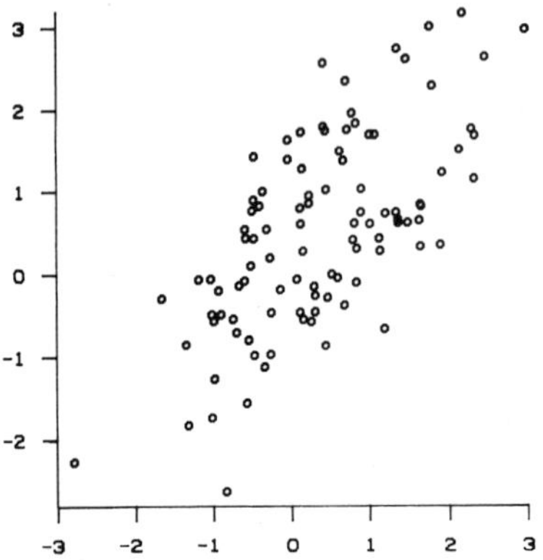

Fig.1b The regression line --- and the digression lines

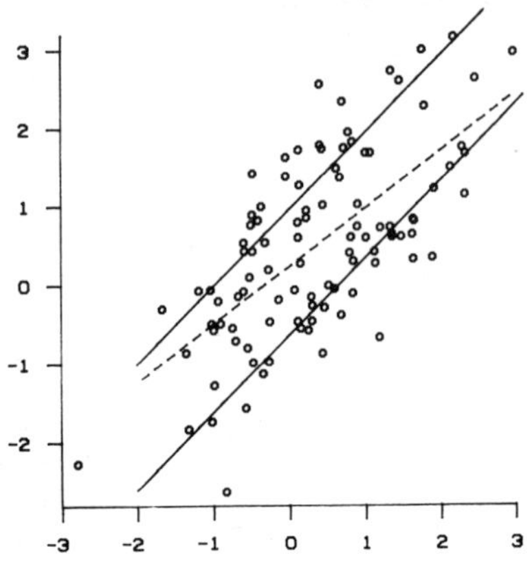

2. Principle of digression analysis

In digression analysis the properties of regression and cluster analysis are combined. Let us have n observations

$$y_j,\ x_{1j}, x_{2j}, \ldots, x_{mj}, \qquad j=1,2,\ldots,n$$

on the variables $y, x_1, x_2, \ldots, x_m$ and assume that these observations are divided in an unknown way into two groups (restriction to two is not essential), and in group i (i=1,2) we have

$$E(y)=f_i(x_1,x_2,\ldots,x_m,\alpha_i)$$

where the form of the regression function f_i is known but possibly different for each group, and α_i is the vector of parameters to be estimated.
Our task is to estimate the parameters α_1, α_2 simultaneously without any previous information on the type of any single observation.

A normal procedure in this situation is to classify the observations using some general clustering algorithm and thereafter the parameters will be estimated by means of regression analysis. This is not, however, efficient since classification and estimation are to be carried out independently of each other.

Simultaneous classification and estimation has occurred at least in econometrics when considering discontinuous parameter changes in time series (Goldfeld and Quandt,1976). In these switching regression problems additional information in a form of a time variable or other extraneous variables is usually available, and it naturally simplifies the problem.

In our approach the parameters are estimated by generalizing the least squares (OLS) criterion

$$\sum_{j=1}^{n}(y_j-f(x_{1j},\ldots,x_{mj},\alpha))^2=\min_{\alpha}$$

to a selective form

$$\sum_{j=1}^{n}\min\{(y_j-f_1(x_{1j},\ldots,x_{mj},\alpha_1))^2,(y_j-f_2(x_{1j},\ldots,x_{mj},\alpha_2))^2\} \tag{1}$$

and this selective least squares (SLS) criterion is to be minimized with respect to α_1,α_2.
Thus each observation will be attributed to the nearest regression curve and the parameters of each submodel f_1,f_2 are determined only by observation points of its own.
We are in fact applying the nearest-mean classification rule (Fukunaga,1972,p.332) in a generalized form.

The digression model defined above will be notated by

$$E(y)=\begin{cases}f_1(x_1,x_2,\ldots,x_m,\alpha_1)\\ f_2(x_1,x_2,\ldots,x_m,\alpha_2).\end{cases} \tag{2}$$

This set up and the corresponding SLS criterion can be easily extended to more than two submodels. The introductory example shows that the submodels may have common parameters. In many potential applications it is natural to expect that the submodels have a similar form and they differ from each other only by a few parameters.

At first it may seem rather odd that this simple selective criterion can work in practice when the subgroups are not distinct but partially overlapped. Then many serious misclassifications occur which may disturb parameter estimation. Let us notice, however, that the misclassifications will usually fall on neutral observations located "between" the regression curves and having no major influence on estimation.
Of course, the estimates obtained by the SLS method may be biased particularly if the data is only slightly heterogeneous and the subgroups are strongly overlapped. This digression bias diminishes rapidly when the heterogeneity grows. The magnitude of the bias depends also on the nature of the parameter. For instance, in the digression model

$$E(y)=\begin{cases}\alpha x+\beta\\ \alpha x+\gamma\end{cases}$$

the location parameters β and γ may have strongly biased estimates while the trend parameter α is always almost unbiased.
In some cases the digression bias can be estimated as well and its detrimental effects may be reduced (Mustonen,1976).

Passing from OLS to SLS means a considerable increase of computational work even in the case of linear submodels f_1,f_2 since minimization of the selective criterion (1) is a nonlinear optimization problem to be solved by iterative methods. It is also difficult to study the SLS principle theoretically, and this may be the reason why it has been ignored.

3. Testing for heterogeneity

In digression analysis it is necessary to make sure that the data in question is really heterogeneous in the intended manner.
One possibility to do this in practice is to fit an ordinary regression model

$$E(y)=f(x_1,x_2,\dots,x_m,\alpha) \qquad (3)$$

and compare the residual sums of squares in (2) and (3).
Let these sums be S_D and S_R, respectively. If $f=f_1$ we have $S_D \leq S_R$ since the digression model is always more flexible than its submodels. As a natural test criterion for heterogeneity the ratio S_D/S_R may be used. Now the crucial question is whether the value of this ratio is small enough to indicate that the digression hypothesis (2) is to be preferred to a plain regression hypothesis (3).
We shall study the behaviour of the statistic S_D/S_R in the simple digression model

$$y=\begin{cases}\mu_1+\varepsilon_1, & \varepsilon_1 \sim N(0,\sigma_1^2)\\ \mu_2+\varepsilon_2, & \varepsilon_2 \sim N(0,\sigma_2^2)\end{cases} \qquad (4)$$

which is equivalent to dissection of a mixture of two normal distributions. Assume that the components of this mixture are presented in our data in the proportions p_1,p_2.
A theoretical counterpart for SLS estimation of this model is to minimize the expected value

$$E(\min\{(y-\lambda_1)^2,(y-\lambda_2)^2\}) \qquad (5)$$

with respect to λ_1,λ_2. The minimum of (5) is denoted by σ_D^2.
In general, it is not possible to write λ_1,λ_2 and σ_D^2 in a closed form. In Table 1 these values are listed for some combinations of $\mu_1=-\mu_2=\mu$, p_2/p_1 and σ_2 ($\sigma_1=1$).

Table 1

μ	σ_2	p_2/p_1	λ_1	λ_2	σ_D^2	σ_D^2/σ_R^2
0.0	1.0	1.0	0.7978	-0.7978	0.3634	0.3634
0.5	1.0	1.0	0.8955	-0.8955	0.4491	0.3593
1.0	1.0	1.0	1.1666	-1.1666	0.6389	0.3195
1.5	1.0	1.0	1.5586	-1.5586	0.8207	0.2525
2.0	1.0	1.0	2.0169	-2.0169	0.9317	0.1864
2.5	1.0	1.0	2.5040	-2.5040	0.9799	0.1352
3.0	1.0	1.0	3.0007	-3.0007	0.9954	0.0995
0.0	0.8	0.8	0.7269	-0.7269	0.3115	0.3709
0.0	0.8	0.6	0.7380	-0.7380	0.3202	0.3703
0.0	0.6	0.8	0.6560	-0.6560	0.2851	0.3985
0.0	0.6	0.6	0.6782	-0.6782	0.3000	0.3948
1.0	0.8	0.8	1.2974	-0.9331	0.5532	0.3027
1.0	0.8	0.6	1.3402	-0.8941	0.5551	0.3080
1.0	0.6	0.8	1.3723	-0.8709	0.4645	0.2728
1.0	0.6	0.6	1.3968	-0.8144	0.4766	0.2808
2.0	0.8	0.8	2.0531	-1.9602	0.7946	0.1659
2.0	0.8	0.6	2.0566	-1.9410	0.8150	0.1766
2.0	0.6	0.8	2.0615	-1.9478	0.6747	0.1446
2.0	0.6	0.6	2.0629	-1.9289	0.7136	0.1582

In the symmetric case $\sigma_1=\sigma_2=\sigma$, $p_1=p_2$, $\mu_1=-\mu_2=\mu$ we have

$$\lambda_1=-\lambda_2=\lambda=(2\Phi(\mu/\sigma)-1)\mu+2\phi(\mu/\sigma)\sigma$$

and $\sigma_D^2=\sigma^2+\mu^2-\lambda^2$, $\sigma_R^2=\sigma^2+\mu^2$. In particular, if the distribution is homogeneous then $\lambda=\sqrt{2/\pi}\sigma$ and $\sigma_D^2/\sigma_R^2=\kappa=1-2/\pi=0.36338$. The ratio σ_D^2/σ_R^2 is clearly a counterpart for S_D/S_R in the model (4) and S_D/S_R tends to κ as the sample size grows if the sample is from a homogeneous normal distribution. It is also obvious that for a homogeneous normal sample the asymptotic distribution of S_D/S_R is normal. To evaluate the mean and variance of this asymptotic distribution, a series of simulation experiments have been carried out. The main results are given in Table 2.

Table 2

number of replicates	n	mean of S_D/S_R	std.dev. of S_D/S_R	skewness	kurtosis
200	50	0.3452	0.0456	-0.07	3.03
1320	100	0.3543	0.0327	0.18	3.19
385	200	0.3587	0.0251	0.12	2.97
210	500	0.3620	0.0156	0.13	2.88
578	1000	0.3633	0.0105	-0.15	2.83

The results indicate that $E(S_D/S_R)$ tends to κ and $Var(S_D/S_R)$ is approximately $0.115/n$.

In fact S_R and S_D/S_R seem to be asymptotically independent variables. In this case it can be shown that the asymptotic variance of S_D/S_R is $8(1-3/\pi)/(\pi n)$. Several tests have been performed for various n showing no significant departure from normality.

In Fig.2 sample distributions of S_D/S_R have been plotted on normal probability paper for n=200,500 and 1000.

Fig.2

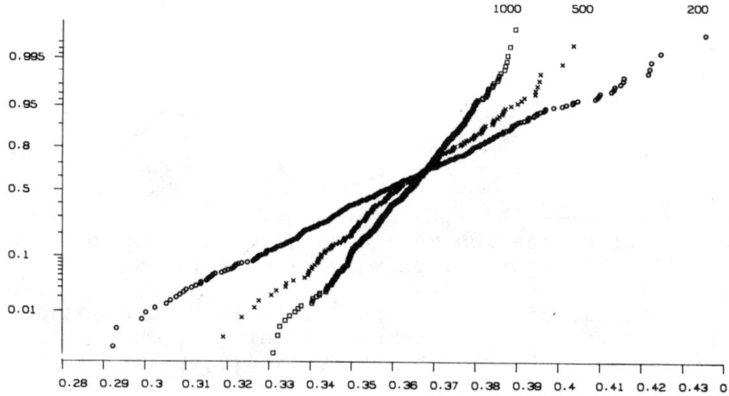

The test, based on the asymptotic distribution of S_D/S_R, can also be used in the more general situation of our introductory example where the digression model can be rewritten in the form

$$y-\alpha x=\begin{cases}\beta+\varepsilon_1\\ \gamma+\varepsilon_2\end{cases}$$

which is same as (4) if α is known. Thus for large n, S_D/S_R has the same asymptotic properties for both models. Also simulations with homogeneous samples for variables x,y support this assertion.

In the introductory example $S_D/S_R=0.248$ and if the data were homogeneous S_D/S_R would be approximately $N(0.35,0.034^2)$. Thus our test indicates that the sample in Fig.1 is very heterogeneous.

In Fig.3 two samples of 1000 observations of the same type are displayed. The first is heterogeneous with $\alpha=1$, $\beta=-\gamma=0.5$ and $\varepsilon_1,\varepsilon_2 \sim N(0,0.5^2)$ but the second sample is homogeneous with $\alpha=0.9$, $\beta=\gamma=0$ and $\varepsilon \sim N(0,0.7^2)$. In this case it is rather difficult to detect the heterogeneity by eye. Here, however, S_D/S_R acquires the value 0.328 for the first sample and 0.366 for the second. In this case S_D/S_R should be $N(0.363,0.0107^2)$ for a homogeneous sample. Thus the homogeneity of the first sample would be rejected.

Fig.3

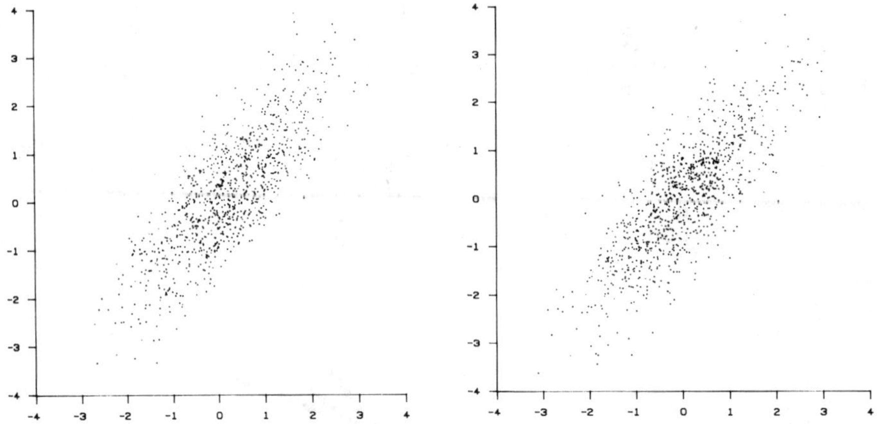

4. Computational aspects

In estimation of digression models we have to minimize the SLS criterion (1). The nature of this problem is illustrated by the following example.

Consider the simple digression model (4). In this case application of the SLS principle means partitioning of observations $y_j, j=1,\ldots,n$ into disjoint subsets $\{y_j, j\in J_1\}, \{y_j, j\in J_2\}$ and selecting the values of μ_1,μ_2 so that

$$\sum_{j\in J_1}(y_j-\mu_1)^2+\sum_{j\in J_2}(y_j-\mu_2)^2$$

is minimized. For each fixed partition J_1, J_2 the minimum is attained when μ_i is the arithmetic mean of y values of J_i, i=1,2. Thus by comparing the minima obtained in various partitions the solution will be found. By sorting the observations only a few comparisons are necessary in practice.
This simple procedure can also be applied to some other digression models, but in general, the solution of the estimation problem must be based on some general iterative algorithm. The task is not easy because the objective function (1) may have unpleasant cusps as illustrated in Fig.4

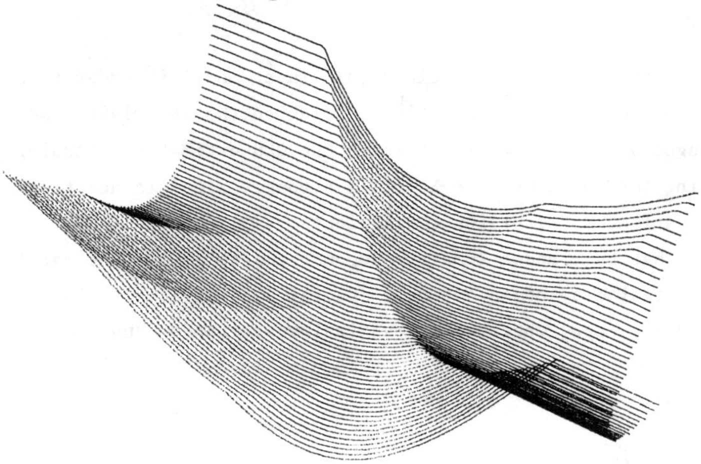

It is important that the algorithm can detect the broad outlines of the function in spite of the cusps. In practice we have experimented with the variable metric method with numerical derivatives and the method of Hooke and Jeeves (1961). The latter method, which is a direct search algorithm, has proved to be reliable in various linear and nonlinear digression models.

References

Fukunaga K., Introduction to Statistical Pattern Recognition, Academic Press, New York, 1972

Goldfeld S.M. and Quandt R.E., Studies in Nonlinear Estimation, Ballinger, New York, 1976

Hooke R. and Jeeves T.A., "Direct search" solution of numerical and statistical problems, J.of the Assn.for Computing Machinery,8,212-229,1961

Mustonen S., Digression analysis, Research Report No.2, Department of Statistics, University of Helsinki, 1976(in Finnish)

Mustonen S., SURVO 76: A statistical data processing system (for Wang 2200), Research Report No.6, Department of Statistics, University of Helsinki, 1977

The Multivariate Approach in Linear Regression Theory

B.M.S. van Praag, Leiden

Summary

In this paper we extend the classical linear model in order that it covers the case of stochastic X. Doing so the underlying model is changed an we have to reinterpret the OLS-estimator accordingly. Admitting for randomness in X puts a stronger significance test on the estimated regression coefficients.
In case that the random X-matrix degenerates to a constant matrix the classical case comes out as a special case. It covers also the intermediate case, where some x-variables are random and some not.

1. Introduction

The standard model in econometric practice is still the classical linear model

(1) $$\underline{y} = \beta_1 x_1 + \dots + \beta_k x_k + \beta_o + \underline{\varepsilon}$$

where the vector of explanatory variables $x = (x_1,\dots,x_k)$ is non-random and the error-term is assumed to be random.[1)] The random character of $\underline{y}$, the variable to be explained, is exclusively due to the randomness of ε. In many practical situations, especially in cross-section analysis, there is considerable doubt (see Wold (1953), Goldberger (1964)) whether the hypothesis that x is non-random can be maintained. In that case the model (1) is replaced by the stochastic model

(2) $$\underline{y} = \beta_1 \underline{x}_1 + \dots + \beta_k \underline{x}_k + \beta_o + \underline{\varepsilon}$$

Sometimes this is also called the multivariate model, (Wold, (1953), Malinvaud (1970), Maddala (1977)), a term we shall sometimes use in the sequel. Although it is mainly assumed that all variables $\underline{x}_1,\dots,\underline{x}_k$ are random we may conceive of mixtures where only $\underline{x}_1$ is random (and $x_2,\dots,x_k$ are non-random), the <u>bivariate</u> model, or models where only $\underline{x}_1,\dots,\underline{x}_j$ $(j < k)$ are random, in which case the term <u>j-variate</u> seems appropiate.
Let $\{ (y_t,x_t) \}_{t=1}^{T}$ be a set of observations.
In the classical and the multivariate model the parameter vector β may be estimated by the linear estimator $\hat{b}= (X'X)^{-1}X'y$ where $y = (y_1,\dots y_t)'$ and X is the T x (k+1) - matrix $X' = (x_{it})'$ with $x_{ot} = 1$ for all t. We decompose $X=(X_b,\iota)$ if needed

In the literature the classical model and the multivariate model are dealt with in separate theories, where the classical model gets much more attention than the multivariate model.
In Section 2 we shall compare the two models.
In Section 3 we derive the large sample-distribution of $\hat{b}$ in the multivariate model and in Section 4 it is shown that the classical results are included as a special case.
In Section 5 we present an application, while Section 6 concludes.

2. The two models compared

a. *The classical linear model.*

It can be summarized as follows. The maintained hypothesis is

(1) $$\underline{y}_t = \beta_1 x_{1t} + \dots + \beta_{kt} + \beta_o + \underline{\varepsilon}$$

under the assumptions

C.1) $E(\varepsilon_t) = 0,\ \sigma^2(\varepsilon_t) = \sigma^2,\ E(\varepsilon_t,\varepsilon_t') = 0$

C.2) the Tx(k+1) - matrix $X' = (x_{it})'$ is fixed <u>in repeated samples</u> (See Goldberger (1964))

----

1) If needed, we underline random variables. Matrices will will be denoted by capitals.

The first assumption deals with intertemporal independence. The second one is somewhat more difficult to interpret. Frequently, it is interpreted as X is non-random, however, it is certainly possible that we do not know before observation which x will occur. But, we know for sure that after T observations we will always have the same observation set $\{x_t\}_{t=1}^{T}$, although the order of appearance may vary. The x-population is exhausted by just T drawings. Using this interpretation we have to add as a specific assumption

C.3) $E(X'\varepsilon) = 0$ (which is implied by C.2 if we assume X to be non-random).

Consider now the sample analogues of $E(\varepsilon_t) = 0$, $E(X\varepsilon) = 0$, they are

$$\frac{1}{T}(\iota' e) = \frac{1}{T}\iota'(y-X\hat{b}) = 0 \tag{2}$$

$$\frac{1}{T}X'e = \frac{1}{T}\left[X'(y-X\hat{b})\right] = 0$$

where $\iota' = (1,\ldots,1)$.

It can be shown that if (X) has full rank, this equation system has just one solution.

Defining all variables as deviations from their mean $\mu_x = \left[\mu_1,\ldots,\mu_k\right]$ and $\hat{\mu}_y$, we may write $\hat{b}$ as

$$\hat{b} = \Sigma_{xx}^{-1}\hat{\Sigma}_{xy}, \quad \hat{b}_o = \hat{\mu}_y - \hat{b}'\mu_x \tag{3}$$

where Σ_{xx} is the population covariance matrix of x and $\hat{\Sigma}_{xy}$ the estimated covariance vector between y and x. We observe that (2) defines $\hat{b}$ completely. If we would specify a specific correlation between X and ε, say $E(X'\varepsilon) = \rho$, equation system (2) would change as well, yielding another $\hat{b}(\rho)$.

We notice also that no "least-squares" argument is involved, although it stands to reason that minimization of $(y-Xb)'(y-Xb)$ yields the same estimator without any further assumption on ε.

b. *The multivariate model.*

In empirical situations it is rarely feasible to draw samples with the same X-matrix. Then assumption C.2 is not met. On the contrary, we have to assume that T observations will

not exhaust the x-population. However, if the hypothesis (1) on (y,x) has any credibility, we have to assume that (y,x) are sampled according to a simultaneous probability density function f(y,x) which does not change during the sampling process.
It implies that our assumptions become
Assumptions

M.1) $E(\varepsilon_t) = 0$, $\sigma^2(\varepsilon_t) = \sigma^2$, $E(\varepsilon_t . \varepsilon_t') = 0$.

M.2) (y,x) is observed from a fixed frequency distribution f(y,x), where fourth-order moments exist.

M.3) $E(X'\varepsilon) = 0$.

Notice that M.2) becomes C.2) if the x-population is assumed to be exhausted by T observations.
In this case $E(\varepsilon_t)$ and $E(X'\varepsilon)$ are estimated as before by their sample analogues and we get system (2) again with the same estimator

(4) $$\hat{b} = \hat{\Sigma}_{xx}^{-1} \hat{\Sigma}_{xy} \qquad \hat{b}_o = \hat{\mu}_y - \hat{b}'\hat{\mu}_x$$

Notice that in this case Σ_{xx}, μ_x are unknown; their values are estimated by $\hat{\Sigma}_{xx}, \hat{\mu}_x$

c. *A Synthesis*

From the above argument it is obvious that the classical model is a specific instance of the stochastic model, where the x-population contains only T different elements. Those elements are different for (X) has full rank. The estimator $\hat{b}$ is identical for both models; only its probability distribution will differ. In the classical case $\hat{b}$ is only random in $\hat{\Sigma}_{xy}$, while in the stochastic case $\hat{\Sigma}_{xx}$ is random as well.

3. The Distribution of $\hat{b}$ in Large Samples

A well-known theorem in statistics (see Cramér (1951), p.354 and 366; Goldberger, (1964) p. 122 a.f.) may be summarized as follows

Let $H(\theta)$ be a twice-differentiable function and let $\hat{\theta}$ be a sample statistic tending to θ_o if T tends to ∞, then

$$\text{plim } H(\hat{\theta}) = H(\theta_o)$$

$H(\hat{\theta})$ becomes normally distributed with

$$E[H(\hat{\theta})] \to H(\theta_o)$$

$$\text{and var } (H(\hat{\theta})) = \left[\frac{dH}{d\theta}\right]^2_{\theta=\theta_o} \cdot \quad \text{var } (\hat{\theta})$$

This theorem can be generalized to vector functions and applied on

$$\hat{b} = \hat{\Sigma}^{-1}_{xx} \; \hat{\Sigma}_{xy} .$$

We get

$$\text{plim } \hat{b} = \Sigma^{-1}_{xx} \; \Sigma_{xy}, \quad \text{plim } \hat{b}_o = \mu_y - \mu_x' \; \Sigma^{-1}_{xx} \Sigma_{xy}$$

$\hat{b}$ is normally distributed about $\Sigma^{-1}_{xy} \; \Sigma_{xy}$ with

$$\text{var } (\hat{b}) = \dot{B}' \hat{\Pi} \dot{B}$$

where

$$(1) \qquad \dot{B} = \underbrace{\begin{bmatrix} \text{vec}\left(\dfrac{\delta \hat{b}_1}{\delta \Sigma_{xx}}\right), \ldots, \text{vec}\left(\dfrac{\delta \hat{b}_k}{\delta \Sigma_{xx}}\right) \\ \Sigma^{-1}_{xx} \end{bmatrix}}_{k} \; \updownarrow k^2+k$$

and where

$$(2) \qquad \hat{\Pi} = E\left[\text{vec}\begin{pmatrix} \hat{\Sigma}_{xx} - \Sigma_{xx} \\ \hat{\Sigma}_{xy} - \Sigma_{xy} \end{pmatrix} \text{vec}\begin{pmatrix} \hat{\Sigma}_{xx} - \Sigma_{xx} \\ \hat{\Sigma}_{xy} \quad \Sigma_{xy} \end{pmatrix}'\right]$$

of order $(k^2+k)x(k^2+k)$

That is, $\hat{\Pi}$ is the <u>covariance</u> <u>matrix</u> of <u>all</u> elements of $\hat{\Sigma}_{xx}, \hat{\Sigma}_{xy}$.

Notice that $\dfrac{\delta \hat{b}}{\delta \sigma_{ij}} = \Sigma^{-1}_{xx} \; I_{ij} \Sigma^{-1}_{xx} \; \Sigma_{xy}$ with I_{ij} the null-matrix except for $\iota_{ij} = 1$.

The elements of $\hat{\Pi}$ are estimated by

(3) $$\text{cov.}\,(\hat{\sigma}_{ij},\hat{\sigma}_{lm}) = \hat{\Pi}_{ij,lm} = \frac{1}{T}\,(\hat{\mu}_{ij,lm} - \hat{\sigma}_{ij}\cdot\sigma_{lm})$$

where

$$\hat{\mu}_{ij,lm} = \frac{1}{T}\sum_{t=1}^{T}(x_{it}-\bar{x}_i)(x_{jt}-\bar{x}_j)(\bar{x}_{lt}-\bar{x}_l)(x_{mt}-\bar{x}_m)$$

a generalization of

$$\text{var}\,(\hat{\sigma}^2) = \frac{1}{T}\,(\mu_4 - \sigma^4)$$ (see Wilks (1962), Goldberger 1964) p. 120).

An expression for var $(\hat{b}_o)$ may be derived in a similar but more complicated way, since we have to employ the just calculated var $(\hat{b})$ as well.

Schönfeld (1971) derives essentially the same result in a condensed form for var $(\hat{b})$ but in an alternative way. (1971, p. 19) He does not present expression (3). nor calculates var $(\hat{b}_o)$.

4. Conformity with Classical Result

In the classical case it is well-known that

$$\text{var}\,(\hat{b}) = \sigma_\varepsilon^2\,(X'X)^{-1} = \frac{\sigma^2}{T}\,\Sigma_{xx}^{-1}\,.$$

Calculating var $(\hat{b})$ according to the multivariate approach all elements in $\hat{\Pi}$ pertaining to Σ_{xx} are zero, when $\hat{\Sigma}_{xx} = \Sigma_{xx}$.

Hence $$\text{var}\,(\hat{b}) = \Sigma_{xx}^{-1}\,\Pi_{22}\,\Sigma_{xx}^{-1}$$

where Π_{22} consists of elements cov $(\hat{\sigma}_{iy},\hat{\sigma}_{jy})$ only.

We have $$\text{cov}\,(\hat{\sigma}_{iy},\hat{\sigma}_{jy}) = \frac{1}{T^2}\,\text{cov.}\,(\Sigma x_{it}y_t,\Sigma x_{jt}y_t)$$

$$= \frac{\hat{\sigma}^2(y)}{T^2}\,\Sigma x_{it}x_{jt} = \frac{\sigma_\varepsilon^2}{T}\,\Sigma_{xx}$$

we get $$\text{var}\,(\hat{b}) = \Sigma_{xx}^{-1}\,\frac{\sigma_\varepsilon^2}{T}\,\Sigma_{xx}\,\Sigma_{xx}^{-1} = \frac{\sigma_\varepsilon^2}{T}\,\Sigma_{xx}^{-1}$$

In case that $\hat{\Sigma}_{xx} \neq \Sigma_{xx}$ all variances will increase. The classical variance is a lower bound to the real variance if $\hat{\Sigma}_{xx}$ is stochastic. It is obvious that the model holds as well when some x's are stochastic and others not. This yields the j-variate model.

5. Application

The previous theory is applied on a dataset which is described extensively in Goedhart, Halberstadt, Kapteyn, Van Praag (1977). A survey was conducted by the Dutch Central Bureau of Statistics in 1975 where 1748 people were asked a.o. the following three questions[1)]:

1. what is your family size? Answer: fs
2. what is your after-tax disposable income; Answer: y
3. what level of net family income would be, in your circumstances, the absolute minimum for you? Answer: y_{min}

The following relationship has been estimated according to the classical model:

$$\underset{}{\ln y_{min}} = \underset{(0.149)}{3.60} + \underset{(0.0126)}{0.12 \ln fs} + \underset{(0.0156)}{0.60 \ln y} \qquad \bar{R}^2 = 0.57 \quad N = 1748$$

The $\bar{R}^2$ is the adjusted correlation coefficient, and the figures between brackets are standard deviations.

In this survey obviously not only y_{min} but also fs and y are random variables.
We apply the multivariate regression model, which yields the same regression coefficient, but the variances increase.

We find according to the multivariate specification

$$\ln y_{min} = \underset{(0.172)}{3.60} + \underset{(0.0141)}{0.12 \ln fs} + \underset{(0.0183)}{0.60 \ln y} \qquad \bar{R}^2 = 0.57 \quad N = 1748$$

In this case the standard deviations increase by about 20%.

REFERENCES

1. Cramér, H., Mathematical Methods of Statistics, Princeton 1951.
2. Goedhart, Th., Halberstadt, V., Kapteyn, A., van Praag, B.M.S., The Poverty Line, Concept and Measurement, The Journal of Human Resources, 12,1977.
3. Maddala, G.S., Econometrics, New York 1977.
4. Malinvaud, E., Statistical Methods of Econometrics, Amsterdam 1970.
5. Schönfeld,P., Methoden der Ökonometrie, Band II, Berlin 1971.
6. Wilks, S.S., Mathematical Statistics, New York 1962.
7. Wold, H. and Jureen, L., Demand Analysis, New York 1953.

----

1) Question abbreviated in this question.

Exact and Approximate Confidence Regions for Functions of Parameters in Non-Linear Models

G.J.S. Ross, Harpenden

Summary

Confidence regions in non-linear models may differ markedly from the quadratic approximations obtained from the asymptotic dispersion matrix of parameters. Exact limits for any parameter or function of parameters may be computed by a sequence of optimisations constrained to a particular value of the function and continued until the maximised likelihood equals a critical value. Approximate limits may be found without optimisation by applying a Lagrange multiplier technique, provided the parameter system is sufficiently stable for the quadratic approximations to apply to the critical contour. An example is discussed.

KEYWORDS: Confidence regions, non-linear models, likelihood, stable parameters, optimisation, Lagrange multiplier.

1. Introduction

Non-linear models are now fitted routinely in a wide variety of applications, but seldom is much attention paid either to the dispersion matrix of the estimated parameters or to the confidence regions within which the parameters may lie. Functions of parameters are required for prediction and interpretation of the fitted model, but confidence limits are seldom evaluated for these, except in the well known analysis of the probit regression line used in biological assay.

The layman is usually sufficiently trained to examine the standard errors of maximum likelihood estimates, and though he is told that the distribution is asymptotically Normal he will disregard the adverb and proceed to test hypotheses and construct confidence regions as if any estimated parameter or function could be treated as a Normal random variable. Joint confidence regions for several parameters will be effectively rectangular and may therefore include combinations of parameters very inconsistent with the data.

The statistician will be aware that for linear models with Normal errors confidence regions will be ellipsoidal and that the covariance structure of the dispersion matrix must be taken into account when computing functions of parameters and their standard errors. For non-linear models he will prefer to test hypotheses by comparing the likelihoods for the general and the specialised model and to assume that a likelihood-ratio test is valid. The exact description of the general set of confidence regions is considered to be both too expensive to compute and too complicated to explain, so that in practice confidence regions do not appear in the majority of applied papers in which statistical methods are used.

The extent to which the naive Normal approximation is misleading may be illustrated even in a simple one-parameter model. If 2 successes are observed in 10 binomial trials then the maximum likelihood estimate of the parameter p is 0.2 with a standard error of 0.127 which might tempt some to assert that 'p is not significantly greater than zero', which is absurd. Fisher and Yates (1963) tabulate a 95% fiducial interval (Table VIII) giving limits of the expectation of p of (0.025, 0.556), and the likelihood-ratio test gives a similar result. In multiparameter models the variety of misleading inferences is much greater.

In many non-linear models the functions of interest, such as interpolated values or maxima, are more precisely estimated than the parameters themselves and it may be computationally inaccurate to estimate standard errors of functions using the dispersion matrix which may be very ill-conditioned. In such cases it is wisest to try to express the model in terms of parameters with low covariances and for which the quadratic approximation to the log likelihood is as widely valid as possible. Such parameterisations also simplify the problem of finding confidence regions, as is shown below. Otherwise it is necessary to impose severe conditions on sample size or error variance which tend to exclude the proper analysis of much of the data that are commonly observed.

Progress in the use of confidence intervals depends on the availability of computer programs to compute them with sufficient speed and accuracy, and the willingness of scientific community to appreciate their advantages in removing some of the apparent paradoxes of conventional statistical analysis.

2. Likelihood based confidence regions

Cox and Hinkley (1974) recommend that confidence regions should be bounded by contours of constant likelihood so that all parameter values within the region are more acceptable than those outside. Such regions are referred to as 'likelihood-based confidence regions' for a parameter set. There is however some confusion about the critical value of the likelihood for an appropriate confidence region, and for confidence limits of functions of parameters. Four such approaches are described below.

(a) Frequency distributions of estimates for the linear model with Normal errors lead to the critical value $p\sigma^2 F(p,n-p,1-\alpha)$ when p parameters are estimated jointly. For non-linear models the probability of generating estimates outside the critical envelope is not necessarily α. However attention is often paid to the marginal distributions of single parameters or functions of parameters, with confidence intervals between the minimum and maximum values of functions on contours with critical value $\sigma^2 F(1,n-p,1-\alpha)$, giving the familiar results based on the t-distribution, and illustrated by Fieller's Theorem for the fiducial limits of a ratio of Normal means.
(b) Likelihood ratio tests of the significance of the estimated parameters compared with fixed values on the critical envelope lead to the same critical value as before for the linear model with Normal errors or a critical sum of squares of

$$\text{R.S.S.}(\hat{\underset{\sim}{\theta}}) \quad (1 + (p/(n-P)F(p,n-p,1-\alpha))$$

and for other distributions such as the Poisson or Binomial, as critical log likelihood of

$$-\log \text{pr}(\theta) \quad + \tfrac{1}{2}\chi^2(p,1-\alpha).$$

A good account of such confidence regions is given by Draper and Smith (1966). The interpretation of likelihood-ratio confidence regions is unchanged by parameter transformations, and since a function of parameters may replace any parameter without loss of generality, the appropriate limits for functions are the upper and lower values attained on the critical envelope. The limits therefore define the widest possible range of values of the function which can arise from parameters not significantly worse fitting than the maximum likelihood estimates. If there is more than one parameter such limits will be wider than fiducial or marginal frequency limits.

This method is valid provided the likelihood-ratio test is valid, where the parameters are few compared with the number of observations.
(c) A pure likelihood interpretation is suggested by Edwards (1972) who defines 'support regions' within contours with critical likelihood ratio k as being at least 1/k times as likely as the maximum likelihood estimates.
(d) Goodness of fit contours are sometimes suggested, using the critical value of the residual log likelihood $-\tfrac{1}{2}\chi^2(n-p,1-\alpha)$ irrespective of the value at the maximum.

The disadvantage of such a criterion is that it may give a null confidence regions if the best fit is itself signficantly poor, or it may give a universal confidence region if all values of the parameters give an acceptable fit.

The difference between these criteria is that they emphasise different statements about the model and its relation to the data. One cannot say that one is correct and the others incorrect, but regions of type (b) appear to be most generally useful.

3. The shape of likelihood contours

Whatever criterion is adopted we require methods of describing likelihood contours at a given level.

Graphical methods consist either of sets of contour plots in two dimension, or curves along one-dimensional transects. Since many important models have more than two parameters several plots are required and therefore graphical methods are unlikely to be used in routine reporting of results. They are however extremely valuable in theoretical studies.

Numerical methods reduce to reporting some numerical characteristics of the likelihood contour. The quadratic approximation to the log-likelihood is

$$\tfrac{1}{2}\,(\underline{\theta}-\hat{\underline{\theta}})'\underline{V}^{-1}(\underline{\theta}-\hat{\underline{\theta}}) \qquad (3.1)$$

where $\underline{V}$ is the estimated dispersion matrix at $\underline{\theta}=\hat{\underline{\theta}}$, and this can be reduced to canonical form by eigenvector methods, noting that the smallest eigenvalue corresponds to the linear function of parameters with least variance. If statements are required about each parameter separately we must find the maximum and minimum value of each parameter on the contour, namely the position of the tangent primes perpendicular to each parameter axis.

For non-linear models or non-Normal errors contours deviate from ellipsoidal form except within some neighbourhood of the maximum likelihood estimate. They may be asymmetric with respect to the solution, curved or they may be in several parts, and they may cross the boundary of the feasible region or be open-ended at infinity. However the shape is a consequence of the parameterisation chosen and it is usually possible to transform the parameters to a more stable system (Ross (1970)) in which contours are more nearly quadratic. Suitable stable parameters are functions of the original parameters easily estimated from the data, transformed if necessary if the errors are non-Normal. For example, stable parameters for curve fitting may be expected height of the curve at suitably chosen values of x, representing different ranges of data points.

A graphical check on the degree to which the approximation holds is to plot the discrepancy between the observed log-likelihood and the approximation given by equation 3.1 (Ross (1975)).

Since stable parameters are not always of direct interest the transformation of the likelihood does not solve the problem of confidence regions unless we may also find the range of any function of parameters on the critical contour.

4. Exact and approximate limits of functions of parameters

Given a routine for evaluating the log likelihood $L(\theta)$, of p parameters and a separate routine to evaluate some single valued function $f(\theta)$ then limits for f must be found subject to $L(\theta)=c$, where c is the critical value chosen.

Formally we have a constrained optimisation problem in which the constraint $L(\underline{\theta})=c$ is certainly not linear, and the objective function to be minimised is either $f(\underline{\theta})$, or $-f(\underline{\theta})$, assuming that only one range of values is involved.

An exact method that is slow to execute is to take trial values of $f(\underline{\theta})$ and to minimise $L(\underline{\theta})$ in the space of p-1 parameters, on each occasion determining the pth parameter from $f(\underline{\theta})$. A secant method is then used to determine the next trial value of $f(\underline{\theta})$ until the minimum value of $L(\underline{\theta})$ is as close to c as possible. Each limit in general requires more optimisation than the original problem of finding the maximum likelihood estimates.

The approximate method to be described assumes that the quadratic form (3.1) is adequate to describe the likelihood contour. Then no optimisations are required, only a routine to evaluate partial derivatives or differences of $f(\underline{\theta})$ with respect to each parameter. Then we can use Lagrange's method of undetermined multipliers to minimise

$$f(\underline{\theta}) - \lambda(L(\underline{\theta})-c) \qquad (4.1)$$

with respect to λ and $\underline{\theta}$ when we solve iteratively the equations

$$\frac{\partial f}{\partial \underline{\theta}} = \lambda \underline{V}^{-1}(\underline{\theta}-\hat{\underline{\theta}}) \qquad (4.2)$$

and $\frac{1}{2}(\underline{\theta}-\hat{\underline{\theta}})'\underline{V}^{-1}(\underline{\theta}-\hat{\underline{\theta}})=c$.

Taking $\frac{\partial f}{\partial \underline{\theta}}$ from the previous iteration and substituting for

$$\underline{\theta}-\hat{\underline{\theta}} = \frac{1}{\lambda}\underline{V}\frac{\partial f}{\partial \theta} \qquad (4.3)$$

we obtain $\lambda^{-2} = 2c/ \left(\frac{\partial f}{\partial \underline{\theta}}\right)' \underline{V} \frac{\partial f}{\partial \underline{\theta}}$

and taking the correct sign of λ we can now estimate new values of $\underline{\theta}$. It is preferable to check that the new value of $\underline{\theta}$ is actually on the contour, and if not, to adjust λ until it is. Convergence can be made to depend on the changes in $\underset{\sim}{\theta}$ at each stage.

The behaviour of the iterative process depends on the nature of $f(\underset{\sim}{\theta})$ in the critical region, both as regards the parallelism of its contours and in the non-linearity of their spacing. Linear functions converge very rapidly. Care should be taken with functions in solving ratios because the confidence interval may include infinity, so that the 'upper' limit is in fact lower than the 'lower' limit. Care should also be taken with many-valued functions such as square roots or inverse trigonometric functions and with functions whose range is restricted. Use of these functions in transformations explains how a model can be well-behaved in terms of its fitted values yet extremely irregular in terms of its defining parameters.

5. A numerical example

The negative exponential curve

$$E(y) = \theta_1 + \theta_2 \exp(-\theta_3 x) \tag{5.1}$$

with Normal errors is commonly fitted to data of which the following is an example:

x	1	2	3	4	6	8
y	3.2	7.9	11.1	14.5	16.7	18.3

The residual mean square is 0.1755 on 3 degrees of freedom giving a critical value of the sum of squares of 5.417 for alternative parameters significantly different from the least squares estimates at the 95% level. The estimated parameters and extreme values on the critical contour are as follows:

	Minimum	Estimate	Maximum
θ_1	16.89	19.77	26.71
θ_2	-28.61	-23.63	-19.45
θ_3	0.164	0.349	0.572

The interval for θ_1 is markedly asymmetrical, and the critical contour deviates sufficiently from the ellipse for the approximate limits for θ_1 to be seriously in error, and the symmetrical interval is found to be (16.06, 23.48).

The time required to compute the exact intervals was over six times that required to fit the model, and so a stable parameter system was used so that the approximate Lagrange technique could be used.

The model was defined by three parameters representing the value of E(y) at x=1, 4 and 7 respectively, these values being chosen to be equally spaced and to span the data range.

These parameters are almost uncorrelated and the critical contour is very close to its predicted quadratic approximation. The Lagrangian procedure was then applied to give the following intervals:

θ_1 (16.90, 26.66)

θ_2 (-28.61, -19.51)

θ_3 (.165, .572)

It would be fair to say that the procedure does not always work as well as this, and the algorithm is capable of refinement. The time reduction is very large, and the slight loss of accuracy is unimportant compared with the serious bias of the symmetrical limits.

6. Practical implementation

Both the exact and the approximate procedures are contained in the author's maximum likelihood program (MLP) which uses the stable parameter method to fit non-linear models with non-normal errors to data. At this stage confidence limits are provided only for users' own models and are optional (Ross, 1978). But it is hoped that they will become more widely used as more efficient algorithms are found for computing them. The program is distributed under licence agreement, and a prospectus may be obtained from the Programs Secretary, Statistics Department, Rothamsted Experimental Station, Harpenden, Herts, England.

7. References

Cox, D.R. & Hinkley, D.V., Theoretical Statistics. Chapman & Hall, London (1974).

Draper, N.R. & Smith, H., Applied Regression Analysis. Wiley, New York (1966).

Edwards, A.W.F., Likelihood. Cambridge, (1972).

Fisher, R.A. and Yates, F. Statistical Tables (6th Edn). Longman (1963).

Ross, G.J.S., The efficient use of function minimisation in non-linear maximum likelihood estimation. Appl.Stats, 19, 205-221.

Ross, G.J.S., Simple non-linear modelling for the general user. Bulletin of the Int.Stat.Inst. Vol 46, Book 2, 585-591 (1975).

Ross, G.J.S., MLP users' manual. Rothamsted Experimental Station (1978).

Nonparametric Regression and Density Estimation

W. Schlee, Munich

SUMMARY:
There are given a nonparametric regression curve and a nonparametric density estimate which are closely adjusted to computational requirements. The regression curve and the density estimator are related to one another as proposed by M.B. Priestley in the discussion of a paper by Boneva et al. (1971). A generalization of the histospline described by Boneva-Kendall-Stefanov seems to be too complicated for computation. Therefore in the present paper a simplified histospline is proposed. Beyond the scope of the paper of Boneva et al. (1971) there are investigated the statistical properties of the density estimate and the empirical regression curve in the multidimensional case: asymptotic normality at the continuity points of the theoretical density resp. regression curve and consistency. Moreover discontinuities of the theoretical curves can be handled too and it is possible to prove weak convergence of the associated multiparametric stochastic processes. The main emphasis of the paper lies on the fact that there are investigated the statistical properties of the really computed regression curve resp. density (besides numerical contamination caused by summation and multiplication). Indeed no further discretization is needed here in contrary to the usual kernel estimates and the functional series expansions. Moreover the required storage capacity for automatic computation only depends on the choice of the parameters in the proposed histospline and does not depend on the sample size. This is an advantage compared with the polynomial estimates too. The given regression curve estimator and the density estimator provide the user with estimators which are easy to handle and which yet have all necessary statistical properties. These estimators may be of special interest if no reasonable hypothesis is available.

KEYWORDS:
nonparametric statistics, density estimation, regression, statistical splines, computational statistics.

1. THREE BASIC LEMMAS.

We start with a function $k: \mathbb{R} \rightarrow \mathbb{R}$ which is assumed to have the following properties:

$$k(x) \geq 0, \quad k(x) \equiv 0 \quad x: |x| > C_x \qquad (1.1.1)$$

k is Riemann-integrable (1.1.2)

$$\int_{\mathbb{R}} k(x)dx = 1 \qquad (1.1.3)$$

$$\sup_x k(x) \leq C_k \qquad (1.1.4)$$

For computational convenience we propose

$$k(x) = \begin{cases} 0 & z \leq -3/2 \\ (z+\frac{3}{2})^2/2 & -3/2 \leq z \leq -1/2 \\ 3/4-z^2 & -1/2 \leq z \leq 1/2 \\ (z-\frac{3}{2})^2/2 & 1/2 \leq z \leq 3/2 \\ 0 & 3/2 \leq z \end{cases} \qquad (1.2)$$

as a basic histospline but all k are admissible which fulfill the propositions (1.1). By suitable transformations of the x-axis one may derive such k's from (1.2) which have a prescribed interval $[a,b]$ as support.

Let be $\beta = \beta(h) \geq 0$, $h = h(n) \geq 0$ and n parameters which are connected by the following limits:

$$\lim_{n\to\infty} h(n) = 0, \quad \lim_{h\to 0} \beta(h)/h = 0 \qquad (1.3)$$

Below n is taken as the sample size.

It is convenient to use the abbreviation

$$\mathfrak{k}^1(x,i) = \prod_{j=1}^{q} k^1\left(\frac{x_j - i_j\beta}{h}\right).$$

In the sequel we assume that there is given a partition of the $\mathbb{R}^q$ into intervals with side length $\beta(h)$. Also the summation

$\sum_{i_1,i_2,\ldots,i_q}$ is taken over all intervals of the partition. If the propositions (1.1) and (1.3) are valid we have:

Lemma 1:

$\forall\ l \geq 1$

$$\lim_{h\to 0} \sum_{i_1,\ldots,i_q} \mathcal{R}^l(x,i)\left(\frac{\beta}{h}\right)^q = \left(\int k^l(y)dy\right)^q \tag{1.4}$$

Lemma 2:

$\forall\ l \geq 1$, g continuous in a neighborhood of x,

$$\sup_x |g(x)| \leq C_g,\ \xi(i) = \xi(i_1,\ldots,i_q) \in \prod_{j=1}^{q}](i_j-1)\beta,\ i_j\beta]$$

$$\lim_{h\to 0} \sum_{i_1,\ldots,i_q} \mathcal{R}^l(x,i)\left(\frac{\beta}{h}\right)^q g(\xi(i)) = g(x)\ \left(\int k^l(y)dy\right)^q \tag{1.5}$$

Lemma 3:

$\forall\ r,s \geq 1,\ (x_1,x_2,\ldots,x_q) \neq (y_1,y_2,\ldots,y_q)\quad \sup_x |g(x)| \leq C_g$

$$\lim_{h\to 0} \sum_{i_1,\ldots,i_q} \left[\mathcal{R}^r(x,i)\ \mathcal{R}^s(y,i)\right] \left(\frac{\beta}{h}\right)^q \times g(\xi(i)) = 0 \tag{1.6}$$

One may consider these three lemmas as discrete versions of the corresponding results of Bochner (1960) which are used already by Parzen (1962) and Cacoullos (1966). The proofs are similar to the ones given in these papers.

2. THE ESTIMATES

Taking into account the above three lemmas we propose as probability density estimator:

$$f_n(x_1,\ldots,x_q) = h^{-q} \sum_{i_1,\ldots,i_q} \prod_{j=1}^{q} k\left(\frac{x_i - i_j\beta}{h}\right) \Delta_\beta(i_1,\ldots,i_q) F_n. \tag{2.1}$$

The additional parameters are explained as follows:

F_n is the empirical distribution function, n the sample size. By F resp. f there is denoted the theoretical distribution function resp. density. $\Delta_\beta(i_1,..,i_q)g = \Delta_\beta(i)g$ denotes the q-folded difference of a function g: $\mathbb{R}^q \to \mathbb{R}$ with respect to the chosen interval partition

$$\Delta_\beta(i)g = \sum_{i_1,..,i_q} g((i_1-j_1)\beta,..,(i_q-j_q)\beta) \times (-1)^{j_1+..+j_q}$$

whereas the summation is taken over all values $j_1,j_2,..,j_q=0,1$.

$\Delta_\beta(i)F_n$ resp. $\Delta_\beta(i)F$ is the empirical resp. the theoretical probability of the corresponding interval.

A regression curve shows some functional relationship between two quantities Y and X. X is assumed to be a q-dimensional continuously varying quantity, Y is a scalar variable. We suppose that y is a random function of x with expectation

$$\mathcal{E}\,Y(x) = g(x) \qquad (2.2)$$

X is a random variable too with a certain density f. In the space of the variable X there is given a partition by intervals with side length β . Again F_n is the empirical d.f. of X.

A sample (y_j,x_j) of size n is given. Let be $\overline{y}_{(i)} = \overline{y}_{(i_1,...,i_q)}$ the arithmetic mean of all measurements with an x lying in the interval $\prod_{l=1}^{q}](i_l-1)\beta, i_l\beta]$. Now the estimate $g_n(x)$ for the regression curve g(x) is given by

$$g_n(x) = (h^q f(x))^{-1} \sum_{i_1,..,i_q} \overline{y}_{(i)} \prod_{j=1}^{q} k\left(\frac{x_j-i_j\beta}{h}\right) \Delta_\beta F_n \qquad (2.3)$$

Using the lemmas 1,2, and 3 the following theorem can be proved and by this the estimators (2.1) and (2.3) are justified.

Theorem 1:

If f is continuous in a neighborhood of z then

$$\lim_{n\to\infty} \mathcal{E} f_n(z) = f(z) \tag{2.4.1}$$

$$\lim_{n\to\infty} \operatorname{Var}\left(\sqrt{nh^q}\; f_n(z)\right) = f(z) \left(\int k^2(u)du\right)^q \tag{2.4.2}$$

If $\mathcal{E}\, y(z) = g(z)$ and $\operatorname{Var} g(z) = \sigma^2(z)$ are continuous in a neighborhood of z then the conditional expectation and variance for the given sample $\mathfrak{X} = (X_1, X_2, \ldots, X_n)$ are

$$\lim_{n\to\infty} \mathcal{E}(g_n(z) \mid \mathfrak{X}) = g(z) \tag{2.5.1}$$

$$\lim_{n\to\infty} \operatorname{Var}\left(\sqrt{n(h/\beta)^q}\; g_n(z) \mid \mathfrak{X}\right) = \sigma^2(z)\left(\int k^2(z)dz\right)^q \tag{2.5.2}$$

For the density estimate the condition $\lim_{n\to\infty} (nh^q(n)) = \infty$ yields consistency, for the curve estimate consistency is already obtained by the last condition of (1.3).

Remark: If the density f of X in (2.3) is unknown, one may use the estimate (2.1). Analogously to Nadaraya (1965) it is possible to prove strong convergence of the estimate (2.1) for continuous f and an appropriate sequence h(n). Therefore the asymptotic properties of this modified $g_n(x)$ are not altered.

Taking into account the well known theorem, that an r-dimensional random variable is normally distributed iff each (non-zero) linear combination of its components is 1-dimensional normally distributed we deduce from the normal convergence criterion in Loève (1977, p. 307) using the lemmas 1,2,3:

Theorem 2:
Let be $\tilde{Z}_n(x) = \sqrt{nh^q}\ (f_n(x) - \mathcal{E}f_n(x))$. For all continuity points $x_1, x_2, .., x_r$ of f the random vector $(\tilde{Z}_n(x_1), .., \tilde{Z}_n(x_r))$ has an asymptotic normal distribution with a diagonal covariance matrix. The expectation is zero and the variance is given by (2.4.2).

Let be $\tilde{G}_n(x) = \sqrt{n(\frac{h}{\beta})^q}\ (g_n(x) - \mathcal{E}g_n(x))$. For all continuity points $x_1, x_2, .., x_r$ of g the random vector $(\tilde{G}_n(x_1), .., \tilde{G}_n(x_r))$ has an asymptotic normal distribution with a diagonal covariance matrix. The expectation is zero and the variance is given by (2.5.2).

Remark: Obviously $Z_n^* = \sqrt{nh^q}\ (f_n(x) - f(x))$ and $G_n^* = \sqrt{n(\frac{h}{\beta})^q}\ (g_n(x) - -g(x))$ are the really applicable quantities (e.g. for confidence intervals), but only with additional assumptions on h(n) it is possible to replace $\tilde{Z}_n$ resp. $\tilde{G}_n$ by Z_n^* resp. G_n^*.

3. COMPUTATION OF THE ESTIMATES

Obviously the estimators f_n and g_n can be written in the following manner:

$$f_n(z) = (nh^q)^{-1} \sum_{j=1}^{m} \prod_{l=1}^{q} k\left(\frac{z_l - i_l(x_j)\beta}{h}\right) \tag{3.1}$$

$$g_n(z) = (nh^q f(x))^{-1} \sum_{j=1}^{m} y_j \prod_{l=1}^{q} k\left(\frac{z_l - i_l(x_j)\beta}{h}\right), \tag{3.2}$$

whereas x_j resp. (y_j, x_j) are the sample values. Now we see that the sample values may be worked up on-line by the computer. To facilitate computation we choose $h = m(n)\beta$ with an integer $m(n)$ according to the above conditions for β and h. Further we take as function k a quadratic spline like (1.2) with knots adjusted to the interval partition given by the side length β . Under

these conditions f_n and g_n are also quadratic splines whereas the knots are the points of the interval partition.
In the case of $q = 1$ we have to store three coefficients of the valid quadratic function for each interval.
In the case of $q > 1$ we have to store 3^q coefficients for each interval.
$i(x) = (i_1(x),..,i_q(x))$ is the index-vector of the interval in which the sample value x lies. In both cases of the density and the regression this index-vector has to be computed. Then
$\prod_{l=1}^{q} k\left(\frac{z_l - i_l(x)\beta}{h}\right)$ resp. $y\prod_{l=1}^{q} k\left(\frac{z_l - i_l(x)\beta}{h}\right)$ are added up considering that these functional summands cover only a finite number of intervals of the partition and are zero outside.
The author has written a computer program. The computer runs were made at the Leibniz-Rechenzentrum München. Numerical examples show the usefulness of the described method which yields rapidly good results.

4. CLOSING REMARKS

Beyond the results of section 2 it is possible to prove weak convergence of the associated stochastic processes even in the case of discontinuities of the theoretical curves. One has to define an appropriate Skorohod space with $\mathbb{R}^q$ as parameter space. According to the papers of Straf (1970) and Neuhaus (1971) the proof can be established. Additional conditions on the function h(n) and some continuity properties of the theoretical curves yield strong convergence analogously to the paper of Nadaraya (1965). Since these statistical results do not influence the computational aspects we do not evaluate these ideas further.

REFERENCES

Bochner, S. (1960), "Harmonic Analysis and the theory of probability ", Univ. of California Press

Boneva, L.I., Kendall, D. and Stefanov, I. (1971) "Spline transformations: three new diagnostic aids for the statistical data-analyst", Journal of the Royal Statistical Society, Serie B, Vol. 33, 1-70

Cacoullos, T. (1966), "Estimation of a multivariate density", Annals of the Inst. of Statistical Mathematics, Japan, Vol. 18, 179 - 189

Loève, M. (1977), "Probability theory I", Springer Verlag, Berlin

Nadaraya, E.A. (1965), "On non-parametric estimates of density functions and regression curves", Theory of Probability and its Appl. Vol 10, 186 - 190

Neuhaus, G. (1971), "On weak convergence of stochastic Processes with multidimensional time parameter", The Ann. Math. Statist. Vol. 42, 1285 - 1295

Parzen, E. (1962), "On estimation of a probability density function and mode", Ann. Math. Statistics, Vol. 33, 1065 - 1076

Straf, M.L. (1970), "Weak convergence of stochastic processes with several Parameters", Proc. Sixth Berkeley Symposium on Math. Statist. and Prob. Vol. II, 187 - 221, University of California Press

Wahba, G. (1975), "Interpolating spline methods for density estimation I. Equispaced knots", The Annals of Statistics 3, 30 - 48.

An Iteration Estimator for the Linear Model

G. Trenkler, Hannover

SUMMARY: The purpose of this paper is to examine a biased estimator of the coefficients in the linear regression model. This so called iteration estimator shares its good properties with the ridge and other competing estimators. It is a linear but shorter transform of the ordinary least squares estimator preferable to the latter with regard to the mean square error criterion.

KEY WORDS

Linear Model; Biased Estimation; Generalized Inverse; Mean Square Error.

1. Introduction

Consider the standard linear regression model

$$y = X\beta + u \tag{1}$$

where y is a Tx1 observed random vector, X is a known Txp nonstochastic matrix of full column rank, β is a px1 vector of unknown parameters and u is an unobservable Tx1 vector with $E(u) = 0$ and $Cov(u) = \sigma^2 I$.

It is widely accepted that the usual least squares (LS) estimator $\hat{\beta} = (X'X)^{-1}X'y$ is unsatisfactory in the case of multicollinearity. Though being unbiased and having minimum variance within the class of linear unbiased estimators the LS-estimator is expected to be far distant from the true parameter vector when X'X is badly conditioned. A number of estimators were proposed to improve on least squares in such circumstances, for example

Ridge estimator	$(k \geq 0)$	$\hat{\beta}^* = (X'X + kI)^{-1}X'y$	Hoerl/Kennard	(1970 a,b)
Shrunken estimator	$(\lambda \geq 0)$	$c_\lambda = \lambda\hat{\beta}$	Mayer/Willke	(1973)
Generalized inverse estimator		$\hat{\beta}^+ = A_r^+ X'y$	Marquardt	(1970)

A_r^+ is a generalized inverse of X'X of assigned rank r.

With these biased estimators a smaller mean square error than least squares can be achieved.

The present paper investigates the linear biased estimator

$$\hat{\beta}_{n,\alpha} = X_{n,\alpha}\, y \tag{2}$$

with $\quad X_{n,\alpha} = \alpha \sum_{i=0}^{n} (I - \alpha X'X)^{i} X'$

where α is a nonnegative constant and n is an integer. It will be shown that the estimator (2) has the virtues (and the deficiencies) of the above mentioned alternatives to the LS-estimator.

2.The Iteration Estimator

Let the eigenvalues of X'X be denoted by

$$\lambda_{max} = \lambda_1 \geq \lambda_2 \geq \ldots . \quad \geq \lambda_p = \lambda_{min} > 0$$

It is well known (Ben-Israel/Greville(1974) or Rao/Mitra(1971)) that for $0 < \alpha < \frac{2}{\lambda_1}$ the sequence

$$X_{o,\alpha} = \alpha X'$$

$$X_{n+1,\alpha} = (I - \alpha X'X)\, X_{n,\alpha} + \alpha X' \tag{3}$$

or equivalently the series

$$X_{n,\alpha} = \alpha \sum_{i=0}^{n} (I - \alpha X'X)^{i} X' \tag{4}$$

converges to the Moore-Penrose inverse $X^{+} = (X'X)^{-1}X'$ of X.
It is worth mentioning that this result also holds when X is not of full column rank (then we have $X^{+} = (X'X)^{+}X'$). The relationship (3) suggests for $\hat{\beta}_{n,\alpha} = X_{n,\alpha}\, y$ the denotation "iteration estimator".

3.Properties of the Iteration Estimator

The estimator $\hat{\beta}_{n,\alpha}$ will be considered for values of α between 0 and $\frac{1}{\lambda_1}$ only. The following results are readily established:

(i) $\quad E(\hat{\beta}_{n,\alpha}) = X_{n,\alpha} X \beta \qquad$, i.e. $\hat{\beta}_{n,\alpha}$ is biased.

(ii) $\quad \mathrm{Cov}(\hat{\beta}_{n,\alpha}) = E\left[(\hat{\beta}_{n,\alpha} - E(\hat{\beta}_{n,\alpha}))(\hat{\beta}_{n,\alpha} - E(\hat{\beta}_{n,\alpha}))'\right] = \sigma^2 X_{n,\alpha} X'_{n,\alpha}$

(variance - covariance - matrix)

(iii) $\quad G(\hat{\beta}_{n,\alpha}) = E\left[(\hat{\beta}_{n,\alpha} - \beta)'(\hat{\beta}_{n,\alpha} - \beta)\right] = \beta'\left[I - X_{n,\alpha} X\right]^2 \beta + \sigma^2 \mathrm{tr}\, X_{n,\alpha} X'_{n,\alpha}$

(mean square error)

(iv) $V(\hat{\beta}_{n,\alpha}) = E\left[(\hat{\beta}_{n,\alpha} - E(\hat{\beta}_{n,\alpha}))'(\hat{\beta}_{n,\alpha} - E(\hat{\beta}_{n,\alpha}))\right] = \sigma^2 \text{tr}\, X'_{n,\alpha}X_{n,\alpha}$

(total variance)

(v) $D(\hat{\beta}_{n,\alpha}) = (E(\hat{\beta}_{n,\alpha}) - \beta)'(E(\hat{\beta}_{n,\alpha}) - \beta) = \beta'\left[I - X_n X\right]^2 \beta$

(squared bias)

For further investigations it is necessary to write X in terms of the eigenvalues of X'X

$$X = Q'\Omega P$$

with orthogonal matrices P and Q,

$$\Lambda = \text{diag}\{\lambda_1, \ldots, \lambda_p\}\ ; \qquad \Omega = \begin{bmatrix} \Lambda^{\frac{1}{2}} \\ \hline 0 \end{bmatrix} .$$

This singular value decomposition is always possible (Rao/Mitra (1971)). Since

$$E(\hat{\beta}'\hat{\beta}) = \beta'\beta + \sigma^2 \text{ tr } (X'X)^{-1} = \beta'\beta + \sigma^2 \sum_{j=1}^{p} \frac{1}{\lambda_j}$$

it follows that small eigenvalues of X'X will lead to unreasonable large absolute values for the coefficients of $\hat{\beta}$. To overcome this one should "shrink" $\hat{\beta}$ by a suitable linear transformation. This shrinking effect is achieved by the ridge estimator and, of course, by the shrunken estimator. As $\hat{\beta}_{n,\alpha}$ can be written in the form $Z_{n,\alpha}\hat{\beta}$ with $Z_{n,\alpha} = X_{n,\alpha}X$ it is a linear transform of the LS-estimator. Before showing the shrinking property of the linear transformation $Z_{n,\alpha}$ a useful lemma is derived.

<u>LEMMA 1</u>

(i) $X'_{n,\alpha}X_{n,\alpha} = Q'\text{diag}\{\lambda^{(1)}, \ldots, \lambda^{(p)}, 0, \ldots, 0\}\, Q$

(ii) $X_{n,\alpha}X'_{n,\alpha} = P'\text{diag}\{\lambda^{(1)}, \ldots, \lambda^{(p)}\}\, P$

with $\lambda^{(j)} = \dfrac{(1-(1-\alpha\lambda_j)^{n+1})^2}{\lambda_j}$, $j = 1, \ldots, p$.

<u>Proof:</u>

(i) Remembering the definition of $X_{n,\alpha}$ it follows at once that

$$X'_{n,\alpha}X_{n,\alpha} = \left[\alpha \sum_{i=0}^{n} (I - X'X)^i\right]^2 X'X \quad \text{or equivalently}$$

$$X'_{n,\alpha}X_{n,\alpha} = Q'\left[\alpha \sum_{i=0}^{n} (I - \alpha\Omega\Omega')^i\right]^2 \Omega\Omega' Q .$$

Using the identity $\alpha \sum_{i=0}^{n} (1-\alpha\lambda)^i = \dfrac{1-(1-\alpha\lambda)^{n+1}}{\lambda}$ the desired result is established.

(ii) Omitted, can be proved on the same lines as (i).

The following theorem shows that $\hat{\beta}_{n,\alpha}$ is shorter than the LS-estimator $\hat{\beta}$.

THEOREM 1

For any values of n and α we have $\hat{\beta}_{n,\alpha}'\hat{\beta}_{n,\alpha} < \hat{\beta}'\hat{\beta}$.

(With probability 1)

Proof:

Since $\hat{\beta}'\hat{\beta} - \hat{\beta}_{n,\alpha}\hat{\beta}_{n,\alpha} = y'X(X'X)^{-2}X'y - y'X'_{n,\alpha}X_{n,\alpha}y$

$$= y'Q'\text{diag}\{\frac{1}{\lambda_1} - \lambda^{(1)}, \ldots, \frac{1}{\lambda_p} - \lambda^{(p)}, 0, \ldots, 0\}Q\,y$$

and α is chosen between 0 and $\frac{1}{\lambda_1}$ it follows that $\frac{1}{\lambda_j} - \lambda^{(j)}$ must be positive $(j = 1, \ldots, p)$. □

Theorem 1 suggests that $\hat{\beta}_{n,\alpha}$ has a smaller total variance than $\hat{\beta}$.

This can readily be seen from Lemma 1:

$$V(\hat{\beta}) = \sigma^2 \text{tr}(X'X)^{-1} = \sigma^2 \sum_{j=1}^{p} \frac{1}{\lambda_j}$$

$$V(\hat{\beta}_{n,\alpha}) = \sigma^2 \text{tr}\, X_{n,\alpha}'X_{n,\alpha} = \sigma^2 \sum_{j=1}^{p} \frac{(1-(1-\alpha\lambda_j)^{n+1})^2}{\lambda_j} \tag{5}$$

From this the conjecture follows at once. Furthermore, equ. (5) shows that with increasing n $V(\hat{\beta}_{n,\alpha})$ is a monotonically increasing sequence (limit $V(\hat{\beta})$). On the other hand with increasing n the squared bias $D(\hat{\beta}_{n,\alpha})$ is monotonically decreasing (limit 0). This result can be derived from the following lemma.

LEMMA 2

(i) $X_{n,\alpha}X = P'\text{diag}\{1-(1-\alpha\lambda_1)^{n+1}, \ldots, 1-(1-\alpha\lambda_p)^{n+1}\}P$

(ii) $\left[I - X_{n,\alpha}X\right]^2 = P'\text{diag}\{(1-\alpha\lambda_1)^{2n+2}, \ldots, (1-\alpha\lambda_p)^{2n+2}\}P$

Proof:

(i) and (ii) follow directly from the identities

$$X_n X = \alpha \sum_{i=0}^{n} (I - \alpha X'X)^i X'X = P'(\alpha \sum_{i=0}^{n} (I - \Lambda)^i \Lambda P .$$ □

Let now γ be the vector $P\beta$ with components $\gamma_1,\ldots,\gamma_p$. Lemma 2 implies that $D(\beta_{n,\alpha}) = \sum_{j=1}^{p} \gamma_j^2 \, (1-\alpha\lambda_j)^{2n+2}$.

Thus with increasing n the squared bias $D(\hat{\beta}_{n,\alpha})$ is monotonically decreasing with limit 0. These properties of $V(\hat{\beta}_{n,\alpha})$ and $D(\hat{\beta}_{n,\alpha})$ lead to the conjecture that there are values of α and n for which the mean square error $G(\hat{\beta}_{n,\alpha}) = V(\hat{\beta}_{n,\alpha}) + D(\hat{\beta}_{n,\alpha})$ is less than $G(\hat{\beta}) = V(\hat{\beta}) = \sigma^2 (X'X)^{-1}$. Next it will be shown that this is actually true for certain integers n. This means that $\hat{\beta}_{n,\alpha}$ is an admissible estimator, i.e. $G(\hat{\beta}_{n,\alpha}) < G(\hat{\beta})$ (see Mayer/Willke(1973)).

THEOREM 2

$$G(\hat{\beta}_{n,\alpha}) = V(\hat{\beta}) + \sum_{j=1}^{p} \frac{(1-\alpha\lambda_j)^{n+1}}{\lambda_j} \left[(1-\alpha\lambda_j)^{n+1} (\sigma^2 + \lambda_j\gamma_j^2) - 2\sigma^2 \right]$$

Proof:

Since
$$G(\hat{\beta}_{n,\alpha}) = \sigma^2 \sum_{j=1}^{p} \frac{1}{\lambda_j} \left(1-(1-\alpha\lambda_j)^{n+1}\right)^2 + \sum_{j=1}^{p} \gamma_j^2 (1-\alpha\lambda_j)^{2n+2}$$

$$= V(\hat{\beta}) + \sum_{j=1}^{p} \left[\frac{-2\sigma^2}{\lambda_j} (1-\alpha\lambda_j)^{n+1} + \frac{\sigma^2}{\lambda_j} (1-\alpha\lambda_j)^{2n+2} + \gamma_j^2 (1-\alpha\lambda_j)^{2n+2} \right]$$

the asserted equality follows after some simple calculations. □

From the theorem it can be seen that there exists an integer $n_o = n(\alpha,\sigma^2,\gamma,\lambda_j)$ such that $(1-\alpha\lambda_j)^{n_o+1} (\sigma^2 + \lambda_j\gamma_j^2) - 2\sigma^2$ is negative $(j=1,\ldots p)$ for all $n \geq n_o$. Since n_o depends on the unknown parameters β and σ^2 it is very difficult if not impossible to determine such a value of n_o without some a-priori knowledge. This problem arises in a similar fashion with the ridge and shrunken estimator.

THEOREM 3

Let there exist a known constant c such that $\beta'\beta \leq c\,\sigma^2$.
Then for all $n \geq n_c$ we have $G(\hat{\beta}_{n,\alpha}) < G(\hat{\beta})$, where n_c is the smallest integer satisfying the inequalities

$$(1-\alpha\lambda_j)^{n_c+1} < \frac{2}{c\lambda_1 + 1} \qquad j=1,\ldots,p . \qquad (6)$$

Proof:

Let n_c be given by the inequalities (6).

Using $\beta'\beta = \gamma'\gamma \geq \gamma_j^2$ for j=1,...,p we conclude that

$$2 > (c\lambda_1+1)(1-\alpha\lambda_j)^{n_c+1} \geq \left(\frac{\beta'\beta}{\sigma^2}\lambda_1+1\right)(1-\alpha\lambda_j)^{n_c+1}$$

which yields $2\sigma^2 > (\sigma^2+\lambda_1\gamma_j^2)(1-\alpha\lambda_j)^{n_c+1}$ for j=1,..,p. As $\lambda_1=\lambda_{max}$

we finally derive that $(\sigma^2+\lambda_j\gamma_j^2)(1-\alpha\lambda_j)^{n_c+1}-2\sigma^2$ is negative (j=1,...p).

It should be pointed out that knowing an upper bound for $\beta'\beta$ and a positive lower bound for σ^2 will guarantee the existence of a constant c from Theorem 3. If there is no such information on $\beta'\beta$ and σ^2 available one should try to select an optimal value for n by inspecting the "iteration trace", i.e. the coefficients of $\hat{\beta}_{n,\alpha}$ and the residual sum of squares $\phi_{n,\alpha} = \hat{u}'_{n,\alpha}\hat{u}_{n,\alpha} = (y-X\hat{\beta}_{n,\alpha})'(y-X\hat{\beta}_{n,\alpha})$ for different values of n.

A good choice for n should be a value for which $\phi_{n,\alpha}$ will not have been inflated, the coefficients of $\hat{\beta}_{n,\alpha}$ have correct signs and reasonable absolute values (cf. Hoerl and Kennard (1970a)).

It seems that with regard to minimizing the mean square error of $\hat{\beta}_{n,\alpha}$ a choice of α near $\frac{1}{\lambda_1}$ is preferable. But when the eigenvalues of X'X are not known a value for α between 0 and 1/tr (X'X) will suffice to assure the convergence of $\hat{\beta}_{n,\alpha}$.

Another iterative method for computing X^+ is given by $X_0 = \alpha X'$; $X_{n+1} = (2I-X_nX)X_n$ $\quad (0 < \alpha < \frac{2}{\lambda_1})$

It can be shown that $X_{2^n-1,\alpha}' = X_n$ (Ben-Israel, Greville (1974)).

This relationship is very helpful for controlling and accelerating the calculation process of $\hat{\beta}_{n,\alpha}$.

REFERENCES

Ben-Israel A. and Greville T.N.E., Generalized inverses: Theory and applications, John Wiley, New York, 1974

Hoerl, A.E. and Kennard, R.W., Ridge regression: Biased estimation for nonorthogonal problems, Technometrics,12,55-67,1970 a

Hoerl, A.E. and Kennard, R.W., Ridge regression: Applications to nonorthogonal problems,Technometrics,12,69-82,1970 b

Marquardt, D.W., Generalized inverses, ridge regression, biased linear estimation and nonlinear estimation, Technometrics,12-591-612,1970

Mayer, L.S. and Willke, T.A., On biased estimation in linear models, Technometrics,15,497-508,1973

Rao, C.R. and Mitra, S.K., Generalized inverse of matrices and its applications, John Wiley, New York,1971

A Comparison of Dynamic Regression Models Based on the Control Test Criterion

Y. Uchida, Kobe

Summary: The control test criterion for the comparison of regression-type models represented by simultaneous equations is proposed in this paper. It is shown analytically as well as computationally that the proposed approach forms optimal feature selection and decision rules, which are not found in the existing methods of comparison of dynamic models.

Key Words: Regression, Model Selection, Optimal Control, Prediction, Econometrics

1. Introduction

During the last decade, considerable statistical efforts,Bayesian and non-Bayesian, have been concerned with development of procedures for comparing models. Also, progress has been made on the related problem of choosing explanatory variables in a single regression model(Mallows, 1973, Akaike, 1970, 1974). Most previous studies have been done based on the prediction test criteria. On the other hand, another test criterion for comparing models must be formed when dynamic models are used to analyze the effects of policy control as developed in the econometric literature.

There have recently appeared various applications of optimal control theory to stabilization policy implemented by the use of econometric models. This paper is an application of optimal control theory to the problem of comparing regression-type models represented by simultaneous equations, which are frequently encountered in econometric models. The control test criterion is proposed for the comparison of dynamic models, and it is observed that the new test is effective in both the prediction and the control.

2. Linear-Quadratic Control Problem

Consider a general linear dynamic system described by

$$s_{t+1} = A_t s_t + B_t x_t + F e_t \tag{1.1}$$

$$y_t = C_t s_t + P_t x_t + e_t \tag{1.2}$$

and suppose that the performance measure is specified by

$$\phi = \Sigma_{t=1}^{T} \phi_t \tag{2.1}$$

$$\phi_t = \| y_t - \hat{y}_t \|_{Q_t}^2 + k \| x_t - \hat{x}_t \|_{R_t}^2 \tag{2.2}$$

where s_t is an NS-vector of the state variables; x_t, an NX-vector of the control variables; y_t is an NY-vector of the output variables; e_t is an NY-vector of the determined input variables; $\hat{y}_t$ and $\hat{x}_t$ are the desired variable vectors; Q_t and R_t are the non-negative definite and positive definite matrices, respectively; k is the positive scalar; $\|x\|_A^2 = x'Ax$.

The problem considered is to solve the tracking problem so as to minimize (2) subject to (1). Let us define

$$\lambda_t = \min_{x_\tau, t \le \tau \le T} \Sigma_{\tau=t}^{T} \phi_t \tag{3.1}$$

By the principle of optimality, λ_t can be represented in the following recursive expression

$$\lambda_t = \min_{x_t} (\phi_t + \lambda_{t+1}) \tag{3.2}$$

Then the results of the solution are given as

$$x_t = \hat{x}_t - x_t^m \tag{4.1}$$

$$x_t^m = g_t - G_t s_t \tag{4.2}$$

for t=T, T-1, ..., 2, 1, where

$$g_t = \hat{R}_t^{-1}(B_t' h_{t+1} + B_t' H_{t+1} \hat{b}_t + D_t' Q_t \hat{d}_t) \tag{5}$$

$$G_t = \hat{R}_t^{-1}(B_t' H_{t+1} A_t + D_t' Q_t C_t) \tag{6}$$

$$h_{t+1} = 0 \tag{7.1}$$

$$h_t = A_t'(H_{t+1} \hat{b}_t + h_{t+1}) + C_t' Q_t \hat{d}_t \tag{7.2}$$

$$H_{T+1} = 0 \tag{8.1}$$

$$H_t = A_t'H_{t+1}(A_t - B_tG_t) + C_t'Q_t(C_t - D_tG_t) \tag{8.2}$$

$$\hat{R}_t = kR_t = B_t'H_{t+1}B_t + D_t'Q_tD_t \tag{9}$$

$$\hat{b}_t = B_t\hat{x}_t + Fe_t \tag{10}$$

$$\hat{d}_t = D_t\hat{x}_t + e_t - \hat{y}_t \tag{11}$$

When performing the optimal control of (4), then λ_t becomes

$$\lambda_t = \| s_t \|^2_{H_t} + 2h_t's_t + \eta_t \tag{3.3}$$

where

$$\eta_{T+1} = 0 \tag{12.1}$$

$$\eta_t = \| \hat{b}_t \|^2_{H_{t+1}} + 2h_{t+1}\hat{b}_t + \eta_{t+1} + \| \hat{d}_t \|^2_{\hat{Q}_t} - \| g_t \|^2_{\hat{R}_t} \tag{12.2}$$

3. Optimization of Multivariate Econometric Models

3.1. The State Variable Form of Econometric Model

Stochastic non-linear econometric model is described by the following structural form:

$$y_t = f(s_t, x_t, y_t, z_t) + u_t \tag{13}$$

where s_t, x_t and y_t are the same as defined in (1); u_t is the disturbance vector. s_t is the lagged variable vector defined by

$$s_t \in \{x_{t-1}, x_{t-2}, \ldots, y_{t-1}, y_{t-2}, \ldots\}$$

Accordingly, s_t can be also expressed as

$$s_t = \Delta_1 s_{t-1} + \Delta_2 x_{t-1} + Fy_{t-1} \tag{14}$$

where Δ_1, Δ_2 and F may be supposed to be zero or to be unity. (13) and (14) denotes the state variable form of econometric model.

We now can approximate the model about $\{s_t^0, x_t^0, y_t^0, z_t^0\}_{t=1}^T$. The deterministic linearized approximation system is given as (1), i.e.,

$$(C_t, D_t, E_t) = (I - \frac{\partial f^0}{\partial y_t})^{-1}(\frac{\partial f^0}{\partial s_t}, \frac{\partial f^0}{\partial x_t}, \frac{\partial f^0}{\partial z_t}) \tag{15.1}$$

$$e_t = E_t(z_t - z_t^0) + y_t^0 - (C_ts_t^0 + D_tx_t^0) \tag{15.2}$$

$$(A_t, B_t) = (\Delta_1 + FC_t, \Delta_2 + FD_t) \tag{15.3}$$

3.2. The Construction of the Weighted Matrices

The weighted matrices Q_t and R_t in the performance index (2) are constructed according to three categories of (i) the time period, (ii) the relative importance between variables and (iii) the autonomy of the model, as we can see in the following.

In the first place, we introduce the element of the weight of

$$\hat{\rho}_t = \frac{(1+\rho_t)^t}{\Sigma_{\tau=1}^{T}(1+\rho)^{\tau}}, \quad \rho \geq 0 \tag{16}$$

for each period, where $\hat{\rho}_t \leq \hat{\rho}_{t+1}$; $\Sigma_{t=1}^{T}\hat{\rho}_t = 1$. Next, the elements of the weights of $\hat{W}_x(i)\hat{x}_t(i)^{-2}$ and $\hat{W}_y(i)\hat{y}_t(i)^{-2}$ are introduced into the endogenous variables, where

$$\hat{W}_x(i) = \frac{W_x(i)}{\Sigma_{i=1}^{NX}W_x(i)}, \quad W_x(i) > 0 \tag{17.1}$$

$$\hat{W}_y(i) = \frac{W_y(i)}{\Sigma_{i=1}^{NY}W_y(i)}, \quad W_y(i) \geq 0 \tag{17.2}$$

where $\Sigma_{i=1}^{NX}\hat{W}_x(i) = 1$; $\Sigma_{i=1}^{NY}\hat{W}_y(i) = 1$. Finally, we introduce the element of the weight implying the autonomy of the model. Assuming that the weighted ratio of the endogenous variables and the control variables is 1 : k, then the value of k becomes small when the autonomy of the model is high.

From the above observations, Q_t and R_t are defined as

$$Q_t(i, j) = \hat{\rho}_t\hat{W}_y(i)\hat{y}_t(i)^{-2}\delta_{ij} \tag{18.1}$$

$$R_t(i, j) = \hat{\rho}_t\hat{W}_x(i)\hat{x}_t(i)^{-2}\delta_{ij} \tag{18.2}$$

where δ_{ij} is the Kronecker delta.

3.3. POEM Algorithm

We describe briefly the POEM algorithm (Policy Optimization using Econometric Models). (For the discussions in some details regarding this algorithm, see Myoken and Uchida, 1978.)

Let the prior value, the posterior value and the historical data be defined by $\mu(0) = \{s_t^0, x_t^0, y_t^0, z_t^0\}_{t=1}^T$, $\mu(*) = \{s_t^*, x_t^*, y_t^*\}_{t=1}^T$ and $\mu(d) = \{s_t^d, x_t^d, y_t^d, z_t^d\}_{t=1}^T$, respectively. Also we assume that $s_1 = s_1^0 = s_1^*$ and $\{z_t = z_t^0 = z_t^\alpha\}_{t=1}^T$. For the prior value and the posterior value, we have

$$y_t^0 = f(s_t^0, x_t^0, y_t^0, z_t) \tag{19.1}$$

$$s_{t+1}^0 = \Delta_1 s_t^0 + \Delta_2 x_t^0 + F y_t^0 \tag{19.2}$$

$$y_t^0 = f(s_t^*, x_t^*, y_t^*, z_t) \tag{20.1}$$

$$s_{t+1}^* = \Delta_1 s_t^* + \Delta_2 x_t^* + F y_t^* \tag{20.2}$$

$$x_t^m = g_t + G_t s_t^* \tag{20.3}$$

$$x_t^* = \hat{x}_t - x_t^m \tag{20.4}$$

For the initial prior value, we use the data to denote $\{x_t^0 = x_t^d\}_{t=1}^T$. Then the prior value $\{s_t^0, y_t^0\}_{t=0}^T$ is calculated from (19). We approximate the system about $\mu(0)$ to obtain $\{A_t, B_t, C_t, D_t, e_t\}_{t=1}^T$. Next, obtain the control law $\{g_t, G_t\}_{t=1}^T$, and then we use (20) to find $\mu(*)$. Thus $\mu(*)$ can be regarded as $\mu(0)$ at the next iteration. Such iterative operation will be repeated until the computation converges.

Since both the prediction and the control are concerned with the course of states in the future, the expected operation may be required. However, the historical data in the past is used for the evaluation of the model, so that the expected operation is not taken. It is then noted that POEM algorithm adopted the procedure by the use of (19) and (20).

4. Comparison of the Models

Before discussing the comparison of the models, let us the following functions be denoted by

$$X(i) = \Sigma_{t=1}^T \hat{\rho}_t \left(1 - \frac{x_t^*(i)}{x_t^d(i)}\right)^2 \tag{21.1}$$

$$X = \Sigma_{i=1}^{NX} \hat{W}_x(i) X(i) = \Sigma_{t=1}^T \| x_t^* - x_t^d \|_{R_t}^2 \tag{21.2}$$

$$Y(i) = \Sigma_{t=1}^T \hat{\rho}_t \left(1 - \frac{y_t^*(i)}{y_t^d(i)}\right)^2 \tag{22.1}$$

$$Y = \Sigma_{i=1}^{NY} \hat{W}_y(i) Y(i) = \Sigma_{t=1}^T \| y_t^* - y_t^d \|_{Q_t}^2 \tag{22.2}$$

4.1. Final Test (Y-Test)

The conventional simulation tests used in the econometric literature have been developed based on the partial, total and final tests. The strongest criterion of them is the final test, but the criterion satisfying the control test is stronger than that of the final test. Let now the final test be denoted by Y-test. Then this test is formulated as follows

$$x^* = \hat{x}_t = x_t^d, \qquad \hat{y}_t = y_t^d \tag{23}$$

$$\beta = 100\sqrt{Y} \tag{24}$$

Y-test is X = 0 and evaluated by the error ratio (%) of the endogenous variables. The parameter β stands for the result of Y-test.

4.2. Inverse Final Test (X-Test)

When Y = 0, we call it inverse final test denoted by X-test. X-test can be expressed by

$$\hat{x}_t = x_t^0, \qquad \hat{y}_t = y_t^d \tag{25}$$

$$\alpha = 100\sqrt{\frac{X+Y}{2}} \quad (\doteqdot 100\sqrt{\frac{X}{2}}\ ) \tag{26}$$

Note that the posterior value x_t^* obtained from the current iteration l is calculated as the posterior x_t^0 and the target value $\hat{x}_t$ at the next iteration $(l + 1)$. Thus we have

$$X^l < X^{l+1}, \qquad Y^l > Y^{l+1}$$

and as $l \to \infty$, $Y^l \to 0$ when the model is perfectly controllable(with 100%). The controllability of the model is calculated as by-products of X-test and is defined as follows. y(i) is γ(i)-controllable (%) if and only if

$$\gamma(i) = 100(1 - \sqrt{Y(i)}\ ) \tag{27.1}$$

And the model is strictly γ-controllable (%) if and only if

$$\gamma \geq \gamma(i) \qquad \text{for } i = 1, 2, \ldots, NY \tag{27.2}$$

Furthermore the model is $\bar{\gamma}$-controllable (%), if and only if

$$\bar{\gamma} = 100(1 - \sqrt{Y}) \tag{27.3}$$

The parameter α in X-test becomes large when the model is ill-conditioned. Thus Y-test implies the criterion of whether the model is fitted to the data. On the other hand, X-test criterion is used to show how the model is appropriate to economic theory.

4.3. Control Test (XY-Test)

XY-test is formulated as

$$\hat{x}_t = x_t^d, \quad \hat{y}_t = y_t^d \tag{28}$$

$$\pi = 100\sqrt{\frac{X+Y}{2}} \tag{29}$$

The following two procedures are considered.

$$X \gtrless Y \rightarrow k^{l} \gtrless k^{l+1} \tag{30.1}$$

$$X \doteqdot Y \Rightarrow \sigma = \frac{k}{1+k}, \quad \text{(stop)} \tag{30.2}$$

where σ stands for the autonomy of the model. $\overline{\gamma} = 0$ when $\sigma = 1$. Inversely $\overline{\gamma} = 100$ when $\sigma = 0$.

5. Concluding Remarks

As was seen in X-test, Y-test and XY-test, we contend that the model is chosen based on the control test criterion, when $\pi < \beta$. XY-test for comparing and choosing among different models is performed by integrating ρ, k, W_x and W_y that indicate the evaluation criteria. In such case, the parameter β is calculated in the process of implementation of XY-test. Decision rule for the choice of models is best given, when π is less than β and minimized. Furthermore this rule can be also applied to the model selection of the simultaneous equations case where size for each model is different.

References

Akaike, H.(1970),"Statistical Predictor Identification," Ann. Inst. Statis. Math., vol.22, 203-217.

Akaike, H.(1974), "A New-Look at Statistical Model Identification," IEEE Trans. Automatic Control, AC-19, 716-722.

Mallows, C. L.(1973), "Some Comments on Cp," Technometrics, vol.15,

Myoken, H. & Uchida, Y.(1978), "System Modelling for Interconnected Dynamic Economy and Decentralized Optimal Control," in Optimization Techniques, Part II, 360-369 (ed. by J. Stoer), Lecture Notes in Control and Information Sciences, Springer-Verlag.

3. Time Series

ARIMA Model or Transfer Function Model; an Empirical Study

J.F. Gorgerat and H. Schiltknecht, Basel

The time series analysis combined to an increasing use of the computer has permitted to realise important progress thanks notably to Arima models and to the transfer functions developped by Box and Jenkins (1970). This paper makes, on the basis of a practical case, a comparison between four models inspired from the works mentionned beforehand.

KEYWORDS: Time series analysis, Arima model,
transfer function

Introductory

Among the practical problems that one meets frequently in the modern management of profit, figure the analysis and the prevision of the future comportment of one or more of these components. During the last fifteen years, important progress has been realised in the field of time series analysis. Paradoxically, problems have not been proportionately simplified. From practical experience, several typical questions come up at each attempt to construct forecasting models of which one (but not the least) remain:

WHAT MODEL TO CHOOSE?

Also, on the strength of the experience accumulated during the realisation of a forecasting model, we have taken the opportunity to devote a certain time for a comparative study of two classes of models: Arima models and transfer functions models. It is also the occasion to present, based on a practical example, the decision (often empirically made) allowing to define the use of leading indicators and to use correctly the seasonal nature of certain behaviors.

Outline of problem

We have been asked to construct a model that will permit the forecast (and the control) of the swiss money stock (2). To do so, we have had at our disposition monthly measures from January 1950 on, i.e. about 330 observations. The study conducted in close collaboration with economicians has permitted to bring out the eventual indicator's role played by what we call here the monetary base (the latter offering the advantage of being partially under the control of the user of the model).

Model definition

Based on the works carried out by Box and Jenkins (1), we have been lead to define a transfer function in the following manner:

$$\hat{y}_t = \sum_{i=1}^{p} \alpha_i y_{t-L_i} + \sum_{j=1}^{q} \beta_j x_{t-L_j} + \sum_{k=1}^{r} \gamma_k \left(\hat{y}_{t-L_k} - y_{t-L_k}\right) + \delta$$

with: $L_i > 0, \quad L_j \geq 0, \quad L_k > 0$

$p \geq 0, \quad q \geq 0, \quad r \geq 0$

where:

$\{y_t\}$: forecast series (money stock)

y_t : value taken by the series $\{y_t\}$ at time t

$\hat{y}_t$: estimation of the value taken by the series $\{y_t\}$ at time t

$\{x_t\}$: leading indicator (monetary base)

$\{L_i\}$, $\{L_j\}$, $\{L_k\}$: represent respectively the sets of lags describing the autoregressive, regressive and moving average part of the model

Model identification

The identification of the model parameters is carried out principally in two stages:
in the first stage, a correlation analysis of the series constituting the model is made. Leaving a large place to the economic intuition, an empirical interpretation of the results permits to define the sets of lags $\{L_i\}$, $\{L_j\}$, and $\{L_k\}$.
At the second stage, the coefficients α_i, β_j, γ_k and δ are estimated based on the past values of the series. This is done by minimising the sum of squares of the residues by means of a non linear optimisation procedure (Levenberg-Marquardt).

Practical case

Four models have been constructed. Two belong to the class of models where the forecast is made from the only information contained in the series itself, the other two using a leading indicator. In each case, one of the models is identified directly from the serie $\{y_t\}$, the other one being identified on the base of the differential serie $\{y_t - y_{t-1}\}$.

Results and conclusions

The analysis of the variance of the residues permits to bring out that:

- it is preferable to identify the model directly from the serie $\{y_t\}$ rather than from the differential serie $\{y_t - y_{t-1}\}$
- when periodical phenomena appear, it is preferable to bring in the model neighbouring terms of the period rather than brutal differentiation (for example $y_t - y_{t-12}$)
- Finally the use of a leading indicator is an important improvement ot the quality of the results. Not only the variance of the residues is sensibly reduced but the model also shows a remarkable stability when used for medium term forecasts.

References

[1] Box G.E.P., Jenkins G.M. 1970
Time Series Analysis Forecasting and Control
San Francisco: Holden-Day

[2] H.J. Büttler, J.F. Gorgerat, H. Schiltknecht, K. Schiltknecht 1977
Ein Multiplikatormodell zur Steuerung der Geldmenge
Diskussionspapier No. 15, Institut für Sozialwissenschaften
Institut für angewandte Wirtschaftsfragen
Universität Basel

The TIBOJ-System

W. Polasek, Vienna

0. SUMMARY

KEYWORDS: Time Series, Box-Jenkins-Method, Forecasting, Interactive Systems.

The name TIBOJ-system stands for "Time Series Interactive Box-Jenkins"-system. In the first step the TIBOJ-system is an interactive program-system for the Box-Jenkins method for identifying, estimating and forecasting univariate time series. This method regards time series as seasonal (SARIMA) and nonseasonal (ARIMA) autoregressive integrated moving average-processes. The system consists of three main parts: The identification-, estimation- and forecasting-program. The data and the parameters for each part of the program can be input interactively in different ways. For long parameter input strings there have been options developed for shortening the input. A special forecast checking routine provides an easier comparison of two or more estimated models. A spectral analysis and an ACF-generation program supports the identification program. The present form of the TIBOJ-system had been implemented by the author at the UNIVAC 1100 computer at the Institute of Advanced Studies in Vienna since 1976.

The following diagram shows the structure of the TIBOJ-system graphically. The arrows indicate the different ways how to go through the system

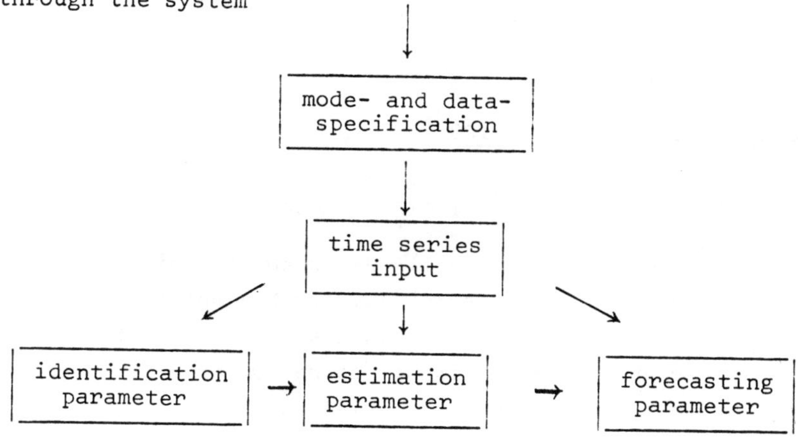

1. THE TIBOJ-STRUCTURE

The TIBOJ-system is divided into the following 5 blocks:

I Mode- and data-specification
II Time series input
III Identification parameters
IV Estimation parameters
V Forecasting parameters

These five blocks are partially ordered and defining different sequences of parameter inputs depending on the kind of analysis to be done.

1) Identification (I, II, III)
   a) for nonseasonal time series
   b) for seasonal time series (seasonal differences)
   c) logarithms (yes or no?)

2) Estimation and/or forecasting
   I, II, IV or I, II, IV, V

3) Updating of forecasts
   I, II, V

2. SPECIAL SYSTEMS CHARACTERISTICS

2.1. The OK-mode

The OK-mode is introduced into the TIBOJ-system to avoid wrong parameter input from terminal. Especially for beginners or for nonpermanent users this procedure should enable the user to ensure whether the right parameter input was done. For skilled users the OK-mode can be set off in order to yield a faster input.

Example: OK-mode on:

```
TIBOJ: NRD NSD IOSD NLOG
user:  1,1,7
TIBOJ: PARAMETER OK?
user:  1
TIBOJ: NRD NSD IOSD NLOG
user:  20,1,,,
TIBOJ: PARAMETER OK?
user:  Ø
TIBOJ: NAC NOACPL NODPL
       :
```

This is the following instruction and the parameter input can continue in the above way.

Example: OK-mode off:

```
TIBOJ: NRD NSD IOSD NLOG
user:  20,1,,,
TIBOJ: NAC NOACPL NODPL
       :
```

The TIBOJ-system continues without the control instruction "PARAMETER OK?".

2.2. The (-1)-mode

The (-1)-mode is implemented with the goal to get further information about the parameters that have to be input at a certain instruction.

If one needs more information about a certain parameter at any input instruction, insert a -1 instead of the true parameter value. The TIBOJ-system then prints out a short description of the admissible parameter values and jumps back to get the right parameter instruction.

Example: (-1)-mode:

```
TIBOJ: NRD NSD IOSD NLOG
user:  Ø,-1,-1,,
TIBOJ: NSD ... number of seasonal differences.NSD.LE.2
```

IOSD ... order of seasonal differences

z(t)=(1-B**IOSD)**NSD*z(t)

NRD NSD IOSD NLOG

user: . . . . .

The TIBOJ-system expects the new parameter input.

2.3. Model strings

To facilitate the input of different ARMA-models it is possible to give an input to the TIBOJ-system in form of a model string. The model string replaces three alternative statements: type of parameters, order of parameters and preliminary values. The model string input to the TIBOJ-system is similar to the operator-equation of the ARMA-model (w_t denotes the appropriate differenced time series), only the powers of the B-operator are not written as exponents. According to the operator-equation

$$\Phi(B^s)\phi(B)w_t = \theta(B)\Theta(B^s)a_t$$

where $\Phi(B^s)$, $\phi(B)$ and $\theta(B)$, $\Theta(B^s)$ are the corresponding seasonal and nonseasonal operators, four types of operators can be distinguished:

E.g.: $(1-\phi_1 B)(1-\phi_{12}B^{12})w_t=(1-\theta_1 B)(1-\theta_{12}B^{12}-\theta_{13}B^{13})$

reads in computer notation:

(1-.3B1)(1-.5B12)=(1-.1B1)(1-.5B12-.1B13)

3. THE FORECAST CHECKING ROUTINE

To observe the forecast performance of an estimated model or between two estimated models, we apply some methods of "forecast-checking". In comparing forecasts, we use the actual values and the percentage change to the previous year:

$$\gamma_t = \frac{z_t - z_{t-s}}{z_{t-s}}$$

where s is the length of the season. For nonseasonal (yearly) time series we have s=1.

To measure the average forecast error for a given forecast period, we calculate the mean square error (MSE) and the root mean square error (RMSE)

$$MSE_L = \frac{1}{L} \sum_{l=1}^{L} (\hat{z}_t(l) - z_{t+l})^2$$

$$RMSE_L = \sqrt{MSE_L}$$

The index L indicates that there is one forecast origin t and L forecasts of the forecast function. For seasonal time series one can choose L=s or L=2s, and then the $RMSE_L$-coefficients between different models can help to decide which model has the better seasonal forecasting performance over one or two seasonal periods.

Besides this procedure, one can compare the one step ahead forecast error over the last K periods. For the sequence of the last K time origins

$$t-k \qquad k=1,\dots,K$$

we estimate the sequence of the one step ahead forecasts

$$\hat{z}_{t-k}(1) \qquad k=1,\dots,K$$

and calculate the MSE of this sequence

$$MSE_1 = \sum_{k=1}^{K} (\hat{z}_k(1) - z_{t-k+1})^2$$

$$RMSE_1 = \sqrt{MSE_1}$$

If the forecast period has the length L then we take for K=L, too. This procedure gives information about the forecasting performance of the model if the most recent amount of information is available.

4. EXPERIENCE WITH THE TIBOJ-SYSTEM

The experience with the Box-Jenkins-method is twofold: Let us concentrate on the question how the estimated parameter or the forecast changes when there are changes in the data.

If some elements of the time series change the estimated parameter can change comparatively high.

Example: The Residential Construction Jan 59-Dec 69: The estimated model is a $\nabla\nabla_{12}z_t=(1-\theta_1 B)(1-\theta_{12}B^{12})a_t$ with the estimated parameters $\hat{\theta}_1$=-.71o (-.845,-.576) and $\hat{\theta}_{12}$=.697 (.552,.842). In parentheses the 95%-confidence intervals are displayed. By typing error two months were wrong: April 62: 19o6 instead of 19o8 and March 65: 1782 instead of 1732. The new correctly estimated parameters are (starting from the same preliminary values) $\hat{\theta}_1$=-.644 (-.781,-.5o6) and $\hat{\theta}_{12}$=.73o (.586,.874).

It is interesting to note that a failure of 3% in one observation causes a change of more than 10% in the estimation of the parameter θ_1. Fortunately, the forecasts are almost not affected by the change of the parameters (base period 60).

Model	Forecasts				
1	1927,0	1755,7	1926,2	2187,7	2409,1
2	1930,6	1763,7	1937,0	2196,1	2412,2

The second experience belongs to the forecast accuracy: The following table gives the forecast percentages (in 4 quarter-distances) and the actual percentages for the private consume (real) in Austria. This forecast check follows an expanding sample scheme with socalled "ex-ante" forecast. The forecast period was four quarters and the forecast performance for the last 11 years had been checked. So the first estimation and forecast was done for the period 54.1-66.4 and the forecasts for 67 are compared with the actual percentages.

Inspite of changing parameter estimates and increasing standard error the forecasts show a surprisingly good behaviour.

TABLE:

PRIVATE CONSUME (REAL)

Model: $\nabla\nabla_4 z_t = (1-\theta_1 B-\theta_3 B^3)(1-\theta_4 B^4)$

time 54.1-	parameters θ_1	θ_3	θ_4	St. err	Forecasts Q1	Q2	Q3	Q4	FC year	actual Q1	Q2	Q3	Q4
66.4	.54	-.29	.67	.194	4.33	2.08	2.55	4.81	67	4.89	1.74	2.64	4.53
67.4	.54	-.30	.68	.186	2.57	3.39	3.65	3.91	68	3.46	4.37	7.59	.69
68.4	.59	$-.25^+$	.60	.198	3.35	4.13	1.16	5.31	69	1.34	2.39	.92	7.69
69.4	.58	$-.19^+$	.64	.197	4.89	4.33	4.74	3.28	70	6.96	4.14	5.87	5.10
70.4	.57	$-.19^+$	.65	.194	4.42	5.90	4.76	4.34	71	4.74	8.03	6.63	5.49
71.4	.57	$-.19^+$	.65	.189	6.20	5.12	5.14	5.60	72	10.30	5.09	7.43	10.14
72.4	.57	-.22	.65	.192	5.52	8.37	7.32	5.89	73	4.09	8.37	1.07	3.50
73.4	.59	-.22	.70	.198	5.08	2.70	6.84	4.09	74	8.53	3.51	3.53	.42
74.4	.61	-.23	.68	.207	.67	2.22	2.91	4.28	75	2.20	.50	2.30	4.60
75.4	.62	-.26	.66	.205	.95	3.47	4.15	2.89	76	1.00	5.20	4.70	4.60
76.4	.62	-.25	.67	.201	5.07	4.11	5.03	4.24	77	5.80	5.90	5.70	9.60

estimates with the subscript "+" indicate non significant parameter estimates.

REFERENCES:

Anderson O.D., Time Series Analysis and Forecasting, London 1976

Box G.E.P. and Jenkins G.M., Time Series Analysis, 2nd ed., San Francisco 1976

Chatfield C., The Analysis of Time Series: Theory and Practice, London 1975

Granger C.W.J. and Newbold P.F., Forecasting Economic Time Series, New York 1977

Polasek W., Das IAZ-System (Interaktives Zeitreihensystem), Institute for Advanced Studies, Vienna 1977 (in German)

Polasek W., Das saisonale Box-Jenkins-Modell, Institute for Advanced Studies, Vienna 1978 (in German)

University of Wisconsin, Computer Center, Box-Jenkins. Computer Programs for the Analysis of Univariate Time Series. Supplementary Program Series No. 517

4. Discriminant Analysis

Methods of Discrimination in Multivariate Binary Data

C.G.G. Aitken, Glasgow

Summary

The analysis of multivariate binary data poses problems especially in terms of measures of dependence and distance. This paper describes five different methods of tackling these problems with examples drawn from medical statistics. Different methods measuring the effectiveness of the results are compared.

KEYWORDS: Discrimination, Generalised Nearest Neighbour Model, Jack-knife Method, Kernel Density Estimation, Multivariate Binary Data, Predictive Logistic Model.

§1 Introduction

The problem of discrimination is one of making an assessment to type of an individual who is assumed to have come from a set T of s mutually exclusive types. Information about the individual is contained in a k-dimensional binary vector. There exists a training set D consisting of the case records, type and binary vector for a set of individuals who have been allocated to type previously by some method not involving the binary vector.

For discrimination in this paper an assessment to type probabilities is provided rather than an allocation rule. Given a new individual, y, a collection of conditional probabilities $p(u/y,D)$ $(u \in T)$ are evaluated and a decision is based on these probabilities. Since

$$p(u/y,D) \propto p(u/D)p(y/u,D) \tag{1}$$

the problem is converted to one of making separate assessments of the two factors on the right hand side of (1). Here the second factor is the main concern. The problem is to use D to estimate the density, $f(y/u)$ say, at y associated with the distribution of the feature vector for each type u. The first factor on the right hand side of (1) is chosen according to the nature of the problem.

§2 Models used for Discrimination

Throughout this section, except in (ii), the conditioning on a particular type u is assumed; the training set D and parameters $\underset{\sim}{\lambda}$ refer only to one type.

(i) Independent Binary Model (Indpt. Bin.)

It is assumed the binary features are independent. Then

$$p(\underset{\sim}{y}/\underset{\sim}{\lambda}) = \prod_{j=1}^{k} \lambda_j^{y_j}(1-\lambda_j)^{1-y_j}$$

where $\underset{\sim}{y}^T = (y_1, \ldots, y_k)$ is a symptom vector and $\underset{\sim}{\lambda}^T = (\lambda_1, \ldots, \lambda_k)$ is the vector of probabilities of each symptom taking the value 1. It is estimated by the sample proportion of 1's.

(ii) Predictive Logistic Model (Pred. Log.)

When $T = (u_1, u_2)$, Cox (1970) proposed the following model for the direct estimate of the probability of type u_1, say, given a symptom vector $\underset{\sim}{y}$ and parameter $\underset{\sim}{\lambda}$

$$\begin{aligned} p(u_1/\underset{\sim}{y},\underset{\sim}{\lambda}) &= \exp(\underset{\sim}{\lambda}^T\underset{\sim}{y})/(1+\exp(\underset{\sim}{\lambda}^T\underset{\sim}{y})) \\ &\simeq \Phi(\underset{\sim}{\lambda}^T\underset{\sim}{y}/\sqrt{b}) . \end{aligned}$$

This may be put in the predictive framework of Aitchison and Dunsmore (1975), where here D refers to all types,

$$\begin{aligned} p(u_1/\underset{\sim}{y},D) &= \int_{\Lambda} p(u_1/\underset{\sim}{y},\underset{\sim}{\lambda})p(\underset{\sim}{\lambda}/D)d\underset{\sim}{\lambda} \\ &= \int_{\Lambda} \exp(\underset{\sim}{\lambda}^T\underset{\sim}{y})/(1+\exp(\underset{\sim}{\lambda}^T\underset{\sim}{y}))\phi(\underset{\sim}{\lambda}/\hat{\underset{\sim}{\lambda}},\hat{\underset{\sim}{v}})d\underset{\sim}{\lambda} \qquad (2) \\ &\simeq \Phi(\underset{\sim}{\lambda}^T\underset{\sim}{y}(\sqrt{b+\underset{\sim}{y}^T\hat{\underset{\sim}{v}}\underset{\sim}{y}}) \end{aligned}$$

since, from the Bayesian version of maximum likelihood theory, $\underset{\sim}{\lambda} \sim N(\hat{\underset{\sim}{\lambda}},\hat{\underset{\sim}{v}})$ where $\hat{\underset{\sim}{\lambda}}$ is the m.l.e. of the coefficients in the logistic discriminant function of Anderson (1972) and $\hat{\underset{\sim}{v}}$ is an estimate of the covariance matrix of the m.l.e. Aitchison and Begg (1976) carried out empirical studies which show that b is best chosen as equal to 2.942.

(iii) Kernel Method

Aitchison and Aitken (1976) suggested a discrete kernel approach analogous to the continuous version of Parzen (1962). The average density function

$$p(\underset{\sim}{y}/D,\lambda) = \frac{1}{n}\sum_{i=1}^{n} K(\underset{\sim}{y}/\underset{\sim}{x}_i,\lambda)$$

is used as an estimate of the density $f(\underset{\sim}{y})$ where $D = (\underset{\sim}{x}_1, \ldots, \underset{\sim}{x}_n)$ and

$$K(\underset{\sim}{y}/\underset{\sim}{x},\lambda) = \lambda^{k-d(\underset{\sim}{x},\underset{\sim}{y})}(1-\lambda)^{d(\underset{\sim}{x},\underset{\sim}{y})}$$

where $\quad d(\underset{\sim}{x},\underset{\sim}{y}) = (\underset{\sim}{x}-\underset{\sim}{y})^T(\underset{\sim}{x}-\underset{\sim}{y})$

the number of disagreements between $\underset{\sim}{x}$ and $\underset{\sim}{y}$. λ is estimated using a jack-knifed likelihood method.

(iv) Generalised Nearest Neighbour Model (GNN)

Hills (1967) proposed a near-neighbour model which can be adapted to the kernel form with a kernel $K_h(./.,\lambda)$ defined as

$$K_h(\underset{\sim}{y}/\underset{\sim}{x},\lambda) = \begin{cases} K(\underset{\sim}{y}/\underset{\sim}{x},\lambda)/B(k,h,\lambda) & \text{if } d(\underset{\sim}{x},\underset{\sim}{y}) \leqslant h \\ 0 & \text{otherwise} \end{cases}$$

where $B(k,h,\lambda)$ is a normalising factor. There is a problem in how to choose h suitably. When h = k this is the kernel method of Aitchison and Aitken.

(v) Multivariate Kernel Method (MVK)

It is possible to have one parameter for each variable and define a kernel

$$K(\underset{\sim}{y}/\underset{\sim}{x},\underset{\sim}{\lambda}) = \prod_{j=1}^{k} \lambda_j^{1-d(x_j,y_j)} (1-\lambda_j)^{d(x_j,y_j)}$$

Each λ_j ($j = 1,2, \ldots, k$) is calculated on its corresponding marginal data and in the binary case may be evaluated analytically, see §6.

In (iii), (iv), (v) there is the further restriction that $\frac{1}{2} \leqslant \lambda \leqslant 1$. A fuller discussion of methods (i), (iii), (iv) may be found in Aitchison and Aitken (1976).

§3 Analysis of Data

The two data sets used came from medical sources. The first is data on Keratoconjunctivitis Sicca (KCS) published by Anderson, Whaley, Williamson and Buchanan (1972). The data used has ten binary symptoms. There are two types, KCS with forty patients and non-KCS with thirty-seven patients. Uniform priors were chosen.

The second data set was provided by the Western Infirmary, Glasgow, and contains information on thrombosis of the leg. There are seven binary symptoms. Two of these tests are expensive and the doctors wish to know their contribution. There were twenty-nine treated and thirty-six untreated patients. Priors proportional to the sample sizes were chosen. This data set was analysed twice, once with the seven symptoms and once with the two expensive test results omitted.

The five methods described in §2 were applied to the two data sets. In the GNN model all orders h from k to 4 are reported and the results are identical. For h less than 4 there are few neighbours and the estimates will be less reliable.

The methods were compared using three different measures. The classification probabilities are measured by the jack-knifed method of Lachenbruch and Mickey (1968). The misclassification rates, expressed as percentages, which were achieved for the three data sets are given in Table 1, where Thrombosis (7) and Thrombosis (5) refer to the numbers of symptoms,

Table 1 : Estimates of misclassification rates, % ages

Method \ Data	KCS	Thrombosis (7)	Thrombosis (5)
Indpt. Bin.	11.7	24.6	30.8
Pred. Log.	11.7	24.6	24.6
Kernel	6.5	26.2	36.9
GNN	6.5	26.2	36.9
MVK	9.1	43.1	27.7

The second method introduces a "doubtful" category. If the odds are 9:1 or greater either way a decision is taken, otherwise the patient is"doubtful" and is referred to further tests. The results are presented in Table 2.

Table 2 : Difference between correct and incorrect classifications at odds of 9:1 with the number of doubtfuls in parentheses

Method \ Data	KCS	Thrombosis (7)	Thrombosis (5)
Indpt. Bin.	57(4)	23(42)	1(62)
Pred. Log.	54(9)	15(48)	8(53)
Kernel	61(10)	28(33)	0(65)
GNN	61(10)	28(33)	0(65)
MVK	53(10)	6(55)	0(65)

The third method is to consider the log likelihood function. Let there be two diagnostic types of size n_1, n_2 respectively, and let $p_s(.)(s=1,2)$ be the probability that an observation is classified correctly. Then the log likelihood of the observations is

$$\ell = \sum_{i=1}^{n_1} \log p_1(i) + \sum_{j=1}^{n_2} \log p_2(j) .$$

If $p_1(.)$ or $p_2(.)$ is less than 10^{-20} then this value is ignored and a note (*) is made of the fact. This stops faults in the computer.

Table 3 : Log likelihood values

Data / Method	KCS	Thrombosis (7)	Thrombosis (5)
Indpt. Bin.	-22.2(***)	-25.4(**)	-37.9(*)
Pred. Log.	-93.4(**)	-30.5	-38.3
Kernel	-17.0	-30.9	-43.9
GNN	-17.0	-30.9	-43.9
MVK	-16.4(***)	-25.2	-36.2

§6 Computational Aspects

The programs were run on IBM 360/370 machines. The c.p.u. times for the various methods are shown in Table 4.

Table 4 : c.p.u. times in seconds

Data / Method	KCS	Thrombosis (7)	Thrombosis (5)
Indpt. Bin.	0.42	0.29	0.27
Pred. Log.	46.4	19.6	8.29
Kernel	68.5	36.9	24.0
GNN	453	142	84
MVK	1.45	0.89	0.70

The values of the parameters for the multivariate kernel were calculated by hand initially, using the following formula.

For one variable let there be n observations, of which r are 1 and s are 0, r + s = n. Then the parameter λ is estimated by

$$\hat{\lambda} = \begin{cases} \dfrac{r^2(r-1-s) + s^2(s-1-r)}{n(r-1-s)(r-s+1)} & |r-s| > 1 \\ 0 & |r-s| < 1 \end{cases}$$

subject to the restriction that $\frac{1}{2} \leqslant \hat{\lambda} \leqslant 1$.

The kernel method is interesting in that the storage is affected linearly by the number of variables and by the square of the number of observations which is the reverse of the more classical methods. This makes the kernel method useful for situations where there are many variables and only a few observations which occur quite often in medical statistics. The figures for the GNN model are for the evaluation of all orders from k to 1; it can readily be seen that as the number of variables increases so the c.p.u. time increases dramatically.

§7 Discussion

This comparison of the five different discrimination methods does not show any particular method to be better or worse than all the others. The analysis of the data sets was carried out with a view to diagnosis. Thus the misclassification rate is not such a useful measure as the criterion of doubt measure. The log likelihood uses more information than the other two but does not provide information about individual patients. If the rough measure of the criterion of doubt is used then the kernel has an advantage over the others. This is not to imply the kernel does not smooth the data effectively. A measure of the smoothing is given by the number of doubtfuls and the kernel has as high a number as the others.

The kernel method has claims to be efficient on practical grounds. It has only one parameter to be estimated which compares favourably with the other methods which have at least as many parameters as there are variables and in the predictive logistic case the number of parameters increases as the square of the number of variables. The main problem with the kernel is the time involved in jack-knifing. This ceases to be a problem in the diagnosis of future patients, a modest desk calculator being all that is necessary to do the calculations.

The methods described here range from the traditional to the modern. It has been shown that the more modern methods compare favourably with the traditional methods and in some aspects have improved on them. There is still plenty of scope, however, for further developments in the variety of kernel methods available and in ways of estimating the parameters.

References

Aitchison, J. & Aitken, C. G. G., Multivariate binary discrimination by the kernel method, Biometrika, 63, 413-20, 1976.

Aitchison, J. & Begg, C. B., Statistical diagnosis when basic cases are not classified with certainty, Biometrika, 63, 1-12, 1976.

Aitchison, J. & Dunsmore, I. R., Statistical Prediction Analysis, Cambridge University Press, 1975.

Anderson, J. A., Separate sample logistic discrimination, Biometrika, 59, 19-35, 1972.

Anderson, J. A., Whaley, K., Williamson, J. & Buchanan, W. W., A statistical aid to the diagnosis of Keratoconjunctivitis sicca, Quart. J. Med., 41, 175-89, 1972.

Cox, D. R., The Analysis of Binary Data, Methuen & Co. Ltd., 1970.

Hills, M., Discrimination and allocation with discrete data, Appl. Statist., 16, 237-50, 1967.

Lachenbruch, P. A. & Mickey, M. R., Estimation of error rates in discriminant analysis, Technometrics, 10, 1-10, 1968.

Parzen, E., On estimation of a probability density function and mode, Ann. Math. Statist., 33, 1065-76, 1962.

One Step Towards a Nonparametric Discriminant Analysis

W. Birkenfeld, Bielefeld

Summary: The practical application of nonparametric procedures in the multivariate analysis, although theoretically well established, is -for computational reasons- restricted to a few samples of very small size, since these procedures are based on permutations of the observations or their ranks.

The paper offers two algorithms which drastically reduce the computational effort and, as a consequence, allow the application as well to practically relevant sample sizes as numbers of samples and variables.

Key words: Nonparametrics. Nonparametric discriminant analysis. Nonparametric correlation estimation. Computational statistics.

1. Introduction.

Considered are $i=1,2,\ldots,c$ samples or classes with $j=1,2,\ldots,n_i$ p-variate observations from sample spaces with distribution function F_i. For fixed i, the $(n_i;p)$-data matrix X_i is given by

$$(1.1) \qquad X_i = (X_{ij}^{(\alpha)}) = (X_i^{(1)}|\ldots|X_i^{(\alpha)}|\ldots|X_i^{(p)}) ,$$

where $X_i^{(\alpha)}$ [$\alpha=1,2,\ldots,p$] is a column vector of length n_i.

Discriminant analysis in its parametric form is associated with an advantage and a disadvantage simultaneously. Advantageous, from a computational point of view, is its simple application because of little programming effort and short computing times. Adverse, from a statistical viewpoint, is a number of premises [e.g. stochastical independence and normality of observation vectors, equality of the covariance matrix for all classes] which impose severe restrictions on the interpretation of its results since these premises are seldom fulfilled in empirical problems.

On the grounds of this situation two problems (a statistical and a

computational one) are to be discussed in this paper.
(1) The statistical point of view: the disadvantage of the restrictive premises in the parametric case can be remarkably reduced by the introduction of nonparametric methods, i.e. the commonly used statistics are replaced by their rank analogon [cf. Section 2]. The only assumptions which are made now are the stochastical independence of the observation vectors [which creates no problems, normally] and the continuity of the corresponding distribution functions F_i [to exclude the problem of ties which is not considered in this first step].
(2) The computational viewpoint: the application of nonparametric procedures seems, for the present, to be restricted to a few samples of very small size because, for given observations x, paired comparisons of the form

$$(1.2) \qquad \Phi_i(x_1,\dots,x_c) = \begin{cases} 1 & \text{if } x_i<x_k \quad k=1,\dots,c;\ \text{except } i \\ o & \text{else} \end{cases}$$

have to be made. Unfortunately, the necessary number of comparisons Φ_i increases tremendously with increasing number of samples, variables and sample sizes.- For a practical problem of moderate size, e.g. c=3 samples each of size n=3o and p=2 variables, the necessary number of comparisons (1.2) is already 123146784o (!).

However, much advantage can be derived from the 2 algorithms presented in this paper. These algorithms are based on rigorous combinatorics and, as a consequence, do not execute the paired comparisons (1.2) at all. Obviously, the reduction in computing effort is enormous.- A more detailed discussion on this subject, including numerical examples, can be found in Birkenfeld [(1978)].

2. Nonparametric discrimination.

With the commonly used notation, the function

$$(2.2) \qquad d_{ik}(X) := [X-\tfrac{1}{2}(\bar{X}_i+\bar{X}_k)]'S^{-1}[\bar{X}_i-\bar{X}_k] \qquad i,k = 1,\dots,c \quad i \neq k$$

serves as a discriminant function [Anderson (1964), pp. 126], where $\bar{X}_i = \sum_{j=1}^{n_i} X_{ij}/n_i$ is the p-dimensional mean vector of sample i and S is the (p;p)-covariance matrix of all samples. On the basis of $d_{ik}(X)$ the location of a concrete p-dimensional observation X is decided either to be the ith or the kth class.

Closely related to discrimination is the several sample location problem which consists of testing

$$(2.2) \qquad H_o: \quad F_1 = F_2 = \ldots = F_c$$

against alternatives $F_i(x) = F(x - d_i)$ with the vectors d_i not all equal. It is well known that the test statistic

$$(2.3) \qquad \sum_{i=1}^{c} n_i(\bar{X}_i-\bar{X})'S^{-1}(\bar{X}_i-\bar{X})$$

is, under H_o, asymptotically χ^2 distributed with p(c-1) degrees of freedom, where $\bar{X} = \sum_{i=1}^{c} n_i\bar{X}_i/N$ with $N = \sum_{i=1}^{c} n_i$ is the mean vector of all samples.

Nonparametric alternatives to (2.3) have been given by Bhapkar [(1961) and (1966)], Tamura [(1966)] and Puri & Sen [(1971)]. In this paper a rank order analogon to (2.3), given by Bhapkar [(1966) equation (2.1)], is discussed in more detail [for the other alternatives [more or less] similar considerations are valid]. It is defined as

$$(2.4) \qquad V = N(2c-1) \sum_{i=1}^{c} p_i(u_i-\bar{u})'E^{-1}(u_i-\bar{u}) \; ,$$

where $p_i=n_i/N$, $u_i^{(\alpha)} = v_i^{(\alpha)}/n_1 n_2 \cdots n_c$, $u_i=(u_i^{(1)},\ldots,u_i^{(p)})'$ and $\bar{u}= \sum_{i=1}^{c} p_i u_i$. Furthermore, E is a nonparametric minimum variance unbiased estimator (MVUE) of a correlation matrix.

The consequent introduction of the above quantities into (2.1) yields the nonparametric version of the discriminant function

$$(2.5) \qquad w_{ik}(X) = (2c-1)[X-\tfrac{1}{2}(u_i+u_k)]'E^{-1}[u_i-u_k] \qquad \begin{matrix} i,k=1,\dots,c \\ i\neq k \end{matrix}$$

As can be seen from (2.4) and (2.5) the computation of the quantities V and w_{ik} mainly consists in determining the quantities u and E, for which the 2 proposed algorithms are designed.

3. The determination of the u's.

The computation of the u's, i.e. $u_i=(u_i^{(1)},\dots,u_i^{(p)})$ in (2.4) and (2.5) with $u_i^{(\alpha)}=v_i^{(\alpha)}/n_1\cdots n_c$ and $\bar{u}=\sum_{i=1}^{c} p_i u_i$ is reducible to the determination of the quantities $v_i^{(\alpha)}$ which are defined as [Bhapkar (1966),p. 3o]

$$v_i^{(\alpha)} := \text{number of c-plets } (X_{1t_1},\dots,X_{ct_c}) \text{ that can be formed by}$$

$$(3.1) \qquad \text{choosing one observation from each sample such that } X_{it_i}^{(\alpha)} \text{ is the smallest among } \{X_{kt_k}^{(\alpha)};k=1,\dots;c\}.$$

The proposed algorithm renounces the consideration of the c-plets and the comparisons given by (1.2). Prior to its presentation a few quantities have to be introduced:

The blockwise collection of the data matrices (1.1) yields

$$(3.2) \qquad X = \begin{bmatrix} X_1 \\ \hline \vdots \\ \hline X_c \end{bmatrix} = [X^{(1)}|\dots|X^{(p)}] ,$$

where $X^{(\alpha)}$ is a column vector with elements $X_{ik}^{(\alpha)}$ $[k=1,\dots,n_1,n_1+1,\dots,n_1+n_2,\dots,N]$. Each column of X is sorted in ascending order to obtain

$$(3.3) \qquad S(X) = [S(X^{(1)})|\dots|S(X^{(p)})] ,$$

where $S(X^{(\alpha)})$ is a column vector of elements $X_{i(l)}^{(\alpha)}$ $[l=1,\dots,N]$. Finally, parallel to the sorted vector $S(X^{(\alpha)})$, one has to maintain a vector $I^{(\alpha)}$ whose elements $I_l^{(\alpha)}$ $[l=1,\dots,N]$ are such that

(3.4) $I_l^{(\alpha)} = i$ if $X_{i(l)}^{(\alpha)}$ came from the ith sample.

This vector $I^{(\alpha)}$ is the basis for the determination of the $v_i^{(\alpha)}$, where certain control variables m_i [cf. algorithm 1] guarantee that the computing procedure stops as soon as all observations from one of the samples are exhausted.

ALGORITHM 1:	Defined by:
begin	
form X	(3.2)
form S(X)	(3.3)
for $\alpha \leftarrow 1$ **to** p **do**	
begin	
form $I^{(\alpha)}$	(3.4)
$l \leftarrow o$	
for $k \leftarrow 1$ **to** c **do** $v_k^{(\alpha)} \leftarrow o$	
for $k \leftarrow 1$ **to** c **do** $m_k \leftarrow n_k$	
repeat	
$l \leftarrow l + 1$	
$i \leftarrow I_l^{(\alpha)}$	(3.4)
$m_i \leftarrow m_i - 1$	
$v_i^{(\alpha)} \leftarrow v_i^{(\alpha)} + [m_1 \cdot m_2 \cdots m_c;$ except $m_i]$	
until $m_1 \cdot m_2 \cdots m_c = o$	
end	
end	

4. The determination of the correlation matrix E.

The elements of $E=(e_{\alpha\beta})$ $[\alpha,\beta=1,\ldots,p]$ are defined [Bhapkar (1966), p. 37-38] as

$f_i^{\alpha\beta}$:= number of (2c-1)-tupels $(X_{ij_1},\ldots,X_{ij_{2c-1}})$ such that

(4.1) $X_{ij_1}^{(\alpha)} < X_{ij_k}^{(\alpha)}$ $k=2,3,\ldots,c$

and

$X_{ij_1}^{(\beta)} < X_{ij_k}^{(\beta)}$ $k=c+1,\ldots,2c-1$ plus

$$(4.2) \qquad e_{\alpha\beta} = \frac{c^2(2c-1)}{(c-1)^2 \sum_{i=1}^{c} n_i(n_i-1)\cdots(n_i-2c+2)} \sum_{i=1}^{c} f_i^{\alpha\beta} - \frac{(2c-1)}{(c-1)^2} \quad .$$

Since the correlation matrix E is symmetrical and because it can be shown [Birkenfeld (1978)] that

$$(4.3) \qquad f_i^{\alpha\alpha} = n_i(n_i-1)\cdots(n_i-2c+2)/(2c-1) \qquad \alpha=1,\ldots,p \quad ,$$

it suffices to compute $f_i^{\alpha\beta}$ for $\alpha=1,\ldots,p-1$ and $\beta=\alpha+1,\ldots,p$.

The following algorithm 2 determines the $f_i^{\alpha\beta}$ without considering (2c-1)-tupels and executing the paired comparisons (1.2) which are contained in (4.1). However, prior to its presentation a few quantities have to be defined:

For fixed i, ranks R must be computed for every column of X_i [given by (1.1)], i.e.

$$(4.4) \qquad R(X_i) = [R(X_i^{(1)})|\ldots|R(X_i^{(p)})] \quad ,$$

where $R(X_i^{(\alpha)}) = (r_{ij_1}^{(\alpha)},\ldots,r_{ij_{n_i}}^{(\alpha)})'$.- On the basis of $R(X_i)$ and for $o\le\gamma\le p-2$ a new $(n_i;p)$-matrix is defined by

$$(4.5) \qquad Y_i(\gamma) = R(X_i;\gamma)$$

so that mathematical operations on $R(X_i)$ will not be executed for the first γ columns of $R(X_i)$.

For α fixed $[\alpha=\gamma+1,\ldots,p-1]$, the rows of $Y_i(\gamma)$ are interchanged in such a way, that the vector $R(X_i^{(\alpha)})$ is sorted in ascending order. The resulting matrix will be denoted by

$$(4.6) \qquad S(Y_i(\gamma)) = [\ldots|r_i^{(\alpha)}|r_i^{(\alpha+1)}|\ldots|r_i^{(p)}] \quad ,$$

where $r_i^{(\alpha)} = (1,2,\ldots,n_i)'$. The set of all $r_{ik}^{(\alpha)} = k$ meeting the first inequality in (4.1) is denoted by m_{ik}^{α}; obviously is

$$(4.7) \qquad m_{ik}^{\alpha} = \{\ j\ |\ k < j \le n_i\ \} \ .$$

ALGORITHM 2:	Defined by:
<u>for</u> $i \leftarrow 1$ <u>to</u> c <u>do</u>	
<u>begin</u>	
<u>form</u> $R(X_i)$	(4.4)
<u>for</u> $\alpha \leftarrow 1$ <u>to</u> p-1 <u>do</u>	
<u>begin</u>	
form $S(Y_i(\alpha-1)$	(4.6)
<u>for</u> $\beta \leftarrow \alpha+1$ <u>to</u> p <u>do</u>	
<u>begin</u>	
$f_i^{\alpha\beta} \leftarrow o$	
<u>for</u> $k \leftarrow 1$ <u>to</u> $n_i-(c-1)$ <u>do</u>	
<u>begin</u>	
form m_{ik}^{α}	(4.7)
form m_{ik}^{β}	(4.8)
form g_{ik}	(4.9)
$a_{ik} \leftarrow \|m_{ik}^{\alpha}\|-g_{ik}$	(4.1o)
$b_{ik} \leftarrow \|m_{ik}^{\beta}\|-g_{ik}$	(4.11)
<u>if</u> $a_{ik}+g_{ik}<c-1$ and $b_{ik}+g_{ik}<c-1$	
or $a_{ik}+b_{ik}+g_{ik}<2(c-1)$	
<u>then</u>	
<u>begin</u>	
compute $F_{ik}^{\alpha\beta}$	(4.12)
$f_i^{\alpha\beta} \leftarrow f_i^{\alpha\beta}+F_{ik}^{\alpha\beta}$	
<u>end</u>	
<u>end</u>	
<u>end</u>	
<u>end</u>	
<u>end</u>	

The set of all $r_{ik}^{(\beta)}$ $[\beta=\alpha+1,...,p]$ that fulfill the second inequality in (4.1) is in the same way

(4.8) $$m_{ik}^{\beta} = \{ j \mid r_{ik} < j \le n_i \} .$$

Furthermore, we need:

$$g_{ik} := \text{number of rank pairs } (r^{\alpha}_{ik};r^{\beta}_{ik}) \text{ so that}$$

$$r^{\alpha}_{ij} \in m^{\alpha}_{ik} \quad \text{and} \quad r^{\beta}_{ij} \in m^{\alpha}_{ik}$$

$$\text{for all } j=k+1,\dots,n_i-(c-1) \;.$$

If the cardinality of a set M is denoted by $|M|$, the quantities a_{ik} and b_{ik} are given by

$$a_{ik} = |m^{\alpha}_{ik}| - g_{ik} \quad \text{and} \tag{4.1o}$$

$$b_{ik} = |m^{\beta}_{ik}| - g_{ik} \quad . \tag{4.11}$$

Finally, it may be shown [Birkenfeld (1978), chapter 6] that

$$F^{\alpha\beta}_{ik} = \sum_{s=o}^{c-1} \sum_{r=o}^{c-1} \frac{g_{ik}!}{[(g_{ik}-s)-r]!} \cdot \frac{a_{ik}!}{[a_{ik}-c+s+1]!} \cdot \frac{b_{ik}!}{[b_{ik}-c+r+1]!} \tag{4.12}$$

and

$$f^{\alpha\beta}_{i} = \sum_{k=1}^{n_i-(c-1)} F^{\alpha\beta}_{ik} \qquad \begin{matrix} i=1,\dots,c \\ \alpha=1,\dots,p-1 \\ \beta=\alpha+1,\dots,p \end{matrix} \tag{4.13}$$

5. References.

ANDERSON T.W. (1964), An introduction to multivariate statistical analysis, 4th pr., John Wiley, New York

BHAPKAR V.P. (1961), A nonparametric test for the problem of several samples, Ann. Math. Stat., 32, 11o8-1117

BHAPKAR V.P. (1966), Some nonparametric tests for the multivariate several sample location problem, in: KRISHNAIAH P.R. (ed.), Multivariate Analysis I, Academic Press, New York, 29-41

BIRKENFELD W. (1978), Praktische Anwendung nichtparametrischer Verfahren in der multivariaten Varianz- und Diskriminanz-Analyse, Diskussionsarbeit Nr. 42 der Fakultät für Wirtschaftswissenschaften an der Universität Bielefeld, Bielefeld, (in German)

PURI M.L. & P.K. SEN (1971), Nonparametric methods in multivariate analysis, John Wiley, New York

TAMURA R. (1966), Multivariate nonparametric several-sample tests, Ann. Math. Stat., 37,1, 611-618

Acknowledgement: The author is greatly indebted to his colleagues Prof. Dr. Peter Naeve and Dipl.-Kfm. J. Felix Hampe for fruitful discussions on the subject and many valuable suggestions.

Use of the Data Analysis to a Cytological Classification of the Non-Hodgkin's Malignant Lymphomas (N.H.M.L.)

P. Caillot and **J.J. Sotto**, Grenoble

Summary : This paper describes what data analysis has brought to an attempt to classify NHML.

KEYWORDS : Canonical analysis, discriminant analysis.

This research has been carried out at the Groupe Hospitalier des Affections Sanguines et Tumorales (G.H.A.S.T.) du Centre Hospitalier Régional et Universitaire, jointly with the U.E.R. d'Informatique et Statistique en Sciences Sociales de Grenoble.

I. Presentation.

1. The problem

In 1974, three simultaneous studies on the NHML - respectively cytological, histopathological and clinico-evolutive - were started at the G.H.A.S.T.

These NHML present a great heterogeneity both for tissue aspects and location, as well as clinical behaviour.

The cytologists were quickly convinced that the fine morphological structure of the cells of the tumors could be linked to the evolution of the disease and so could provide an efficient means of forecasting this evolution with a good reliability.

For 2 years the cytologists compared their observations on a selection of 120 preparations. Over these two years they come to agree both on the qualitative and quantitative criteria to be applied and on the relevance of some of their associations. This led them to a first classification into 10 cytological classes, published in 1976 (5).

But the need was felt to found this classification more firmly and the cytologists called for a statistical approach. The aim was :

- to prove the statistical reality of this new classification (another one does exist).
- to suppress the frequent trap in this problem to overvalue the importance of some criteria and to forget others that can provide a better definition.
- to determine the most reliable and significant criteria to insure the good reproducibility of this classifying.
- eventually to sharpen this classification and question it.

2. The data

We started from cytological descriptions. With the cytologists we brought to light each criterion or character they effectively used (i.e. shape of the nucleus) and for each, every one of their specific values (i.e. regular, cleaved, convoluted). We so selected 19 characters, every one them being qualitative and taking from 2 to 5 values (see table 1). For each character, the cytologist, scanning its preparation through the microscope, adopted the attitude of an investigator wanting to estimate the distribution of this character in a population of cells (issued from a tumor). Thus he had to evaluate the frequency of each specific value. Table 2 gives an idea of the data matrix we so obtained ; the greatest table we had, was 144 x 60. On every patient, the cytologists observed about the same number of cells (200) so that an equal weight was given to each individual.

Added to the terms character and specific value (of a character) that we have just defined, we shall use the following terminology through out this article :

- individual i will be the ith observation ; that is to say the smear from the ith patient examined by the cytologist. It will also be used for the ith row X_i of table 2.

- variable j will refer to vector X^j, the matrix of which is the jth column of table 2 divided by the sum of its coordinates. It can be interpreted as the distribution of the ith specific value on the set of the individuals.

- X_i^j will be the percentage of the ith individual's cells having the jth specific value divided by $\sum_{i=1}^{N} X_i^j$, being the number of individuals.

We would like to point out a troublesome confusion, we shall discuss later, between the data analysis notion of individual, that coincides with the observations gathered on the cells of one patient, and the statistical notion of individual which refers to the unit of observation that is here every cell from a patient's tumor.

II. Statistical analysis.

1. General framework :

- We have followed two opposite approaches:

. On the one hand we have not taken in account the cytological classification ; we have performed automatic classification program such as hierarchical clustering methods (1), dynamic clusters (2) and descriptive technics such as correspondance analysis (1), canonical analysis. The general term of cluster analyses that may be used in the paper will refer to this way.

. On the other hand we have founded the statistical analysis on the given cytological classification and we have used discriminant analyses to test the ability of the variables to separate these 9 given classes.

We have choosen to developp here the results of two analyses : first as an example of the cluster analysis we present the canonical analysis we performed, because it has provided with interesting results, second we present the results of the stepwise program of discriminant analysis (performed by using the biomedical computer program BMD07M) which proved to be the best to perform this analysis. In the conclusion we will say a few words about the other technics we used.

The first results we obtained led us to lightly modify the classification : two classes that were seriously overlopped were fused into one and the nine classes obtained were named such a way to make clear 3 groups (1, 2, 3,) formed by three classes (A, B, C). The classes were so-called 1A, 1B,... 3C (the reason for doing so will appear later). Moreover 24 new individuals were added.

The common material for these two analysis is the N x p-data matrix X where N is the number of individuals and p is the number of the variables associated with the specific values of the characters. We suppose there are K characters, the specific values of the character k being numbered from k_1 to k_k. If we refer to tables 1 and 2: N = 144 , p = 51, K = 19 (in fact we will have p = 60). For the second character (N/P ratio), $k_1 = 6 \ldots k_k = 8$.

2. Canonical analysis

We have performed a canonical analysis of K sets of variables each of these sets being composed of the variables connected with the specific values of a given character (i.e. from table 2, the first and the second set of variables are respectively formed of five diameter sizes, and three N/P ratio levels). The reason to do so is the following :

The links which eventually exist between the different characters observed on any cell, are destroyed by the observation for, as we have seen, it is only possible to observe one character at a time (for any individual, cytologists have to see about 200 cells). This being so, we think that if correlations do exist between the characters from our data, this must be due to the presence of homogeneous individual groups on which distribution of specific values are similar. And we hoped these homogeneous individual groups were precisely the classes defined by the cytologists.

But, it is clear that we are speaking about links between characters although we worked with correlations between their specific values. From this point of view , correlations between the specific values of a given character are nuisance correlations we attempt to weed out by means of the canonical analysis.

Concerning the theoritical aspect of the canonical analysis of several sets of variables, we refer the reader to Kettenring (3) for a general statement and to Saporta (4) for a detailed presentation of the method we used (according to Kettenring it is the sum of squared correlations methods).

The aim of the canonical analysis we performed here, was not so much to find canonical correlations but to give a description of the individual so as to see how they are established. Moreover we wanted to plot both individuals and variables all the more so as the variables(as defined above) are distributing weight over the individuals. This provides a good help to interpret the results, any variable being at the gravity center of the cluster of the individuals (with respect to the weight the variable defines). To obtain the outputs we wanted, we finally wrote our own program.

The results

We have here 144 individuals, 60 variables, 16 sets of variables.

- In fact we have only 44 (60-16) independant variables -.

Let F_1 be the first factor we obtain and λ_1 its associated first eigenvalue, let $p_1, \ldots, p_k$ be the multiple coefficient correlation of F_1 with each of the K sets. We know that

$$\lambda_1 = \sum_{k=1}^{K} p_k{}^2 = \max \sum_{k=1}^{K} r_k{}^2$$

where r_i is the multiple coefficient correlation of any other variable with each of these K sets.

We obtain here $\lambda_1 = 4.05$, thus the mean of the squared coefficient correlation is about 0.25 (in fact p_2 varies from .08 to.77). At first glance, this may appear a rather low level. However the analysis provides some interesting results :

- the first canonical factors either put some groups (generally two groups) in opposition or separate one group from all the others. Moreover we can easily see what the variables that are responsable of this situation are.

For instance the 1st factor opposes class 1A to class 3B and 3C. It associates class 1A with diameter 10-13 μ, well formed blocks of chromatin, poor basophilia cytoplasm and absence of mitoses. It individualizes classes 3B and 3C associated with more than 18 μ diameter, several nucleoli, strong basophilia and increase of mitoses.

It seems meaningful (although it is not statistically significant) to go on till the 11th factor.

Primarily to obtain a two dimensionnal Enclidean representation of these results, and secondarily to see how the canonical factors could discriminate the classes, we performed the BMD70M of linear discriminant analysis program, using these 11 canonical factors and the previous nine classes as input (this analysis must not be confused with the discriminant analysis we will present hereunder). This gave us Figure 1 where the plot of the first two discriminant factors (linear compounds of the 11 canonical factors) is stratified on the basis of the third.

We can clearly see 3 groups, each of them composed of 3 classes. These groups are well marked by their extremities. Class 1A, the whole of group 2 and class 3C are very well isolated. Classes 3A and 3B are discriminated by the third discriminant factor. Only 1B and 1C overlap.

This good separation of classes and unexpected formation of three groups led the cytologists to adopt this definite nomenclature. However the most interesting result is the fact that classes gathered in a given groups are associated to a given evolution pattern (see table IV).

As regards to the hypothesis we made at the beginning of this section on the meaning of the correlations we could observe, it is quite important to remark the order in which the canonical factors were chosen by the stepwise procedure :

it took successively (we are only writing here the number of the factor) 1, 3, 2, 5, 4, 11, 6, 10...

So it seems quite obvious that these correlations are very strongly linked with the given classification.

3. Linear discriminant analysis

We wanted to test the accuracy of the 51 variables we had defined to discriminate between the 9 given classes. We used several programs but the linear discriminant analysis performed through the BMD70M program provided good results.

For each analysis, by random sampling we pointed out about 20 % of individuals to constitute a group that is deleted from the computation of the program except for classification and plotting. This group was used to test the classification functions (it is so called test-group) ; it would not be reasonable to use likelihood ratio tests, some of distribution being multinodal. The set of the other 80 % are called the active group. We did several tests and always we obtained similar results, especially in the order of the choice of variables in the course of the stepwise procedure.

In table III.1 we can see an example of the process. Here, there are 27 individuals in the test-group and 117 in the active group. We have drawn only the principal flows to make the network clear : large diameters definitely separate class 3C at the first step, then basophilia points out class 2B, etc...

While from 50 to 60 variables (here 51) were used to describe the observations, we can see at the 7th stem 80 % of the active group well-classified, 62 % for the test-group ; it becomes respectively 88 % and 78 %, at the eleventh step. Table III.2 describes the classification of the test-group at this stage ; we can see 85 % of these individuals in their right groups.

4. Other methods

The other analyses we used gave results that were in heeping with those obtained through the previous ones. The results of the correspondance analysis are close to those of the canonical analysis. But hierarchical clustering methods and dynamic clusters do not appear so well adapted.

The former have scattered the less concentrated classes to the benefit of the most concentrated ones ; the latter turned out to prouve to be unstable by change in initial conditions.

III. Conclusion

To conclude we would say that this study has truly led to a more accurate definition of the classification proposed as well as made the cytologists confident in its reliability. This classification is now routinely used by the physicians of the GHAST in order to adapt the therapeutic schedule to the forecasted evolution.

REFERENCES

1. BENZECRI J.P., l'analyse des données, Dunod, Paris, 1973 (in French)

2. DIDAY E., optimization in non hierarchical clustering, Pattern reconition, 6, 17, 1974.

3. KETTENRING J.R., canonical analysis of sets of variables, Biometrika, 58, 433, 1971.

4. SAPORTA G., liaisons entre plusieurs variables et codage de données qualitatives, thèse de 3è cycle, Université Paris VI, 1975 (in French)

5. SOTTO J.J., SOTTO M.F., BRAMBILLA E., MARTIN H., MICHALLET M., BENSA J.C., VROUSOS C., HOLLARD D., non-Hodgkin's lymphoma (NHL). Multifactorial analysis of prognostic factors ; special value of cytology, 16th int. Congr. Hemat., Kyoto, 1976.

Cytological elementary characters	Specific values: Number	Specific values: Description
Diameters of cells	5	< 10, 10-13, 14-17, 18-25, > 25 μ
N/P ratio	3	High, intermediate, low
Shape of the nucleus	3	Regular, cleaved, convoluted
Chromatin density	3	Pale, intermediate, dense
Homogeneous chromatin	3	0, punctuated, in network
Non homogeneous chromatin	3	0, well formed blocks, irregular thickenings
Nucleoli number	3	0, one, several
Nucleoli outline	2	Circled, non circled
Nucleoli size	2	Large, small
Nucleoli color	2	Pale, blue
Cytoplasm outline	3	Distinct, irregular, blurred
Cytoplasm basophilia	4	Poor, fair, strong, "hyperbasophilia"
Cytoplasm homogeneity	2	Homogeneous, non homogeneous
Cytoplasm peripheral reinforcement	2	Present, absent
Naked nuclei	2	Percentage
Cytoclasia	2	Present, absent
Cytoplasm vacuoles	3	0, some, numerous
Mitosis	2	Percentage
Normal lymphocytes	2	Percentage
TOTAL	51	

TABLE I

Individuals (144) \ Cytological characters (51)	Data in percentage: Diameters of cells μ: < 10	10 - 13	14 - 17	17 - 25	> 25	N/P ratio: High	Intermediate	Low
1	11	65	24	0	0	70	28	2
2	4	20	62	4	0	62	38	0
3	0	0	5	31	64	0	18	82

TABLE II

Cytological allocation \ Statistical allocation	1A	1B	1C	2A	2B	2C	3A	3B	3C	TOTAL
1A	5									5
1B		1				1				2
1C		1	2							3
2A				2						2
2B					3					3
2C			1			2				3
3A							3			3
3B			1					2		3
3C				1				1	1	3
TOTAL	5	2	4	3	3	3	3	3	1	27

TABLE III 2

FIGURE 1

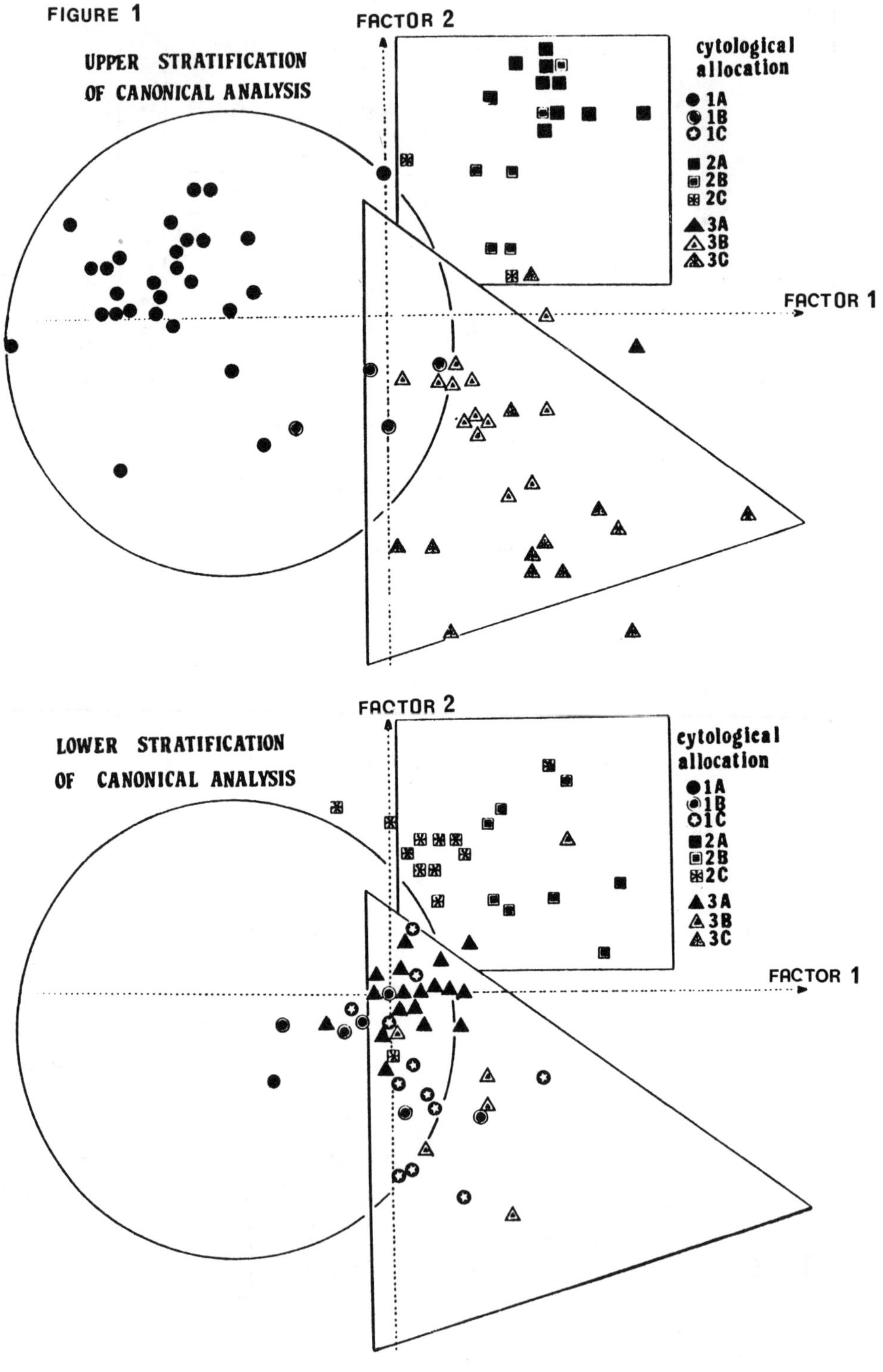
UPPER STRATIFICATION
OF CANONICAL ANALYSIS
FACTOR 2
FACTOR 1
cytological
allocation
1A
1B
1C
2A
2B
2C
3A
3B
3C
LOWER STRATIFICATION
OF CANONICAL ANALYSIS
FACTOR 2
FACTOR 1
cytological
allocation
1A
1B
1C
2A
2B
2C
3A
3B
3C

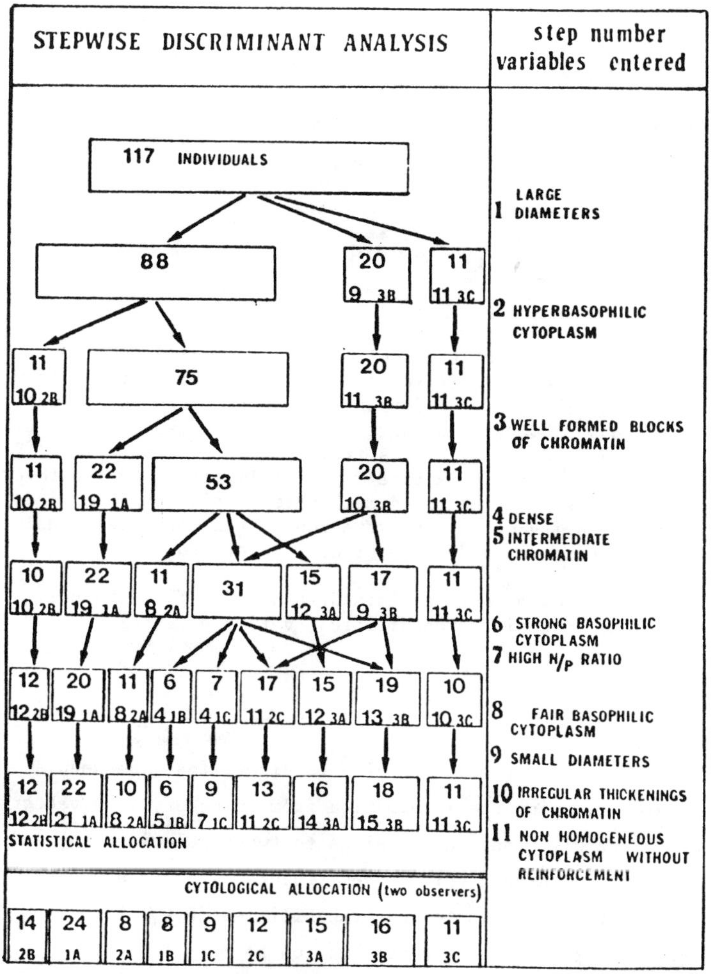

TABLE III-1

EVOLUTIVE GROUPS	A LEUKEMIC	B BAD AND METASTATIC	C GOOD CHRONIC AND DIFFUSED	D GOOD AND LOCALIZED
% OF PATIENTS FROM CYTOLOGICAL CLASSES 1A + 1B + 1C	5 %	21 %	81 %	80 %
% OF PATIENTS FROM CYTOLOGICAL CLASSES 2A + 2B + 2C	90 %	3 %	3 %	0
% OF PATIENTS FROM CYTOLOGICAL CLASSES 3A + 3B + 3C	5 %	76 %	16 %	20 %
TOTAL	100 %	100 %	100 %	100 %

REPARTITION OF CYTOLOGICAL CLASSES IN THE CLINICAL AND EVOLUTIVE FOUR GROUPS.

TABLE IV

Variable Kernel Density Estimation in Discriminant Analysis

J.D.F. Habbema, J. Hermans and J. Remme, Leiden

Summary

The performance of the variable kernel method is studied, and compared with the fixed kernel. The variable kernel method seems to bring nearly no improvement in discriminatory performance in quite a few situations. For skew distributions, however, the performance may increase substantially. The variable kernel depends on distances from data points to their k'th nearest neighbour; the choice of k appears to be important, but not very critical. The pseudo maximum likelihood method for estimating the window size seems to perform quite well. The extension of the variable kernel method from continuous to mixed data is briefly described.

KEYWORDS: Choice of window size; discriminant analysis; fixed kernel; mixed data; posterior probabilities; variable kernel.

1. Introduction

In discriminant analysis (D.A.) one aims to discriminate between a number of populations, using the information from an observation vector $X = (x_1, \ldots, x_p)$. We will confine ourselves to two populations, A_1 and A_2, and we follow the D.A. approach using Bayes' theorem: for an element with unknown population of origin, posterior probabilities (P.P.'s) for the populations are estimated, given the observation X:

$$\hat{P}(A_i|X) \propto \hat{P}(A_i)\hat{f}(X|A_i) \qquad i = 1,2 \qquad (1)$$

It is assumed that the estimates of the population incidences, $\hat{P}(A_i)$, and of the population conditional densities, $\hat{f}(X|A_i)$, are based on so-called training samples from the two populations, with a sample size of N_1 resp. N_2.

The density estimate $\hat{f}(X|A_i)$ is the most critical problem in Bayes D.A. Linear and quadratic D.A. are based on rigorous assumptions about the distribution of the variable X: multinormal distributions with equal resp. unequal covariance matrices. But experimental data are usually of a far more irregular nature. A radical alternative to the linear- and quadratic methods is the kernel estimation method: a probability mass is placed around each training sample point X_{ij}, $i=1,2$, $j=1,\dots,N_i$, and the resulting density estimate is just the average of the N_i kernels:

$$\hat{f}(X|A_i) = \frac{1}{N_i} \sum_{j=1}^{N_i} K(X;X_{ij}) \qquad i = 1,2 \qquad (2)$$

The kernel method requires a choice for the functional shape of K and a choice of a smoothness parameter or window size, say h. The functional shape is not very important, but the value of smoothness parameter is, see e.g. Wegman (1972). The D.A. package ALLOC is based on multinormal shaped kernels with diagonal covariance matrix, and a pseudo maximum likelihood method for the estimation of the smoothness parameter h, see Habbema et al (1974a) and Hermans and Habbema (1976). This kernel method seems to be more generally applicable than the linear and quadratic D.A., see Remme et al (1977, 1978). However, rather disappointing results were obtained for D.A. with lognormal distributed variables. This is probably caused by the fixed smoothness of each of the N_i kernels within an estimate (2). In the lognormal case a variation in the degree of smoothness leading to sharper kernels around the mode and smoother kernels in the tail might be preferrable. Such a variable kernel approach is recently discussed in some detail by Breiman et al (1977). They take as smoothness for the kernel around X_{ij}:

$$h_{ij} = h_i d_{ijk_i} \qquad (3)$$

with h_i an overall window-size for A_i and d_{ijk_i} the after-standardization distance of X_{ij} to its k_i'th nearest neighbour in the training sample from A_i.

Using (3), two parameter values (h_i,k_i) have to be assessed for each density estimate instead of one (h_i) for the fixed kernel. The pair (h_i,k_i) can be attacked by methods of simultaneous estimation. This is discussed by Raatgever and Duin (1978), who use density estimation criteria.

The present paper uses a two step estimation procedure in stead of a simultaneous one: for pre-chosen values of k_i, the value of h_i will be optimized according to the ALLOC-method of pseudo maximum likelihood. The aim of this paper is to present relevant results for the choice of k_i, and to compare results of the variable kernel with those of the fixed kernel. The criteria in the present paper will be of a D.A.-nature: they refer to posterior probabilities. Section 2 describes some simulation results, and section 3 a medical application. Section 4 gives the extension of the variable kernel from continuous to mixed data. In section 5, at last, some prudent conclusions will be drawn.

2. Results from simulation studies

The results from this section are from a simulation study whose main results are presented in Remme et al (1978), and the reader is referred to that paper for detailed information about the study. The advantage of a simulation study is knowledge of true posterior probabilities $P(A_i|X)$. So posterior probabilities as estimated by the kernel (K) resp. variable kernel model (VK), say $\hat{P}_K(A_i|X)$ resp. $\hat{P}_{VK}(A_i|X)$ can be compared with those true ones. This comparison can be restricted to A_1, because with two populations only one of the P.P.'s yields independent information. It will be done by using the cross tabulation in Table 1.

Table 1. Cross tabulation of true and estimated posterior probabilities.

$P(A_1\|X)$				
	[.9-.1]	E_1	e_2	a_3
	(.1-.9)	e_1	a_2	e_3
	[0-.1]	a_1	e_4	E_2
$\hat{P}_j(A_1\|X)$, j=K,VK		[0-.1]	(.1-.9)	[.9-1]

The P.P.'s are subdivided into low [0-.1], medium (.1-.9) and high [.9-1], with the values .1 and .9 of course arbitrarily chosen. The regions [0-.1] and [.9-1] represent sharp probability judgments; the region (.1-.9) represents a state of relative doubt. The three cells a_1, a_2, and a_3 measure agreement between true and estimated P.P.'s; their sum will be indicated by a; e_1, e_2, e_3 and e_4 measure moderate disagreements (sum is e); E_1 and E_2 measure grave errors (sum is E). Using loss-functions considerations, it can be argued that for the threshold .9 a grave error must be valued as about ten times as grave as a moderate disagreement, compare Habbema et al (1974b). When we attribute one unit of loss to a small disagreement and ten units of loss to a grave error, we get as an overall loss value:

$$L = e + 10E \tag{4}$$

2.1 Comparison of fixed kernel and variable kernel

Table 2 gives the a, E and L scores for situations where the variable X is drawn from multinormal distributions with equal (EQ) resp. unequal (UNEQ) covariance matrices, from lognormal distributions (LOG) and from a mixture of three multinormal distributions (MIX). All situations are two-dimensional except UNEQ2 which is six-dimensional.

The training sample sizes were $N_1=N_2=15$ (upper table) resp. $N_1=N_2=35$ (lower table), k_1 and k_2 were taken equal. The a, E and L values are calculated from 100 independent test samples, 50 from each population. Table 2 gives

Table 2 (a)

N=15	Fixed Kernel			Variable Kernel k = 1			k = 2			k = 5			k = 10			k = 13		
	a	E	L	a	E	L	a	E	L	a	E	L	a	E	L	a	E	L
EQ	78	0.1	23	71	0.3	32	75	0.6	30	77	0.4	27	77	0.0	23	80	0.1	21
UNEQ1	76	0.0	24	68	0.3	35	70	0.3	33	73	0.4	31	75	0.1	26	76	0.1	25
UNEQ2	85	0.5	20	79	0.7	27	80	0.6	25	82	0.6	23	83	0.6	22	84	0.6	21
LOG	44	1.3	68	63	1.0	46	62	1.2	49	60	1.1	50	53	1.1	57	45	1.3	67
MIX	63	0.4	41	61	0.9	47	64	0.8	43	66	0.5	38	64	0.1	37	65	0.4	39

Table 2 (b)

N=35	Fixed Kernel			Variable Kernel k = 1			k = 2			k = 5			k = 10			k = 20			k = 33		
	a	E	L	a	E	L	a	E	L	a	E	L	a	E	L	a	E	L	a	E	L
EQ	81	0.0	19	78	0.0	22	80	0.0	22	83	0.0	17	84	0.0	16	85	0.0	15	84	0.0	16
UNEQ1	78	0.0	22	74	0.0	26	76	0.1	25	77	0.1	24	78	0.1	23	80	0.0	20	80	0.0	20
UNEQ2	89	0.0	11	84	0.0	16	85	0.0	15	86	0.0	14	86	0.0	14	87	0.1	14	89	0.1	12
LOG	48	0.4	56	67	0.1	34	69	0.2	33	71	0.1	30	70	0.2	32	65	0.2	37	49	0.4	55
MIX	75	0.2	27	68	0.0	32	73	0.0	27	75	0.2	27	75	0.0	25	75	0.2	27	74	0.1	27

Table 2. Percentage elements with a resp. E score, and the resulting loss measure L, for fixed kernel model and for variable kernel model. The variable kernel model is used for a number of values for k ($=k_1=k_2$). Table 2 (a) is based on training samples of size 15, Table 2 (b) on size 35. The k-value for which the loss L is minimized is underlined.

averages of these values over 25 such runs.

As is seen from this table, there is no pronounced optimum for k_i. For lognormal distributions the VK is superior to the K model. For the other three cases there is no clear superiority for either the K or the VK model.

2.2 A detailed study of performance as a function of (h_i,k_i)

In Tables 3 (a) and 3 (b) the quality as measured by L is studied as a function of (h_i,k_i) combinations for the lognormal distributions as studied in Tables 2 (a) and 2 (b). The results are averages over 50 runs (see section 2.1).

Table 3 (a)

value of h

N=15	.1	.15	.2	.3	.4	.45	.5	.6	.75	.8	.9	1.0	1.3	1.5	1.6	2.0	3.5
k=13	66	63	64	70			77										
k=10	75	60	56	53			60			71							
k=5			56	47	45			48			52		61				
k=2				55		44		42				44	46		49		
k=1							57		45			44		44		46	52
Fixed	82		71	64	62			66			73						

Table 3 (b)

value of h

N=35	.05	.1	.15	.2	.25	.3	.35	.4	.45	.5	.55	.6	.7	.9	1.0	1.5	2	3.5
k=33	50	48	54	61														
k=20			35		33		36		39									
k=10					30			29			33		34					
k=5						32				29			29	31				
k=2						51				32		30			30	32	33	
k=1								60				37			29	31	33	37
Fixed		49		43		45			49			57		68				

Table 3. L-values for selected (h,k) combinations. Table 3 concerns the LOG example of Table 2; N=15 in (a) and N=35 in (b). For each value of k, the minimal L-values are underlined, and the L-values with the ALLOC-method for estimating h can be found in Table 2. The bottom rows present the fixed kernel results.

3. A medical example

As a medical example, consider the problem of discriminating between two kinds of hypercalcaemia, see for a short description Habbema et al (1974b). With a doubt level of .90, the fixed kernel model made 5 gross errors and 17 cases of doubt and 53 agreements, upon the 75 patients. So the performance can be indicated by the triplet (5,17,53). For the variable kernel model, the (k_1,k_2) values of (2,2), (5,5), (10,10), (20,20), (30,30), (2,5), (5,10), (10,5), (8,20) and (10,20) were tried. The performance was surprisingly constant for all (k_1,k_2) combinations, being (2,23,50) or (3,20,52), with as only exception the (2,5) case with (3,23,49). So the choice of (k_1,k_2) does not much matter in this example, and the variable kernel yield better results than the fixed kernel, which is in accordance with the skew, lognormal like, distribution of the sample data.

4. Extension to mixed binary-nominal-ordinal-continuous data

The variable kernel approach can also be applied to mixed data, together with a suitable distance measure. In the recently developed ALLOC-program for D.A. with mixed data, the kernel (5)-(12) is used:

$$K(X;X_{ij}) = \prod_{r=1}^{p} K(x_r;x_{ijr}) \tag{5}$$

with as kernel for the r'th component

$$K(x_r;x_{ijr}) = \frac{1}{C_r(\mu)}\,\mu^{d^2(x_r;x_{ijr})} \tag{6}$$

with μ the smoothness parameter, $0 \leq \mu \leq 1$. (Equivalently μ could be transformed as $\mu=\exp(-1/2h^2)$, $0 < h < \infty$, with h as smoothness parameter). The normalizing constant $C_r(\mu)$ depends on the type of the variable and the value of μ. The distance measure $d^2(x_r;x_{ijr})$ also depends on the type of variable.

For the normalizing constant one has to take

$$x_r \text{ binary} \quad : C_r(\mu) = 1 + \mu^{1/s_{ir}^2} \tag{7}$$

$$x_r \text{ nominal} \quad : C_r(\mu) = \{1 + (t_r-1)\mu^{1/s_{ir}^2}\} \tag{8}$$

$$x_r \text{ continuous} \quad : C_r(\mu) = s_{ir}\sqrt{-\pi/ln(\mu)} \tag{9}$$

$$x_r \text{ ordinal} \quad : C_r(\mu) = \sum_{l=1}^{t_r} \mu^{d^2(x_r(l);x_{ijr})} \tag{10}$$

with $x_r(1), \ldots, x_r(t_r)$ the t_r possible values for the ordinal variable x_r. Note that (10) also depends on x_{ijr}.

For the distance measure we take:

$$d^2(x_r;x_{ijr}) = (x_r - x_{ijr})^2/s_{ir}^2, \tag{11}$$

with s_{ir}^2 the usual expression for the variance. The exception is the nominal case with (x_r-x_{ijr}) equal to zero for equal categories x_r and x_{ijr} and equal to 1 for unequal categories, and with as variance, see Burr (1968),

$$s_{ir}^2 = \{N_i^2 - \sum_{u=1}^{t_r} n_{iu}^2\}/\{2N_i(N_i-1)\} \tag{12}$$

with n_{iu} the number of elements from sample i in cell $x_r(u)$.

The overall distance between the two points X and X_{ij} equals $d^2(X,X_{ij}) = \sum_{r=1}^{p} d^2(x_r,x_{ijr})$. This distance can be used for a variable kernel approach in exactly the same way as is done before for continuous data only, see eq. (3). The equal range $[0,1]$ of the smoothness parameter μ for all different types of variables is, in our opinion, an improvement over the proposals of Aitchison & Aitken (1976), who get different ranges, and, consequently, problems in combining different types of variables.

5. Discussion and conclusions

The problem of variable kernel density estimation is considered here from the point of view of discriminating between populations. This is reflected in the choice of performance measures. A number of conclusions can be drawn, of course with the limitations as implied by the examples and methods as studied in this paper:

- The variable kernel methods lead to substantial improvement over the fixed kernel method for skew distributions, as examplified here by lognormal ones. For symmetric distributions and mixture distributions, nearly no improvement is made.
- The l.o.o. method of Habbema et al (1974a) for estimating the window-size leads to reasonably good results, admittedly a bit prudent (too much smoothed).
- The exact values of (k_1,k_2) are not very critical: the performance may be nearly optimal for a large range of k-values. However, this range may be quite different for different situations. For skew

distributions, where improvement over the fixed kernel is made, the optimal k-values are low (k=1 resp. 5 for N=15 resp. 35); for the other situations the k-values are rather large. See Table 2. Good overall guesses for k are k=5 for N=15 and k=10 for N=35.

- Also the example studied in section 3 gives surprisingly similar results for a large range of (k_1,k_2) values.
- The variable kernel method can, without substantial problems, be extended towards kernels for mixed binary-nominal-ordinal-continuous data.

Acknowledgements

J.F.M. Kaasenbrood is acknowledged for his contribution to section 2, and T. van Rijn for his contribution to section 4. Mrs. E. Arents did the lay-out and typing.

References

Aitchison J. and Aitken C.G.G., Multivariate binary discrimination by the kernel method, Biometrika,63,413-420,1976

Breiman L, Meisel W. and Purcell E., Variable kernel estimates of multivariate densities, Technometrics,19,135-144,1977

Burr E.J., Cluster sorting with mixed character types: I. Standardization of character values, Australian Computer Journal,1,97-99,1968

Habbema J.D.F., Hermans J. and van den Broek K., A Stepwise Discriminant Analysis Program, Using Density Estimation, in G. Bruckmann (ed.) COMPSTAT 1974, Proceedings in Computational Statistics, Physica Verlag, Wien,1974a

Habbema J.D.F., Hermans J. and van der Burgt A.T., Cases of Doubt in Allocation Problems, Biometrika,61,313-324,1974b

Hermans J. and Habbema J.D.F., Manual for the ALLOC discriminant analysis programs, Technical Report, Dept. of Medical Statistics, University of Leiden,1976

Raatgever J.W. and Duin R.P.W., On the variable kernel model for multivariate nonparameteric density estimation, this volume

Remme J., Habbema J.D.F. and Hermans J., A comparison of the performance of two discriminant analysis models, in Data Analysis and Informatics, IRIA symposium, Rocquencourt,269-279,1977

Remme J., Habbema J.D.F. and Hermans J., A simulative comparison of linear, quadratic and kernel discrimination, submitted for publication, 1978

Wegman E.J., Nonparametric probability density estimation: II. A comparison of density estimation methods, J. Statist. Comput. Simul.,1,225-245, 1972

Computational Problems in Predictive Diagnosis

I.J. Lauder, Hong Kong

0. Summary

Computational methods of predictive diagnosis are developed for the case when the feature vectors are inaccurate. The likelihood approach is taken and the role of multi-dimensional integral approximation, the EM algorithm and Monte Carlo methods in arriving at the final assessment for a new case are described.

KEYWORDS: Predictive diagnosis, maximum likelihood, integral approximation, EM algorithm, Monte Carlo Methods.

1. Problem

The diagnostic paradigm (Dawid, 1976) specifies the statistical diagnostic assessment for a new case with accurate feature vector x, disease type variable t and accurate training set $D = \{x_i, t_i : i=1,\dots,n\}$ in the form of the conditional probability $p(t|x,D)$. 1.1

If the model underlying the data is parametric with unknown parameter vector δ, then the predictive approach specifies $p(t|x,D)$ as

$$p(t|x,D) = \int_\Delta p(t|x,\delta)\ p(\delta|D)\,d\delta \qquad 1.2$$

whereas the estimative approach is to replace δ by an efficient estimate $\hat{\delta}$ based on D so $p(t|x,D) = p(t|x,\hat{\delta})$, (Aitchison, 1977). 1.3

When the feature vectors are inaccurate but the typing is still accurate, we excounter two problems:

(i) The estimation of δ from $D = \{y_i, t_i : i=1,\dots,n\}$ where y_i are the inaccurate feature vectors with p.d.f.'s $p(y|x)$ (or equivalently $p(x|y)$) where x is accurate. This problem involves evaluation of

$$p(t|y_i,\delta) = \int_X p(t|x,\delta)\ p(x|y_i)\,dx \qquad 1.4$$

(ii) If the full predictive approach is taken, then for a new observed inaccurate y, it is necessary to evaluate $p(t|y,D) = \int_\Delta p(t|y,\delta)\ p(\delta|D)\,d\delta$. 1.5

We consider the computational aspects of these two problems for the case of two types (t=1 or 2) and when the method of maximum likelihood is used.

2. Computational Methods for the Likelihood Approach

In this section we consider problem 1(i). For the ith case in the training set with inaccurate feature vector y_i with error variance covariance matrix S_i, $p(t|y_i,\delta) = \int_X p(t|x,\delta)\; p(x|y_i,S_i)dx$. 1.6

For the rest of the paper we make the not very restrictive assumption that $S_i = S,\ \forall_i$. The generalisation to individual S_i is straightforward.

The likelihood of the observations in the training set D is

$$\ell = \prod_{i=1}^{n} p(t|y_i,\delta) = \prod_{i=1}^{n} \int_X p(t|x,\delta)\; p(x|y,S)dx \ .$$

Any maximization technique used to obtain the m.ℓ. estimate will require at the rth iteration, the evaluation of $\int_X p(t|x,\delta)\; p(x|y_i,\delta)dx$, $i=1,\ldots,n$.

To avoid direct numerical integration which is a tedious if not impossible task we consider two possible alternatives:

(i) A functional approximation to $p(t|y_i,\delta)$.

If $p(t|y_i,\delta) \simeq q(t|y_i,\delta)$ where q is an explicit function that can be easily evaluated and differentiated, then the problem reduces to a reasonably straightforward case of functional maximization.

(ii) The "EM algorithm" (Dempster, 1977).

If the data set D can be regarded as incomplete relative to some underlying set of complete data sufficient statistics C with corresponding model, then the application of the EM algorithm could produce a computationally simpler method of obtaining $\hat{\delta}$.

Even if it is not possible to obtain an exact representation for C, it may be possible to apply an "approximate EM algorithm" that produces an acceptable approximation to $\hat{\delta}$.

3. Application to Two Models

(i) Logistic Model with Normally Distributed Error

The logistic model for accurate data is

$$\begin{aligned} p(t=1|x,\delta) &= \psi(\delta^T x) \\ p(t=2|x,\delta) &= 1-\psi(\delta^T x) \end{aligned} \quad \text{where } \psi(v) = \frac{e^v}{1+e^v} \quad \text{(Cox, 1970)} . \qquad 3.1$$

When inaccurate y is observed with normally distributed error,

$$p(t=1|y,\delta) = \int_X \psi(\delta^T x)\; \phi(y|x,S) \qquad 3.2$$

This integral can be reduced to the form

$_{-\infty}\int^{\infty} \psi(v)\ \phi(v|\mu,\sigma^2)$, where $\mu = \delta^T y$, $\sigma^2 = \delta^T S\delta$ (Aitchison, 1976). 3.3

It is not possible to obtain a closed form for this integral.

Following 2(i), an approximation to 3.3, can be found in the form

$$I = \int\psi(v)\ \phi(v|\mu,\sigma^2) \simeq \psi\left(\frac{\mu}{\sqrt{1+\sigma^2/k^2}}\right). \qquad 3.4$$

This approximation derives from the normal-logistic c.d.f. approximation $\Phi(v) \simeq \psi(kv)$ for suitable k, 3.5

so the integral 3.3 $\simeq \int\Phi\left(\frac{v}{k}\right)\ \phi(v|\mu,\sigma^2) = \Phi\left(\frac{\mu}{\sqrt{k^2+\sigma^2}}\right)$. 3.6

Applying 3.5 to 3.6 gives 3.4. Why the integral approximation is not left in the Φ form will become apparent in 3(iii).

The value of k depends on the criterion used in the approximation. Various choices are available and are summarised as follows:

Tocher, 1963 gives a value of k based on a Taylor series expansion around the origin. The value is $k = \sqrt{\frac{8}{\pi}} \simeq 1.60$. 3.7a

The minimax value of $|\psi(kv) - \Phi(v)|$ is given by $k = 1.70$. 3.7b

The best value in terms of the Kullback-Liebler information measure is

$$k = \frac{\pi}{\sqrt{3}} \simeq 1.81. \qquad 3.7c$$

Numerical investigation in the μ, σ plane with the central value of $k = 1.7$ in 3.4 gives the maximum absolute deviation of the approximation from the integral as 1×10^{-2}. The behaviour of the approximation for different values of k in various regions of the μ, σ plane is currently under investigation.

Following 2(ii), if we take as approximate complete data sufficient statistics (x,t) where x is the true value of y, then the appropriate form of the EM algorithm is (Aitchison, 1978) at the (r+1)th iteration:

E-stage: $E\left(x_i|y_i,\delta^{(r)}\right) \simeq$

$$x_i^{(r+1)} = y_i \pm \frac{S\delta^{(r)}}{\sqrt{k^2+\delta^{(r)^T}S\delta^{(r)}}} \cdot \phi\left(\pm\frac{\delta^{(r)^T}y}{\sqrt{k^2+\delta^{(r)^T}S\delta^{(r)}}}\right) \Big/ \left(\Psi\left(\pm\frac{\delta^{(r)^T}y}{\sqrt{k^2+\delta^{(r)^T}S\delta^{(r)}}}\right)\right)$$

+ for t=1, - for t=2 3.8

M-stage: Determine $\delta^{(r+1)}$ by applying ordinary logistic m.ℓ. analysis to $\{x_i^{(r+1)}, i=1,\dots,n\}$.

(ii) Cumulative Normal Model with Normally Distributed Error

The form of this model for exact x is

$$p(t=1|x,\gamma) = \Phi(\gamma^T x), \qquad p(t=2|x,\gamma) = 1-\Phi(\gamma^T x) \qquad 3.9$$

where Φ is the c.d.f. of the standard normal distribution.

When inaccurate y is observed with normal error,

$$p(t=1|y_i,\gamma) = \int_X \Phi(\gamma^T x)\ \phi(y_i|x,S)\,dx = \Phi\left(\frac{\gamma^T y_i}{\sqrt{1+\gamma^T S\gamma}}\right) \qquad 3.10$$

From 3.10 we see it is possible to estimate γ directly.

The approximate EM algorithm with (x,t) as before leads to (Aitchison, 1978):

E-stage:

$$x_i^{(r+1)} = y_i \pm \frac{S\gamma^{(r)}}{\sqrt{1+\gamma^{(r)T} S\gamma^{(r)}}} \cdot \phi\left(\pm \frac{\gamma^{(r)T} y}{\sqrt{1+\gamma^{(r)T} S\gamma^{(r)}}}\right) \Bigg/ \left(\Phi\left(\pm \frac{\gamma^{(r)T} y}{\sqrt{1+\gamma^{(r)T} S\gamma^{(r)}}}\right)\right) \qquad 3.11a$$

+ for t=1, - for t=2

M-stage: Estimate $\gamma^{(r+1)}$ by m.ℓ. from $\ell = \prod_{i=1}^{n} \ell_i$ where

$$\ell_i = \Phi\left(\gamma^T x_i^{(r+1)}\right) \text{ for } t=1, \qquad = 1-\Phi\left(\gamma^T x_i^{(r+1)}\right) \text{ for } t=2 \qquad 3.11b$$

An exact and computationally straightforward EM algorithm for the normal c.d.f. model is given in Aitchison, 1978. To summarise, the complete data sufficient statistics are (x,v) where

$$\begin{aligned} p(v|x) &= N(\gamma^T x,1) \\ p(x|y) &= N(y,S) \\ p(v|y) &- N(\gamma^T y,1+\gamma^T S\gamma) \end{aligned} \qquad \begin{aligned} &t=1 \text{ corresponds to } v > 0 \\ &t=2 \text{ corresponds to } v \leqslant 0 \end{aligned} \qquad 3.12$$

The appropriate form of the EM algorithm is

E-step: Given $\gamma^{(r)}$ compute

$$v_i^{(r+1)} = \gamma^{(r)T} y_i \pm \sqrt{1+\gamma^{(r)T} S\gamma^{(r)}} \cdot \phi\left(\pm \frac{\gamma^{(r)T} y_i}{\sqrt{1+\gamma^{(r)T} S\gamma^{(r)}}}\right) \Bigg/ \left(\Phi\left(\pm \frac{\gamma^{(r)T} y_i}{\sqrt{1+\gamma^{(r)T} S\gamma^{(r)}}}\right)\right)$$

$$x_i^{(r+1)} = y_i \pm \sqrt{1+\gamma^{(r)T} S\gamma^{(r)}} \cdot \phi\left(\pm \frac{\gamma^{(r)T} y_i}{\sqrt{1+\gamma^{(r)T} S\gamma^{(r)}}}\right) \Bigg/ \left(\Phi\left(\pm \frac{\gamma^{(r)T} y_i}{\sqrt{1+\gamma^{(r)T} S\gamma^{(r)}}}\right)\right)$$

+ for t=1, - for t=2 3.13a

M-step: Regress $v_i^{(r+1)}$ or $x_i^{(r+1)}$ assuming unit variance to obtain $\gamma^{(r+1)}$. 3.13b

This is an exact procedure and does not require numerical differentiation of the normal c.d.f.

(iii) Numerical Example

The example is based on data from Cox, 1976 and is given in table 1. The results of fitting the logistic and cumulative normal models to these data with simulated normal errors are given in table 2.

For the logistic model with errors it was possible to evaluate the exact estimates by one-dimensional numerical integration for this simple case. The integral approximation 3.3 gives values closer to these than and the approximate EM algorithm 3.8. The pre-assigned values of k was 1.70.

Fitting the normal model verifies that the (x,v) form of the EM algorithm in 3.13 is exact when x is accurate. However, in the exact case the algorithm is sensitive to starting values. When it is applied to the inaccurare data it diverges. These properties have been born out in more recent trials with other data.

The comparison of the approximation to $\hat{\delta}$ obtained by the use of the integral approximation 3.4 for the logistic model with $\hat{\gamma}$ obtained from the use of 3.10 for the normal model demonstrates why the logistic form of the approximation is much preferable to the normal c.d.f. approximation in 3.6. The approximation to δ is much closer to the actual value than $1.70 \times \hat{\gamma}$.

Both models are very similar in terms of goodness of fit to the data and support. However it is not possible to approximate the parameter estimates of one model by transforming estimates for the other model.

A comparison of the algorithms for each model in terms of timing for each iteration and the number of iterations to convergence is given in table 1. Newton-Raphson iteration with analytic differentiation was employed where appropriate. The EM algorithm 3.13 converges very slowly and obviously does not posess the quadratic convergence properties of Newton-Raphson iteration. All computations were made on a Wang 2200, 16K mini-computer using Wang Basic.

4. Determination of $p(t|y,D)$ in the Predictive Case

This second problem is under current investigation and is considered only briefly here.

For the full predictive model $p(t|y,D) = \int_\Delta p(\delta|D) \int_X p(t|x,\delta)\, p(x|y)dx\, d\delta$ 4.1

If $\int_X$ can be evaluated analytically or if a good function approximation can be found, then $p(t|y,D) = \int_\Delta p(t|y,\delta)\, p(\delta|D)d\delta$ 4.2

where $p(t|y,\delta)$ has an explicit form.

e.g. for the logistic model, $p(t|y,\delta) \simeq \Psi\left(\frac{\mu}{\sqrt{1+\sigma^2/k^2}}\right)$ as in 3.4

and the normal model $p(t|y,\gamma) = \Phi\left(\frac{\mu}{\sqrt{1+\sigma^2}}\right)$ as in 3.10.

If we consider m.ℓ. estimation for δ as in 2, 3, then asymptotic m.ℓ. theory in its Bayesian form gives $p(\delta|D) \simeq N(\hat{\delta}, V(\hat{\delta}))$ 4.3
where $V(\hat{\delta})$ is the usual inverse of the information matrix. If an EM algorithm is used to obtain $\hat{\delta}$, then one evaluation of the first and second derivatives of the likelihood function is necessary to obtain V.

4.2 and 4.3 give $p(t|y,D) = \int_\Delta p(t|y,\delta)\ \phi(\delta|\hat{\delta},V(\delta))\,d\delta$.

This integral can be estimated by a Monte Carlo Method (Hammersley and Handscomb, 1964).

e.g. Importance Sampling.Sample δ_j,i=1,...,m from MVN $(\hat{\delta}, V(\hat{\delta}))$

Estimate p by $\Sigma p(t|y,\delta_j)/m$, with appropriate estimated variance.

5. Discussion

The straightforward numerical example presented here demonstrates the basic properties of the current models and algorithms under investigation in this area. Current research is on their applicability to small sample, multi-attribute clinical data (Aitchison, 1978).

References

Aitchison, J. and Begg, C.B., Statistical diagnosis when basic cases are not classified with certainty, Biometrika, 63, 1-12, 1976.

Aitchison, J., Habbema, D.Y., Kay, J.W., A critical comparison of two methods of statistical discrimination, Appl.Statist., 26, 15-25, 1977.

Aitchison, J. and Lauder, I.J., Statistical diagnosis with imprecise data, 1978.

Cox, D.R., The analysis of binary data, Methuen, London, 1970.

Dawid, A.P., Properties of diagnostic data distribution, Biometrics, 33, 647-658, 1976.

Dempster, A.P., Laird, N.M., Rubin, D.B., Maximum likelihood via the EM algorithm, R.J. Statist. Soc. B, 39, 1-38, 1977.

Hammersley, J.M. and Handscomb, D.C., Monte Carlo methods, Methuen, London, 1964.

Tocher, K.D., The art of simulation, England universities press, 1963.

Table 1 (from Cox (1970), p.86)

Time	x	7	14	27	51
No. of units produced		55	157	159	16
No. of failures		0	2	7	3

Table 2

M.L. Fit of Logistic and Normal Model to exact data and data with simulated error. $y = x + \varepsilon$, x is as in table 1, $\varepsilon \simeq N(0,s^2)$.

s	Algorithm for ψ model	Estimate of δ	Algorithm for Φ model	Estimate of γ
0	Exact M.L.	$-5.4152,\ 8.0696\times10^{-2}$	Exact M.L. EM algorithm 3.13 }	$-2.8004,\ 3.9076\times10^{-2}$
1	Exact M.L. by integration	$-5.3775,\ 7.9355\times10^{-2}$	Exact M.L. 3.10	$-2.7796,\ 3.8312\times10^{-2}$
	Functional approxn. 3.4	$-5.3794,\ 7.9399\times10^{-2}$	EM algorithm 3.13	Diverges
	Algorithm 3.8	$-5.3886,\ 7.9756\times10^{-2}$	Algorithm 3.11	$-2.7699,\ 3.8008\times10^{-2}$
5	Exact M.L.	$-5.1279,\ 6.7796\times10^{-2}$	3.10	$-2.6419,\ 3.1956\times10^{-2}$
	3.4	$-5.1658,\ 6.866\times10^{-2}$	3.13	Diverges
	3.5	$-5.3576,\ 7.7310\times10^{-2}$	3.11	$-2.5019,\ 3.1350\times10^{-2}$

Table 3 Efficiency of Algorithms

Model	Algorithm	Time per Iteration*	No. of iterations to convergence	
	Exact M.L.	54		3
	3.4	1		3
	3.8	1.6	EM stage } 1	4
			2	2
			3	2
	3.10	2.2		3
	3.13	1.6		50
	3.11	2.2	EM stage } 1	2
			2	2
			3	1

* Expressed relative to algorithm 3.4.

An Algorithm for Sequential Unsupervised Classification

U.E. Makov, London

Summary

Unsupervised Bayes sequential learning procedures for classification and estimation are often useless in practice because of computational restraints. In this paper a composite algorithm is presented for a particular multiple-class decision problem. The proposed algorithm begins using a coherent Bayes procedure switching to a Quasi-Bayes procedure when computational limits are met. Some numerical illustrations are provided.

Keywords: Unsupervised learning, sequential Bayes classification, Quasi-Bayes.

1. Introduction

Problems of unsupervised learning arise when attempts are made to learn about parameters using sequential unclassified observations each stemming from any of k classes ($k \geq 2$). A general discussion of such problems in the context of Statistical Pattern Recognition is given by Young and Calvert (1974) and Makov and Smith (1976) and references there cited.

Computationally, formal Bayesian procedures become hopelessly impractical when the number of observations or classes becomes large. Approximating procedures while having fast and good asymptotic behaviour are inferior in the short run. Advantages can accrue from creating composite learning algorithms and this paper describes and reports experience of one such algorithm.

Our problem is as follows. A sequence of (possibly vector-valued) observations, $x_1, \ldots, x_n, \ldots$ are received, one at a time, and each has to be classified as coming from one of a known number of k of exclusive classes $H_1, \ldots, H_k$ before the next observation is received. Each decision is made with the knowledge of all the previous observations, but without knowing whether previous classification were correct or not.

We shall consider a situation in which the mixing probabilities, $\pi = (\pi_1, \ldots \pi_k)$, that an observation belongs to class H_i, $i = 1, \ldots k$, are <u>unknown</u> while the conditional probability densities $f_i(x) = f(x|H_i)$ are completely <u>specified</u>. These assumptions may be appropriate when large training sets are available for each individual class, but there is little initial information regarding the "mix" of observations. We further assume that, conditional on π, the x_n are independent with probability density

$$f(x_n|\pi) = \sum_{i=1}^{k} \pi_i f_i(x_n) \quad . \tag{1}$$

Let $X_n = (x_1, \ldots, x_n)$. The Bayesian algorithm for learning about π involves the specification of a prior density for π, and the subsequent recursive computation of the posterior density $p(\pi|X_n)$ using

$$p(\pi|X_n) \propto f(x_n|\pi)p(\pi|X_{n-1}) \quad . \tag{2}$$

Classification of x_n is dependent on the loss structure specified, and the values of $P_r(x_n \in H_i|X_n)$ $i = 1, \ldots k$. These probabilities are computed using

$$P_r(x_n \in H_i|X_n) \propto f_i(x_n) \cdot \int \pi_i p(\pi_i|X_{n-1})d\pi_i = f_i(x_n)\hat{\pi}_i^{(n-1)} \quad , \tag{3}$$

where $\hat{\pi}_i^{(n-1)}$ is the best current estimate of π_i.

Clearly, an efficient classification procedure requires an efficient procedure for the estimation of π. However, due to the mixture form inherent in (1) there exists no reproducing (natural conjugate) densities for unsupervised Bayes classification (in (2)). This results in a rapid increase in computer and memory requirements with increasing n.

An alternative is the Quasi-Bayes procedure (see Smith and Makov, (1978)) which confines the posterior density function (2) to a single density in a way which retains the natural conjugacy. The resulting procedure is computationally efficient and asymptotically identical to the formal Bayes solution. However, under various conditions the short ran Quasi-Bayes performance may be greatly inferior to that of the coherent Bayes. This leads us to propose an algorithm which starts off using the Bayes procedure and which switches to the Quasi-Bayes when a predetermined criterion is reached. In §2 we give more details on the calculation of $p(\pi|X_n)$ using both procedures. In §3 we discuss possible criteria and give an illustration.

2. The Bayes and Quasi-Bayes procedures

We assume that $p(\pi)$, the prior density for π, has the form of a Dirichlet density

$$p(\pi) = \frac{\Gamma(\alpha_1^{(0)} + \alpha_2^{(0)} + \ldots + \alpha_k^{(0)})}{\Gamma(\alpha_1^{(0)})\Gamma(\alpha_2^{(0)})\ldots\Gamma(\alpha_k^{(0)})} \prod_{i=1}^{k} \pi_i^{\alpha_i^{(0)}-1} \tag{4}$$

which we denote by $D(\pi;\ \alpha_1^{(0)}, \alpha_2^{(0)}, \ldots, \alpha_k^{(0)})$, where $\alpha_i^{(0)} > 0$, $i = 1, 2, \ldots, k$.

We further assume a zero-one loss function for the misclassification of an observation. This implies that x_n is classified as belonging to H_j, say, if $p_r(x_n \varepsilon H_j|X_n) \geqslant p_r(x_n \varepsilon H_i|X_n)$ for $i = 1, \ldots, k$, $i \neq j$.

From (1), (2) and (4) it follows that in the coherent Bayes procedure $p(\pi|X_n)$ is a weighted mixture of Dirichlet densities, each corresponding to a certain partition of the observations among the classes. It is the storing of these mixtures, whose number of terms increases as ${}^{k+n-1}C_n$ and the updating following the introduction of a new observation, which creates difficulties. When ${}^{k+n-1}C_n$ is within 'core limits', an efficient way to represent $p(\pi|X_n)$ is by using the following mixture

$$p(\pi|X_n) = \sum_{i_1=0}^{n} \sum_{i_2=0}^{n-i_1} \sum_{i_3=0}^{n-i_1-i_2} \cdots \sum_{i_{k-1}=0}^{n-i_1-i_2-\ldots-i_{k-2}} \cdot\, \omega^{(n)}[\mathrm{IND}(n, i_1, i_2, \ldots, i_k)]\, D(\pi;\ \alpha_1^{(0)} + i_1, \ldots, \alpha_k^{(0)} + i_k), \tag{5}$$

where $i_k = n - i_1 - i_2 - \ldots - i_{k-1}$

Here $\omega^{(n)}[\mathrm{IND}(n, i_1, i_2, \ldots, i_k)]$, $\sum_j i_j = n$, is the posterior probability that the first n observations are partitioned as follows: i_1 from H_1, i_2 from $H_2, \ldots, i_k$ from H_k IND(*) is an integer counting function, which gives the serial position of each of the densities in the mixture (5), and which allows the evaluation of $\omega^{(n)}[*]$ from $\omega^{(n-1)}[*]$ through the relation

$$\begin{aligned}\omega^{(n)}&[\mathrm{IND}(n, i_1, i_2, \ldots, i_k)] \propto \\ &\omega^{(n-1)}[\mathrm{IND}(n-1, i_1 - 1, i_2, \ldots, i_k)] f_1(x_n)(\alpha_1 + i_1 - 1) \\ &+ \omega^{(n-1)}[\mathrm{IND}(n-1, i_1, i_2 - 1, \ldots, i_k)] f_2(x_n)(\alpha_2 + i_2 - 1) \\ &+ \ldots + \omega^{(n-1)}[\mathrm{IND}(n-1, i_1, i_2, \ldots, i_k - 1)] f_k(x_n)(\alpha_k + i_k - 1) . \qquad (6)\end{aligned}$$

(Note that whenever $i_j - 1 < 0$, $\omega^{(n-1)}[\mathrm{IND}(n-1, \ldots\, i_j - 1 \ldots,)]$ must be set equal to zero as such a partition is infeasible, and that unless equal to zero, $\omega^{(0)}[*] = 1$) .)

The classification of x_n is carried using (3), where $\hat{\pi}_i^{(n)}$ is given by

$$\hat{\pi}_j^{(n)} = \sum_{i_1=0}^{n} \ldots \sum_{i_{k-1}=0}^{n-i_1-\ldots-i_{k-2}} \omega^{(n)}[\mathrm{IND}(n, i_1, i_2, \ldots i_k)] \frac{\alpha_j^{(0)} + i_j}{\alpha_0 + n} \qquad (7)$$

and $\alpha_0 = \alpha_1^{(0)} + \alpha_2^{(0)} + \ldots + \alpha_k^{(0)}$.

When 'core limits' are reached, the Quasi-Bayes procedure can easily take over. Here the posterior distribution $p(\pi|X_n)$ is given by a single Dirichlet density with parameters $\alpha_i^{(n)} = \alpha_i^{(n-1)} + p_r(x_n \varepsilon H_i|X_n)$, $i = 1, 2, \ldots, k$, where $\alpha_i^{(n-1)}$ are the parameters of $p(\pi|X_{n-1})$, and the calculation of $p_r(x_n \varepsilon H_i|X_n)$ proceeds through (3). The $\hat{\pi}_j^{(n)}$ are calculated sequentially using

$$\hat{\pi}_j^{(n)} = \hat{\pi}_j^{(n-1)} - \frac{1}{\alpha_0 + n} \left[\hat{\pi}_i^{(n-1)} - p_r(x_n \varepsilon H_i | X_n)\right] \qquad (8)$$

where

$$\hat{\pi}_j^{(0)} = \frac{\alpha_j^{(0)}}{\alpha_0}$$

3. Discussion and numerical example

The computational attractiveness of the Quasi-Bayes is certainly preferable whenever k and n are of a reasonable size. Though the Quasi-Bayes procedure for estimating π (equation (8)) guarantees convergence to the true parameter with probability one (for proof see Smith and Makov, (1978)) it has two short run drawbacks: (a) It is order dependent and thus could be ill effected by the data, and (b) it could be painfully slow when the f_i's domains of support overlap.

By marrying the two procedures, i.e., classifying $x, \ldots, x_{N*}$ using the Bayes procedure and the rest of the data using the Quasi-Bayes, we can enjoy the particular advantages of the two procedures. This way, we start by improving our knowledge on π using a reliable and relatively fast procedure (and thus reducing the probability of misclassification at a higher rate), switching to an approximated procedure which is easy to compute and which is asymptotically optimal.

The choice of $N*$, the transition point, is dependent on several parameters. We should aim at large $N*$ whenever the f_i's domains of support overlap and when the cost of misclassification is high. The maximum value ascribed to $N*$ is a function of the computer core and the maximum time we allow for each classification, (critical in some on-line processes).

In the Figure below, we show the paths of the first 100 successive estimates of π(true value 0.75), for a simulated example of the 'Signal versus Noise' problem. Here f_1 and f_2 are both Gaussian with means 0.75 and 0 respectively, and variances equal to one; starting point $\hat{\pi}_1^{(0)} = \frac{\alpha_1^{(0)}}{\alpha_1^{(0)} + \alpha_2^{(0)}} = \frac{1}{4}$ and $N*$, the transition point, equal to 30.

Due to the considerable overlap between f_1 and f_2 (low 'signal to noise ratio'), the Quasi-Bayes estimates are lagging well behind the Bayes solution. The composite procedure, switching from Bayes to Quasi-Bayes after 30 observations, mimics the formal Bayes procedure until n = 70, after which the Bayes solution is clearly superior.

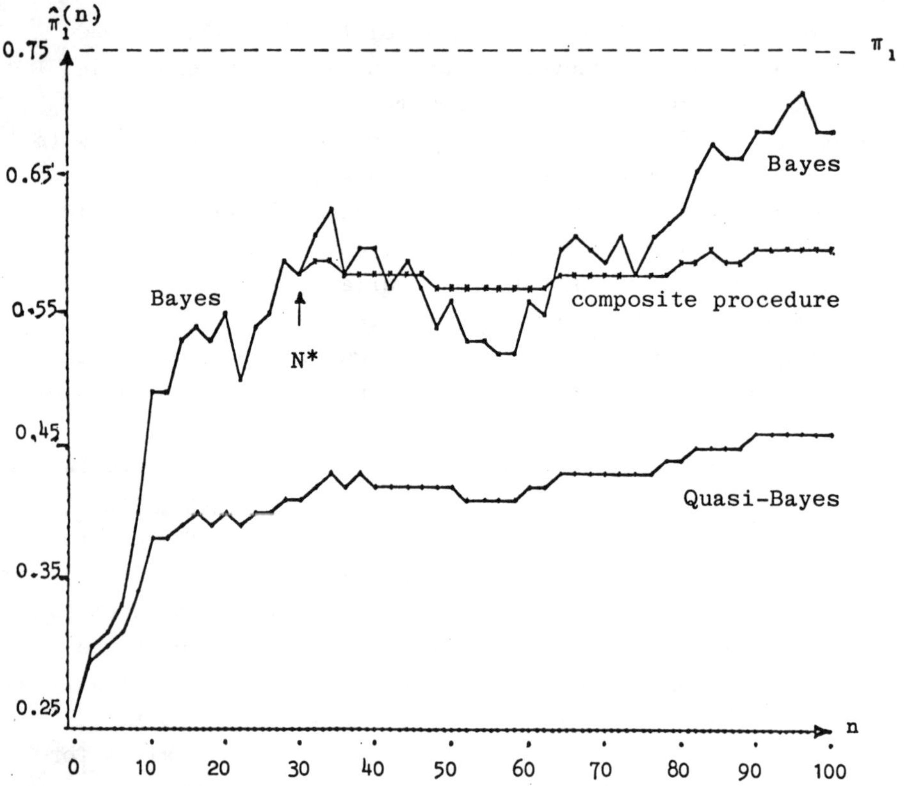

Acknowledgement

The author would like to thank Dr. A.M. Skene for his helpful comments and discussions.

References

Makov, U.E. and Smith, A.F.M., Quasi-Bayes procedures for unsupervised learning. Proc. of the 1976 IEEE Conf. on Decision and Control, pp. 408-411, 1976.

Smith, A.F.M. and Makov, U.E., A Quasi-Bayes sequential procedure for mixtures, J. Roy. Statist. Soc. Ser. B, 40, 1978.

Young, T.Y. and Calvert, T.W., Classification, Estimation and Pattern Recognition. New York: American Elsevier, 1974.

Discrimination Using Latent Structure Models

A.M. Skene, London

SUMMARY

A latent structure model may be used for discrimination when the observable variables are both discrete and continuous. Such a model allows the calculation of probabilities of class membership even when components of the training data are missing or when the feature vector of a new item is incomplete. Parameter estimation is achieved using the EM algorithm.

KEYWORDS: ALLOCATION, DISCRIMINATION, EM ALGORITHM, LATENT STRUCTURE MODEL.

1. INTRODUCTION

When an item is to be assigned to one of I classes $C_1, \ldots, C_I$ on the basis of an observed K dimensional vector of features, $\underset{\sim}{w}$, one approach is to calculate the probability that the item is a member of each class using Bayes' theorem. This requires knowledge of the prior probabilities $p(C_i)$ and of the conditional distributions $p(\underset{\sim}{w}|C_i)$. For the latter it is usual to assume a particular model and then use training data to estimate the model parameters. However, for many choices of model, such an approach involves many computational difficulties especially when $\underset{\sim}{w}$ contains both discrete and continuous variables, K is large, or items in the training data are incomplete.

Here we describe an extension of the latent structure model which avoids some of these problems. While the precise assumptions necessary for the model's derivation are rarely satisfied in practice, the model is sufficiently highly parameterised to afford an approximation to $p(\underset{\sim}{w}|C_i)$ which is useful for allocation.

2. THE LATENT STRUCTURE MODEL

Suppose that, in addition to the K manifest variables available, there exists a discrete latent variable y taking values $n = 1, \ldots, N$, which contains all the information provided by $\underset{\sim}{w}$. Thus $\underset{\sim}{w}$ and C_i are independent, given y. Furthermore, the levels of y define classes of items with similar feature vectors, hereafter known as latent classes, which are sufficiently homogeneous that within each latent class the manifest variables can be assumed to be independent. Thus

$$p(\underset{\sim}{w}|C_i) = \sum_{n=1}^{N} \prod_{k=1}^{K} p_k(w_k|\underset{\sim}{\theta}_{kn})pr(n|C_i) \quad . \qquad (1)$$

Each conditional distribution is thus expressible as a mixture of distributions which are independent of the C_i. Only the mixing probabilities depend on which class is being considered. Each component distribution of the mixture is a product of independent densities whose functional form depends on w_k and whose parameters $\underset{\sim}{\theta}_{kn}$ depend only on the level of the latent variable.

When the marginal densities $p_k(\cdot|\cdot)$ are all multinomial, (1) is recognisable as a simple generalisation of a latent class model; if all are continuous, (1) describes a latent profile model (Lazarsfeld and Henry, 1968). However (1) may also be used when a different functional form is assumed for each k.

The validity of (1) in any particular application depends on the value chosen for N since the independence assumptions become more realistic as N increases. In practice, N may be chosen by repeatedly fitting (1) to the training data for increasing N until no significant improvement in model fit is observed.

One useful way of envisaging a discrimination procedure which incorporates (1), is to view the calculation of class membership probabilities as a two stage process. First, for each new item the probabilities of latent class membership are calculated using

$$pr(n|\underset{\sim}{w}) \propto \prod_{k=1}^{K} p_k(w_k|\underset{\sim}{\theta}_{kn})pr(n) \qquad (2)$$

where $$\mathrm{pr}(n) = \sum_{i=1}^{I} \mathrm{pr}(n|C_i)\mathrm{pr}(C_i) \quad . \tag{3}$$

Secondly

$$\mathrm{pr}(C_i|\underset{\sim}{w}) = \sum_{n=1}^{N} \mathrm{pr}(C_i|n)\mathrm{pr}(n|\underset{\sim}{w}) \quad . \tag{4}$$

Expressed in this form it can be seen that the probabilities $\mathrm{pr}(n|\underset{\sim}{w})$ $n = 1,\ldots, N$ are a transformation of $\underset{\sim}{w}$ which preserves the information relevant to the allocation, when the model is true. Furthermore the assumption of independence within latent class means that the calculation of $\mathrm{pr}(n|\underset{\sim}{w})$ is not complicated when elements of $\underset{\sim}{w}$ are missing. It is interesting to note that when $N = I$ and a one-to-one correspondence exists between the latent classes and the C_i, $i = 1,\ldots, I$, (1) reduces to the so-called Bayes Independence Model (Lusted, 1968, p. 32)

3. PARAMETER ESTIMATION

Prior to the allocation of a new item to a class, estimates must be obtained for the parameters, $\underset{\sim}{\theta}_{kn}$ and the mixing probabilities $\mathrm{pr}(n|C_i)$. Given a set of training data, $\underset{\sim}{w}_{ij}$ $i = 1,\ldots, I$, $j = 1,\ldots, J_i$, maximum likelihood estimates can be computed for these quantities using the EM algorithm (Dempster et al. 1977).

In general, the EM algorithm provides a means of obtaining maximum likelihood estimates when a model in which such computation is normally straightforward is complicated by missing data. Each iteration of the algorithm requires two distinct steps. In the first, the Expectation step, estimates of the missing data are calculated using current estimates of the model parameters. Secondly, in the Maximisation step, new estimates are obtained for the model parameters by maximising the full data model.

In the present context, parameter estimation would be straightforward if the latent class to which each item of training data belonged was known. Let $\underset{\sim}{T}_{ij} = (T_{ij1},\ldots, T_{ijN})$ be an indicator vector whose n^{th} element is 1.0 and whose remaining elements are 0.0 when the ij^{th} item belongs to latent class n. Thus the T's are 'missing'.

It is easy to show that the 'full-data' log likelihood for the training data is given by

$$\sum_{i=1}^{I} \sum_{j=1}^{J_i} \sum_{n=1}^{N} T_{ijn} \log pr(n|C_i)$$

$$+ \sum_{i}^{I} \sum_{j}^{J_i} \sum_{n=1}^{N} T_{ijn} \sum_{k=1}^{K} \log p_k(w_{ijk}|\underset{\sim}{\theta}_{nk}) \quad . \qquad (5)$$

The M step is thus trivial as

$$\hat{pr}(n|C_i) = \sum_{j=1}^{J_i} T_{ijn}/J_i \qquad (6)$$

and we can maximise

$$\sum_{i=1}^{I} \sum_{j=1}^{J_i} T_{ijn} \log p_k(w_{ijk}|\underset{\sim}{\theta}_{nk}) \qquad (7)$$

separately for each n and k, yeilding $\hat{\underset{\sim}{\theta}}_{nk}$.

As Dempster et al. observe, (5) is also linear in the T's and thus at the E step we may estimate each T_{ijn} separately. As $E(T_{ijn}|data) = pr(T_{ijn} = 1|data)$, by Bayes' theorem

$$E(T_{ijn}|data) \propto \prod_{k=1}^{K} p_k(w_{ijk}|\hat{\underset{\sim}{\theta}}_{kn})\hat{pr}(n|C_i) \quad . \quad n = 1, \ldots, N \; . \qquad (8)$$

The algorithm may be initiated by choosing starting values for the T's. Thereafter the M and E steps are repeated alternately until convergence. It is straightforward to extend (6), (7) and (8) to allow for an arbitrary number of replications of each observation w_{ijk}, including the case when w_{ijk} is missing.

In practice the EM algorithm provides slow but sure convergence to a local maximum of the likelihood

$$\prod_{i=1}^{I} \prod_{j=1}^{J_i} \left[\sum_{n=1}^{N} (pr(n|C_i) \prod_{k=1}^{K} p_k(w_{ijk}|\theta_{nk})) \right] \quad . \qquad (9)$$

Repeating the exercise with several different starting values gives an indication of the strength of the data in relation to the number of parameters being estimated. A choice can be made between local maxima by evaluating (9) at each point. However, limited experience suggests that different local maxima have very similar predictive performance when the corresponding discriminant procedures are tried on test data.

In common with factor analytic models, (9) has several equal global maxima corresponding to different enumerations of the latent classes. Clearly in the present context this ordering is immaterial, as the latent classes are not intended to have any physical interpretation. They are simply artifacts introduced to obtain a flexible yet parsimonious parameterisation of the distribution $p(\underset{\sim}{w}|C_i)$.

4. EXAMPLE

The latent structure model finds application in medical diagnosis and prognosis. Jennett et al. (1976) discuss the difficulties in predicting outcome following severe head injury, using the Bayes independence model. A very simple and somewhat artificial example drawn from that study is considered here. Four features recorded for each patient within the first day of coma are used to predict whether the patient will survive a six month period. Two of the features, age and a coma score (measured on a twelve point scale) were assumed to be normally distributed within a latent class. Two further features had a binomial and multinomial distribution respectively. Table 1 gives estimates of the mixing probabilities and the model parameters, when three latent classes are assumed . Two training samples each of 250 patients were used.

On 500 test cases, 382 were accurately predicted using a 0-1 loss function. Latent class 2 gives a clue why accurate prediction is difficult. Whereas 24% of all patients who died were characterised by this class, so too were 16% of those patients who survived.

TABLE 1

Mixing probabilities:

Outcome	Latent Class 1	Latent Class 2	Latent Class 3
Death	.715	.242	.041
Survival	.021	.160	.818

Parameter estimates:

Variable	Distribution		Latent Class 1	Latent Class 2	Latent Class 3
1) Age	Normal	$\hat{\mu}$	38.3	48.3	23.9
		$\hat{\sigma}^2$	453	367	242
2) Coma score	Normal	$\hat{\mu}$	3.16	4.9	5.85
		$\hat{\sigma}^2$	2.07	1.03	5.78
3) Operated haematoma	Binomial*	No(0)	.488	.199	.648
		Yes(1)	.512	.801	.352
4) Pupil response	Multinomial*	Good(0)	.155	.556	.665
		Med.(1)	.261	.342	.315
		Poor(2)	.584	.102	.020

* Table entries are estimates of pr(response ℓ | latent class n).

References

Dempster, A.P., Laird, N.M, and Rubin, D.B. Maximum likelihood from incomplete data via the EM algorithm (with discussion), J. Roy. Statist. Soc. B, 1-38, 1977.

Jennett, B., Teasdale, G., Braakman, R., Minderhoud, J. and Knill-Jones, R. Predicting outcome in individual patients after severe head injury, Lancet, i, 1031-34, 1976.

Lazarsfeld, P.F. and Henry, N.W. Latent structure analysis, Houghton Mifflin, Boston, 1968.

Lusted, L.B. Introduction to medical decision making, Thomas, Springfield, Illinois, 1968.

Classical Discriminant Analysis and Lancaster Models for Qualitative Data

H.-J. Trampisch, Giessen

SUMMARY

The performance of the two classical discriminant functions, the linear and quadratic discriminant function is compared with three elements of the LANCASTER models, the independent model, the 2-nd order LANCASTER model and the multinomial model. The LANCASTER models are one of those model families for discrimination introduced by TRAMPISCH (1978).

KEYWORDS: classical discriminant analysis, LANCASTER models, reachable error, qualitative data.

1. INTRODUCTION

The well-known problem in discriminant analysis is to allocate a n-dimensional random variable $X = (X_1,...,X_n)$ with minimal risk of disallocation to one of m populations $D_1,...,D_m$. For a mathematical description of the problem see e.g. TRAMPISCH (1978), for a more practical presentation - also of the arising problems - see HABBEMA and HERMANS (1978).
In the case of a continuous random variable X besides the classical discriminant functions many procedures, mostly based on non-parametric density estimation (e.g. see VICTOR, 1976), exist.
If the variable consists of qualitative data (symptoms) only two well known allocation rules especially for this case exist:

(1) The multinomial model (M)
For an allocation rule based on this model all cell probabilities are to be estimated.

(2) The independent model (I)
For this model independence of all components of the random variable is assumed. Therefore the cell probabilities could be estimated only by use of the 1-dimensional marginals.

In practice often the classical allocation rules are used, too, although this procedure seems to be very dubious, especially for nonbinary data. VICTOR et al. (1974) proposed an introduction of model families, TRAMPISCH (1978) specified this idea. In this paper three elements of the LANCASTER models are studied. We do not want to go into details (for a comprehensiv discussion see TRAMPISCH (1978) or TRAMPISCH (1978a)). The first order LANCASTER model corresponds to the independent model. The second order LANCASTER model takes into account the 2-dimensional marginals. The n-order LANCASTER model is the full multinomial model.

2. DEFINITION OF DIFFERENT ERROR RATES

In this paper we confine ourselves to the case of two groups Π_1 and Π_2 and equal a priori probabilities. For the components of the qualitative random variable $X = (X_1,\dots,X_n)$ the values $X_i = 1,2$ $(i=1,\dots,n)$ are permitted. The problem of finding a discriminant function is strongly bound up with the problem of estimation of the error rate. We need three different kinds of errors which we want to introduce in this section. We take $D(P_1,P_2,x)$ as a discriminant function. P_1,P_2 are the two probability measures of the groups Π_1 and Π_2 (the underlying distributions), x is an element from the mixed group Π. D divides Π into two disjoint sets D_1 and D_2. For $x \in D_1$ we assign x to Π_1, otherwise to Π_2. We name

(3) $$F(D) = 0.5\ (P_1(D_2)+P_2(D_1))$$

the conditional error rate of the discriminant function D.
The error (3) is of interest only by complete information (i.e. by known probability measures P_1 and P_2). In practice, however, the measures P_1 and P_2 are unknown. A discriminant function $\hat{D}$ has to be estimated from a training sample. In the following we assume, that for each of the two groups ℓ training elements are available. With $\hat{D}_\ell$ we denote a discriminant function which is estimated from such a training sample. Now the discriminant function as well as the conditional error rate $F(\hat{D}_\ell)$ are random variables. To characterize the quality of $\hat{D}_\ell$ we use the expected value of $F(\hat{D}_\ell)$ which we call expected error rate. The expectation is to be taken over all training samples with size 2ℓ.
The third error rate needed in the following is the reachable error rate for a model. The reachable error for a model J (e.g. J=I for the independent model) is the stochastic limit of the conditional error $F_J=F_{J(\ell)}$ for increasing sample

size ℓ (if it exists).
TRAMPISCH (1978) has shown that in many cases the reachable error for a model J is the conditional error calculated under the model restrictions J based on the true probabilities.

3. PERFORMANCE OF THE SIMULATION STUDY

In the present simulation study the performance of five allocation rules for qualitative data has been analysed under the following restrictions:

(4) the number of variables has been fixed at 5 (n=5),
(5) only binary variables have been used,
(6) only the 2-group case has been studied (m=2),
(7) equal a priori probabilities have been assumed,
(8) the optimal error rate has been fixed at 0.15,
(9) the expected error was calculated for sample sizes, 3, 5, 10, 15, 30, 50, 100, 500 and 1000 per group.

To fulfill the demand (8) the following algorithm was performed:

(i) two contingency tables P_1 and P_2 have been simulated at random,
(ii) the cells of these contingency tables have been iteratively altered at random as long as the optimal error is 0.15.

These contingency tables, P_1 and P_2 have been then used as populations (underlying distributions). Under these restrictions 5 different situations have been studied which have a great practical importance. These 5 situations result from the following three assumptions:

(10) there is no information about the structure of the underlying distributions,
(11) it may be suggested that for both contingency tables the hypothesis of independence holds,
(12) it may be suggested that a dependency exists only between pairs of variables.

Because in practice the assumptions (11) and (12) will never be fulfilled exactly, 3 situations have been selected for which the following are used as underlying distributions:

(a) at random simulated contingency tables,
(b) ε-almost L_1 contingency tables,
(c) ε-almost independent contingency tables.

For an ε-almost independent contingency table there exists an independent contingency table such that the sum of the absolute values of the differences of the cell probabilities of these two contingency tables is equal to ε. One can show (see TRAMPISCH, 1978) that if one uses as underlying distributions two ε-almost independent contingency tables the difference of the reachable error of the independent model and the optimal error is less than or equal 0.5 ε.

L_1 contingency table is defined as a contingency table which meets the requirements for the 2-nd order LANCASTER model; ε-almost L_1 contingency table is defined equivalent to the above mentioned independent case. One can also show that for two ε-almost L_1 contingency tables as underlying distributions the difference of the reachable error for the 2-nd order LANCASTER model and the optimal error is less than or equal 0.5 ε.

For situation (12) L_1 contingency tables are only one of many possibilities to describe dependency between pairs of variables, for example, you could also use the definition of the log-linear model.

For these 3 situations the following 5 allocation rules are used:

(13) the multinomial model (M),

(14) the 2-nd order LANCASTER model (L),

(15) the independent model (I),

(16) the linear discriminant function (D),

(17) the quadratic discriminant function (Q).

The linear discriminant function is based on the inverse of the pooled covariance matrix of the two groups. Because of the singularity of the covariance matrix for sample size 3 per group, this function could not be computed. Because the quadratic discriminant function is based on the inverse of the covariance matrix for each group, this function could not be computed for sample sizes 3 and 5.

Each simulation starts with the generation of two contingency tables with restriction (8). Then the reachable error rates F_M, F_L and F_I, F_U, F_Q for the multinomial model, the 2-nd order LANCASTER model, the independent model, the linear discriminant function and the quadratic discriminant function are calculated. F_M is the optimal error rate, that is F_M=0.15. These errors are shown in fig. 1-3. For these two contingency tables (the underlying distributions), a training sample with size 2ℓ will be simulated; where ℓ elements from the training sample are from the first group and the others from the second group. From this training sample the cell probabilities are to be estimated under the different model conditions, and the conditional error rates for the estimated

discriminant functions are to be determined.
The means from twenty different samples are used as estimators for the expected error rates. These means depend on the sample size are shown in fig. 1-3.

4. DISCUSSION OF THE RESULTS

Before discussion the results in more detail we will state two general remarks:

(18) For all situations there is a very great conformity between the errors of the linear discriminant function and the independent model as well as between the errors of the quadratic discriminant function and the 2-nd order LANCASTER model. One could say it does not matter which procedures are used, the classical or the two first LANCASTER models give the same overall performance.

(19) In contradiction to the most previous simulation studies the multinomial model gives a very good overall performance even for very small sample sizes. These result supports the theoretical results of GOLDSTEIN and WOLF (1977).

Because of (18) we have used the following style of representation for the figures: for the corresponding classical discriminant function and LANCASTER model we have used the same symbol and that filled in for the classical case and not filled in for the corresponding LANCASTER model. If the absolute value of the errors of the classical discriminant function and the corresponding LANCASTER model is less than 0.03, only the symbol for the classical case is drawn. This has been done to avoid too many graphs which would make the figures too complicated.
Fig. 1 shows that the independent model and the linear discriminant function should not be used for any sample size if the structure of the underlying contingency tables is generated at random (situation a). Even if there is a more stable estimation of the parameters, the two allocation rules do not work well because their reachable errors are to high. For this situation, the application of the multinomial model is always recommended.
Fig. 2 (situation b) shows different graphs. The reachable errors of the five allocation rules are close together. Therefore, for all sample sizes one allocation rule is not always the best; it depends upon the particular sample size. For this case, only for very large sample sizes, the multinomial model

is to be chosen.
Fig. 3 shows the expected results for situation (c). The underlying distributions are of such a special kind that for almost all sample sizes the independent model and the linear discriminant function are preferred.

5. CONCLUSIONS

The performance of the 5 allocation rules strongly depends on their reachable error rates. If the distance between the reachable error for a model and the optimal error is large, this model will not have a good performance for any sample size. If the distance is small, a selection of one model dependent upon the sample size is reasonable. A different performance of the classical discriminant functions and the corresponding LANCASTER models could not be established for any situations.

6. REFERENCES

Goldstein, M., Wolf, E. (1977): On the Problem of Bias in Multinomial Classification. Biometrics 33, 325-331.

Habbema, J.D.F., Hermans, J.M.H. (1978): Statistical Methods for Clinical Decision Making. Ph.D. Dissertation (unpublished), University of Leiden.

Trampisch, H.-J. (1978): Untersuchungen zu Fehlerraten von Trennverfahren aus Modellfamilien. Ph.D. Dissertation (unpublished), University of Giessen.

Trampisch, H.-J. (1978a): Some Results for Allocation Rules Based on a Model Family. J. Clinical Computation (in print).

Victor, N., Trampisch, H.-J., Zentgraf, R. (1974): Diagnostic Rules for Qualitative Variables with Interactions. Meth. Inf. Med. 13, 183-186.

Victor, N. (1976): Non-parametric Allocation Rules. In: F.T. de Dombal, F. Gremy (eds): Decision Making and Medical Care. North-Holland, Amsterdam.

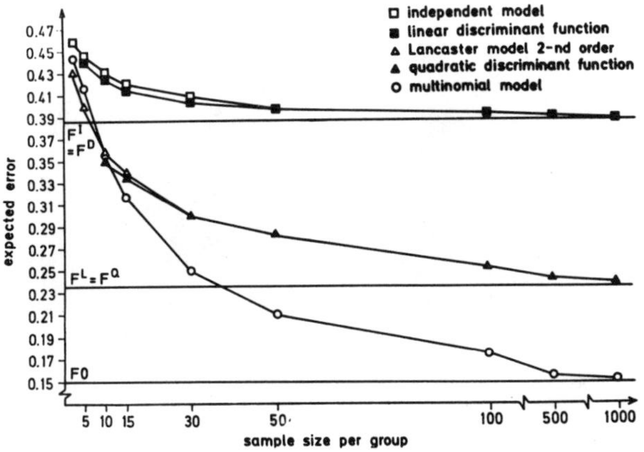

Fig.1:

Expected and reachable error for two at random simulated contingency tables

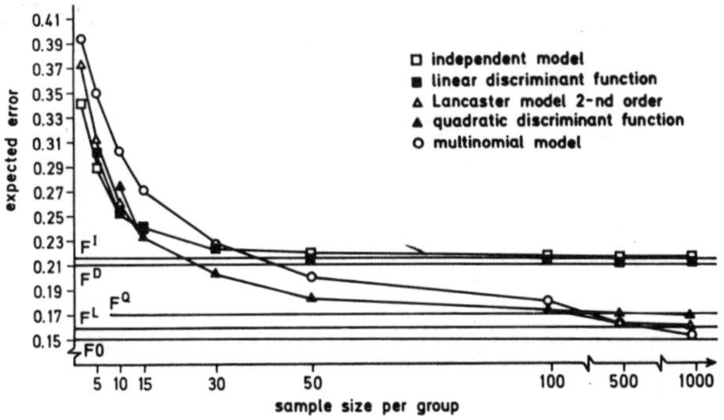

Fig. 2:

Expected and reachable error for two 0.05-almost L_1 contingency tables

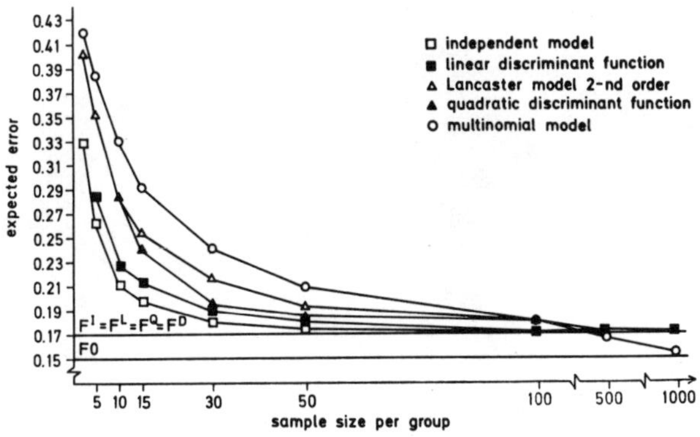

Fig. 3:

Expected and reachable error for two 0.05-almost independent contingency tables

5. Contingency Tables

On the Treatment of Truncated Contingency Tables and Incomplete Experimental Designs

D. Collombier, Toulouse

SUMMARY : *Some results on the treatment of truncated contingency tables and incomplete experimental designs are given, especially for the two way tables and designs. These results concern the detection of the connected components and of the non-interactive cells, the formulation of the hypotheses, the computation of the degrees of freedom and the estimation in (quasi) log linear models.*

KEYWORDS : *Contingency tables, log linear models, experimental designs, linear models.*

1 - INTRODUCTION

The analysis of truncated contingency tables by means of log linear models and of incomplete experimental designs by means of linear models presents some difficulties. These arise when trying :

1/ to formulate briefly the hypotheses of the analysis, for instance in terms of a basis of a subspace in an appropriate vector space ;

2/ to find the connected components ;

3/ to compute the degrees of freedom of the usual test statistics ;

4/ to estimate the parameters of a log linear model when some cell counts are nul.

In this communication we present some theoretical and practical results (algorithms and subprograms) related to the preceding topics. It summarizes and completes the matter of several articles of the author.

More specifically we are dealing with :

1/ detecting automatically the connected components and the non-interactive cells of a table (resp. a design) under a quasi-independence (resp. an additivity) hypothesis with two terms ;

2/ analysing tables with some cell counts nul under the quasi independence hypothesis by means of a quasi linear model.

DEFINITIONS AND NOTATIONS

Consider the set, E, of the cells, e, of a contingency table or an experimental design. It is a subset of the cartesian product $E_I = \Pi\{E_i \mid i \in I\}$, where E_i is the set of the levels of the qualitative variable or the factor i and I their set. If $E = E_I$ the table or the design is said complete. If $E \subset E_I$ the table is said truncated (or incomplete) and the design incomplete.

Consider a subset, J, of the variables or the factors and $\bar{J}$ its complementary in I. Each element of E_I may be regarded as a couple $(e_J, e_{\bar{J}})$ where $e_J \in E_J = \Pi\{E_i \mid i \in J\}$ and $e_{\bar{J}} \in E_{\bar{J}} = \Pi\{E_i \mid i \in \bar{J}\}$. Given e_J, with $J \neq \emptyset$ and $J \neq I$, we call *section of* E the subset $E_{\bar{J}}(e_J) = \{(e_J, e_{\bar{J}}) \mid e_{\bar{J}} \in E_{\bar{J}} : (e_J, e_{\bar{J}}) \in E\}$. By extension we call section each $\{e\} \subset E$ and E itself. We note them $E_\emptyset(e)$ and $E_I(e_\emptyset)$ respectively.

Given $J \neq \emptyset$ we call *J-contrast on* E a numerical function defined on E, constant and equal to $\nu_J(e_J)$ on each section $E_{\bar{J}}(e_J)$, the average of the function ν_J being nul on each section $E'_{J\setminus\{i\}}(e_i)$ of $E'_J = \{e_J \mid e_J \in E_J : E_{\bar{J}}(e_J) \neq \emptyset\}$ for $e_i \in E_i$ and $i \in J$. In the vector space of the numerical functions defined on E : $\mathbb{R}^E$ we note Ω_J the subspace spanned by the J-contrasts on E and $\Omega_\emptyset$ or $\Theta_\emptyset$ the space of the constant functions.

Given an element $e^0 = (e_i^0 \mid i \in I)$ of E_I we note Θ_J the subspace of R^E spanned by the indicators of the sections $E_{\bar{J}}(e_J) \neq \emptyset$ for $e_J \in \Pi\{E_i \setminus \{e_i^0\} \mid i \in J\}$.

2 - THE FORMULATION OF THE INDEPENDENCE HYPOTHESES IN THE ANALYSIS OF A TABLE OR A DESIGN.

Let $\mu(e)$ the expected mean of the random variable observed in e. Generally speaking, when we analyse a table (resp. a design) under a hypothesis of independence or of no-interaction we suppose that the vector $\theta = (\theta(e) = \operatorname{Log} \mu(e) \mid e \in E)$ (resp. $\mu = (\mu(e) \mid e \in E)$) belongs to the subspace $\Omega_{\mathcal{H}} = \Sigma\{\Omega_J \mid J \in \mathcal{H}\}$ where $\mathcal{H}$ is a class of subsets of I. Considering a table it is further assumed that $\mu(e) > 0$ for $e \in E$.

It is not always easy to use this formulation - although standard -: computations become cumbersome and results difficult to interpret. In such cases the following modified formulation may be considered θ or $\mu \in \Theta_{\mathcal{H}} = \Sigma\{\Theta_J \mid J \in \mathcal{H}\}$ This modification is often implicit but might be wrong if $\mathcal{H}$ is not a hierarchical class.

PROPOSITION 1 : If $\mathcal{H}$ is a hierarchical class - that is $(J \in \mathcal{H} \wedge J' \subset J) \Rightarrow (J' \in \mathcal{H})$ - then $\Omega_{\mathcal{H}}$ and $\Theta_{\mathcal{H}}$ are both spanned by the indicators of the sections $E_J^-(e_J) \neq \emptyset$ for $e_J \in E_J$ and $J \in \mathcal{H}^g$, where $\mathcal{H}^g$ verifies $(J \in \mathcal{H}^g \subset \mathcal{H} \wedge J \subset J') \Rightarrow (J' \notin \mathcal{H})$ - Hence $\Theta_{\mathcal{H}} = \Omega_{\mathcal{H}}$

Proof cf D. COLLOMBIER [1978 a]

In practice if $\mathcal{H}$ is hierarchical this result has several consequences. For instance the restriction to E of a J-contrasts basis on E_I, with $J \in \mathcal{H}$, is a spanning family of $\Omega_{\mathcal{H}}$. It also simplifies the extraction of a basis from a spanning family of $\Omega_{\mathcal{H}}$ (using indicators instead of contrasts) and the computation of the usual test statistics' degrees of freedom (functions of the codimension of $\Omega_{\mathcal{H}}$ in $\mathbb{R}^E$).

More information on that topic, an algorithm and a subprogram FORTRAN using this approach may be found in D. COLLOMBIER [1977,78 a].

THE CASE OF QUASI-INDEPENDENCE OR ADDITIVITY HYPOTHESIS

Considering the particular case where $\mathcal{H}$ is hierarchical with $|\mathcal{H}^g| = 2$ hypothesis above reduces to the two terms quasi independence hypothesis for a table or to the two terms additivity hypothesis for a design. The following result simplifies the treatments :

PROPOSITION 2 : If $\mathcal{H}$ is a hierarchical class with $|\mathcal{H}^g| = 2$. Consider the hypergraph $\mathcal{G} = (E, \{E_J^-(e_J) \mid e_J \in E_J : E_J^-(e_J) \neq \emptyset ; J \in \mathcal{H}^g\})$. Note t the number of its edges, c that of its connected components and A its incidence matrix. Then $\mathcal{G}$ is totally unimodular. A has rank $r = t - c$ and it is always possible to find in A a square block $r \times r$ triangular with the diagonal coefficients equal to 1.

N.B. The column vectors of A are the indicators of the spanning family of $\Omega_{\mathcal{H}} = \Theta_{\mathcal{H}}$ defined in the proposition 1.

Proof cf D.COLLOMBIER [1978] and [1978 a] (for the rank and the form of A)
To demonstrate this proposition we use the properties of the dual hypergraph $\mathcal{G}^*$ of $\mathcal{G}$. These are : 1/ $\mathcal{G}^*$ is a bipartite graph, hence it is totally unimodular;

2/ for each tree of $\mathcal{G}^*$ there exists in A a square block of full rank, triangular with diagonal coefficients equal to 1 (and its vertices are those of a connected component).

In the analysis of a table or a design under the above hypotheses this result is useful for :

1/ detecting the connected components, defining a basis of $\Theta_{\mathcal{H}} = \Omega_{\mathcal{H}}$ and computing the codimension of this subspace of $\mathbb{R}^E$,

2/ defining a basis of the subspace orthogonal to $\Theta_{\mathcal{H}}$ in $\mathbb{R}^E$ and detecting the non interactive cells.

The first treatment requires two algorithms : the first constructs a tree of a graph and the second - included in the first - scans the cells. Then a basis of $\Omega_{\mathcal{H}}$ is extracted from the spanning family of the column vectors of A. Its vectors are the indicators of the vertices (except one of them) of trees of $\mathcal{G}^*$. For the second treatments this basis is completed by the indicators of the cells which form cycles from the trees of $\mathcal{G}^*$. The matrix of this set of vectors is totally unimodular, regular and triangular. This matrix is then easily inverted . Some of the line vectors of its inverse define a basis of the subspace orthogonal to $\Omega_{\mathcal{H}}$. Let $\{\beta_i \mid i \in [1,p]\}$ $(p = \text{Codim}\,[\Omega_{\mathcal{H}}])$ this basis, the set of the non-interactive cells is $E^* = \cap\{\{e \mid e \in E : \beta_i(e) = 0\} \mid i \in [1,p]\}$.

The algorithms and the subprograms FORTRAN in D.COLLOMBIER [1978 b] perform present treatments according to these methods.

3. THE ESTIMATION OF THE PARAMETERS IN A QUASI LOG LINEAR MODEL

In a contingency table when some cell counts are nul it may arise that a M.L.E. (maximum likelihood estimation) does not exist.

> *PROPOSITION 3 : Consider a contingency table n_I and a parametric space $\Theta \subset R^E$. A M.L.E. of the parameter μ - with $\theta = (\theta(e) = \text{Log}\,\mu(e) \mid e \in E) \in \Theta$ - exists if and only if there is a vector δ orthogonal to Θ such that $n_I(e) + \delta(e) > 0\ \forall e \in E$.*

Proof cf S.J. HABERMAN [1974]

There are two types of situations in which a M.L.E. does not exist. For instance consider each of the following tables and suppose we have to analyse them under a quasi-independence hypothesis.

1	2		
3	4	0	
		5	6
		7	8

1	2	0	
3	4	0	
		5	6
		7	8

In the first table a cell count is nul in a non-interactive cell (that is in a cell where all the vectors orthogonal to Θ are nul). In the second table there are several vectors orthogonal to Θ with non-nul but of opposite signs coordinates in the cells where the counts are nul. In these two cases the condition of proposition 3 does not hold.

Here the difficulties lie in the fact that all the $\mu(e)$ must be strictly positive in the log linear models. Therefore we were lead to consider an extension of these models in which such a contraint disappear in part. This extension was first formulated by J.P. BENZECRI [1967] for the complete tables. It is different from the quasi-log linear models of Y.M.M. BISHOP and others [1975] which are log linear models for truncated tables.

Given a vector θ of R^E let Support $[\theta]$(resp. $Half_+ [\theta]$, $Half_- [\theta]$) the set of the cells where $\theta(e) = 0$ (resp. $\theta(e) > 0$, $\theta(e) < 0$). Let also Support $[\Theta_\perp] = \cup \{\text{Support } [\theta] \mid \theta \perp \Theta\}$. We call quasi-log linear a model in which :

1/ $\mu(e) \geq 0 \quad \forall e \in E$ and $E^* = \{e \mid e \in E = \mu(e) > 0\}$ is such that $(e \in E \setminus E^*)$

$\iff (e \in E \setminus \text{Support } [\Theta_\perp]) \vee (\forall \theta \perp \Theta : e \in Half_+[\theta] \Rightarrow \exists e' \in E \setminus E^* : e' \in Half_-[\theta])$

2/ $\forall \theta \perp \Theta \quad \Pi \{\mu(e)^{-\theta(e)} \mid e \in Half_-[\theta]\} = \Pi \{\mu(e)^{\theta(e)} \mid e \in Half_+ [\theta]\}$.

PROPOSITION 4 : *A M.L.E of the parameter always exists in a quasi-log linear model.*

Proof : The proof outlines are :

1/ on $E \setminus E^*$ the second hypothesis is trivialy satisfied, then the expected and observed counts are equal ; on E^* the model is log linear ;

2/ for any table n_I there is always a set of cells which verifies the conditions of the first hypothesis and a vector δ orthogonal to Θ such that

$$n_I(e) = \delta(e) = 0 \quad \forall e \in E \setminus E^* \text{ and } n_I(e) + \delta(e) > 0 \ \forall e \in E^*.$$

In some cases a second property simplifies the computations.

PROPOSITION 5 : *Note $\{\beta^e \mid e \in E\}$ the canonic basis of R^E ($\beta^e(e') = 0$ if $e \neq e'$ and 1 if $e = e'$). Consider*

1/ the convex set $\mathcal{C}$ intersection of the manifold containing n_I orthogonal to Θ and of the cone of the positive functions on E,

2/ the linear hull $L[\mathcal{C}]$ of $\mathcal{C}$ (that is the intersection of all the manifolds containing $\mathcal{C}$).

Then the M.L.E. $\hat{\mu}$ of the parameter is such that $\hat{\mu} \in \mathcal{C}$, $\hat{\mu}(e) = n_I(e)$

$\forall\ e \in E\backslash\tilde{E} = \{e \mid e \in E : \beta^e \perp L[\mathcal{C}]\}$ and $\hat{\mu}(e) > 0$ $\forall\ e \in \tilde{E}$. The degrees of freedom of the usual test statistics is equal to the dimension of $L[\mathcal{C}]$.

Proof : We deduce the proof from the two following remarks: on $E\backslash\tilde{E}$ the model implies no constraints, on $\tilde{E}$ it is a log linear model.

When $\mathcal{C}$ is a convex polyedron $L[\mathcal{C}]$ is equal to the linear hull of each polyedral convex cone containing $\mathcal{C}$ and spanned by all the half straight lines which support all the edges of $\mathcal{C}$ issued from one of its vertices. If the directions β_j, $j \in [1,q]$, of these half straight lines are known then their number is the dimension of $L[\mathcal{C}]$ and

$$E\backslash\tilde{E} = \cap\{\{e \mid e \in E : \beta_j(e) = 0\} \mid j \in [1,q]\}.$$

In the case of the two terms quasi-independence hypothesis $\mathcal{C}$ is a convex polyedron. In a connected component of the table each vertex of $\mathcal{C}$ is associated with a tree of the hypergraph $\mathcal{G}^*$ of proposition 2 and each direction issued from this vertex is associated with an elementary cycle constructed from this tree.

Using these properties and an estimation procedure in the log linear models we may define an algorithm for detecting the cells of $\tilde{E}$, for estimating the parameters of a quasi-log linear model and for computing the degrees of freedom of the usual test statistics cf. D.COLLOMBIER [1978 b].

REFERENCES

Benzécri J.P., *Lois de probabilité sur un ensemble produit : les diverses notions d'indépendance et le critère d'entropie maximale*, Institut de Statistique de l'Université de Paris, document C20, 1967.

Bishop Y.M.M., Fienberg S.E. and Holland P.W., *Discrete multivariate analysis : theory and practice*, the M.I.T. Press, Cambridge (USA), 1975.

Collombier D., Procedures FORTRAN pour l'analyse de tables de contingence. *Publications du laboratoire de Statistique de l'Université Paul Sabatier*, Toulouse (France), 01-77, 1977.

Collombier D., Un algorithme d'aide à l'analyse des tables de contingence et des plans d'expériences incomplets, *Annales de l'Institut Henri Poincaré*, Paris, 14(2), 1978 a.

Collombier D., Sur le traitement des tables de contingences à deux dimensions, *Publications du Laboratoire de Statistique de l'Université Paul Sabatier*, Toulouse (France), 03-78, 1978 b.

Haberman S.J., *The Analysis of Frequency Data*, University of Chicago Press, Chicago, 1974.

On some Procedures for Identifying Sources of Dependence in Contingency Tables

D. Pokorny and **T. Havranek**, Prague

The question of identifying sources of dependence in,in a sense,multidimensional contingency tables intractable by classical methods is considered.Some general features of efective computer procedures are presented and then ilustrated on the case of 2X2X ...X2 tables.Finally,a procedure for a representation of an RXC table is described.

KEY WORDS: contingency tables,derived and collapsed tables, chi-square statistic,hypotheses formation.

GENERAL REMARKS

In statistical practice,we frequently meet contingency tables which are multidimensional and hence troublesome in two directions;the first concerns the number of variables entering the table,the second the range of values of variables.We shall consider for a moment the first case,but our remarks can be applied also to the second one.Such a multidimensional table with,for example, 30-60 variables and 1000-5000 objects could not be analysed by usual theoretically developed statistical methods,for example methods based on log-linear models (see Bishop at al.(1975) and Dixon (1977)).Reasons are clear - the big dimension of computer space needed (we must use the whole frequency table for hypotheses testing) and problems with zero and small frequencies in the table (cf.Havránek,1978).In practice,the way using derived,collapsed and marginal tables is used in spite of its poor theoretical foundation.Clearly,the number of such tables which are to be analysed, given a big source table,is extremely big again.Hence we need some optimized computer procedures for generating and investigating these tables.

Hájek,Havel and Chytil (1966) and Hájek and Havránek (1978) suggested procedures using the following features:

1.Effective syntactical way of describing the set of tables needed. 2.Printing only such generated tables on which a statistic (e.g.chi-square)exceeds a limit. 3.Use of the possibility to *deduce* from the value of a statistic on a table information on the value of this statistic on a set of other generated tables.

Clearly,these hints are based only on properties of statistics as functions on data (not their probabilistic properties). Hence sometimes one speaks about *observational properties* of statistics.Strict logical and mathematical theory of such deduction and respective procedures is given in Hájek and Havránek (1978a). These general (and vague) principles are not restricted to applications in contingency tables: some references to another applications can be found in Hájek and Havránek (1978b).

1. MULTIDIMENSIONAL TWO-VALUED CONTINGENCY TABLES

Consider 2X2X...X2 tables and chi-square statistic. The basic underlying observational property is the following: Let $T=\langle a,b,c,d\rangle$ and $T'=\langle a',b',c',d'\rangle$ be 2X2 tables. If $a\leq a', b\geq b', c\geq c', d\leq d'$ then $\chi^2(T)\leq\chi^2(T')$. Now if we generate tables (for a given set of derived tables) in an appropriate linear ordering $\prec$ we can *see* from the fact that for a table $\chi^2(T)\geq c$ (or $\chi^2(T)<c$) and a simple auxiliary computation that $\chi^2(T')\geq c$ (or $\chi^2(T')<c$) for each T' from a certain segment of the ordering $\prec$. Hence in the first case T and $\chi^2(T)$ are printed only (with some information concerning the length of the segmen) and, in the second case, neither T nor any T' from the segment is printed. In any case, we need not to generate tables from the segment, i.e. to compute the appropriate frequencies; we can "overjump" the segment. Moreover, in some situation we know, that if $\chi^2(T)<c$ then $\chi^2(T')<c$ for each $T'\succ T$; in such a case the procedure stops its work before generating all tables.

Let us remark three things concerning realized programs for these procedures called GUHA procedures (authors of programs: J. Rauch and I. Havel; see Hájek and Havránek (1978a,b)): 1. Procedures are "robust" in the sense that istead of the chi-square test we can use a wide variety of tests and estimators having similar observational properties. 2. On the other hand, only tables of particular form are generated, namely tables concerning association between "derived" properties, e.g. *male* and *health control* and *non-smoker* affects *mortality* , where *male, health control, non-smoker, mortality* are input properties (variables) of the table. 3. Tables are generated (frequencies computed) not from the base 2X...X2 table but successively from source matrix with rows corresponding to objects and columns to variables. Columns are represented as binary strings and boolean operations on binary strings are used. The number of summations and searching steps in the table is then limited. For more information see Appendix A by J. Rauch to Hájek and Havránek (1977).

An example of application (with comparison to BMDP) can be found in Havránek at al. (1977). The procedure checked, for example, 10^3 2X2 tables derived from a 2^{19} table in the time 3 min. (using Fisher exact test statistic with the limit 0.05, 34 tables were printed) and 10^4 tables derived from a 2^{54} table in the time 17 min. (399 tables printed).The computer used was IBM 370/135.

It is clear that such results are unreliable from theoretical point of view.They can serve as *hypotheses* for further investigation.Hence we speak on hypotheses formation methods.

2. RXC CONTINGENCY TABLES

In the present case,the rejection of hypothesis of independence gives very little information concerning the structure of dependence in the table.Hence some methods are used for a characterization of this structure,namely,sign schema based on Haberman's adjusted residuals,smooth tables,finding the most significant Goodman's logarithmic interaction (Anděl,1974),Brown's departures from independence (Brown,1976).Computational complexity of all these methods,measured in the number of arithmetic operations,is polynomial in R,C.Output of all methods (excluding the Brown's one) is a RXC matrix of numbers or symbols.To obtain a useful information, the user has to read all the RXC output table.The output of Brown's procedure can be shorter and,moreover,output information is ordered with respect to its importance; i.e. relevant information can be obtained by reading an initial segment of the output.Our procedures have the same advantage.

Our procedures are based on the testing of 2X2 tables collapsed from the given RXC table.Let the range of the first variable be $V=\{1,\dots,R\}$,of the second one $W=\{1,\dots,C\}$.Let $A\subseteq\mathcal{P}(V)$,$B\subseteq\mathcal{P}(W)$.We shall consider tables given by a pair $\langle X,Y\rangle$,where $X\in A, Y\in B$.If $T=\{a_{ij}\}$ is the original RXC table,the collapsed table given by $\langle X,Y\rangle$ is the 2X2 table with frequencies $a=\sum_{i\in X, j\in Y}a_{ij}$, $b=\sum_{i\in X, j\in W-Y}a_{ij}$, $c=\sum_{i\in V-X, j\in Y}a_{ij}$, $d=\sum_{i\in V-X, j\in W-Y}a_{ij}$. By $v\langle X,Y\rangle$ we denote the value of a statistic on the table (given by) $\langle X,Y\rangle$;we suppose that a statistic for evaluating positive association is used.Clearly,for χ^2 statistic we consider

$$v\langle X,Y\rangle= (am-(a+c)(a+b))\sqrt{m/((a+c)(a+b)(d+c)(d+b))} \qquad (1)$$

where $m=a+b+c+d$.The aim of the procedure is to find,for a given RXC table,all"interesting" tables $\langle X,Y\rangle$.Interestingness is formalized as follows: Order all pairs from the set $\{\langle X,Y\rangle; X\in A, Y\in B\}$ with respect to the decreasing value of $v\langle X,Y\rangle$.The obtained sequence (factorized w.r.t. =) is denoted as $F_1,\dots,F_p$. (2)
Let three numbers N,K,Q are given (N natural, K,Q real,$K\geq 0, 0\leq Q\leq 1$). $\langle N,K,Q\rangle$ -interesting tables (or,if one likes,hypotheses,cf.Hájek and Havránek,1977) are tables from an initial segment of (2): $F_1,\dots,F_l$ where l is the greatest natural number such that $l\leq p$, $l\leq N$, $v(F_l)\geq K$ and $v(F_l)\geq v(F_1)\cdot Q$.

I.e.for a given table we try to find at most N collapsed tables,ordered with respect to the value of a statistic and such that the value of the last of them is greater than a limit and not much less than the value of the first printed table.

In the following we work with the worst case when $A=P(V)-\{V,\emptyset\}$ and $B=P(W)-\{W,\emptyset\}$,i.e. no nontrivial limitation of the form of generated tables.If we use a general statistic v,the search of the list $F_1,\dots,F_l$ of output tables has time complexity $O(2^{R+C})$ (note: $O(f(n))$ denotes the set of all functions such that for some $c_1>0$, $c_2>0$ and n_0,for each $n\geq n_0$,$c_1 f(n)\leq g(n)\leq c_2 f(n)$).For this reason we consider in the further a special form of v,namely χ^2.Note that trivially $v\langle X,Y\rangle = v\langle V-X,W-Y\rangle$. (3)

3. A HIERARCHICAL PROCEDURE

By XxY we denote the table obtained from the given RXC table by omitting rows and columns not in X and Y respectively.We use iteratively a recursive procedure based on three steps:

For a given RXC table:
(1) find the best collapsed table $F_1=\langle X,Y\rangle$(note the fact (3));
(2) create the subtable XxY and if it is non degenerate (i.e. at least 2X2) call recursively the procedure;
(3) create the subtable (V-X)x(W-Y) and if it is non degenerate call recursively the procedure.

As output we obtain a binary tree of tables (or a deblocking structure of the table);see the example.For an interactive version of this procedure see procedure COLLAPS as described in Pokorný (1978). Now we shall consider some facts that can substantially speed up the procedure.All of them are of the form

condition for X and Y $\Rightarrow$ $v\langle X,Y\rangle\leq D$. (4)

The usefulness of these facts for speeding up the computation is based on the following:If a segment of tables,which are to be evaluated,satisfies the left hand condition,an auxiliary test can be done:D<CRIT? where CRIT is a "critical" value for v in the present stage of computation (it depends on values of previous tables in sequence).If D<CRIT then for each table in the segment $v\langle X,Y\rangle<CRIT$ and all the segment can be overjumped without evaluating tables of it.This feature can be in a very clear way described in an appropriate logical theory;see Hájek and Havránek (1978a).

For an RXC table a_{ij} denote $a_{XY}=\sum_{i\in X,j\in Y} a_{ij}$, $m=a_{VW}$, $r_X = \sum_{i\in X} a_{i.}$, $k_Y=\sum_{j\in Y} a_{.j}$,$r=\min a_{i.}(m-\min a_{i.})$,$k=\min a_{.j}(m-\min a_{.j})$, $d_{XY}=a_{XY}m - r_X k_Y$.For any number x denote $x'=x$ if $x\geq 0$,else $x'=0$. Then put $t_j=\sum_{i\geq 2} d'_{ij}$, $m_j = d_{2j}+\sum_{i\geq 3} d'_{ij}$ and $t_Y=\sum_{j\in Y} t_j$, $m_Y = \sum_{j\in Y} m_j$ and,finally $s = r_{12}(m-r_{12})$,where $r_{12} = \min(a_{1.},a_{2.})$.Order

$k_1,\dots,k_C$ in the sequence $k_1,\dots,k_C$, $t_1,\dots,t_C$ in the sequence $t_1,\dots,t_C$ and $m_1,\dots,m_C$ in the sequence $m_1,\dots,m_C$. Put $G_j^* = \min(K_1(m-K_1), K_2(m-K_2))$, where $K_1 = \sum_{q=1}^{j} k_q$ and $K_2 = \sum_{q=C-j-1}^{j} k_q$. Moreover, put $t_j^* = \sum_{q=1}^{j} t_q$ and $m_j^* = \sum_{q=1}^{j} m_q$. Then we can state the following facts of our RXC table: C1. $v\langle X,Y\rangle = v\langle V-X, W-Y\rangle$; C2. $v\langle X,Y\rangle \le m$; C3. $v\langle X,Y\rangle = m$ iff $a_{X,W-Y} = a_{V-X,Y} = 0$; C4. $v\langle X,Y\rangle\ \sqrt{(\sum\sum d_{ij}^2 m/(r_i k_j))}$; C5. (i) $v\langle X,Y\rangle \le \sum_j t_j \sqrt{m/(rk)}$, (ii) if $1 \notin X$, $2 \in X$ (*), then $v\langle X,Y\rangle \le \sum_j m_j \sqrt{m/(rk)}$; C6. (i) $v\langle X,Y\rangle \le \max_{j=1,\dots,C-1} t_j^* \sqrt{m/(rG_j^*)}$; (ii) if (*), then $v\langle X,Y\rangle \le \max_{j=1,\dots,C-1} m_j^* \sqrt{m/(rG_j^*)}$; C7. (i) $v\langle X,Y\rangle \le \max_{\emptyset = Y \subsetneq W} t_Y \sqrt{m/(rk_Y(m-k_Y))}$; (ii) if (*), then $v\langle X,Y\rangle \le m_Y \sqrt{m/(rk_Y(m-k_Y))}$. The following two facts hold for 2XC tables only. Denote $H = \{j; d_{1j} \ge 0\}$. For sets M,N put $M \Delta N = (M-N)(N-M)$. Now denote $G_Z = \min\{k_Y(m-k_Y); Z\Delta H \subseteq Y\Delta H, \min((Y\Delta H)-(Z\Delta H)) > \max(Y\Delta H), \emptyset = Y \subsetneq W\}$. Two auxiliary statements: (i) If $Z\Delta H \subseteq Y\Delta H$, then $d_{1Z} \ge d_{1Y}$; (ii) put $z = \max(Z\Delta H)$, then $G_Z = \max\{k, \min(L_z(m-L_z), P_z(m-P_z))\}$, where $L_z = k_z - k_L$ and $P_z = k_z - k_P$ for $L = \{j; j>z, j \in H\}$ and $P = \{j; j>z, j \notin H$. (I.e. for a given table G_Z depends only on z.)

Now the promised useful facts: C8. If $Z\Delta H \subseteq Y\Delta H$ and $\min((Y\Delta H)-(Z\Delta H)) > \max(Y\Delta H)$, then $v\langle\{1\},Y\rangle \le d_{1Z}\sqrt{m/(r_1 r_2 G_Z)}$; C9. if $\langle X,Y\rangle$ is the "best" table, then for Y the following conditions hold: $a_{1j} = 0 \Rightarrow j \notin Y$, $a_{1j} = a_{.j} \Rightarrow j \in Y$.

Note that right-hand sides of C1-C9 are simple expressions except C7, but decision about this inequality can be speeded up by similar tools as for 2XC table.

4. REALIZATION OF THE PROCEDURE

A boolean tree for a set $V = \{1,\dots,v\}$ is a tree with domain $P(V)$ and with the sequence of succesors for an $X \subseteq V$ given by $X \cup \{x+1\}$, $X \cup \{x+2\}, \dots, X \cup \{v\}$, where $x = \max(X)$ (put $\max(\emptyset) = 0$). For ordering in which collapsed tables are to be generated we can give the following hints, wanting to generate "hopeful" tables as soon as possible and to use facts C1-C8 effectively. (On the beginning of work we use C2-C4.). Hints:

H1. If R>C transpose the frequency table. H2. Permute rows according decreasing value of $\sum_j |d_{ij}|$ and columns according decreasing value of $a_{.j}$. H3. Use depth-first search in the boolean tree for $\{1,\dots,R-1\}$. In each node apply successively C5-C7. (If N=1, apply C9 and use the result for a reduction of generated sets Y for this node.) H4. For each generated $X \subseteq V$ create relatively "hopeful" $Y_0 = \{j;\ d_{Xj} > 0\}$. Then use depth-first search for the boolean tree of symmetric difference $Y \Delta Y_0$. (At each not-leaf node apply C8.)

Space complexity of the suggested procedure is O(RC)+O(N), time complexity $O(2^{R+C})$ for the worst case. Effectivity for a work on concrete data can be measure by "speed up factor" = (number of tests computed + number of auxiliary tests C1-C9 computed) / number of tables to be tested (investigated) .

The procedure COLLAPS is now implemented in PL/I (OS IBM 370). It has input parameters N,K,Q defining "interestingness" (see §2), parameters for restriction of the set of tables to be generated (cf.sets A;B) and parameters for restriction of the input table. Output tables are in file LIST and they are printed by another procedure after COLLAPS stops. The present implemented version uses facts and hints C1,C2,C8,H1-H4. But even the slightly older version using C8,H3,H4 only and used in the following example was satisfactorily quick for all reasonable applications.

5. EXAMPLE

Investigating cultural interests of population,we meet a sample of 1224 people (in categories with respect to employment in 1.industry,2.building industry,3.agriculture,4.transport,5.bussiness,6.health and social services,7.state administration,8.education,arts and science,9."others",10.students) and,among others, the question:What is the main obstacle to your cultural interests? Choose on of the following answers: 1.nothing,2.marriage and family,3.having a baby,4.change of the living place,5.loss of interest 6.illness,7.shortage of opportunities in the living place,8.pressure of work,9.political and social activity,10.recognizing own inability for such activities,11.financial reasons.12.other.Usual chi-square statistics gives in the 10X12 table the value 379.1. Hierarchical COLLAPS procedure gives the following results:

Step 0.<{9.students,10.otheres},{1.nothing,5.no interest,6.illness, 11.finances,12.other}> (or equivalently <{1 - 8},{2,3,4,7-10}>). *Step 1.*For subtable {9,10} × {1,5,6,11,12} we have <{10},{5,6}>(or <{9},{1,11,12}>). *Step 2.* For {1 - 8} ×{2,3,4,7-10} we have: <{2,4,5,6,7,8},{3,7,9,10}> (or <{1,3},{2,4,8}>). *Step 2.1.* For {2,4,5,6,7,8}×{3,7,9,10}we have<{2},{7}> (or<{4,5,6,7,8},{3,9,10}>) *Step 2.2.* For {1,3}×{2,4,8} we have<{1},{2,4}> (or<{3},{8}>). *Step 2.1.1.* For{4,5,6,7,8} × {3,9,10} we have <{5},{3,9}> (or <{4,6,7,8},{10}>.

Results can be summarized in a "block" table or a tree (Fig.1). They are clearly interpretable (note that"others"are mainly retireds).*For the permition of presenting the data we are obliged to dr.Miloš Chyba,Institute for the research of culture,Prague.*

Now some statistics concerning the work of COLLAPS:In the step 0. from 2^{22} tables of interest 13 397 tables were tested.The entire evaluation v<X,Y> was needed in 1 925 cases and only in 4 cases v<X,Y>≥CRIT and LIST was changed.The effectiveness is due to C8, which was used in 12 435 cases and in 10 510 succesfully,i.e. a segment of tables to be evaluated can be "overjumped".Speed up factor is hence 272.9 . By our opinion,the results of the present example illustrate well the advantages of our approach.

Fig.1:

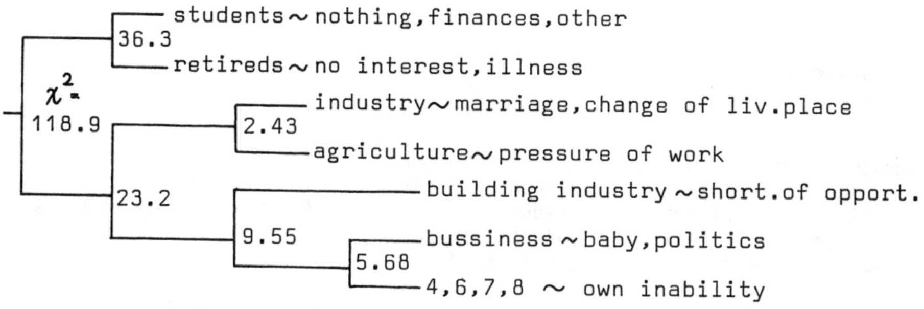

REFERENCES:

Anděl J.,The most significant interaction in a contingency table, Aplikace matematiky, 19, 246-253, 1974

Bishop Y.M.,Fienberg S.E.,Holland P.W.,Discrete multivariate analysis, MIT Press, Cambridge, Massachsetts, 1975

Brown M.B., The identification of sources of significance in two-way contingency tables, Appl.Statistics, 23, 405-413, 1976

Dixon J.W., Ed., BMDP - biomedical computer programs, sec.ed., Univ. of California Press, Los Angeles, 1977

Hájek P.,Havel I.,Chytil M., The GUHA method of automated hypotheses determination, Computing, 1, 293-308, 1966

Hájek P.,Havránek T., On generation of inductive hypotheses, Int. J.Man-Machine Studies, 9, 415-438, 1977

Hájek P.,Havránek T., Mechanizing hypothesis formation - mathematical foundations for a general theory, Universitext, Springer Verlag, Berlin-Heidelberg-New York, 1978a

Hájek P.,Havránek T., The GUHA method - its aims and techniques (with full bibliography and information on programs), Int.J. Man-Machine Studies, 10, 3-22, 1978b

Havránek T., Statistics of multidimensional contingency tables and the GUHA method, Int.J.Man-Machine Studies, 10, 87-93, 1978

Havránek T.,Chyba M.,Pokorný D., Processing sociological data by the GUHA method - an example, Int.J.Man-Machine Studies, 9, 439-447, 1977

Havránek T.,Pokorný D., GUHA style processing of mixed data, Int. J.Man-Machine Studies, 10, 47-58, 1978

Pokorný D., The GUHA method and desk calculators, Int.J.Man-Machine Studies, 10, 75-86, 1978

Exact Comparison of Several Estimating Procedures in 2 x 2 Contingency Tables

H. Yassaee, Teheran

Summary Under independence model, parameters of an rxc contingency table are estimated by maximum likelihood, minimum X^2_p, minimum X^2_N, and minimum discrimination information procedures. These procedures produce estimators which are asymptotically equivalent. In separate papers we have derived formulas for estimators and have shown computational methods generate stable solutions for parameters under investigation. In this paper, by the use of each method of estimation we study on biasedness and mean square error of estimators for parameters of a 2x2 contingency table under the model mentioned earlier. Although our program is written in general, we generate all possible 2x2 contingency tables whose total frequency is specified. Then we compute exact mean and expected mean square according to almost all values of parameters and several values of total frequency. We compare estimators obtained by different procedures in terms of exact values of parameters and total frequency.
KEY WORDS: Contingency tables, Biasedness, Mean square error, Minimum discrimination information statistic, Iterative method.

1. Methods of estimation and derivations

We assume that an experiment is performed and outcomes are categorized in the form of an rxc contingency table (especially in a case that r=c=2). Let x(ij) be the frequency of outcomes belonging to (i,j)th cell of the table, i=1,2,...,r; j=1,2,...,c. Let $x(i.) = \sum_j x(ij)$, $x(.j) = \sum_i x(ij)$, $n = \sum_i \sum_j x(ij)$. We denote the probability that an observed outcome is categorized in (i, j)th cell by p(ij). We also denote marginal probabilities $\sum_j p(ij)$ and $\sum_i p(ij)$ by p(i.) and p(.j), respectively. Then we can write the model of independence in the form

$$p(ij) = p(i.)\, p(.j) \quad \forall i \;;\; i=1,2,\ldots, r;\; j=1,2,\ldots,c$$

$$\sum_i \sum_j p(ij) = 1. \tag{1.1}$$

Likelihood function for a given rxc contingency table with cell frequencies 0 < x(ij)'s and cell probabilities p(ij)'s is written as

$$L = \frac{n!}{\prod_i \prod_j [x(ij)]!} \{\prod_i \prod_j p(ij)^{x(ij)}\} \;;\; n = \sum_i \sum_j x(ij), \quad \sum_i \sum_j p(ij) = 1, \tag{1.2}$$

To estimate parameters we make use of the method of Lagrange multiplier. We maximize ℓnL with respect to p(i.) and p(.j)'s and get the estimators for them. Thus maximum likelihood (ML) estimator for p(ij) is given by

$$\hat{p}(ij) = \frac{x(i.)}{n} \cdot \frac{x(.j)}{n} \quad \forall\ (i, j)$$

$$= \hat{p}(i.)\ \hat{p}(.j) \tag{1.3}$$

In this procedure estimators are obtained without using an iterative procedure.

Under model(1.1) X^2_p is defined as

$$X^2_p = \sum_i \sum_j \frac{[x(ij) - n\ p(i.)\ p(.j)]^2}{n\ p(i.)\ p(.j)} = \frac{1}{n} \sum_i \sum_j \frac{x^2(ij)}{p(i.)p(.j)} - n$$

By minimizing X^2_p with respect to p(i.) and p(.j) we come up to the following system of equations

$$\frac{p(i.)}{p(r.)} = \left[\frac{\sum_{j=1}^{c} \frac{x^2(ij)}{p(.j)}}{\sum_{j=1}^{c} \frac{x^2(rj)}{p(.j)}} \right]^{\frac{1}{2}} \quad , i = 1,2, \ldots, r-1 \tag{1.4}$$

$$\frac{p(.j)}{p(.c)} = \left[\frac{\sum_{i=1}^{r} \frac{x^2(ij)}{p(i.)}}{\sum_{i=1}^{r} \frac{x^2(ic)}{p(i.)}} \right]^{\frac{1}{2}} \quad , j = 1,2,\ldots, c-1. \tag{1.5}$$

To solve equations (1.4) and (1.5) we initialize $\hat{p}(.j) = \frac{x(.j)}{n}$ and used it in (1.4) to get initial value for $\frac{p(i.)}{p(r.)}$ and consequently p(i.)'s, i = 1,2,...,r. Then we introduce these p(i.)'s in (1.5) to get second value for p(.j)'s.

This completes the first cycle of iteration. We continue repeating the cycle of iteration until we get stable results for p(i.)'s and p(.j)'s. In Yassaee (1977a) we have given another way of computing estimates along with a proof for the convergence of iterative procedure. In Yassaee (1978) we have proved the convergence of iterative procedure mentioned in this paper.

Under model (1.1) X^2_N is defined as

$$X^2_N = \sum_i \sum_j \frac{(x(ij) - n\,p(i.)\,p(.j))^2}{x(ij)}$$

$$= n^2 \sum_i \sum_j \frac{p^2(i.)\,p^2(.j)}{x(ij)} - n \qquad (1.6)$$

Statistic X^2_N is minimized by p(i.) and p(.j) that satisfy in the system of equations

$$\frac{p(i.)}{p(r.)} = \frac{\sum_{j=1}^{c} \frac{p^2(.j)}{x(rj)}}{\sum_{j=1}^{c} \frac{p^2(.j)}{x(ij)}} \quad ; i = 1,2,\ldots, r-1 \qquad (1.7)$$

$$\frac{p(.j)}{p(.c)} = \frac{\sum_{i=1}^{r} \frac{p^2(i.)}{x(ic)}}{\sum_{i=1}^{r} \frac{p^2(i.)}{x(ij)}} \quad ; j = 1,2,\ldots, c-1 \qquad (1.8)$$

We use the same iterative procedure as that mentioned earlier to get estimates for p(i.) and p(.j)'s. In Yassaee (1978) a proof for the convergence is given. Finally we introduce a version of discrimination information as defined by Kullback (1959):

$$I = \sum_i \sum_j n\,p(i.)\,p(.j)\,\ell n \frac{n\,p(i.)\,p(.j)}{x(ij)} .$$

Estimates for p(i.) and p(.j)'s that minimize I are solutions of the nonlinear system of equations given by

$$\ell n \frac{p(i.)}{p(r.)} = \sum_{j=1}^{c} p(.j)\,\ell n \frac{x(ij)}{x(rj)} \quad ; i = 1,2,\ldots, r-1 \qquad (1.9)$$

$$\ell n \frac{p(.j)}{p(.c)} = \sum_{i=1}^{r} p(i.) \ \ell n \frac{x(ij)}{x(ic)} \quad , \ j = 1,2,\ldots, c-1 \qquad (1.10)$$

We use iterative procedure as mentioned for solving equations (1.4) and (1.5) to solve equations (1.9) and (1.10). For proof of convergence see Yassaee (1978). We have provided a program which computes estimates for p(i.) and p(.j), in general. However due to limited budget on computations, we restricted ourselves to the case that r = c = 2. For exact comparison of estimators in rxcx2 contingency tables especially 2x2x2 and 2x3x2 contingency tables see Odoroff (1966), and Yassaee (1977b).

2. Generation of tables

Given $n = \sum_i \sum_j x(ij)$, we have provided a program which generates all possible rxc tables with cell frequencies x(ij)'s, exactly-not by simulation. By using theory of occupation one may compute the number of different tables with $n = \sum_i \sum_j x(ij)$. For example, if r = 2, c = 2 this number equals $\binom{n+3}{3}$. For computing estimates, we took n = 5(5), 10, ..., 25, r = c = 2.

3. Bias and mean square error

In this paper we study biasedness and mean square error of estimators for various values of parameters and sample sizes, n. By bias of an estimator $\hat{p}$ for parameter p whose exact value is p_0 we mean $B = E(\hat{P}) - p_0$, where E stands for expectation or mean. Mean square error of this estimator is defined by $MSE = Var(\hat{p}) + B^2$, where $Var(\hat{p})$ is the variance of $\hat{p}$. Our study is based on absolute value of bias and mean square errors in four different procedures of estimation mentioned in section 1.

4. Description of results

As we mentioned in section 2, we generated all possible rxc (in our study r=c=2) tables whose total cell frequencies are n. That is, we find all rxc tables with frequencies x(ij) such that $\sum_i \sum_j x(ij) = n$. Then we think of these tables to be deduced from the model p(ij) = p(i.) p(.j), i = 1,2, j=1,2,. For each table we apply four methods of estimation mentioned in section 1 and get estimate for p(i.) and p(.j). We assign specific values to set (p(1.), p(.1)) starting (.05, .50), (.06, .49), (.07, .48), ...,(.05, .50). We take n=5(5), 25. In each method of estimation, we think all tables generated by n, do come from the model of independence whose $p_{1.}$, $p_{.1}$ are what given in set $(p_{1.}, p_{.1})$. Thus the probability of having a 2x2 table whose p_{ij} and x(ij) are known is given by

$$L_a = \frac{n!}{\prod_{i=1}^{2}\prod_{j=1}^{2} x(ij)!} \prod_{i=1}^{2}\prod_{j=1}^{2}\left[p(i.)\ p(.j)\right]^{x(ij)}.$$

We compute $E(\hat{p}(i.)) = \sum_{a\epsilon J} \hat{p}(i.)L_a$, where J is the set of all possible tables that can be generated and $\hat{p}(i.)$ is the estimate for p(i.) that is obtained by one of four methods of estimation. Variance of $\hat{p}(i.)$ is computed by $\sum_{a\epsilon J} [\hat{p}(i.)]^2 L_a - [E(\hat{p}(i.))]^2$. We repeate these steps of computations for all parameter set values (p(1.), p(.1)). We also compute mean and variance - consequently absolute value of bias and mean square error - according as each n, each p(1.), p(.1), and each method of estimation. We give details for bias in absolute value and mean square error of estimator $\hat{p}(1.)$. Similar details can be given for estimator $\hat{p}(.1)$.

In results obtained by using our computer program, we see that bias and mean square error of estimator like $\hat{p}(1.)$ is a function of sample size, true value of parameter, and the method of estimation. In the case of bias, it seems that $E(\hat{p}(1.))$ is a linear function of p(1.) approximately for X^2_P, X^2_N, and I method. The linear relation is exact for the method of maximum likelihood. When exact value of parameter p(1.) is close to .5, the bias value is almost zero for almost all methods.

Mean square error is a function of sample size, n, and p(1.) and p(.1). According as our computer outputs, it is almost certain that this function is a polynomial in terms of variance.

As the size of the sample increases, the value of bias gets smaller. This situation is almost the same for all cases. Due to large production of computer outputs, we give some results obtained for n=10, and a figure for two $\widehat{MSE1.}$'s. —. We ask interested reader to write to author for more information on computational results.

TABLE of $E(\hat{p}(1.))$, $E(\hat{p}(.1))$, MSE(1.),MSE(.1)
L: ML; $P = X^2_P$, $N = X^2_N$, n = 10.

	$E(\hat{p}(1.))$	$E(\hat{p}(.1))$	MSE(1.)	MSE(.1)	(p(1.), p(.1))
L	.0500	.5000	.0048	.0250	
N	.0493	.5000	.0045	.0252	.05 .50
P	.0630	.5000	.0069	.0241	
I	.0496	.5000	.0046	.0251	
L	.1000	.4500	.0090	.0248	
N	.0974	.4493	.0083	.0255	.10 .45
P	.1194	.4519	.0110	.0231	
I	.0987	.4496	.0086	.0251	
L	.1500	.4000	.0128	.0240	
N	.1447	.3974	.0117	.0254	.15 .40
P	.1713	.4051	.0137	.0219	
I	.1474	.3987	.0122	.0246	
L	.2000	.3500	.0160	.0228	
N	.1924	.3448	.0152	.0242	.20 .35
P	.2203	.3591	.0158	.0206	
I	.1963	.3474	.0156	.0234	
L	.2500	.3000	.0188	.0210	
N	.2415	.2925	.0188	.0219	.25 .30
P	.2673	.3134	.0175	.0191	
I	.2459	.2963	.0187	.0214	
L	.3000	.2500	.0210	.0188	
N	.2925	.2415	.0219	.0188	.30 .25
P	.3134	.2673	.0191	.0175	
I	.2963	.2459	.0214	.0187	
L	.3500	.2000	.0228	.0160	
N	.3448	.1924	.0242	.0152	.35 .20
P	.3591	.2203	.0206	.0158	
I	.3474	.1963	.0234	.0156	
L	.3600	.1900	.0230	.0154	
N	.3554	.1828	.0245	.0145	.36 .19
P	.3683	.2107	.0208	.0154	
I	.3577	.1865	.0237	.0149	
L	.4000	.1500	.0240	.0128	
N	.3974	.1447	.0254	.0117	.40 .15
P	.4051	.1713	.0219	.0137	
I	.3987	.1474	.0246	.0122	
L	.4500	.1000	.0248	.0090	
N	.4493	.0974	.0255	.0083	.45 .10
P	.4519	.1194	.0231	.0110	
I	.4496	.0987	.0251	.0086	
L	.4900	.0600	.0250	.0056	
N	.4899	.0590	.0253	.0053	.49 .06
P	.4902	.0747	.0239	.0079	
I	.4900	.0595	.0252	.0055	
L	.5000	.0500	.0250	.0047	
N	.5000	.0493	.0252	.0045	.50 .05
P	.5000	.0630	.0241	.0069	
I	.5000	.0496	.0251	.0046	

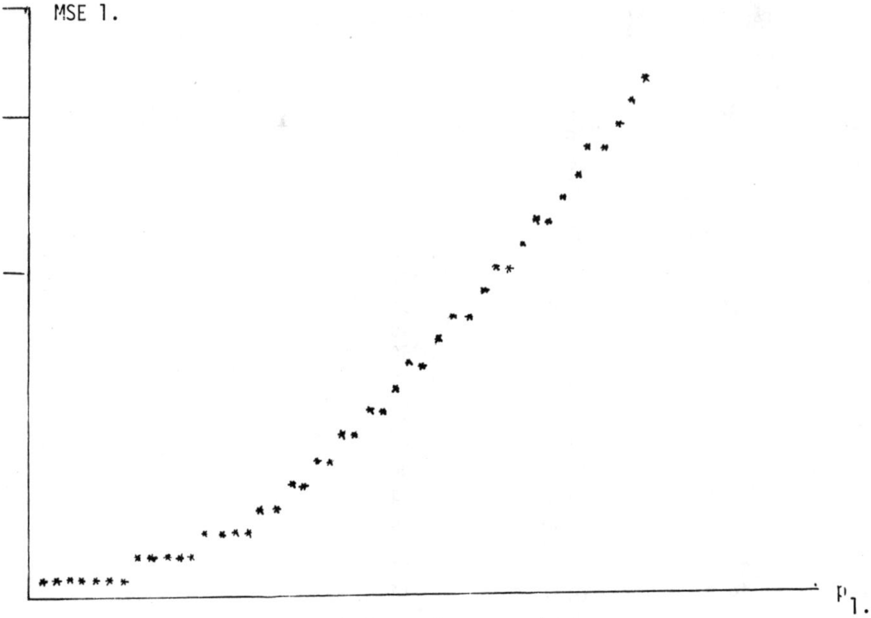

Figure 1. n=10; MSE1. of information procedure.

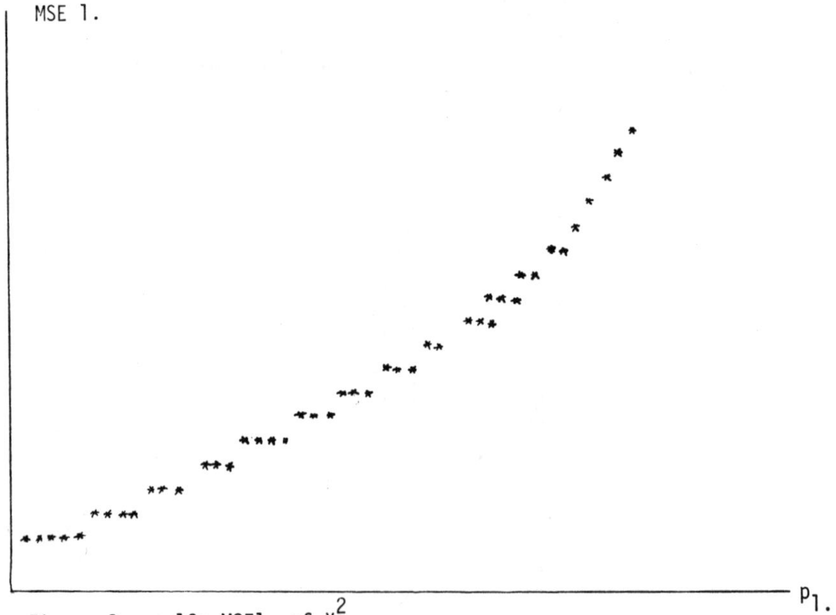

Figure 2. n=10; MSE1. of X^2_p.

REFERENCES

Kullback, S. (1959), Information Theory and Statistics, John Wiley & Sons, New York(also Dover Publishing Co.(1968)).
Odoroff, C.L. (1966), A comparison of minimum logit chi-square and maximum likelihood estimation for multidimensional contingency tables:Ph.D. Thesis, Harvard University, Cambridge, Mass.
Yassaee, H.(1977a), On Estimating Parameters of rxc Contingency Tables Under Independence Model. Statistical Computing , ASA, Washington, D.C, 382-5.
_________ (1977b), On Properties of Estimators in rxcx2 Contingency Tables: Logit Linear Model;Colloques IRIA, Data Analysis and Informatics, Vol.1, 329-37.
_________ (1978), Computing Estimates of Marginal Probabilities of rxc Contingency Tables Under Independence Model: Technical Report, Arya-Mehr University of Technology, Tehran, Iran.

6. Cluster Analysis

Large Data Set Clustering Methods Using the Concept of Space Contraction

M. Bruynooghe, Aix-en-Provence

SUMMARY

A number of the usual algorithms of hierarchical classification are quite hopeless to apply to more than a comparatively small number of objets. The graph theoretical clustering methods based on the concept of "space-contraction", which are presented, are able to handle a large multivariate data set and are optimal methods for the know sorting strategies: single linkage, complete linkage, mean linkage, variance...

KEYWORDS hierarchical classification, contracting sorting strategy, large data set.

I - *INTRODUCTION*

The classical algorithm of ascending hierarchical classification (AHC) makes it possible to build a binary hierarchy on the basis of any given aggregation criterion, but its application is excluded for any table with more than a thousand items, Ward(1963), Sokal and Sneath(1963), Wishart(1969), Cormack(1971)...

At the same time, other hierarchical algorithms which are able to deal with a greater number of items have some drawbacks : obligation to use the single linkage aggregation strategy, Gower and Ross(1969), Jarvis and Patrick(1973), or heuristic construction of the hierarchy according to any given aggregation strategy, Bruynooghe(1977).

The new methods of classification, which are presented, use the concept of "contracting aggregation strategy" and surpasses the limits of the usual classification algorithms by generating an exact hierarchy on a large data set, Bruynooghe(1977).

II - THE CONTRACTING AGGREGATION STRATEGIES

Let ρ be a stratification threshold, Q a partition of the I set of items,"a" a class of Q ; we denote δ (t, a) the dissimilarity index between classes t and a, the definition of which depends on the sorting strategy used, and V (a, ρ) the neighborhood of the a class :

$$V(a, \rho) = \{t \mid t \in Q \; ; \; \delta(t, a) \leqslant \rho, \; t \neq a\}$$

By definition, a contracting aggregation strategy is such that :

$$V(a \cup b, \rho) \subset V(a, \rho) \cup V(b, \rho) \text{ for } \forall (a,b) \text{ such that } \delta(a,b) \leqslant \rho$$

It can be shown that the aggregation methods using the single linkage, the complete linkage, the mean linkage or the variance strategy are contracting, Bruynooghe(1977).

III - EXACT ASCENDING HIERARCHICAL CLASSIFICATION BY THE "REDUCIBLE CLUSTERS METHOD"

The "*reducible clusters method*", Bruynooghe(1977), generates an exact total binary hierarchy on the set I of items to be classified, by building a series of binary trees A_0 , A_1 , ... A_h ... $A_{|I| - 1}$ and a series of similarity graphs G_0 , G_1 ... G_h ... $G_{|I| - 1}$ such that, $A_{|I| - 1} = A$.

Let $\{\rho^*_k \mid k = 0, 1, 2, \ldots\}$ be a series of stratification threshold values, fixed in advance or during the classification procedure.

Initialization : Do $h = o$, $k = o$, $A_o = \{\{i\} \mid i \in I\}$

Phase 0 : Construction of the similarity graph on the set Som(A_h) of the upper nodes of the binary tree A_h.

Do, $\rho_h = \rho^*_k$

Let, $U_h = \{(s,s') \mid s,s' \in \text{Som}(A_h), \; s \neq s' \; , \; \delta(s,s') \leqslant \rho_h\}$

$X_h = \{s \mid s \in \text{Som}(A_h), \; \exists \; s' \in \text{Som}(A_h) \text{ such that } (s,s') \in U_h\}$

$G_h = (X_h, U_h)$

If, $X_h = \emptyset$ and $U_h = \emptyset$, do $k = k + 1$ and go to phase 0.
Otherwise, go to phase 1.

Phase 1 : Aggregation of the two closest nodes.

Do, $h = h + 1$ and let (s_h, s'_h) be a pair of nodes on the A_{h-1} tree, connected by an arc of the G_{h-1} graph and separated by the least possible dissimilarity.

$$\delta(s_h, s'_h) = \inf \{\delta(s,s') \mid s,s' \in X_{h-1}, (s,s') \in U_{h-1}\}$$

Phase 2 : Construction of the A_h tree from the A_{h-1} tree.

Denote : $a_h = s_h \cup s'_h$

$A_h = A_{h-1} \cup \{a_h\}$ $\quad$ $\mathrm{Som}(A_h) = \mathrm{Som}(A_{h-1}) \cup \{a_h\} - \{s_h, s'_h\}$

Phase 3 : Stop test : if $h = |I| - 1$, then $A_{|I|-1} = A$ END
Otherwise, go to phase 4.

Phase 4 : Construction of the G_h graph from the G_{h-1} graph.

Do, $\rho_h = \rho_{h-1}$

Determine $V(s_h, \rho_h) = \{t \mid t \in X_{h-1}, (t, s_h) \in U_{h-1}\}$

$V(s'_h, \rho_h) = \{t \mid t \in X_{h-1}, (t, s'_h) \in U_{h-1}\}$

Denote, $E(a_h, \rho_h) = V(s_h, \rho_h) \cup V(s'_h, \rho_h) - \{s_h, s'_h\}$

Determine $V(a_h, \rho_h) = \{t \mid t \in E(a_h, \rho_h), \delta(t, a_h) \leqslant \rho_h\}$

and, $U_h = U_{h-1} - \{(t,s_h) \mid t \in V(s_h,\rho_h)\} - \{(t,s'_h) \mid t \in V(s'_h,\rho_h)\} + \{(t,a_h) \mid t \in V(a_h,\rho_h)\}$

$$X_h = \{s \mid s \in \mathrm{Som}(A_h), V(s,\rho_h) \neq \emptyset\} = \{s \mid s \in \mathrm{Som}(A_h), \exists s' \in \mathrm{Som}(A_h) \text{ such that } (s,s') \in U_h\}$$

If, $X_h = \emptyset$ and $U_h = \emptyset$, de $k = k + 1$ and go to phase 0, otherwise, go to phase 1.

It can be shown that the proposed method generates an exact hierarchy which is not dependent upon the series of stratification threshold values, Bruynooghe(1977). The use of the neighborhood contracting property allows the implicit elimination of a large number of node pairs during the search for the two classes to be agglomerated at each step of the binary tree construction. In this way, $1.59\ 10^6$ distances have been calculated in order to generate a binary tree on a set of 1561 items. This can be compared with the $0.56\ 10^9$ distances that would have been computed by the classical AHC algorithm to establish the same tree, that is 350 times more !

IV - EXACT ASCENDING HIERARCHICAL CLASSIFICATION BY THE "ADAPTATIVE CLUSTERS METHOD"

The "*adaptative clusters method*" which generates an exact total hierarchy A on the set I of items to be classified is based on a local definition of the stratification thresholds, capable of improving the efficiency of the classification process.

For any $s \in X_0$, a local stratification threshold $\rho(s)$ is determined so that the corresponding neighborhood $V(s,\rho(s))$ is not empty (by looking for the p nearest neighbors of s, for example).

$$V(s,\rho(s)) = \{t \mid t \in X_o - \{s\},\ \delta(t,s) \leqslant \rho(s)\}$$

$$U_o = \{(s,t) \mid s \in X_o,\ t \in V(s,\rho(s))\}$$

To update the similarity graph, after aggregation of the two closest clusters, one must denote $\rho(a_h) = \inf\{\rho(s_h)\ ;\ \rho(s'_h)\}$ and determine the corresponding neighborhood $V(a_h,\rho(a_h))$. The arcs of the similarity graph being oriented, it may be necessary to update the neighborhoods of some upper nodes of the A_h tree, other than the newly created node a_h, Bruynooghe(1977).

V - EXACT ASCENDING HIERARCHICAL CLASSIFICATION BY THE "RECIPROCAL CLUSTERS METHOD"

The "*reciprocal clusters method*" is a decomposition method of a large classification problem, which enables to generate an exact total hierarchy on the set of items to be classified, according to any contracting aggregation strategy.

This method determines at first the pairs of reciprocal neighboring elements on the set of items, so that each element of a pair is the nearest neighbor to the other element. Then, the reciprocal neighboring elements inside the connex components of the reciprocity linkage graph are progressively aggregated. After reduction of connex components, the pairs of the reciprocal neighboring connex components are to be found in order to generate the similarity graph on the upper nodes set of the tree which is being built. The aggregation process and the reciprocal neighboring clusters determination process are alternately continued until all the items are united in a single cluster.

The similarity graph is defined as follows : let s and t be two clusters of a partition Q of the set I of the items to be classified,

Denote, $\forall s \in Q : d(s) = \inf \{\delta(s,t) \mid t \in Q,\ t \neq s\}$

and $B(s) = \{t \mid t \in Q,\ t \neq s,\ \delta(t,s) = d(s)\}$

By definition, s and t are two reciprocal neighboring clusters if : $t \in B(s)$ and $s \in B(t)$, the pair (s,t) is then represented by a non oriented arc of a similarity graph built on the set of the Q clusters.

$$G = (Q,U) \text{ with } U = \{(s,t) \mid s,t \in Q,\ s \neq t,\ t \in B(s),\ s \in B(t)\}$$
$$= \{(s,t) \mid s,t \in Q,\ s \neq t,\ d(s) = d(t)\}$$

From the data processing point of view, the possible existence, in the similarity graph, of large connex components, may need the introduction of global stratification thresholds, as in the "*reducible clusters methods*", to take into account the limitation of the available memory space and to anable classification of a large data set on a mini-computer, Bruynooghe(1977).

VI - FAST GENERATION OF A NEIGHBORHOOD SET

The experiments carried out show that the variation in computing time required for the new algorithms is approximately proportional to the number of items to be classified, provided this number is below 1,000. For a set containing several thousands of items, the computing time needed for classification increases approximately as the square of the number of items.

Nethertheless, the implementation of a branch and bound algorithm for computing the similarity graphs would reduce the computing time needed for classification, by eliminating the necessity of calculating many pair-wise distances, Fukunaga and Narendra(1974), Bruynooghe(1977).

CONCLUSION

The new clustering algorithms using the *"neighborhood contracting porperty"* makes it possible to surpass the limits of the usual clustering algorithms and thus to undertake the hierarchical analysis of a large data set, using very little computing time.

REFERENCES

BRUYNOOGHE M., Méthodes nouvelles en classification automatique de données taxinomiques nombreuses. Colloque International de Taxonomie numérique 6 septembre 1977, Orsay et Bulletin de l'Association des Statisticiens Universitaires, Statistique et Analyse des données, 3, 24-42, 1977 (in French).
Classification ascendante hiérarchique des grands ensembles de données : un algorithme rapide fondé sur la construction des voisinages réductibles. *Les cahiers de l'Analyse des Données, Vol. III* - 1978 - n° 1 - pp 7 - 33 (in French).

CORMACK R.M., A review of classification. *J.R. Statist. Soc., A 134*, Part 3, 321-367, 1971.

FUKUNAGA K. and NARENDRA P.M., A Branch and Bound Algorithm for computing k - nearest neighbors. *IEEE Transactions on Computers*, 750-753, July 1975.

GOWER J.C. and ROSS G.J.S., Minimum spanning trees and single linkage cluster analysis. *Appl. Statist*, 18, 54-64, 1969.

JARVIS R.A. and PATRICK E.A., Clustering using a similarity measure based on shared near neighbors. *IEEE Transactions on Computers*, Vol. C-22, n° 11, 1025-1034, 1973.

SOKAL R.R. and SNEATH P.H.A., Principles of Numerical taxonomy. London *Freeman*, 1963.

WARD. J.H., Hierarchical grouping to optimise an objective function. *J. Am Statist. Ass.*, 59, 236-244, 1963.

WISHART D., An algorithm for hierarchical classifications. *Biometrics* 25, 165-170, 1969.

A Monte Carlo Study on Agglomerative Large Sample Clustering

P.O. Degens and **H. Federkiel**, Munich

Summary

From a statistical point of view cluster analysis should be consistent. In $\mathbb{R}^1$ a simple criterion is the consistency of a split point. It was shown in a Monte Carlo study, that the complete link algorithm is inconsistent. Moreover, for distributions on [0,1] with a density $f \geq \eta > 0$ the distribution of the split point is asymtotically independent of f.

KEYWORDS: cluster analysis, consistency, asymptotic distribution, complete link clustering, median clustering.

Introduction

Cluster analysis has been applied in wide spread fields of data analysis. In this paper we will deal only with hierarchical agglomerative cluster analysis for object classification. There are a lot of algorithms for hierarchical clustering, but only a few criteria for a critical examination of these methods, and there is no consensus about the importance of these criteria - see for example the disscussion between Jardine & Sibson (1968), Lance & Williams (1967) and Sibson (1970).

If we look at cluster analysis from a statistical point of view, it is important to note, that we can apply such algorithms only on random samples. But if an algorithm works on a sample of objects, and not on the whole population, it is necessary, that the result of the procedure depends for large samples of the same population mainly on the real probability distribution and not on the random fluctuations of special samples. For large samples the clusters should be a good approximation of the (not yet well-defined) clusters of the population. Moreover, only if the clusters of the samples converge in a reasonable sense, it is possible to define 'clusters of the real distribution' in terms of this convergence. So, one criterion for the quality of a clustering algorithm can be seen in its consistency and stability properties. That is, for similar samples the result must be similar too. By the way, it is possible to give formal definitions for partitions of distributions within a suitable topological space and to show the consistency of a lot of known cluster methods via this topology , see Degens (1978). In this paper however, we will only show the inconsistency of some well known algorithms. This will be done in an elementary manner.

Consistency of the split point

To begin with, let us consider a multidimensional data space. There are a lot of possible spaces, but in many instances the observations are represented in an Euclidean space $\mathbb{R}^k$. Then you have to face the question: is there consistency in $\mathbb{R}^k$. But this problem is difficult to cope with, if there is no precise definition of a topological space. Fortunately, there is a simple interpretation for consistency and (still better) for inconsistency in $\mathbb{R}^1$. Evidently inconsistency in $\mathbb{R}^1$ yields inconsistency in $\mathbb{R}^k$ for special distributions. Let us look for the sake of simplicity only at partitions into two classes (clusters). Most of the known clustering algorithms give in $\mathbb{R}^1$ two connected clusters, i. e. clusters which are split by one split point.

```
(. ..  .....  . . ... ... .. )X(. .. ..  ..  ... .. ...   .)
     cluster                 split        cluster
                             point
```

Note, however, the split point depends on the actual sample and not only on the real distribution; that means the split point itself is a random variable with a probability distribution. The distribution of the split point provides the basis for a criterion of consistency or inconsistency: We will call a clustering algorithm consistent, if the distribution of the split point is asymptotically concentrated in one point, which is the split point of the real distribution of the population. We should at least accept this definition for populations which are distributed with a positive density , i.e. $f \geq \eta > 0$, on an interval, say $[0,1]$. In this case the cluster limits are unique, and the split point is consistent, if it is consistent as a parameter in the usual sense. In the special examples disscussed here, we will see, that the inconsistency of the clustering algorithms is quite obvious.

The Monte Carlo study on [0,1].

We did some Monte Carlo studies to investigate the asymptotic behavior of two well known clustering algorithms.

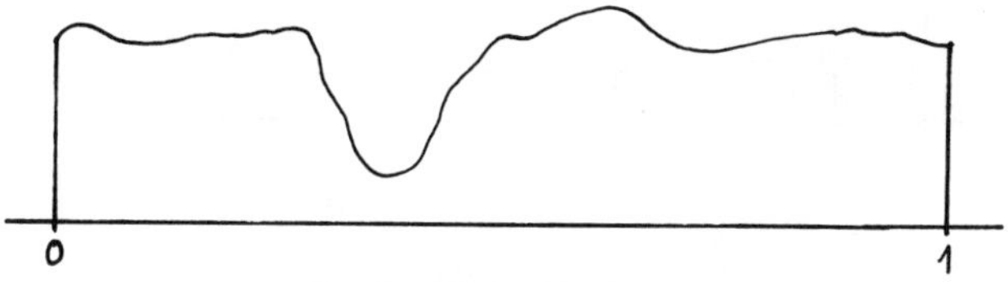

Real distribution

Take 1000 large samples of say 4000 points, and apply the algorithm to all 1000 samples. You will have 1000 split points and a histogram of the distribution of the split points. If you are lucky, your histogram will look like this:

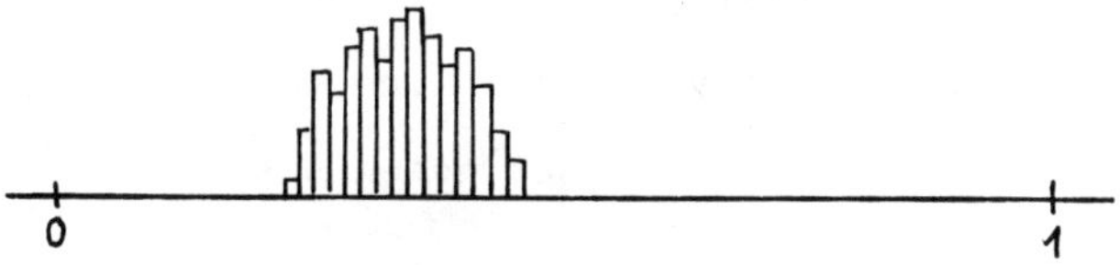

(1000 split points of 1000 samples from the above distribution)

Heuristical considerations led us to the supposition, that the complete link and the median algorithms are inconsistent. In a Monte Carlo study for the following four distributions:

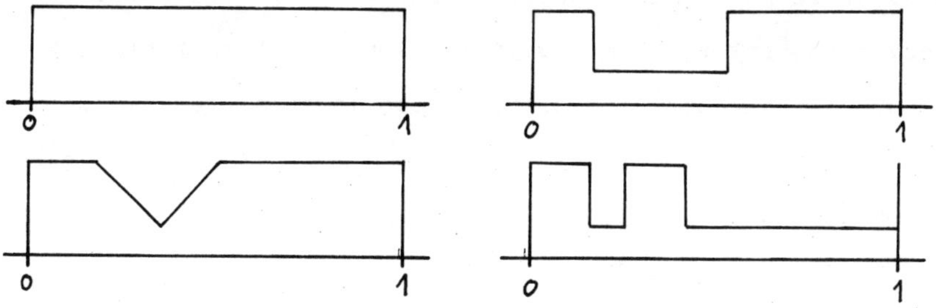

each with about 1000 samples consisting of 4000 points we obtained essentially the same histogram for the split points.

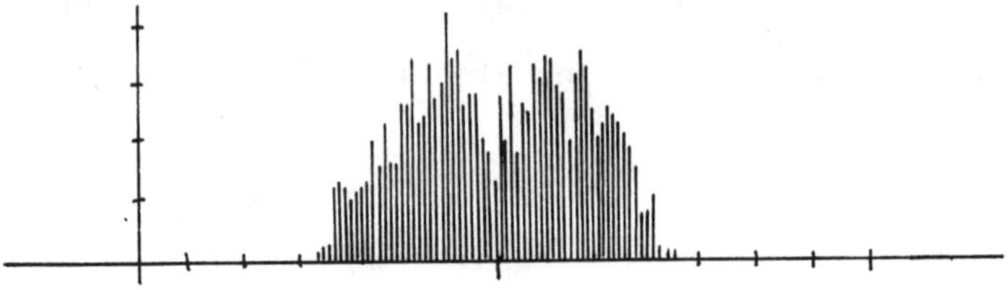

(Asymptotic distribution for complete link clustering on [0,1])

With a χ^2-test (for 16 classes) even at the 10% level the histograms for the four chosen distributions were not statistically different. As a result, when the sample size approaches infinity, the complete link method at the last level of the clustering hierarchy gives two clusters for distributions with positive density, $f \geq \eta > 0$, on an interval. These clusters have a split point varying in the range from 1/4 to 3/4 on the interval independent of the chosen distribution.

Thus, the results of this Monte Carlo study are the following:

1. An asymptotic split point distribution exists.
2. The complete link algorithm is inconsistent, because the asymptotic split point distribution has a positive variance.
3. Moreover the split point distribution is asymptotically independent of the underlying distribution in the data space.

Essentially the same results are valid for the median method. An independence of the asymptotic split point distribution was

found in the complete link method and in the median method. The single link method and similar methods show a better asymptotic behavior, in that the split point distribution is related to the regions of relatively low density in the underlying distribution in the data space.
For theoretical as well as for practical reasons it is interesting to investigate the behavior of cluster algorithms like the complete link method for distributions on the circle. In this case , two clusters have two split points, that are dependent from one another. If one of these points is chosen either randomly or by some appropriate criterion, its asymptotical distribution is the uniform distribution on the circle.

Heuristic considerations.

All distances between neighbours in the ranked order of observations approaches zero, if the sample size approaches infinity. Therefore, it is heuristically sufficient to cope with partitions of the given interval [0,1]. Roughly speaking the interval partitions are defined by the split points. The split points seperate adjacent clusters. The cluster criterion for the complete link algorithm is at each level the diameter of the new cluster. The diameter is approximately equal to the sum of the diameters of the two joining clusters. It is easy to show, that the diameter of two neighbouring clusters (intervals) is not greater than 3:1, so that the last split point must lie in 1/4 to 3/4 of the given intervall [0,1].

The split points are determined by the complex complete link algorithm, they are mostly unique, but small random fluctuations of one sample point may shift the split point essentially at larger and later levels. Thus the uniting of the neighbouring clusters depends strongly on random fluctuations and not on the real distribution. Therefore, the algorithm asymptotically leads to a special distribution independent of the original observation, if the procedure is extended over a sufficiently large number of computational steps.

Hartigan (1978) shows in his paper, that the split point distribution for (non hierarchical) clustering with a special criterion (variance - criterion) is asymptotically consistent. For a lot of (non hierarchical) clustering methods this is also an immediate consequence of the results of Degens (1978).

Degens, P.O.	Clusteranalyse auf topologisch mass - theoretischer Grundlage, Dissertation, Universitaet Muenchen, to appear 1978 (in german)
Hartigan, J.A.	Asymptotic distributions for clustering criteria, The Annals of Statistics, 6, 117-131, 1978
Jardine,N.,Sibson,R.	Construction of hierarchic and non hierarchic classifications, Computer Journal ,11 , 177-183, 1968
Lance,G.N., Williams,W.T.	A general theory of classificatory sorting strategies 1. hierarchical systems, The Computer Journal, 9, 373-380, 1967
Sibson,R.	Some observations on a paper by Lance and Williams, The Computer Journal, 14, 156-157, 1970

The Distribution and Power Properties of the AID Criterion

R. Ecob, London

SUMMARY
Recent work on the distribution and power of the AID criterion can now provide the user of AID with guidelines for the choice of stopping rules and with help in the interpretation of his results. Mention is made of theoretical work by Kass (1975), Scott & Knott (1976) and of the results of simulations (which extend their conclusions to finite sample sizes) of the distribution of the AID criterion on null population models. Investigations of the power properties of the criterion are also resported using two models of the population.

KEY WORDS

1. THE DISTRIBUTION

When the A.I.D. technique (see Appendix 1 for description) was developed by Sonquist & Morgan (1964) the distribution of the BSS/TSS criterion (c) when there is no relation between the dependent variable and predictors was not known. This resulted in the recommended values at which to set the stopping rules being fixed and having little explicit meaning.

More is now known about the distribution of c under certain null population models (where there is no relation between the dependent variable and the predictors). The fact that c is related by a constant factor to the likelihood ratio criterion (λ) for the test of the null hypothesis that population mean values for all categories are the same versus the alternative that they form two groups with different means, the mean values being the same within each group (Scott & Knott (1974) has results on the distribution of λ) provides a link with cluster analysis.

In particular it is known that c is inversely proportional to the sample size and roughly proportional to the number of categories for the case of one free predictor and for one monotonic predictor the relation is of an increase in criterion value with number of predictor categories where the slope reduces as the number of categories increases (Fielding, O'Muircheartaigh and Ecob (1978)Chapter 4; hereafter referred to as FOE).

In addition the null asymptotic permutation distribution of the criterion K = nc (n = sample size) has been found (Kass (1975)) when the categories of the (one) predictor are of equal size which depends only on the number of categories and the proportion of the sample within each category. Also a χ^2 approximation for K has been given for use in this situation for the free predictor case (Scott & Knott (1976)) which agrees closely both with that of Kass and with the results of simulations for sample sizes of 2000 and over, assuming a constant normal error structure with constant variance in each category (FOE, 1978, Chapter 4). Further simulations with smaller sample sizes suggest that as the sample size decreases the agreement is reasonably good for 90% and 95% points at least down to samples of size 200. This is illustrated in Table 1.

Table 1 : Critical values of K for one free predictor

sample sizes	2 90%	2 95%	4 90%	4 95%	6 90%	6 95%	8 90%	8 95%	10 90%	10 95%
50	3.30	3.55	4.90	6.70	7.20	8.50	9.10	11.10	9.90	11.30
100	2.40	4.00	5.50	6.40	7.10	9.50	8.60	10.00	10.60	12.60
200	2.72	3.60	5.28	6.82	7.20	8.82	9.00	10.70	10.82	12.52
300	2.91	3.66	5.82	7.26	7.41	8.94	9.00	11.04	10.74	12.33
400	2.68	3.68	5.24	6.56	7.24	8.24	8.64	10.16	11.36	13.88
1000	2.71	3.92	5.32	6.93	7.67	9.25	9.15	10.63	11.07	12.89
2000	2.78	3.92	5.26	6.88	8.06	9.54	9.38	10.62	11.20	12.90
(1) ∞	2.71	3.84	5.39	6.76	7.30	8.80	9.10	10.80	10.80	12.60
(2) χ^2			5.70	6.90	7.50	8.90	9.20	10.80	10.90	12.60

(Column headings: No. of categories 2, 4, 6, 8, 10.)

Table 2 suggests that the value recommended by Sonquist (1971) of 0.6% of the variance (BSS/TSS = 0.006) as a cut off rule is too low except in the case of large samples, leading often to spurious splits.

Table 2 : 95% critical value of c for one predictor, free and monotonic, for sample sizes n = 512, 1024, 2048, number of categories, k, between 2 and 64

No. of categories	Sample size n=512 Free	Sample size n=512 Monotonic	Sample size n=1024 Free	Sample size n=1024 Monotonic	Sample size n=2048 Free	Sample size n=2048 Monotonic
2	<u>0.006</u>	<u>0.006</u>	<u>0.004</u>	<u>0.004</u>	<u>0.002</u>	<u>0.002</u>
3	0.009	0.009	<u>0.005</u>	<u>0.005</u>	<u>0.003</u>	<u>0.002</u>
4	0.014	0.010	<u>0.006</u>	<u>0.005</u>	<u>0.003</u>	<u>0.003</u>
6	0.018	0.012	0.008	<u>0.005</u>	<u>0.004</u>	<u>0.003</u>
8	0.021	0.012	0.010	<u>0.006</u>	<u>0.005</u>	<u>0.003</u>
16	0.036	0.015	0.019	0.008	0.008	<u>0.004</u>
27	0.052	0.016	0.027	0.007	0.013	<u>0.004</u>
64	0.112	0.017	0.052	0.007	0.027	<u>0.004</u>

Underlined values are those less than or equal to the recommended value of Sonquist.

This knowledge allows us in certain simplified situations to set the cut-off rules for the BSS/TSS criterion at such a value that a split will only take place (or only be deemed significant, through later considerations of the tree) when the decision is made with a preset Type 1 error.

Further aspects such as the number of predictors being greater than one and not containing equal numbers of categories, the categories not being of equal size, the error distribution not being normal, and the presence of two other cut-off rules make the splitting at any one stage with preset Type 1 error less of a real possibility. However, Kass (1975) and Scott & Knott (1976) suggest approximations for the case of unequal size categories and the simulations of FOE (1978); Chapter 4 give guidelines for the case of two, three and five predictors each having the same number of categories per predictor (2,3,4,8) for certain sample sizes, and in addition in some cases for different number of categories in each predictor.

One real problem remaining is that of the hierachical operation of the technique. As the child groups of each split are themselves split further, we have a situation similar to sequential testing. On certain assumptions we can set the probability of a split on null data at such a level as to have a preset probability of obtaining a tree, all branches being of the same length. Considering a tree containing a split of each child group of the initial split, and assuming that each child group has the same degree of heterogeneity as the original group, the probability of this tree or a longer continuation of it emerging on null data is $P = p^3$ where p is the probability of one split on null data. The probability of this tree and no other type is $p' = p^3(1-p)$. Setting this (P or p') to a chosen value will give a value of p to use. For example setting P = 0.05 gives $p = \sqrt[3]{0.05} = 0.368$. This shouldn't be read as suggesting that the use of AID be other than exploratory: it is widely held (e.g. Cox (1978)) that significance tests are of proven value in the exploratory stage of data analysis when used to suggest rather than test a model of the data. A case could also be put here for a value of $P > 0.05$ giving a more lenient, but more powerful test in the exploratory context.

2. RELIABILITY AND VALIDITY

a) Reliability

However, the cut-off rules are set, questions about the reliability or sampling stability of AID may well be asked. How similar are the results found on different samples from the same population? Work on this is reported by FOE (1978) Chapter 5 on samples from two real data sets. Qualitative analysis in terms of the predictor chosen for the first few splits and the variance accounted for by the predictor (Fielding & Sheperd (1973)) suggest cause for concern, especially for small sample sizes (less than 500 cases). More recently, with the use of measures of difference between the structures of two trees and of two (final) partitions (Ecob (1978), FOE (1978) Chapter 10) it has been possible to quantify the sampling stability and to relate it to sample size. This makes it possible to investigate the effect of variation in the value of the cut-off rules (or a change in the BSS/TSS criterion) on the sampling stability though this has not yet been done.

b) Validity

Even if fully reliable, AID may be regarded as putting an interpretation on the data stemming from the nature of the algorithm (sequential dichotomisation with a certain criterion), and one may thus be sceptical whether the output reveals the data in its full light. It is known, for instance: 1) that a predictor which is highly associated with one already used for a split is unlikely to be used, and 2) that the splits being dichotomies, there is a tendency to split data (in the free case) into approximately equal groups. This tendency increases the stronger the relation between the predictor and dependent variable (FOE (1978) Chapter 4) . Finally, 3) that when a dependent variable is highly skewed the extreme part is liable to be split off (FOE (1978) Chapter 9).

3. POWER

In addition we may question the power of AID: that is the probability of making a split when there are real differences in values of the dependent variable in different predictor categories. Two possible population models are considered here:

Model 1: Linear regression with one predictor

Both free and monotonic predictors were considered over 500 samples of sizes 200, 500, 1000, 2000. The relation between the two variables was chosen to be that of linear regression with constant error variance, the distribution of the predictors being normal, and categorised into 10 categories. Five cases were considered: no relation (null case), marginal relation (the 95% confidence interval for the regression coefficient (B) just included the value 0), and also with regression coefficient taking values 2B, 4B, 10B.

By comparing the distributions of the BSS/TSS criterion for each strength of regression the Type II error, β corresponding to a given Type I error, α could l found (Fig. 1) for each sample size and criterion type (free or monotonic). These results refer to the marginal relation case only.

Fig. 1

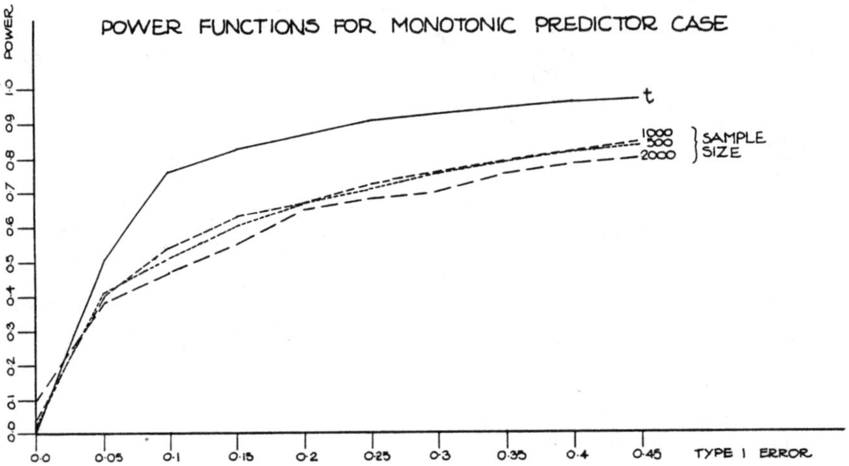

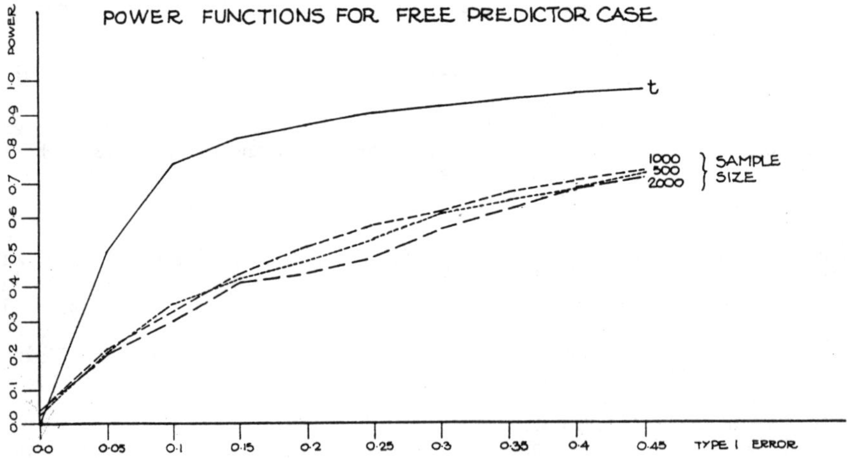

The upper curve in each set of graphs is the characteristic function for the uniformly most powerful test that based on the sample regression coefficient itself.

The precision of these results is limited by the fact that the values were interpolated using 20 order statistics. However it is seen that for both the monotonic and free predictor cases the characteristic function for the AID criterion is independent of the sample size. In the free case it falls further short of the optimal value given by the uniformly most powerful test.

Model 2 : Two groups with different dependent variable values; 1 predictor.

Sample sizes are as before, but the predictor categories are divided into 2 groups with adjacent categories. The population mean in each category within a group has the same value but is different in each group. The observations are normally distributed with the same variance in each category. Each category has the same number of observations and the proportion of categories (and therefore observations) in each group is systematically varied. Also the number of categories is varied having values 3,4,5,6,8,10, and the extent of difference in dependent population variable means in each group takes 3 values corresponding to the critical value of the t statistic for testing the differences between the two groups at the 0.05, 0.01, 0.001 levels.

These simulations were designed to test both the power of the AID criterion in this context (a split not being in the correct position leading to non optimal power) and the validity. The latter is measured by the extent of difference between the population model and that revealed by AID, this being measured by a normalised entropy measure (Ecob (1978)). This enables us to compare the relative difference in models over samples of different sizes, having different group division points and having different numbers of categories. It is conjectured that loss of validity will be most marked when the proportion of the population in one group is small. Results will be given in the verbal presentation.

REFERENCES

Ecob, J.R. (1978) An empirical examination of the behaviour of selected measures of tree and partition similarity in relation to the sampling stability of AID.
Paper read at Cairo conference on Statistics, Computing and Operational Research.

Fielding, A., O'Muircheartaigh, C.A., and Ecob, J.R. (1978) An investigation of the sampling properties of the Automatic Interaction Detector.
Report on Grant HR2647/1 from the SSRC.

Fielding, A. & Shepard (1973) The sampling stability of AID. Contributed paper to the 39th Session International Statistics Institute.

Kass, G.V. (1975) Significance testing in automatic interaction detection. Applied Statistics 24, 178-189.

Lindsey (1973) Inferences from Sociological Survey data. Amsterdam.

Scott, A.J. & Knott, M. (1974) A cluster analysis method for grouping means in the analysis of variance. Biometrics 30 507-512.

Scott, A.J. & Knott, M. (1976) An approximate test for use with A.I.D., Applied Statistics, 25, 103-106.

Sonquist, J.A., Baker, E.L. and Morgan, J.N. (1971) Searching for Structure Ann Arbor : Institute for Social Research, University of Michigan.

Morgan, J.N. and SONQUIST, J.A. (1963). Problems in the analysis of survey data. Journal of the American Statistical Association, 58, 415-434.

Sonquist, J.A. and Morgan, J.N. (1964). The Detection of Interaction Effects. Michigan: Institute for Social Research.

Appendix 1: Description of AID and of the Terminology associated with it.

AID (Automatic Interaction Detector) was devised at the Institute for Social Research at the University of Michigan and grew out of a paper of Sonquist and Morgan (1963) which aimed to show some limitations of existing survey analysis techniques and suggested the development of AID in this context.
AID is applicable to data sets consisting of one dependent variable and a number of predictors, the dependent variable being on an interval scale and the predictors on categorical scales. It is a hierachical binary segmentation technique, at each stage dividing the data set on a chosen predictor into two groups chosen so as to maximise a certain criterion. This criterion is the ratio of the between groups sum of squares variation to the total sum of squares (on the dependent variable), called BSS/TSS. The predictor chosen for the split at any stage is that which gives the highest maximum value of the criterion subject to the constraints on the groups which can be formed.
The group to be split at any stage is termed the parent group. This is split into two child groups which in turn form the parent groups for the next splits. The whole structure produced is a (labelled) tree where each node corresponds to a particular group and (apart from the first) can be labelled by the characteristics of the split producing the group and the predictor categories selected. This is called the tree structure. By analogy with graph theory, the final groups are sometimes called terminal groups (corresponding to terminal nodes).
Two modes of operation are possible. The free case reorders the categories of the predictor (in terms of increasing values of the dependent variable for the adjacent categories). The splitting point used is that which maximises the criterion value. No combination of predictor categories into two groups can increase the criterion value in this case. The monotonic case eliminates the reordering stage and so constrains the new groups to the original adjacencies.
Three cut-off rules operate to limit the extent of splitting. The size of the child groups has to be greater than a specified value (minimum group size) for a split to occur; the total sum of squares, TSS of the parent group must be greater than a fixed proportion of the original TSS; and the BSS/TSS (where TSS is the original TSS) must be greater than a fixed value. Recommended values are given for those by Sonquist and Morgan but they can be set at any level by the user. Without any cut-off rules the technique would be of little use in terms of the final groups produced as these would correspond to cells in the original cross-classification of predictors. This suggests the use of AID as a data reduction device (see Lindsey 1973) forming the set of final groups at any specified stage of the splitting process.
The ratio of the sum of all BSS produced at each stage to the TSS is called the Explanation of AID. Sometimes it is preferred to express this as a ratio of the total between cell sum of squares, called the explainable variation, which when the cut-off rules are varied would give an upper bound of 1 for the explanation, this occuring when all values of the cut-off rules are set to zero.
An extended version of AID (AID3) allows a tree arising in one context to be used in another context to define the natures of the preliminary splits. This is called a forced tree.

Inferences Concerning Cluster Structure

O. Frank, Lund

Summary

A model of cluster structure is considered in which observational errors occur in determining whether or not two objects belong to the same cluster. The true cluster structure can be represented by a transitive undirected graph, and the observed structure is generally not transitive. It is possible to make inferences concerning various parameters in the unknown cluster structure by using a set of subgraph count statistics. The first- and second-order moments of these statistics are investigated and estimators are suggested for the number of clusters, the mean cluster size and some other parameters. Some properties of the estimators are illustrated by simple computer experiments.

Key words: Subgraph counts, partitions, cluster inferences, elementary symmetrical functions of integers.

1. Introduction

Assume that a set of N objects is partitioned in an unknown way into subsets which will be called clusters. By making paired comparisons between the objects it is possible to obtain uncertain information about which objects belong to the same cluster. A simple stochastic model is specified by assuming that the $\binom{N}{2}$ paired comparisons are affected by independent disturbances which provide false results with probabilities α and β within and between the clusters, respectively.

We can consider the cluster structure as a transitive unordered graph having N vertices and edges between vertices which represent objects in the same cluster. This graph cannot be observed without errors. The errors are caused by independent removals and additions of edges. Each edge is removed with probability α, and with probability β a new edge is inserted where none existed before.

The cluster structure can be characterized by the numbers of clusters of different sizes, the total number of clusters, the mean and variance of the cluster sizes, etc. We shall consider the problem of estimating the cluster sizes and some other parameters of the cluster structure by using subgraph counts from the observed graph. Subgraph counts are convenient statistics for summarizing the information given by a graph structure (Bloemena 1964, Frank, 1971, 1977 a).

In the next section we derive some properties of dyad and triad counts in the graph observed. Section 3 discusses various parameters of the cluster structure, and shows that it is possible to identify all the cluster sizes by some of their power sums. For $N \leq 13$ it is sufficient to know the sum of squares and the sum of third powers of the cluster sizes. Section 4 brings together the results from Sections 2 and 3, thereby obtaining estimators for various parameters of the cluster structure by using the dyad and triad counts. Some illustrative numerical results are reported. Section 5 gives some concluding remarks.

2. Subgraph count statistics

The adjacency matrix of the graph observed is given by a matrix X with entries satisfying $X_{ii}=1$ and $X_{ij}=X_{ji}$ for $i=1,\ldots,N$ and $j=1,\ldots,N$. For $i<j$ the X_{ij} are stochastically independent and have the expected values

$$E\, X_{ij} = A_{ij}(1-\alpha) + (1-A_{ij})\beta \ , \qquad (1)$$

where A_{ij} are the entries of the adjacency matrix A of the cluster structure.

Let Z_{2r} and Z_{3r} denote the numbers of dyads and triads (subgraphs with two and three vertices, respectively) having r edges. The dyad counts Z_{20} and Z_{21} add up to $\binom{N}{2}$. The triad counts Z_{30}, Z_{31}, Z_{32} and Z_{33} add up to $\binom{N}{3}$. According to our model Z_{2r} is distributed as a sum of two independent binomially-distributed variables which have the parameters $(C_{20}, \beta^r(1-\beta)^{1-r})$ and $(C_{21}, \alpha^{1-r}(1-\alpha)^r)$, where C_{20} and C_{21} are the dyad counts in the cluster structure given by A. It follows that Z_{2r} has the expected value

$$E\, Z_{2r} = C_{20}\beta^r(1-\beta)^{1-r} + C_{21}\alpha^{1-r}(1-\alpha)^r \ , \quad r=0,1. \qquad (2)$$

By examining the possible ways to generate triads it can be shown that

$$E\, Z_{3r} = C_{30}\binom{3}{r}\beta^r(1-\beta)^{3-r} + C_{31}[(1-\alpha)\binom{2}{r-1}\beta^{r-1}(1-\beta)^{3-r} +$$

$$+ \alpha\binom{2}{r}\beta^r(1-\beta)^{2-r}] + C_{33}\binom{3}{r}(1-\alpha)^r\alpha^{3-r} \ , \quad r=0,1,2,3, \qquad (3)$$

where C_{3r} are the triad counts in the cluster structure given by A. Variances and covariances can also be obtained but will not be considered here. We refer to Frank (1977 a) for such moment calculations.

3. Cluster structure parameters

Assume that there are K clusters, and let $N_1,\ldots,N_K$ denote their sizes in nonincreasing order $N_1 \geq \ldots \geq N_K$. The number of clusters of size n is denoted K_n for $n=1,\ldots,N$. We have that

$$N = \sum_{k=1}^{K} N_k = \sum_{n=1}^{N} K_n, \quad K = \sum_{n=1}^{N} K_n . \tag{4}$$

Moreover, it follows that nK_n is the number of row sums of A which are equal to n, and K is the sum of the inverted row sums of A.

The sums of the rth powers of the cluster sizes are given by

$$S_r = \sum_{k=1}^{K} N_k^r = \sum_{n=1}^{N} n^r K_n = \sum_{i=1}^{N} \left(\sum_{j=1}^{N} A_{ij} \right)^{r-1} \tag{5}$$

for r=0,1,... , In particular, $S_0 = K$ and $S_1 = N$. The cluster sizes $N_1,\ldots,N_K$ (or their frequencies $K_1,\ldots,K_N$) are uniquely determined by the power sums $S_1,\ldots,S_K$. In fact, the cluster sizes are often uniquely determined even by S_1, S_2 or S_1 , S_2, S_3. For example, an examination of the 15 partitions of N=7 shows that there are 11 partitions which are uniquely determined by S_2, and there are no partitions which are not uniquely determined by (S_2, S_3). Table 1 gives the numbers of partititons of N and the numbers of S_2- and (S_2, S_3)-values which are unique or common to 2, 3, 4 or more partitions of N for $N \leq 30$.

The elementary symmetrical functions of the cluster sizes are given by

$$C_r = \sum_{i_1 < \ldots < i_r} \cdots \sum N_{i_1} \ldots N_{i_r} \tag{6}$$

for r=1,...,K. We also define $C_0=1$. The sum defining C_r contains $\binom{K}{r}$ terms, and the mean value of the terms is denoted $\bar{C}_r = C_r/\binom{K}{r}$. According to a classical result by Newton (see e.g. Hardy, Littlewood, Pólya 1952, p. 52) we have

$$\bar{C}_{r-1}\bar{C}_{r+1} \leq \bar{C}_r^2 \tag{7}$$

for r=1,...,K-1. There is equality in (7) if and only if all the clusters are of the same size. From (7) it follows that

$$K \geq [r^2C_r^2-(r-1)(r+1)C_{r-1}C_{r+1}]/[rC_r^2-(r+1)C_{r-1}C_{r+1}] , \tag{8}$$

provided $C_r \neq 0$, i.e. provided $K \geq r$. By substituting

$$C_1 = S_1, \quad C_2 = (S_1^2 - S_2)/2, \quad C_3 = (S_1^3 - 3S_1S_2 + 2S_3)/6 \tag{9}$$

we obtain

$$K \geq \lfloor N^2/S_2 \rfloor , \tag{10}$$

and

$$K \geq \lfloor [N^2(N^2-S_2)-2(NS_3-S_2^2)]/[S_2(N^2-S_2)-2(NS_3-S_2^2)] \rfloor \tag{11}$$

where $\lfloor t \rfloor$ denotes the smallest integer not smaller than t. Equality holds in (10) if all the clusters are of the same size, or if there are only two clusters. Equality holds in (11) if all the clusters are of the same size, or if there are at most three clusters. Equalities in (10) and (11) also occur in many other cases.

4. Estimators based on dyad and triad counts

Since the cluster sizes are often uniquely determined by the power sums S_1, S_2, S_3 we shall consider the problem of estimating S_2 and S_3 for given $S_1=N$.

Consider first estimation based on dyad counts. The dyad counts in the cluster structure are given by

$$C_{20} = C_2, \quad C_{21} = \sum_{k=1}^{K} \binom{N_k}{2} = \binom{N}{2} - C_2 , \tag{12}$$

and it follows from (2) and (9) that S_2 has an unbiased estimator

$$S_2^* = [2Z_{21} + (1-\alpha)N - \beta N^2]/(1-\alpha-\beta) \tag{13}$$

if $\alpha + \beta \neq 1$. Let $\hat{S}_2$ be the modified estimator defined as the value in the range of S_2 which is nearest to S_2^* . Then we can define $(\hat{K}_1,\ldots,\hat{K}_N)$ as the randomization over the set of values on $(K_1,\ldots,K_N)$ which satisfy $\sum_{n=1}^{N} n^2 K_n = \hat{S}_2$; i.e., the unknown partition is estimated by a partition which is randomly drawn from the set of partitions which are consistent with $\hat{S}_2$. The number K of clusters, and other cluster parameters as well, can be estimated by using $(\hat{K}_1,\ldots\hat{K}_N)$, e.g. the total number of clusters is estimated by $\hat{K} = \sum_{n=1}^{N} \hat{K}_n$ and the mean cluster size is estimated by $N/\hat{K}$. Alternatively, an estimator of K suggested by (10) is given by $\hat{K} = \lfloor N^2/\hat{S}_2 \rfloor$.

Estimation based on triad counts can be treated in a similar way. The triad counts in the cluster structure are given by

$$C_{30} = C_3, \; C_{31} = \sum_{k=1}^{K} \binom{N_k}{2}(N-N_k), \; C_{32} = 0, \; C_{33} = \sum_{k=1}^{K} \binom{N_k}{3}, \tag{14}$$

and they satisfy the general equalities

$$C_{30} + C_{31} + C_{32} + C_{33} = \binom{N}{3}, \quad C_{31} + 2C_{32} + 3C_{33} = (N-2)C_{21} . \tag{15}$$

It follows from (9), (12), (14) and (15) that the triad counts can be given as linear functions of S_2 and S_3, and by substituting these in (3) and replacing EZ_{3r} with Z_{3r} we obtain an over-determined equation system. After choosing a solution (S_2^*, S_3^*) we can proceed as above and define estimators $(\hat{S}_2, \hat{S}_3)$

taking values in the proper range of (S_2, S_3). Now $(\hat{K}_1,\dots,\hat{K}_N)$ is randomly drawn from the set of values on $(K_1,\dots,K_N)$ which satisfy $\sum_{n=1}^{N} n^2 K_n = \hat{S}_2$ and $\sum_{n=1}^{N} n^3 K_n = \hat{S}_3$. Again, K can be estimated by $\hat{K} = \sum_{n=1}^{N} \hat{K}_n$, or, alternatively, by an estimate of the right-hand side of (11).

In order to illustrate the estimation procedures we will report some results obtained in a computer experiment for the case N=12, K=4, $(N_1,\dots,N_4) = (4,3,3,2)$, $\alpha=\beta= 0.2$. These results are representative for a series of similar experiments which have been made. We simulated 200 observations on the adjacency matrix X. The estimates S_2^* and S_3^* were calculated as the mean-square solutions to the over-determined equation system which is obtained if the moment method is applied to (Z_{21},Z_{30},Z_{33}). The empirical distribution of (S_2^*,S_3^*) was found to be well concentrated around the true value $(S_2,S_3) = (38, 126)$. For each value of (S_2^*,S_3^*) we calculated the closest (in the sense of L^1-metric) value $(\hat{S}_2,\hat{S}_3)$ attainable by some partition of N=12. This value determines a unique partition (see Table 1), and its parts are the estimates of the cluster sizes. Table 2 gives the empirical distribution of the estimates of the cluster sizes.

5. Some remarks

The combinatorial problem of determining how many power sums are required in order to achieve unique cluster sizes does not seem to have been studied in any detail in the literature. This problem is essentially one concerning the coefficients in polynomial equations with integer roots.

The estimators suggested for S_2 and S_3 are obtained by application of the moment method to the dyad and triad counts in the observed graph. The maximum-likelihood method applied to the dyad and triad counts leads to difficulties except in the simplest case of estimating S_2 from the dyad counts.

The maximum-likelihood method can also be applied to the entire data matrix X. The logarithm of the likelihood function can then be given by

$$L(s,t) = s \log \frac{\beta}{1-\alpha} + t \log \frac{\alpha}{1-\beta} + c, \tag{16}$$

where s and t are the numbers of added and removed edges, respectively, $0<\alpha<1$, $0<\beta<1$, and c is independent of A. If $\alpha+\beta<1$, then L(s,t) is maximized for those admissible (s,t) which are reached first by the line L(s,t)=c when it is parallel-translated upwards in the (s,t)-plane. For instance, it is found for the graph in Figure 1 that the optimal (s,t) are those shown in Figure 2, and the maximum-likelihood estimates of the cluster sizes are 222211 if $\gamma\leq 1$,

32221 if $\gamma=1$, 3322 if $1\leq\gamma\leq5$ and 532 if $\gamma\geq5$, where

$$\gamma = \log \frac{\beta}{1-\alpha} \ / \log \frac{\alpha}{1-\beta} \ . \tag{17}$$

Generally, the computational problems appear prohibitive with this linear programming approach.

The problem of estimation of cluster sizes in other stochastic graph models has been considered by Capobianco (1972) and Frank (1971, 1977 b). The idea exploited here, that the cluster sizes are often uniquely determined by their power sums S_1, S_2, S_3, might be useful also in some of these models.

References

Bloemena A.R., Sampling from a graph, Math. Centre Tracts, Amsterdam, 1964

Capobianco M., Estimating the connectivity of a graph. In Graph Theory and applications, D.R. Lick, A.T. White, Eds., Springer, Berlin , 1972

Frank O., Statistical inference in graphs, Swedish Research Institute of National Defence, Stockholm, 1971

Frank O., Moment properties of subgraph counts in stochastic graphs, Dept. of Statistics, Univ. of Lund, 1977 a. (To appear in Annals of the New York Academy of Sciences.)

Frank O., Estimation of the number of connected components in a graph by using a sampled subgraph, Dept. of Statistics, Univ. of Lund, 1977 b

Hardy G.H., Littlewood J.E., Pólya G., Inequalities, University Press, Cambridge, 1952

Figure 1. A graph and its optimal cluster structures.

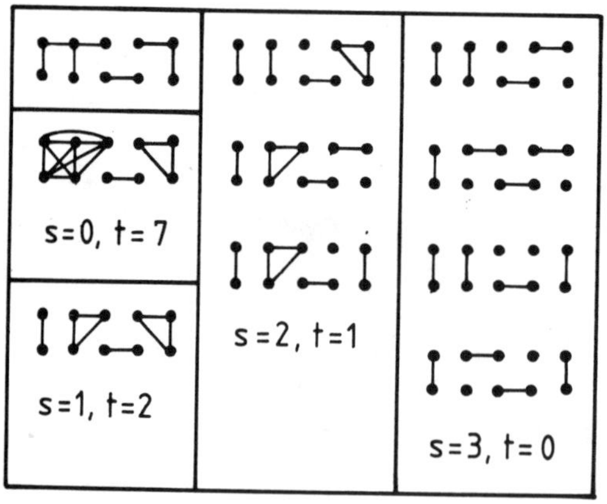

Figure 2. Optimal (s,t) and estimates of the cluster sizes.

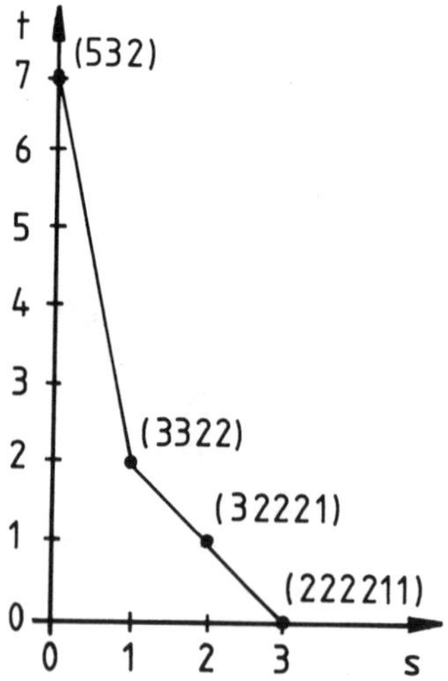

Table 1. Number of partitions of N and numbers of outcomes of S_2 and (S_2,S_3) which are common to different numbers of partitions.

N	Number of partitions	Number of S_2-outcomes with frequency					Number of (S_2,S_3)-outcomes with frequency				
		1	2	3	4	≥5	1	2	3	4	5
2	2	2					2				
3	3	3					3				
4	5	5					5				
5	7	7					7				
6	11	7	2				11				
7	15	11	2				15				
8	22	14	4				22				
9	30	13	7	1			30				
10	42	15	9	3			42				
11	56	19	8	7			56				
12	77	17	12	4	6		77				
13	101	17	13	7	8	1	101				
14	135	20	10	9	7	8	133	1			
15	176	19	12	8	10	12	172	2			
16	231	22	14	6	9	21	221	5			
17	297	26	12	8	9	28	283	7			
18	385	27	14	5	10	36	357	14			
19	490	31	15	9	8	43	450	20			
20	627	32	17	8	9	52	561	33			
21	792	34	18	5	10	63	694	49			
22	1002	37	19	9	8	72	851	74	1		
23	1255	45	12	15	9	81	1044	104	1		
24	1575	47	14	10	14	91	1253	155	4		
25	1958	47	19	10	13	104	1523	204	9		
26	2436	49	21	8	13	118	1823	279	17	1	
27	3010	50	23	12	10	131	2185	358	35	1	
28	3718	52	25	12	14	143	2596	462	62	3	
29	4565	52	26	16	16	155	3065	597	94	6	
30	5604	59	24	13	15	173	3578	755	153	13	1

Table 2. Empirical distribution of the cluster size estimates.

Estimates of the cluster sizes	Frequency in per cent
4332	7
543	6
42222	6
5322	5
44211	5
3333	5
33321	5
43311	4
5331	4
Various other partitions	None larger than 3

Experiments with Cluster Analysis Criteria Based on the within Groups Scatter Matrix

P. Korhonen, Helsinki

Summary: Many optimality criteria suggested for use in cluster analysis are based on the within groups scatter matrix. The most widely known criteria in this family are Minimum variance, Wilks´ lambda and Hotelling´s trace. In this paper these three criteria are being studied, both theoretically and experimentally: A number of representative data sets is construed and the results suggested by the various criteria are described. The best results are found to be given by the Wilks´ lambda criterion.

KEYWORDS: Cluster analysis, grouping, invariant clustering criteria and within groups scatter matrix

1. Introduction

The problem of clustering (grouping) multivariate observations can be approached in several ways. The viewpoint depends on assumptions about the observations and the underlying population. When no assumptions about the form of the population have been made, cluster analysis can be regarded as a purely descriptive method with an aim to find information for more formal methods.

In this paper we assume that the population is composed of distinct categories and each observation in the sample may arise from any one of different distributions. Furthermore, we assume that the distributions are p-variate normal with a common covariance matrix Σ and that the number of the distributions is g. The purpose of cluster analysis is to group together all observations originated from the same distribution (Scott and Symons (1971)).

In several articles (Friedman and Rubin (1967), Fukunaga and Koontz (1970), Scott and Symons (1971) etc.) there are proposals to solve the above-mentioned clustering problem, using one or more criteria based on the within groups scatter matrix (commonly denoted by W). The most common of these are: Minimum variance, Wilks´ lambda and Hotelling´s trace.

Although these three criteria have been mentioned in many articles, comparative theoretical and experimental studies have been presented only occasionally. Some useful comparisons are studied in papers by Friedman and Rubin (1967).

In this paper we have studied

- group structures that are characteristic for each criterion and
- performance of the criteria to find real groups under various group structures.

The above three criteria are commonly used also as test statistics in multivariate analysis of variance and many articles (e.g. Olson (1976) and Schatzoff (1966)) have been published, in which behavior of these test criteria have been examined under various alternative hypotheses. Power considerations presented in these articles can be utilized also in clustering problems.

2. Theoretical considerations

Assume that we have at our disposal an observation matrix X (n x p), where the row vectors X_i stand for observations and the column vectors x_j for variables. Thus the grouping of the observations means a partition of the row vectors of X. Without loss of generality we may assume that the total mean vector of the n observations is a zero vector. Thus the total scatter matrix is given by $T=X'X$.

Let us now suppose a given partition of g groups, with the number of observations $n_1, n_2, \ldots, n_g$ and with groupwise sum vectors $S_1, S_2, \ldots, S_g$. A diagonal matrix with $n_1, n_2, \ldots, n_g$ in the main diagonal will be denoted by N. Further, a matrix of the order g x p with the groupwise sum vectors in rows will be denoted by S.

The between groups scatter matrix is defined by $B = S'N^{-1}S$. Because of the well known matrix identity $T=W+B$ we can define the within groups scatter matrix by $W = X'X - S'N^{-1}S$

The criteria mentioned in the introduction may be defined in terms of scatter matrices as follows:

(2.1a)	$F_1 := \operatorname{tr} WT^{-1}$	->	min	(Minimum variance)
(2.1b)	$F_2 := \lvert W\rvert / \lvert T\rvert$	->	min	(Wilks´ lambda)
(2.1c)	$F_3 := \operatorname{tr} BW^{-1}$	->	max	(Hotelling´s trace)

The criterion functions F_1, F_2 and F_3 can be presented by means of eigenvalues of the matrix BW^{-1}.

$$F_1 = \sum_{i=1}^{q} (1+r_i)^{-1} \qquad (2.2a)$$

$$F_2 = \prod_{i=1}^{q} (1+r_i)^{-1} \qquad (2.2b)$$

$$F_3 = \sum_{i=1}^{q} r_i \qquad (2.2c)$$

The criterion functions F_i (i=1,2,3) for a given partition are commonly used in test theory as multivariate analogies of F test. These analogies are used, for example, in multivariate analysis of variance for testing the null hypothesis of no differences between the group mean vectors. In the general multivariate case the tests are most powerful in different situations, depending on the nature of the departure from the null hypothesis.

Power of these test criteria has been examined e.g by Schatzoff (1966) and Olson (1976) under various group structures from highly concentrated to very diffuse allocations of noncentrality. The group (noncentrality) structure is called concentrated, if the mean vectors of the population are confined to one of the q (=min(p,g-1)) dimensions. If the population mean vectors are equally pronounced in all of the q dimensions, the structure is called diffuse. The power considerations have indicated that in the concentrated structure, the tests tend to be ranked F_3, F_2 and F_1 from most powerful to least powerful. In the diffuse structure the ordering is reversed.

Power considerations in clustering problems have been utilized in section 4 by examining experimentally the dependence between group structures and criterion functions. We shall show, for example, that the criterion F_1 usually produces the most diffuse group structures, while F_3 tends to most concentrated group structures.

The group structures of the sample can be illustrated with the aid eigenvalues of the matrix BW^{-1}. It is a well known, that the group means can be described by means of the eigenvectors associated with the eigenvalues $r_1 >= r_2 >= ... >= r_q > 0$, where $q = \min(p, g-1)$, provided that n>p. (The terms concentrated and diffuse are used for a sample, too). Furthermore, the eigenvalue r_i is the ratio of the between groups scatter to the within groups scatter as measured in one dimension along the direction of the eigenvector associated with r_i. If $r_1 >> r_2 >= ... >= r_q > 0$, the structure is highly concentrated. On the other hand, if all eigenvalues are roughly equal the structure is diffuse. Intermediate structures, between the concentrated and diffuse extremes, are of course possible as well.

3. Computational considerations

As an algorithm for finding the optimal grouping with respect to a given criterion we have used a widely known method that by processing a single observation at a time generates a sequence of groupings converging to a local optimum. For processing observations the author (Korhonen (1977) and (1978)) has developed an efficient technique. By means of this technique the efficiency of the algorithm in using the Wilks´ lambda criterion and the Hotelling´s trace criterion has been improved essentially. For instance, the grouping of 100 observations with any number of variables (<=10). required only about three times more computing time with the Wilks´ lambda criterion than with the minimum variance one.

This technique is based on the use of the pivotal operation and certain dual expressions for the grouping criteria. Using the pivotal operation the transformation formulae have been derived to "sift" the changes in the values of the criterion functions due to the possible move of a single observation. The pivotal operation is also used to update the stage of the grouping, when a single observation is "shifted" into a new group.

The efficiency of the procedure has been increased by using an alternative expression, called a dual expression, for the criterion functions:

$$(3.1a)\quad \mathrm{tr}\, HN^{-1} = \mathrm{tr}\, WT^{-1} - (p-g)\ ,\ \text{where } H=N-ST^{-1}S'$$
$$(3.1b)\quad |H|/|N| = |W|/|T|$$
$$(3.1c)\quad \mathrm{tr}\, NH^{-1} = \mathrm{tr}\, BW^{-1} + g$$

The identities (3.1a-c) are based on the fact that the matrices HN^{-1} of order g x g and WT^{-1} of order p x p have the same eigenvalues less than 1.

The procedure described above has been implemented into our statistical program package HYLPS. HYLPS has been developed at the University of Helsinki and is widely used by Universities and state departments in Finland. All following simulation experiments were run by HYLPS.

4. Simulation experiments

For experimental purposes we constructed at first a random data matrix X consisting of 100 observations and 20 normally distributed variables. For these variables we computed the standardized principal components and denoted by Y the new sample data matrix, that consists of principal component scores. The standardization was made so that $Y'Y=I$. This transformed matrix can be used as well as the original one for grouping experiments purposes, because the criteria (2.1a-c) are invariant under nonsingular linear transformations of the observations.

4.1 Characteristic group structures

By grouping the homogenous data (Y) we try to find the characteristic group structures for each of the criteria (2.1a-c). By varying the number of variables p and of the desired groups g different grouping results can be produced. The group structures have been studied by grouping the data matrix Y with p=2,4,6,8,10 and g=4,6,8,10 by using criteria (2.1a-c). Four initial partitions were generated randomly for each grouping task. The eigenvalues of BW were computed with respect to each best grouping among four attempts.

Because we are interested in only relative differences between eigenvalues, we use in the sequel only the proportional values for these:

$$f_k = 100*r_k\left(\sum_{i=1}^{q} r_i\right)^{-1},\ k=1,\dots,q$$

In describing group structures we use the following quantities:

- o the first "normalized" eigenvalues f_1
- o the 90% percentages points c_1 for the cumulative distribution of the eigenvalues

$$c = \min(k \mid \sum_{i=1}^{k} f_i > 90\%)$$

By using these quantities we can clearly enough find the related ratios of the eigenvalues, for describing group structures.

The results are described in table 1. The table is partitioned so that in each partition the number of eigenvalues q = min(g-1,p) is identical.

TABLE 1: Eigenvalue analysis for groupings $(f = f_1)$

g		4		6		8		10	
p	Crit.	f	c	f	c	f	c	f	c
		q=2							
2	F_1	69.4	2	66.6	2	62.8	2	56.7	2
	F_2	86.1	2	83.4	2	70.0	2	76.2	2
	F_3	99.5	1	99.6	1	99.9	1	99.9	1
		q=3		q=4					
4	F_1	56.0	3	43.5	3	36.9	4	32.4	4
	F_2	54.9	2	63.1	2	61.8	3	60.1	2
	F_3	99.8	1	99.8	1	99.4	1	99.6	1
				q=5		q=6			
6	F_1	49.2	3	37.0	5	32.8	5	27.1	5
	F_2	82.6	2	51.0	3	75.0	2	73.7	2
	F_3	98.5	1	99.1	1	99.6	1	99.4	1
						q=7		q=8	
8	F_1	40.7	3	33.3	4	27.8	5	27.1	6
	F_2	70.5	2	61.5	3	53.5	3	61.0	3
	F_3	99.4	1	99.1	1	99.4	1	99.3	1
								q=9	
10	F_1	45.1	3	31.6	4	25.3	5	25.5	6
	F_2	59.1	2	56.4	3	36.5	4	48.2	4
	F_3	99.1	1	96.5	1	99.3	1	99.4	1

In table 1 we see that the first eigenvalues with respect to the grouping produced by the Hotelling's trace criterion are very high indicating highly concentrated structures. Respectively, the first eigenvalues with respect to the grouping produced by the minimum variance criterion are the smallest. From this and information included in column c we can conclude that the group structures in this case are the most diffuse.

4.2 Performance of the criteria

A number of authors (e.g. Friedman and Rubin (1967), Fukunaga and Koontz (1970), Scott and Symons (1971), Späth (1977) etc.) have examined the criteria (2.1a-c) and some useful comparisons have been presented in their papers. In these comparisons the theoretical advantages of Wilks' lambda criterion have been brought up. We, too, believe that the Wilks' lambda criterion is superior to the other two (Minimum variance and Hotelling's trace), as a rule, but we are also interested in its performance, when the real group structures are either very concentrated or very diffuse. In the sequel we examine this problem experimentally.

Various group structures were generated by grouping the basic data matrix Y into g (g=3,4,5,6) groups randomly and by moving these groups more separately in desired directions. For moving the transformations $z_{ij} = (y_{ij} - \bar{y}_k) + d_j\bar{y}_k$ were used, where d_j is a constant choosed for each variable.

Concentrated group structures are found by setting some $d_j > 0$ and $d_1=d_2=\ldots=d_{j-1}=d_{j+1}=\ldots=d_p=0$. Diffuse group structures can be found by setting $d_1=\ldots=d_p$, respectively. In this case the eigenvalues of BW^{-1} are roughly equal, because $W = Y'Y = I$ by our construction.

The experimental results found by grouping the concentrated structures are presented in table 2, as misgrouping percentages. Values 2, 5 and 8 were used for p. The parameter d_p was set to 3.5 and all the other parameters were set to zero. We denote by "*" the misgrouping percentages exceeding 50 %.

TABLE 2: The misgrouping percentages for highly concentrated group structures

p	cr. g	3	4	5	6
2	F_2	2	0	8	39
	F_3	1	0	8	34
5	F_2	5	36	*	46
	F_3	8	19	*	39
8	F_2	28	50	*	*
	F_3	48	*	*	*

The corresponding misgrouping percentages for diffuse structures are presented in table 3. The values $2.5p^{-0.5}$ have been used for the parameters d_j, j=1,...,p.

TABLE 3: The misgrouping percentages for very diffuse group structures

p	cr. g	3	4	5	6
2	F_1	5	23	3	19
	F_2	4	4	2	21
5	F_1	2	0	1	12
	F_2	1	0	0	3
8	F_1	0	0	0	1
	F_2	0	0	0	24

On the basis of the results in tables 2 and 3 we can conclude that the performance of the Hotelling's trace criterion is not worse than that of the Wilks' lambda criterion, if the group structure is concentrated, and the minimum variance criterion is not worse than the Wilks' lambda criterion, if the group structure is diffuse.

5. Concluding remarks

We found that the minimum variance criterion produced the most diffuse group structures and ,respectively, the Hotelling's trace criterion produced the most concentrated group structures. On the other hand we can not assert that the minimum variance criterion would be working better in grouping data with a diffuse grou structure or that the Hotelling´s trace criterion would be workin better in grouping data with a concentrated group structure.

On the basis of these inspections we recommend the Wilks´ lambd criterion, at least, if we can assume that

- o the covariance matrices are (roughly) equal and
- o the number of observations in groups are (roughly) equal

Unfortunately we are so far unable to demonstrate the performanc of these three criteria, if the above-mentioned assumptions ar violated.

Finally we would like to remind you that the criteria (2.1a-c) ca also be applied in purely descriptive studies,when our aim i simply to group the data in some sensible way without trying t find the real groups. Because the group structures are not fixe in advance, we can not present any general recommendations for th choice of the criterion. Of course, we can suggest "special" criteria (Minimum variance or Hotelling´s trace), if a user wants to produce "special" group structures. Sometimes, for example, a user might want to find a grouping, where the group means are approximately concentrated on a line. For this problem Hotelling´s trace criterion will be recommended, because it appears to have a clear tendency to reveal this sort of group configurations.

References:

Friedman H.P and Rubin J., On some invariant criteria for grouping data, J. Am. Statist. Ass. 62, 1159-1178, 1967

Fukunaga K. and Koontz W.L.G., A criterion and algorithm for grouping data, IEEE Trans. on Comp.,vol. c-19,No 10,917-923,1970

Korhonen P.J., Tilastollinen ryhmittelyanalyysi, lisensiaattitutkielma sovelletussa matematiikassa, Helsinki, 1977 (in Finnish)

Korhonen P.J., A stepwise procedure for a multivariate clustering problem, Helsinki, (will be published 1978)

Olson C.L., On choosing a test statistic in multivariate analysis of variance, Psychological Bulletin, vol.83, No 4, 579-586, 1976

Schatzoff M., Sensitivity comparisons among tests of the general hypothesis, J. Am. Statist. Ass., vol. 61, 415-435, 1966

Scott A.J. and Symons M.J., Clustering methods based on likelihood ratio criteria, Biometrics 27, No 2, 387-398, 1971

Späth H., Computational experiences with the exchange method; applied to four commonly used partitioning cluster analysis criteria, European Journal of Operational Research 1, 23-31,1977

Steinhausen D. und Langer K., Clusteranalyse,Einfuhrung in Methoden und Verfahren der automatischen Klassifikation, Walter de Gruyter, Berlin-New York, 1977

Correspondence Clustering by Paradigms

P.P. Sint, Vienna

Abstract

Assume we have given information about objects in two spaces x,y which allow to determine similarities in these two domains. Then determine the k-linkage lists for all elements (lists of k next neighbours in domain x and next k in y). If l of those k-neighbours in the x domain and the y domain are equal we call this object a (k,l) paradigm. If the spaces x,y allow to define densities paradigms are cases for which $h(x,y)/f(x) \cdot g(y)$ is high. A correspondence cluster is a region with values of this fraction consistently higher than in the surrounding area. Each of the l objects common to the two k-linkage lists is a "case" of the paradigm. Two paradigms which are cases of each other are "strongly connected". If only one is a case of the other they are connected. If there exists a chain of n intermediate connected paradigms objects are called weakly connected of order n + 1. Correspondence clusters may also be defined as in some way connected paradigms together with their cases. Conditional clusters are clusters which have a "connected" criterion domain.

1. The Problem

One of the key questions in statistics is the problem, how two sets of data are related to each other. Which values in one domain (space) correspond to which values in the other domain ? What inferences may be drawn concerning their correlations ? Exist regularities in the relationships between the properties an individual has in one domain and other properties of the individual ?
Very often there is also a direction of the possible relationship defined :
A set of predictor variables is used in an attempt to determine values of a set criterion variables. One hopes to

explain psychological measurements by somatic variables. Or one tries to predict demographic behavior by economic and political factors.

A traditional way to do this is to look for functional relationships between the criterion variables (y) and the predictor variables (x) : multiple regression, linear and nonlinear, is the method of choice. One may also look for an intermediate (latent) variable between the two sets : canonical correlation studies may produce such intermediate variables. We may show this in a simple graphical form.

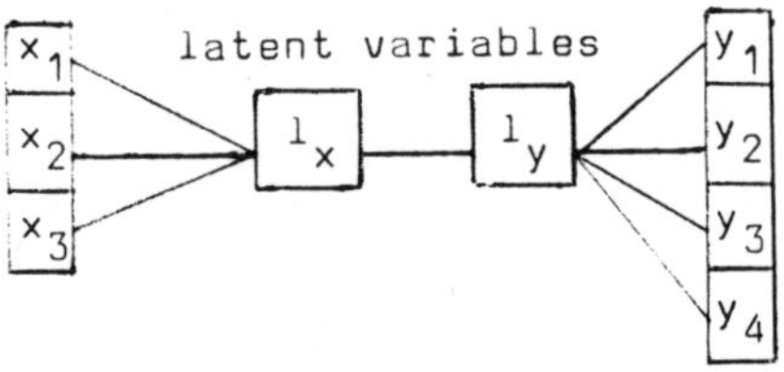

Fig.1 Predictor variables Criterion variables

Path models with latent variables generalize this to more than two sets of data (H. Wold, 1978)

A more modest approach tries to look for a classification of the objects characterised by the predictor variables and hopes that the resulting clusters may be formed in such a way that they allow to make inferences about the values which correspond them in the criterion domain. The one intermediate latent variable is in this case a multistate variable defining different classes of the individuals characterized by the predictor variables.

Traditional cluster analysis and latent class analysis (Lazarsfeld,Henry,1968)take all variables together (x,y) and study inhomogenities in this variable domain. For our problem the information concerning the division of the different character of the variables is lost.(e.g.Sneath-Sokal)

In earlier work (Sint 1971,1974) the predictor variables x were used to define classes such that they give maximum transformation for the description of the criterion variables

y. Each other optimiality criterion of the resulting clusters in domain y may also be used. The optimality criterion had to be optimized "conditional" to the fact that the classes had to be identifiable by the predictor variables.
A similar approach was taken by E. Diday (1975). He allocated objects to clusters if they were near to their corresponding kernels in the domains x and y :
Each cluster defined kernels in the domain x and y (e.g. its centroids;the domain x could be reduced to a subset of its variables). The sum of weigthed distances to this pair of kernels over all individuals studied gave an optimiality function.
The Diday method is a generalization of a monothetic division method by Sonquist and Morgan (1974) which tried to optimize the split in the criterion variables.
Sint and Diday optimized by iterative procedures.
The Diday computational method seems to be more efficient and needs less effort to reach the optimum.
However both methods try to classify each object and force therefore individuals in clusters without justification.

2. Paradigms

This paper tries to show another approach.
We start by looking at each individual if it is a "typical" case of some sort. For this reason we look for its next neighbours in the two domains.Therefore it is only necessary to know similarities in the two spaces (s_x, s_y) up to monotonical transformations.
Let out of theknext neighbours in the two domains l be equal, then we will call such an object a (k,l) paradigm. This is by definition also a (k,j) paradigm for all $j \leqq l$. Given a total number of objects n and assuming representability of their distribution $F(x), G(x)$ in the spaces x and y by densities $f(x), g(x)$ we may write

$$c = \frac{k}{n}$$

$$\int_u f\,(x)\,dx = c$$

Where u is the neighbourhood-defined by some distance measure approximated by the similarity - which contains k neighbours. And similar

$$\int_v g(y)\,dy = c$$

Then a point in the joint space corresponds to a paradigm if

$$\frac{\int_{u \times v} h(x,y)\,dx\,dy}{\int_u f(x)\,dx \int_v g(y)\,dy} \geqq \frac{1}{k^2}\,n = d \qquad (1)$$

More general a (k,m,l) paradigm would have l common neighbours out of k neighbours in the predictor and m in the criterion domain.

The probability to obtain l or more common neighbours in case of independence of x and y would be

$$\sum_{j=1}^{m} \binom{k}{j}\binom{n-k}{m-j} \Big/ \binom{n}{m}$$

The probability of obtaining no common neighbours beeing rather high as long as k=m is small against n

$$\frac{(n-k)}{n} \frac{(n-k-1)}{(n-1)} \cdots\cdots \frac{(n-2k+1)}{(n-k+1)}$$

3. Cluster concepts

Formula (1) suggests the following mathematical formulation of the problem :
Look for connected regions for which

$$\frac{h(x,y)}{f(x)g(y)} \qquad (2)$$

is consistently higher than in its neighbourhood.

Locally sensitive clustering methods-Kittler (1975,1976) may be used to determine the connected regions defined by (2), which should be called "correspondence clusters". Naturally this assumes a rather large number of individuals, or another form of determining the densities rather directly. "Conditional clusters" would have to be connected only in y and not necessarily in x.
The (k,l) paradigm formulation bears resemblence to the "dense" points in Wisharts (1969,1975) mode analysis and may be determined with help of the k-linkage lists determined in this context.
Because of the often rather sparse appearance of individuals, the fact that densities are not available in multistate - nominal scale spaces, or the availability of similarities only, we have to use the (k,l) paradigm formulation to achieve some similar concepts of correspondence and conditional clusters.

We define :
Case : The l individuals which are the common next neighbours in both spaces considered are "cases" of the paradigm.
Strongly connected: two paradigms are strongly connected if each is a case of the other.

Connected : Two paradigms are connected : One paradigm is a case of the other. Weakly connected of order n : two

paradigms are weakly connected if there exists a chain of n-1 paradigms connecting them. Predictor neighbour : paradigm which is one of the k next neighbours in the predictor domain.
Criterion neighbour : Paradigm which is one of the k next neighbours in the criterion domain.
Paradigmatic class : Class of (strong, weak) connected paradigms togehter with their cases.
Pure paradigmatic class : Members do not have predictor or criterions neighbours which are not members. This is a proxy of a correspondence cluster.
Criterion class : members do not have criterions neighbours which are not members of the class. A class may be augmented by its criterion neighbours which results in a cluster which is approximately what we have called a conditional cluster above. Its paradigms define a connected region in the criterion domain (space). But they may combine different regions of the predictor space.
Experiments with artificial data (normally distributed clusters in x and y) show that it is possible to identify corresponding regions in the two domains. Already the identification of the paradigms gives some insight into the structure of the data. In the case of higher number of individuals n, very low l (even l=1) may be necessary to give meaningful results for small k. There is hardly any guidance for the choice of k, upper limits are however determined by computational restrictions. The maximum number l of common neighbours determines where to start the analysis. One looks what may be explained by the paradigms whith maximum l, and uses other paradigms later on. After identification of regions in x, the corresponding regions in y may be investigated and the individuals not used to define the x region could give a statistical measure on the quality of the class found.
This concept of paradigm seems to be very near the procedure we use by intuitively forming classes or notions. In practice we encounter individual cases and compare them with earlier experience. If a "typical" case, a paradigm, appears all of a sudden it becomes clear that this one is representative for a

larger number of cases. However a large number of units under study will still remain unclassified.
To make the facts which may be brought out by our approach visible we give a two dimensional example. Fig. 2

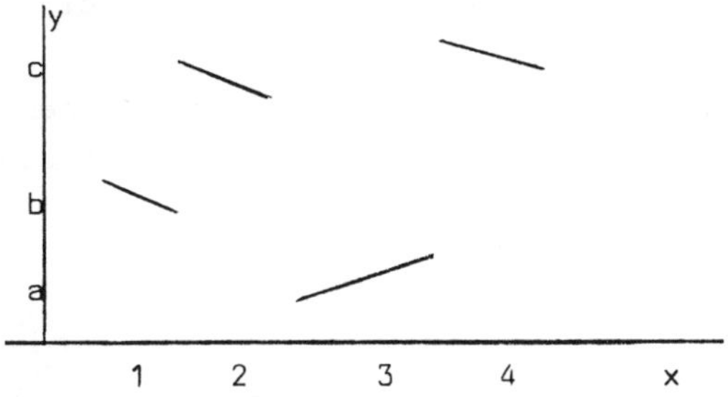

Fig.2

Fig.2 shows that it may be hard to find a functional dependence between two variables. But we can identify regions which may be connected in domain x and y .

4. Outlook

One obvious extension may be the use of more than two sets or types of variables.
Fig. 3 shows how the complexity rises in this case

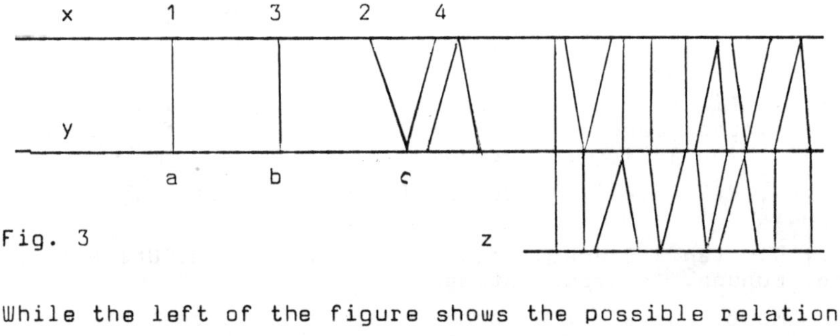

Fig. 3

While the left of the figure shows the possible relationships in the two dimensional case (using partly the example of fig.2) the right hand side shows the possible relationship between classes in 3 groups of variables. (x,y,z may e.g. represent data in different time intervals). Probably one would have to choose a model after looking at the pairwise relationships (x,y), (y,z) and possibly (x,z).

Fig. 2 shows another possibility : The different classes obtained may themself show identifiable relationships between the variables concerned. One could look for dependencies between predictor and criterion variables for the neighbours in the predictor domain only. This would result in an even more improved association analysis - correspondence analysis - correlation analysis - dependence analysis - between variables of different domains.

References :

Diday E., Classification automatique et selection de parametres sous contrainte floue, Comptes Rendus Acad.Science Franc., t 281,24 nov. 1975,ser.A (in French)

Kittler J., A comparative study of five locally sensitive clustering techniques, Proc. Int.Comp.Symp., North Holland, Amsterdam 1975

Kittler J., A locally sensitive method for cluster analysis, Pattern recognition 8 , 23-33 (1976)

Lazarsfeld P.L, N.W.Henry, Latent Structure Analysis, Boston Houghton Mifflin Co., 1968

Morgan J.N., R.C. Messenger, A Sequential Analysis Program for the Analsis of Nominal Scale Dependent Variable, Survey Res.Ctr. Inst. Social Res.,Univ.Michigan, USA 1974

Sint P., Conditional Clustering, 39th session of the International Statistical Institute, Contributed Papers, 2, 940-946, Wien 1973

Sint P., Klassifikation und Information, Mitteilungsblatt der Österreichischen Gesellschaft für Statistik und Informatik, 1 (4) 1-9, Wien 1971 (in German)

Sneath P.H.A., R.R. Sokal, Numerical Taxonomy , Freeman, San Francisco 1973

Wishart D., Clustan 1 C User Manual, computer centre, University College, London, 19,Gordon Street, WC 1H 0AH, 1975

Wishart D., Mode Analysis : A Generalisation of Nearest Neighbours which Reduces Chaining Effects, in : Numerical Taxonomy , ed A.J.Cole, Academic Press London, New York 1969

Wold H., Ways and means of multidisciplinary studies, 6th international conference for the unity of science, Fairmont Hotel, San Francisco, 25-27 nov. 1977

Treatment of Missing Values in Cluster Analysis

D. Wishart, Edinburgh

Five practical treatments for missing values in cluster analysis are discussed with reference to the euclidean sum of squares. Case list deletion is rejected as inappropriate; pairwise deletion and mean substitutions are shown to introduce bias. However, an unbiased estimate of the euclidean sum of squares is derived from an assumption that missing values are distributed with the same mean as the complete data. Algorithms which cater for missing values are outlined for Ward's method, k-means and monothetic divisive cluster analysis. A maximum likelihood method for estimating missing values using partial regression is described.

KEYWORDS: missing values; cluster analysis; euclidean sum of squares; Ward's method; k-means; monothetic division; multivariate normal; partial regression; estimation

Multivariate statistical methods such as cluster analysis usually make reference to a "data matrix". This is an array of numbers $\underline{x}$ where x_{ij} represents the ith observation (row) on the jth variable (column), there being N observations on M variables. When some x_{ij}'s are missing the following treatments can be employed:

a. Case list deletion. Delete any row or column containing a missing value.
b. Pairwise deletion. Calculate values from complete data; ie by deleting all paired comparisons involving missing values.
c. Mean substitution. Calculate cluster averages of complete data and substitute these for any missing values. Then proceed as if data matrix complete.
d. Estimation of cluster statistics. Assume that the missing values are distributed with the same mean as the complete

values, and estimate cluster statistics from the distribution of the complete values.

e. Estimation of missing values. Assume each cluster is multivariate normal and use maximum likelihood regression to estimate missing values.

Some statistical packages adopt solution (a) as the missing value treatment. However, since the usual purpose of a cluster analysis is to obtain a grouping of observations into classes, deletion of any observations which are incomplete is not a very satisfactory solution. Treatment (a) can therefore be dismissed as inappropriate for use with cluster analysis methods.

Calculating distances

The general euclidean distance between two observations i and k is usually calculated under treatment (b) from all pairs of complete values in rows i and k of $\underline{x}$ and scaled to an average value for cross-comparison; thus:

$$d_{ik}^2 = \frac{1}{m_{ik}} \sum_j (x_{ij} - x_{kj})^2 \qquad (1)$$

where the summation is across all pairs of complete values in i and k, there being m_{ik} such pairs altogether. There are $\frac{1}{2}n(n-1)$ such distances, which form a lower triangular distance matrix $\underline{d}$.

While it is acceptable to use $\underline{d}$ as calculated above with cluster methods defined as transformations of similarities or distances (eg single linkage, average linkage, etc), theoretical problems can arise when it is desirable to minimise an objective function which expresses the scatter or disorder within a given overall classification. The rest of this paper considers the implications of approaches (b)-(e) in the particular case of cluster analysis methods designed to minimise the euclidean sum of squares.

Euclidean sum of squares

When the data are complete and the sample of N observations has been divided among a number of clusters, the euclidean sum of squares E_c for a cluster c is defined by:

$$E_c = \sum_{i \varepsilon c} \sum_{j=1}^{M} (x_{ij} - \bar{x}_{cj})^2$$

$$= \sum_{i \varepsilon c} \sum_{j} x_{ij}^2 - n_c \sum_{j} \bar{x}_{cj}^2 \qquad (2)$$

where $\bar{x}_{cj} = \sum_{i \varepsilon c} x_{ij}/n_c$ is the mean of variable j for cluster c.

This statistic measures the scatter about cluster means; therefore small values are indicative of a homogeneous classification, in which the members of each cluster are all closely grouped about the cluster mean.

If the data are not complete, equation (2) can be partitioned into "observed" and "missing" components, as follows:

$$E_c = \underbrace{\sum_{i \varepsilon c} \sum_{j=1}^{M} (x_{ij} - \bar{x}_{cj})^2}_{\text{observed component}} + \underbrace{\sum_{i \varepsilon c} \sum_{j=1}^{M} (\hat{x}_{ij} - \bar{x}_{cj})^2}_{\text{missing component}} \qquad (3)$$

where summation of the first component is over all observed values x_{ij}, summation of the second component is over all missing values $\hat{x}_{ij}$, and the sample mean $\bar{x}_{cj}$ is not known exactly if there are any missing values. Instead, the mean is estimated from complete data

$$\bar{x}_{cj} = \sum_{i \varepsilon c} x_{ij}/n_{cj} \qquad (4)$$

where summation is across the n_{cj} complete observations of variable j within cluster c. If the equivalent mean of the missing values is available (or estimated) from:

$$\tilde{x}_{cj} = \sum_{i \varepsilon c} \hat{x}_{ij}/(n_c - n_{cj}) \qquad (5)$$

then equation (3) reduces, after substitution of (4), (5) to:

$$E_c = \sum_{i\varepsilon c}\sum_j x_{ij}^2 - \sum_j n_{cj}\bar{x}_{cj}^2 + \sum_{i\varepsilon c}\sum_j \hat{x}_{ij}^2 - \sum_j (n_c - n_{cj})\tilde{x}_{cj}^2 + \sum_j \frac{n_{cj}(n_c - n_{cj})}{n_c}(\bar{x}_{cj} - \tilde{x}_{cj})^2 \qquad (6)$$

The above expression is the sum of three components: the first is the sum of squares of the complete data; the second is the sum of squares of the missing values; and the third component is a weighted distance between the means of the observed and missing values. If missing data treatment (b) is chosen E_c is estimated by the first component only. Similarly, if treatment (c) is adopted, namely missing values are replaced by the cluster mean, then $\tilde{x}_{cj} = \bar{x}_{cj}$ and the second and third components of (6) become zero. These substitutions are clearly unsuitable, since they result in E_c being underestimated.

Most cluster methods designed to minimise E compute the increase I_{pq} in E resulting from the union of two clusters p,q to form a new cluster r. This takes the form:

$$I_{pq} = E_r - E_p - E_q \qquad (7)$$

The observed mean for the new cluster is obtained from:

$$\bar{x}_{rj} = (n_{pj}\bar{x}_{pj} + n_{qj}\bar{x}_{qj})/(n_{pj} + n_{qj}) \qquad (8)$$

An expansion of (7) by which I_{pq} is expressed in terms only of the complete data for clusters p and q does not seem possible. However, if it can be assumed that the missing values are distributed in clusters p and q with the same mean as the complete values, ie if:

$$\tilde{x}_{pj} = \bar{x}_{pj} \quad \text{and} \quad \tilde{x}_{qj} = \bar{x}_{qj} \qquad (9)$$

then after substitution of equation (8) for $\bar{x}_{rj}$ and similarly for $\tilde{x}_{rj}$ equation (7) simplifies to:

$$I_{pq} = \frac{n_p n_q}{n_p + n_q} \sum_j (\bar{x}_{pj} - \bar{x}_{qj})^2 \tag{10}$$

which is the same result irrespective of whether there are any missing values. It is somewhat remarkable that all the terms n_{pj}, n_{qj} cancel in the expansion of (7) to derive the simple expression (10) under the distribution assumption (9).

Treatment of missing values in Ward's method

The above result now suggests a generalisation of Ward's method of hierarchical agglomerative clustering to minimise E (see, for example, Ward, 1963; Wishart, 1969). The distance matrix $\underline{d}$ is calculated using (1) and the first union involves the two observations which are closest. At this and each subsequent union the mean of the resulting cluster r is calculated from (8). The subsequent increase in E resulting from the union of any other cluster s with the new cluster r can be obtained from

$$I_{rs} = \frac{2n_r n_s}{m_{rs}(n_r + n_s)} \sum_j (\bar{x}_{rj} - \bar{x}_{sj})^2 \tag{11}$$

where the summation is across all complete pairs of centroid coefficients in r and s, there being m_{rs} such pairs altogether. The factor $2/m_{rs}$ is introduced to (11) so that the calculation is consistent with that of d_{ik}^2 from (1).

The coefficients $\{I_{rs}\}$ calculated from (11) replace each d_{rs}^2 for all other clusters s, and the algorithm proceeds to the next fusion by finding the next lowest coefficient in $\underline{d}$.

Treatment of missing values in k-means

The partitioning cluster method known as "k-means" and generally attributed to Macqueen (1967) seeks to move observations from one cluster to another if the move reduces E. Specifically, a reduction in E is achieved if an observation i belonging to a cluster p is moved to another cluster q when

$$E_p - E_{p-i} > E_{q+i} - E_q$$

ie if $$I_{p-i,i} > I_{qi} \tag{12}$$

Upon substitution of (8) and (10), the test (12) reduces to:

$$\frac{n_p-1}{n_p} \sum_j \frac{n_{pj}^2}{(n_{pj}-1)^2}(\bar{x}_{pj} - x_{ij})^2 > \frac{n_q}{n_q+1} \sum_j (\bar{x}_{qj}-x_{ij})^2 \tag{13}$$

where the summations are across the observed values x_{ij} only. Since each move satisfying (13) will reduce E by the difference between the two sides of the inequality, the above algorithm must terminate.

Treatment of missing values in monothetic divisive clustering

Williams and Lance(1977) describe a monothetic divisive method for the efficient division of a cluster to minimise the euclidean sum of squares. All possible splits into two groups defined by a cut-off value on each variable are considered, and that split which reduces E by the greatest amount is chosen. However, when the data are incomplete a method for allocating missing x_{ij}'s must be devised. It is suggested that the optimum split on a variable j should first be found from the ordered list of complete values; next, each observation for which x_{ij} is missing should be allocated to the sub-cluster for which the smallest further increase in E results. The above procedure is then repeated for each variable, and partition is on that variable which minimises E.

Estimation of missing values

There may be instances in which assumption (9) underlying equation (10) seems unreasonable. This could happen if the observations for which values are missing are atypical or of special interest. In such situations it may be important to provide a reliable estimate of each missing value.

Hartigan(1975) has proposed substitution of the cluster mean as an estimate of each missing value. However, as has been shown in equation (6), this will cause the euclidean sum of squares to be underestimated. Orchard and Woodbury(1972) have proposed a convenient method for estimating missing values in continuous data which can be adapted to a classification problem as follows:

1. Under the simplifying assumption (9) use k-means to obtain k reasonable clusters. For each cluster p, substitute the cluster mean $\bar{x}_{pj}$ as a trial value for any missing data.
2. Estimate the covariances a_{jh} for each cluster using the full data matrix after the above substitutions.
3. Compute partial regression coefficients β_{jh} from the provisional means and covariances for each cluster, and estimate missing values using

$$\hat{x}_{ij} = \bar{x}_{pj} + \sum_{h=1}^{M} \beta_{jh}(x_{ih} - \bar{x}_{ph})$$

4. Compute new means and covariances for each cluster, and iterate until no further changes occur in any $\bar{x}_{pj}$ or a_{jh}.

Orchard and Woodbury have shown that the use of appropriate correction terms for $\bar{x}_{pj}$, a_{jh} at each iteration give maximum likelihood estimates of the missing values when each cluster is multivariate normal.

References

Hartigan J.A., Clustering algorithms, Wiley, 1975.
Macqueen J., Some methods for classification and analysis of multivariate observations, Proceedings 5th Berkeley Symposium on Mathematical Statistics and Probability, University of California Press, Berkeley, 281-298, 1967.
Orchard T. and Woodbury M.A., A missing information principle: theory and applications, Proceedings 6th Berkeley Symposium on Mathematical Statistics and Probability, University of California Press, Berkeley, 697-715, 1972.
Ward J.H., Hierarchical grouping to optimise an objective function, J.Am.Statist.Ass., 58, 236-244, 1963.
Williams W.T. and Lance G.N., Hierarchical classificatory methods, In Statistical Methods for Digital Computers (Edited by K. Enslein et al), Wiley, 269-295, 1977.
Wishart D., An algorithm for hierarchical classifications, Biometrics, 22, 165-170, 1969.

7. Exploratory Techniques

Structures to be Considered in the Reduction of Large Data Sets

D.S. Blohm, Hopewell Junction

Summary

When designing statistical software, one should consider the importance of tables, the man-machine interface, matrix data structures, a half-open cell assertion, and a facility for maintaining sequential files.

KEYWORDS: statistics packages, data analysis, data reduction, data structures, large data sets, matrix structure.

Introduction

We will consider the design of data analysis software.

The typical user and the operator of statistical software are assumed to be the same person. "He wants answers for his problem and assistance with the whole situation of data analysis" ...Hill (1976)... He is an active but somewhat casual operator. He has a fair interest in learning new tools, but is unskilled in computer terminal usage.

Design Priority

Most of the methods used are basic. Our experience has shown that about 72% of the methods are descriptive in nature, such as histograms, two-way plots, percentiles, correlations, listings, and summaries, and about 28% of the runs do simple or multiple regression. Neither normality testing nor principal component procedures are frequently used. Therefore, priority should be given to providing basic calculations which can be extended to the more advanced methods. Also, analysis of computer performance, a specific problem, requires handling large data sets.

Man-Machine Interface

We will assume that an adequate central processing unit (CPU) is available and only I/O hardware devices are of serious concern. With large data sets, we suggest that a high-speed input be used and a high-speed printer be available for the output.

In the design of output devices, one should consider the need to facilitate the analysis of exploratory data; this is done best at a terminal. There are discrete character devices and graphics devices. The discrete character device is restricted by less characters per line, resulting in a crowded format display design which makes one contend with plot granularity ... Velleman et al. (1976)... The graphics device, however, does not implicitly meet the requirement for control input. If possible, a multi-colored functional keyboard should be used with the graphics panel for the interaction of control functions. The keyboard must still be available for the input of labels, names, and titles. If the designer decides to use a functional keyboard, then his "dialogue design" will be similar to an interactive graphic menu approach ...Martin (1973)...

Tables

All of the users know what tables are (Fig. 1), and the typical user prefers them to matrices (Fig. 2). Advanced users also prefer matrices; therefore, the design should address both tables and matrices.

ATTRIBUTES OR VARIABLES (COLUMNS)

Samples, entities, or observations (rows)

No.	Age	Sex	Years of Service
1	48	M	15
2	32	M	7
3	29	M	4
4	37	F	9
5	35	M	3
6	49	M	20
7	29	M	4
8	43	M	13

Fig. 1. Example of a table.

ATTRIBUTES OR VARIABLES (COLUMNS)

Samples, entities, or observations (rows)

1	48	M	15
2	32	M	7
3	29	M	4
4	37	F	9
5	35	M	3
6	49	M	20
7	29	M	4
8	43	M	13

Fig. 2. Example of a matrix.

Matrix Data Structure

The matrix must be understood because the more advanced user prefers it, statistics algorithms usually use matrix notation, I/O tables map to matrices, files map to matrices, and output plots are matrices. See the equivalence of the contents among the table, file, and matrix in Figs. 1-3. Files and matrices have some operations in common: file concatenation vs matrix augmentation, and file inversion vs matrix transposition (Figs. 4 and 5).

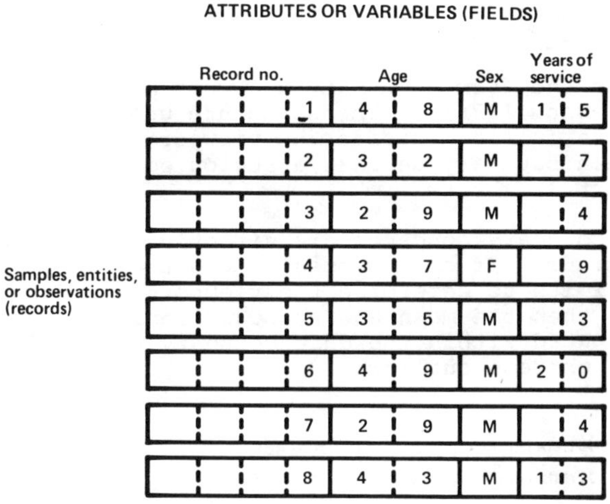

Fig. 3. Example of a file.

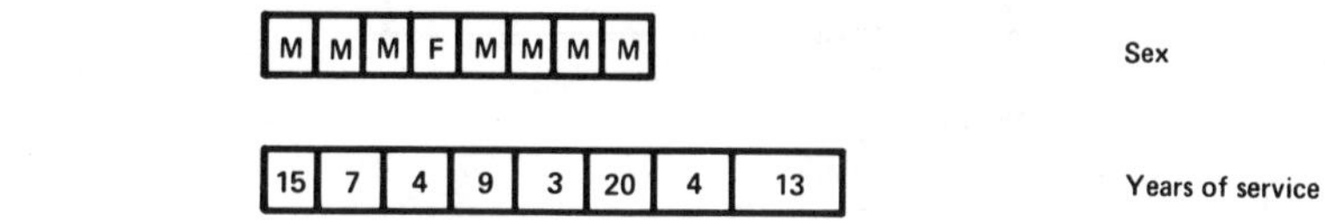

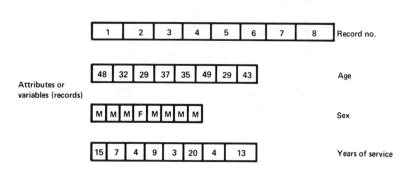

Fig. 4. Example of an inverted file.

SAMPLES, ENTITIES, OR OBSERVATIONS (COLUMNS)

	1	2	3	4	5	6	7	8
Attributes or variables (rows)	48	32	29	37	35	49	29	43
	M	M	M	F	M	M	M	M
	15	7	4	9	3	20	4	13

Fig. 5. Example of a transposed matrix.

Output Display Structures

Output plots are in the form of a matrix. This matrix is the "viewport" ...Velleman (1976)... The structure used to monitor and display the data falling outside the viewport is the "data boundary". The data boundary defines a region equal to or containing the viewport.

Viewport and data boundary concepts are directly applicable to the histogram (Fig. 6). If one chooses to use the "three sigma" and "four sigma" limits to determine the viewport and data boundary, respectively, then the mean and standard deviation statistics should be computed within the data boundary to avoid the adverse effects of extreme outliers.

X data boundary lower limit = $\overline{X} - 4Sx$

X data boundary upper limit = $\overline{X} + 4Sx$

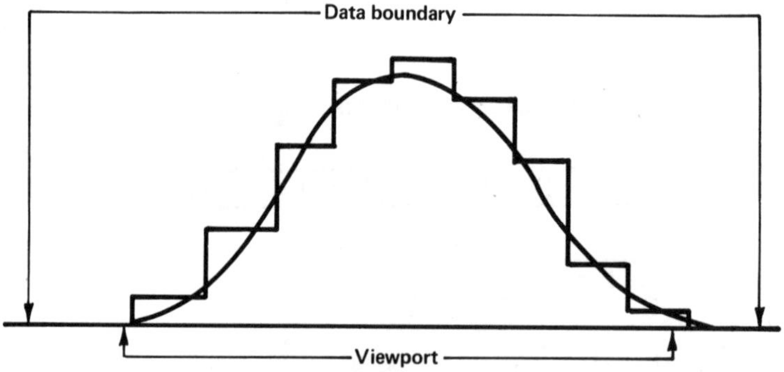

X viewport lower limit = $\overline{X} - 3Sx$

X viewport upper limit = $\overline{X} + 3Sx$

Fig. 6. A schematic representation of a histogram plot showing the viewport and data boundary.

Another structure to be considered is the cell boundary (Fig. 7). Let a histogram, two-way frequency cells, and all data limits be represented as half-open intervals. This avoids misallocating a datum that falls on a boundary, a frequent occurrence in general systems that process large data sets. The following equation shows the relationship among viewport, data boundary, and cell boundary, and may be used as an assertion:

$$[D_l, D_u) \subseteq [V_l, V_u) \subseteq \bigcup_{k=o,n} [V_l + k\Delta h, V_l + (k+1)\Delta h)$$

where $\bigcup_{k=o,n} [V_l + k\Delta h, V_l + (k+1)\Delta h)$ is the cell partition, $[V_l, V_u)$ is the viewport, and $[D_l, D_u)$ is the data boundary. From this equation, it follows that: $D_l \leq V_l < V_l + \Delta h < V_l + (n-1)\Delta h < V_u \leq D_u$, and if there is at least one cell per histogram, $D_l \neq D_u$ and $V_l \neq V_u$.

HISTOGRAM

Cell boundary problem

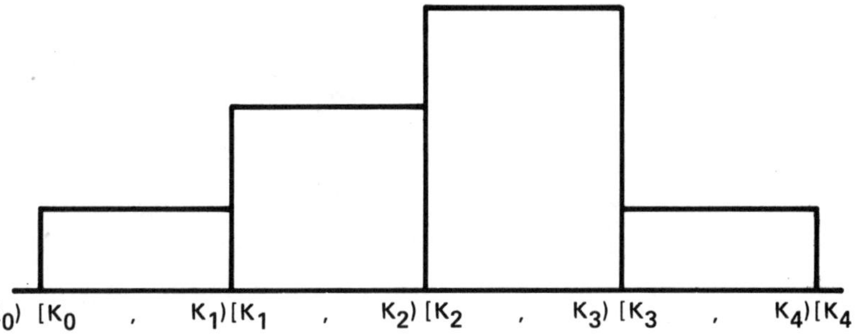

Fig. 7. Histogram cell boundaries.

Large Data Sets

Although an interactive terminal is ideal for the user who has to do exploratory data analysis, its use presents a serious problem for the system design of large data sets. Large data sets usually contain 500 or more variables (columns) and 5,000,000 or more observations (rows). These data cannot be held in the main storage, a requirement of interactive system designs. The solution is to design a hybrid system with the capability of using a large sequential file. Thus certain aspects of batch mode operation, such as processing and diagnosing command statements, will have to be retained prior to processing against the sequential data set.

References

Hill M., "Workshop on Evaluation of Statistical Program Packages," Proceedings of the Ninth Interface Symposium on Computer Science and Statistics, p. 149.
Martin, J., Design of Man-Computer Dialogues, Prentice Hall, 1973.
Velleman P.,"Some Criteria for Evaluating Data Analysis Graphics Software," Proceedings of the Ninth Interface Symposium on Computer Science and Statistics, p. 149.

Multidimensional Scaling: a Short Critique and a New Method

F. Critchley, Glasgow

SUMMARY

The methods of classical and Kruskal nonmetric multidimensional scaling are briefly reviewed, attention being focussed upon the relationship between symmetric dissimilarities δ_{ij} observed for all distinct pairs i,j from a set of n objects and their representation by Euclidean distances d_{ij}. A new and intermediate approach is proposed in which each d_{ij} is approximated by $f(\lambda, \delta_{ij})$ where $f(\lambda,\cdot)$ is a nondecreasing function and λ is a possibly vector-valued parameter. Considerations of parsimony lead naturally to a constrained and nonlinear eigenvalue optimisation problem whose solution is then discussed together with an example. Various complements and extensions of this approach are indicated.

Keywords : EIGENVALUES; MULTIDIMENSIONAL SCALING; OPTIMISATION.

1. INTRODUCTION

The definitive treatment of the classical multidimensional scaling method occurs in Torgerson (1958) but occupies only one chapter of a book devoted largely to unidimensional methods. An important emphasis in many of these latter methods is upon the form of relation between two measurements, made upon each of a set of objects, for example true and perceived weights. The multidimensional analogue is the form of relation between Euclidean distances (for all pairs of objects) and the observed dissimilarities which they represent. In practice, this D-Δ relation is rarely discussed, emphasis being placed instead upon aspects of the corresponding Euclidean configuration. With a few early exceptions in say Shepard (1962) and Kruskal (1964), this remains true of the more recent nonmetric methods, the reasons for this omission being quite straightforward as we note below.

Nevertheless, for Euclidean distances, specification of the D-Δ relation characterises a scaling method and it is unsurprising then that the general properties of such methods can usually be traced back to this specification. In what follows, we first review the general properties of classical and Kruskal nonmetric scaling before introducing a new approach which parameterises the D-Δ relation. Some of the complements and extensions of this approach are indicated briefly in the final section. They will be reported upon elsewhere. In a paper of the present length, no claim is made to an exhaustive treatment of any of the above topics.

2. CLASSICAL AND NONMETRIC METHODS: A SHORT CRITIQUE

The classical multidimensional scaling method restricts attention a priori to the relationship d_{ij} (or d_{ij}^2) = δ_{ij} and consequently may be computed with high efficiency, requiring only a simple algebraic transformation and one full eigensolution of a real, symmetric n×n matrix. By orthogonality, no extra computation is required to obtain solutions in all real Euclidean dimensionalities $p < n$.

However, by imposing a particular D-Δ relation upon the data, the method cannot be used as it stands to analyse the form of that relation (although it can of course be used to falsify the particular relation postulated). In particular cases this may be desirable. In others, the form of the D-Δ relation may itself be of intrinsic interest and it would be advantageous then to have a method which permits examination of this relation. Further, unless there are strong a priori reasons for imposing a particular D-Δ relation, considering a more general parameterised relation has the advantage of offering a gain in parsimony through a lower dimensional representation, even after allowing for any loss due to the parameterisation.

The more recent nonmetric or order-invariant methods naturally allow the $\{d_{ij}\}$ to be approximated by any nondecreasing function of the corresponding $\{\delta_{ij}\}$ and so are tailor-made for dissimilarities of only ordinal significance. Nevertheless, under certain conditions, they can produce remarkably accurate reconstructions of configurations from apparently scanty data (e.g. Shepard (1966), Kendall (1971)). Considering such an extremely general form of D-Δ relation, many more data sets can be well represented by low dimensional Euclidean configurations than would otherwise be the case. This general applicability is further widened by the ability to handle tied, weighted, replicated and missing data and also, if desired, non-Euclidean distance functions although this can give rise to problems of interpretation.

However, the very general form of D-Δ relation admitted has certain drawbacks. Unlike the classical method, there is no known relation between solution configurations in differing dimensionalities. This makes an appropriate choice of dimensionality p more difficult and also requires a nontrivial optimisation to be performed for each of a range of values of p. For each fixed p, the optimum is sought among all possible configurations. It is unsurprising then that local optima are a difficulty and, as always, tactics to avoid them involve additional computing. Using only the rank order information in Δ, these methods are inherently prone to certain forms of degeneracy, for example when p is near n and when the data exhibits a high degree of clustering (Shepard, 1962). Further, whenever the $\{\delta_{ij}\}$ possess more than just ordinal significance, there is a loss of information in using these methods. In particular, questions such as the concavity or convexity of the D-Δ relation cannot meaningfully be discussed. Since an optimum is sought regardless of the implied D-Δ relation, these methods only exceptionally produce a regular relation. Indeed, with Kruskal's method, a step-function and hence, in general, irregular relation is necessarily obtained because of the reliance solely upon the ordinal information in Δ.

There are then converging lines of argument in favour of a D-Δ relation intermediate between those admitted by classical and nonmetric methods. One possibility is discussed in the following section. Roskam (1972) has earlier considered the case of linear and logarithmic D-Δ relations.

3. A NEW METHOD

3.1 NOTATION

We use the following notation. All matrices involved have real elements:

$X = (x_{i\alpha})$: $n \times p$ Euclidean configuration of n points in p dimensions with $r(X) = p < n$ and $n \geq 2$.

$B = (b_{ij})$: $n \times n$ symmetric, nonnegative definite matrix defined by: $B = XX^T$

$D_{(2)} = (d_{ij}^2)$: $n \times n$ symmetric matrix of squared Euclidean inter-point distances for X.

$\Delta = (\delta_{ij})$: $n \times n$ symmetric matrix of observed dissimilarities with $\delta_{ii} = 0$ and $\delta_{ij} \geq 0$ for all $1 \leq i, j \leq n$.

$\underline{1}$: $n \times 1$ vector each of whose elements is unity.

J : $n \times n$ symmetric matrix defined by $J = \frac{1}{n}\underline{1}\,\underline{1}^T$. Note that J and hence I-J are also idempotent, with $r(J) = tr(J) = 1$ corresponding to $J\underline{1} = \underline{1}$.

X is sometimes identified without confusion with the partitioned $n \times n$ matrix $(X|0)$ where here 0 denotes an $n \times (n-p)$ matrix of zeroes. $D_{(2)}$ is invariant under an arbitrary shift of the origin of X and under postmultiplication of X by any $p \times p$ orthogonal matrix. These indeterminacies may with the exception noted be removed by the normalisations:

(1) centroid at origin: $X^T\underline{1} = \underline{0}_p \iff B\,\underline{1} = \underline{0}_n$, where $\underline{0}_p$ denotes a $p \times 1$ vector of zeroes

and (2) principal axes: let B have spectral decomposition $B = QMQ^T$ where Q is $n \times n$ orthogonal and $M = \text{diag}(m_1, \ldots, m_p, 0, \ldots 0)$ with $m_1 \geq m_2 \geq \ldots \geq m_p > 0$. Choose $X = QM(\frac{1}{2})$ where $M(\frac{1}{2}) = \text{diag}(\sqrt{m_1}, \ldots, \sqrt{m_p}, 0, \ldots 0)$, so that $X^TX = M$. Note, however, that arbitrary reflections in the origin are still allowed.

Following Kruskal, the overall scale of X is normalised by the choice:

(3) RMS Euclidean distance of the points to the origin = 1.
Given (1), this is equivalent to:

$$\underline{1}^T D_{(2)}\underline{1} = 2n^2 \iff tr(B) = n \iff \Sigma_{i=1}^n \Sigma_{\alpha=1}^p x_{i\alpha}^2 = n.$$

Lastly, for any $n \times n$ matrix A, we define a new $n \times n$ matrix $\tau(A)$ by the relation: $\tau(A) = -\frac{1}{2}(I-J)\,A(I-J)$. Note that $B = \tau(D_{(2)})$.

3.2 DESCRIPTION OF THE NEW METHOD

An intermediate approach is proposed in which either d_{ij} or d_{ij}^2 represents $f(\lambda, \delta_{ij})$, where $f(\lambda, \cdot)$ is a nondecreasing function but otherwise may be freely chosen and λ is a possibly vector-valued parameter belonging to some index set Λ. For example, $f(\lambda, \delta_{ij}) = \delta_{ij}^\lambda$ for $\lambda > 0$. Let $\Delta(\lambda)$ be the $n \times n$ matrix with general element $f(\lambda, \delta_{ij})$ and $\Delta(\lambda)_{(2)}$ that with general element $(f(\lambda, \delta_{ij}))^2$. Then $\Gamma(\lambda) = \Delta(\lambda)_{(2)}$ or $\Delta(\lambda)$ is to approximate $D_{(2)}$ and $\beta(\lambda) = \tau(\Gamma(\lambda))$ is to approximate B. Let $\mu_1(\lambda) \geq \ldots \geq \mu_n(\lambda)$ be the eigenvalues of $\beta(\lambda)$. Then we seek $\hat{\lambda} \in \Lambda$ to maximise the target function:

$$T(\beta(\lambda)) \equiv T(\lambda) = \Sigma_{i=1}^n (\mu_i(\lambda))^2/n^2$$

subject to the constraints:

(a) $\mu_n(\lambda) = 0$, so that $\beta(\lambda)$ is nonnegative definite and $\exists\, X = X(\lambda)$ obeying $\beta(\lambda) = X X^T$. (Equality due to centroid at origin).

and (b) $\bar{\mu}(\lambda) \equiv \frac{1}{n} \Sigma_{i=1}^{n} \mu_i(\lambda) = 1$, so that the scale constraint (3) is satisfied.

It can readily be proved that if $f(\lambda,\delta_{ij})$ is continuous as a function of λ then so is $T(\lambda)$. In the sense illustrated in Figure 1, maximising $T(\lambda)$ under the above constraints is then a continuous analogue of the discrete notion of minimising the Euclidean dimensionality p. In this sense, $\hat{\lambda}$ is the most parsimonious parameter value.

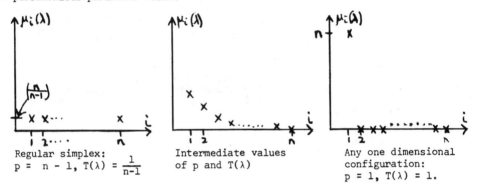

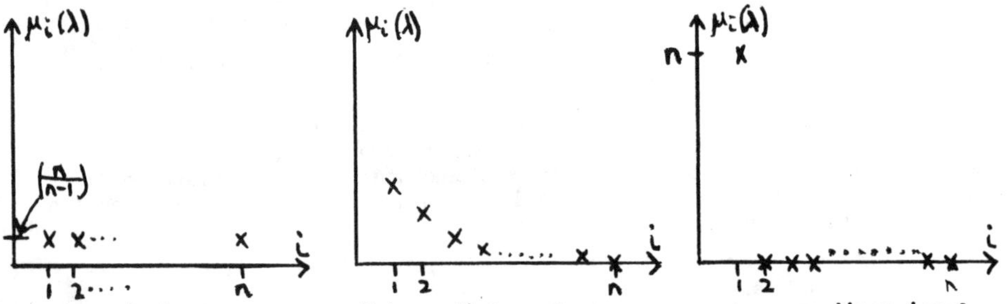

Regular simplex: $p = n - 1$, $T(\lambda) = \frac{1}{n-1}$

Intermediate values of p and $T(\lambda)$

Any one dimensional configuration: $p = 1$, $T(\lambda) = 1$.

(direction of p decreasing and $T(\lambda)$ increasing)⟶

Figure 1: Relation between $T(\lambda)$ and p.

In practice, for whatever reason (rounding, errors of measurement,..), negative eigenvalues of $\beta(\lambda)$ are to be expected even when $\Gamma(\lambda)$ approximates $D_{(2)}$ closely. Their presence can of course be accommodated in more than one way. In particular, the following approach may be adopted:

Let $k = -\mu_n(\lambda) \geqslant 0$. Transform $\beta(\lambda)$ to the nonnegative definite matrix $\beta(\lambda) + kI$ and then renormalise as at (1) and (3) above. The matrix $\beta_*(\lambda) = \alpha\{\beta(\lambda) + k(I - J)\}$ results, where $\alpha = \alpha(n,k) = n/(n + (n-1)k)$, so that $0 < \alpha \leqslant 1$. Further, $T_*(\beta_*(\lambda)) \equiv T_*(\lambda) = \alpha^2 T(\lambda) + n^{-1} k\, \alpha(\alpha+1)$, so that $T_*(\lambda) < T(\lambda)$ unless $k = 0$ and $T_*(\lambda)/T(\lambda) \to 0$ as k^{-2} when $k \to \infty$.

In short $T_*(\lambda)$ is a rather natural extension of $T(\lambda)$ from nonnegative definite matrices to any symmetric matrix, and it may be sensible then to replace the original problem by the now unconstrained one of finding $\lambda_* \in \Lambda$ to maximise $T_*(\lambda)$.

When λ has a modest number of components, this approach is readily programmed requiring only the use of some sensible search procedure among all $\lambda \in \Lambda$. For each trial value of λ, we can compute $T(\lambda)$ as $n^{-2} \Sigma_{i=1}^{n} \Sigma_{j=1}^{n} \beta_{ij}^{2}(\lambda)$ and $\mu_n(\lambda)$ by a standard algorithm so yielding $T_*(\lambda)$. For the optimal λ_* the full eigensolution of $\beta_*(\lambda_*)$ is obtained (ignoring eigenvectors associated with nonpositive eigenvalues) and thence the required configuration $X(\lambda_*)$.

3.3. *AN EXAMPLE*

This example is here given merely as an illustration of the new method. Using data from Benjamin (1958), the Blau-Duncan measure of inflow dissimilarity is computed for all distinct pairs of the 13 socio-economic groups used in the 1951 census. For $\lambda > 0$, δ_{ij}^{λ} is used to approximate d_{ij}. Figure 2 shows the graphs of $T_*(\lambda)$ and $\mu_n(\lambda)$ (above and below the horizontal axis respectively) for $\lambda \in [0.1, 10]$. Over this range, $\lambda_* = 1.4$ maximises $T_*(\lambda)$ the corresponding eigenvalues $\{\mu_i(\lambda_*)\}$ being, in nonincreasing order, 7.67, 3.71, 1.22, 0.40 down to -0.27 so that a two, or at most three, dimensional solution seems adequate. The configuration $X(\lambda_*)$ is in broad agreement with that obtained by nonmetric methods. Using the relation $d_{ij} = \delta_{ij}^{1.4}$ relative distances between points in $X(\lambda_*)$ can be converted back into relative dissimilarities which have substantive meaning.

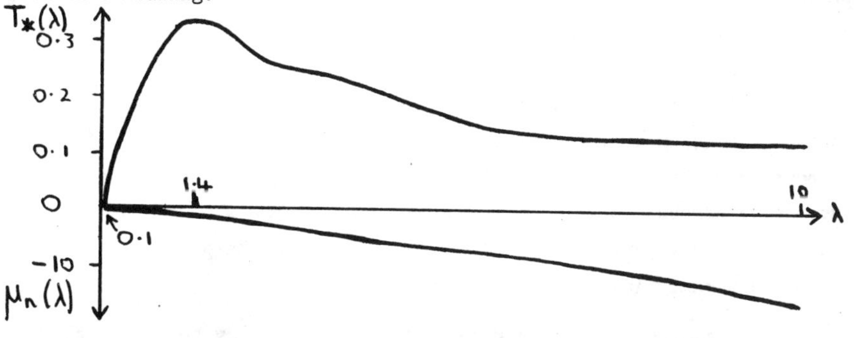

Figure 2: Graphs of $T_*(\lambda)$ and $\mu_n(\lambda)$

3.4 *DISCUSSION*

Although different in its emphasis on parsimony, the new method in restricting attention to a parametric family of D-Δ relations is intermediate between classical and nonmetric methods both in this sense and, consequently, in terms of its applicability. This parameterisation aids the search for a parsimonious optimum within a given family, retains more than just the ordinal information in Δ and so helps to avoid the degeneracies to which nonmetric methods are prone. The method retains the advantages of the classical approach of choice of dimensionality and ease of computation due to the orthogonal nesting of solutions. It permits examination of the D-Δ relation. In some cases, an appropriate family of relations may be apparent contextually and interest then centres upon the value of λ. In others, a model-fitting approach involving perhaps several families may be adopted.

However, the method like classical scaling is limited to Euclidean distances, and, currently, to complete, unweighted and unreplicated data. Although not a problem in limited practical experience to date, general conditions for the existence of a unique solution have not yet been obtained. Neither has the robustness of the method to departures from $\Gamma(\lambda) = D_{(2)}$ been studied in detail.

Finally, we note that the new method is, for multidimensional scaling, intermediate between classical and nonmetric methods in the same sense that the Box and Cox (1964) methods are, for the linear model with a possibly transformed dependent variable, intermediate between the standard approach and that of Kruskal (1965).

4. COMPLEMENTS AND EXTENSIONS

In section 3.2 above it can be shown that the transformation $\beta(\lambda) \to \beta_*(\lambda)$ is equivalent to $\Gamma(\lambda) \to \Gamma_*(\lambda) = \alpha[\Gamma(\lambda) + 2k\,(\underline{1}\,\underline{1}^T - J)]$ being the familiar result that any symmetric matrix with zero diagonal entries can be transformed into a squared Euclidean distance matrix merely by adding the same sufficiently large constant to each of its off-diagonal elements.

Our procedure for the display of residuals, originally developed as an aid to interpreting stress (formula one), can be applied here when dimensions with small positive eigenvalues are discarded. This can help in detecting those points naturally lying in higher dimensions.

When the data is in the form (β_{ij}) rather than (δ_{ij}), it may be preferable to parameterise the $b_{ij} - \beta_{ij}$ relation directly, rather than first transforming (β_{ij}) to (δ_{ij}) form.

Under appropriate assumptions, we may consider models in which the least-squares or maximum-likelihood principle can be used to determine λ. In particular cases, an explicit solution has been obtained. See also Ramsay (1977).

REFERENCES

Benjamin B., Inter-generation differences in occupation, Population Studies, 11, 262-268, 1958.

Box G.E.P. and Cox D.R., An analysis of transformations (with Discussion), J. Royal Statist. Soc., B, 26, 211-252, 1964.

Kendall D.G., Construction of maps from "odd bits of information", Nature, London, 231, 158-159, 1971.

Kruskal J.B., Multidimensional scaling by optimising goodness of fit to a nonmetric hypothesis, Psychometrika, 29, 1-27, 1964.

Kruskal J.B., Analysis of factorial experiments by estimating monotone transformations of the data, J. Royal Statist. Soc., B, 27, 251-263, 1965.

Ramsay J.O., Maximum likelihood estimation in multidimensional scaling, Psychometrika, 42, 241-266, 1977.

Roskam E.E., MRSCAL: an algorithm for multidimensional scaling by metric transformation of data, Program Bulletin No. 23, University of Nijmegen, 1972.

Shepard R.N., The analysis of proximities: multidimensional scaling with an unknown distance function: II, Psychometrika, 27, 219-246, 1962.

Shepard R.N., Metric structures in ordinal data, J. of Mathematical Psychology, 3, 287-315, 1966.

Torgerson W.S., Theory and methods of scaling, John Wiley, New York, 1958.

Lower Rank Approximation of Matrices by Least Squares with Any Choice of Weights

K.R. Gabriel and **S. Zamir**, Rochester

Reduced rank approximation of matrices has hitherto been possible only by unweighted least squares. This paper presents iterative techniques for obtaining such approximations when weights are introduced. The techniques involve criss-cross regressions with careful initialization. Possible applications of the approximation are in modelling, biplotting, contingency table analysis, fitting of missing values, checking outliers, etc.

KEYWORDS: Reduced rank approximation; least squares; criss-cross regression; Householder-Young theorem; biplot; contingency table; outliers.

1. INTRODUCTION: Approximation of matrices by other matrices of lower rank plays a useful role in fitting models to data (Mandel, 1969, 1971; Bradu and Gabriel, 1978), in graphical representation of data (Gabriel, 1971, 1972), in principal component analysis (Whittle, 1952) and in other multivariate techniques. The method of approximation used in all these applications is least squares, with the solution due to Householder and Young (1938) for which a variety of special computational routines are available (Golub and Reinsch, 1970).

The need for approximation by weighted least squares also arises frequently. For example, a table of means based on samples of widely varying sizes should be fitted with weights proportional to sample sizes. In the extreme case of zero size samples, an "entry" should play no role in fitting. This would also take care of missing values by assigning zero weights.

This paper considers iterative methods of fitting lower rank least squares approximations for a general choice of weights. (For more detail see Gabriel and Zamir, 1978.) For an (nxm) matrix Y of elements $y_{i,j}$ it considers least squares fitting subject to weights $w_{i,j}$. Fitting by a matrix of rank ρ or less is equivalent to fitting by a matrix product AB' where A and B are n$\times\rho$ and

$m \times \rho$, respectively (Gabriel, 1978a). The minimizing criterion can therefore be written

(1.1) $$\Phi(A,B) = \{\sum_{i=1}^{n} \sum_{j=1}^{m} w_{i,j}(y_{i,j}-\underline{a}_i'\underline{b}_j)^2\} ,$$

where $\underline{a}$ and $\underline{b}$ denote rows of A and B, respectively.

2. THE CASE OF EQUAL WEIGHTS: Householder and Young (1938) dealt with equal weights, $w_{ij}=1$, and minimized $\Phi = ||Y-AB'||^2$, the Euclidean norm of the matrix of residuals. A convenient method of solution (see, e.g., Good, 1969, p. 827) deals with the columns of A, and the corresponding columns of B, one at a time. The solutions for $\underline{a}_{,r}$ and $\underline{b}_{,r}$--the r-th columns of A and B, respectively--are obtained after solutions for $\underline{a}_{,1},\ldots,\underline{a}_{,r-1}$ and $\underline{b}_{,1},\ldots,\underline{b}_{,r-1}$ are available and subtracted out of Y to give residuals

(2.1) $$Y^{(r-1)} = Y - \sum_{t=1}^{r-1} \underline{a}_{,t}\underline{b}'_{,t}.$$

The equations determining $\underline{a}_{,r}$ and $\underline{b}_{,r}$ are

(2.2) $$(\Sigma_i a_{i,r}^2)^{1/2} b_{j,r} = \Sigma_i a_{i,r} y_{i,j}^{(r-1)}$$

and

(2.3) $$(\Sigma_j b_{j,r})^{1/2} a_{i,r} = \Sigma_j b_{j,r} y_{i,j}^{(r-1)} .$$

These are iterated, from same initial $\underline{a}_{,}$ until they converge. Equivalently, one could omit the square roots in both equations and introduce some other normalization. The method then becomes one of criss-cross regression of columns of $Y^{(r-1)}$ onto $\underline{a}_{r,}$ to obtain $\underline{b}_{,r}$ as coefficients, and regression of rows of $Y^{(r-1)}$ onto $\underline{b}_{r,}$ to obtain $\underline{a}_{r,}$ as coefficients.

This unweighted least squares fit proceeds by dyadic (i.e., rank one) steps, from fitting dyadic $\underline{a}_{,1}\underline{b}'_{,r}$ to Y, through fitting dyadic $\underline{a}_{,2}\underline{b}'_{,2}$ to $Y^{(1)}=Y-Y_{(1)}$ and on to fitting $\underline{a}_{,\rho}\underline{b}'_{,\rho}$ to $Y^{(\rho-1)}$. At each step the sum of the dyadic residual fits gives the overall fit of that rank, that is,

(2.4) $$Y_{(r)} = \sum_{t=1}^{r} \underline{a}_{,t}\underline{b}'_{,t}.$$

This stepwise fitting is possible because successive $\underline{a}_{,}$'s, and also successive

$\underline{b}_{,}$'s, are orthogonal (or, in the case of multiple eigenvalues of Y'Y, they can be chosen so as to be orthogonal).

3. CRISS-CROSS REGRESSIONS AND SUCCESSIVE DYADIC FITS: The method of criss-cross regressions of columns and rows of $Y^{(r-1)}$ onto, respectively, $\underline{a}_{,r}$ and $\underline{b}_{,r}$ is readily generalized to arbitrarily weighted least squares. The iteration equations generalize to

$$(3.1)\qquad (\Sigma_i w_{i,j} a_{i,r}^2) b_{j,r} = \Sigma_i w_{i,j} a_{i,r} y_{i,j}^{(r-1)}$$

and

$$(3.2)\qquad (\Sigma_j w_{i,j} b_{j,r}^2) a_{i,r} = \Sigma_j w_{i,j} b_{j,r} y_{i,j}^{(r-1)} .$$

Successive solution of these equations for $r=1,\ldots,\rho$ has been referred to as the NIPALS procedure (Wold, 1966; Wold and Lyttkens, 1969).

This is perfectly adequate for rank 1 fits, but when used for rank 2 or more it does not generally yield the fit with minimal weighted sum of squared deviations. The orthogonality properties of the unweighted case break down and the sum of the dyadic fits to successive residuals does not produce the desired reduced rank fit--as can be verified by counterexamples.

However, one may attempt to arrive at a reduced rank (≥ 2) fit by iterating the dyadic fits of the ρ columns. Thus, one would repeat each step of NIPALS on residuals from fits of all other columns until the entire matrices A and B converged. This will be referred to as successive dyadic fits.

4. CRISS-CROSS MULTIPLE REGRESSIONS: A more direct approach deals with the entire factor matrices $A_{(n\times\rho)}$ and $B_{(m\times\rho)}$, rather than separately with each column. Thus, for a given matrix A one would obtain B as coefficients of the weighted multiple regressions of the columns of Y onto those of A. Similarly, for given B, one would obtain A as coefficients of the weighted multiple regression of the rows of Y onto the columns of B. The equations are

$$(4.1)\qquad ((\Sigma_i w_{i,j} a_{i,g} a_{i,g'}))\underline{b}_j = ((\Sigma_i w_{i,j} a_{i,g} y_{i,j}))$$

and

(4.2) $$((\Sigma_j w_{i,j} b_{j,e} b_{j,e'}))\underline{a}_i = ((\Sigma_j w_{i,j} b_{j,e} y_{i,j}))$$

for the rows of B and of A, respectively.

Since neither A nor B are given, one starts with some initial guess $A_{(0)}$ and iterates from A to B then from B to A, etc.

The least squares properties of multiple regression can be used to show that this method of iteration must converge, though it does not prove that it converges to the minimum value of Φ. However, the convergence point of the iterations, say (A*,B*), satisfies

(4.3) $$\min_A \Phi(A,B^*) = \min_B \Phi(A^*,B) = \Phi(A^*,B^*)$$

which is a necessary, though not sufficient, condition for (A*,B*)'s being the minimum point of Φ.

5. INITIALIZATION: Two iterative procedures have been introduced. Both need an initial $(n\times\rho)$ matrix $A_{(0)}$ to begin the first iteration. No choice was obvious so we started with NIPALS, initializing each step, arbitrarily.

When some weights were zero, these fits occasionally converged well away from the least squares fit. If, $w_{i,j}=0$ for some given i,j and the dyadic fit iteration reached approximately

(5.1) $$\underline{a}, \doteq \frac{1}{\alpha}(y_{1,j}, y_{2,j}, \ldots, y_{i-1,j}, \alpha\beta, y_{i+1,j}, \ldots, y_{n,j})'$$

and

(5.2) $$\underline{b}, \doteq \frac{1}{\beta}(y_{i,1}, y_{i,2}, \ldots, y_{i,j-1}, \alpha\beta, y_{i,j+1}, \ldots, y_{i,m})$$

for some constants α and β, then it converged to these vectors with infinitely increasing α and β. This provided perfect fit in all cells of row i and of column j, except cell (i,j) whose fitted value $\alpha\beta$ increased indefinitely (which did not affect the goodness of fit since $w_{i,j}=0$). The fit outside these columns could be extremely poor, as each fitted value decreased indefinitely to zero. The sum of squared deviations therefore converged to

(5.3) $$\Phi^*_{i,j} = \sum_e \sum_g w_{e,g} y^2_{e,g} - \sum_e w_{e,j} y^2_{e,j} - \sum_g w_{i,g} y^2_{i,g} \ .$$

In all the numerical experiments that we ran with various initial vectors $\underline{a}_{(0),}$ this was <u>the only type</u> of above-minimal convergence that we came across. In view of this we tried to eliminate this undesirable phenomenon by a suitable choice of the initial vector $\underline{a}_{(0),}$.

Note that on the i-th row and j-th column the same sum of squared deviations, namely zero, is obtained for any values α and β in the above vectors $\underline{a}_{,}$ and $\underline{b}_{,}$. These two values may therefore be chosen so as to minimize the deviations outside the i-th row and j-th column. Φ will then be reduced below $\Phi^*_{i,j}$--except in the special case when it remains equal to $\Phi^*_{i,j}$ because all values in Y outside the i-th row and j-th column are zero.

An obvious way to choose α and β with this purpose is to regress the values $(y_{e,g};e\neq i,g\neq j)$ onto the products $a_e b_g;e\neq i,g\neq j)$. Thus, one may solve

$$(5.4)\qquad (\sum_{e\neq i}\sum_{g\neq j} w_{e,g}y^2_{e,j}y^2_{i,g})/\alpha\beta = \sum_{e\neq i}\sum_{g\neq i} w_{e,g}y_{e,j}y_{i,g}y_{e,g}$$

for α and β, where either of these can be given any arbitrary non-zero value. Putting $\alpha=1$, the regression coefficient in (5.4) is $1/\beta$ and the initial column becomes

$$(5.5)\qquad \underline{a}_{(0),} = (y_{i,j},\ldots,y_{i-1,j},\beta,y_{i+1,j},\ldots,y_{n,j})' \ .$$

Unless $1/\beta=0$, the initial fit must be at least as good as, and in non-trivial cases strictly better than, that of (5.1) and (5.2) and the process must converge to a sum of squares below $\Phi^*_{i,j}$.

Motivated by this observation, we start the initialization with the calculation of $\Phi^*_{i,j}$ for each (i,j) with $w_{i,j}=0$ (and also for (i,j)'s with weights which are close to zero). The (i,j) with the highest

$$(5.6)\qquad \Psi_{i,j} = \sum_{e,g} w_{e,g}y^2_{e,g} - \Phi^*_{i,j} = \sum_{e} w_{e,j}y^2_{e,j} + \sum_{g} w_{i,g}y^2_{i,g}$$

is chosen and the appropriate vector $\underline{a}_{(0),}$ calculated from (5.4) and (5.5). Clearly, the iteration must converge to a lower sum of squares than that of any pair $\underline{a}_{,}$ and $\underline{b}_{,}$ of (5.1) and (5.2). All those above-minimum convergences are therefore improved upon.

If no $w_{i,j}$ is zero or very small our initialization consists simply of choosing the column with the longest weighted norm

(5.7) $$\theta_j = \sum_i w_{i,j} y^2_{i,j}$$

and putting

(5.8) $$\underline{a}_{(0),} = (y_{1,j},\ldots,y_{i,j},\ldots,y_{n,j})' \quad .$$

This initialization has converged to the true minimum of Φ in all the examples we have tried. We conjecture that it does so for all except perhaps some highly pathological cases.

6. ROUTINES AND PROGRAMS: Seven alternative programs for weighted least squares approximation were built up from a small number of routines which carry out the computations described in the preceding sections. Rank one, two and three fits were computed for several data sets. In all instances the seven programs converged to the same fit.

This is strong evidence that all the programs work and reach the true least squares approximation. Additional evidence to this effect was obtained by trying weights which factored into column and row components and finding that the present programs arrived at the true minimum as obtained by an extension of the Householder-Young method (Haber and Gabriel, 1977). In particular, for equal weights, the programs always yielded the Householder-Young approximation.

When fits of both rank 2 and 3 were calculated it was found cheapest (fastest) to run the program which uses criss-cross multiple regressions. Next fastest were programs which use successive dyadic fits. Double checking programs were slower. The difference in costs of the two programs was not large enough to warrant an unequivocal recommendation.

ACKNOWLEDGEMENT

The authors express their appreciation of Israel Einot's (Jerusalem) and Janet Gough's (Rochester) thoughtful and patient programming of successive versions of these procedures. Much of the success of this work is due to their efforts. Computer programs in FORTRAN are available on request from the Division of Biostatistics, University of Rochester Medical Center, Rochester, NY 14642.

REFERENCES

Bradu, D. and Gabriel, K.R., The biplot as a diagnostic tool for models of two-way tables, Technometrics,20,47-68,1978.

Christofferson, A., The one-component model with incomplete data, Ph.D. Thesis Uppsala University, Institute of Statistics,1969.

Gabriel, K.R., The biplot-graphic display of matrices with application to principal component analysis, Biometrika,58,453-467,1971.

Gabriel, K.R., Analysis of meteorological data by means of canonical decomposition and biplots, J. App. Meteor.,11,1071-1077,1972.

Gabriel, K.R., Least squares approximation of matrices by additive and multiplicative models, J.Roy.Statist.Soc.,B, 1978, to appear.

Gabriel, K.R., The complex correlational biplot, In Theory Construction and Data Analysis in the Behavioral Sciences (S. Shye ed.)., San Francisco, Jossey-Bass (in press), 1978.

Gabriel, K.R. and Zamir, S., Reduced rank approximation of matrices by least squares with any choice of weights, Technometrics,(to appear),1978.

Good, I.J., Some applications of the singular value decomposition of a matrix, Technometrics,11,823-831,1969.

Golub, G.H. and Reinsch, C., Singular value decomposition and least square solution, Numer. Math.,14,403-420,1970.

Haber, M. and Gabriel, K.R., Weighted least squares approximation of matrices with applications to canonical correlation and biplot display, mimeographed, 1977.

Householder, A.S. and Young, G., Matrix approximation and latent roots, Am.Math. Monthly,45,165-171,1938.

Mandel, J., A method of fitting empirical surfaces to physical and chemical data, Technometrics,11,411-430,1969.

Mandel, J., A new analysis of variance model for non-additive data, Technometrics, 13,1-18,1971.

Whittle, P., On principal components and least square methods of factor analysis, Skand.Aktuar.,34,232-239,1952.

Wold, H. and Lyttkens, E., Nonlinear iterative partial least squares (NIPALS) estimation procedures, Bull.Inter.Statist. Inst.,43,29-51,1969.

Wold, H., Nonlinear estimation by iterative least squares procedures. In Research Papers in Statistics (F.M. David, ed.), New York, Wiley, 1966.

On Seriation and Multidimensional Scaling

E. Pleszczyńska, J. Cwik, T. Papagorasz, E. Palinkas, Warszawa

Some special class of families of distributions is discussed and shown to be applicable in building seriation and multidimensional scaling models. Models concerning Plato dating problem are considered as an illustration. Moreover, a new approach towards the connections between multidimensional scaling and measures of positive dependence in bivariate distributions is presented.

KEYWORDS: multidimensional scaling, seriation, dating, positive dependence, dissimilarity, Kullback-Leibler divergence.

1. Evolution schemes in seriation and multidimensional scaling

Seriation and multidimensional scaling often involve rather vague assumptions about the phenomena investigated. For example, in problems concerning datting of some Plato works it was assumed that Plato's style was changing with time in some vaquely specified way (Boneva(1971)). More precisely, attention was restricted to changes of the distribution of the succession of long and short syllables among the five last ones in particular sentences. Let Λ bo tho known interval of time in which the works in question were written and, for any $\lambda\in\Lambda$, let C_λ denote the succession distribution at time λ on the set $U=\{0,1,\ldots,31\}$ consisting of all possible sentence-endings under consideration. Denote $C=(C_\lambda,\lambda\in\Lambda)$ and let $\mathcal{C}$ be a chosen class of such "evolutionary" families of distributions. It is obvious that a choice of $\mathcal{C}$ is practically equivalent to a choice of the model for the chronology of Plato's works. We show in Sec.2 that this is also true in general in seriation and multidimensional scaling provided that the sets U and Λ are suitably specified and interpreted.

The intuitive idea concerning any C in $\mathcal{C}$ is usually the following one: for any λ_1,λ_2 in Λ, the more "distant" the points λ_1 and λ_2 are the more "different" the distributions C_{λ_1} and C_{λ_2} will be. Let d be some chosen distance for pairs of λ's and let Φ be some chosen real-valued measure of discrepancy between pairs of distributions. Then the relations between d and Φ can be used to characterize C_s' in $\mathcal{C}$. To fulfil the intuitions, the points in the set

$H=\{(d_{\lambda_1,\lambda_2},\Phi_{\lambda_1,\lambda_2});\lambda_1,\lambda_2\in\Lambda\}$, where $\Phi_{\lambda_1,\lambda_2}:=\Phi(C_{\lambda_1},C_{\lambda_2})$ and $d_{\lambda_1,\lambda_2}=d(\lambda_1,\lambda_2)$, should be concentrated along the graph of a non-decreasing relation. It is natural to measure the concentration in H as positive dependence between random variables $d_{\lambda',\lambda''}$ and $\Phi_{\lambda',\lambda''}$ where λ' and λ'' are independent random variables uniformly distributed on Λ. The restrictions are that Λ admits an uniform distribution and that d and Φ are measurable; that will be assumed in the sequel.

Let K be a specified class of bivariate distributions with a "sufficiently strong" positive dependence of the first component on the second one. We shall say that for any d, Φ and K a family $C=(C_\lambda,\lambda\in\Lambda)$ is of the type (d,Φ,K) if the distribution of $(d_{\lambda',\lambda''},\Phi_{\lambda',\lambda''})$ belongs to K. Then the set $\mathcal{C}$ can be chosen as a set of families C of the type (Φ,d,K).

Let us consider more detailly the case when $\Lambda=(0,1)$ and $U=\{0,1,\dots,r\}$. This includes the Plato problem with the time interval suitably normalized and r=31. Let $c_{i\lambda}=C_\lambda(\{i\}),\lambda\in\Lambda$, $i=0,\dots,r$. Two discrepancies will be discussed, namely

(1) $$\Phi^{(1)}_{\lambda_1,\lambda_2}=\sum_{i=0}^{r}(c_{i\lambda_1}-c_{i\lambda_2})\ln(c_{i\lambda_1}/c_{i\lambda_2})$$

introduced by Kullback and Leibler and

(2) $$\Phi^{(2)}_{\lambda_1,\lambda_2}=1-\sum_{i=0}^{r}\min(c_{i\lambda_1},c_{i\lambda_2})$$

used by D.G.Kendall(1971) and L.Boneva(1971). The distance d is standard: $d_{\lambda_1,\lambda_2}=|\lambda_1-\lambda_2|$.

It is easy to notice that for any C such that

(3) $$c_{i\lambda}=a_i\lambda+b_i,\quad i=0,\dots,r,\quad \lambda\in(0,1),\quad a_i\neq 0$$

$\Phi^{(2)}_{\lambda',\lambda''}$ is linearly dependent on $d_{\lambda',\lambda''}$. Indeed, by (2) for any $\lambda_1,\lambda_2\in(0,1)$ and any C there exists a non-empty subset $I(C,\lambda_1,\lambda_2)$ of $\{0,\dots,r-1\}$ such that $\Phi^{(2)}_{\lambda_1,\lambda_2}=\sum_{i\in I(C,\lambda_1,\lambda_2)}|c_{i\lambda_1}-c_{i\lambda_2}|$. If C fulfils (3) then $I(C,\lambda_1,\lambda_2)$ is the same, say $I(C)$, for any (λ_1,λ_2) and hence $\Phi^{(2)}_{\lambda',\lambda''}=\sum_{i\in I(C)}|a_i|\,d_{\lambda',\lambda''}$.

We discuss below two families $C^{(1)}$ and $C^{(2)}$ related with the Plato problem, each of them depending on the distributions C_0 and C_1 corresponding to the extreme points $\lambda=0$ and $\lambda=1$. In the Plato problem as considered by Cox and Brandwood (1959) C_0 and C_1 are the distributions of endings when respectively Republic and Laws were written, since the works subject to dating were known to belong to this period of time. An approximation of C_0 and C_1 given by Cox and Brandwood is used in the numerical examples below. The family $C^{(1)}$ which was considered by Cox and Brandwood is defined by

$$c_{i\lambda}^{(1)} = (c_{io})^{1-\lambda}(c_{i1})^{\lambda} \Big/ \sum_{j=0}^{r} (c_{jo})^{1-\lambda}(c_{j1})^{\lambda}. \tag{4}$$

The family $C^{(2)}$ is defined analogously with λ in the right-hand side of (4) replaced by λ^5 to show the effect of a monotone change of the speed of time-flow.

Figure 1 presents sets H corresponding to families $C^{(1)}$ and $C^{(2)}$ arranged in pairs with discrepancies $\Phi^{(1)}$ and $\Phi^{(2)}$. In the case of $C^{(1)}$ there is practically a functional relationship between $d_{\lambda',\lambda''}$ and $\Phi^{(i)}_{\lambda',\lambda''}$ which is close to a linear one (specially for $\Phi^{(2)}$). Indeed, the values of the correlation coefficient ϱ are 0.95 and 0.99, respectively. In the case of $C^{(2)}$ the dependence is considerably weaker (ϱ=0.61 and 0.68).

However, the correlation coefficient is not in general a proper measure of positive dependence and it is not desirable to choose the class K as that consisting of distributions with correlation coefficients sufficiently large. This is due to the fact that large values of the coefficient can be achieved by good correspondence of extremely large values of d and Φ while small and medium values are only vaguely related. For instance, the value of the correlation coefficient in the set H on fig.3 consisting of then points, with one outlier being solely responsible for the positive relationship, is equal to 0,906. This drawback cannot be sufficiently corrected by the choice of a more robust real-valued measure of concentration. To show the scheme of dependence thoroughly enough, a function-valued measure is needed in order to evaluate the tendency of the values of one component larger than its p-th quantile to coappear with large values of another component, for every $p\in(0,1)$. For the set H_0 from fig.3

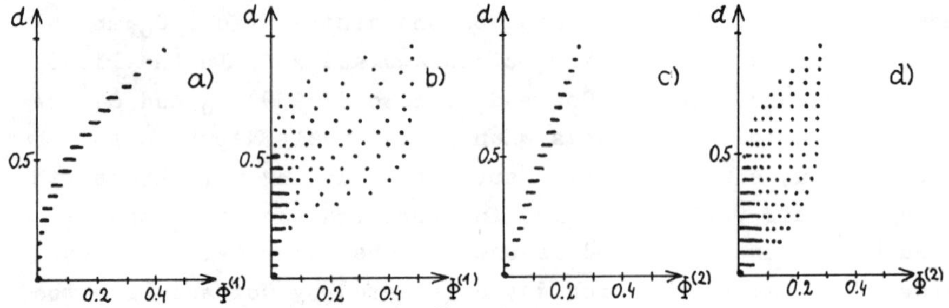

Fig.1

Sets H for a) $C^{(1)}$ and $\Phi^{(1)}$, b) $C^{(2)}$ and $\Phi^{(1)}$, c) $C^{(1)}$ and $\Phi^{(2)}$ d) $C^{(2)}$ and $\Phi^{(2)}$.

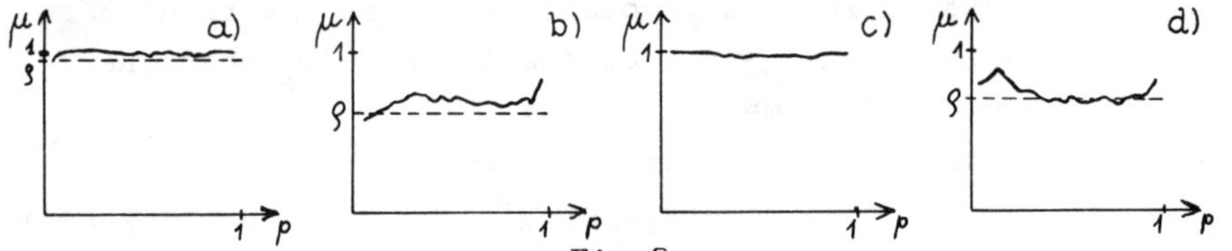

Fig.2

Monotone depend. curves μ and corr.coeff. ϱ of sets H from fig.1

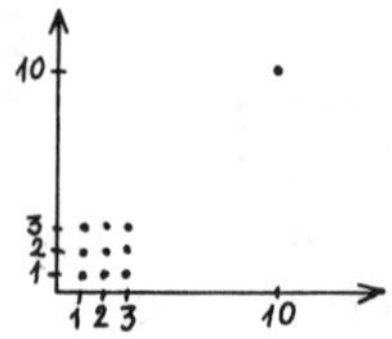

Fig.3

Set H_0: 10 points with 1 outlier.

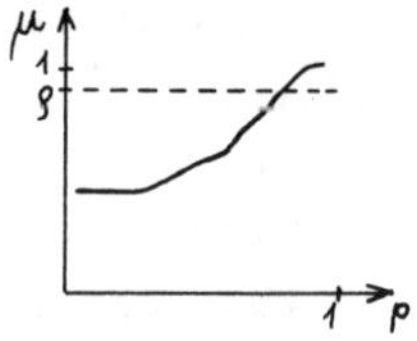

Fig.4

Monotone dependence curve for set H_0 from fig.3.

a measure of this kind is presented on fig.4. One can see that the intensity of correspondence sharply increases for large p's which provides the required information about the set H_0. The so called monotone dependence curve appearing on fig.4 is the graph of the monotone dependence function introduced in Kowalczyk and Pleszczyńska(1977) and Kowalczyk(1977) in order to measure the positive dependence of bivariate distributions. The computer program for the function is given in Ćwik(1978).

Fig.2 presents the monotone dependence curves for sets H given on fig.1. They inform us that in each of the investigated cases the positive relationship between distances and discrepancies is almost "uniform" in p. It is very strong in the case of $C^{(1)}$ and weaker in the case of $C^{(2)}$ and it is approximately linear (especially for $\Phi^{(2)}$) since the monotone dependence functions are close to constant ones identically equal to the corresponding correlation coefficients. Then the curves seem to be a good descriptive statistic summarizing the information about positive dependence in an impressive graphical form. Consequently, it seems that the class K mentioned before could be satisfactorily fixed as consisting of distributions with monotone dependence functions suitably chosen.

2. Multidimensional scaling problems and measures of dependence

Rigorously treated, proper multidimensional scaling problems are realized to be special cases of prediction problems in which the "true" value of an unobservable random element X is estimated from the observed value of an observable random element Y. The model specifies a family $\mathcal{P}$ of joint distributions of X and Y which includes the "true" one. What distinguishes multidimensional scaling problems from other prediction problems is the special form of $\mathcal{P}$.

Usually, one has in mind n objects and the corresponding vectors of values of k unobservable and m observable features so that $(X,Y)=((X_{ij},Y_{it});\ i=1,\dots,n;\ j=1,\dots,k;\ t=1,\dots,m)$. The random vectors $(X_i=(X_{i1},\dots,X_{ik}),\ Y_i=(Y_{i1},\dots,Y_{im}))$ for different objects $i=1,\dots,n$ are assumed i.i.d. Let Λ and Γ denote the sets of values of X_i and Y_i, respectively. The elements of Λ^n are called "configurations" (and the "true" configuration is searched). The marginal distributions of any X_i are one-point and any point λ_i in Λ is admitted. Then $\mathcal{P}$ is determined if one specifies families $(Q_\lambda,\lambda\in\Lambda)$ of conditional distributions Q_λ of Y_i when $X_i=\lambda$. Now, $(Q_\lambda;\lambda\in\Lambda)$ should be an "evolutionary" family of some kind and turning back to Sec.1 one can put $U=\Gamma$ and $C_\lambda=Q_\lambda$; if however for any i $Y_{i1},\dots,Y_{im}$ are assumed i.i.d. with values from some set say Γ_0 then it is more convenient to put

$U=\Gamma_0$ and $C^m_\lambda=Q_\lambda$. In any case, $\mathcal{P}$ is determined by a class $\mathcal{C}$ of evolutionary families $(C_\lambda,\lambda\in\Lambda)$, which can be introduced as in Sec.1 or in a related way.

One of the alternative but closely related ways is as follows. Instead of Φ,d and K one can specify δ,d and K, where the "dissimilarity" δ is a function from Γ^2 onto R^+ playing the role of a counterpart of the distance $d:\Lambda^2\rightarrow R^+$. To formalize the duality of δ and d, one can introduce four random variables $(\lambda',\lambda'',\eta',\eta'')$ such that λ' and λ'' are (as before) independent and uniformly distributed on Λ while the conditional distribution of η' when $\lambda'=\lambda$ and of η'' when $\lambda''=\lambda$ is equal to Q_λ(i.e. is C_λ or C^m_λ). The family $C=(C_\lambda;\lambda\in\Lambda)$ is said to be of the type (δ,d,K) if the distribution of $(d_{\lambda',\lambda''},\delta_{\eta',\eta''})$ belongs to K, i.e. distances are sufficiently strongly positively dependent on dissimilarities. Obviously, the same remarks about the choice of K as those in Sec.1 are applicable here.

In Kruskal's solution of multidimensional scaling problems the sets $W_{\lambda_1,\dots,\lambda_n}=\{(d(\lambda_u,\lambda_v),\ \delta(y_u,y_v));\ u,v=1,\dots,n;\ u<v\}$ are considered for any configuration $(\lambda_1,\dots,\lambda_n)\in\Lambda^n$ and any vector of observations $(y_1,\dots,y_n)\in\Gamma^n$. The points in W (as those in H) should concentrate along the graph of a non-decreasing relation and similar troubles arise with suitable measuring of the concentration. Kruskal's choice of such a measure (or more precisely of a measure of the lack of concentration) was the real-valued stress, which cannot provide the information about the shape of W according to the previous remarks. The value of the stress for the set H_0 from fig.3 would be very small indicating a strong positive relationship between distances and dissimilarities in the same way as the correlation coefficient does. It seems advisable to calculate monotonic dependence curves at least for sets W corresponding to configurations selected as the solution, to possess a better recognition of the scheme of dependence between distances and dissimilarities. This is in accordance with D.G.Kendall's remark (1971) that the lack of "uniformity" of dependence of d's and δ's is the reason of the horse-shoe shaped solutions in the case of models with linear realtionship of X_i on Y_i. It seems that the shape of the

monotone dependence curve of $d_{\lambda',\lambda''}$ on $\delta_{\eta',\eta''}$ determines the shape of the solutions of MDSCAL.

The same remarks apply also to improper multidimensional scaling problems, in which no "true" configurations exist and the respective algorithms are treated as descriptive statistics providing a "simpler numerical representation" of observable data.

3. Conclusion

The goals of the present paper are

(i) to contribute in presenting proper multidimensional scaling as rigorously stated statistical problem with suitably chosen family of distributions,

(ii) to illustrate the importance of a proper choice of Φ or δ,

(iii) to stress the importance of the choice of parameters that are measuring positive dependence of bivariate distributions and to suggest some possibilities connected with the monotone dependence curves.

References

Boneva L.I., A new approach to a problem of chronogical seriation associated with the works of Plato. Mathematics in the Archaeological and Historical Sciences, 173-85 (eds Hodson F.R., Kendall D.G., Tautu P.). Edinburgh 1971

Cox D.R., Brandwood L., On a discriminatory problem connected with the works of Plato. J.Roy. Stat. Soc. (Ser.B),21,195-200

Cwik J., Algorithm of the monotone dependence function. Submitted to Information Processing Letters

Kendall D.G., Seriation from abundance matrices. Mathematics in the Archaeological and Historical Sciences, 215-52 (eds Hodson F.R., Kendall D.G., Tautu P.). Edinburgh 1971

Kowalczyk T., General definition and sample counterparts of monotonic dependence functions in the bivariate case. Math. Operationsforsch. Statist. (Ser. Statistics)8,351-369,1977

Kowalczyk T., Pleszczyńska E., Monotonic dependence functions of bivariate distributions. Ann. Statist. 5, 1221-27, 1977

Exploratory Selection of Groups of Variables Using Marginal Associations

H.v. Rechenberg and **H. Skuginna**, Giessen

0. SUMMARY

With large sets of data containing many qualitative variables the simultaneous treatment of the characteristics is the only possibility for a sufficiently small and proper selection of variables. The purpose of this examination was to formalize such a selection of variables according to specific criteria. The underlying association structure among all possible pairs of variables of the data set is represented by an association matrix.
After choosing an assignment instruction for associations among variables a non-directional graph is generated. It is a model of the pairwise interaction structure of all variables of the data set. The structure of the graph is analysed by graph theory methods.
Results are discussed by example of a clinical study.

Keywords: Exploratory techniques, automatic classification, graphtheory methods.

1. INTRODUCTION

In the analysis of clinical and epidemiological studies association structure analysis has a great importance, for example, in search of common background factors, syndroms, and types (KRAUTH and LIENERT (1973)). Usually data sets consist of many more qualitative single variables that can be analysed simultaneously with the usual contingency analysis programs. E.g. BMDP 3F works simultaneously up to 7 variables at most. Therefore it is obvious that you should check a data set tentatively in the beginning for special aspects of the underlying association structure.
While using a rough method you can simultaneously work up a big quantitiy of variables. ROMMEL et al. (1976), for instance, have undertaken for 58 collected single variables a preliminary examination (1653 different) χ^2-tests of depen-

dence for each pair of variables to decide on different α-levels if an association exists or not.
Because several tests are made on the same data set, a statement on the significance of the represented assignment structure is not possible. Furthermore marginal associations among pairs of variables represent only one aspect of the underlying association structure for the influence of associations of higher order is not indicated by this.
Therefore, it seems wise, independent of detailed analysis, to examine the rough structure of all variables of one data set altogether. Such a rough structure analysis which works with the data set as a whole is the aim of this paper whereby the crucial point lies in qualitative variables.

2. REPRESENTATION OF THE ASSOCIATION STRUCTURE TO A GRAPH

In this examination we restrict ourselves exclusively to representation of the marginal association structure that is given by relations among pairs of variables. Therefore, it has to be pointed out that in this case no information can be gained about the influence of associations of higher order although with qualitative variables such influences do exist, as for instance, KRAUTH and LIENERT (1973) have discussed.
Under this restriction we gain a computer model of the association structure in the following steps.

1. We proceed from the assumption that in general the data existing of qualitative variables is coded in the following form: The levels of each variable are, if necessary, numbered in an arbitrarily determined increasing sequence. Each individual case is represented by the number of observed levels.

2. For each pair of variables is constructed one contingency table. With n variables there exist n(n-1)/2 different tables. We construct all contingency tables simultaneously by reading in the data matrix once, case by case, from the peripheral data storage.
   The contingency tables are held in core. With the IBM 370/158 it is possible to work in the 192 K-region with 100 different variables or 50 variables each with 4 levels.

3. For each contingency table, for the i-th and j-th variable one value χ^2_{ij} (i<j) is calculated under the usual null hypothesis, and the cells in

one level are occupied corresponding to a binomial or multinomial distribution. After this the contingency tables are not used any more for we only go on working with χ^2-dependent association measures. Only the total frequencies of each table are saved, because the missing values are included in the single observation.

4. After the definition of an assignment function the association structure is represented on a graph G(V,E) (LAUE (1971)). The estimation instruction for the connection of two variables v_i, v_j has the form

$$C(v_i,v_j) = \begin{cases} 1 & \text{if } c(\chi^2_{ij}) \geq c\{\chi^2(f;\alpha)\} \\ 0 & \text{if } c(\chi^2_{ij}) < c\{\chi^2(f;\alpha)\} . \end{cases}$$

c is a χ^2-dependent non-directional association measure for multi-compartment tables; a review is given in LIENERT (1973) for instance. $\chi^2(f;\alpha)$ is the upper limit for the confidence interval of the χ^2-dependence test with f degrees of freedom and the significance level α. Instead of $c\{\chi^2(f;\alpha)\}$ you can choose arbitrarily a bound for the association measure. If individual relations are different, in order to assess you can introduce an "assignment-matrix" $\{\alpha_{ij}\}$ instead of using α.
We define the graph G(V,E) in the following way: The variables are identified with the node set $\{V:v_i, i=1,...,n\}$. The edge set E we state in the conventional manner

$$C(v_i,v_j) = \begin{cases} 1 \rightarrow e_{ij} \in E \\ 0 \rightarrow e_{ij} \notin E . \end{cases}$$

We store the graph in the form of its adjacent matrix. It is symmetric since $C(v_i,v_j) = C(v_j,v_i)$. Once the graph representing the structure model is set then its structure can be analysed in a purely formal way without bothering with the relations of the underlying data.

3. ANALYSIS OF THE STRUCTURE OF THE GRAPH

We are interested in a decomposition of the graph into more or less homogeneous structural elements; in this case we look for the decomposition in combined components or the solution of the path problem. The transitive closure of the graph represents the desired solution. MEHLHORN (1977) gives the following definition:

The cells of the 253 different four-compartment tables were occupied sufficiently so that the assumption of the asymptotic χ^2-dependence test is satisfied (LIENERT (1973)). Figures 1a-c show three adjacent matrices which were constructed by application of different estimation instructions out of the $\{\chi_{ij}^2\}$-matrix. Figures 2a-c show the corresponding matrices H* after variable groups have been rearranged. In the figures, for each case the highest edge number is given which was obtained by reaching out the farthest point on the shortest path. It is $H^* = H^{(K)} = H^{(K+1)} = \ldots = H^{(n)}$.

In spite of different assignment instructions, one recognizes analog characteristic complexes of variables by comparison of the figures 2a-c. On the other hand, with the possibilities of selection fitting assignment instructions lies a wide latitude that permits the efficient utilization of preknowledge in relation to the proof of special hypotheses concerning the content of special data.

REFERENCES

DÜRRE, K., LINDENTHAL, U., THOMA, H.: Interaktive Anwendung graphentheoretischer Methoden. In: Applied Computer Science 4: Graphen, Algorithmen, Datenstrukturen (Ed. Noltemeier, H.), München 1976 (Hanser-Verlag) pp 233-250.

KNÖDEL, W.: Graphentheoretische Methoden und ihre Anwendungen. Heidelberg 1969 (Springer Verlag), pp 26-59.

KRAUTH, J., LIENERT, G.A.: Die Konfigurationsfrequenzanalyse und ihre Anwendung in Psychologie und Medizin. Freiburg, München 1973 (K. Alber-Verlag).

LAUE, R.: Elemente der Graphentheorie und ihre Anwendungen in den biologischen Wissenschaften. Braunschweig 1971 (Vieweg-Verlag), pp 23-73.

LIENERT, G.A.: Verteilungsfreie Methoden in der Biostatistik, Bd. I. Meisenheim 1973 (2) (A. Hain-Verlag), pp 557-579.

MEHLHORN, K.: Effiziente Algorithmen. Stuttgart 1977 (Teubner-Verlag), pp 142-186.

ROMMEL, K., STEINHARDT, B., ÜBERLAG, K.: Modell-Vorsorgeuntersuchung in zwei Betrieben. III. Zusammenhänge zwischen Meßwerten und Antworten im Fragebogen. Klin. Wochenschrift 54, pp 1187-1192, 1976.

Fig. 1a-c: Adjacentmatrices of graphs, representing some models of association structure

Fig. 2a-c: Transitive closure in matrix representation, regarding to graphs on the left. Rows resp. columns have been interchanged

a. χ^2-Tests: α = 0.01, f = 1, 5 edges

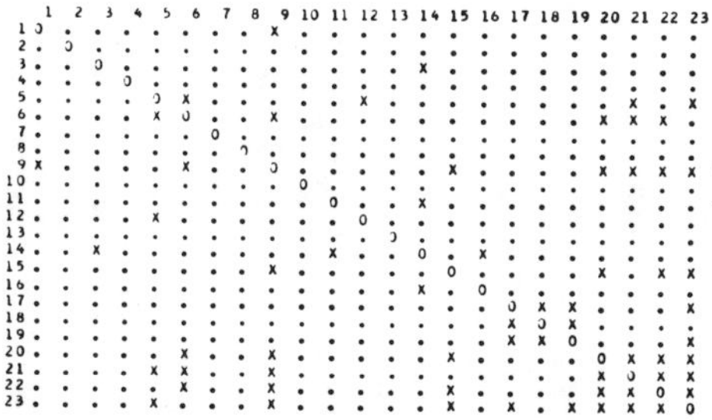

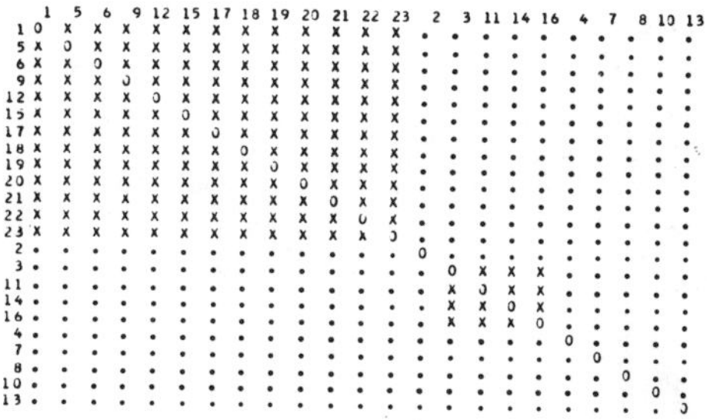

b. Cramers c.: c_α = 0.30, 2 edges

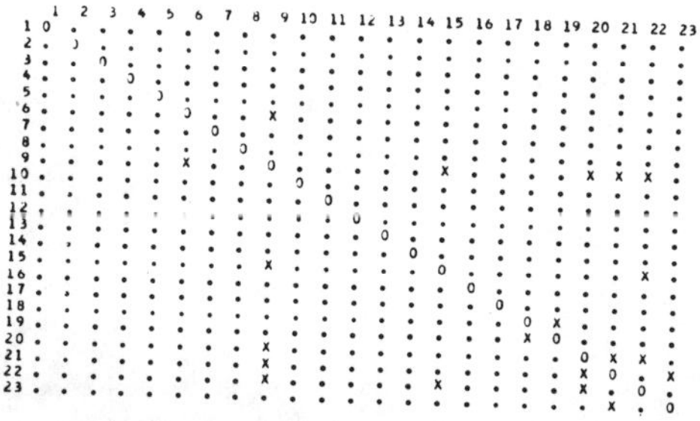

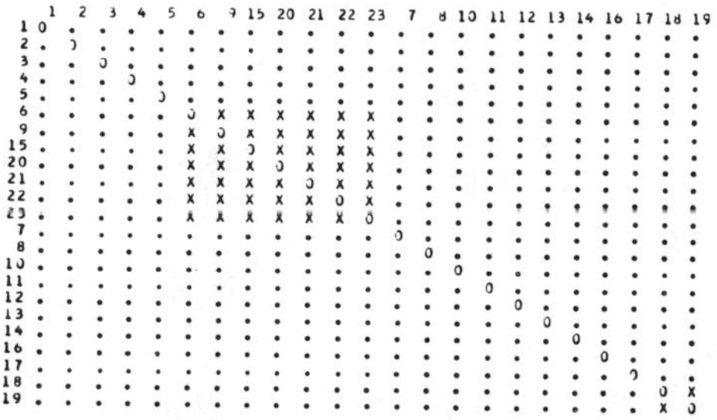

c. Pearsons c.: c_α = 0.30, 4 edges

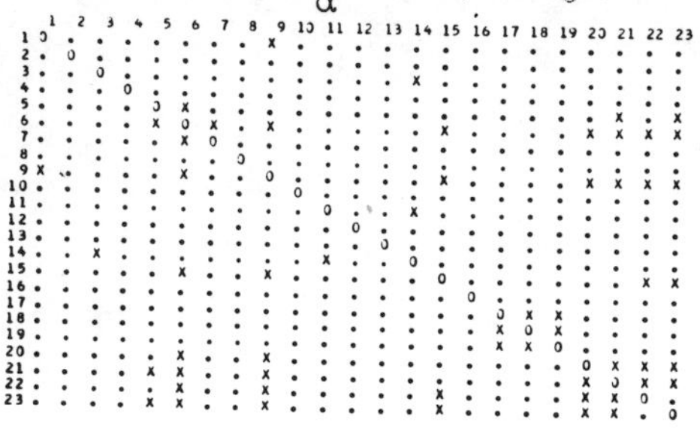

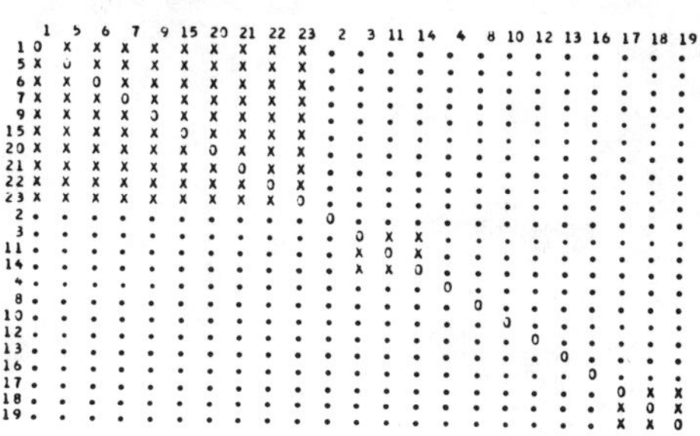

<u>Theorem 2.3</u> The rank of submatrix $T_k(c_k \times r_k)$ is $r_k - 1$, i.e.

$$\text{rank}\,[\,T_k(c_k \times r_k)\,] = r_k - 1 \,. \tag{2.8}$$

<u>Proof</u> Since the categories $t_{(k)1}, \cdots, t_{(k)r_k}$ are connected with each other, the r_k-1 rows $[1, -1, 0, \cdots, 0]$, $[1, 0, -1, 0, \cdots, 0]$, $\cdots$, $[1, 0, \cdots, 0, -1]$ are linearly dependent to the rows of T_k.
Hence

$$\text{rank}\,(T_k) \geq r_k - 1 \,. \tag{2.9}$$

On the other hand the number of linearly independent contrasts of r_k variables is at most r_k-1, i.e.

$$\text{rank}\,(T_k) \leq r_k - 1 \,. \tag{2.10}$$

From (2.9) and (2.10) we obtain (2.8) . Q.E.D.

<u>Corollary.</u> The rank of the transformation matrix $T(c \times r)$, which is composed of m submatrix $T_1, T_2, \cdots, T_m$, is $r-m$, i.e.

$$\text{rank}\,[\,T(c \times r)\,] = r - m \,. \tag{2.11}$$

Letting $M(T_k)$ be the linear manifold spanned by the row vectors of T_k, the r_k-1 rows in the proof of Theorem 2.1 construct a basis of $M(T_k)$. Then, if we add a row which corresponds to a transformation

$$z_{(0)k} = t_{(k)j}\,, \quad \text{for any } j, \tag{2.12}$$

we can obtain a transformation submatrix with rank r_k. For the sake of simplicity we may choose $j=1$ in (2.12) without loss of generality. Now we obtain

<u>Theorem 2.4</u> We can construct a transformation matrix $T[(c+m) \times r]$ of rank r, by augmenting m rows through (2.12) corresponding to the subset $\mathcal{J}_1, \mathcal{J}_2, \cdots, \mathcal{J}_m$. The augmented transformation matrix $T[(c+m) \times r]$ is expressed as

$$T[(c+m) \times r] = \begin{array}{c} \\ c_1 \\ c_2 \\ \vdots \\ c_m \\ m \end{array} \begin{array}{|c|c|c|c|} \multicolumn{1}{c}{r_1} & \multicolumn{1}{c}{r_2} & \multicolumn{1}{c}{\cdots} & \multicolumn{1}{c}{r_m} \\ \hline T_1 & 0 & \cdots & 0 \\ \hline 0 & T_2 & \cdots & 0 \\ \hline \vdots & \vdots & \ddots & \vdots \\ \hline 0 & 0 & \cdots & T_m \\ \hline \multicolumn{4}{|c|}{T_0} \\ \hline \end{array} \tag{2.13}$$

where

$$T_0 = [n^0_{ij}],$$

$$n^0_{ij} = \begin{cases} 1 & \text{for } t_j \in \mathcal{J}_0\,, \\ 0 & \text{otherwise,} \end{cases}$$

and $\mathcal{J}_0$ is a set of elements selected for (2.12).

From Theorem 2.4, the transformation is expressed as

$$z[(c+m) \times 1] = T[(c+m) \times r]\,t(r \times 1), \tag{2.14}$$

where

$$z[(c+m) \times 1] = [z'_{(1)}, z'_{(2)}, \cdots, z'_{(m)}, z'_{(0)}]',$$
$$t(r \times 1) = [t'_{(1)}, t'_{(2)}, \cdots, t'_{(m)}]',$$
$$t_{(k)} = [t_{(k)1}, t_{(k)2}, \cdots, t_{(k)r_k}]',$$
$$z_{(k)} = [z_{(k)1}, z_{(k)2}, \cdots, z_{(k)c_k}]', \quad k=1, 2, \ldots, m.$$
$$z_{(0)} = [z_{(0)1}, z_{(0)2}, \cdots, z_{(0)m}]'.$$

According to the problem to maximize Q, the location of scores may be arbitrarily determined. Therefore, withou loss of generality, we may specify a score $t_{(m)1}$ zero. Then the criterion is expressed as

$$Q = \tilde{\mathbf{t}}' \tilde{A} \tilde{\mathbf{t}} / \tilde{\mathbf{t}}' \tilde{B} \tilde{\mathbf{t}} , \qquad (2.15)$$

where $\tilde{A}$, $\tilde{B}$ and $\tilde{t}$ indicate the matrices made from A, B and t by eliminating a row and/or column corresponding to the specified score. Thus letting

$$t_{(m)1} = 0, \qquad (2.16)$$

we obtain the transformation

$$\tilde{\mathbf{z}}[(c+m-1)\times 1] = \tilde{T}[(c+m-1)\times(r-1)]\tilde{\mathbf{t}}[(r-1)\times 1], \qquad (2.17)$$

where the rank of $\tilde{T}$ is r-1 and the meaning of the symbol (~) is same as in the case of $\tilde{A}$, $\tilde{B}$ and $\tilde{t}$.

Since the transformation matrix $\tilde{T}$ is of full rank, it has a left inverse matrix $(\tilde{T}' \tilde{T})^{-1}\tilde{T}'$. From (2.17), we obtain

$$\mathbf{t} = (\tilde{T}' \tilde{T})^{-1} \tilde{T}' \tilde{\mathbf{z}}. \qquad (2.18)$$

Hence,

Theorem 2.5 The problem of optimal scaling under arbitrary order restrictions can be always transformed to the following form of optimization.

$$Q(z) = \tilde{z}' C \tilde{z} / \tilde{z}' D \tilde{z} \rightarrow \max \qquad (2.19)$$

subject to

(i) $z_{(k)} = [z_{(k)1}, z_{(k)2}, \cdots , z_{(k)c_k}]' \geq 0, \quad k=1, 2,\ldots, m,$ (2.20)

(ii) $a'_{(kj)}z_{(k)} = 0, \quad j=1, 2,\ldots, c_k-r_k+1, \quad k=1, 2,\ldots, m,$ (2.21)

where

$$C = \tilde{T}(\tilde{T}' \tilde{T})^{-1} \tilde{A}(\tilde{T}' \tilde{T})^{-1} \tilde{T}' , \qquad (2.22)$$

$$D = \tilde{T}(\tilde{T}' \tilde{T})^{-1} \tilde{B}(\tilde{T}' \tilde{T})^{-1} \tilde{T}' \qquad (2.23)$$

and where $a_{(kj)}$ is coefficient vector with 0's and ±1's for $z_{(k)}$ in the equality restrictions corresponding to linear dependecies among $[z_{(k)1}, z_{(k)2}, \cdots , z_{(k)c_k}]$, k=1, 2,..., m. The number of equality restrictions is given as the difference between the number of transformed variables $\{z_{(k)j}\}$ and the number of linearly independent variables. The equality restrictions are obtained through the procedure based on graph theory.

By the way, both of the cases discussed by Bradley, Katti and Coons[1] and by Nishisato and Arri[5] are special cases with categories mutually connected and with no equality restriction.

3. Application of a nonlinear programming technique to the optimization problem

3.1 Wolfe's reduced gradient method

As shown above the problem of optimal scaling under generalized order restrictions reduces finally to (2.19) ∿ (2.21), i.e. the problem of maximizing a nonlinear objective function under linear equality restrictions. For such a problem available is the Wolfe's reduced gradient method[9] as a nonlinear programming technique for solving efficiently the following type of problem.

$$M(x) \rightarrow \min., \quad \text{subject to } A\,x = b \text{ and } \mathbf{x} \geq 0. \qquad (3.1)$$

3.2 Numerical investigation

Let us apply the generalized method to the data for a five-treatment experiment with a five-point scoring scale, which is taken from the study of Bradley, Katti and Coons[1] (p. 366, example 3). Suppose there exist order restriction $t_1 \geq \{t_2, t_3\} \geq t_4 \geq t_5$, where $a \gtrless \{b,c\}$ denotes $a \gtrless b$ and $a \gtrless c$. These restrictions are expressed by a graph in Fig. 3.1. Since this is a connected graph, we cannot classify into smaller subsets any more, i.e. m=1 by the notation of preceding section.

initial approximations are not always sufficiently near the optimal values. Thus required are to choose mesh points and initial values carefully and to solve a large scale linear programming problem.

Because of these difficulties of separable programming we applied the wolfe's reduced gradient method. It is known as a very efficient algorithm to solve a special type of nonlinear programming problem with linear equality constraints for non-negative variables. Thus it may be said that the method is just suitable for our problem (2.19) $\sim$ (2.21). In fact the procedure converges rapidly to the optimal values, starting from arbitrary chosen initial values $z_1 = z_2 = \cdots = 1.0$

References

[1] Bradley, R.A., Katti, S.K. and Coons, I.J.: Optimal scaling for ordered categories, Psychometrika 27 (1962), 355-374.

[2] Busacker, R.G. and Saaty, T.L.: Finite Graphs and Networks: An introduction and applications, McGraw-Hill (1965).

[3] Fisher, R.A.: Statistical Methods for Research Workers, 13th ed. Oliver & Boyd (1958).

[4] Hayashi, C.: On the prediction of phenomena from qualitative data and the quantification of qualitative data from the mathematico-statistical point of view, Ann. Inst. Statist. Math. Vol. 3, No. 2 (1952).

[5] Nishisato, S. and Arri, P.S.: Nonlinear programming approach to optimal scaling of partially ordered categories, Psychometrika 40 (1975), 525-548.

[6] Tanaka, Y.: On quantification theory with ordered categorical outside variable, Standardization and Quality Control 25 (1972), 31-9, Japanese Standards Association (In Japanese).

[7] Tanaka, Y. and Asano, Ch.: Statistical Inference about effects of factors based on a method of optimal scaling, paper presented at the 4th meeting of Japanese Behaviometric Society (1976).

[8] Tanaka, Y.: Some generalized methods of optimal scaling and their asymptotic theories, (I) The case of single response-multiple factors, (II) The case of multiple response-multiple factors, to appear.

[9] Wolfe, P.: Methods of nonlinear programming, in R.L. Graves and P. Wolfe (eds.), Resent Advances in Mathematical Programming, McGrow-Hill (1963).

Two-Way-Table Analysis by Biplot-Methods (According to K.R. Gabriel [+]) Using a Three-Dimensional Display

E. Weber and J. Berger, Heidelberg

S u m m a r y

The biplot technique is a very useful graphical method to display the relationships between row and column characteristics in two-way tables. This method is applicable as long as the rank-2 approximation explains a large part (e.g. 95 %) of the whole variability. However, since in large tables only a rank-3 approximation will yield such a high degree of explanation, a three-dimensional biplot technique has been introduced, using a 3d-screen as a matter of presentation.

Keywords: Graphical Methods, Three-Dimensional Display, Biplot Techniques, Singular Value Decomposition (SVD).

Introduction

The coordinates for a 3d-display of a 2-way table Y with n rows and m columns can be computed from the Singular Value Decomposition (SVD) $Y_{n\times m} = P_{n\times r}\,\Lambda_{r\times r}\,Q'_{r\times m}$; r = rank of Y. Q and Λ can be computed from the Eigenvalue problem $(Y'Y-\lambda_i I)q_i = 0$.
Let us assume

$$\Lambda^2 = \begin{bmatrix} \lambda_1 & & 0 \\ & \ddots & \\ 0 & & \lambda_r \end{bmatrix} \quad \text{with } \lambda_1 \geq \lambda_2 \geq \ldots \geq \lambda_r > 0 \text{ and } P = YQ\Lambda^{-1}.$$

Then the coordinates for a three-dimensional biplot can be computed from $P_{n\times 3}\,\Lambda_{3\times 3}\,Q'_{3\times m}$. The coordinates of the vectors which represent the n rows (=individuals) of Y are the n rows of $P_{n\times 3}$ and the coordinates of the vectors which represent the m columns (=variables) of Y are the m rows of $Q_{m\times 3}\,\Lambda_{3\times 3}$.
Considering the degrees of freedom

$$\sqrt{(n-1)}\; P_{n\times 3} = G = (\underline{g}_1, \underline{g}_2, \ldots, \underline{g}_i, \ldots, \underline{g}_n)' \text{ and}$$

$$\sqrt{1/(n-1)}\; Q_{m\times 3}\,\Lambda_{3\times 3} = H = (\underline{h}_1, \underline{h}_2, \ldots, \underline{h}_j, \ldots, \underline{h}_m)'$$

one can spot the following approximations in the biplot:

+ We wish to express our gratitude to Prof. Dr. K.R. Gabriel, Rochester, N.Y. for his initiative and helpful comments.

Because this relative complex data matrix - 73 vectors for the rows and 18 vectors for the columns - is difficult to survey, (see Fig. 2) all vector vertices were projected on a globe (in the following called "data globe"). The disadvantage of this projection is that the lengths of the vectors are made equal, but the approximations regarding the angles between the vectors remain unchanged which alone is of importance for the following questions.

2.2. Are there correlations between the 18 laboratory determinations?

Fig. 3 (below) shows two sides of the data globe. The vertex positions are marked from A to R. Some correlation coefficients are listed below. The closer the neighbourhood of two capitals, the higher the correlation coefficients. Since these pictures are opposite hemispheres, it is also possible to recognize negative correlations because the 3d-screen allows to look at the front - and backside of the globe at the same time.

FIG. AND TABLE 3:
DISPLAY OF THE RANK-3 APPROXIMATIONS OF THE CORRELATIONS BETWEEN 18 LABORATORY DETERMINATIONS A,B,...,R ON THE DATA GLOBE

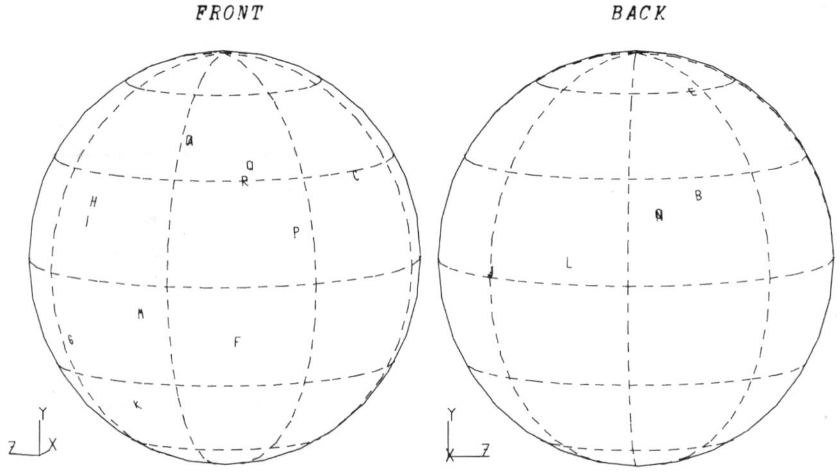

FULL-RANK CORRELATIONS

POS. CORRELATIONS		*NEG. CORRELATIONS*		*POS. CORRELATIONS*	
A-B:	.98	*M-L:*	-.98	*N-O:*	.99
Q-R:	.90	*F-B:*	-.92	*B-N:*	.92
H-I:	.68	*I-J:*	-.90	*B-O:*	.90
F-M:	.68	*M-N:*	-.89	*B-L:*	.51
K-D:	.14	*M-O:*	-.89	*B-J:*	.31
K-A:	.15	*B-K:*	-.49	*E-J:*	.21

2.3. Are there separate clusters on the data globe due to the groups GI and GII based on the 18 laboratory determinations?

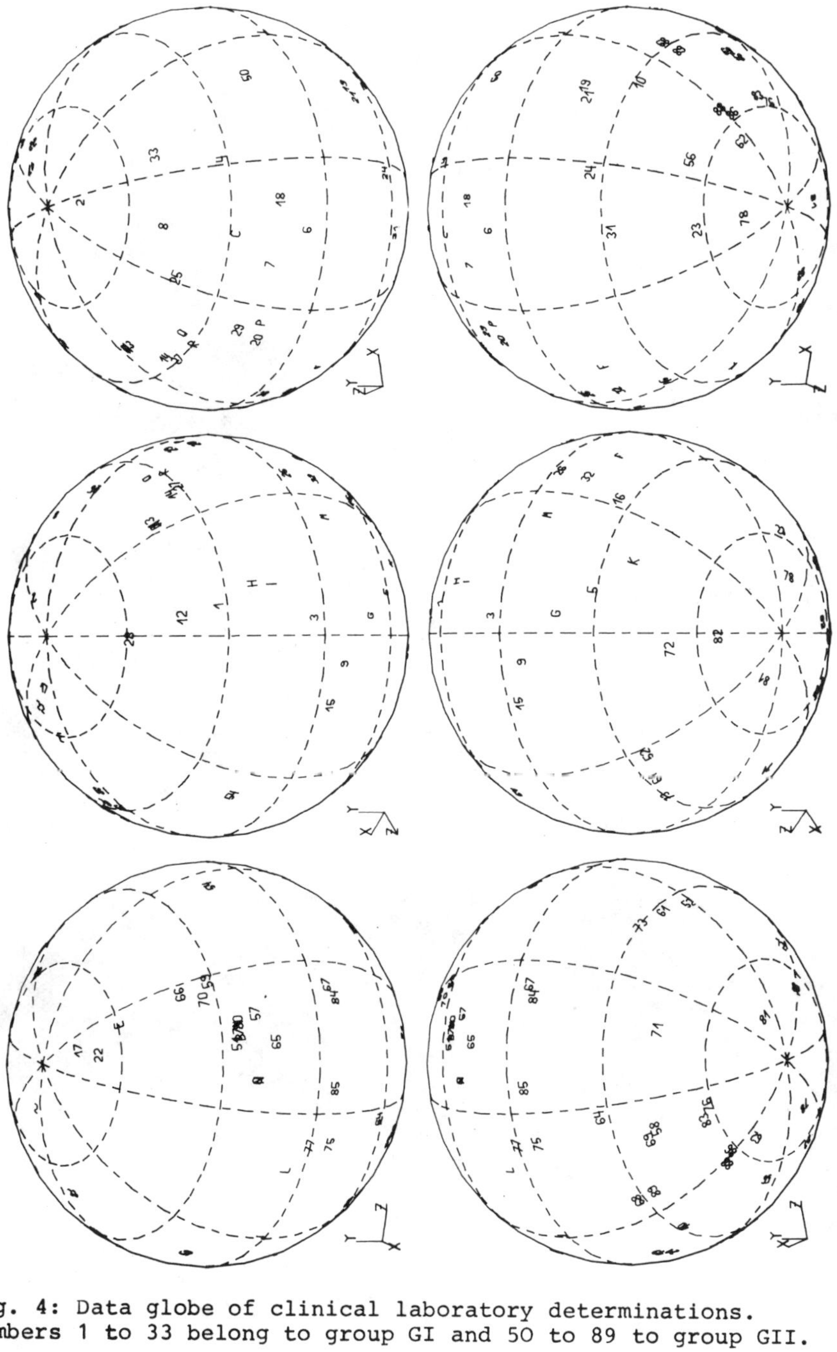

Fig. 4: Data globe of clinical laboratory determinations. Numbers 1 to 33 belong to group GI and 50 to 89 to group GII.

II. Example for absolute frequencies

Connections between criminal offence, age and sex of the offenders in the Federal Republic of Germany in 1974

In large contingency tables which due to their complexity, are difficult to analyse, connections between row and column characteristics may well be displayed by a biplot with standardized residuals of the absolute frequencies

$$y_{ij} := \left[y_{ij} - (y_{i.}\; y_{.j})/y_{..}\right] \Big/ \sqrt{y_{i.}\; y_{.j}/y_{..}} \;.$$

The figures below show the connection between several offences and 25-40 year old males. The group of males between 35-30 years of age (G) is associated with "aggravated assault", "resisting a public officer in the execution of his office", "murder" and "non-negligent manslaughter". With same associated is the age group I 30-40 years of age as well as with "assault", "disorderly" conduct", "offence at duty" and "offences against family and children". The offences "fraud" and "imbezzlement" are close to each other. The offence "white collar crime" is close to "fraud" (disloyality) and "offences against family and children".

On the opposite side of the globe we find near the "south pole" women of all ages and men over 60 years of age. The only offence in this region is "shoplifting" without aggravating circumstances.

Fig.5: Criminal Statistics 1974, Federal Republic of Germany, Age, Sex and Offences

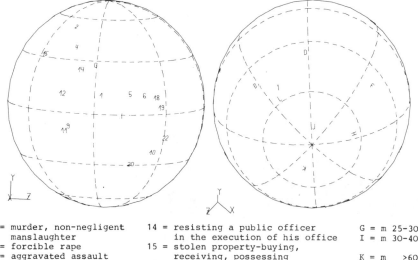

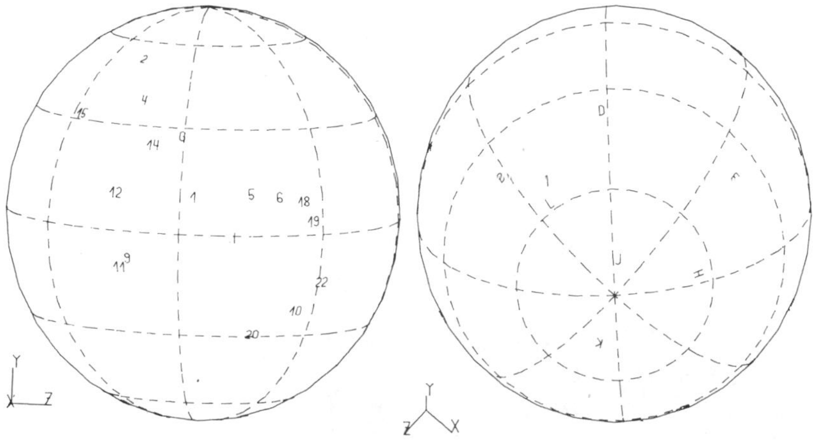

1 = murder, non-negligent manslaughter
2 = forcible rape
4 = aggravated assault
5 = assault
6 = disorderly conduct
9 = fraud
10 = fraud (disloyality)
11 = imbezzlement
12 = forgery

14 = resisting a public officer in the execution of his office
15 = stolen property-buying, receiving, possessing
18 = offence at duty
19 = offences against family and children
20 = insult
22 = white collar crime
7 = shoplifting

G = m 25-30
I = m 30-40
K = m >60
B = w <15
D = w 15-20
F = w 20-25
H = w 25-30
J = w 30-60
L = w >60

Due to restricted space, literature can be taken from:

Bradu, D. and Gabriel, K.R., The biplot as a diagnostic tool for models of two-way tables, Technometrics 20, 47-68, 1978

8. Simulation and Optimization

A Simple Algorithm for the Computer Generation of Random Samples from a Student's t or Symmetric Beta Distribution

D.J. Best, Sydney

Summary

An acceptance-rejection algorithm for the generation of random samples from a Student's t Distribution will be presented. Besides being considerably faster than previous algorithms the present algorithm has the advantage of being easily modified to produce standard normal and symmetric beta random samples.

Keywords: Random deviates, Student's t, Standard normal, Symmetric Beta, Binomial

Introduction

In a recent paper Kinderman, Monahan and Ramage (1977) describe a number of algorithms for the computer generation of random samples from a Student's t distribution with probability density function, $\{\alpha^{\frac{1}{2}}B(\frac{1}{2},\alpha/2)(1+x^2/\alpha)^{(\alpha+1)/2}\}^{-1}$, $-\infty<x<\infty$, $\alpha>1$. They conveniently separated their algorithms into two classes - those which calculate constants depending on α once, before the generation of a sequence of random samples having the same α, and those which do not use such a "setting up" of constants. This paper presents an algorithm for the case $\alpha>3$, which is simpler to program, requires no constants to be set up, and is faster than any of the Kinderman, Monahan and Ramage (1977) algorithms. The algorithm also allows the generation of standard normal deviates as efficiently as Margsalia and Bray's (1964) modification to the polar method of Box and Mueller (1958).

A further advantage of this algorithm is that it allows, with a slight modification, the generation of random symmetric beta samples with probability density function $(x-x^2)^{\beta-1}/B(\beta,\beta)$, $0<x<1$, $\beta>1.5$. This sampling method is simpler to program and is as fast as algorithm BS given by Ahrens and Dieter (1974) for the case when β is constant from call to call. For the no "set-up" case, when β varies from call to call, it is faster than algorithm BS. This means that the new symmetric beta algorithm can be used to make the binomial sampling method of Relles (1972) exact and possibly always as fast as algorithm BC, the fastest of the binomial algorithms given by Ahrens and Dieter (1974).

The Generation of Random Normal Samples

Put $f(x) = (2\pi)^{-\frac{1}{2}}e^{-\frac{1}{2}x^2}$ and $g(x) = \{3^{\frac{1}{2}}B(\frac{1}{2},3/2)(1+x^2/3)^2\}^{-1}$, $-\infty<x<\infty$.

Following the adaptation of the envelope rejection technique given, for example, in Cheng (1977) it is required to find $M = \max_x \{\frac{f(x)}{g(x)}\}$ where M is finite. It is easy to show that $M = 8(1.5\pi/e)^{\frac{1}{2}}/9$ and that for this M, $x^2=1$.

Suppose now that x is a random sample from the distribution with density g(x) and u is a random sample from U(0,1), the uniform distribution on [0,1], then x is acceptable as a random sample from the density f(x) if $T(x) \equiv f(x)/(Mg(x)) > u$, i.e. if $\ln(T(x)/u) > 0$. Most computers have software for sampling from such a uniform distribution while the distribution of g(x) -Student's t with 3 degrees of freedom - may be sampled following Kinderman and Monahan (1977). To avoid the use of the logarithm function the inequality $T^2(x) > 0.86 - x^2/8.6$ can be used.

A FORTRAN function T3N based on this method is given in the Appendix. FUNCTION T3N is slightly faster on a CDC 7600 (which is used for all comparisons in this paper) than PO, also given in the Appendix, which is based on the improved Box-Mueller (1958) method given by Margsalia and Bray (1964). PO, however, requires slightly less storage and so the two algorithms involved can be thought of as about equally efficient.

The Generation of Random Student's t Variates

Suppose g(x) is defined as above but now f(x) is given by $f(x) = \{\alpha^{\frac{1}{2}}B(\frac{1}{2},\alpha/2)(1+x^2/\alpha)^{(\alpha+1)/2}\}^{-1}$, $-\infty<x<\infty$, $\alpha>3$. Then it is easy to show that $M = \max_x \{\frac{f(x)}{g(x)}\} = 8\pi 3^{\frac{1}{2}}/\{9\alpha^{\frac{1}{2}}B(\frac{1}{2},\alpha/2)(1+1/\alpha)^{(\alpha+1)/2}\}$ and that $T(x) = 9(1+x^2/3)^2\{((\alpha+1)/(\alpha+x^2))^{(\alpha+1)/2}\}/16 > 9e^{\frac{1}{2}-\frac{1}{2}x^2}(1+x^2/3)^2/16$, i.e. $T^2(x) > 0.86 - x^2/8.6$ as before.

A FORTRAN function T3T based on this method is given in the Appendix. Note that T3T is only T3N with a few additional lines of programming. Table 1 below compares execution times of T3T and TAR based on the algorithm given by Kinderman, Monahan and Ramage (1977). These comparisons and those of Table 2 following are based on 10,000 DO loop calls to the functions. The comparisons of Table 1 suggest T3T is faster than any of the algorithms given by Kinderman, Monahan and Ramage (1977).

TABLE 1

Central processing time required on a CDC 7600 to generate one t sample (in μ secs)

α	5	10	30	100
TAR	17.0	17.6	17.7	17.9
T3T	9.6	9.8	10.0	10.2

For completeness it may be noted that Kinderman and Monahan (1977) give a special algorithm for $\alpha=1$ and that for $\alpha=2$ a random sample is $(u-\frac{1}{2})\{\frac{1}{2}(u-u^2)\}^{-\frac{1}{2}}$. For $1<\alpha<3$ TAR or one of the other algorithms given by Kinderman, Monahan and Ramage (1977) is applicable. For $\alpha<1$ Jöhnk's (1964) method can be used to generate a beta sample and hence by transformation a t sample.

The Generation of Symmetric Beta and Binomial Samples

If the variate T has a Student's t distribution with 2β degrees of freedom then the variate X defined by $X = \frac{1}{2}+\frac{1}{2}T(2\beta+T^2)^{-\frac{1}{2}}$ can be shown to have a symmetric beta distribution with parameter β. Thus the algorithm given in the last section may also be used as the basis for an algorithm to generate symmetric beta variates. A FORTRAN function T3B based on this method is given in the Appendix. Table 2 compares execution times of T3B with those of function BS which is based on the method of Ahrens and Dieter (1974). Note that neither of these functions assumes any "set-up". A "set-up" version of BS is about as fast as T3B but requires almost twice the storage space.

Comparisons of non "set-up" functions are also appropriate because these are useful in making the algorithm of Relles (1972) for generating random binomial samples exact. In the Appendix, a version of Relles algorithm with the symmetric beta variates generated as in T3B is given as function IBINOM.

Besides sampling exactly the desired binomial distribution and not just an approximation to this distribution IBINOM also has the advantage of not needing to call a random normal generator as Relles original algorithm did.

TABLE 2

Central processing time required on a CDC 7600

to generate one symmetric beta sample (in μ secs)

β	10	30	50	70	100
T3B	14.6	14.6	14.8	14.8	14.7
BS	19.4	18.9	18.9	18.8	18.8

Acknowledgement

The author is grateful to Dr A.J. Miller, DMS, CSIRO, for a number of helpful comments.

Appendix

This appendix contains FORTRAN listings of the algorithms discussed in the paper. Note that RANF(DUMMY) returns a different U(0,1) sample each time it is called and that on computers other than a CDC 7600 some other function will need to be used.

(a) Normal Generators

(i)

```
      FUNCTION PO(DF)
      DATA IA/0/
      IF(IA.NE.0) GO TO 100
      IA=1
    5 U=RANF(D)
      V=RANF(D)
      U=U+U-1.0
      V=V+V-1.0
      SUM=U*U+V*V
      IF(SUM.GE.1.0) GO TO 5
      SLN=ALOG(SUM)
      SLN=SQRT((-SLN-SLN)/SUM)
      PO=U*SLN
      RETURN
  100 IA=0
      PO=V*SLN
      RETURN
      END
```

(ii)

```
      FUNCTION T3N(D)
    1 U=RANF(D)
      V=RANF(D)-0.5
      IF(U*U+V*V.GT.U) GO TO 1
      T3N=1.732050807*V/U
      U=RANF(D)
      T=T3N*T3N
      IF(0.86-T/8.6.GE.U*U) RETURN
      V=1.0+T/3.0
      IF(ALOG(V*V*0.9274057147/U).GE.0.5*T) RETURN
      GO TO 1
      END
```

(b) Student's t Generators

(i)

```
      FUNCTION TAR(V)
      TAR=0.0
      IF(V.LE.1.0) RETURN
    1 U=RANF(D)
      IF(U.LT.0.5) GO TO 2
      TAR=4.0*U-3.0
      RR=TAR*TAR
      VV=RANF(D)
      GO TO 3
    2 TAR=0.25/(U-0.25)
      U1=RANF(D)
      RR=TAR*TAR
      VV=U1/RR
    3 IF(VV.LT.1.0-0.5*ABS(TAR)) RETURN
      IF(ALOG(VV).GE.-0.5*(V+1.0)*ALOG(1.0+RR/V)) GO TO 1
      RETURN
      END
```

(ii)

```
      FUNCTION T3T(A)
      T3T=0.0
      IF(A.LE.3.0) RETURN
    1 U=RANF(D)
      V=RANF(D)-0.5
      IF(U*U+V*V.GT.U) GO TO 1
      T3T=1.732050807*V/U
      U=RANF(D)
      T=T3T*T3T
      IF(0.86-T/8.6.GE.U*U) RETURN
      V=1.0+T/3.0
      U=2.0*ALOG(V*V*0.9274057147/U)
      IF(U.GE.T) RETURN
      DF=A+1.0
      IF(U-1.0.GE.DF*ALOG((T+A)/DF)) RETURN
      GO TO 1
      END
```

(c) Symmetric Beta Generators

(i)

```
      FUNCTION BS(V)
      BS=0.0
      IF(V.LE.1.5) RETURN
      A=V-1.0
      T=SQRT(A+A)
    1 S=PO(D)
      BS=0.5*(1.0+S/T)
      IF(BS.LT.0.0.OR.BS.GT.1.0) GO TO 1
      U=RANF(D)
      S4=S*S*S*S
      A8=8.0*A
      IF(U.LE.1.0-S4/(A8-12.0)) RETURN
      A8=A8-8.0
      S5=S4/A8
      IF(U.GE.1.0-S5+0.5*S5*S5) GO TO 1
      IF(ALOG(U).GT.A*ALOG(4.0*BS*(1.0-BS))+S*S/2.0) GO TO 1
      RETURN
      END
```

(ii)

```
      FUNCTION T3B(D)
C     D/2.0 IS THE SYMMETRIC BETA PARAMETER
      T3B=0.0
      IF(D.LT.3.0) RETURN
      U=RANF(D)
      V=RANF(D)-0.5
      IF(U*U+V*V.GT.U) GO TO 1
      T3B=1.732050807*V/U
      U=RANF(D)
      T=T3B*T3B
      IF(0.86-T/8.6.GE.U*U) GO TO 2
      V=1.0+T/3.0
      U=2.0*ALOG(V*V*0.9274057147/U)
      IF(U.GE.T) GO TO 2
      DF=D+1.0
      IF(U-1.0.GE.DF*ALOG(((T+D)/DF)) GO TO 2
      GO TO 1
    2 T3B=0.5+0.5*T3B/SQRT(D+T)
      RETURN
      END
```

(d) Binomial Generator

```
      FUNCTION IBINOM(NN,PP)
      IBINOM=0
      N=NN
      P=PP
    1 IF(N.LT.38) GO TO 6
    2 IF(MOD(N,2).EQ.1) GO TO 3
      N=N-1
      IF(RANF(D).LE.P) IBINOM=IBINOM+1
    3 N=N/2
      A=FLOAT(2*(N+1))
   10 U=RANF(D)
      V=RANF(D)-0.5
      IF(U*U+V*V.GT.U) GO TO 10
      T3B=1.732050807*V/U
      U=RANF(D)
      T=T3B*T3B
      IF(0.86-T/8.6.GE.U*U) GO TO 30
      V=1.0+T/3.0
      U=2.0*ALOG(V*V*0.9274057147/U)
      IF(U.GT.T) GO TO 30
      DF=A+1.0
      IF(U-1.0.LT.DF*ALOG((T+A)/DF)) GO TO 10
   30 R=0.5+0.5*T3B/SQRT(A+T)
      IF(R.LE.P) GO TO 5
    4 P=P/R
      GO TO 1
    5 IBINOM=IBINOM+N+1
      P=(P-R)/(1.0-R)
      GO TO 1
    6 IF(N.EQ.0) GO TO 8
      DO 7 I=1,N
    7 IF(RANF(D).LE.P) IBINOM=IBINOM+1
    8 RETURN
      END
```

References

Ahrens, J.H. and Dieter, U., Computer methods for sampling from gamma, beta, Poisson and binomial distributions, Computing, 12, 223-46, 1974.

Box, G.E.P. and Muller, M.E., A note on the generation of normal deviates, Ann. Math. Statist., 29, 610-11, 1958.

Cheng, R.C.H., The generation of gamma variables with non-integral shape parameters, Applied Statistics, 26, 71-5, 1977.

Jöhnk, M.D., Erzeugen von betaverteilten und gammaverteilten Zufallszahlen. Metrika, 8, 5-15, 1964.

Kinderman, A.J., Monahan, J.F. and Ramage, J.G., Computer methods for sampling from Student's t distribution, Mathematics of Computation, 31, 1009-1018, 1977.

Kinderman, A.J., and Monahan, J.F., Computer generation of Random Variables Using the Ratio of Uniform Deviates, A.C.M. Transactions on Mathematical Software, 3, 257-60, 1977.

Margsalia, G. and Bray, T.A., A convenient method for generating normal variables, SIAM Rev., 6, 260-4, 1964.

Relles, D.A., A simple algorithm for generating binomial random variables when N is large, J. Am. Statist. Ass., 67, 612-3, 1972.

Spectral Analysis of Stochastic and Analytic Simulation Results for a Nonlinear Model for the Italian Economy

C. Bianchi, G. Calzolari and **E.M. Cleur**, Pisa

When dealing with nonlinear econometric models, resort is often made to simulation techniques for the investigation of their dynamic properties. A spectral analysis using stochastic and analytic simulation is carried out on a nonlinear model of the Italian economy. The two approches are empirically compared.

KEYWORDS: stochastic simulation, nonlinear econometric models, analytic simulation, spectral analysis, Monte Carlo methods.

1. *Introduction*

It is a well known result that an analytical description of the properties of a system of simultaneous difference equations can be obtained in a straightforward manner by the use of the spectral representation of a stochastic process. Such an approach is also known to have several advantages over a direct estimation of the spectra of the endogenous variables generated by a stochastic simulation of the system. Unfortunately it is not possible to obtain such a description in the nonlinear case.

In order to overcome this problem alternative estimates of the spectra may be obtained through a linearization of the nonlinear model as in Howrey(1971). However, apart from the difficulties implicit in such an approach, if the model is highly nonlinear the linear approximation could be misleading. Hence it is often necessary to resort to a stochastic simulation approach, as in several contributions in Hickman(1972).

Alternatively Howrey and Klein(1972) have proposed overcoming this difficulty by means of a simulation approach which, strictly speaking, is not stochastic, but is a combination of numerical simulation and an analytic evaluation of the spectrum; they often refer to this approach as an "analytic simulation", whereas Klein(1973) terms it as an "evaluation of the spectrum by empirical nonstochastic simulation".

After a short description, the stochastic and analytic simulation approaches will be applied to a nonlinear macroeconometric model for Italy. It should be remembered that the main purpose of this paper is to compare the performance of the two approaches just mentioned rather than make inferences on the cyclical properties of the model or on the economic meaning of the results.

2. *Spectrum evaluation by means of stochastic simulation*

The basic idea underlying this method is that of applying spectral analysis to the "time series" or "observations" generated by means of a stochastic simulation of the model beyond the sample period. The reason for introducing stochastic shocks over a long period is that of determining, as suggested by Adelman and Adelman(1959), whether business cycles with realistic characteristics are found in the simulated results. As in other Monte Carlo experiments, the simulation (e.g. each stochastic simulation run) is replicated many times over the same period; the spectrum is computed for each run and averaged over the number of replications.

Even though this methodology is not new in applied econometrics, there is no uniqueness of consensus about the way in which such an experiment should be performed.

Several problems arise which are related to the use of a short-term model for long-run simulations, so that it is often necessary to modify the structure of the model in order to take into account long-run factors. In such a context there is no direct interest in the results of the long-run forecast itself, but a reasonable forecast should in any case be produced, and hence, in order to obtain a control deterministic solution which could be regarded as a base-line solution for the stochastic simulation runs, a realistic projection of all the exogenous variables is required.

Other problems arise due to the very nature of spectral analysis. For instance, spectral analysis generally requires very long time-series, so that, at least in principle, more reliable spectral estimates can be obtained only from a very long simulation period; this could raise the difficulty of obtaining a realistic control solution especially for large dynamic nonlinear econometric models, in which convergence and stability problems can be present. Further, classical spectral analysis can only be applied to stationary series, and hence, for each shocked run, it is necessary to filter any trend; generally in these experiments the detrending is performed by subtracting out the control deterministic solution, but in some cases the paths of the control and stochastic solutions suggest the use of other filters.

The way in which all these aspects have been faced in our experiment on the ISPE model will be briefly discussed in Section 4. It must be recalled here that, for each replication, the random shocks have been generated by means of McCarty's(1972) procedure and, after control solution detrending, spectrum densities have been computed using the formula:

$$f(\lambda_j) = 1/(2\pi)\left\{C_0 + 2\sum_{s=1}^{M-1} C_s w_s \cos(\lambda_j s)\right\} \tag{1}$$

where:

$C_s = 1/(N-s)\sum_{t=1}^{N-s}(x_t-\bar{x})(x_{t+s}-\bar{x})$ is the autocovariance function,

w_s is the Parzen window, M the truncation point and $\lambda_j = \pi j/M$.

3. *Spectrum evaluation by means of analytic simulation*

As mentioned above, this technique was suggested by Howrey and Klein(1972). Even if it can be proved to be asymptotically exact only for linear systems, from a computational point of view it can be applied exactly in the same way also to nonlinear systems. Briefly the method is as follows. Let

$$A(L)Y(t) = B(L)X(t) + U(t) \tag{2}$$

be a linear econometric model in structural form, where A(L) and B(L) are matrices of polinomials in the lag operator L; Y(t), X(t) and U(t) are, respectively, the vectors of endogenous and exogenous variables and of the structural disturbances at time t. Making explicit Y(t) on the left hand side provides:

$$Y(t) = A^{-1}(L)B(L)X(t) + A^{-1}(L)U(t). \tag{3}$$

We are interested in computing the spectral matrix of the second term on the right hand side, which represents the deviations from the control solution corresponding to the random disturbance process U(t). The straightforward solution is:

$$S_y(\lambda) = A^{-1}(e^{-i\lambda})S_u(\lambda)A^{-1*}(e^{-i\lambda}) \tag{4}$$

where $*$ means conjugate transpose and $S_u(\lambda)$ is the spectrum matrix of U(t).

The method proposed by Howrey and Klein starts from the representation of the vector $A^{-1}(L)U(t)$ as a weighted average of the residuals, that is:

$$D_0U(t) + D_1U(t-1) + \ldots = \sum_{s=0}^{\infty} D_sU(t-s) \tag{5}$$

where D_s is the matrix of the partial derivatives of the elements of Y(t) with respect to the elements of U(t-s). These derivatives can be computed by means of numerical simulation for both linear and nonlinear models by computing deviations of disturbed solutions from a control solution. More exactly, the procedure for computing the elements of D_s (for any s) is the following (see also Chow(1975),pp.134-136).

1) A dynamic simulation run must be performed for s+1 periods with all the values of U(t)=0 ($t=t_0,t_0+1,\ldots,t_0+s$); this is taken as the control solution.
2) The j-th component of the vector $U(t_0)$ is set equal to ϵ, an arbitrarily small number, while all the other components are again set to zero; to zero are also set all the components of the vectors U(t) at time $t \neq t_0$.
3) The dynamic simulation run is performed as above; the difference between the values of the endogenous variables computed at time t_0+s and the corresponding values of the control solution supplies the desired deviations. These deviations, divided by ϵ, provide the values of the partial derivatives of the endogenous variables with respect to the j-th element of the disturbance vector lagged of s periods.

Steps 2 and 3 must be repeated for all the values of j (all the components of the $U(t_0)$ vector) completing, in this way, the computation of the matrix D_s.

The process must be repeated from step 1 for values of s=0,1,2,... up to a reasonable truncation point in the sum (5).

An optimal choice of the value for ϵ can be made in such a way as to guarantee at least 3-4 exact decimal digits for each derivative in the case of nonlinear model (if the model is linear, it is well known that any value of ϵ leads always to the same result).

The analytic simulation approach can be usefully used in place of equation (4) even in linear models when the dimensions of the matrix A(L) are such that it could be difficult to enter the correct input, i.e. to write the coefficients in the right position. On the other hand the Gauss-Seidel solution procedure generally also used in the simulation of large linear models can be easily adapted to handle this problem, rather than have the computing burden involved in inverting large complex-valued matrices at each frequency.

4. *Spectral analysis of the ISPE model*

The nonlinear model used in the experiment is the annual model of the real and fiscal sector of the Italian economy developed by a team led by ISPE (Istituto di Studi per la Programmazione Economica), and described in Sartori(1977). The version of the model used in both the stochastic and analytic simulation experiments consists of 34 equations, 19 of which are stochastic; the model was estimated by two stage least squares with principal components according to method 4 of Kloek and Mennes(1960) for the sample period 1955-1976. The choice of this method was based on the dynamc simulation behaviour of the model in the sample period, as described in Bianchi, Calzolari and Sartori(1978).

As carried out by Fitzgerald(1973), and in order to avoid the heteroschedasticity induced by the nonlinearities of the model, the stochastic simulation was undertaken by keeping the exogenous variables fixed, and the spectra were calculated from the residuals from the control (deterministic) solution after having eliminated the first 20 observations; such a procedure helps eliminate respectively trend and the transitory component. The simulation period, after several trials, was set at 110 years into the future. This was suggested by the fact that, in longer simulation periods, the control solution path reached values unreasonable from an economic point of view.

The analytic simulation procedure, after previous tests on linear models (Klein-I and Samuelson-Hicks), was applied to the ISPE model. The simulation run, that is the truncation point in the sum (5), was 100 periods; in fact after 90 periods, the results remain constant up to the first 2-3 significant digits. Even here the exogenous variables were kept fixed over all the simulation period. An optimal choice of ϵ was made for each component of the vector $U(t_0)$; in order of magnitude, its value was approximately equal to the standard deviation of the corresponding element of $U(t_0)$ divided by 10^4, hence requiring a great precision (small tolerance at the convergence point) in the Gauss-Seidel iterative solution algorithm.

The figures below display, for the Total Private Production, respectively the average power spectrum computed on 50 replicated stochastic simulations and the power spectrum computed by means of analytic simulation.

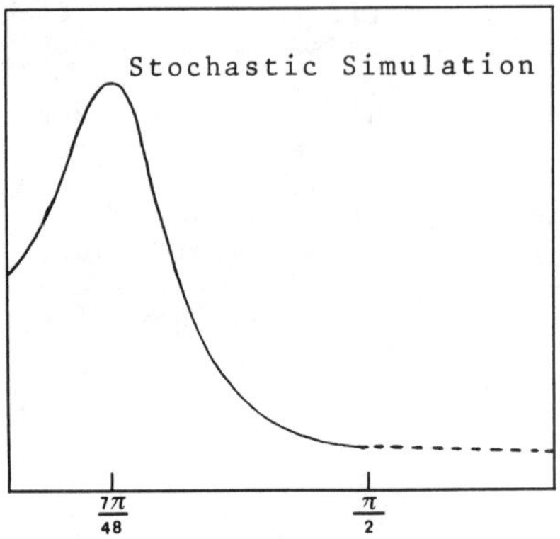

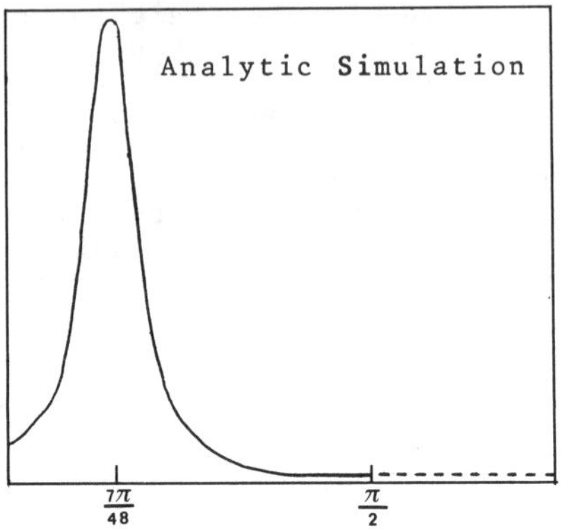

All the endogenous variables have well defined peaks at frequency 0.073 cycles/year, when using the analytic simulation, thereby indicating the generation of an overall 14 year cycle by the model. A few of the variables also contain substantial power at zero frequency, which means that trend or very long cyclical components are also present. On the other hand, the spectra of the series obtained from the stochastic simulation procedure have slightly higher power at zero frequency and the peaks are still well defined in the neighbourhood of frequency 0.073 cycles/year even if slightly less pronounced.

From a qualitative point of view, the two approaches give the same information and, on the basis of this concordance, we may conclude that the ISPE model helps generate a reasonably long cyclical pattern, but does not reproduce the well known business cycles which are generally said to have periodicity of between 7 and 10 years.

We have also calculated cross-spectra between some of the endogenous variables with the intention of analysing the relationship between the 14 year cycles previously identified. We may thus note that the 14 year cycles which dominate the stochastic components of Employment in the Industrial Sector and Industrial Production, of Private Consumption Deflator and Wages per Employee in the Industrial Sector, and of Private Investment and Net Private Consumption are all very highly correlated (the coherence in all three cases is higher than 0.95), with the following lead-lag relationships:

1) Private Consumption Deflator lags Wages by a little less than one year;
2) Investment lags Consumption by about half a year;
3) Industrial Employment lags Production by about one year.

5. *Concluding remarks*

With respect to the stochastic simulation approach, the analytic simulation was empirically found to have the following advantages.

The experimental error due to random number generation is avoided.

It is unnecessary to replicate the stochastic solutions of the model many times; more exactly, we require only one control solution and as many disturbed solutions as the number of stochastic equations (19, in our case), instead of at least fifty replications as was found necessary in our case to get reliable results from the stochastic simulation approach. Therefore the cost of computation was smaller (5 minutes of CPU time for the ISPE model, instead of 10 minutes).

The length of the simulation period in the analytic simulation depends only from the choice of a reasonable truncation point in the sum (5), while in the stochastic simulation approach, to improve the resolution of the spectrum estimator, the simulation period and the truncation point in (1) must be increased (see, for example, the considerations by Jenkins and Watts(1968) on the problems of bias and inconsistency of the spectrum estimates (pp.245-247)). Using 100 periods in the analytic simulation approach we obtained results that were exact up to 2-3 significant digits (in the sense that they did not change when the number of periods was further increased); in order to get the same precision with the stochastic simulation approach, in previous experiments with linear models several hundreds of replications had to be performed on a simulation period of a few thousand years and truncation point of about 400, requiring, in this way, more than one hour of CPU time for the Klein-I model. For the ISPE model it was practically impossible to get the same precision in the stochastic simulation results, since, as already mentioned, simulation runs longer than 110-120 periods led to meaningless results.

All these considerations seem to stress, in the particular case considered here, a preference in the use of analytic simulation. In a more general case, given a larger model with, say, one hundred stochastic equations, the number of necessary (disturbed) solutions in the analytic simulation approach should be one hundred, i.e. greater than the number of replications required to get reliable results with the stochastic simulation, which would then turn the balance in favour of stochastic simulation. However, this may only be true in qualitative terms since, from our above mentioned experiment on linear models, in order to obtain the same resolution in the spectral estimates from the stochastic simulation approach, the simulation period would probably have to be much longer and the number of replications much greater.

A possible drawback in the use of the analytic simulation approach however, could be found in what Howrey and Klein point out (p.600) on the fact that such a method can be easily proved to be exact in the case of linear models, while "no attempt is made at this point to justify this approach to the analysis of nonlinear systems beyond the analogy with linear systems". Chow also notes that (p.136): "It seems reasonable to suppose that the method will work well only if the system, net of the effects of random disturbances and of the exogenous variables, has a stable equilibrium"; this however is not a drawback, as the same criticism can be made of the stochastic simulation approach.

All the simulation experiments have been carried out by means of the program by Bianchi, Calzolari and Corsi(1978) on a computer IBM/370 model 168; some special features have been added to this program to allow analytic simulation as well.

References

Adelman,I. and F.L.Adelman, "The Dynamic Properties of the Klein-Goldberger Model", Econometrica, 28, 596-625, 1959.

Bianchi,C., G.Calzolari and P.Corsi, "A Program for Stochastic Simulation of Econometric Models", Econometrica, 46, 235-236, 1978.

Bianchi,C., G.Calzolari and F.Sartori, "Stima e Simulazione di un Sistema Nonlineare di Equazioni Simultanee: una Applicazione al Modello ISPE del Metodo dei Minimi Quadrati a Due Stadi con Componenti Principali", Quaderni ISPE, Roma, 1978, (in Italian, forthcoming).

Chow,G.C., "Analysis and Control of Dynamic Economic Systems" John Wiley & Sons, New York, 1975.

Fitzgerald,V.W., "Dynamic Properties of a Non-Linear Econometric Model", in "Econometric Studies of Macro and Monetary Relations", ed. by A.A.Powell and R.A.Williams, 169-193, North Holland, Amsterdam, 1973.

Hickman,B.G., editor, "Econometric Models of Cyclical Behavior", Studies in Income and Wealth n.36, NBER, New York, 1972.

Howrey,E.P., "Stochastic Properties of the Klein-Goldberger Model", Econometrica, 39, 73-87, 1971.

Howrey,E.P. and L.R.Klein, "Dynamic Properties of Nonlinear Econometric Models", International Economic Review, 13, 599-618, 1972.

Jenkins,G.M. and D.G.Watts, "Spectral Analysis and its Applications", Holden-Day, San Francisco, 1968.

Klein,L.R., "Dynamic Analysis of Economic Systems", Int. J. Math. Educ. Sci. Technol., 4, 341-359, 1973.

Kloek,T. and L.B.M.Mennes, "Simultaneous Equations Estimation Based on Principal Components of Predetermined Variables", Econometrica, 28, 45-61, 1960.

McCarthy,M.D., "Some Notes on the Generation of Pseudo-Structural Errors for Use in Stochastic Simulation Studies", in "Econometric Models of Cyclical Behavior", ed. by B.G.Hickman, Studies in Income and Wealth n.36, 185-191, NBER, New York, 1972.

Sartori,F., "An Economic Model for Italy", presented at the IBM UK/IIASA Seminar on "Models for Regional Planning and Policy Making", Laxenburg, Vienna, 1977.

A Stochastic Method for Global Optimization

L. de Biase and **F. Frontini**, Milano

SUMMARY. In this paper a method is proposed for the minimization of a function $f:S\subset R^N \to R$. The root of a suitable approximation $A(\xi)$ of the level set measure yields an approximation β^* to f^*, the minimum value. $A(\xi)$ is obtained by a recursive spline technique, smoothing the data found by a sequential uniform random sampling both on S and on the expected range of function values.
To obtain the actual value and coordinates of the global minimum, some local searches are performed.
The problem of choosing the proper number of local searches and their starting points is solved by means of cluster analysis techniques.

KEYWORDS. Stochastic methods. Global Optimization. Cluster analysis. Nonlinear parameter estimation.

INTRODUCTION. We propose a global optimization method for continuous real valued functions $f(x)$, defined on a compact set $S\subset R^N$.
At first we construct a function $\psi(\xi)=m(E(\xi))$, where $E(\xi)$ is the set

$$E(\xi)=\{x\varepsilon S:\ f(x)\leq\xi,\quad \xi\varepsilon R\}$$

and $m(\cdot)$ is the normalized Lebesgue measure on S.
Obviously the minimum value f^* of the function is such that

$$\psi(\xi)=0 \text{ for } \xi\leq f^* \quad \text{and } \psi(\xi)>0 \text{ for } \xi>f^*,$$

provided the minimum point is isolated.
It can be proved (Archetti-Betrò (1976)) that $\psi(\xi)$ has the following regularity properties: it is non decreasing in R, it is a.e. differentiable and, if no set H exists such that $m(H)>0$ and $f(x)$ constant on H, it is a.e. continuous.

PREVISION OF THE MINIMUM VALUE. Unfortunately, a part for trivial cases, $\psi(\xi)$ is not available in analytical form; it is then necessary to set up a stochastic sampling technique to provide an approximation of it in analytical form. This is possible because, if the sampling distribution in S is uniform, $\psi(\xi)$ turns out to be the probability of hitting the region $E(\xi)$.

We perform a sample θ_q of q points ($q\geq 1$) in S and evaluate f(x) at every point of it. Set:

$$\theta_\ell = \min\{f(w_i),\quad i=1,2,\ldots,q\}$$

and

$$\theta_u = \max\{f(w_i),\quad i=1,2,\ldots,q\}\ ,$$

it can be proved that, as $q\to\infty$, $\theta_\ell\to f^*$ and $\theta_u\to \|f\|_\infty$ with prob. 1.

Let's then choose ξ out of a uniform distribution in $[\theta_\ell\ ,\ \theta_u]$ and let p be the number of sampled points hitting $E(\xi)$; the number $\tilde{\psi}=\frac{p}{q}$ is assumed as an approximation of $\psi(\xi)$ and it can be proved that

$$P\{\frac{p}{q}\to\psi(\xi)\quad \text{for } q\to\infty\}=1$$

and that $\tilde{\psi}$ is an unbiased estimate of $\psi(\xi)$.

Thus $\psi(\xi)$ is an unknown regression function and we look for its root ξ^* such that $\psi(\xi^*)=0$ and $\psi(\xi)>0$ for $\xi>\xi^*$.

This problem is in fact a stochastic extrapolation problem and then stochastic techniques are likely to fail.

To avoid these difficulties we provide for $\psi(\xi)$ a uniform as regular as possible approximation; this can be obtained by means of a least squares approximation with spline functions of odd degree as basic functions. Let ϕ_ℓ, $\ell=1,2,\ldots,k$ be such splines and

$$\sum_1^k \lambda_\ell\phi_\ell(\xi)$$

be the approximation. The coefficients λ_ℓ, $\ell=1,2,\ldots,k$ are found by minimizing the empirical risk function

$$J(\lambda)=\sum_1^r\{\tilde{\psi}_i-\sum_1^k\lambda_\ell\phi_\ell(\xi_i)\}\ ,$$

where r is the number of samples θ_q performed and $\tilde{\psi}_i=\psi(\xi_i)=p_i/q$,

and p_i is the number of points hitting $E(\xi_i)$ in θ_q^i.
As $\{\theta_q^i, i=1,2,\dots,r\}$ are independent samples, we obtain an independent sample

$$\{(\xi_i, \tilde{\psi}_i), i=1,2,\dots,r\}$$

for the construction of $\psi(\xi)$.
Obviously when the number of knots of the spline approximation increases, the approximation is improved, but of course there is a limit to this increasing due to the number of points by means of which the spline itself is constructed. It can be proved (see Mikhal'skii (1974)) that, if the increase law is such that

$$\lim_{r\to\infty} \frac{N^2(r)\log r}{r} = 0,$$

where $N(r)=N+2m$ (being N the number of knots of the spline approximation and $2m-1$ its degree), the spline approximation converges uniformly to $\psi(\xi)$ on $[f^*, \|f\|_\infty]$ with probability 1.
The minimization of $J(\lambda)$ is obtained by solving a linear system of the form $C_i\lambda=b$.
Computations for this solution may be reduced from $\frac{N^3(r)}{3}$ to $2N^2(r)$ by an updating technique for C_i^{-1} which can be applied whenever the number of knots does not increase:

$$C_{i+1}^{-1} = C_i^{-1} - \frac{C_i^{-1}\Phi(\xi_{i+1})\Phi^T(\xi_{i+1})C_i^{-1}}{1+\Phi^T(\xi_{i+1})C_i^{-1}\Phi(\xi_{i+1})}$$

where $\Phi(\xi_{i+1})=\{\phi_1(\xi_{i+1}), \phi_2(\xi_{i+1}),\dots, \phi_k(\xi_{i+1})\}$ (see Betrò De Biase (1976)).
At every sample we check whether the λ coefficients have reached convergence, namely if

$$\frac{|\lambda_j^i - \lambda_j^{i-1}|}{|\lambda_j^{i-1}|} \leq \eta$$

where λ_j^i is the j-th component of the vector of λ coefficients obtained at the i-th sample and $\eta>0$ is a fixed precision.
At any convergence of λ coefficients we evaluate the root β of

the approximating function and the mean value β^i_{mean} of all of the roots obtained until sample i.

<u>TERMINATION CRITERIA</u>. At the moment termination criteria are completely heuristic and deterministic. There are two levels of tests: at the first we check if the values β^i_{mean} converge; if

$$\frac{|\beta^i_{mean} - \theta^i_\ell|}{|\theta_u - \theta^i_\ell|} \leq \varepsilon$$

where $\varepsilon>0$ is a fixed precision, we proceed to local searches. Another test is performed, at the first level, on the value of the empirical risk function, namely

$$J(\lambda) < \delta,$$

where $\delta>0$ is a fixed precision.
For the most part of cases this criterion has less relevance than the others. Only for Shekel's test family this is the criterion which leads to local searches.
The second level of tests is performed after local searches in order to check whether the prevision β^* (i.e. the last β^i_{mean}) was good enough, namely if

$$\frac{|F_c - \beta^*|}{|\theta_u - F_c|} \leq \alpha,$$

where $\alpha>0$ is a fixed precision and F_c is the value of f(x) after local searches.

<u>CLUSTER ANALYSIS AND LOCAL SEARCHES</u>. To decide the number and the starting points for local searches, a cluster analysis procedure is set up, based on a local evaluation of the density of the r best points obtained along sampling. The idea for this procedure has been suggested by a paper of Torn's (1975).
A cluster is characterized by a density of points in a subset of S greater than the average density ρ in S ($\rho=V/r$, where V is the

hypervolume of S).

Briefly, the process is as follows: chosen a seed point u^o, the first cluster is widened enclosing new points until the density of points in hyperspheres centred at u^o is greater than ρ. As soon as such density becomes less than ρ, we assume that the first cluster is exhausted and, chosen a new seed point, we start the construction of the subsequent cluster. The process terminates when every point has been considered.

To select the hyperspheres centred at the seed points we calculate their "critical radii" in such a way that, if V_n is the volume of the n-th hypersphere, the relation $\rho V_n=n$ is verified, $n=1,2,...,d$, where d is the number of hyperspheres needed to cover S. With this choice the construction of clusters is very simple: we enumerate the points whose distance from the selected seed is less than the n-th radium; if the n-th hypersphere contains at least n points, we proceed to the (n+1)-th; otherwise the present cluster is exhausted.

A device is constructed, based on an adjustement of the average density, to avoid that the number of clusters be too low or large with respect to a priori information on the function.

The determination of the global minimum is then obtained by means of local searches with starting points at the seed of each cluster.

<u>CONSTRAINED MINIMA</u>. If the minimum point is restricted to lie in some subset of S we set up a penalty procedure; let the constraints be: $g_i(x)\leq 0$, $i=1,2,...,m$; $h_j(x)=0$, $j=1,2,...,n$; $\ell_k(x)>0$, $k=1,2,...,s$. Then, following Lootsma's approach (Lootsma(1972)), we minimize the function

$$F(x)=f(x)+A\sum_{i=1}^{m}\{\max[0,g_i(x)]\}^2+B\sum_{j=1}^{n}h_j^2(x)-\frac{1}{C}\sum_{k=1}^{s}\log(\ell_k(x)),$$

where A, B, C are sufficiently large coefficients, chosen at first proportional to the expected amplitude of the range of f(x).

If the found minimum point does not satisfy the constraints within a prefixed precision, the algorithm is started again with increased value of the proper coefficients.

We show here the results obtained for four classical test functions.

1. Shekel's family:

$$f(x) = -\sum_{i=1}^{m} \frac{1}{\|x-a^i\|^2+c^i}$$

where $x=(x_1,x_2,\ldots,x_N)^T$, $a^i=(a_1^i,\ldots,a_N^i)$, $c^i>0$, $i=1,2,\ldots,m$, where N is the dimension of the problem and m the number of minima of coordinates a^i and levels determined by c^i, $i=1,2,\ldots,m$.

2. Hartman's family:

$$f(x) = -\sum_{i=1}^{m} c_i \exp\left(-\sum_{j=1}^{N} \alpha_{ij}(x_j-p_j^i)^2\right)$$

where N is the dimension of the problem, m is the number of minima of coordinates p^i. Shape and amplitude of attraction regions are determinad by the coefficients α_{ij}.

3. Branin's RCOS:

$$f(x_1,x_2)=a(x_2-bx_1^2+cx_1-d)^2+e(1-f)\cos x_1+e$$

where $a=1$, $b=5.1/(4\pi^2)$, $c=5/\pi$, $d=6$, $e=10$, $f=1/(8\pi)$. This function has 3 global minima in the region $-5\leq x_1\leq 10$, $0\leq x_2\leq 15$.

4. Goldstein&Price:

$$f(x_1,x_2)=\{1+(x_1+x_2+1)^2(19-14x_1+3x_1^2-14x_2+6x_1x_2+3x_2^2)^2\}\cdot\{30+$$
$$+(2x_1-3x_2)^2(18-32x_1+12x_1^2+48x_2-36x_1x_2+27x_2^2)\} .$$

In the region $-2\leq x_i\leq 2$, $i=1,2$, this function has 4 local minima. The global minimum is at $x^*=(0,-1)$ with $f(x^*)=3$.

Function	N	q	r	FE	TFE	cl	β^*	F_c
1. Shekel (4,7)	4	4	91	364	604	10	-1.2010	-10.393
2. Shekel (4,10)	4	4	41	164	327	6	-1.531	-10.915
3. Hartman (4,3)	3	2	35	70	147	3	-3.740	-3.860
4. Hartman (4,6)	6	2	150	300	404	6	-3.191	-3.3223
5. Branin RCOS	2	2	71	142	208	4	2.360	1.250
6. GOLDPR	2	2	36	72	144	3	3.5513	2.9997

REMARKS. As noticed previously, cases 3., 4., 5. reached termination by test 2). From the table we observe that in these cases the prevision β* is not very satisfactory, even if F_c is good. The reason of it can be ascribed to the particular shape of attraction regions for Shekel's family. It can also be observed that the number of function evaluations (FE) is independent of the number of minima and the dimension of the problem; it depends, on the contrary on the shape of attraction regions, namely it increases noticeably when they are extremely sharp.

REFERENCES.

Archetti F. - Betrò B., Recursive stochastic evaluation of the level set measure in global optimization problems, Quaderni del Dipartimento di Ricerca Operativa e Scienze Statistiche,A21, 1976.

Betrò B. - De Biase L., A recursive spline technique for uniform approximation of sampled data, Quaderni del Dipartimento di Ricerca Operativa e Scienze Statistiche, A31, 1976.

De Biase L. - Frontini F., A stochastic method for global optimization: its structure and numerical performance, Towards Global Optimization, North Holland Press, to appear.

Lootsma F.A., A survey of methods for solving constrained minimization problems via uncostrained minimization, Numerical Methods for Nonlinear Optimization, Academic Press, 1972.

Mikhal'skii A.J., The method of averaged splines in the problem of approximating dependencies on the basis of empirical data, Autom. Rem. Control,35 N.3, 1974.

Torn A., Cluster analysis as a tool in a global optimization model, preprint, Abo, Finland, 1975.

Simulation with Bedsocs; Teaching Aid and Research Tool

B.D. Bunday, Bradford

Summary

Bedsocs is a simulation language. It is an extension of the language Basic and contains facilities for the integration of sets of simultaneous differential equations. The solutions of the equations can be displayed on a visual display unit, printed copies of which can be obtained. In addition the dependent variables can be tabulated at specified intervals of the independent variable. The examples discussed are from the field of stochastic processes and show how the language can be used to illustrate difficult ideas in this area, as well as to obtain numerical solutions to hitherto unsolved research problems.

KEYWORDS: SIMULATION, STOCHASTIC PROCESSES, QUEUES, MACHINE INTERFERENCE, BUSY PERIOD, IMBEDDED RANDOM WALK.

1. Introduction

Bedsocs is an acronym for Bradford Educational Simulation language for Continuous Systems. It is an extension of the language Basic and as implemented on the Hewlett Packard 2100 series of computer it is upward compatible with H.P. Basic. It is a continuous system simulation language which is simple to use and easy to learn and is therefore very valuable as a teaching aid.

Bedsocs contains facilities for the automatic sorting and solution of systems of equations and for the integration of sets of simultaneous differential equations. In the latest version, a variable step fourth order Runge-Kutta-Merson integration method and a fixed step second order Runge-Kutta integration method are available. The latest version is a multi-user system and enables a number of users to run their simulation programs concurrently on a Hewlett-Packard 2100 series computer which has a minimum of 16k of core store. Full details of the language and its facilities together with other examples of its application can be obtained from the Reference Manual by G. Brown and J. Stephenson (1976).

Bedsocs is an interactive language. Program and data can be input by using a keyboard terminal or a paper tape reader. Output of results from the computer in numerical form can be made via a teletype. The solutions of the differential equations can also be displayed on a visual display unit, the graphs scaled to any required accuracy, and printed copies of the display obtained. In addition, the dependent variables can be tabulated at specified intervals of the independent variable. In the sections which follow examples chosen from the field of stochastic processes are discussed. The equations governing the systems are stated and the output from programs written in Bedsocs is given.

2. The Single Server Queue

For a single server queue with random arrivals at rate λ, and exponential service at rate μ, if $p_n(t)$ denotes the probability that there are n customers in the system at time t, the equations for the $p_n(t)$ are given by:- [e.g. Saaty (1961)]

$$\frac{dp_0(t)}{dt} = \lambda p_0(t) - \mu p_1(t),$$
$$\frac{dp_n(t)}{dt} = \lambda p_{n-1}(t) - (\lambda + \mu)p_n(t) + \mu p_{n+1}(t); \qquad n \geqslant 1. \qquad 2.1$$

If we make the transformation $\tau = \mu t$ so that the unit of time is equal to the mean service time the equations become:-

$$\frac{dp_0(\tau)}{d\tau} = \rho p_0(\tau) - p_1(\tau),$$
$$\frac{dp_n(\tau)}{d\tau} = \rho p_{n-1}(\tau) - (1 + \rho)p_n(\tau) + p_{n+1}(\tau); \qquad n \geqslant 1, \qquad 2.2$$

where $\rho = \frac{\lambda}{\mu}$ is the so called traffic intensity.

The transient solution of this set of differential-difference equations was first obtained by Clarke (1953) and involves a complicated sum of Bessel functions. Since it is an infinite set we need to truncate the system in order to be able to use Bedsocs which only deals with finite systems. For the case $\rho = 0.1$, the first ten equations of this set were solved using Bedsocs. The output graphs for $p_0(\tau)$ and $p_1(\tau)$ are shown in Figure 1.

The initial conditions used were $p_0(0) = 1$ and $p_n(0) = 0$ for $n \neq 0$. The vertical scale is from 0 to 1 and the horizontal scale is from 0 to 20. The output which is drawn on the screen as the integration progresses clearly indicates the (rapid in this case) convergence to the steady state solution:- $p_n = (1 - \rho)\rho^n$. This is confirmed by the column of figures at the side which are the values of $p_0(20)$, $p_1(20)$,... etc., the final valuss of the $p_n(\tau)$'s on the horizontal scale.

RUN
.9
9.00000E-02
8.99987E-03
8.99973E-04
8.99816E-05
8.99662E-06
8.98608E-07
8.96854E-08
8.85364E-09
8.02703E-10

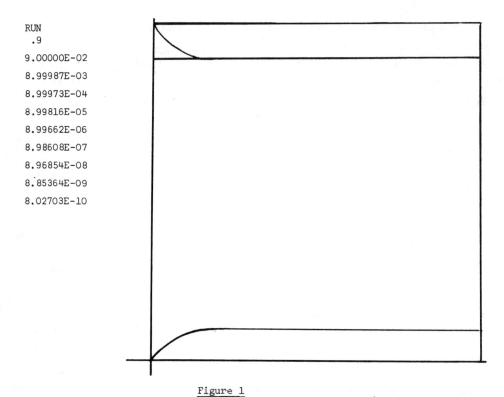

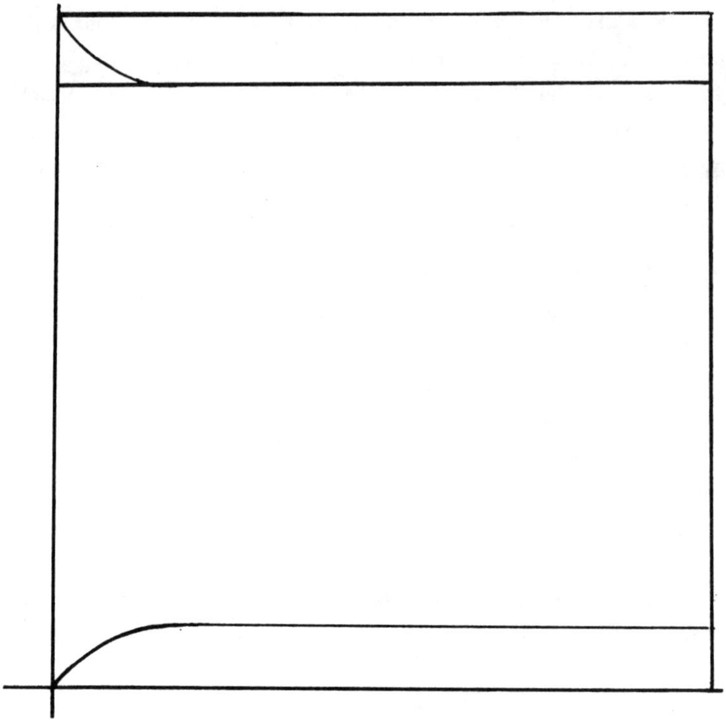

Figure 1

3. The Machine Interference Problem

One operative is in charge of a group of N identical automatic machines which break down independently at random at rate λ in running time for each machine. Repair times are independently distributed and have an exponential distribution with mean $1/\mu$. Then if $p_n(t)$ denotes the probability that n machines are stopped at time t, and the unit of time is taken to be the mean repair time, the equations for the $p_n(t)$ as given by Benson and Cox (1951) are:-

$$\frac{dp_0(t)}{dt} = N\rho\ p_0(t) + p_1(t),$$

$$\frac{dp_n(t)}{dt} = (N - n + 1)\rho\ p_{n-1}(t) - [(N - n)\rho + 1]p_n(t) + p_{n+1}(t), \quad 1 \leqslant n \leqslant N - 1, \qquad 3.1$$

$$\frac{dp_N(t)}{dt} = \rho\ p_{N-1}(t) - p_N(t),$$

where $\rho = \dfrac{\lambda}{\mu}$.

No transient solution to these equations has been reported to date although Benson and Cox used the steady state solution in their later calculations. If

$$F(N, \rho) = 1 + N\rho + N(N - 1)\rho^2 + N(N - 1)(N - 2)\rho^3 + \ldots N!\rho^N$$

the steady state solution is given by

$$p_n = N(N - 1) \ldots (N - n + 1)\rho^n/F(n, \rho).$$

Bedsocs had few problems in dealing with this finite set of equations. For different values of N and ρ it drew the graphs for the $p_n(t)$, tabulated the functions and indicated the rate of convergence to the steady state solution. The case N = 10, $\rho(\equiv K) = 0.1$, with all machines running at time zero, is shown in Figure 2. The vertical scale is from 0 to 1, the horizontal scale from 0 to 20 and the graphs and tabulated values of $p_0(t)$, $p_1(t)$ and $p_2(t)$ are shown.

RUN
N
?10
K
?0.1

TIME	P(0)	P(1)	P(2)
0	1	0	0
3	.337734	.294115	.200855
6	.265602	.252564	.205392
9	.239589	.23397	.200757
12	.22761	.224851	.19747
15	.221554	.220119	.195543
18	.218361	.217594	.19446

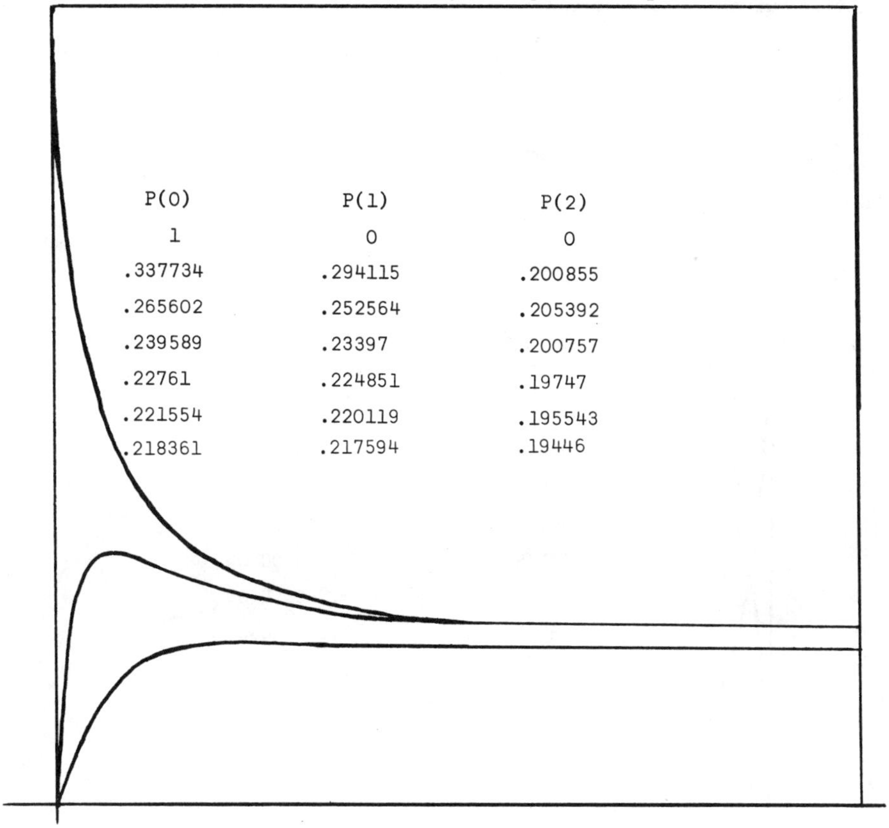

Figure 2

The distribution of the operative's busy period can be dealt with in like fashion. The busy period commences with 1 machine stopped and ends when there are no machines stopped. Thus the equations to be solved are:-

$$\frac{dp_0(t)}{dt} = p_1(t),$$

$$\frac{dp_1(t)}{dt} = -[1 + (N - 1)\rho]p_1(t) + p_2(t),$$

$$\frac{dp_n(t)}{dt} = (N - n + 1)\rho\, p_{n-1}(t) - [1 + (N - n)\rho]p_n(t) + p_{n+1}(t), \quad 2 \leqslant n \leqslant N - 1 \qquad 3.2$$

$$\frac{dp_N(t)}{dt} = \rho\, p_{N-1}(t) - p_N(t),$$

with $p_1(0) = 1$ and $p_n(0) = 0$ for $n \neq 1$. $p_0(t)$ and $p_1(t)$ represent the distribution function and probability density function of the duration of the busy period. The case $N = 5$, $\rho\ (\equiv K) = 0.2$ is shown in Figure 3.

RUN
N
?5
K
?0.2

TIME	P(0)	P(1)
0	0	1
2	.667597	.109938
4	.80748	4.58207E-02
6	.876826	2.62619E-02
8	.918793	1.66324E-02
10	.945896	1.09171E-02
12	.963815	7.26091E-03
14	.975755	4.85300E-03
16	.98376	3.24955E-03
18	.989115	2.17737E-03
20	.992704	1.45932E-03

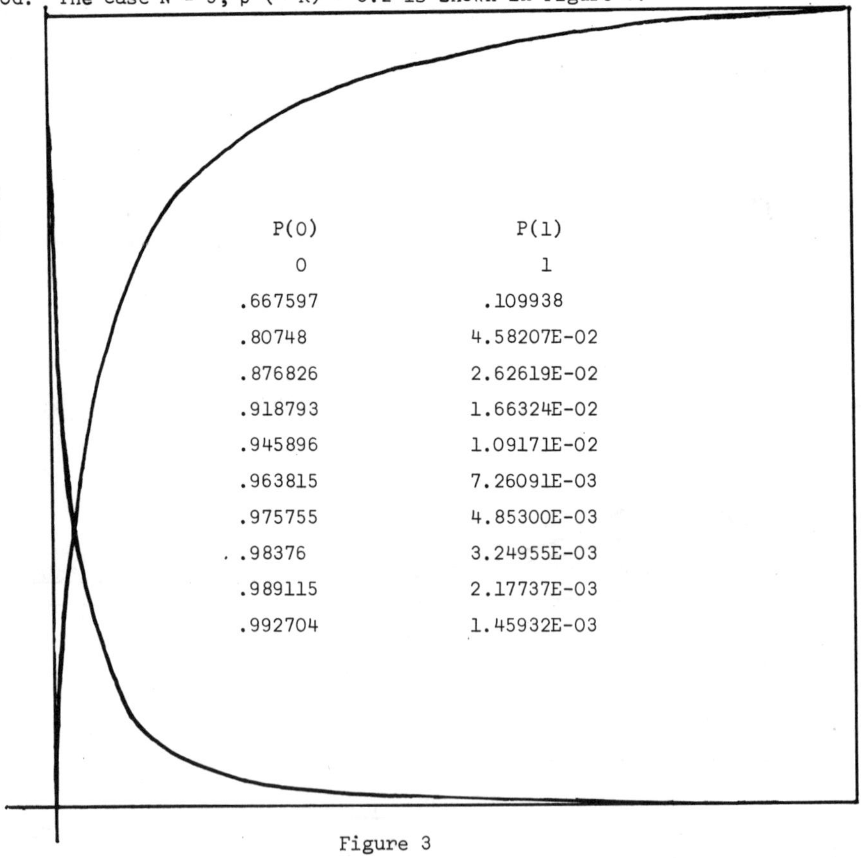

Figure 3

4. The Random Walk for the Imbedded Process

For the problem just considered, if attention is restricted to those epochs at which a machine stops or a repair is completed, then the behaviour of the system during a busy period can be represented by a random walk on a two dimensional lattice. If y denotes the number of machines running and x the number of repairs completed,

$$\Pr\{(x, y) \to (x+1, y+1)\} = \frac{\mu}{\mu + \lambda y} = \frac{P}{P + y}, \qquad \Pr\{(x, y) \to (x, y-1)\} = \frac{\lambda y}{\mu + \lambda y} = \frac{y}{P + y}, \qquad \begin{pmatrix} 0 \leq x \leq \infty; \\ 0 \leq y \leq N; \end{pmatrix} \tag{4.1}$$

where $P = \frac{\mu}{\lambda}$, and all other transitions have zero probability.

The busy period commences at (0, N - 1) and terminates at (Z, N) where Z represents the number of repairs completed in a busy period. If $\Pr(Z|x, y)$ represents the probability that starting from (x, y) absorption occurs at (Z, N) then the backward equations give

$$\Pr(Z|x, y) = \frac{P}{P + y} \Pr(Z|x + 1, y + 1) + \frac{y}{P + y} \Pr(Z|x, y - 1), \tag{4.2}$$

subject to the boundary conditions

$$\Pr(Z|x, N) = \delta_{Z,x} \quad \text{for } x \leq Z,$$

$$\Pr(Z|x, y) = \delta_{Z-x, N-y} \cdot \frac{P \,.\, P}{(P + y)(P + y + 1)} \cdots \frac{P}{(P + N - 1)} \text{ for } Z - x \leq N - y.$$

For the case N = 5, P = 10 (i.e. $\rho = 0.1$) values of $\Pr(12|x, y)$ are given in table 1. Table 2 gives the values of $\Pr(Z|0, 4)$, i.e. the distribution of the numbers of repairs during a busy period.

Table 1 Pr(12|x, y)

y \ x	0	1	2	3	4	5	6	7	8	9	10	11	12
4	.000	.000	.001	.001	.002	.004	.008	.016	.031	.065	.157	.714	0
3	.001	.001	.002	.004	.008	.015	.029	.056	.109	.226	.549	0	0
2	.001	.003	.005	.010	.019	.037	.071	.137	.258	.458	0	0	0
1	.003	.006	.011	.021	.041	.078	.149	.272	.416	0	0	0	0
0	.006	.011	.021	.041	.078	.149	.272	.416	0	0	0	0	0

Table 2 Pr(Z|0, 4)

Pr(Z|0, 4) =	.714	.157	.065	.031	.016	.008	.004	.002	.001	.001	.000	.000
Z =	1	2	3	4	5	6	7	8	9	10	11	12

Random walks for this situation based on 4.2 and as simulated and drawn by Bedsocs are shown in Figure 4.

```
RUN
P
?10
N
?5
IN. VAL. Y
?4
HOR. SC.
?20
RUNS
?100
MEAN TO N
= 1.47
```

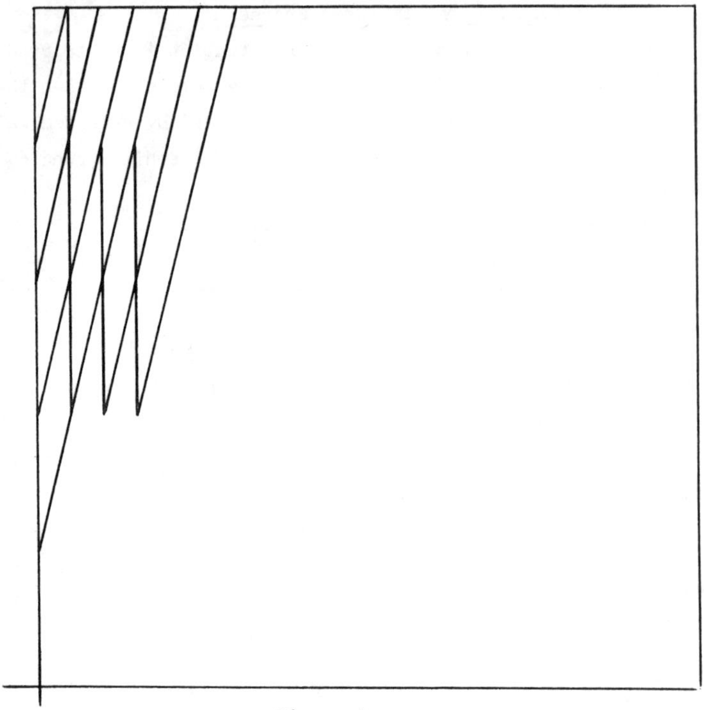

Figure 4

5. Further Applications

The examples given in this paper show Bedsocs used to advantage as a teaching aid, dramatically illustrating difficult concepts, and also as a research tool, giving numerical solutions when analytical solutions do not exist. The problems considered reflect the author's research interests as well as the areas of concern of this conference. They are by no means exhaustive, and the language has been utilised to obtain solutions to problems in stochastic epidemiology and stochastic models for chemical reactions, as well as being used to deal with sets of differential equations arising from many fields of engineering.

References

Benson, F. and Cox, D.R., The productivity of machines requiring attention at random intervals, J.R.S.S., B, 13, 65-82, 1951.

Brown, G. and Stephenson, J., Bedsocs Reference Manual, Univ. of Bradford, 1976.

Clarke, A.B., The Time Dependent Waiting Line Problem, Univ. of Michigan, Report M720-IR39, 1953.

Saaty, T.L., Elements of Queueing Theory, Chapter 2, McGraw-Hill, 1961.

Multivariate Data Analysis in Analytic-Simulation Modeling: a Case Study

W.W. Chiu and H.P. Friedman, Yorktown Heights

Measurement and data analysis are necessary for the development and effective use of analytic queueing or discrete event simulation models. This paper presents a case study that describes the use of multivariate data analysis in the development of a hybrid analytic/simulation model of an IBM MVS operating system. Graphical methods of data analysis, cluster analysis, principal component analysis, and regression analysis are used.

KEYWORDS: Computer performance modeling, multivariate statistics.

I. Introduction

Analytic queueing or discrete event simulation techniques have been widely employed for computer performance prediction. The construction of such models for complex systems often requires an understanding of system behavior under changing workload conditions. The insight and understanding is best obtained by measurement and data analysis of the system to be modeled. This paper describes some aspects of measurement and multivariate data analysis used in the development of a model of an IBM MVS operating system.

For a system as complex as MVS there are several hundred possible variables to be measured. An initial choice of variables to study was made by first constructing a conceptual model of the system logical structure. A simple view of this model is shown on figure 1. Within the framework of this model we grouped the variables into three classes: (1) system activity counts, (2) queue sizes, (3) resource utilization variables. A list of these variables is given in **page 3.**

The paper is divided into the following: section II describes the system and the discussion of the measurements; section III describes the use of scatter plots, principal components analysis and clustering analysis procedure of the resource utilization data to characterize the dynamics of system behavior; section IV describes the use of multiple regression analysis on the activities counts to provide estimates of the rates of resource utilization as parameters for use in the model.

II. The System Description and Measurements

MVS is a virtual storage paged operating system. In this section we provide an overview of the work flow through major components of MVS and the factors that delay their progress through the system (figure 1). For more detailed description the readers are referred to Scherr (1973) and Lynch and Page (1974).

In the model development process we are particularly interested in factors that delay the progress of work units through the system. There are in general three types of work units or transactions, namely, batch jobs, TSO commands and data base applications.

A batch transaction enters the JES component (Job Entry Subsystem) either from local or remote stations, and is queued by its job class parameters. A TSO command (transaction) when entered by a user from a terminal into the system is first received by the telecommunications component of MVS. The SRM schedules the workload for execution in addition maintains resource utilizations within desired levels. The mechanism that SRM uses to achieve this goal is by swapping address spaces in and out of main storage, i.e., control of the multiprogramming set, since transactions can only make progress when executing on the CPU. The Real Storage Manager (RSM) allocates real storage page frames on demand in the MVS virtual storage environment.

Since program behavior is dynamic in nature, the same MPL sometimes may cause unacceptably high page fault rates that reduce actual throughput. To prevent overcommitment of main storage, the SRM monitors the paging rates between main storage and secondary paging devices (such as drums or disks). If the rate exceeds some threshold, the target MPL Of some domain is decreased by one. On the other hand, if resources are under utilized the reverse happends.

A measurement tool, called RESMON, Chiu and Galatil (1977), which is capable of capturing and outputting both system and user statistics at fixed time intervals and event occurrences, was developed. The output of RESMON is a multivariate time series together with asynchronous event traces. Benchmark experiments were conducted on an IBM 370/158 with three megabytes of memory under different loads. Each experiment lasts about half an hour. The monitor sampling frequency is 2 seconds. In the next sections we describe the data analysis procedures using the data from the experiment of 30 TSO users and 5 batch initiators.

III. Exploratory Data Analysis

The variables selected for the analysis are as follows:

1. user swap out rate (per second (SOUT);
2. TSO arrival rate (URDY);
3. memory shortage rate (AVQL);
4. rate of paging operations into memory (PIN);
5. count of TSO users on CPU queue (TSOCQ);
6. count of batch users on CPU queue (BATCQ);
7. average multiprogramming level (MPL);
8. CPU utilization (CPU);
9. uncharged CPU (UNCPU);
10. TSO CPU (TSOCPU);
11. batch I/O rate (BATIO);
12. batch cpu (BATCPU);
13. total I/O rate (TSIO);
14. master scheduler task CPU (MASTCPU);
15. telecommunication task CPU (TCAMCPU);
16. TSO I/O rate (TSOIO);
17. number of active users (ACTIVE);
18. count of domain 1 users (batch+system) in memory (I1);
19. count of domain 2 users (short TSO) in memory (I2);
20. count of domain 3 users (long TSO) in memory (I3).

These variables represent the major components of resource utilization, queue sizes as well as some indication of the activities responsible for the resource utilizations as indicated by the conceptual model. The data consists of 120 samples of consecutive ten second intervals. The average CPU utilization is nearly 100 percent throughout the run and that UNCPU (mostly system overhead) is about 15 percent. UNCPU includes the overheads of task switching, scheduling functions, interrupt handling and various system services. Summary statistics do not give any indication of the system dynamics. Relationships between variables have been explored with numerous scatter plots, figure 2. A subset of the original 20 variables are shown. These six variables reflect the CPU and I/O utilizations: (1) UNCPU, (2) TSOCPU, (3) BATCPU, (4) TSIO, (5) MASTCPU, and (6) TCAMCPU. The scatter plots indicate that batch CPU usage decreases as TSO CPU usage increases. This is to be expected since TSO users in general have priority over batch users. There is also a strong relationship between UNCPU, TSIO and MASTCPU. Also indicated by these plots are small groups of outliers of atypical behavior when the master scheduler task was dominant.

To gain further understanding of the behavior of the system the following analyses were performed. A data matrix, called UTIL, consisting of 120 rows representing the intervals and six columns containing the CPU and I/O utilization variables, the same as in figure 2, was the input for the analyses.

Some preliminary cluster analysis was done using a variety of procedures. In particular a single linkage clustering was done after standardizing the columns of UTIL, Hartigan (1975). There was no evidence of strong clustering of the ten second intervals. Further the data were clustered by minimizing the determinant of the pooled within group covariance matrix, Friedman and Rubin (1967). Again there was no evidence of strong clustering found. However, both these procedures were picking out small groups of outliers reflecting the anamolies seen in the scatter plots relating to master scheduler activities (MASTCPU).

We then decided to do a principal component analysis of the standardized data matrix. This analysis was done with caution with the view towards handling the outliers. Initially we found that we required three components to account for 90 percent variation of the data. Residual plot showed the third component was primarily due to a single outlier with unusually high MASTCPU as well as high TSOCPU. Removal of this outlier gave two components accounting for 92 percent of the variation. The eigen values were 3.04, 1.8, .70, .36, .079 and .024 respectively. A table of the eigen vectors scaled by the square root of the corresponding eigen values is given below for the two largest values:

.94	-.58	.07	.89	.86	.54
.12	.80	-.98	.18	.06	.38

A plot of the columns of this matrix is shown in figure 3. This plot shows that the first eigen vector direction is controlled by the variables 1, 4, 5 and 6. The second eigen vector direction reflects the difference between variables 2 and 3 (TSOCPU-BATCPU). A plot of the projection of the standardized data matrix onto these two eigen vector directions is shown in figure 4.

As can be seen from figure 4 there was no evidence of distinct clusters in this plane. Even though there are no distinct clusters we decided to look for dominant modes. A KMEANS cluster analysis, Hartigan (1975), was performed on the standardized UTIL. The algorithm was chosen because at this stage in the analysis we thought that the data was well described by the principal components. This algorithm will partition the data to minimize the within group sum of squares. We decided that 3 clusters best described the principal components analysis. The center of cluster A was above average on variables1, 4, 5 and 6. Cluster B was above average on TSOCPU. Cluster C was above average on BATCPU. Projections of the 6 dimensional cluster centers onto the space of principal components is shown in figure 4 as A, B and C. The remaining components are uninformative. Figure 5 depicts the cluster centers in wrapped profile diagrams as in Friedman, et al. (1975).

Our conclusions from this analysis is that one could characterize the CPU and I/O activities in this two dimensional plane. In particular, samle intervals falling around A represent a contention state of high I/O, MASTCPU and UNCPU activities (about 36% of all the samples). Those samples falling around B and C represent high TSO and BATCH CPU activities respectively (36% and 28%). The high percentage of cluster A samples indicated that the UNCPU and MASTCPU activities were important factors to be dealt with in the model. They would have to be allocated to various activities accounting for them. Details of this analysis are described in the next section.

IV. Parameter Estimation

In this section we describe multiple regression analysis on counts data to account for UNCPU and MASTCPU. Multiple regression analysis with UNCPU and the dependent variable was straight forward. Backward elimination procedures, Hocking (1976), gave the following equation:

UNCPU = A0 + al SOUT + a2 PIN + a3 TSIO
a0 = 26.4 millisecond per second real time
al = 25.5 millisecond per SOUT
a2 = 1.4 millisecond per PIN
a3 = 1.7 millisecond per TSIO
T values = 6.5, 10.6, 4.8, 22.3
DF of residuals = 116 R squared = .92

The residual plots show no strong evidence of either lack of fit or nonnormality. UNCPU is the fitted uncharged CPU time in milliseconds of CPU time per second of real time. The coefficients provide us with the cost of each of these operations and are used as inputs to the model.

The MASTCPU was regressed on SOUT (swap out rate) and PIN (page in rate) only. Since the other counts data do not functionally relate to the master scheduler task. Initial regression analysis and subsequent Q-Q plot of the residuals, Gnanadesikan (1977), figure 6, gave strong evidence of several outliers in the data. A review of the circumstances indicated that these anamolies in the master scheduler activities were related to operator communications.

After 5 outliers have been removed the following equation was obtained for MASTCPU:

MASTCPU = a0 + al SOUT + a2 PIN
a0 = 9.48 millisecond per second real time
al = 13.1 millisecond per SOUT
a2 = 3.6 millisecond per PIN
T values = 2.6, 5.1, 14.9
DF of residuals = 112 R squared = .79

Subsequent Q-Q plot of the residuals of this equation is shown in figure 7.

V. Conclusions

We have described the use of multivariate data analysis in the development of a hybrid analytic/simulation model of an IBM MVS operating system. For details of the model, see Chiu and Chow (1978). Graphical methods were used to expose unusual overhead CPU usages. Principal components and cluster analysis were used to characterize the dynamics of system behavior or over time. Regression procedures were used to provide rates of overhead usage for the model. As a result a more parsimonious hybrid model was developed that combined computational efficiency of an analytic model with the flexibility of a simulation model.

VI. References

Chiu, W. and Chow, W., A Hybrid Hierarchical Model of a Multiple Virtual Storage (MVS) Operating System, IBM Research report RC6947, 1978.

Chiu, W. and Galati, G., Resmon: a software measurement tool for MVS, IBM Research, 1977.

Friedman, H. and Rubin, J., On some invariant criteria for grouping data, J. Am. Stat. Assoc., 62, 1159-1178, 1967.

Friedman, H., Goldwyn, R. and Siegel, J., The use and interpretation of multivariate methods in the classification of stages in serious infectious disease processes in the critically ill, Perspectives in Biometrics, Academic Press, Vol. 1, 82-122, 1975.

Gnanadesikan, R., Methods for statistical data analysis of multivariate observations, Wiley, N. Y,, 1977.

Hartigan, J., Clustering Algorithms, Wiley, N. Y., 1975.

Hocking, R., The analysis and selection of variables in linear regression, Biometrics, 32, 1-49, 1976.

Lynch, W. and Page, J., The OS/VS2 Release 2 System Resources Manager, IBM Systems Journal, Vol. 13, No. 4, 1974.

Scherr, A., Functional Structure of IBM Virtual Storage Operating Systems Part II: OS/VS2-2 concepts and Philosophies, IBM Systems Journal, Vol. 12, No. 4, 1973.

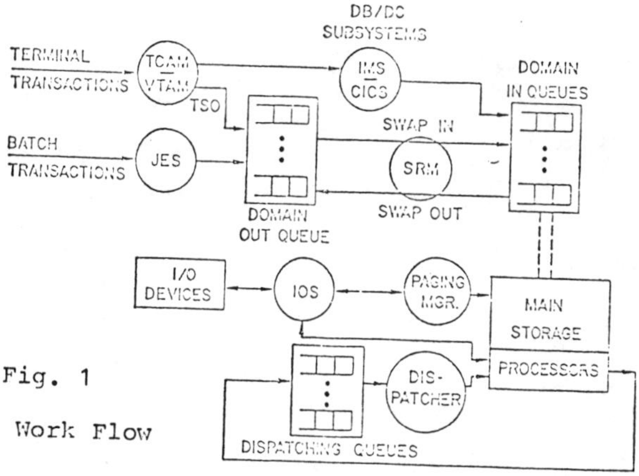

Fig. 1

MVS Work Flow

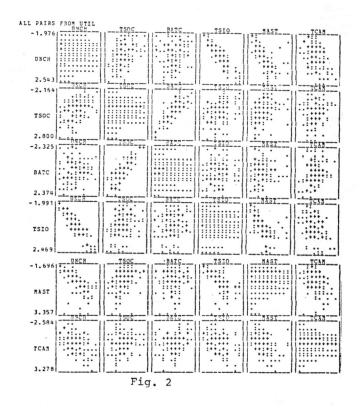

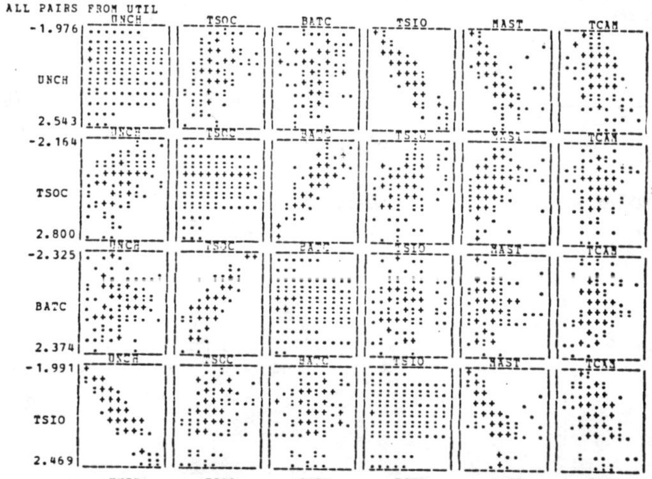

Fig. 2

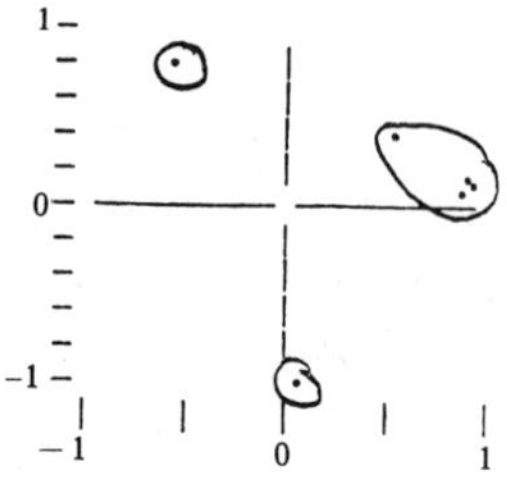

Fig. 3

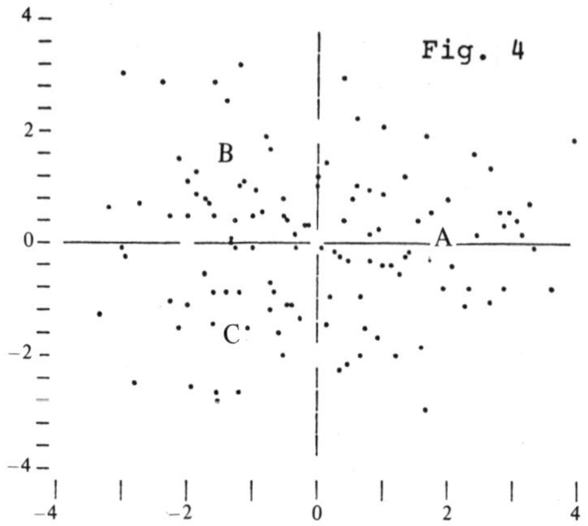

Fig. 4

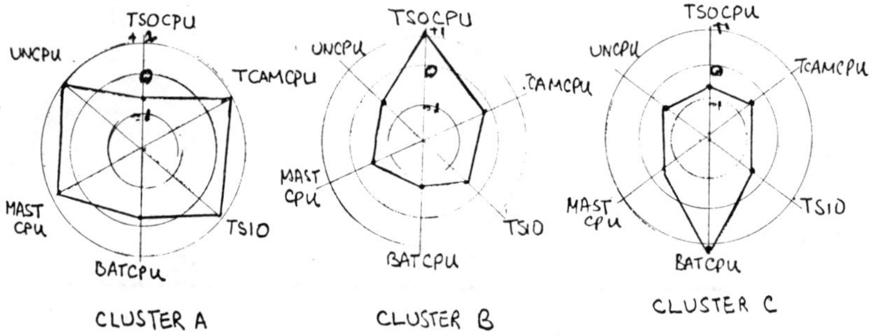

Fig. 5

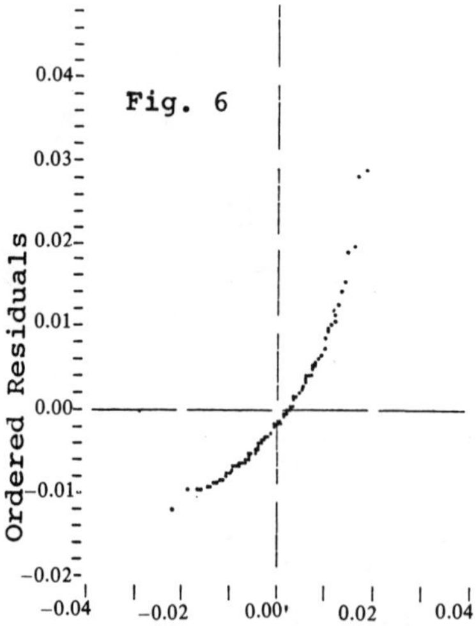

Fig. 6

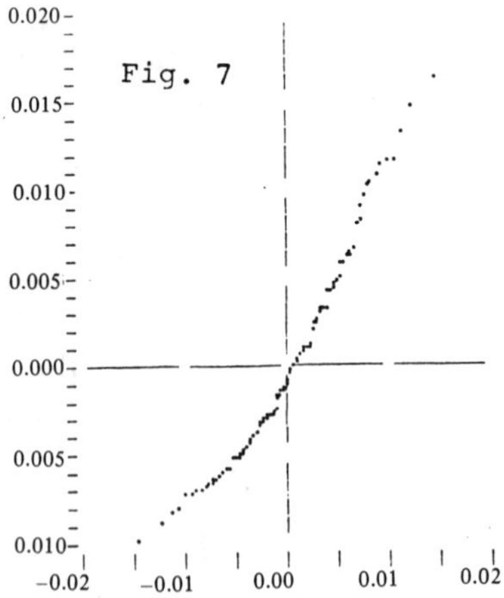

Fig. 7

Expected Values of Normal Order Statistics

Monte Carlo Integer Programming Applied to Nonlinear Oil Refinery Problems

W.C. Conley and D.S. Tracy, Green Bay

SUMMARY

A computer technique is presented for solving nonlinear optimization problems in oil refineries. An example is presented. A discussion of some of the special difficulties encountered in refinery work follows. Then it is shown how to use current and future computer technology and statistics to solve an optimization problem in any field of endeavor.

"KEYWORDS" Oil Refinery, Nonlinear, Optimization, Computer, General Technique

1. INTRODUCTION

Monte Carlo integer programming is a computer technique that performs a random search for the optimum of the mathematical programming problem in question. Until recently this solution approach was rarely tried. However two new developments have made Monte Carlo optimization attractive. The first is the tremendous improvements and advances in speed, capacity, and availability of computers. This frequently makes random samples in the millions possible. The second is the study of sampling distributions of feasible solutions of a wide variety of optimization problems by Conley and Tracy (1977) and Conley (1978). The technique used was developed by Conley and Tracy (1976). The results of these studies show that any practical optimization problem has so many nearly optimal solutions that a random search is extremely effective in solving the problem.

We present a nonlinear oil refinery problem as an illustration.

2. THE REFINERY PROBLEM

An oil refinery can obtain five grades of crude oil. It uses the crudes to make three products. They need to make 400 units of Product 1,

450 units of product 2, and 550 units of Product 3. The following table shows what percentage of a unit of each crude becomes Product 1, Product 2, and Product 3. For example, 1 unit of crude oil 1 yields .3 units of Product 1, .35 units of Product 2, and .30 units of Product 3. It is required to produce 400 units of Product 1, 450 units of Product 2 and 550 units of Product 3.

YIELDS OF THE FIVE CRUDES

	1	2	3	4	5
Product 1	.30	.25	.30	.25	.35
Product 2	.35	.30	.25	.25	.25
Product 3	.30	.40	.40	.40	.30

In addition the refinery can obtain at most 600 units of Crude 1, 1500 units of Crude 2, 600 units of Crude 3, 200 units of Crude 4, and 400 units of Crude 5. Also, the limited supply and demand factors cause the prices for the crudes to be nonlinear (vary with the amount purchased). If x_i is the number of units purchased of crude i, the cost equation is given as $C=\$4.02x_1^{1.06}+\$5.18x_2^{1.09}+\$4.58x_3^{1.11}+\$3.82x_4^{1.15}+\$4.48x_5^{.94}$

The problem is to select the right amounts of the various crudes to satisfy the yield requirements of 400, 450, and 550 units and at the same time minimize C. Therefore, the problem can be stated as

$$\text{Minimize } C=4.02x_1^{1.06}+5.18x_2^{1.09}+4.58x_3^{1.11}+3.82x_4^{1.15}+4.48x_5^{.94}$$

subject to

$$.30x_1+.25x_2+.30x_3+.25x_4+.35x_5=400$$

$$.35x_1+.30x_2+.25x_3+.25x_4+.25x_5=450$$

$$.30x_1+.40x_2+.40x_3+.40x_4+.30x_5=550$$

$$0\leq x_1\leq 600,\ 0\leq x_2\leq 1500,\ 0\leq x_3\leq 600,$$

$$0\leq x_4\leq 200 \text{ and } 0\leq x_5\leq 400.$$

In this case a Monte Carlo search is not needed because (after solving the system of equations) there are only 80,601 feasible solutions. Therefore our computer program is written to search all combinations for the minimum cost. The solution is:

$$x_1=436.84,\ x_2=705.26,\ x_3=142.11,\ x_4=200,\ x_5=0$$

and minimum C=$11,935.40.

3. DISCUSSION

However in larger problems (with billions and trillions of answers) a random search is necessary. But the well behaved nature of sampling distributions of integer programming problems (no isolated optimums) guarantees a good "optimal" solution from the simulation approach. Figures 1 through 4 present some examples. Figure 1 is the actual sampling distribution of the oil refinery problem discussed in section 2.

Oil refinery problems (and other applications) that deal with systems of equations face the additional difficulty of having to exclude negative values from any of the solution variables. Many times this can be handled by reading in random numbers in a sequence, where each number takes into account what the values of the previous random numbers were. This and the other programming details are available from the authors.

4. CONCLUSION

The power and usefulness of the simplex technique for linear programming and the modified distribution technique for "linear" transportation problems is demonstrated by their wide acceptance in applications. This should continue for decades to come.

However they were developed before today's and tomorrow's "super" computers were available. These computers make possible the solution of optimization problems, by previously inefficient techniques, with tremendous efficiency and speed. This frees the quantitative worker to develop more

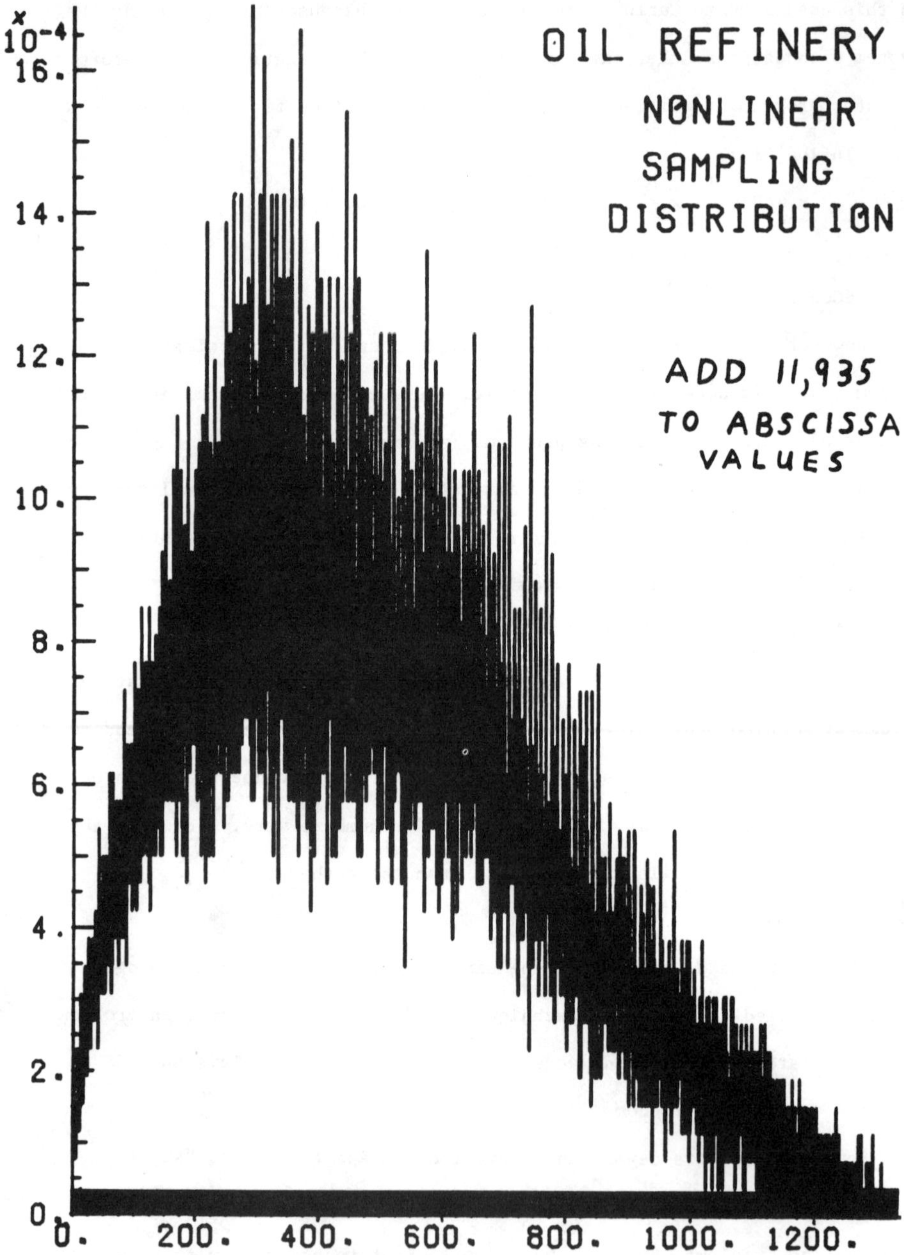
OIL REFINERY
NONLINEAR
SAMPLING
DISTRIBUTION
ADD 11,935
TO ABSCISSA
VALUES
x 10^-4
16.
14.
12.
10.
8.
6.
4.
2.
0
0.
200.
400.
600.
800.
1000.
1200.

FIGURE 1

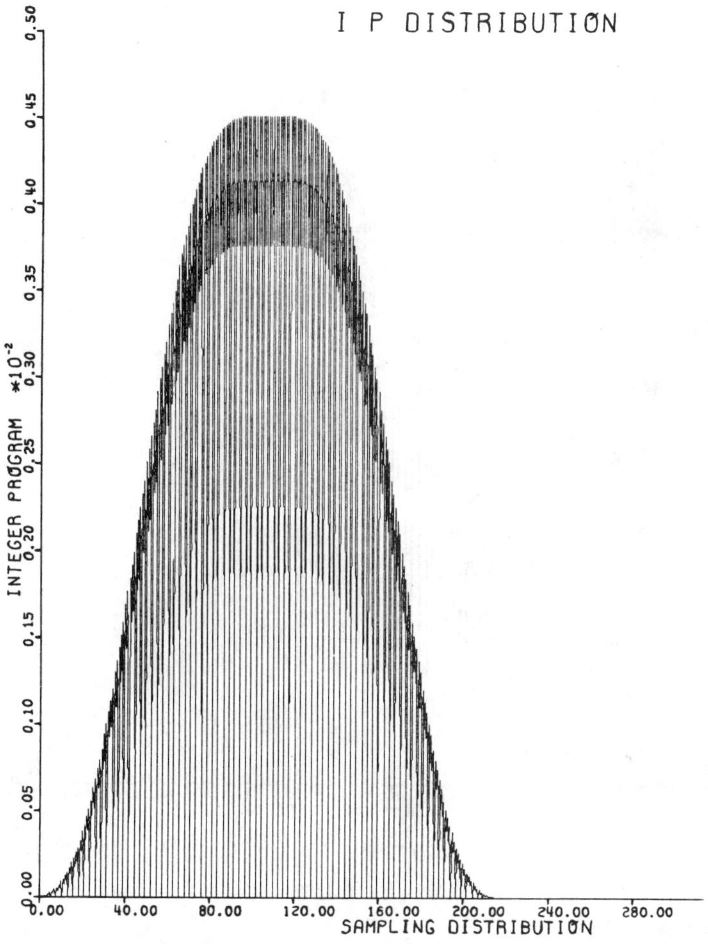

of $P = x_1 + 2x_2 + 2.5x_3 + 5x_4 + 11x_5$ subject to $0 \le x_i \le 10$ $i = 1, 5$

Figure 2

accurate models in business, industry, and science, and allows the computer to worry about finding the optimal solution. With this point of view non-linear problems present few difficulties.

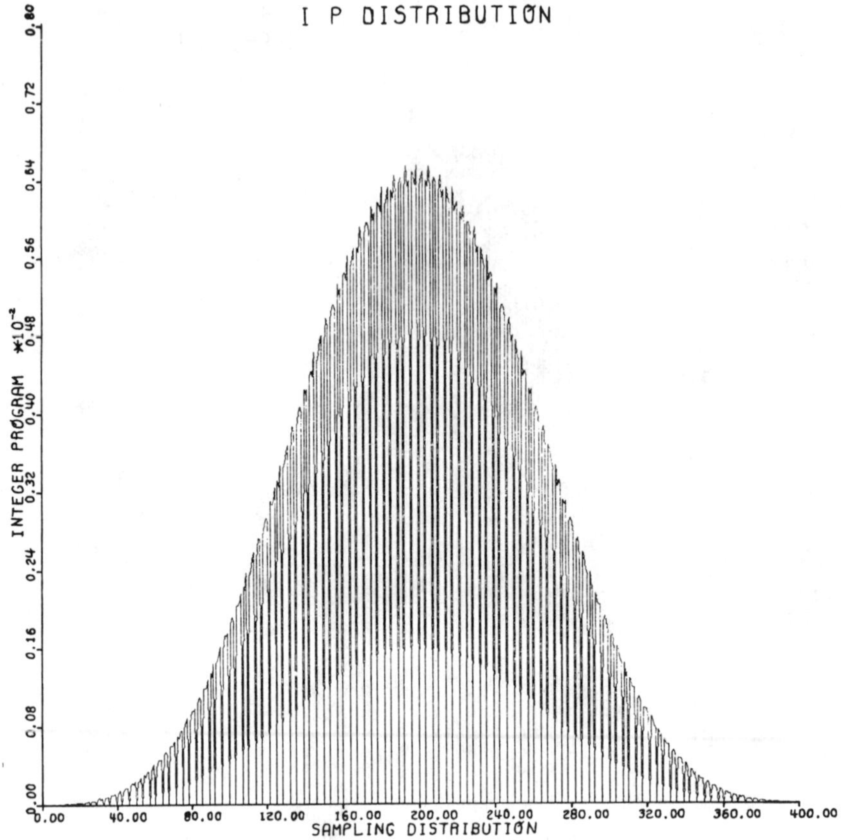

of $P = 9x_1 + 8x_2 + 12x_3 + 6x_4 + 5x_5$ subject to $0 \le x_i \le 10$ $i = 1, 5$

Figure 3

5. NOTE ON GRAPHS

The graphs are plots of the sampling distributions of selected integer programming problems. They were drawn on a Calcomp plotter attached to an I.B.M. 360-65 and a Xerox Sigma 6 computer. Sampling distributions of integer programming problems are produced by treating the objective function as a statistic, and plotting the histogram of all the feasible solutions. The computer programs were written in FORTRAN IV.

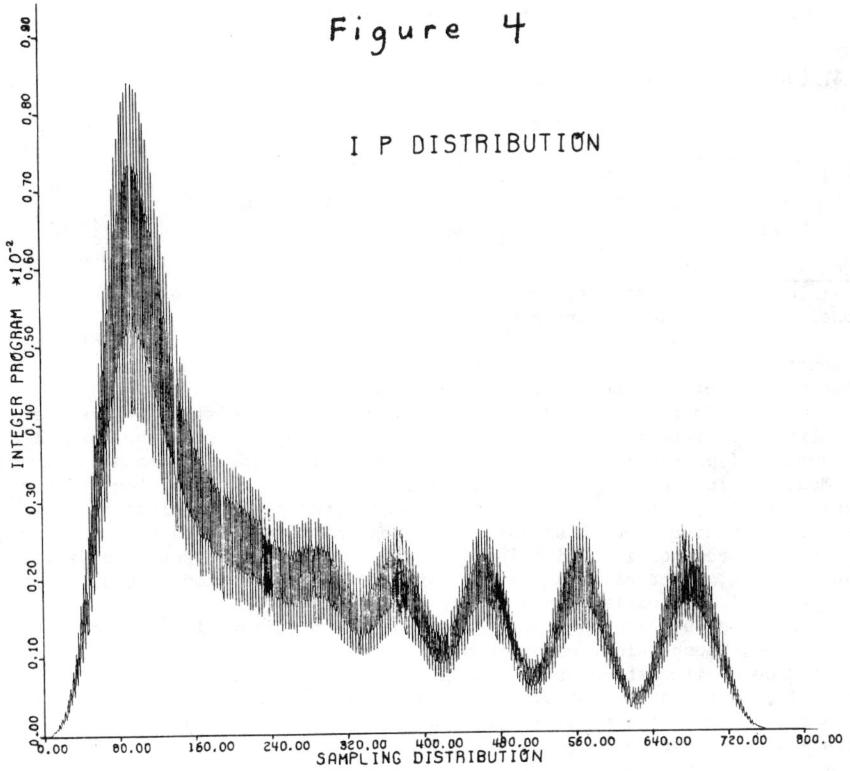

of $P = 3x_1 + 5x_2 + 6x_3^2 + 5x_4 + 3x_5$ subject to $0 \le x_i \le 10$ $i = 1,5$

REFERENCES

Conley, W.C., Simplifying the teaching of integer programming, Int. J. Math. Educ. Sci. Technol., 9, 1978.

Conley, W.C. and D.S. Tracy, Integer Programming with a Computer: A Statistical Approach, Proceedings of Computer Science and Statistics: Tenth Annual Symposium on the Interface, National Bureau of Standards, Gaithersburg, Maryland, 362-366, 1977.

Conley, W.C. and D.S. Tracy, Small Sample Sampling Distributions, COMPSTAT 1976 Proceedings in Computational Statistics, Physica-Verlag, Wurzburg-Vienna, 239-246, 1976.

Stochastic Simulation of a Space-Time Dependent Predator-Prey Model

D.M. Dubois and **G. Monfort**, Liege

SUMMARY.

In 1957, Bartlett performed an artificial realization of a stochastic model of the Lotka-Volterra predator-prey system.

The paper deals with a generalization of the Bartlett work in taking into account not only the time dependent behavior of the predator-prey system but also spatial effects due to random walks (spatial diffusion).

One developed a new method for the stochastic simulation of a system of non-linear differential equations describing the dynamics of the spatial distribution of populations in predator-prey relationship. This method belongs to Monte-Carlo techniques : by generations of random numbers, the horizontal (one dimension) distribution of prey and predator concentrations is simulated.

The computer simulation shows the spontaneous emergence of very strong spatial heterogeneities which is called the patchiness effect. One assists to the creation, propagation and annihilation of concentrations waves, and this, independently of initial and boundary conditions.

The fundamental mechanism of this spatial structuration can be explained as follows. Stochastic fluctuations drive the system very far from equilibrium and induce a bifurcation within the predator-prey system which is structurally unstable. In the phase space, one has a stable stochastic limit cycle. This effect belongs to the temporal dissipative structures class defined by Prigogine and to Thom's morphogenesis theory.

KEYWORDS: Lotka-Volterra model, predator-prey system, stochastic simulation, spatial heterogeneities, dissipative structure, morphogenesis.

The Lotka-Volterra predator-prey model.

Classical Lotka-Volterra predator-prey model is given by two differential equations

$$\frac{dN_1}{dt} = k_1N_1 - k_2N_1N_2$$

$$\frac{dN_2}{dt} = -k_3N_2 + \alpha k_2N_1N_2$$

where t is the time, N_1 and N_2 the prey and predator populations, respectively, k_1 the growth rate of the prey, k_3 the decay rate of the predator, k_2 the predator-prey interaction rate and α the utilisation coefficient.
Properties and solutions of these equations can be found in the excellent book of Pielou (1969).

In 1957, Bartlett performed a stochastic simulation on computer (artificial

realizations) of the above Lotka-Volterra system. Let us summarize his technique.
Three possible events are considered at any time : (i) the birth of a prey, (ii) the death of a predator, and (iii) the attack of a prey by a predator. The probability of occurence of each of these events is given in table I.

Table I.

EVENT		PROBABILITY
$N_1 \to N_1 + 1$	$N_2 \to N_2$	$P_1 = Ck_1N_1$
$N_1 \to N_1$	$N_2 \to N_2 - 1$	$P_2 = Ck_3N_2$
$N_1 \to N_1 - 1$	$N_2 \to N_2 + 1$	$P_3 = Ck_2N_1N_2$

The constant C is such that the probabilities sum to unity. In table I, $\alpha = 1$; it means that the birth of a predator always coincides with the death of a prey. If it is not the case, then the event $N_1 \to N_1 - 1$ will have two possible accompaniments : either $N_2 \to N_2 + 1$, with probability equal to $C\alpha k_2N_1N_2$, or $N_2 \to N_2$, with probability equal to $C(1 - \alpha)k_2N_1N_2$. This would happen if some predator attacks were unsuccessful so that, though the prey was killed by the attack, no predator was born as a result. The simulation on computer is made as follows. One generates a random number R in the range (0,1(. If $R \leqslant P_1$ let the next event be the birth of a prey, if $P_1 < R < P_1 + P_2$ the next event will be the death of a predator, and so on. Once the event has happened and the populations sizes have been adjusted accordingly we may calculate the new probabilities (which depend on the new populations sizes) for the next event and proceed as before. Thus we have a sequence of events. Next consider when the events occur, assuming that simulation begins at time zero. We require the probability density function (pdf) of t, the time to the next event. We assume that, so long as the populations remain of sizes N_1 and N_2, the probability of an event in any time interval is independent of the probability in an earlier interval. If we write $p_0(t)$ for the probability that no event will occur in an interval of length t, it then follows that :

$$p_0(t + \Delta t) = p_0(t)p_0(\Delta t) = p_0(t)(1 - \frac{1}{C} t)$$

Letting $\Delta t \to 0$, we have

$$\frac{dp_0(t)}{dt} = - \frac{1}{C} p_0(t)$$

Since we take $p_0(0) = 0$, one has $p_0(t) = \exp(- \frac{t}{C})$ which represents the probability that at time t no event will occur.
The cumulative distribution function of the time elapsed before the next event is thus :

$$F(t) = Pr(\text{time to next event } \Delta t)= 1 - p_0(t) = 1 - \exp(- \frac{t}{C})$$

and the pdf is

$$f(t) = F'(t) = \frac{1}{C} \exp(- \frac{t}{C})$$

For simulation of the process we select as before one random number R and set it equal to F(t). Solving for t, we get $t = -C \ln(1 - R)$ the random value of t desired.

Bartlett performed simulation of the Lotka-Volterra model in such a way. He has showed that one of the population dies after a few oscillations. Thus, the stochastic system is unstable : this can be explained by the fact that no internal mechanism yields to the regression of random fluctuations. Let us generalize Bartlett's work in taking into account the spatial diffusion of populations.

Simulation of predator-prey populations spatial patterns.

In 1975, Dubois proposed the following generalization of the Lotka-Volterra predator-prey model in the framework of marine populations

$$\frac{\partial N_1}{\partial t} + \underline{w}.\nabla N_1 = k_1 N_1 - k_2 N_1 N_2 + \nabla.(K \nabla N_1)$$

$$\frac{\partial N_2}{\partial t} + \underline{w}.\nabla N_2 = -k_3 N_2 + \alpha k_2 N_1 N_2 + \nabla.(K \nabla N_2)$$

where K is a diffusion coefficient (i.e. diffusivity of the sea), $\underline{w}$ the velocity of the advection current of the sea. This system was numerically simulated for describing the spatial repartition of phytoplankton (prey) and herbivorous zooplankton (predator) populations in the North Sea (Dubois, 1975). The equations were integrated upon the depth so that only the horizontal pattern was obtained (in the North Sea, depth is very small in comparison with horizontal dimensions). The spatial operator was then given by $\nabla = \underline{1}_x \partial/\partial x + \underline{1}_y \partial/\partial y$ (x and y representing the horizontal coordinates). Contrary to experimental data for plankton populations, the asymptotic solution of this deterministic system is given by a quasi-uniform repartition of both populations.
Surprisingly, the stochastic simulation leads to the spontaneous emergence of very strong spatial heterogeneities like the real situation in the sea.

The stochastic simulation of the above system is a generalization of Bartlett's technique. Before giving the full algorithm, let us make a few remarks.
Due to the prohibitive computer time, only the one-dimensional spatial problem was simulated stochastically. Dubois showed that the deterministic solutions at one and two spatial coordinates give the same type of spatial pattern.
The stochastic simulation of the spatial system is unstable like Bartlett's simulation (Dubois and Monfort, 1978). In view of stabilizing the system, the equations are slightly modified in taking into account the experimental fact that the predator-prey interaction rate k_2 is zero when the concentration of the prey becomes smaller than a critical threshold N_1^*.
The 1-D spatial domain is divided in n cells of length equal to Δx and each cell is noticed by the index i (i=1,...,n). The probabilities corresponding to the diffusion and advection effects are given by the well-known finite differences schemes formula of the diffusion and adection operators, respectively, in the deterministic equations. Let us notice that the finite differences scheme for the advection operator depends on the sign of the adection current w. For satisfying the Von Neumann criterium of numerical stability, we use an alternating method for simulating the velocity field w : during the time inter- ΔT, all w_i are positive and during the following ΔT, all w_i are negative. The w_i's are assumed to be randomly distributed following a Gaussian curve. As the scheme introduces a numerical viscosity, the value of the coefficient of diffusion K (which is taken constant) is adjusted so that it fits with experimental values. This numerical viscosity is related to the cell length.

Table II describes the different events we consider as well as their probabilities. An event is by definition a modification of one unit of concentration of a population inside one and only one cell of the spatial domain.

Starting at time t = 0, with a uniform distribution of both populations, Figure 1 shows, at time 5 (one time period later), the spontaneous emergence of one patch of prey. In Figure 2, a high density prey patch is created (1)

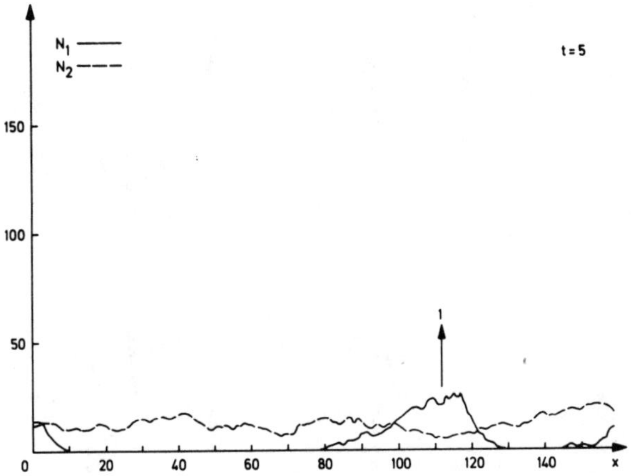

Figure 1.

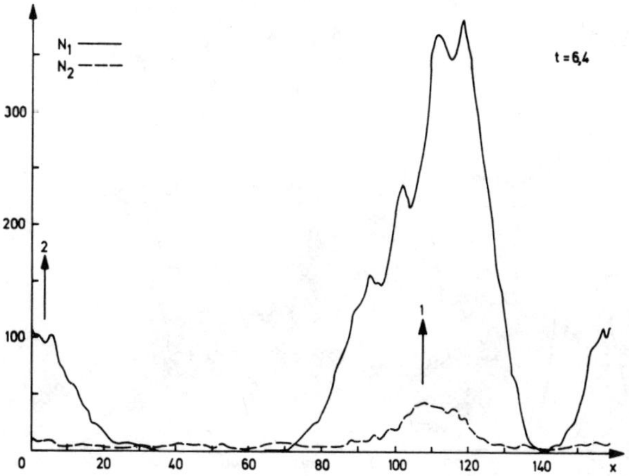

Figure 2.

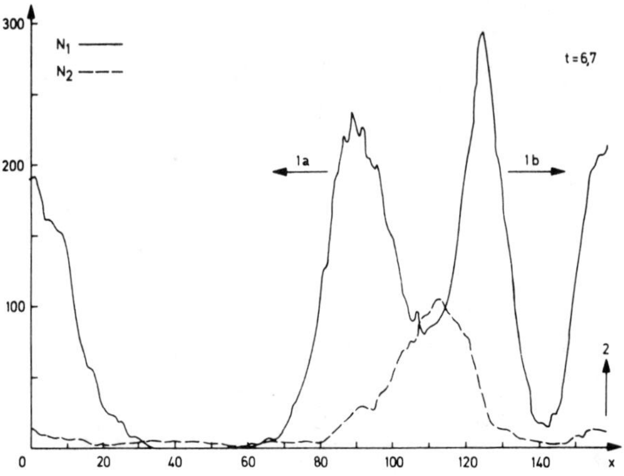

Figure 3.

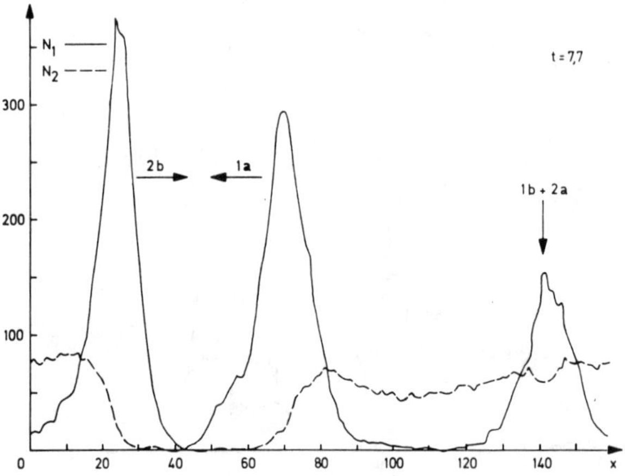

Figure 4.

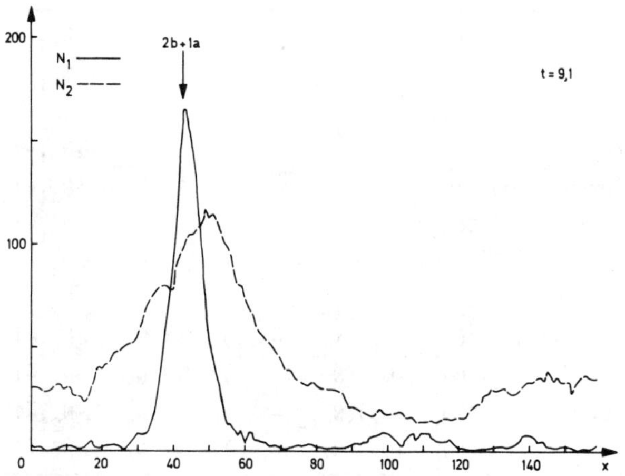

Figure 5.

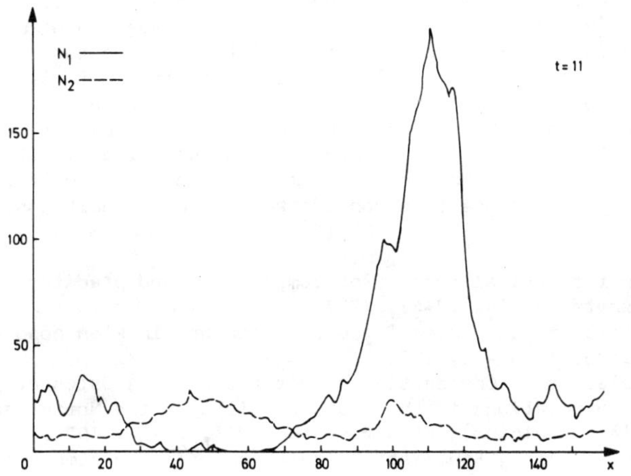

Figure 6.

Table II.

	PROBABILITY (1)	EVENT
Birth of a prey	$Ck_1^+ N_{1i}$	$N_{1i} \rightarrow N_{1i}+1$
Death of a prey	$Ck_1^- N_{1i}$	$N_{1i} \rightarrow N_{1i}-1$
Birth of a predator	$Ck_3^+ N_{2i}$	$N_{2i} \rightarrow N_{2i}+1$
Death of a predator	$Ck_3^- N_{2i}$	$N_{2i} \rightarrow N_{2i}-1$
Decay of a prey (predation)	$Ck_2 N_{1I} N_{2i}$	$N_{1i} \rightarrow N_{1i}-1$
Growth of a predator (,,)	$C\alpha k_2 N_{1i} N_{2i}$	$N_{2i} \rightarrow N_{2i}+1$
Diffusion of a prey	$\pm CK(N_{1i+1}+N_{1i-1}-2N_{1i})/\Delta x^2$	$N_{1i} \rightarrow N_{1i}\pm 1$
Diffusion of a predator	$\pm CK(N_{2i+1}+N_{2i-1}-2N_{2i})/\Delta x^2$	$N_{2i} \rightarrow N_{2i}\pm 1$
Advection of a prey: $w > 0$	$\pm C(w_{i-1}+w_i)(N_{1i-1}-N_{1i})/2\Delta x$	$N_{1i} \rightarrow N_{1i}\pm 1$
$w < 0$	$\pm C(w_{i+1}+w_i)(N_{1i}-N_{1i+1})/2\Delta x$	$N_{1i} \rightarrow N_{1i}\pm 1$
Adv. of a predator: $w > 0$	$\pm C(w_{i-1}+w_i)(N_{2i-1}-N_{2i})/2\Delta x$	$N_{2i} \rightarrow N_{2i}\pm 1$
$w < 0$	$\pm C(w_{i+1}+w_i)(N_{2i}-N_{2i+1})/2\Delta x$	$N_{2i} \rightarrow N_{2i}\pm 1$

(1) : In the case of diffusion and advection, the sign + or - is chosen so that the probability is always positive. As a consequence, the event is the increase or decrease of one unit of population (prey or predator).

and a second one is beginning to create (2). A predator patch is also created (due to its growth with a time lag). The creation of 2 prey waves (1a and 1b) is well-shown in Figure 3 as a consequence of the increase of predator populations in the center of the prey patch. Noticed also the development of the second prey patch. The first wave (1a) propagates to the left with a velocity given approximately by $v = 2(k_1 K)^{1/2}$. Due to the same process, patch 2 splits also in two waves (2a and 2b). Figure 4 shows the propagation of waves 2b (to the right) and 1a (to the left) and the annihilation of the two meeting waves (1b and 2a). When waves 2b and 1a meet, one assists also to their annihilation, as given in Figure 5. Finally, Figure 6 shows the creation of a new prey patch and the spatial pattern looks very similar to the spatial pattern of Figure 2. In fact, the same type of spatial pattern appears periodically with a slight modification. It may be remarked that the emergence of these patterns is independent of boundary conditions : we considered periodic conditions.

REFERENCES.

Bartlett M.S., On theoretical models for competitive and predatory biological systems, Biometrika, 44, 27-42, 1957.

Dubois D.M., A model of patchiness for prey-predator plankton populations, Ecol. Modelling, 1, 67-80, 1975.

Dubois D.M., Simulation of the spatial structuration of a patch of prey-predator plankton populations in the Southern Bight of the North Sea, Mém. Soc. Roy. Sci. Liège (Belgium), 6° série, tome VII, 75-82, 1975.

Dubois D.M. and G. Monfort, Stochastic simulation of space-time dependent predator models, Lecture Notes in Control and Information Sciences, Springer-Verlag, 6, 400-410, 1978.

Pielou E.C., An introduction to mathematical ecology, Wiley-Interscience, 1969.

Volterra V., Leçon sur la théorie mathématique de la lutte pour la vie, Gauthier-Villars, Paris, 1931.

Network Design and Control by Simulation Experiments

W. Grossmann, G. Pflug and **W. Schimanovich**, Vienna

SUMMARY: A complex algorithm for the evaluation of network performance, including simulation, mathematical programming and optimization by iteration is presented. This algorithm is especially suitable for the study of urban street networks.

KEY WORDS: traffic simulation, flows on transport networks, mathematical programming.

1. INTRODUCTION

We will consider a network (directed graph) with given numbers of nodes and edges. Furthermore a demand matrix is given whose elements y^{ab} are the demand between origin node a and destination node b. One problem is to find the system optimal flow for this demand (normative assignment) in the network. Another problem is that of comparing two different networks as to how far they differ in their optimal performance.

As a special case we will investigate traffic networks. In that case we have to distinguish between two different kinds of problems:

(i) Highway networks: Here the flow is almost determined by the performance on the edges. The behavior on the nodes and the control system is therefore only of secondary importance for the optimization. An extensive treatment of the problem can be found in Steenbrink (1974).

(ii) Urban networks: The flow is primarily determined by the nodes and the control system and the optimal flow depends on the control system. A review of the principles and problems of traffic assignment in that case can be found in Akcelik and Maher (1977).

In the following we will consider urban networks. Because of the complexity of these systems simulation plays an important rôle and very complex simulation models for urban networks have been developed (See e.g. Liebermann et al. 1972). All these models do simulation of a given flow pattern. The aim of this paper is to show how simulation can play an active rôle in solving the optimal routing and optimal control problems. Simulation has the advantage of not only giving mean values of the flow, which are used in theoretical investigations, but some idea of the shape of the probability distributions.

Ideas of that kind have also been used by Maher and Akcelik (1977). These authors use an incremental loading technique for the traffic assignment, which has the disadvantage that the traffic which has been loaded to a special route cannot be relocated to another route. We therefore propose another algorithm.

2. THE MODEL

We consider an urban network graph G which consists of intersections I and links L between the intersections. Different directions are represented by different links. Let $\mathfrak{I} = \{I_1 \ldots In_I\}$ be the set of all intersections with card $(\mathfrak{I}) = n_I$ and $\mathcal{L} = \{L_{ij}\}$ be the set of all links between the intersections with card $(\mathcal{L}) = n_L$. Furthermore two subsets $\mathbb{O}$ and D of $\mathfrak{I}$ are defined which represent the origins and destinations of the traffic. The matrix $\mathbb{O}D = \{y^{ab} \mid 1 \leq a \leq n_{\mathbb{O}},\ 1 \leq b \leq n_D\}$ gives the demand between the origins and destinations. Fig 1 gives an example of a network graph G with 8 intersections and 14 links. The intersections I_1-I_5 are considered as origins and destinations with the demand matrix $\mathbb{O}D$ given in Fig 2. If we are interested in finding the optimal flow between the inner intersections I_6-I_8 it is useful to distinguish between three possible types of flow at each intersection, namely the flow straight ahead, the flow turning right and the flow turning left. If we assume that each type of flow follows laws which are typical for each direction it is easier to consider an associated graph $\tilde{G}$

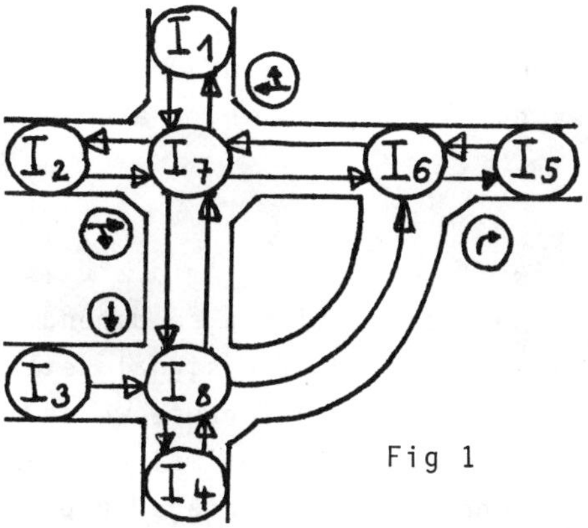

Fig 1

O \ D	I_1	I_2	I_3	I_4	I_5
I_1	0	400	-	800	200
I_2	-	0	-	900	2000
I_3	400	-	0	200	700
I_4	1200	300	-	0	500
I_5	600	1400	-	-	0

Fig 2 DEMAND MATRIX

instead of the original graph G. The nodes of the new graph $\tilde{G}$ are located in the center of the links between the intersections and the edges are the possible directions which can be taken from that point. We call the set of nodes of $\tilde{G}$ $N = \{1,...n_N\}$ with $card(N) = n_N = n_L$ and the set of edges of $\tilde{G}$ the set of pseudolinks $PL = \{p_{ij}\}$ with $card(PL) = n_{PL} \leq 12n_I$. Fig 3 gives the associated graph $\tilde{G}$ for the network of Fig 1. The demand matrix is the same as in Fig 2 except for the node numbers. In order to keep the information of the original network we introduce equivalence classes of pseudolinks $\pi_m, 1 \leq m \leq n_I$, which are the sets of pseudolinks which belong to the same intersection I_m. This concept has also the advantage that $\tilde{G}$ contains only allowed paths through the network and no set of forbidden paths has to be kept in mind.

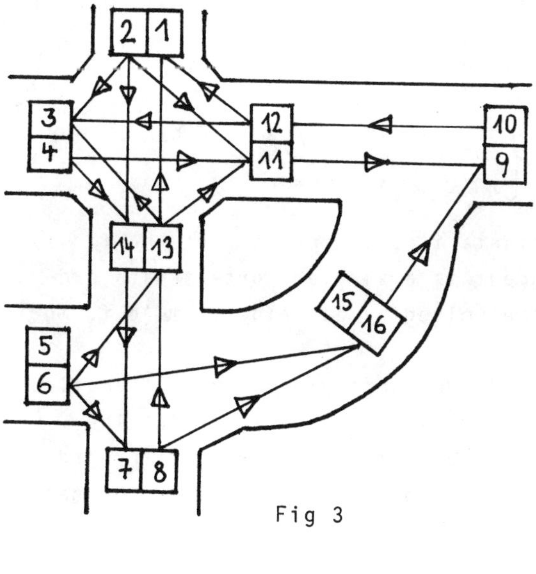

Fig 3

If x_{ij} is the flow between the nodes i and j on the pseudolink p_{ij} we consider the time a vehicle needs to pass the pseudolink as a function depending on all flows on pseudolinks which are in the same class as p_{ij}.

$$t_{ij} = f_{ij}(\{x_{kl} | p_{kl} \sim p_{ij}\}) \tag{2.1}$$

In general the functions f_{ij} and so the traffic time also depends on the special choice of the control system, i.e. the signal setting for the intersections. We omit this parameter because we assume that for given flows the signal setting is an optimal one. Optimization of signal setting can be done by mixed integer programming as in Gartner et al. (1975).

The problem of finding the optimal traffic assignment to the network is to find the value $X = (x_{ij})$ which minimizes

$$F(X) = \Sigma x_{ij} \cdot t_{ij} = \Sigma x_{ij} \cdot f_{ij}(\{x_{kl} | p_{kl} \sim p_{ij}\}) \tag{2.2}$$

This minimum search has to be done under the following two types of flow restrictions in order to fulfill the demand (c.f. Steenbrink (1974)):

$$\sum_{a,b} x_{ij}^{ab} = x_{ij} \tag{2.3}$$

where x_{ij}^{ab} is that part of the flow from origin a to destination b that uses the pseudolink p_{ij} and

$$\sum_i x_{ij}^{ab} - \sum_k x_{jk}^{ab} = \begin{cases} 0 & \text{if } j \neq a \quad j \neq b \\ -y^{ab} & \text{if } j = a \\ y^{ab} & \text{if } j = b \end{cases} \tag{2.4}$$

If the functions f_{ij} are constant, i.e. independent of the flows, the problem of optimal assignment is a simple shortest path problem of graph theory and can be solved by any algorithm (c.f. Mori and Nishimura 1967).

In its general form (2.1) - (2.4) define a problem of mathematical programming but the size of the problem and the fact that the functions f_{ij} are not known in general makes a straight forward solution almost impossible. We therefore use an iterative procedure which is described in the following.

3. THE ALGORITHM

The algorithm described below consists of a series of very complex subalgorithms, which are nested within a loop. These subprocedures are independent modules and can be replaced by better ones, if invented in the future. Since e.g. new graph theoretic algorithms are still found and published, this may be important.

1. Set $n := 1$, $X^{(0)} = (\ 0\ )$, $t_{ij}^{(0)} = 0$
2. Find the starting solution $X^{(1)} = (x_{ij}^{ab})$
3. Compute optimal traffic control
4. Simulate the traffic behavior on each intersection, yielding the passing time $t_{ij}^{(n)}$ for each pseudolink
5. If $\Sigma\,|x_{ij}^{(n)} \cdot t_{ij}^{(n)} - x_{ij}^{(n-1)} \cdot t_{ij}^{(n-1)}|$ is small, go to 9
6. Compute the minimum distance flows $Z = (z_{ij}^{ab})$ based on the "lengths" $t_{ij}^{(n)}$
7. Compute the new iteration of the solution as
   $$X^{(n+1)} = (1-\alpha)X^{(n)} + \alpha Z$$ with α a relaxation factor
8. Set $n: = n + 1$ and go to 3
9. Compute the performance index $P = \Sigma x_{ij}^{(n)} . t_{ij}^{(n)}$
10. Stop

ad 2: The starting solution is found when traffic is assigned to the shortest routes, the distances being defined as the geometrical lengths of the pseudolinks. For shortest path algorithms, Floyd's algorithm is used, [see Mori & Nishimura (1967)].

ad 3: The optimal signal setting is found according to an algorithm due to Gartner et alii (1975) which is conceptually simple and easily implemented. The flows on each pseudolink are the input data of this procedure and the output consists of a computed common cycle time, the green splits and the relative offsets per intersection.

ad 4: The great advantage of this concept is that one does not need a simulation of the whole network. For every intersection (and its neighbours) a discrete event (microscopic) traffic simulation is done during this step and the expected passing times for each pseudolink are found successively. It is worth mentioning that the time loss for asynchronous turning into a green wave street is clearly taken into consideration. As a byproduct, some interesting probabilities (complete breakdown of the traffic, of overcrowding a lane, etc.) can be computed.

ad 6: The minimum distance flow is found when traffic is assigned to the shortest routes. From the second to the last iteration run, distances are defined by the travel times.

ad 7: The relaxion factor α is introduced to avoid infinite loops and oszillation of the solution.

ad 9: The network performance index is a tool for the comparison of network alternatives.

4. CONCLUDING REMARKS

The program system as presented here is conceptually a compound of simulation, optimization and iteration. The whole system evaluates the performance for network alternatives as described, whereas the included subsystems can be used independently for different tasks. A pure simulation study can be carried out using only section 4, optimal signal setting for given flows is found with section 3. Optionally, the simulation can be replaced by the computation of traffic flow equations when the functional dependencies are known. But simulation is indispensable for the evaluation of probabilities.

The presented algorithm has been implemented on a CDC Cyber 74 Computer using SIMULA Programs for simulation and graph theoretic procedures, since this is the only programming language which provides both simulation routines and a highly developed pointer structure concept. The optimal control is computed with the help of the MPOS system based on FORTRAN. The interface between the FORTRAN and SIMULA sections is done by a special assembler program and operating system routines.

5. REFERENCES

Akcelik R., Maher M.J., Route control of traffic in urban road networks, Transp. Res. Vol. 11, 15-24, 1977

Christofides N., Graph theory - an algorithm approach; Academic Press, 1975

Dahl O., Myhrhaug B., Nygaard U., Simula 67, Common base language, Norwegian Computing Center, Oslo, 1967

Gartner N., Little J., Gabbay H., Optimization of traffic signal settings by mixed-integer linear programming, Trans. Sci. 9, 321-343, 1975

Hu T., Integer programming and network flows, Addison Wesley, 1970

Liebermann E. et alii, Logical design and demonstration of UTCS-1 network simulation model, Highway Research Record 409, 46-56, 1972

Maher M., Akcelik R., Route control-simulation experiments, Transp. Res. Vol 11, 25-31, 1977

Mori M., Nishimura T., Solution of the routing problem through a network by a matrix with auxiliary nodes. Transp. Res. Vol. 1, 165-180, 1967

Steenbrink P., Optimization of transport networks, John Wiley & Sons, 1974.

Statistical Tests for Linear Congruential Pseudo-Random Numbers

H. Niederreiter, Urbana

Summary. This is a report on recent progress in the study of the statistical properties of the most commonly used pseudo-random numbers, namely those generated by the linear congruential method. The results pertain to Kolmogorov-type tests and to the statistical independence of successive terms in a sequence of such pseudo-random numbers. Effective criteria are developed for the optimal choice of parameters producing the desired statistical independence properties.

KEYWORDS. Pseudo-random numbers, linear congruential method, equidistribution test, serial test, Tausworthe generators.

1. Introduction. Let $m \geq 3$ and r be integers, let y_0 be an integer in the least residue system mod m, i.e., $0 \leq y_0 < m$, and let λ be an integer relatively prime to m with $2 \leq \lambda < m$ and $(\lambda - 1)y_0 + r \not\equiv 0 \pmod{m}$. A sequence $y_0, y_1, \ldots$ of integers in the least residue system mod m is generated by the recursion $y_{n+1} \equiv \lambda y_n + r \pmod{m}$ for $n = 0, 1, \ldots$. A sequence $x_0, x_1, \ldots$ of linear congruential pseudo-random numbers (abbreviated LCPRN) in the interval $[0,1]$ is derived by setting $x_n = y_n/m$ for $n = 0, 1, \ldots$. In this context, m is referred to as the *modulus* and λ is called the *multiplier*. In practice, m is taken to be a large prime or a large power of 2. One distinguishes the *homogeneous case* $r \equiv 0 \pmod{m}$ and the *inhomogeneous case* $r \not\equiv 0 \pmod{m}$. In the homogeneous case, one may, w. l. o. g., choose y_0 to be relatively prime to m, for otherwise the same sequence of LCPRN could be produced with a smaller modulus. The sequence $x_0, x_1, \ldots$ is always purely periodic. Let τ denote the length of the least period.

The parameters $m, \lambda, y_0,$ and r have to be chosen in such a way that the resulting LCPRN will pass appropriate statistical tests for randomness. The modulus m is selected in accordance with machine capabilities, typical choices being $m = 2^{32}$, $m = 2^{35}$, or the Mersenne prime $m = 2^{31} - 1$. The numbers r and y_0 have comparatively little influence on the behavior of the LCPRN. The properties of a sequence of LCPRN are, in fact, mainly governed by the choice of the multiplier λ. For accounts of classical results on LCPRN, see [2, Ch. 3] and [10, §7].

2. Equidistribution test. Since the linear congruential method is intended as a uniform pseudo-random number generator, the sequence $x_0, x_1, \ldots$ should be subjected to the equidistribution test, i.e., to a measurement of the deviation of its empirical distribution from the uniform distribution on [0,1]. For this purpose, we use a Kolmogorov-type test based on the so-called *discrepancy*

$$D_N = \sup_J \left| F_N(J) - |J| \right| \qquad \text{for } N \geq 1,$$

where the supremum is extended over all subintervals J of [0,1], $F_N(J)$ is N^{-1} times the number of terms among $x_0, x_1, \ldots, x_{N-1}$ falling into J, and $|J|$ denotes the length of J. The general theory of discrepancy is expounded in [3, Ch. 2].

Information about D_τ, i.e., about the discrepancy of the full period, is easily obtained (see [10, §9] for a summary). The range $1 \leq N < \tau$ is of great practical interest since only an initial segment of the sequence of LCPRN is actually used in calculations. Let $m = p^\alpha$ with p prime and $\alpha \geq 1$. For $h \geq 1$, let $\mu(p^h)$ be the exponent to which λ belongs mod p^h. We define an integer β as follows: if p is odd, let $\beta = 0$ for $\alpha = 1$, and for $\alpha \geq 2$ let β be the largest integer such that p^β divides $\lambda^{\mu(p)} - 1$; if $p = 2$, let β be the largest integer such that 2^β divides $\lambda^{\mu(4)} - 1$.

Furthermore, let κ be the largest integer such that p^{κ} divides $\lambda - 1$ and let ω be the largest integer such that p^{ω} divides $(\lambda - 1)y_0 + r$. We set $\gamma = \beta + \omega - \kappa$. Then a simplified version of results from [4], [6] reads as follows.

Theorem 1. For a sequence of LCPRN with $m = p^{\alpha}$, p prime, $\alpha \geq 1$, and $\gamma < \alpha$ we have

$$ND_N \leq C\left(\frac{m\tau}{\mu}\right)^{\frac{1}{2}} \log^2 m \quad \text{for} \quad 1 \leq N < \tau,$$

where $\mu = \mu(p^{\alpha})$ and C is an absolute constant.

It should be noted that $\gamma = 0$ for a prime modulus m and for the commonly employed choice $m = 2^{\alpha}$, $\alpha \geq 3$, $\lambda \equiv 5 \pmod 8$, and r odd. In the homogeneous case we have $\tau = \mu$ and $\gamma = \beta$. The above estimate is best possible apart from the logarithmic factor by results in [6, §5], [10, §9].

3. Serial test. As a test for the statistical independence of successive terms in a sequence $x_0, x_1, \ldots$ of LCPRN we use the so-called *serial test*. For fixed $s \geq 2$, consider the s-tuples $\underline{x}_n = (x_n, x_{n+1}, \ldots, x_{n+s-1})$, $n = 0, 1, \ldots$. We determine the empirical distribution of these s-tuples and compare it with the uniform distribution on the s-dimensional cube $[0,1]^s$. The original sequence $x_0, x_1, \ldots$ passes the s-dimensional serial test if the deviation between these two distributions is small. This deviation is measured by the discrepancy $D_N^{(s)}$ which is defined like D_N, but where J now runs through all subintervals of $[0,1]^s$, $F_N(J)$ is N^{-1} times the number of terms among $\underline{x}_0, \underline{x}_1, \ldots, \underline{x}_{N-1}$ falling into J, and $|J|$ denotes the volume of J. The serial test was studied in [7], [8], [9], [10, §11].

To describe the results, we need some definitions. For a nonzero lattice point $\underline{h} = (h_1, \ldots, h_s) \in \mathbb{Z}^s$, let $r(\underline{h})$ be the absolute value of the product of all nonzero coordinates of $\underline{h}$. We set

$$\rho^{(s)}(\lambda,m) = \min r(\underline{h}),$$

where the minimum is extended over all nonzero lattice points $\underline{h}$ with $-m/2 < h_j \leq m/2$ for $1 \leq j \leq s$ and $h_1 + h_2\lambda + \cdots + h_s\lambda^{s-1} \equiv 0 \pmod{m}$. We use C_s to denote an effectively computable positive constant which depends only on s and whose exact value may be different in each occurrence.

Theorem 2. For a sequence of LCPRN with prime modulus m we have

$$D_\tau^{(s)} \leq \frac{1}{\tau}(m-\tau)^{\frac{1}{2}}\left(\frac{2}{\pi}\log m + \frac{7}{5}\right)^s + \frac{C_s \log^s m}{\rho^{(s)}(\lambda,m)},$$

and if, in particular, λ is a primitive root mod m, then

$$D_\tau^{(s)} \leq \frac{C_s \log^s m}{\rho^{(s)}(\lambda,m)}.$$

Theorem 3. For a sequence of LCPRN with $m = p^\alpha$, p prime, $\alpha \geq 2$, and $\gamma < \alpha$ we have

$$D_\tau^{(s)} \leq \frac{C_s(1 + 2\gamma\log p)^s \log^s m}{\rho^{(s)}(\lambda,p^{\alpha-\gamma})}.$$

Theorem 4. For a sequence of LCPRN with $m = 10^\alpha$, $\alpha \geq 4$, λ belonging to the largest exponents mod 2^α and mod 5^α, and $r = 0$ we have

$$D_\tau^{(s)} \leq \frac{C_s \log^s m}{\rho^{(s)}(\lambda,m/80)}.$$

Similar estimates can be shown for parts of the period. For instance, by combining results in [9], [10, §11] one obtains the following.

Theorem 5. For a sequence of LCPRN with prime modulus m we have

$$D_N^{(s)} \leq C_s \left(\frac{m^{\frac{1}{2}} (\log m)^{s+1}}{N} + \frac{\log^s m}{\rho^{(s)}(\lambda,m)} \right) \quad \text{for} \quad 1 \leq N < \tau.$$

4. Figures of merit. The results of Section 3 suggest that in the cases of interest the reciprocal of $\rho^{(s)}(\lambda,m)$ may be taken as a measurement for the amount of statistical dependence among s successive terms in a sequence of LCPRN. The fact that this is really the correct indicator is shown by the following result.

Theorem 6. For a sequence of LCPRN with arbitrary modulus m and corresponding multiplier λ, we have

$$D_N^{(s)} \geq C_s/\rho^{(s)}(\lambda,m) \quad \text{for} \quad 1 \leq N \leq \tau.$$

Here we may take $C_s = s^{-s}$ for $2 \leq s \leq 3$ and $C_s = (\pi/2)(\pi + \frac{1}{2})^{-s}$ for $s \geq 4$. This is an improvement on a lower bound in [9]. The proof relies on an auxiliary result of independent interest.

Lemma. For any points $\underline{t}_0, \ldots, \underline{t}_{N-1}$ in $[0,1]^s$ with discrepancy $D_N^{(s)}(\underline{t}_0, \ldots, \underline{t}_{N-1})$, any nonzero lattice point $\underline{h} \in \mathbb{Z}^s$, and any real θ we have

$$\left| \frac{1}{N} \sum_{n=0}^{N-1} \cos 2\pi(\underline{h} \cdot \underline{t}_n - \theta) \right| < \frac{2}{\pi}(\pi + \frac{1}{2})^s \, r(\underline{h}) \, D_N^{(s)}(\underline{t}_0, \ldots, \underline{t}_{N-1}).$$

It is now justified to call $\rho^{(s)}(\lambda,m)$ the (s-dimensional) *figure of merit* of λ (relative to m). A good multiplier λ is then characterized by the properties that it yields a large period τ and a large figure of merit. It should be emphasized that $\rho^{(s)}(\lambda,m)$ depends strongly on the dimension s. For instance, for Jansson's generator $m = 2^{35}$, $\lambda = 2^{24} + 5$, $r = 1$ we have $\rho^{(2)}(\lambda,m) \approx m^{2/3}$, but $\rho^{(3)}(\lambda,m) = 250$. Thus, the choice of an optimal multiplier can only be made relative to the desired number of statistically independent successors in the Monte Carlo problem at hand. There is no universally optimal multiplier. This can be made explicit by showing, on the basis of the pigeonhole principle, that $\rho^{(s)}(\lambda,m) = 1$ whenever $s \geq \log_2(m+1)$.

For the case $s = 2$, Borosh and Niederreiter [1] developed a systematic search procedure for those λ which maximize $\rho^{(2)}(\lambda,m)$ given the modulus m. For $m = 2^\alpha$, $6 \leq \alpha \leq 35$, it transpires that there is always a multiplier $\lambda \equiv 5 \pmod 8$ with $\rho^{(2)}(\lambda,m) \geq m/5$. Exceptionally good multipliers relative to the 2-dimensional serial test are $\lambda = 657759677$ for $m = 2^{30}$ and $\lambda = 1812433253$ for $m = 2^{32}$, with odd r in both cases.

5. Tausworthe generators. For a prime modulus p and an integer $k \geq 2$, the kth order linear recurrence

$$y_{n+k} \equiv a_{k-1} y_{n+k-1} + \cdots + a_0 y_n \pmod p \qquad \text{for} \qquad n = 0, 1, \ldots,$$

with $y_0, y_1, \ldots$ in the least residue system mod p, $(y_0,\ldots,y_{k-1}) \neq (0,\ldots,0)$, and $x^k - a_{k-1}x^{k-1} - \cdots - a_0 \in \mathbb{Z}[x]$ a primitive polynomial mod p, was proposed by Tausworthe as a pseudo-random number generator (cf. [11], [2, §3.2.2]). The derived sequence $x_n = y_n/p$, $n = 0, 1, \ldots$, of pseudo-random numbers has period $\tau = p^k - 1$. In the full period, this sequence shows an excellent distribution of s-tuples for $1 \leq s \leq k$ (cf. [10, §7]). For parts of the period, one uses an estimate for exponential sums in [5] to obtain the following result, where we write $D_N^{(1)}$ for D_N.

Theorem 7. For a sequence of kth order Tausworthe pseudo-random numbers we have

$$D_N^{(s)} < \frac{s}{p} + \left(\frac{p^{k/2}}{N}\left(\frac{2}{\pi}\log\tau + \frac{2}{5}\right) + \frac{1}{\tau}\right)\left(\frac{2}{\pi}\log p + \frac{7}{5}\right)^s$$

for $1 \leq N < \tau = p^k - 1$ and $1 \leq s \leq k$.

References

1. Borosh I., Niederreiter H., Optimal multipliers for pseudo-random number generation by the linear congruential method (to appear).

2. Knuth D. E., The art of computer programming, vol. 2: Seminumerical algorithms, Addison-Wesley, Reading, Mass., 1969.

3. Kuipers L., Niederreiter H., Uniform distribution of sequences, Wiley-Interscience, New York, 1974.

4. Niederreiter H., On the distribution of pseudo-random numbers generated by the linear congruential method. II, Math. Comp., 28, 1117-1132, 1974.

5. Niederreiter H., Some new exponential sums with applications to pseudo-random numbers, Topics in Number Theory (Debrecen, 1974), Colloq. Math. Soc. János Bolyai, vol. 13, pp. 209-232, North-Holland, Amsterdam, 1976.

6. Niederreiter H., On the distribution of pseudo-random numbers generated by the linear congruential method. III, Math. Comp., 30, 571-597, 1976.

7. Niederreiter H., Statistical independence of linear congruential pseudo-random numbers, Bull. Amer. Math. Soc., 82, 927-929, 1976.

8. Niederreiter H., Pseudo-random numbers and optimal coefficients, Advances in Math., 26, 99-181, 1977.

9. Niederreiter H., The serial test for linear congruential pseudo-random numbers, Bull. Amer. Math. Soc., 84, 273-274, 1978.

10. Niederreiter H., Quasi-Monte Carlo methods and pseudo-random numbers, Bull. Amer. Math. Soc., 84, 1978 (to appear).

11. Tausworthe R. C., Random numbers generated by linear recurrence modulo two, Math. Comp., 19, 201-209, 1965.

9. Teaching of Statistics

The Importance of Statistical Computing to the Curricula of Secondary Schools

G. Darnton and S.M. Leverett, Chelmsford

SUMMARY

The uses of statistics and computing have pervaded the Western world to such an extent that both are intrinsic to our modern way of life. This premise, coupled with pure educational arguments, form the basis for including statistical computing in the "compulsory curricula" of today's secondary schools. By so doing, some fundamental educational and sociological problems, caused by a naive perception of the world, may be overcome. The authors assert that the primary aims for education should be humanity, literacy and numeracy, and that statistical computing is *the* vital ingredient in curricula in order for students to achieve these aims.

KEYWORDS: Statistical Computing; Complexity; Teaching/Learning Process; Educational Objectives; Data; Information Processes; Socially Pervasive, Intrinsic and Covert; Literacy; Numeracy; Humanity/Citizenship.

1. INTRODUCTION

The uses, applications and implications of statistics, computing and as we shall suggest, statistical computing, have now pervaded Western culture specifically and cultures all over the world generally, to such an extent that we postulate the need and urgency of introducing statistical computing to secondary school curricula.

Systems are elemental to human social existence and development. The development of systems theory has led to a greater awareness on the part of some teachers of the need for education to present opportunities for young people to become aware of, and learn how to handle, complexity within many disciplines.

It is far beyond the scope of this paper to consider what should be the rôle of schools, so we summarise our position by suggesting that schools should not be used specifically for the purposes of social engineering to a specification determined by some narrow ideology or group of interests - rather schools should be viewed and organised as resources to be used as part of learning and other related cultural and developmental processes.

Any conscientious teacher will be concerned with the efficacy of the teaching/learning process in order to maximise the achievment of defined educational objectives. This concern is evident by the search for effective innovatory techniques of teaching style and of use of auxilliary educational technology to enhance the learning process. During the course of these developments there has emerged a prevailing school of thought which sees the teaching/learning process as a "complex interdependent system" within which modern technology in general and computer systems in particular can play a vital rôle (*see:* OECD, 1976; CET, 1975a, 1975b, 1977a, 1977b, 1978).

2. STATISTICAL COMPUTING WITHIN THE TEACHING/LEARNING PROCESS

Viewing the student at the centre of the teaching/learning process, the teacher and the multifarious teaching/learning resources may be seen jointly as the "teaching/learning environment". Fig. 1(a) depicts the interactive relationship between the student (*S*) at the centre of the process, with the teacher (*T*) and the resources (*R*) on the periphery, where the arrows indicate the "information flow" of the interaction.

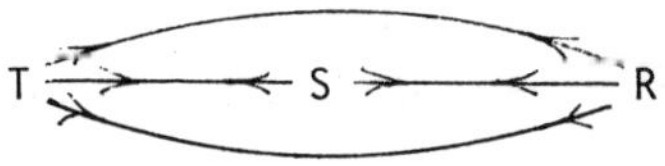

Fig. 1(a)

R is where educational technology can play a part, and since we have isolated the rôle of the computer within this technology, we may logically extend the *TSR* model (Fig. 1(a)) to that shown in Fig. 1(b). In the extended *TSR* model, *T* (which may be a *team* of teachers) will use the computer system (*C*) in conjunction with other resources (*O*) to enhance the overall teaching/learning process. Within this process *T* will attempt to present *C* and *O* in a variety

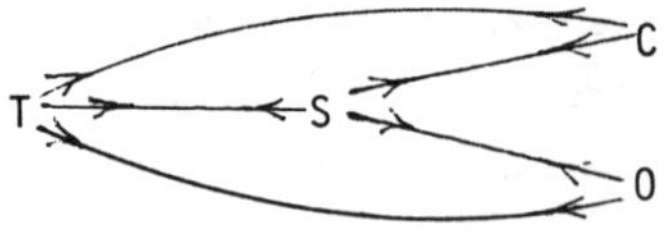

Fig. 1(b)

of ways to assist *S* in achieving pre-defined objectives, such as *knowledge*, *awareness* or *understanding* (*see:* Bloom, 1956; Krathwohl, 1964; Ormell, 1974).

Whatever an educational objective may be, the raw material in the teaching/learning process is *data* and the *process* is the treatment of that data in such a way as to facilitate the provision of information for the realisation of a particular objective (see Fig. 2(a)). It is of the utmost importance for people to have the opportunity and resources to investigate the relationship between data, information processes and objectives.

DATA ⟶ PROCESS ⟶ OBJECTIVE

Fig. 2(a)

By the very nature of computers, both the handling of the data and the process itself may be enhanced by the effective use of these machines (Fig. 2(b)).

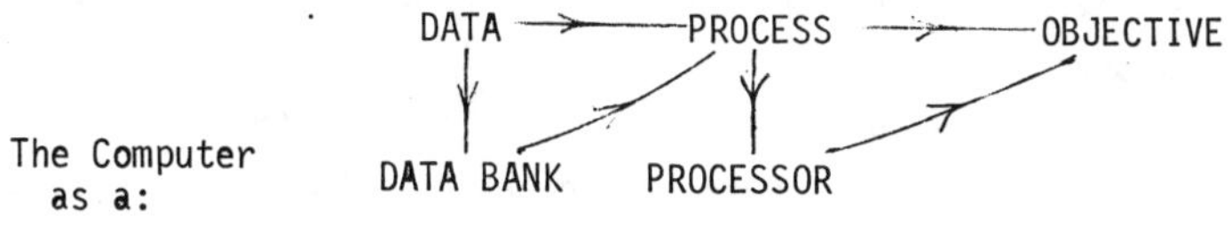

Fig. 2(b)

Thus, the use of a computer system within the teaching/learning process, both as a data bank and as a processor of data, may be classified under four heads:

1. To simulate experiments, systems and scenarios, which would otherwise be too dangerous, complex, expensive, fast or slow to undertake in a classroom.
2. To facilitate the storage and retrieval of data.
3. To facilitate the processing of data (literal, numeric or both), and for problem-solving in general.
4. To develop logical thought processes and to reinforce logical and numerical concepts through the experience of computer programming.

3. PHILOSOPHICAL CONSIDERATIONS

Participation in a complex society involves tacit support for the mechanisms of government, control, allocation of resources, power, and so on, which in turn poses individuals with some terrible moral dilemmas that can only be dealt with satisfactorily on an initial basis of good factual information and understanding. Statistical and computer activity are socially pervasive, intrinsic and covert all at the same time and this implies a necessity for an awareness on the part of our citizens of the nature and uses of modern computer systems and statistical methods. While there are many other aspects of our modern world which are equally important we suggest that none has to the same extent such fundamental implications for privacy and democracy. To ask whether or not the late Sir Ronald Fisher would be correct in describing statistics as the key technology of the century is, of course, to miss the point; not only is statistics the key to understanding much development in theory and technology in so many disciplines, but also statistics and statistical computing can provide people with the means to convert the mass of data around them into manageable information, along with developing some useful paradigms and heuristics. There are many reasons why nowadays the ability to cope with masses of data and overdetermined systems may be crucial to long-term survival for individuals and cultures.

The teaching/learning process we have depicted does form a complex interdependent system. We take this opportunity to suggest some educational priorities. Adopting the same position as the Council of the Royal Statistical Society (RSS, 1951), that the purpose of education is "to help each individual to realise the full powers of his personality - body, mind and spirit - in and through active membership of a society", is helpful. In terms of understanding the culture we are in, we would suggest the first layer of priorities to be a combination of basic literacy, basic numeracy, and basic humanity/citizenship, with the emphasis on the latter. Once these basic skills are established, we propose a second layer of priority, statistical computing, through which other disciplines can be approached to enhance understanding.

We seek to justify the proposal for giving such priority to statistical computing under two major heads:

1. the cultural pervasiveness of statistics and computer systems and the need for related "literacy";

2. the major contribution which statistical computing can make to the teaching/learning process.

The term "statistical computing" is meaningful within the context of three broad based interpretations: (1) learning *about* statistics and computers (arguments for learning about computers have been made elswhere; Leverett, 1978); (2) learning *with* statistics and computers; and (3) using statistics and computers as an aid to the management and administration of learning. Hence, we seek a very broad meaning to the term "statistical computing", which embraces statistics, computer systems, and possible interrelations between the two.

4. STATISTICS IN SCHOOLS

Statistics is now taught in many schools as a separate subject. A detailed description of examinations and syllabuses currently available appears elsewhere (Darnton, 1978).

However, in practice the subject follows rather traditional lines of requiring the usual mechanical calculations within various statistical topics - very few questions appear which encourage a deeper study of statistical concepts, the assumptions underlying various models, or real-life situations. Some topics often seem to be included in syllabusus because of their simple mathematical elegance rather than after a careful consideration of real-life data or uses of statistics.

In recent years there have been statistics books directed primarily at other disciplines, such as History (Floud, 1973), Technology (Chatfield, 1975), Economics (Thomas, 1973; Mayes and Mayes, 1976), Biology (Campbell, 1967; Bishop, 1966), Geography (Gregory, 1973; Smith, 1975), Health (Larsen, 1975), Human Sciences (Hammerton, 1975), Sociology (Blalock, 1972) and Management (Cass, 1973; Broster, 1972). This list is, of course, purely illustrative and obviously by no means exhaustive. All of these books, however, contain substantial sections which are capable of being incorporated into school courses in the UK.

Within the literature there appears to be much discussion around whether statistics should be a separate discipline or taught within and supplementary to other subjects. These positions are well exemplified by Rao who adopts both positions (Rao, 1975). We take the position of suggesting that statistical computing should be both a separate discipline to impart essential core skills, knowledge and ideas, and also well integrated with most other disciplines.

5. COMPUTING IN SCHOOLS

Historically, computing in UK secondary schools has been orientated towards mathematics as a discipline. In recent years there have been decisive moves by those concerned with computing in schools to broaden the basis of school computing (even though most of these teachers are traditionally teachers of mathematics). Nevertheless, fewer than a third of schools are significantly involved with computing at the curriculum level, and within these probably no more than 10% of their students follow any computing course.

6. STATISTICAL COMPUTING IN SCHOOLS: The Future

The relationship of statistics to other subjects has already been considered. In many ways, both computing and statistics have very similar relationships to other subjects; furthermore, the two complement one another: computing may be seen as the "hardware" for implementing the "software" of statistics.

Whether education in the future is subject-orientated or multidisciplinary statistical computing should form an essential basis. Whenever data are reduced or summarised, ideas put forward about relationships between variables, complexity studied, theories postulated, and so on statistical computing, as we have defined it, is elemental. For all areas of the school curriculum data bases should be established along with a wide range of statistical and computer-based models of behaviour, etc.. This provides pupils with essential opportunities to enhance their learning process.

An important objective in presenting these opportunities is to enable students to obtain at least an intuitive understanding of the nature of systems. We reiterate that a combination of statistics and computing: will introduce students to quite complex problems through simulation techniques; will facilitate the analysis and manipulation of data appertaining to systems; and will ease problems in storing and accessing large amounts of such data. With these points in mind, "statistical computing" should be construed accordingly.

In conclusion, the authors are currently engaged on an on-going programme involving the intuitive relationship between computers and statistics to establish some research designs to formulate: further aims and objectives; the levels at which certain ideas and concepts discussed can be introduced into the school curriculum; and the problems associated with teaching/learning about complexity and systems. The authors have some preliminary findings, which can be discussed with interested parties, but space precludes further presentation within this paper.

THE AUTHORS: G. Darnton, teacher at Mayflower School, Billericay;
S.M. Leverett, Advisory Teacher, Chelmer Institute,
Chelmsford, Essex, UK.

REFERENCES

Bishop, O.N. (1966) *Statistics for Biology* LONDON: Longman Group Ltd
Blalock, H.M. (1972) *Social Statistics* NEWYORK: McGraw-Hill Book Co
Bloom, S. (ed) *et al*(1956) *Taxonomy of Educational Objectives. Handbook I: Cognitive Domain* NEWYORK: David McKay Co Inc
Broster, E.J. (1972) *Management Statistics* LONDON: Longman Group Ltd
Campbell, R.C. (1967) *Statistics for Biologists* LONDON: Cambridge University Press
Cass, T. (1973) *Statistical Methods in Management* LONDON: Cassell & Co Ltd
CET (1975a) *Computer Assisted Learning in the UK* LONDON: CET
CET (1975b) *Two Years On - The National Development Programme in Computer Assisted Learning* LONDON: CET
CET (1977a) *The National Development Programme in Computer Assisted Learning - Final Report* LONDON: CET
CET (1977b) *Technical Report No. 15: Educational Computing in the Local Authority Area - the Next Ten Years* LONDON: CET
CET (1978) *The Cost of Learning with Computers* LONDON: CET
Chatfield, C. (1975) *Statistics for Technology* LONDON: Chapman & Hall
Darnton, G. (1978) "'O' and 'A' level statistics Syllabuses", *Statistics Teaching* Summer 1978
Floud, R. (1973) *An Introduction to Quantitative Methods for Historians* LONDON: Methuen & Co Ltd
Gregory, G. (1973) *Statistical Methods and the Geographer* LONDON: Longman Gp Ltd
Hammerton, M. (1975) *Statistics for the Human Sciences* LONDON: Longman Group Ltd
Krathwohl, D.R., *et al* (1964) *Taxonomy of Ed. Objectives. Handbook II: Affective Domain* NEWYORK: David McKay Co Inc
Larsen, R.J. (1975) *Statistics for the Allied Health Sciences* COLUMBUS: Charles E. Merrill Publishing Co
Leverett, S.M. (1978) "The Green Paper and Computer Education", *Computer Education*, 28, p.29
Mates, A.C., and Mates, D.G. (1976) *Introductory Economic Statistics* LONDON: John Wiley & Sons
OECD (1976) *The Use of the Computer in Teaching Secondary School Subjects* PARIS: OECD Publications
Ormell, C.P. (1974) "Bloom's Taxonomy and the Objectives of Education", *Educational Research*, 5(1), pp.33-43
Rao, A. (1975) in *Statistics at the School Level* (L. Råde, *ed*), pp 93, 121-140; STOCKHOLM: Almqvist and Wiskell
Smith, D.M. (1975) *Patterns in Human Geography* HAMMONDSWORTH: Penguin Books
RSS (1951) *Journal of the Royal Statistical Society* Series A, CXV(1), 1952
Thomas, J.J. (1973) *An Introduction to Statistical Analysis for Economists* LONDON: Weiderfeld and Nicolson

NPSTAT – A Software Package for Teaching Nonparametric Statistics

H.-J. Lenz, Berlin

NPSTAT (Nonparametric Statistical Package) is a collection of APL programs designed for teaching nonparametric statistics and for assisting nonparametric data analysis as well as methodological research in this area. The last updated version of NPSTAT consists of five main groups of methods. Group 1 covers general programs like plots, prints, random generators, distribution functions and its inverses. Group 2 contains the classical descriptive statistics as well as some orderstatistics. Group 3 handels the single-sample tests, group 4 presents the corresponding two-sample tests for paired and unpaired data while group 5 generalises these methods to the k-sample problem.

KEY WORDS: APL, Nonparametric Statistics, Software Packages, Teaching Statistics

1. INTRODUCTION

Teaching nonparametric statistics for graduate students at a faculty of economics includes in general the phases of motivation by real life problems, the developping of the theory, some reasoning on computational statistics and some studies , say by means of simulation, on the robustness of the discussed tests.

No doubt, the phases motivation, computing and simulating are best done by computer aided instruction (CAI). It is a pity that anybody knows what a computer is like but nobody knows what computer aided instruction is actually, cf. NAEVE(1976). Therefore NPSTAT is designed as a software package highly suitable for lecturing combined with an appropriate data-base system.

The main design criteria have been:

- o Interactivity
- o Manual Job control
- o Semantic & Structural Indentity
- o Modular Programming Technique

2. DESIGN CRITERIA

With APL a fully interactive system is available. As the APL community is increasing and going on to exchange their (one line?) programs APL looks like to be one of the best languages for teaching purposes.

The facet 'Manual Job Control' seems necessarily in order to force the students to run step by step through the phases of doing → thinking → computing → thinking → discovering → ...

Just quite opposite to common CAI-software packages NPSTAT should assist you in

- o problem solving (data analysis)
- o teaching (learning,drilling,discovering)
- o research (methodolocical analysis).

Let us turn to the design criteria of semantic and structural identity. When you are teaching nonparametric statistics referring to special textbooks as for example of GIBBONS(1971), CONOVER(1971) or BUENING&TRENKLER(1978) it would be very unpleasant for your students and yourself to use subroutines for the exercices on the computer like

```
STDEV(X)    Standard deviation of series X
FPRT(X)     FISHER-PITMAN Randomtest on X
```

Moreover, the shorthand X for the very well known time series 'Sales of Company X', cf. CHATFIELD & PROTHERO (1973), seems to be rather nasty espescially for non-guinea pigs. Although its typing may be tedious I nevertheless would like to vote for commands like

```
STANDARDDEVIATION SALESOFCOMPANYX
FISHERPITMANRANDOMTEST SALESOFCOMPANYX.
```

Again, this identity is only aimed at for the learners sake. Notice, that sending off a command of that calibre at a terminal is just spelling out the name of a method introduced into your lecture some times before.

This learning by doing is easily supported in APL when using groups as a set of functions(methods). For example you will find in NPSTAT such major groups as

GROUP 2 CLASSICAL DESCRIPTIVE STATISTICS,ORDERSTATISTICS
GROUP 3 SINGLE-SAMPLE TESTS
GROUP 4 TWO-SAMPLE TESTS
GROUP 5 K-SAMPLE TESTS.

Picking out one subgroup for illustrating purposes you will find

SUBGROUP 31 ONE-SAMPLE LOCATION TESTS
SIGNTEST
MEDIANTEST
WILCOXONSIGNEDRANKTEST.

Each time your students inform themselves about the contents of their workspaces copied from NPSTAT they rerun the headlines of the contents of your lecture on nonparametric statistics, cf. GIBBONS(1971). Because the groups are structural identical to the main subjects of your lecture, such an approach causes learning by doing again.

3. DATA INPUT

As everybody knows about the benefits of APL - the saying goes that APL is the most efficient desc calculator- the only thing you have to do when running NPSTAT at a terminal are two things : Typing messages as data, commands etc. and waiting for the system response - hoping that the host doesn't break down.

As it seems to be clear now how to compute special statistics and/or how to run special test procedures with NPSTAT some notes on how the data come in might be desirable.For instance you may wish to generate 100 extremally and independently distributed random numbers. Use the command, cf.WHEELER(1973)

```
DATA←NEXTREME 100
```

Secondly, if you are really a fun of the time series 'Sales of Company X' - as I am- the following command makes this series available for your data analysis

```
)COPY 1124 DATEN SALESOFCOMPANYX
```

Of course, if you are anxious about information retrieval try the direct input by typing item by item

```
DATA ← 154 96. 73. 49    etc.,
```

but don't forget to press the end-of-text key just when you finished the last (77th) item.

4. SOME EXAMPLES OF HOW TO USE NPSTAT

Using NPSTAT is principially as simple as using a COMMODORE, HP-XX,TEXAS INSTRUMENTS etc - again, a design criteria was to assist teaching statistics but not to teach applied computer science-, let us have a look at how to compute some simple nonparametric statistics and how to perform some tests. For the sake of simplicity we restrict ourselves to the one-sample case.

We are starting with looking at the generated random numbers. As there is only limited space we select the first 9 items from the one-dimensional array DATA and print them out using only up to 3 significant decimals

```
DATA[19]
2.03  .197  1.16  1.97  1.09  1.5  1.06  1.21  ¯1.38
```

Plotting is in when making data analysis. Therefore use the command

```
10 50 PLOT DATA
```

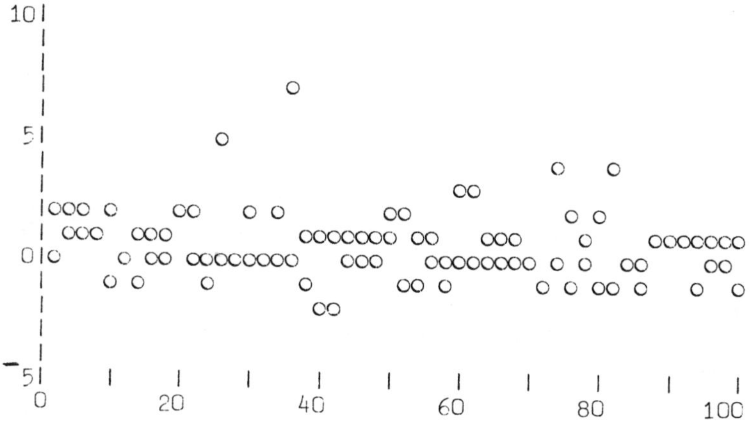

The plot is not very informative in this case. Therefore try

to estimate the histogram of DATA. Wishing a width of 1 for all the class intervals you should send off the command

1 HISTO DATA

and with a delay of about 4 seconds you will get the response

```
ABS   REL    MIN   MAX  |
  2  2.00  ¯2.5  ¯1.5  |□□
 15 15.00  ¯1.5  ¯0.5  |□□□□□□□□□□□□□□□
 34 34.00  ¯0.5   0.5  |□□□□□□□□□□□□□□□□□□□□□□□□□□□□□□□□□□
 30 30.00   0.5   1.5  |□□□□□□□□□□□□□□□□□□□□□□□□□□□□□□
 13 13.00   1.5   2.5  |□□□□□□□□□□□□□
  2  2.00   2.5   3.5  |□□
  2  2.00   3.5   4.5  |□□
  1  1.00   4.5   5.5  |□
  0  0.00   5.5   6.5  |
  1  1.00   6.5   7.5  |□
```

If you are not satisfied with the shape of the estimated density it is simple enough to start the estimating procedure again. At that moment you will get a better understanding of truly interactive systems when making error and trial attacks on data.If not, are you sure about the effect of decreasing the class width to 0.5 ?

Let us now turn to the computing of some classical descriptive statistics,i.e mean,variance and standard deviation called 'Standardabweichung' in the German language.

MEAN DATA

```
.622
```

VARIANZ DATA

```
1.91
```

STANDARDABWEICHUNG DATA

```
1.38
```

Perhaps you will find it more cumbersome to compute the following orderstatistics without any help by NPSTAT:

ORDSTAT DATA

```
¯2.01  ¯1.95  ¯1.5   ¯1.38  ¯1.06  ¯1     ¯.921  ¯.918  ¯.858
       ¯.827  ¯.762  ¯.689  ¯.679  ¯.628  ¯.613  ¯.549
       ¯.501  ¯.495  ¯.477  ¯.46   ¯.44   ¯.434  ¯.433  ¯.428
       ¯.417  ¯.394  ¯.374  ¯.344  ¯.306  ¯.272  ¯.235
       ¯.23   ¯.142  ¯.134  ¯.133  ¯.0074  .057  .0598  ...
```

```
                MEDIAN DATA
 .468
                (ORDSTAT DATA) [1]
 ¯2.01
                (ORDSTAT DATA) [100]
 7.03
                RANGE DATA
 9.04
```

Truncating the output of the series of ranks corresponding to the series 'DATA' one receives

```
                RANK DATA
 90  43  73  89  71  82  68  74  4  92  50  46  6  70 ...
```

Let us switch over to some few one-sample testproblems. A well known test for randomness (linear trend as H_2-hypothesis) is the COX&STUART Test. The appropriate command will produce

```
                COXSTUARTTEST DATA
 N=50
 X=18
 Z=¯1.98
 50  18  .5  ¯1.98  0
```

Of course, you will recognise some difficulties in executing the test. But this was exactly the effect the designer of NPSTAT wanted to cause by design. Computing without thinking doesn't make any sense. Therefore NPSTAT was designed and implemented making use of a manual job control approach instead of creating one new fully automatic method base. So help yourself commanding

```
                0 1 NORMAREA ¯1.98
 .0239
                NORMPCP 0.01 0.05 0.95 0.99
 ¯2.33  ¯1.65  1.65  2.33
```

To pick up only one test for randomness more let us try

```
                FISHERPITMANRANDOMTEST DATA
 8.51  100
```

The tour d'horizon should be closed with a goodness-of-fit test, say the KOLMOGOROV-SMIRNOV-test introduced in the modern literature as KS-test. Performing this test is easily illustrated by testing a series of 100 (0,1)-uniformally and independently random numbers on their uniform distribution.

```
'0 1 UNIAREA'KSTEST NUNIFORM 100
1.06
```

Let us close with an example of the self-documentation abilities of NPSTAT again referring to the KS-test.

```
KSTESTHOW

              DN←F KSTEST X
              STATISTIK DES KOLMOGOROFF-SMIRNOV-
              ANPASSUNGSTESTS.

    X SEI DIE STICHPROBE IM UMFANG N UND F DIE
UNTER HO VOLL SPEZIFIZIERTE VERTEILUNGSFUNKTION
FO(X). DANN LIEFERT DER AUFRUF DN← P1 P2 FO KSTEST X
 DEN WERT DN DER KS-STATISTIK
    DN=(N*.5)×SUP|FN(X)-FO(X)|,
WOBEI FN(X) DIE EMPIRISCHE VERTEILUNGSFUNKTION IST.
    P1 UND P2 SIND MOEGLICHE FUNKTIONSPARAMETER
DIESE SIND MIT FO ZUSAMMEN MITHILFE VON QUOTE EINZUGEBEN

    METHODE: NPSTAT-VORLESUNG,LENZ,SS1977, S.32
```

5. GROUPS & SUBGROUPS OF NPSTAT

GROUP 1: PLOT; LOGNORMAL, NCAUCHY, NEXPONENTIAL, NEXTREME, NLAPLACE, NLOGISTIC, NNORMAL, NUNIFORM; BINOMIALPROB, HYPERGEOMETRICPROB, MATCHPROB, NEGBINOMIALPROB, POISSONPROB, RUNSPROB, SIGNEDRANKPROB, TAUPROB, UTESTPROB, GAUSSPROB, FAREA, TAREA, NORMAREA, NORMPCP

GROUP 2: MEAN, STANDARDABWEICHUNG, VARIANZ; ORDSTAT, MEDIAN, RANGE, RANK, RANKCOR, RUNS, CONCORDANCE, TIES, CTAB, CHI2; BINOMTEST, NORMBINOMTEST, XPCONFINT, PCONFINT

GROUP 3: KSTEST, CRAMERVONMISESTEST; FISHERPITMANRANDOMTEST, RANDOMTEST, COXSTUARTTEST, RUNSTEST, UTEST; SIGNTEST, MEDIANPERMUTATIONSTEST, WILCOXONSIGNEDRANKTEST; INTERQUARTILSRANGETEST;

GROUP 4: SIGNTEST, WILCOXONSIGNEDRANKTEST, MCNEMARTEST; CHI2TEST, FISHERYATESTEST, BLOMQUISTWESTENBERGTEST; WALDWOLFOWITZTEST, KSTWOSAMPLETEST, MEDIAN2TEST; FISHERPITMANTEST, WILCOXONTEST, UTEST, TERRYHOEFFDINGTEST, VANDERWAERDENTEST, GASTWIRTHTEST; MOODTEST, FABDBTEST, SIEGELTUKEYTEST, KLOTZTEST, GASTWIRTHTEST, SUKHATMETEST

GROUP 5: KRUSKALWALLISTEST, MEDIANKTEST, FRIEDMANTEST, QTEST, CATANOVA

ACKNOWLEDGEMENTS

I would like to thank my colleague Assistant Professor Dr. B. Streitberg for his persistent support in collecting quite a lot of APL functions used now in NPSTAT.

REFERENCES

Buening,H.,Trenkler,G.,Nichtparametrische statistische Methoden, de Gruyter, Berlin 1978

Chatfield,C.,Prothero,D.L., Box-Jenkins seasonal forecasting: problems in a case-study, JRSS, ser.A, vol.136, 295-336, 1973

Conover,W.J., Practical Nonparametric Statistics, Wiley, New York etc., 1971

Gibbons,J.D., Nonparametric Statistical Inference,Mc Graw Hill, New York etc, 1971

Naeve,P, CAI and Computational Statistics, Discussion Paper N° 16/76, Inst.f.Quant.Ökonomik & Statistik, Freie Universität Berlin, Berlin, 1976

Wheeler,R.E., Random Variable Generators, APL Quote Quad, vol.4, 7-16, 1973

The Utilization of the Computer in the Teaching of Statistics at Elementary Level

T. Pukkila, Tampere

SUMMARY: The paper describes the utilization of the computer in the teaching of elementary level statistical courses consisting yearly of 200-250 students. An example is also given of the use of the statistical data-processing system SURVO developed in the Computer Centre of Tampere University.

KEYWORDS: Computer in the teaching of statistics, SURVO.

1. INTRODUCTION

In the year 1971 the Computer Centre of Tampere University placed the statistical data-processing system SURVO at the disposal of users in the time-sharing system HONEYWELL 1644. The first version of SURVO was already implemented in 1966 on an ELLIOTT-803, the computer using mainly paper tape as its input and output device.

Originally the system was developed to offer statistical data-processing tools e.g. for social scientists in their empirical investigation problems. As in other statistical computer packages also in SURVO it is possible e.g. to transform variables, to make tabulations, to compute sampling characteristics and to apply the usual statistical multivariate analysis methods. During the years 1975 and 1976 the time-sharing version was enlarged by a number of time series analytical operations, so that in the SURVO system it is possible e.g. to build univariate Box and Jenkins models and also transfer function noise models with several correlated inputs.

In spite of the fact that in planning the SURVO system account was not taken of the special needs of the teaching of statistics, the system has been used from the very beginning e.g. in courses on multivariate methods. In these courses the number of students has usually been rather small. However, because it was found that for the students it is very easy to learn to use the system even with no previous knowledge of computers, after a few experiments with small groups of students the system was taken into use in the year 1975 also on the first course in statistics usually consisting of 200-250 students.

The elementary course comprises students from administration, economics and the mathematical sciences. Altogether the whole year course consists of 112 hours lectures and 56 hours exercises, the teaching being divided evenly over 28 weeks. The content of the course is roughly: measurement of variables, classification and tabulation, sample characteristics, probability, random variables, theoretical distributions, estimation, confidence intervals and testing of hypotheses, correlation and regression, analysis of variance, some of the non-parametric methods and time series analysis.

The task of the course is twofold. On the one hand it has to form the basis for later and more advanced studies in statistics. On the other hand for most students the course is the first and the last in statistics and therefore during the course these students must attain such competence that they can deal satisfactorily with their practical statistical problems in later studies. For these reasons the bulk of the course is in practical considerations, without however forgetting important theoretical aspects.

2. THE PRACTICE IN THE UTILIZATION OF THE COMPUTER

From the viewpoint of computer utilization the contents of the elementary statistical course can be divided into two different parts. The first consists of theoretical matters and the second those which are empirical i.e. connected with a real data-matrix. For some time now in the University of Tampere the computer has been used to a large extent at elementary level in the handling of empirical statistical problems.

In the elementary statistical course the computer is employed in that some of the weekly exercises are solved by students using SURVO. These empirical exercises are connected with real data-matrices collected at various times by students and teachers of statistics. Often these practical exercises are formulated rather loosely by the teachers. The aim is that the student has to deliberate what kind of statistical problems are relevant for the data studied. Of course among the empirical exercises there are also more technical problems to be solved by the SURVO system. However, the main purpose is that the students learn to raise real statistical problems and to solve them. The role of a computer in this activity is to work mainly as a calculator. As a by-product the students are familiarized with the nature of computers. A further advantage of the utilization of the computer is that the practical work e.g. in the terminal rooms and in students finding their ability to solve real problems with the aid of a computer seems to motivate and inspire students more than without the computer to study statistics and not to feel the course merely as a "necessary evil".

During the course every student also makes two fairly small written treatises with the aid of the computer. For these two papers they can either use an existing data-matrix on computer disc, or they can settle their problems themselves, gather the data, move them into the computer, solve the problems and finally report the results.

It is clear that all students have to be familiarized with the SURVO system and the use of the computer via time-sharing terminals. This necessary computer-oriented teaching takes place after a short introduction to statistical concepts. Experience during the last few years has shown that two lectures of two hours on the system and two terminal exercises each of one hour is a sufficient amount of computer teaching in the beginning. Thereafter the students can manage alone e.g. in the terminal rooms in their own time. Later in the course when the teacher of statistics is talking e.g. on classification of variables in his lectures, in this connection he also tells briefly how to define classifications in the SURVO system. It has been found that after one has learned the principles of the system e.g. in the context of calculating means and making frequency tables, one has usually no difficulties in learning also other operations in the system. The only presumption is that the user of the system knows the underlying statistical ideas and concepts.

As said earlier the SURVO system is implemented in Tampere University on a HONEYWELL 1644, which is a small time-sharing system based on two minicomputers. The size of the core storage is 32K a' 16 bit. At the disposal of the students and investigators there are nowadays about 40 time-sharing terminals. These can be used 8.00-21.00 from Monday to Friday.

3. AN EXAMPLE OF A SURVO PROGRAM

SURVO programming is not computer-programming in the usual sense. Preferably to make a SURVO program means defining the statistical task by discussing with the computer. After writing the last SURVO-operation END the system generates the corresponding FORTRAN program that will be executed. The results of the program are written on lineprinter. An example will clarify the definition of the SURVO program.

One of the data-matrices which has been used in the teaching of statistics is SAIDIT. It is composed of 120 normal births in Finland 1965-1969, and the variables of the matrix are concerned with the mother and the new-born. For example the variable PAINO gives the weight of the child in grammes and the variable AIDINPAI the weight of the mother in kilogrammes. We make by SURVO "the regression analysis" such that the dependent variable is PAINO and the explaining variable is AIDINPAI. In the following the text after the mark ! comprises the replies of the user.

```
?SURVO

      STATISTICAL DATA PROCESSING SYSTEM SURVO/71
                UNIVERSITY OF TAMPERE
                   COMPUTER CENTRE

THIS PROGRAM
!LEIDEN TARMO PUKKILA

IS A SEQUEL TO THE PROGRAM
!

THE OBJECT OF OPERATIONS IS DATAMATRIX
!SAIDIT/880

HARJOITUSAINEISTO
STAT
TILASTOTIEDE/SAIDIT

LIST OF SURVO-OBJECTS
!NO



NEXT OPERATION IS
!CLASS

POSSIBLE CLASSIFYING SPECIFICATIONS ARE
   INT  FOR EQUAL INTERVALS
   TAB  FOR CLASSTABLE
!TAB

EACH CLASS IS DEFINED BY CLASSIDENTIFIER AND CLASSLIMITS
!I 54 64 II 64 69 III 69 74 IV 74 94;

ERROR MESSAGES OF UNDEFINED VALUES
!NO

THE NAME OF THIS CLASSIFICATION IS
!WEIGHT



NEXT OPERATION IS
!TABLE

CLASSIFIED COLUMN VARIABLE IS
!WEIGHT(AIDINPAI)

AND CLASSIFIED ROW VARIABLES ARE
!

OPTIONAL SPECIFICATIONS
!YES
```

```
THESE RESULTS ARE STORED UNDER THE NAME
!

POSSIBLE OUTPUT SPECIFICATIONS ARE
    COL%  FOR PER CENT OF COLUMN SUMS
    ROW%  FOR PER CENT OF ROW SUMS
    TOTAL%  FOR PER CENT OF TOTAL SUM
    NO    FOR NO FREQUENCY TABLE
!

THESE CLASSES TABULATE VARIABLES
!PAINO

POSSIBLE OUTPUT SPECIFICATIONS ARE
    SUM  FOR SUMS
    MEAN  FOR MEANS
    STDDEV  FOR MEANS AND STANDARD DEVIATIONS
!STDDEV

THE TITLE OF THESE RESULTS IS
!THE MEANS OF THE VARIABLE PAINO IN THE FOUR CLASSES
!OF THE VARIABLE AIDINPAI DEFINED BY THE CLASSIFICATION
!WEIGHT



NEXT OPERATION IS
!END
```

The above SURVO program produces the following results:

```
TARMO PUKKILA
*****************************************************************


         STATISTICAL DATA PROCESSING SYSTEM SURVO/71
                   UNIVERSITY OF TAMPERE
                      COMPUTER CENTRE

PROGRAM...: LEIDEN        PERSON.......: HARJOITUSAINEISTO
LISTING...: LLEIDE        DEPARTMENT...: STAT
DATA......: SAIDIT/880    SUPERVISOR...: TILASTOTIEDE/SAIDIT


DATE......: 78-04-11      NUMBER OF OBSERVATIONS...:    120

*****************************************************************
```

THE MEANS OF THE VARIABLE PAINO IN THE FOUR CLASSES
OF THE VARIABLE AIDINPAI DEFINED BY THE CLASSIFICATION
WEIGHT

TABLE
****

NUMBER OF OBSERVATIONS: 120
COLUMN VARIABLE.......: AIDINPAI
CLASSIFICATION........: WEIGHT

	I	II	III	IV	TOTAL
FREQ	31	23	29	37	120
MEANS OF PAINO	3257.74	3625.22	3652.76	3679.73	3553.75
STDDEVS OF PAINO	398.787	425.044	442.750	532.418	486.320

4. THE EVALUATION OF THE COMPUTER UTILIZATION

When the computer was taken into use already for the elementary level teaching of statistics in the University of Tampere, the aim was, of course, to better the teaching of statistics. The positive results can be seen e.g. in the two small practical treatises which the students write during the course.

In practice it has been important that the computer use on large elementary level statistical courses has become everyday practice such that this activity needs not more attention from teachers than any other work during the usual lectures. In fact SURVO has made all of the above performances possible in practice. It is quite natural that a student of the elementary level statistical course goes now and then to a terminal and begins to define a SURVO program. In practice it has also been very important that the utilization of the computer has not increased work for either the Computer Centre staff or the teachers. In fact the elementary statistical course consisting of 200-250 students has only increased the work of the computer. The course produces weekly 250-750 SURVO programs. It is to be remembered that the computer is not only for students and research workers of statistics. The Computer Centre of Tampere University has also to serve other members of a university consisting of about 10 000 students.

In some contexts when talking about the use of computers in the teaching of statistics some teachers of statistics have stated that students do not learn to calculate manually when a computer is used already at elementary level. Why so? It is really quite unnecessary to forget previous and good teaching methods the moment a computer is taken into use in the teaching of statistics. Secondly, it is also said that at elementary level in statistics students can very easily produce with the aid of a computer a lot of figures with no sensible meaning, misuse statistical methods and so on. It is true that these kinds of results are possible. The fact is, however, that it is very difficult to study theoretically the handling of empirical data. Therefore especially every student of statistics also needs a place where he can learn to handle real data and also to make his first mistakes. And is it not really the case that a statistical course is one of the safest surroundings to learn to handle data, draw inferences on it, and also make unavoidable mistakes and misuse statistical methods and computers?

10. Statistical Software

The Statistical Principle and Methodology in NISAN System

C. Asano, K. Wakimoto, T. Shohoji, T. Komasawa, K. Jojima, M. Goto, Y. Tanaka, T. Tarumi and N. Ohsumi, Fukuoka

Summary NISAN system is a new interactive statistical analysis program package constructed by an organization of Japanese statisticians. The package is widely available for both statistical situations, confirmatory analysis and exploratory analysis, and is planned to obtain statistical wisdom and to choose optimal process of statistical analysis for senior statisticians.

Keywords: Statistical program package, data investigation, quantification, cluster analysis, inference process, graphic representation, NISAN system

1. System Modules

NISAN system has the following diversity functions: 1) highly portability, 2) serviceable interactive, 3) data base, 4) inquiry, 5) documentation and 6) abundant data investigation. The computer language used in NISAN system is FORTRAN only, and the system mainly consist of four big modules which are interlaced one another.

Most STAT modules introduce several adequate processes of statistical analysis, which include current and newly-developed statistical methods in exploratory or confirmatory situations. Therefore it may be said at present that the modules attempt to give us the most progressive methodology for the practical use of statistical program packages.

NISAN system files consist of a data file for analysis, and a document file for records. DATA modules control the data file, and DOC modules control the document file. Without any considering the file structures, all computational modules can easily access any files through DATA and DOC modules. HELP modules have the complete inquiry functions for giving answers to the users for dispelling their questions on interpretation and utilization of NISAN system. It is also aimed that even if the user is beginner, he will easily access the NISAN system by the guide of HELP modules. The minimum equipment, as a terminal, is a character display or a teletype terminal to access NISAN system.

2. Statistical Principle

In view of statistical methodology, the most emphasized functions are as follows; 1) data investigations, 2) graphic representations, 3) generalized methods of optimal scaling, 4) various methods of cluster analysis and multidimensional scaling, and 5) studies on successive processes of statistical inference.

Generally speaking, on applying the statistical methods in practice, it is very important for us to know the features and properties of input data in advance, and we cannot neglect such investigations. Thinking that the current statistical program packages have not enough data investigation function, we studied and strengthened the contents of data investigation, especially the examinations of multivariate normality, the transformation of variables, the check of outliers and so on. Thus we enable data investigation before statistical analysis.

According to visual features, i.e. inspecting on graphical representation at every stage of analysis, we obtain occasionally important insights, effective suggestions and interpretation not only on the input data but also on the way of analysis and the results. NISAN system can give us arbitrarily such graphical representations by users' request.

For categorical input data, the NISAN system includes generalized methods of optimum quantification, newly-developed by us, as well as the ordinary nonparametric methods. We are able to choose any of them, depending on the existence of external criterion and on the ordered relations among item-categories.

The methods of cluster analysis and multidimensional scaling give us some of the exploratory methodology in data analysis. These are also widely included with our newly-developed, and are applicable with relation to the quantity and properties of input data and to the hierarchical or nonhierarchical structure of clustering.

Concerning the situations of statistical inference, methodologies of testimating, testipredicting and testitesting are included in view of the unspecified mathematical model of data, e.g. pooling methodology is available in cases of ANOVA and MANOVA with the resultant estimations. Facing the statistical data analysis, we can obtain statistical wisdom on the accuracies and precisions for estimates, the powers of test for various alternative hypotheses and so on, by applying a simulation function in NISAN system. Thus, as a whole process of statistical inference, we can consider and examine the performances and strategies, and can finally proceed with the optimal procedure of statistical analysis.

3. Emphasized Functions for Methodology in NISAN

3.1 Data investigation

In order to investigate the features and properties of input data, NISAN system includes two kinds of examinations, for basic and simple data inspection and for further investigations on mathematical assumptions, in face of applying the methods of statistical analysis. The former is related to mis-rewriting, mis-input, missing values, extraordinary data and so on. The latter concerns mainly the type of distribution, transformations of variables, trend, strata and so on. Especially, since many statistical methods require the normality of distribution, the system includes the tests of skewness and kurtosis, Geary test, Gap test, Shapiro-Wilks test, Shapiro-Francis test and D'agstino test for univariate normality, and Mardia test for multivariate normality, because of the convenience to obtain the global feature, asymptotic property and easy algorithum of computation for the frequency distribution. For the different types from normal distribution, the NISAN system provides two kinds of normal-transformations of variables, i.e. variance-stabilizing transformations and power-transformations. Severally speaking, the transformations are square-root method, angular method, log-transformation, log log-transformation, logit-transformation, probit-transformation, rankit-transformation and so on. Naturally after transformation, if necessary, the performance of transformed distribution is examined by the normality tests mentioned above. The examination for outliers may depend largely on the identification of population, the feature of distribution type, the choice of variables and so on. Actually it may be rather complicated for us to define and treat such outliers, especially in multi-vatiate cases. Therefore the NISAN system includes the omnibus methods, i.e. FUNOP and FUNOM proposed by J.W. Tukey for single variate and the influence method proposed by F.R. Hample for multivariate.

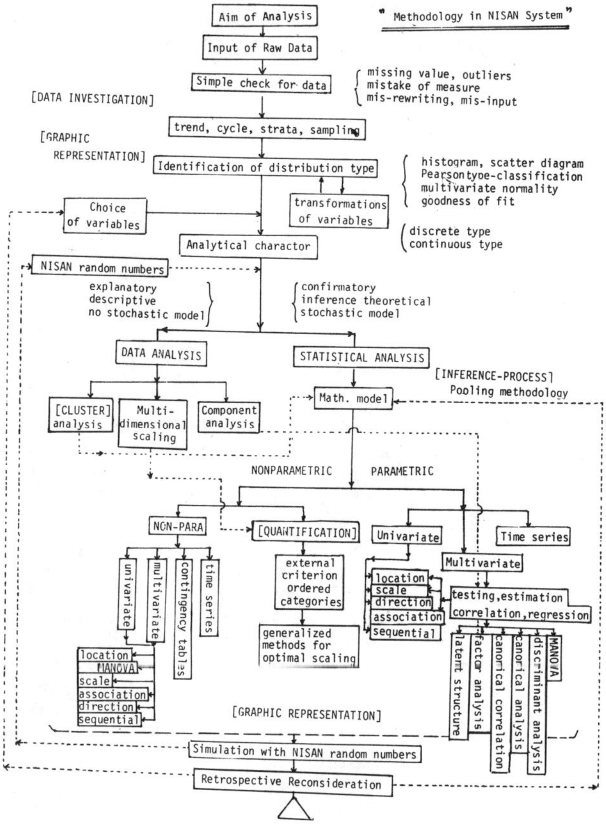

3.2 Graphic representations

Inspecting the feature of observations gives us some important insights, effective suggestions and interpretation not only on the input data but also on the way of analysis and the results. Generally speaking, such trials are less confining, descriptive and rather informal, and still they are fruitful. In view of such advantages in practice of statistical data analysis, NISAN system contains various kinds of graphic representation as follows; Histogram, Hanging rootgram, Stemleaf graph, Scatter diagram, Radar chart, Face graph, Body graph*, Constellation graph*, Tree graph*, Linked vector graph*, Biplot graph, Statistical ellipse, Non-linear mapping graph, Dendrogram, etc., where the symbol * shows new graphs proposed by NISAN group. Setting each variable or composite variable to each part defined on graph, we are able to get quickly figures as we like.

Therefore, these graphs are selected on the basis of the aim of analysis, the field of application, and the character of data. Naturally it will be expected that graphic representations and analytical methods complement mutually on a sound statistical data analysis. Particularly, our graphic representations are suitable for multi-dimensional observations to grasp visually the structures as a whole, and simultaneously are helpful to investigate characteristics of individuals. Some of them are demonstrated as below. Body graph

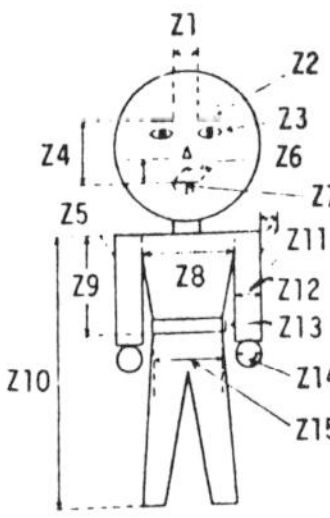

Body Graph

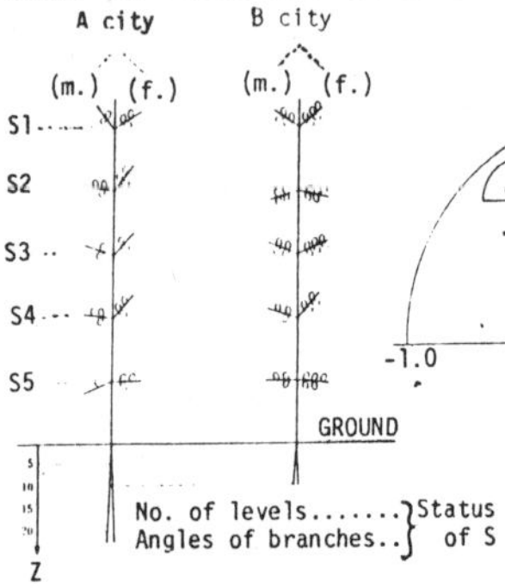

Tree Graph

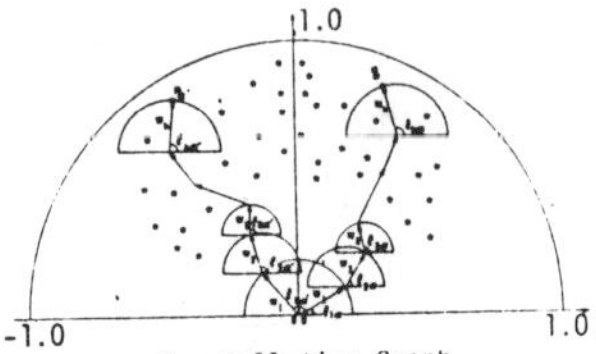

Constellation Graph

may represent the global status of subjects effectively rather than the face graph like in case of investigation of physique, physical strength and other latent structures. The above graph illustrated depends on obsevations for body weight, chest circumference, sitting height and so on. Tree graph may represent multi-items or multi-traits by the branches roots, fruits, leaves, heights and shapes of tree, and thus it may be recognized globally the characteristics and profiles of the subjects. It seems to us that the tree graph is particularly superior to other graphs in grasping the global correlation relationship among items, latent traits and time-dependent changes, too. The physical characteristic of constellation graph is to show data in the upper half circle. For the construction of constellation graph, after transforming the original data $\{x_{j\alpha}\}$ to standardized values $\{\xi_{j\alpha}\}$ for location and scale, $j=1,2,\ldots,p$ and $\alpha=1,2,\ldots,n$, the graph is drawn by a set of complex numbers $\{P_\alpha\}$, where $P_\alpha = \Sigma_j w_j \exp(i\xi_{j\alpha})$, $i = \sqrt{-1}$ and $\Sigma_j w_j = 1$. Further details, (Wakimoto-Taguri, 1978), may be presented at the poster session of the present symposium.

3.3 Extensive methods of optimal scaling

The methods of optimal scaling, or quantification, are classified into two types. The methods of the first type are for the cases with external criterion and may be applied to an explained variable, using information related to the qualitative attributes of each subject, and may analize the contribution or influence of each attribute to the explained variable. The methods of this type include those proposed by Fisher(1948), Johnson(1950), Hayashi (1952), Bradley, Katti and Coons(1962), Nishisato and Arri(1975), and Tanaka and Asano(1978) recently developed and generalized. The methods of the latter type are only based on the relationships within data and are applied to represent relatively the data set by locating themselves in an appropriate multidimensional space and occasionally to classify the data. Those proposed by

Guttman(1941, 1968), Hayashi(1952, 1954, 1974), Okamoto and Endo(1973) belong to the latter type.

Thus in the NISAN system, a variety of optimal scaling methods, which are widely used in various fields, is going to be available systemically. The characteristics of these methods, including in the NISAN system, will be to give those generalized for unordered item-categories and those developed for ordered item-categories, and also to give the evaluation for reliability of the optimal scores, if necessary, and also to complete detailed inference about the contributions of factor items on the explained variables, by the use of asymptotic theories. As a matter of course, since the system has full functions of preliminary analysis and editing data and graphical representations, it may be very convenient and reliable for us to search the optimal model and to interpret the results of analysis. The generalized methods (Tanaka and Asano, 1978) will be presented with the case of ordered categories at another session of the present symposium.

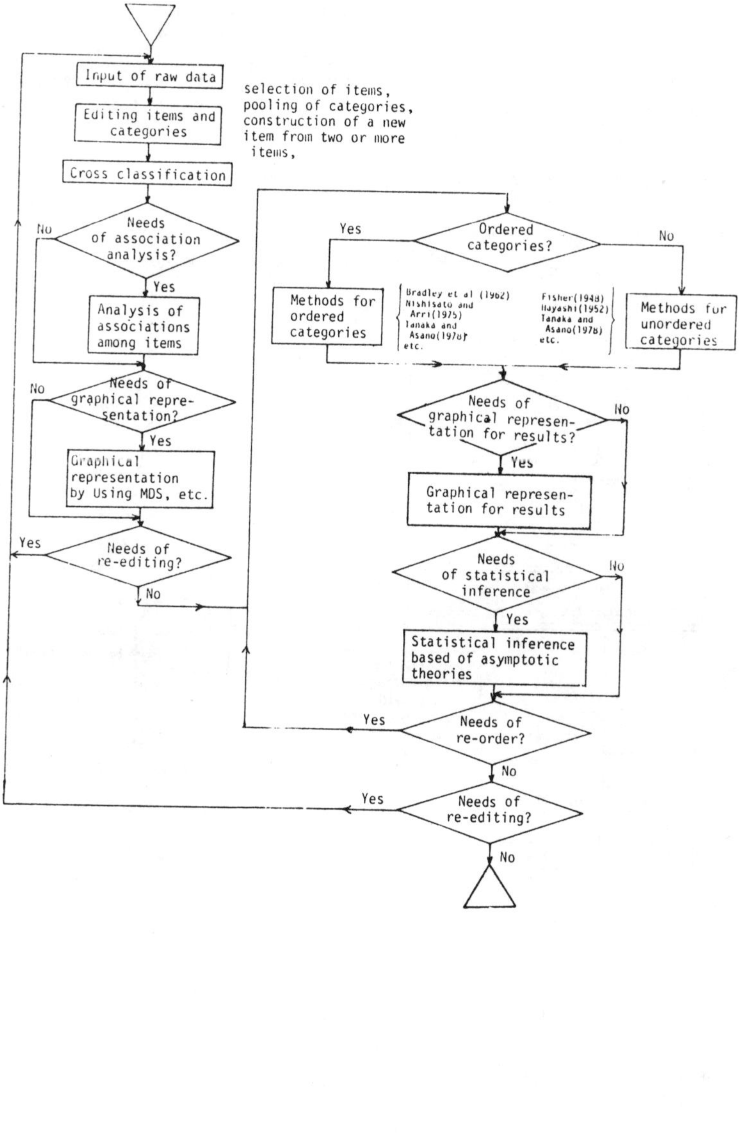

3.4 Systemical techniques for cluster analysis and multidimentional scaling

The techniques of cluster analysis are nowadays popular for data analysis. Although there exist a lot of techniques of cluster analysis, systemical techniques are included in NISAN system, in view of those objectively defined with clear algorithm and frequently refered with wide adaptability for various kinds of data. The techniques may be generally classified into three categories. (i) Hierarchical types with agglomerative type and divisive type, including Automatic Interaction Detector type, (0,1) Association Analysis and their modified types by us. (ii) Nonhierarchical types with k-means method, Iterative Self-Organizing Data Analysis method and the modified for outlines. (iii) Other types with Fuzzy clustering and two-way clustering. Naturally these techniques are interactively connected each other and also connected to the next step to analyze. It may be the advantage of the present system for statisticians to evaluate the criteria of measures of similarity or distance, of numbers of clustering, and of the optimization. Also it may be worth to say that a number of sensitivity analysis is available on the basis of simulations by the use of NISAN random numbers. Concerning the methods of multidimensional scaling included are based on MDA-OR and MDA-UO, proposed by Hayashi(1974). These also give us effective methods for exploratory data analysis.

3.5 Studies on processes of statistical inferences

Studies on Statistical Inference Process in NISAN system

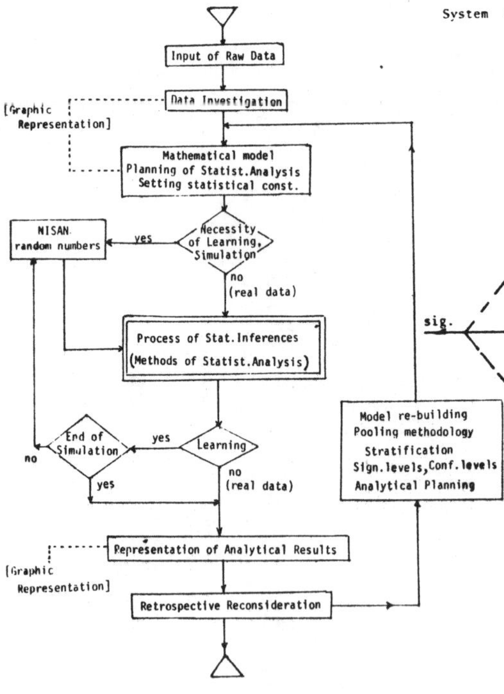

System of Successive Process of Statistical Inference

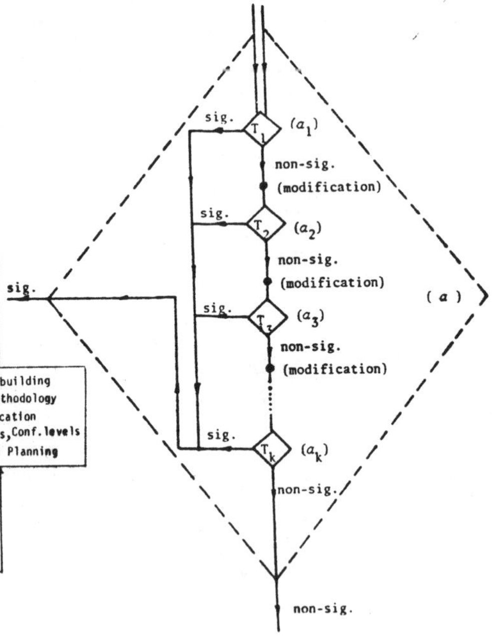

In order to specify adequate mathematical model(s) for statistical data, statisticians may apply their systematic processes of statistical methods to their data in accordance with their inference logics. From the viewpoints of such uses of statistical methods in a package, statisticians tend to examine objectively the performance of a total system of statistical inferences on the validity, the reliability, the sensibility, the efficiency and so on. The NISAN system enables statisticians to evaluate their inference processes. For instance, pooling methodology may be applied. Keeping away from awfully complicated formulations and the numerical computation for a multiple-stage process, the NISAN system is able to obtain numerical evaluation on the basis of simulating the process by NISAN random numbers implemented. The NISAN random numbers were generated physically and transformed as 2.4 million physical random figures. The characteristics were assured of good properties by fifteen tests for randomness (Goto and Asano, 1978). According to such studies on inference process, statisticians may obtain several important comments for statistical analysis as follows; (i) improvement on bias, precision, or the combined risk for parameter estimation, (ii) improvement or adjustment for the power of tests, (iii) investigations for various associations among statistical methods, (iv) choice of a serial process of statistical methods and a mathematical model, fitting better to the given data, and (v) estimation of the additional number of samples.

Conclusion NISAN system has been planned and constructed by a statisticians' organization in Japan, since 1976, and will be finished the first version by the end of 1978. The attempts, principle and methodology, of NISAN system are considerably different from those of the ordinary statistical program package being used already.

References Only Related to NISAN Members' Works

[1] Asano, Ch. and Jojima, K.: An Investigation Report on Statistical Program Packages in Europe, Report of B-1 Section in the Special Research Project "Formation Process of Information System and Organization of Scientific Informations", July (1977). (in Japanese)

[2] Tarumi, T.: Serveys on Statistical Program Packages Used in Japan, Research Report Connected with Grant (A) in Aid for Encouragement of Scientist, March (1978). (in Japanese)

[3] Goto, M., Uesaka, H. and Asano, Ch.: Methodology of data investigation in NISAN system; multivariate normality tests, Res. Rep. No. 90, Res. Instit. Fund. Infor. Sc., Kyushu University (1978).

[4] Goto, M., Inoue, T. and Asano, Ch.: Confirmatory studies of NISAN random numbers, Res. Rep. No. 91, Res. Instit. Fund. Infor. Sc., Kyushu University (1978).

[5] Wakimoto, K. and Taguri, M.,: Constellation graphical method for representing multidimentional data, Ann. Instit. Statist. Mathem. Vol. 30 (1978), 77-84.

[6] Wakimoto, K.: Tree graph method for visual representation of multidimentional data, J. Jap. Statist. Soc. Vol. 7 (1977).

[7] Tanaka, Y. and Asano, Ch.: A generalized method of optimal scaling for partially ordered categories, Res. Rep. No. 76, Res. Instit. Fund. Infor. Sc., Kyushu University (1977). Also see their references at another session of this Symposium.

[8] Matsusita, K. and Ohsumi, N.: Evaluation procedure of clustering techniques, Franco-Japan Seminary, Paris, March 13-20 (1978).

[9] Hayashi, C.: Minimum dimension analysis - MDA, Behaviormetrika No. 1 (1974).

Macros in GENSTAT with Special Reference to Multivariate Analysis

C.F. Banfield and J.C. Gower, Harpenden

Summary

The Genstat macro facility has been more used for multivariate analysis than for other branches of statistics. We report on our experiences in writing Genstat macros that are both efficient and easy to use. We think that some of our findings will be useful to writers of other statistical systems, all of which should have a macro-type facility.

KEYWORDS: MACROS, MULTIVARIATE ANALYSIS, GENSTAT, STATISTICAL SYSTEMS, SUBROUTINES.

1. Introduction

This paper is about macros in Genstat, with implications about the place of macros in any statistical computing system. To understand our remarks, which are primarily stimulated by our experiences in writing multivariate-analysis macros, we must first give a brief account of the Genstat language, especially those aspects of it that concern multivariate analysis.

The full specification of Genstat is given by Nelder et al (1977). The operands of Genstat are termed structures and may be single values (SCALAR); one-way arrays (UNIT, VARIATE, FACTOR, NAME, INTEGER, POINTER); matrices (MATRIX, SYMMAT, DIAGMAT) and a sums-of-squares-and-products structure (DSSP); multi-way tables (TABLE); or text (HEADING, CAPTION). The values contained in these structures are usually of numerical type and mode real, but the multiplicity of one-way arrays provides (in part) facilities for defining other types (see Gower & Hill (1971) for a discussion of terminology). The names and attributes of structures are declared by special directives, written as in the above upper case characters. Structures can be dimensioned by constants, SCALARs or any of the one-way arrays (dimension = array's length). Only SCALARs with numerical values already assigned and arrays with assigned lengths can dimension other structures. Structures may be stored on and retrieved from files on backing store.

Further directives operate on structures to produce new structures and/or printed output. Arithmetic operations are covered by the CALCULATE directive, which includes most of the standard mathematical functions amongst its facilities. All Genstat structures with real values (including matrices) may be added, subtracted, multiplied (element by element) or divided. Important for multivariate analysis are the special matrix functions, which enable most matrix operations to be programmed easily in Genstat. These include TRACE, TRANS(transpose), DET(determinant), PDT(productXY), PDTT(XY^T), TPDT(X^TY), INV(inverse), RSYMRI(XSX^T, S symmetric), CHOL(giving lower-triangular L for a symmetric $S = LL^T$) and SUBMAT (extracting a submatrix from a bigger matrix). The special matrix directive LRV (latent roots and vectors) solves $BX=AX\Lambda$, or $BX=X\Lambda$ where B and A are symmetric and Λ diagonal, and SVD (singular value decomposition) solves $C=U\Lambda V^T$ where U, V are orthogonal and Λ diagonal.

Many standard multivariate problems could be tackled with these matrix facilities but we have thought it worthwhile to provide standard directives for the more popular analyses, partly to facilitate ease of use, partly to improve efficiency, and partly to output information that is not easily handled by standard Genstat structures. Special directives are easier to use because:

(a) If printed output only is required many fewer structures need be declared. Simple standard print-option facilities can be used to control output. Parameterisation is simple.
(b) Efficiency is improved because Genstat compiles code that is interpreted. Hence a single multivariate directive is interpreted rather than many matrix ones.
(c) Some calculations are not easily compatible with operations on the standard Genstat structures. They are better (and more efficiently) coded as parts of directives.

The multivariate directives in Genstat (see Banfield (1978)) are PCP (principal components analysis), CVA (canonical variate analysis), PCO (principal coordinate analysis), ROTATE (Procrustes analysis), FACROT (factor rotation), CLASSIFY (forming non-hierarchical classes), and ADPT (add new points to a previous principal coordinate analysis). A suite of twelve directives, of which the principal is HIERARCHY (forming hierarchical classes), is available for cluster analysis.

We use PCP to illustrate the scope of these directives. Users may input either a list of VARIATEs from which an SSP-structure is derived, or the SSP-structure itself. Derived structures that may be formed and passed on to other directives include the roots and vectors (the loadings), the trace, the scores and the residuals. Any of these may be, independently, printed under the control of the standard Genstat print-option consisting of a series of letters following the directive name. Additionally approximate χ^2 significance tests may be printed. The user may specify how many dimensions he requires in printed structures and independently how many in stored structures; he can specify whether he is interested in the largest or smallest roots and he can operate on normalised data or raw data.

To obtain plots of the scores or loadings, to do further calculations on the residuals or to compute the scores of new data not included in the original data, users must follow a PCP statement by further Genstat statements. Such additional calculations may be included in one program or they may be performed at a later date, having filed the PCP output-structures on backing store.

The other Genstat multivariate directives give similar freedom to users. Output is not fixed but very much under users' control and none is given unless it is asked for specifically. Users are encouraged to keep output-structures and perform extra calculations.

2. The Macro facility

The freedom and efficiency given by providing special directives for each multivariate facility is expensive in time spent in writing Fortran code (the language in which Genstat itself is written) and in space taken by this code. For rarely used multivariate (and other) methods such expense cannot be justified. There is, in any case, the important consideration that any system like Genstat should be stable if users are not to be bombarded by frequent updates of the system code and documentation. Changes of this kind are a continuing frustration both to users and computer managers and may lead to disaffection.

Accordingly we decided that rather than include new directives the best way to extend the multivariate side of Genstat would be to write macros for an official Genstat macro library. Although formally different, operationally the process is very similar to constructing a subroutine library. In Genstat the macro takes the simple form:

```
'MACRO' macro-name ∅
(body of the macro)
'ENDMACRO'
```

and the body of the macro is stored by the compiler as characters, just as if it were text. When USE macro-name is encountered, the compiler reads and compiles the stored text. The macro text may have been stored on a totally different occasion to when it is used. Macros may call other macros, to depth eight.

Figure 1 is an example of a simple macro. Given two lists of variates named VARP and VARQ, the macro calculates and prints the canonical correlations between them and the loadings of both lists of variates. The annotation to Figure 1 explains briefly the function of individual statements, some of which are described in greater detail below. The CALCULATE instructions are mainly matrix operations giving the familiar canonical correlation matrix calculations.

3. Parameterisation of Macros

It is essential that a library macro can be parameterised to analyse sets of data of different dimensions. Those structures used internally by the macro, not explicitly declared as local to the macro by a LOCAL directive, are automatically treated as being global and as such are parameters of the macro. Global structures can have values and lengths set prior to the macro being compiled and, if SCALARs or one-way arrays, can be used to dimension local structures. In the CANCOR macro of Figure 1 the two lists of variates VARP and VARQ are specified by the user. The POINTERs P,Q and PQ have lengths equal to the number of their associated variates and hence satisfactorily dimension following structures.

Genstat statements		Explanation
'MACRO'	CANCOR ∅	Declares the macro name
'LOCAL'	P,Q,PQ,SSP,C,R,T,S,D,E,A	Declares which structures are local
'POINTER'	P=VARP:Q=VARQ	The sizes of the variate-lists
:	PQ=VARP,VARQ	pointed to are p,q and p+q respectively
'DSSP'	SSP ∅ PQ	Declares an SSP-structure for the p+q variates
'MATRIX'	C ∅ Q,P	Declares C (q,p)
:	M ∅ P,Q	" M (p,q)
:	L ∅ Q,Q	" L (q,q)
'SYMMAT'	S ∅ PQ	" S (p+q,p+q) symmetric
:	D ∅ P	" D (p,p) symmetric
:	E,A ∅ Q	" E and A (q,q) symmetric
'DIAGMAT'	R,RR ∅ Q	" R and RR (q,q) diagonal
'SCALAR'	T	Required by LRV (below) but not otherwise needed
'SSP'	SSP	Evaluates the SSP-structure
'EQUATE'	S = SSP	Copies the SSP-matrix into S
'CALCULATE'	C,D,E = SUBMAT(S)	Extracts sub-matrices C,D,E from S
:	D = INV(D)	Inverts sub-matrix D
:	A = RSYMRI (C;D)	$A = CD^{-1}C'$
'LRV'	A,E;L,RR,T	Evaluates L and RR (squared canonical correlations r^2)
'CALCULATE'	RR=SQRT(RR)	Compute RR with elements r

```
'CALCULATE/ZDZ=ZERO'  R=(RR/RR)/RR          Compute R with elements 1/r,
                                            allowing for possible zeros
'CALCULATE'           C=PDT(C;D)            C=CD-1
    :                 M=TPDT(C;L)           M=D-1C'L
    :                 M=PDT(M;R)            M=D-1C'LR
'PRINT/S'             RR,L,M $ 10.4         Print RR, L and M
'DEVALUE'             SSP,C,S,D,E,A,R       Recovers the space occupied by
                                            the values of the structures
'ENDMACRO'                                  Ends the statements of the macro
```

Figure 1. Macro CANCOR for canonical correlation analysis.

Not all the calculations and printed output of a macro may be required by a user. The values of global structures, can be used to indicate what is or is not required. Conditional jumps in the macro will then ignore the unwanted parts of the macro's statements. In macro CANCOR there are no such indicators so all the correlations and loadings are calculated and printed without option.

Many multivariate analysis directives allow structures of limited dimensions to be specified e.g. to keep only the first few principal components. If these directives are used in a macro, such structures can be dimensioned by global structures. The labelling of printed output from the macro can also be controlled by the user if the structures holding the labels are made global to the macro. However, providing many global structures throws a burden onto users, giving more room for errors and could be a serious imposition for those users requiring simplicity. In macro CANCOR the number of global structures has been kept to an absolute minimum. The global structures L, M and RR, which the macro prints, have been declared inside the macro preventing the user from providing labels for these structures but relieving him from, possibly erroneous, declarations.

Careful thought by writers as to what structures should be global can make macros just as flexible as individual directives, but as usual the best balance between flexibility and simplicity is debatable.

4. Available Macros for Multivariate Analysis

Of the eleven macros provided in release 4.01 of the Genstat macro library five concern the analysis of multivariate data. These include the macro CANCOR, described in Sections 2 and 3, and macro CLASSF (Section 5). Macro GENPROC performs a generalised Procrustes analysis (Gower (1975)). Given n matrices holding the coordinates of n configurations of p points in multidimensional space the macro obtains by translation, rotation and dilation the best fit (in a least squares sense) of n configurations to a 'consensus' configuration. The coordinates of the configurations after fitting and an analysis of variance are output. Macro MULTMISS obtains estimates of missing values in multinormal data using iterative multiple regression (Beale and Little (1974)). Macro MANOVA performs a multivariate analysis of variance and obtains the hypotheses and error sums-of-squares-and-products matrices as well as various test criteria and canonical variables for the wide class of experimental designs handled by Genstat.

Release 4.02 will have further multivariate analysis macros. These include macro ASYMANAL for the analysis of asymmetric matrices (Gower(1977)), macro CORRESP for correspondence analysis (Hill (1974)) and macro CVAID which produces a more comprehensive output for canonical variate analysis than the CVA directive, including dispersion matrices, tests of homogeneity, canonical variate plots and a table showing any misallocation. Four macros DSQUARE, MISALLOP, MISALLOG and ALLOCATE relating to problems of allocation in discriminant analysis will also be included.

5. Problems arising in producing Macros

Macros must be both efficient and simple to use. Minimising the number of global structures can make macros easier to call but can seriously reduce efficiency and the user's control (Section 3). For example if the number v of variates to be analysed is given as the value of a global SCALAR V then all statements in the macro requiring the value of v explicitly can use V. But if this single global structure is not provided, then the value v has to be obtained inside the macro by extricating the dimension of a global structure with length v, always provided that such a structure exists. This extrication may involve Genstat statements that must be compiled and executed as a 'block', commenced by a START and ended by a RUN, before the substance of the macro can be compiled and it is this switching between the compile and execution (run) phase within a macro that can prove inefficient.

Another important feature of macro efficiency is to minimise the number of both named and unnamed structures that are local to the macro. Unknowingly a macro user may quickly exhaust the available directory space. If the macro is called more than once a complete set of local named structures is added to the directory with every call. Unnamed structures are unnecessarily accumulated when a FOR directive is used for looping over a list of constants.

(a)
```
'FOR' X = 1...N
Genstat statements
'REPEAT'
```

(b)
```
'SCALAR' L:X=1
'LABEL' L
Genstat statements
'CALC' X = X+1
'JUMP' L*(X.LE.N)
```

In (a) the program will set up N unnamed structures in the directory, these being SCALARs holding the constants 1,2...N. When N happens to be large the inefficiency can be serious and, as usual, N has to be known before the FOR statement can be compiled. By declaring just two SCALARs and using the CALCULATE, LABEL and JUMP directives as in (b), these unnecessary unnamed structures and the need for a compile/run phase can be avoided. Similarly, if a constant is used more than once in a macro it is preferable to declare a SCALAR having the constant as its value and to use this SCALAR. Experience familiarises a macro writer with the directives which set up unnamed structures most liberally. Named structures however are easily kept to a minimum by using the same structure for as many purposes as possible. Thus in CANCOR D holds a matrix and later its inverse, M is used to hold intermediate values before it contains the final loadings, and RR contains successively, values r_i^2 and r_i. The last directive of a macro should be DEVALUE followed by the names of structures. This will recover the space occupied by the values of those structures, although not their other attributes. It will also clear from the directory the values and the attributes of all superfluous unnamed structures. Failure to DEVALUE may cause the macro to use more space than is necessary, possibly to run out of space altogether.

Macro CLASSF (Figure 2) classifies N units into K classes, which may then be used to initialise iterations of the CLASSIFY directive. K class nuclei are accumulated by successively finding the unit most distant from the space spanned by the nuclei already found (the two initial nuclei being the two units furthest apart). The remaining N-K units are assigned to their nearest nucleus. The values of SCALARs N and K, and of the list of VARIATEs VSET are given, and to hold the output classification a FACTOR named START must be declared. Some of the features mentioned above are exemplified in this macro. For instance, SCALARs N1 (=N-1) and K1 (=K-1) are computed in the first block and then used in the compilation of the second block. Here the inclusion of this first block was thought preferable to having N1 and K1 as global structures. The constant 1 is required several times in the macro and to avoid several unnamed

Genstat statements	Explanation
'MACRO' CLASSF ∅	Declares the macro name CLASSF
'LOCAL' L1,K1,RCN(1...N),M,L2,N1,PROW,DISTS, PSUB,D2,S,LAB,DDR(1),RORD,RORD2,PROW2,D3, RES,RESD2,INN,VECTS,ROOTS,CD,VART, ONE,I,J,II	Declares which structures are local
'SCALAR'J,K1,RCN(1...N),M,N1:ONE=1	Declares various scalars
'START'	Defines start of first block
'CALCULATE' N1=N-ONE:K1=K-ONE	Calculates scalars N1 and K1
'RUN'	Executes the first block
'START'	Defines start of a second block
'POINTER' PROW=RCN(ONE...N)	PROW points to scalars RCN(1...N)
'SYMMAT' DISTS ∅ PROW	Declares symmetric matrix DISTS indexed by PROW
'MATRIX' RES ∅ N,ONE	Declares matrix RES(N,1)
'VARIATE' VART=1...K:RESD2 ∅ N : INN ∅ ONE	Declares variate VART having values 1 to K, variate RESD2 having N values and variate INN having 1 value
'PCO' VARI=VSET;DIST=DISTS	Calculates Pythagorean distance matrix,DISTS from VSET
'CALCULATE' RCN(1)=MAX(DISTS)	Puts maximum distance into RCN(1)
'POSITION' INN=RCN(1) ∅DISTS	and its address into INN
'CALCULATE' RCN(1,2)=INN,ONE	Puts address into RCN(1), and value one into RCN(2)
'LABEL' L1	Declares label L1
'CALCULATE' RCN(1)=RCN(1)-RCN(2)	Subtracts RCN(2) from RCN(1)
:RCN(2)=RCN(2)+ONE	Adds one to RCN(2)
'JUMP' L1*(RCN(1).GT.RCN(2))	Jumps to L1 if RCN(1) > RCN(2)
'JUMP' L2*(K1.LE.ONE)	Jumps to L2 if K1 ⩽ 1
'CALCULATE' DISTS=DISTS**2	Squares distances
'FOR' I=2...K1:II=RCN(3...K)	Loops I from 2 to K1 and II from RCN(3) to RCN(K)
'USE/R' MAC1 ∅	Calls macro MAC1 at run-time
'MATRIX' VECTS ∅ I,I	Declares matrix VECTS (I,I)
'DIAGMAT' ROOTS, CD ∅ I	Declares diagonal matrices ROOTS, CD (I,I)
'CALCULATE' S,D2=SUBMAT(DISTS)	Forms submatrices S and D2 of DISTS
: S=-0.5*S	Multiplies S by $-\frac{1}{2}$
'PCO' S;RESU=VECTS,ROOTS,M;CENT=CD	Obtains principal coordinates and centroid distances

Genstat statements	Explanation
'ADPT' CD;VECTS,ROOTS,M;D2;;RES	Obtains residual distances
'CALCULATE' II=MAX(RES)	Puts maximum residual into II
'POSITION' II=II ∅ RES	and its address into II
'REPEAT'	Ends FOR loop
'LABEL' L2	Declares label L2
'DEVALUE' D2,VECTS,ROOTS,S,CD,RES	Devalues several structures
'VARIATE' DDR(1),RORD2 ∅ K	Declares variates DDR(1) and RORD2 having K values
: RORD =ONE...K	Declares variates RORD having values 1 to K
'RUN'	Executes the second block
'POINTER' PROW2=RCN(RCN(1...K))	PROW2 points to scalars RCN(RCN(1)) to RCN(RCN(K))
'MATRIX' D3 ∅ PROW,PROW2	Declares matrix D3 indexed by PROW and PROW2
'CALCULATE' D3=SUBMAT(DISTS) : J=ONE	Extracts submatrix D3 from DISTS and puts value one into J
'LABEL' LAB	Declares label LAB
'COPY' DDR(1)=D3 ∅ VART	Copies certain values of D3 into DDR(1)
'CALCULATE' VART=VART+K	Adds K to VART
: RORD2=ORDER(RORD;DDR(1))	Reorders values of RORD as DDR(1)
: ELEM(RESD2;J)=ELEM(RORD2;ONE)	Puts Jth value of RESD2 equal to first value of RORD2
'CALCULATE' J=J+ONE	Adds one to J
'JUMP' LAB*(J.LE.N)	Jumps to LAB if J ⩽ N
'GROUP' START=RANK(RESD2)	Ranks values of RESD2
'DEVALUE' D3,RESD2,DISTS,RORD,RORD2,DDR(1)	Devalues several local structures
'ENDMACRO'	Ends statements of macro CLASSF
'MACRO' MAC1 ∅	Declares the macro name MAC1
'POINTER' PSUB=RCN(RCN(1...I))	PSUB points to scalars RCN(1...I)
'MATRIX' D2 ∅ PROW,PSUB	Declares matrix D2 indexed by PROW and PSUB
'SYMMAT' S ∅ PSUB	Declares symmetric matrix S indexed by PSUB
'ENDMACRO'	Ends statements of macro MAC1

Figure 2 Macro CLASSF for initialising iterations in non-hierarchical classification.

structures being set up, a single SCALAR (named ONE) having value 1, is used. Writing USE/R macro-name delays the compilation of a macro until run-time. Here we use this facility to declare POINTER PSUB, and the matrices D2 and S it indexes, which cannot be compiled until the values of SCALARs RCN(1...I), augmented at each pass of a FOR-loop, are known. So the declarations have been put into a macro, MAC1, and are compiled within the loop by writing USE/R MAC1. Although this switching between compiling and running is slow, it is preferable to declaring as many POINTERs and pairs of matrices as there are passes of the loop, which would be both time consuming and wasteful of directory space. Towards the end of the second block, DEVALUE has been inserted to recover space occupied by several redundant structures; this then becomes available for structures declared in the last section of the macro.

Features such as those discussed above often stretch the Genstat language to its limits revealing, and so eliminating, esoteric bugs and other shortcomings.

6. Discussion

Gower (1969) forsaw the time when statistical systems, in their present form, might be absorbed into subroutine packages written in a powerful General Purpose Language (GPL) usable at increasing levels of complexity. That time has not come, but our experiences illustrate how the development of extendable statistical systems requires the same kind of considerations as for developing GPLs. In particular the macro or subroutine facility (the dividing line between the two is not always sharp) with parameter-passing ability is essential for any statistical (or other) system with any claim to generality and a need is often felt for an ability to drop down from a high-level language to a GPL (see for example Bernard (1977)). Understandably writers of statistical systems are reluctant to get embroiled with sophisticated programming techniques used by writers of GPLs, and the result is that even when general facilities are provided, they are usually crude and/or inefficient.

Elements of crudeness and inefficiency in Genstat macros have been cited above, but nevertheless we encourage their use. They provide a viable means for extending the language indefinitely and are especially useful for complicated calculations done insufficiently frequently to make it worthwhile to write a special efficient program; many statistical calculations fall into this class. While waiting for the hoped-for GPL, macros are an acceptable alternative.

References

Banfield C.F., Multivariate analysis in Genstat, J.Statist.Comput.Simul., 6, 211-222, 1978.

Beale E.M.L. and Little R.J.A., Missing values in multivariate analysis, J.R.Statist.Soc., B, 37, 129-145, 1975.

Bernard G., Écriture d'un algorithme en langage Genstat, First international symposium on data analysis and informatics, Institut de Recherche d'Informatique et d'Automatique, Rocquencourt, Le Chesnay, 2, 851-856, 1977 (in French)

Gower J.C., Autocodes for the statistician, In: Statistical computation, (R.C. Milton and J.A. Nelder, eds.), Academic Press, New York, 1969.

Gower J.C., Generalized Procrustes analysis, Psychometrika, 40, 33-51, 1975.

Gower J.C., The analysis of asymmetry and orthogonality, In: Recent developments in statistics, (J.Barra, ed.), North Holland, Amsterdam, 1977.

Gower J.C. and Hill I.D., Internal data structures, Appl.Statist., 20, 32-45, 1971

Hill M.O., Correspondence analysis: a neglected multivariate method, Appl. Statist., 23, 340-354, 1974.

Nelder J.A. and members of the Rothamsted Statistics Department, Genstat Manual, Rothamsted Experimental Station, Harpenden, Herts, U.K., 1977.

A Comparison of three Statistical Packages: GENSTAT, BMDP, and SPSS

G. Bernard, Saint Denis

SUMMARY

The comparison of three statistical packages (GENSTAT, BMDP and SPSS) has revealed different performances. The main reason lies in the different basic choices made by the designers of the packages, and especially the choices relating to the basic structure of the data matrix and to the ability, given or not, to name and store structures other than variates. However, the different performances are also explained by the shortcomings in the choice of the algorithms and the input-output routines inparticular. In other respects, the comparison has revealed the importance of the kind of user and the kind of use to which it will be put in choosing a statistical package.

KEYWORDS : software packages

1 - INTRODUCTION

Many statistical packages are put on the market to-day. Very often, when a user has to choose a package, the criterion is the availability of the package in the computer centre ; the possibilities of the package, its potential users and the use to which it can be put are given too little consideration. This paper will try to contribute to help the statistical software user to choose, if not the package itself, at least the kind of package most suited to the problems to be solved and to the training of the user.

2 - CRITERIA OF COMPARISON SELECTED

They were divided into four groups :

1. Influence of the system on the implementation and the use of the packages (kind of equipment needed - source language - portability and material supplied by the dealer - ease of implementation - extensibility and bringing up to date - interactive use)

2. Technical comparison (methodological comparison : organization and storage of the data, methods of analysis available, output of the results - numerical comparison - possibility of linking several analysis - amount of data which can be analyzed - costs of implementation and use)

3. Possibilities of linking with other packages

4. Aid given to the user (ease of learning of the control languages - ease of writing the models - documentation - aid for the correction of errors - help for a better understanding of the structures - "intelligence" of the packages).

The criteria selected are those decided by the Statistical Computing Section of the American Statistical Association (Francis et al., 1975) ; however, the third group of criteria (linking with other softwares) was added, since no package, however complete it may be, can lay claim to universality, and thus it may be interesting to link a statistical package, upstream or downstream, with another specialized package or with a general programming language ; furthermore, the fourth group of criteria was extended, in particular by the inclusion of the ease of learning and use, and of the "intelligence" of the packages.

3 - CHOICE OF THE PACKAGES

The packages to be compared were choosen from the packages with interpretive language, since systems of this kind relieve the user most of the constraints of programming, while requiring only one job step. One of the poles of the comparison was GENSTAT (Nelder, 1975). As a matter of fact, this as yet not very widely distributed package offers the user an interpretive language which is both a language for calling statistical procedures and a language which permits the writing of algorithms. Thus, GENSTAT (like some other packages of the same design) is different from the most used packages, and it was interesting to compare GENSTAT with them.

The choice of the packages other than GENSTAT was determined by several considerations :

- it must be possible to link easily several statistical analysis on the same data (a condition essential to the carrying out of a serious statistical study) ;
- the selected packages must be widely distributed ;
- it must be possible to use them at the Centre Inter-Régional de Calcul Electronique (Paris XI University) equipped with two IBM 370/168 computers, where all our programs are run, so as to be able to run test-programs.

Finally, BMDP (Dixon, 1975) and SPSS (Nie et al., 1975) were selected. Of course, this choice does not claim to be the best possible - one could have thought of SAS (Service, 1972) in particular - ; however, it offers the advantage of comparing three packages of clearly different designs : a powerful language (GENSTAT), a classical package (SPSS), a coherent set of independant programs (BMDP). Thus, the results of the comparison do not apply only to the three particular packages studied, but concern to a large extent the kinds of packages which they stand for.

4 - PRESENTATION OF THE VERSIONS USED

GENSTAT was developed by the Statistical Department of Rothamsted Experimental Station, Harpenden, Herts, England, under the direction of J.A. Nelder. GENSTAT is a general purpose package, but it shows however a rather pronounced "analysis of experimental designs" orientation, due to the area of activity of the Rothamsted team. It is a set consisting of a single program and about three hundred subroutines. The 3.08 version was used.

The BMDP package is the new series of the BMD programs designed by W.J. Dixon and his team at the University of California. The July 1975 version. which we used, contains 26 programs calling 72 subroutines. From the point of view of the user, BMDP can be used like a set of subroutines with an interpretive language, thanks to a system of files permitting - to some extent - the transmission of the results from one program to another in the same job. BMDP is a general purpose package, directed more especially to survey analysis however.

SPSS is developed by the National Opinion Research Center of Chicago University. It is, like GENSTAT, a single program using a few hundreds of subroutines. The 6.02 (1975) version was used. SPSS is a package directed towards the resolution of the statistical problems arising in social sciences (handling of files containing a great deal of data).

5 - COMPARISON

5.1 - influence of the basic choices

The choices made by the designers of the packages and relating to the kind and the organization of data structures which the user can operate on, store, name, determine to a large extent the packages' performances (Nelder, 1974). So, the basic structure of the data matrix may be the unit (BMDP, SPSS) - this permits operations on tables containing a great deal of data -, or else the variate (GENSTAT) - this permits the easy addition of new variates, such as predictors, scores and residuals, to the initial ones ; the user may be able to name structures other than variates (GENSTAT), such as sums of squares and products matrices - this permits operations on these structures, their storage and editing in a suitable form -, or else the only structures which can be handled are the variates (BMDP, SPSS) ; the program instructions may be kept in core (GENSTAT) - this leads to the possibility of branching and writing an algorithm -, or else the instructions are, one after another, interpreted, executed and then lost (BMDP, SPSS). Due to these different basic choices, one can expect different performances for GENSTAT, BMDP and SPSS.

5.2 - results

5.2.1. The first group of criteria did not reveal any major differences between the three packages. They are easy to implement (the distributors deliver load modules together with a satisfactory documentation) ; they can be transported from one computer to another, quite easily ; finally, it is difficult for a user to modify the package himself, because this operation implies a thorough knowledge of the system, which is not given by the documentation.

The comparison of the three packages included the running of test-problems for most of the statistical routines. These test-problems permitted the evaluation of the performances of the packages in the area of statistical analysis itself, but also in the areas corresponding to the last three groups of criteria of comparison. The results obtained relate to the versions which were used, but the versions or releases distributed since this study have not brought any fundamental change to the packages, so that the inferences derived are still valid for the main points.

Individual superiorities for each package have been pointed out : for instance, GENSTAT offers the most flexible analysis of variance routine, BMDP offers the most complete factor analysis routine, the SPSS manuals are the clearest, etc.

However, we have taken care not to assign an average score to each package, by the means of a set of coefficients, and thus to establish a final rating. As a matter of fact, the importance of the different criteria varies according to the kind of user and the kind of use of the packages (Francis, 1975 ; Francis and Valiant, 1975 ; Gentle, 1975 ; Heiberger, 1975 ; Blashfield, 1976).

Concerning the area of use, though the three packages are general-purpose ones, the choice of the basic structure of the data matrix and its consequences help to adapt GENSTAT more particularly to the analysis of experimental designs, and BMDP and SPSS to the analysis of surveys.

Concerning the kind of user, the use of GENSTAT, which calls up the notions of compilation, execution, loop, branching..., is made easier by the knowledge of a general programming language, much less useful for BMDP and SPSS, which are easier to use than GENSTAT ; with respect to the statistical training of the user, SPSS the manual of which includes statistical reminders, applies more particularly to novices, while GENSTAT and BMDP suppose the user to be familiar with the statistical methods which he wishes to use.

Moreover, it is important to take into account the continuity of the planned use of the package. The BMDP manual is designed so as to be used by opening it at the page of a particular program ; what is more, the ease of learning the general conventions of the language allows a new user to handle BMDP very quickly. This is not true for SPSS and especially for GENSTAT, which require a much longer learning. Now many statistical package users are not regular users, so it is unthinkable to impose GENSTAT programming courses on them before they are able to solve their straightforward regression problem. This aspect is seldom taken into account in the comparisons of packages ; nevertheless, statistical analysis are not carried out by statisticians only.

5.2.2. Each basic choice mentioned in 5.1. has its advantages and disadvantages. There is no ideal solution. However, whatever the options of the software builders may be, the users are entitled to expect :

- the use of reliable and well-documented algorithms ;
- the ability to edit (on printer or on any device which enables further reading), at least in a fixed format, the structures which are computed by the statistical algorithms ;
- the ability to read, in a user-specified format, any structure allowed as input for a statistical algorithm (variates, correlation matrix...) ;
- the homogeneousness of the language (specification of the options of the different instructions) and the output of the results (number of digits).

Are these well-founded demands met by GENSTAT, BMDP and SPSS?

- the SPSS factor analysis procedure sometimes gives erroneous results for the elementary computing of standard deviations or correlations (particularly bad results have been obtained with Longley's data (Longley, 1967) : for instance, the printed standard deviation for the 16-values variate 1947, 1948... ...1962 was 4.50, whereas the true value is 4.76) ; the BMDP orthogonal regression program deals with multicollinearity very badly, whereas orthogonal regression is a particularly interesting method in this case (with Longley's data the results were wrong or absurd (correlations greater than 1, negative sums of squares) according to whether correlations or covariances were used). The SPSS manual never gives the description of the algorithms used and does not even give references, so that the user only knows how to use the procedure, and not its content ;

- though the printing of results is generally satisfying, so it is not with the formatted output on magnetic devices or with punching : BMDP never gives this feature and SPSS only allows the output of variates and (sometimes) of some matrices ; only GENSTAT permits the output of any computed structure, in any specified format, on any selected device ;

- for the three packages, the reading of variates is done in the user-chosen format ; on the other hand, only one BMDP program (factor analysis, BMDP4M) allows the formatted reading of structures other than variates, and when SPSS allows matrix reading, the format is determined by the package ;

- in two different GENSTAT directives, the same option is not always coded in the same form ; amongst the various BMDP regression programs, the one which carries out computing with the greatest precision, prints the smallest number of digits. Though it does not reduce the packages' performances, this lack of homogeneousness is a constraint upon the user.

5.2.3. The quality of the documentation is very important (it must be clear and complete). The layout of the SPSS documentation is one of the factors of the success of this package, while the documentation of GENSTAT is no invitation to use this language. The "marketing" of a package, and consequently the importance of its distribution, is also a factor of use.

However, whatever the quality of the next GENSTAT manual may be, this package will certainly always be more difficult to use than SPSS and BMDP, owing to its very design (language permitting the writing of algorithms). So, to ensure the distribution of a package such as GENSTAT, a great effort must be made to promote it (teaching) by its authors and by the computing centres ; it would not be enough to place the documentation at the users' disposal for the package to be actually used.

5.2.4. GENSTAT, BMDP and SPSS each present a system of self-describing files allowing the transmission of results from one analysis to the next. However, GENSTAT is the only package which actally allows a multi-stage statistical analysis : its conditional branching instructions, its ability to name and store any analysis result and thus to use them again at a later stage, set GENSTAT, from this pointof view, on a quite different level from BMDP and SPSS, which very often allow transmission of only the data matrix from one step to another, and which present no branching feature. Furthermore, BMDP and SPSS make it difficult to use results obtained by another package (statistical package or general programming language), since controlled- format reading is generally only possible for variates.

5.2.5. Statistical packages are not used by statisticians only. Very often, the users have only a limited training in statistics and a poor conception of statistical analysis (reading - computing - printing - stop) ; furthermore, many of them are occasional users, who wish to obtain results very quickly, without devoting a lot of time to the learning of a package. It is reasonable that they should turn to SPSS, or more often to BMDP, rather than to GENSTAT. Easy-to-use packages, with consequently reduced possibilities, are thus still useful, along with more sophisticated packages. But they should not be designed so as to encourage the failings of the user and to allow him to do any analysis in any conditions ; on the contrary, they should incite the user to think about his data and supply him with safety devices, being thus "intelligent" (Nelder, 1976).

6 - CONCLUSION

GENSTAT presents different features from BMDP and SPSS, since it offers the user not only a language to call statistical procedures, but also a powerful programming language which permits the writing of algorithms. Yet these higher possibilities lead to greater difficulty in learning and to clumsier programming. The family of interpretive language packages includes packages with widely different performances ; the differences are mainly explained by the basic choices made by the designers of the packages. It is important for the user who wonders which package to choose, to be clearly informed of the performances that he may expect from each package, so that he may select the package most fitted to the kind of work to be done. Moreover, no matter what the basic choices of the designers may be, the input-output routines do not always present the flexibility needed, and unfortunately, doubtful algorithms are still used. These shortcomings can be easily eliminated by the designers of the packages.

7 - REFERENCES

Bernard G., Ecriture d'un algorithme en langage Genstat - Exemple de l'analyse des correspondances, Premières journées Internationales Analyse des données et Informatique, Versailles, 7-9 sept. 1977, 851-856, 1977(in french)

Bernard G., Comparaison de trois logiciels spécialisés pour l'analyse statistique : Genstat, Bmdp, Spss, Thèse 3ème cycle, Université de Paris XI, 1977 (in french)

Blashfield R.K., A consumer report on the versatility and user manuals of cluster analysis software, Proc. of the Statistical Computing Section, American Statistical Association, 24-30, 1976

Dixon W.J., BMDP : Biomedical Computer Programs, Berkeley : University of California Press, 1975

Francis I., Design for evaluation of statistical program packages, Bull.I.S.I., 46, 2, 573-584, 1975

Francis I., Heiberger R.M., Velleman P.F., Criteria and considerations in the evaluation of statistical program packages, Amer. Stat., 29, 1, 52-56,1975

Francis I., Valiant R., The novice with a statistical package : performance without competence, Proc. of Computer Science and Statistics : Eighth annual symposium on the Interface, University of California, Los Angeles, 110-114, 1975

Gentle J.E., Comparisons of Statistical Packages by users having some familiarity with computing and statistics, Proc. of the Statistical Computing Section, American Statistical Association, 114-117, 1975

Heiberger R.M., A procedure for the review of statistical packages and its application to the user interface with regression programs, Proc. of Computer Science and Statistics : Eighth Annual Symposium on the Interface, University of California, Los Angeles, 115-121, 1975

Longley J.W., An appraisal of least squares programs for the electronic computer from the point of view of the user, Amer. Stat. Assoc. Journal, 62, 819-841, 1967

Nelder J.A., A user's guide to the evaluation of statistical packages and systems, Int. Stat. Rev., 42, 3, 291-298, 1974

Nelder J.A. et al., GENSTAT Reference Manual and User's Guides, Statistics Department, Rothamsted Experimental Station, Harpenden, Herts, England, 1975

Nelder J.A., Intelligent programs : the next stage in statistical computing, Congrès Européen des Statisticiens, Grenoble, France, 143-145, 1976

Nie N.H. et al., Statistical Package for the Social Sciences, 2nd ed., Mac Graw Hill, New York, 1975

Schucany W.R., Minton P.D., A survey of statistical packages, Computing Surveys, 4, 2, 65-79, 1972

Service J., A users guide to the Statistical Analysis System, Carolina State University, 1972

A TPL to SAS Communication

K. Buckley, Clifton

SUMMARY

The TPL-SAS linkage program provides researchers and analysts with an efficient, generalized method of analyzing TPL cell values. The cell values from up to ten TPL tables can be transformed into SAS readable data sets. Complex data structures can be accessed by SAS through TPL. The criteria established for selecting the TPL-SAS linkage provided useful guidelines for insuring the quality of the program. The linkage is integrated into the SAS system to provide a consistent command language structure. The extensibility of the SAS system has been exercised by incorporating its data management utilities into the linkage. The variety of statistical routines provided by SAS and the ancillary feature of using BMDP procedures satisfies the analytical demands of TPL researchers.

KEYWORDS: Communication, Extensibility, Linkage, SAS, TPL

1.0 INTRODUCTION

The Bureau of Labor Statistics' Table Producing Language (TPL) was developed to provide a quick, inexpensive, and efficient method for researchers to tabulate data. Analysts can generate tables rapidly to meet changing specifications in their research. The TPL CODEBOOK system allows one to define and store the structure of data files for reference by any TPL request. Researchers can accesss complex data files without concerning themselves with the physical structure of the records. Instead, the analyst need only know the names of the variables defined in the corresponding CODEBOOK. TPL is able to filter data from sophisticated data structures, such as hierarchical files, that are often too difficult to define directly in some statistical programs. Aggregating and recoding features in TPL allow data to be "massaged", i.e. condensed, summarized, or edited, before input into a statistical program. An outgrowth of such a convenient tabulating system was the demand for a convenient and reliable method of analyzing the table cell values. Re-entry of the data as input to statistical software systems either manually or by ad-hoc application programs was not viewed as acceptable solutions for meeting this requirement.

In 1973, a TPL-SOUPAC linkage program was developed. The linkage converted TPL table cell values into SOUPAC (Statistically Oriented Users Programming and Consulting) readable files. The output from any TPL table construct could be transformed into a SOUPAC data set for direct input into SOUPAC statistical procedures. The linkage successsfully served the Bureau's analytical requirements until the summer of 1976.

The installation used for Bureau research efforts utilizes International Buisness Machine (IBM) computers and in the spring of 1976 implemented the Multiple Virtual Storage (MVS) Operating System. Analysts using SOUPAC under the MVS Operating System experience "random program failures", SOUPAC programs run successfully or terminate in abnormal endings (ABEND) without any apparent pattern. The University of Illinois supports SOUPAC but was in the process of transferring SOUPAC to Control Data Corporation (CDC) machines at the time of our problem. Consequently, they were only able to provide limited support for our situation. The system analysts at our computer center suggested that we attempt to re-create the SOUPAC program library under the MVS operating System using their compilers. In attempting to reconstruct the SOUPAC system, it was discovered that certain "compiler release dependent code", prevented programs from successfully executing in the new computer environment. The program failures as well as the uncertainty of continued support from the University of Illinois for SOUPAC on IBM equipment convinced the Bureau that an alternative statistical software system must replace SOUPAC.

The purpose of this paper is to discuss the criteria used in selecting the Statistical Analysis System (SAS) as a replacement statistical system and the development of the TPL-SAS linkage. Section 2 will develop the criteria considered for evaluating statistical software systems to replace the TPL-SOUPAC linkage and briefly discuss justifications for using SAS. Section 3 will be devoted to the mechanics of the actual linkage program. The reader is assumed to be familiar with the SAS and TPL systems.

2.0 SELECTION CRITERIA FOR THE STATISTICAL SOFTWARE SYSTEM

In selecting a new software system to replace SOUPAC, the considerations offered by Francis, Heiberger, and Vellman (1975) were used as foundations for the evaluation guide lines. The following factors provided a general framework for our analysis:

1. Statistical reliability of the software.
2. Documentation and support provided by the software vendor.
3. Stability of the software to upgrades in the computer system.
4. Extensibility of the software and complexity of adding new procedures.
5. Ease of use.
6. Ability to save intermediate files in machine readable form.

Accurate documentation and vendor support for a system is an asset to maintaining statistical software for analysts. Users often discover "bugs" in a software system that are not apparent to the authors. Many outstanding statistical procedures and routines are offered that are easily acquired and inexpensive. However, sometimes support for such may not be available because the authors are no longer associated with the facility. Such problems not only inconvenience those responsible for maintaining the system, but also users who must learn a new, and often foreign, command language structure should the system be discontinued.

Software stability should not be overlooked when investigating a new system. The software ought to be free of code that is dependent upon operating system releases or undocumented peculiarities of a compiler or programming language release. Upward compatibility is of even greater inportance when the software is to be maintained at a computer installation not under one's control, as in time sharing environments. Under these circumstances, system improvements are often implemented without customer knowledge. As with SOUPAC, problems occur when source code utilizes specific attributes of the "home computer facility". Although such code may increase the efficiency of the system, it may also cause problems in maintaining the system under a new computer environment.

Extensibility, as in Francis, Heiberger, and Vellman (1975), was a strong factor in the evalution of the new linkage. SOUPAC had many features which distinguished it from other packages - notably its econometric procedures. It was expected that any substitute system would have comparable, but not necessarily duplicate, statistical procedures. Thus an important issue in any system considered was the mechanics involved in adding new procedures or modifying existing routines. As examined by Lurie (1976), "The ability to extend a package allows the user to take advantage of the data management capabilities of the package, thus leaving him only with the task of programming the statistical technique." The asset of such extensibility allows the basic algorithm to remain somewhat detached from the structures of the software system. This allows the procedure to be easily adapted into new releases of the parent system without extensive re-writing of data management portions. Data management routines and utilities necessary for incorporation into the additional program need to be well documented and clearly explained. System programmer's guides should be unambiguously written so that the logic and overall flow of the system can be maintained in any new procedures that are added. Extensibility allows a software system to be tailored to the individual needs of the user community.

Several widely used statistical packages were considered as replacements for the TPL-SOUPAC linkage. Aside from the obvious consideration of numerical accuracy and stability of system algorithms and methodology, the range of econometric procedures was evaluated. The regression procedures needed to be sensitive to multi-collinearity in the data. Autocorrelation procedures, weighting options, and generalized least squares procedures were important considerations since most Bureau analyses are of a time-series nature. The system needed to provide methods of saving intermediate results in a user directed format, allowing results to be saved for future use either in the same system or in another statistical software system.

2.1 Selection of SAS

The Statistical Analysis System (SAS) was developed at North Carolina State University. It is presently supported and maintained by the SAS Institute. The command language uses mnemonics for specifying programs and parameters. A number of TPL users had expressed dissatisfaction with the SOUPAC command grammar. Gentle (1975) discusses this aspect of SAS and SOUPAC from a users perspective. Two other articles, Bryce and Hilton (1975) and Weingarten (1977), evaluate installation and computational qualities of the SAS package.

The SAS Programmer's Guide documents the various data management and utility routines used in its system. The guide discusses all SAS subroutines and MACROS as well as provide examples of incorporating these into new procedures for the SAS library. Useful insight is gained into the mechanics of SAS as well as the conventions and standards for expanding capabilities in SAS. The philosophy of the manual was consistent with the extensibility objective established for our evaluation since the basic program code for transmitting the TPL cell values could remain independent from the SAS system management routines.

A useful feature of SAS which distinguished it from other systems under consideration was the provision to access BMDP (Biomedical Computer Programs) via SAS at installations having the BMDP system. Such a feature is very useful for TPL researchers since access to two powerful statistical systems could be provided with a single linkage.

3.0 TPL-SAS LINKAGE

In discussing the actual linkage program, an overview will describe the overall structure, flow, and mechanics of the linkage. Seperate sections will discuss the parsing module and the procedure code.

3.1 OVERVIEW

The TPL-SAS linkage program is designed to transform the cell values from the output of up to ten TPL tables into SAS data sets. The linkage program is called in the SAS commmand stream with the procedure name PROC TPLSAS. The linkage reads two intermediate files generated by the TPL system. These two files are &&TBCELLS, containing the cell values of all tables produced in the TPL request, and &&TPLSTR, containing records describing the structure of the TPL tables (see figures 3.1 and 3.2).

The &&TBCELLS file is sorted by table/wafer/stub/header in ascending order, while the &&TPLSTR file is in ascending order by table number only. In the &&TBCELLS file, table numbers are initialized at one while the wafer, stub, and column numbers are initialized at zero. The first two records from the &&TBCELLS file appear as:

```
0001000000000000000000000nnnnnnnn
0001000000000000100000000nnnnnnnn
```

The output of the TPL-SAS linkage is a series of SAS data sets each containing the output of a corresponding TPL table. Wafers are stacked ordinally within each data set so that the cell values of wafer 1 appear first and that of wafer n appear last. The rows of each wafer within a table are treated as SAS observation vectors and columns are treated as SAS variables. Since it was not possible to preserve the column labels within each table request as variable names in the corresponding SAS data set, column 1 is named VAR1, column 2 is named VAR2, up to column N being named VARN. The SAS RENAME command allows selection of more suitable names for the variables. In order to determine the table and wafer number of each observation, two additional variables are attached to the observation vectors. The first variable is TABLENO, the table number of the TPL row, and the second variable is WAFERNO, the wafer number of the TPL row. These two extra variables allow the user to enjoy various data set manipulations within SAS and still be able to keep track of the observations.

FIGURE 3.1 - &&TBCELLS Record

Bytes	Content	Form
1-4	Table Number	Full Word Binary Integer
5-8	Wafer Number	Full Word Binary Integer
9-12	Stub Number	Full Word Binary Integer
13-16	Heading Number	Full Word Binary Integer
17-20	Post Compute Zero Divide Switch	Full Word Binary Integer
21-24	Field Not Used in the Linkage	
25-32	Cell Value	Double Word Floating Point Number

FIGURE 3.2 - &&TPLSTR Record

Bytes	Content	Form
1	Not-toggle ID	Zoned Decimal
2-16	Table Number	Zoned Decimal
17-31	# of Wafers	Zoned Decimal
32-46	# of Rows	Zoned Decimal
47-61	# of Columns	Zoned Decimal
62-76	# of Cells	Zoned Decimal
77-80	blank	
81-95	# of Cross Tabulations	Zoned Decimal
96-110	# of Cells Generated	Zoned Decimal

TPL automatically deletes tables, wafers, and rows that are completely composed of missing values. However, it is often desirable to maintain a symetric relationship among the wafers in the data set. By using the "$¬" toggle in the TPL request, all missing tables, wafers, and rows are included as missing values in the resultant data sets. Such missing values follow the SAS convention of being denoted by a single decimal ".". Once the table cell values have been processed, the resulting data sets can be directly used in subsequent SAS procedures.

3.2 THE PARSING MODULE

The Parsing Module communicates the options and parameters from the command language to the actual SAS procedure. New commands must conform to the grammatical constructs of the system. As an example, the word "PROC" prefixes all procedure names to signify its beginning in the command stream. The module is assembled using SAS MACROS and loaded into the SAS library. The format of PROC TPLSAS is shown in figure 3.3.

The CELLSDD and STRDD are positional parameters that must, if used, appear in the correct order before the SAS data set names. The following PROC TPLSAS command would be used to transfer the cell values of two TPL tables to SAS data sets with the names ABLE and BAKWR:

```
PROC TPLSAS OUT1=ABLE OUT2=BAKER;
```

FIGURE 3.3 - PROC TPLSAS Command

```
PROC TPLSAS CELLSDD=ddname1
            STRDD=ddname2
            OUT1=sasdsn1
            .
            .
            .
            OUT10=sasdsn10;
where,
ddname1   =  The ddname of the &&TBCELLS file with
             a default ddname of TBCLS
ddname2   =  The ddname of the &&TPLSTR file with a
             default ddname of STR
sasdsn1   =  The SAS data set name for up to 10
             output SAS data sets.  The default data
   .         set name being DATAn . . . DATAn+9,
   .         where n is the number of the last data
   .         set created in the SAS run prior to calling
             PROC TPLSAS.  All data set names must
sasdsn10 =   conform to SAS naming conventions.
```

Although only ten tables may be transmitted from a single TPL request, the intermediate files from more than one request may be processed by pointing to the appropriate "ddnames" in subsequent PROC TPLSAS statements.

3.3 The LINKAGE PROCEDURE

The linkage procedure is written for the PL/I Optimizer Compiler and designed to be incorporated into release SAS-76.5. The procedure utilizes the SAS core management, data set construction, input/output, and buffer management utilites. Incorporating these utilities into the linkage allows concentration of effort on the actual linkage code and on setting up the arguments for the subroutines. Should SAS change any of the internal machine code requirements or formats for these utilities in future releases, the linkage program would, at most, need only change the required subroutine arguments.

When PROC TPLSAS is invoked, the parsing module passes the ddnames for the TPL files and the SAS data set names to the linkage procedure. A record is read from the &&TPLSTR file to determine the number of columns in the TPL table request. The number of table columns dictates the number of variables to be included in the subsequent SAS data set. The SAS core management utilities are called for each new TPL table. Once it has been determined that enough core is available to process the table cell values, initialization of the SAS data set begins. A descriptor record is created to document the names, types, and lengths of the variables to be contained in the data set. The descriptor record is used by SAS as a directory for fetching information from the data set into other procedures. Additional core is allocated for the output buffers based upon the length of the observation vector. If enough core is available, cell value processing begins by reading the &&TBCELLS file. If the not toggle identifier is set in the &&TPLSTR record, the SAS output data set is written precisely to the specifications listed on that record. Missing values are generated for the blank rows, wafers, and tables. If the not toggle identifier is not set, checks are only made on whether counts exceed those specified on the &&TPLSTR record. Cell value processing is completed when an "end of file" condition is detected in the &&TBCELLS file or the table number value changes. Upon completion of cell value processing for a particular table, buffer and core space are released and a new record is read from the &&TPLSTR file to transmit an additional table. All messages from the linkage procedure are routed through the SAS output management utilities. As a result, messages from the linkage follow the flow of normal SAS system output. Information concerning the number of variables and observations contained in each new data set is displayed as part of the SAS log.

BIBLIOGRAPHY

Barr, J. A., Goodnight, J. H., Sall, J.P., Helwig, J. T., A User's Guide to SAS 76, SAS Institute, 1976.

Barr, J. A., Goodnight, J. H., Sall, J.P., Helwig, J. T., SAS Programmer's Guide, SAS Institute, 1977.

Bryce, G. R., Hilton, H. G., "Local Installation of Packages", Proceedings Statistical Computing Section, American Statistical Association (1975), 13-16.

Bureau of Labor Statistics, Office of Systems and Standards, Table Producing Language Version 4.0 User's Guide, U. S. Department of Labor, Washington, D. C., February 1978

Francis, I., Heiberger, R.M., and Vellman, P., "Criteria and Considerations in the Evaluation of Statistical Program Pakages", American Statistican 29, 1, (1975), 52-56.

Gentle, J.E., "Comparisons of Statistical Packages by Users Having Some Familiarity With Computing Statistics", Proceedings Statistical Computing Section, American Statistical Association, (1975) 114-117.

Lurie, D. S., "Comments on the Extensibility of the Statistical Package for the Social Sciences (SPSS)", Proceedings Statistical Computing Section, American Statistical Association, (1976), 213-217.

Weingarten, H., "A Note on the Accuracy of Computer Algorithms for Least Squares", Agricultural Economic Research, 29, 3, (1977), 49-51.

Improvements in Data Display in P-STAT 78

R. Buhler and **S. Buhler**, Princeton

SUMMARY

P-STAT 78, the newest version of the P-STAT statistical computing system, is considerably improved in areas of data display, particularly in file listing and crosstabulation formats. Examples are shown and related programming issues are discussed.

KEYWORDS: statistical packages, file listing, crosstabulation.

1. INTRODUCTION

All of us have seen pages of output that qualify as bad data display. It is usually not worth the trouble to format attractive output for programs that are only used occasionally. The reverse is true for the major packages, where widespread use makes it necessary to invest the effort for attractive output.

P-STAT 78, the newest version of P-STAT, is being tested this summer and will be fully released in October. It has a number of improvements; an interactive text editor that can modify commands or data; a stepwise discriminant program, etc, but the largest amount of effort has gone into data display in the LIST and TABLES commands. This paper will show examples of output from these programs and will discuss some of the design trade-offs and programming techniques involved.

2. LISTING A SIMPLE FILE

READ is a new data input command for entering free format data. A P-STAT file named F can be made as follows....

```
READ = F, VAR = SEX / VAR1 / VAR2 / 'AGE OF MOTHER' $
2  1.1  71.123  33
1  2.2  12.234  37
2  3.3  -3.345  29
2  4.4  14.456  31
1  5.5  65.678  38
    (a blank or null record defines the end of data)
```

Now, we would like to display (i.e., print, type, etc.) this file (which was given default row labels) in an efficient but readable form.

LIST = F $ will produce the following output...

```
                                      AGE
                                       OF
   ROW                                MOT
 LABEL    SEX  VAR1      VAR2         HER

    L1      2   1.1   71.123           33
    L2      1   2.2   12.234           37
    L3      2   3.3   -3.345           29
    L4      2   4.4   14.456           31
    L5      1   5.5   65.678           38
```

Several things are evident; the precision of each variable is replicated, the labels are quite readable and very little space is used.

"Response time" is a well known measure of how quickly an interactive system begins a reply. Once the reply has begun, the line speeds and the length of the reply determine how long it takes until the response is done. Limiting the response space, a measure of the output produced by the replying program, is an important criterion when programming for interactive use.

The goals of attractive layout and maximum information in the least amount of space are not always compatible, causing a variety of programming trade-offs. The default settings in LIST are designed to minimize the response space, but a number of options have been provided to increase the attractiveness of the layout when that is important.

The first issue is how much space does each variable need. The LIST program begins by making a pass through the data file to determine the largest absolute value found in each variable and the apparent number of decimal places in each variable. If X is the largest value on some variable, we can set N to the spaces needed to print its real part as follows....

```
    N  = 0
    AX = ABS(X) + 0.5
200 IF ( AX .LT. 1. )   done
    N = N + 1
    AX = AX / 10.
    GO TO 200
```

These Fortran examples illustrate the technique but do not show all the checks and tests that are actually done. For example, we must apply this procedure to the smallest value, increase its N by 1 if it is negative (to hold the minus sign), get a similar N for the largest value and then use the larger N.

To complete the allocation of printing space for a variable, we need to know how many decimal places it has. Since that can vary, we examine each value during the data pass and note the largest number of apparent decimal places found for each variable. The first step, for a value X, is to see if it has a fractional part at all. The neatest way we know of to see if a real number has decimal places is....

```
    IF ( AMOD ( X, 1. ) .EQ. 0. )      it has no places.
```

There are, of course, other ways of doing the same thing....

```
    IF ( FLOAT ( IFIX ( X ) ) .EQ. X ) it has no places.
```

```
or....    K = X
          T = K
          IF ( T .EQ. X )              it has no places.
```

The AMOD form is easier to read, faster (by 70 percent) and avoids integer overflow problems. If the number has a fractional part, we divide the value by a constant to get a starting noise level and progressively test remainders against noise levels.

At this point we know the printing width needed for each variable. A variable which had nothing but integer values from 0 to 9 could print in a single column, however the variable label at the top would look silly if it were only one column wide. For this reason, the minimum width is 4 columns. A 16 character label can fit in a 4 by 4 grid at the top and will probably be readable. The default gap between variables is 2, but it can be changed by using the option GAP=.

```
      LIST = F, GAP = 4 $     produces....

        ROW                              AGE OF
      LABEL     SEX    VAR1       VAR2   MOTHER

         L1       2     1.1     71.123       33
         L2       1     2.2     12.234       37
         L3       2     3.3     -3.345       29
         L4       2     4.4     14.456       31
         L5       1     5.5     65.678       38
```

Another feature of LIST allows score labels to appear in place of values.

```
LIST = F, LABELS, GAP = 4 $
SEX (1) MALE (2) FEMALE /
*END                                  would produce....
```

ROW LABEL	SEX	VAR1	VAR2	AGE OF MOTHER
L1	FEMALE	1.1	71.123	33
L2	MALE	2.2	12.234	37
L3	FEMALE	3.3	-3.345	29
L4	FEMALE	4.4	14.456	31
L5	MALE	5.5	65.678	38

When this label feature is used, the LIST program notes the widest score label found for each variable and uses that information in making space allocations.

The formatting of labels is much improved in P-STAT 78. Previous versions would, in some situations, take a 16 character label and, if only two lines were available, break it blindly so that the first 8 characters appeared on one line and the rest on the second line. Now a general subroutine is called by any program (LIST, TABLES, etc.) that needs to print a label.

In the first LIST example, there was a 4 line by 4 character area available for each label. When GAP=4 is used, two spaces are still needed as empty spaces to separate the variables, but the two extra spaces are used for better label layout. Thus, there is a 4 by 6 area and the word "MOTHER" can fit on a single line.

The subroutine tries to break labels in sensible ways, given the grid area that is available. It first tries to break a label using internal blanks. If that fails (i.e., if a section is too large for a line) it breaks on dots, and then on any non letter/number. It can be told to right or left justify or to center the label in the available space. The label can be thick (use as few lines as possible) or thin. A 9 character label like EDUCATION, being placed into a 3 by 8 area, will be broken in the middle to avoid having just one letter in one of the lines.

If a sorted file is supplied, LIST can be told to separate the printout into subgroups, identifying each as it occurs. Other options include specifying a margin on the left, controlling the number of decimal places to be printed, supplying a row number, and omitting the row labels.

3. IMPROVEMENTS IN CROSSTABULATION

P-STAT 78 has three new table formats. These are indicated in table definitions by the use of WITHIN, THEN and "..".

```
T = AGE BY RACE WITHIN SEX,
```

will create a nested table in which the rows represent the values of the variable AGE. The columns, however, represent the values of the variable RACE within each value of SEX. The row variable can also be nested. (See the example below.)

```
T = AGE BY RACE THEN SEX,
```

provides a format for side by side tables. A mixture of these two formats can also be used, i.e.,

```
T = AGE THEN EDUCATION BY RACE WITHIN SEX,
```

The third new format displays a series of adjacent variables by their scores. This is useful for viewing the frequencies of a large number of variables within a compact space.

```
T = AGE TO RACE BY .., or
T = .. BY AGE TO RACE,
```

Each variable will be a row in the first table and their scores (indicated by the ..) will be columns. In the second table the scores will be rows and the variables will be columns.

WIDTH=n, where n is the maximum width needed for the cell contents, can be used to control cell widths. With a narrower cell, more cells will fit on an output surface. The default is 9 columns per cell, 6 or 12 can be requested.

A number of new options have been added to give the user more control over appearance. Several heading records can be used. They will be centered one below the other. The outlining cell boxes can be removed. Selected parts of the boxes, such as the top and left edges, can be chosen. The page number can be specified. The number of places used to print a MEANS= variable can be controlled.

Consider the following table definition and its output.

```
T = (P-STAT TEST VERSION) (MAY 26, 1978)
    SEX WITHIN EDUCATION BY WORK.STATUS WITHIN OCCUPATION,
    MEANS = HRS.LAST.WEEK, WIDTH=6 $  will produce this table....
```

P-STAT TEST VERSION
MAY 26, 1978

CELL CONTENTS ARE....
CELL COUNTS
---MEAN SCORE OF VARIABLE -HRS.LAST.WEEK--

WORK.STATUS WITHIN OCCUPATION

EDUCATION	SEX	..PROFESSIONAL.. FULL TIME	PART TIME	..WHITE COLLAR.. FULL TIME	PART TIME	.. BLUE COLLAR.. FULL TIME	PART TIME	ROW TOTALS
GRADE SCHOOL	MALE			7	3	11		21
				44.4	15.0	44.8		40.4
	FEMALE			3	1	3	1	8
				31.3	25.0	40.0	20.0	32.4
HIGH SCHOOL	MALE	3		24	2	26	8	63
		46.7		45.5	10.5	43.7	20.1	40.5
	FEMALE		1	23	5	16	5	50
			15.0	38.7	28.0	37.2	30.6	35.9
COLLEGE	MALE	14	2	32	2	6	3	59
		44.5	28.5	47.5	40.0	50.2	21.3	44.8
	FEMALE	14	3	8	4	2	2	33
		40.1	20.3	45.3	15.0	40.0	16.0	35.0
TOTAL N		31	6	97	17	64	19	234
MEAN		42.7	22.2	44.0	21.8	42.6	22.6	39.5

This illustrates both the economical use of space and the attention given to formatting the output. Because both the row and column variables are nested, this single surface contains the information normally produced by 9 surfaces (i.e., pages) in the older SEX BY WORK.STATUS BY EDUCATION BY OCCUPATION form.

The WIDTH option is used to control the cell size because we wanted the output to fit within the narrow constraints of this paper. The labels are formatted in a very readable fashion. The headings are centered. The interior vertical and horizontal bars are automatically removed in a nested table to emphasize the nested relationships. When the nested tables code was first written, the boxes were complete and it was difficult to see the groupings. It took considerable experimenting with different characters (such as dots and semi-colons) to decide that the clearest format had no divider separating the within fields at all.

In P-STAT 78, there are several new features that are available to interactive users of the TABLES command. The tables are saved on a scratch unit and can be individually retrieved and modified in a variety of ways. The rows, columns or table surfaces (in n-way tables) can be combined, deleted and re-ordered. New headings can be supplied and score labels can be changed. Many of the options, such as row percents, chi square, etc., can either be selected or turned off.

4. CONCLUSIONS

It is difficult to display data both attractively and efficiently. Defaults must be acceptable in most situations but there must be sufficient user options so the result can be fine-tuned if the situation warrants. It takes a great deal of code to do this - LIST is about 2,500 Fortran statements - and it takes time and usage for this type of program to mature.

These programs must respond to changes in hardware capabilities. It has become important to fit as much information as possible in the widely used 24 by 80 screen. It is unlikely to be many years before intensity variation and color selection also become a part of good data display.

Survey Analysis: Retrieval Algorithm and Table Specifications

C. Clunies-Ross, London

Summary:

The file organisation and data retrieval-accumulating algorithm are described for a survey analysis programme dealing with tree structured data. Minimal extensions necessary to the table specification language are illustrated with examples.

KEYWORDS Tree structured data, survey analysis programme design

Section 1 : Basic Procedure

Survey analysis programmes have two specific characteristics: they produce tables (cross-tabulations) and are run through specifications rather like a very high level "report-writer" language. Much survey data has a fixed format. Even when there is some variation (e.g. because of "skips" in the questionaire) it has usually been adequate to retain the fixed format with allowance for "not asked/not answered" codes. However, when the not answered codes account for the majority of the data the computing procedures become inefficient. Further, some surveys have the data collected with a more variable format and are not readily converted into a fixed format. Consequently tree structured data may be required either for efficiency or because of the nature of the data.

The following comments arise out of the design of a programme suite for dealing with tree structured data. The data is considered to have been built up from blocks of fixed format data which constitute the branches of the tree. The occurence of multiple response questions (e.g. "Which of these have you heard of?") are treated as an extension of the tree structure. Each branch generates a control variable on the parent branch which is the count of the branches. This variable can also be used as a data variable in its own right; it is often a useful one e.g. the number of people in a household.

Tabulations typically deal with relatively few variables but all of the cases. The data is stored physically as an inverted file so that a table does not need access to all of the data. The relationship between the logical structure of the tree and the file structure is illustrated in Figure 1 which is a very small tree. The data is stored in a single random access file. The data on one variable is contiguous. The variables on a branch are usually contiguous but not necessarily so.

Figure 1: Tree and File Structures (A Small example)

1.1. Tree Structure

Household ---- Person

-- Car

1.2 File Structure

[n] = number of cases (households)

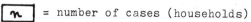

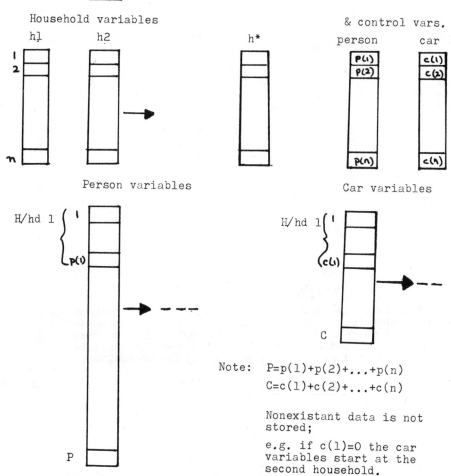

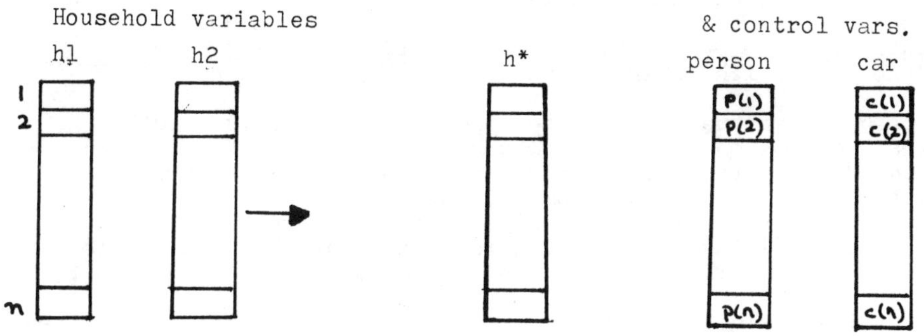

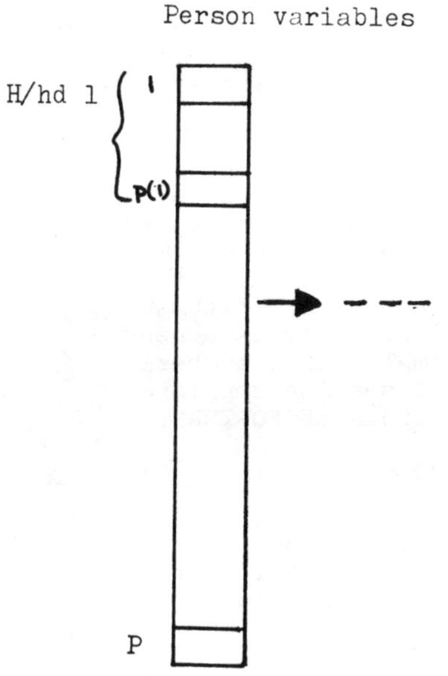

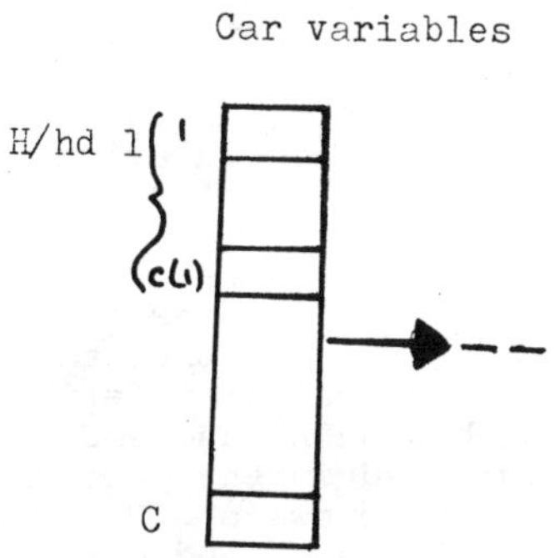

Note: P=p(1)+p(2)+...+p(n)

C=c(1)+c(2)+...+c(n)

Nonexistant data is not stored;

e.g. if c(1)=0 the car variables start at the second household.

Retrieval of the data on variables in bulk from a backing store is easy enough because of the inverted form of the file. Interlocking the individual values with the accumulation is a more interesting problem.

The syntax of table specifications is:

Tabulate variable 1 by variable 2

but with a tree, or even a linearchy, the specification is not complete. A further distinction may be required. If, for example, one is tabulating age by social class one may want to know the distributions of individuals or to know something about households (say the % with children). This can be dealt with by extending the syntax to include the idea of <u>units</u> used in the tabulation i.e. UNIT = household or UNIT = person.

The programme actually tabulates groups of tables (subject to restrictions on the same units and certain structural and space limitations). Consequently there can be several variables involved in an accumulation rather than just two. Whilst the vast majority of tables do not require the complications illustrated in Figure 2, it would be undesirable to limit which variables could be tabulated against each other.

The retrieval algorithm starts with the list of variables required for the tabulation (v1, v2,..v8) in the example shown in Figure 2. The list is extended to include the necessary control variables (cA, cB,...,cL) as indicated in Figure 2.2. This information is recalled if necessary from the backing store ready for the accumulation.

In programming terms the cumulation can be shown as a set of nested DO loops as shown in Figure 2.3. The actual structure of the nesting depends on the inter-relationship between the tree structure and the table. The term 'get variables' may involve physical transfer, within core movements or just setting beginning and end indices. The actual algorithm used is programmed in the pattern shown in Figure 2.4. as a nested downward tree sweep. Using a Dewey decimal branch numbering system (within a single word) the control section consists of about a couple of dozen closely knitted lines of FORTRAN.

Section 2 : Limitations and Extensions

The emphasis in Section 1 was on data organisation. The implication was that a specification syntax suitable for fixed format would be the basis of one for tree structured data with the retrieval/accumulation algorithm taking care of the other considerations. The one extension was to include the notion of units. However certain further points need examination.

Figure 2: Retrieval & Accumulation (Example)

2.1 Tree structure with eight variables needed for table

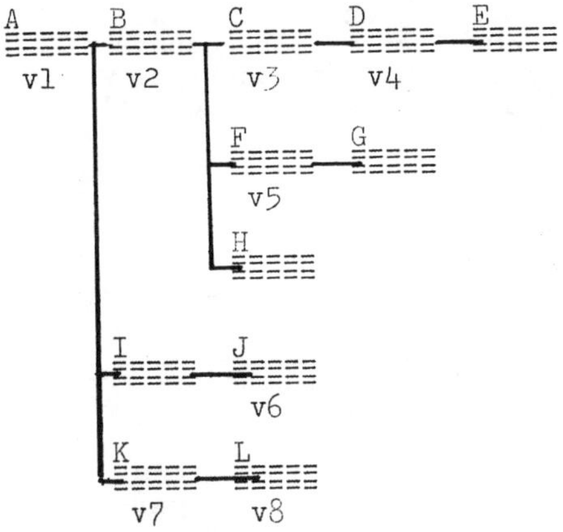

Units = Branch C

2.2 Including implied control variables, omitting unused variables

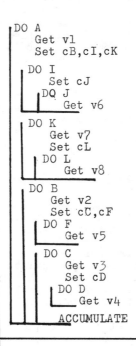

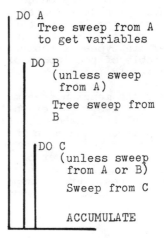

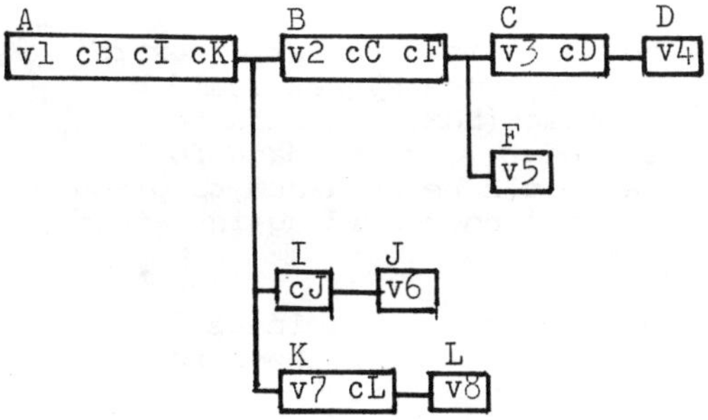

2.3 Organisation as DO loops

```
DO A
  Get v1
  Set cB,cI,cK
  DO I
    Set cJ
    DO J
      Get v6
  DO K
    Get v7
    Set cL
    DO L
      Get v8
  DO B
    Get v2
    Set cC,cF
    DO F
      Get v5
    DO C
      Get v3
      Set cD
      DO D
        Get v4
      ACCUMULATE
```

2.4 Algorithm structure

```
DO A
  Tree sweep from A
  to get variables
  DO B
    (unless sweep
     from A)
    Tree sweep from
    B
    DO C
      (unless sweep
       from A or B)
      Sweep from C

      ACCUMULATE
```

2.1 Agglomeration

All the variables are single valued. But by the time that an accumulation is being formed some of the variables may be multi valued. In the example shown in Figure 2 the variables v1, v2 and v3 are single valued but the others are all multiple valued. Some method of treatment of such multi valued variables must be incorporated into the accumulation routine. The possibilities are clarified when one considers a more concrete example : tabulations of income (person branch of Figure 1) when units are households. The tables that could be intended include ones showing:

total household income
average income per earner
average income per household member
number of households with earners in specified ranges
maximum individual income

All of these would require a different cumulation routine, none of them can be derived from another.

The general policy followed in developing the programme has been to keep the syntax simple. In effect this means separating areas of complexity. The way that agglomeration is carried out is as a multiple mention (corresponding to the fourth one above). This is also influenced by the fact that multiple mention is never totally inappropriate and is sometimes the only appropriate treatment (e.g. for much verbal data). Moreover the other possibilities can be handled with a different programme to generate further variables. The syntax can overlap

```
e.g. UNIT = household
          incomehd = SUM income
```

and then the table can be specified in terms of the new variable.

It would be easy enough to allow for a limited number of extra tabluation treatments of agglomerations. The syntax could be extended to include terms such as income (SUM) although this could raise problems in the allocation of working space for certain types of table. This syntax would be strained to produce a table of the income of the head of the household against total household income.

Multiple mention treatment does not completely eliminate ambiguities. For example there is a difference between the accumulation needed to find the proportion of households with earners earning more than £100 per week and that for the average number of such earners per household. Put more generally it is a matter of whether or not to suppress duplicates which arise through agglomeration. It is much easier not to suppress duplicates. Proper suppression requires a much greater extension to the syntax as it should be flexible enough to cover duplication within grouped data (e.g. income ranges) as well as the raw data. On the other hand it is also a bit more complicated to produce extra multi valued variables as this involves modifying the tree structure.

2.2 Different Tree Structures for the same Data

It should not be thought that there is a unique tree representation for a set of data. This can be illustrated in terms of a market research survey providing background information on a particular product field. As well as general information there will also be sections on brand awareness, brand usage, brand image and advertising recall. Such a survey may be treated in a fixed format (admittedly with some limitations). This can be considered as tree A. The next structure that could be inferred is:

```
Tree B = Respondent -- Brand
```

where the brand branch covers all areas. If, however, the range of brands aware of is in general much higher than the level of questioning on usage, image and recall the structure could be extended to:

```
Tree C = Respondent -- Brand -┬ Usage
                              ├ Image
                              └ Adrecall
```

Both trees B and C will require considerable reorganisation of the input data. A tree description based on the input data could be:

```
Tree D = Respondent -┬ Usage
                     ├ Image
                     └ Adrecall
```

which differs from Tree C in that the brand identification is a separate variable on each of the tree branches.

Tabulations of the usage of a brand are simplest in tree A but can be done using a filter on the brand with the other trees. Tabulations of usage by brand can be readily specified for trees B, C and D but have to be treated as a composite set of tables for the fixed format tree A. Tables of usage by image for a particular brand can be specified for tree A, also for B and C by filtering on the brand. But filtering does not work for tree D. This can be achieved by an extension to the syntax:

```
usage (brandu=X) by image (brandi=X)
```

which extends the idea of filtering to variables rather than just tables. This is not just an elaborate way of getting round a poor tree definition: any of the tree structures will need it to tabulate the images of one brand against another.

image (brand=X) by image (brand=Y)

It is possible to design a tree structure which does not require such extensions to the syntax. This is based on the fixed format allowing for all information on all brands. Each brand is taken as a logical branch of the tree. The only structuring is to allow the branches to be present or not: i.e. all the control variables would have value one or zero. This would look like:

```
Tree E = Respondent -┬- Brand1 -┬- Usage1
                     |          ├- Image1
                     |          └- Adrecall1
                     |
                     ├- Brand2 -┬- Usage2
                     |          ├- Image2
                     |          └- Adrecall2
                     |
                     |  ...................
                     |
                     └- Brandk -┬- Usagek
                                ├- Imagek
                                └- Adrecallk
```

and may be the most suitable one as far as efficiency is concerned.

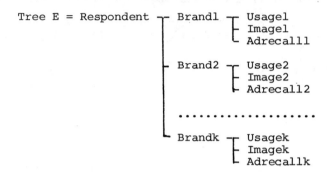

Towards a Bayesian Package

T. Fearn, London

SUMMARY

The analysis of the hierarchical normal linear models studied by Lindley and Smith (1972) involves only simple matrix computations when all the dispersion parameters are assumed known. When this assumption is relaxed, as it must be in practice, one must either resort to quadrature to obtain the desired posterior densities or use approximations such as posterior modal estimates. This paper describes a program which performs the quadrature for a particular model, discusses the range of applicability of the techniques used, and finally comments on the computation of approximate solutions.

KEYWORDS: BAYES, EXCHANGEABILITY, LINEAR MODEL, ONE-WAY TABLE, PROGRAM, QUADRATURE.

1. INTRODUCTION

A typical, three-stage, model of the type studied by Lindley and Smith (1972) may be written in standard notation as

$$\underset{\sim}{y} \mid \underset{\sim}{\theta}_1 \sim N(\underset{\sim}{A}_1 \underset{\sim}{\theta}_1,\ \underset{\sim}{C}_1)$$

$$\underset{\sim}{\theta}_1 \mid \underset{\sim}{\theta}_2 \sim N(\underset{\sim}{A}_2 \underset{\sim}{\theta}_2,\ \underset{\sim}{C}_2)$$

$$\underset{\sim}{\theta}_2 \mid \underset{\sim}{\theta}_3 \sim N(\underset{\sim}{A}_3 \underset{\sim}{\theta}_3,\ \underset{\sim}{C}_3)$$

where the matrices $\underset{\sim}{A}_1$, $\underset{\sim}{A}_2$, $\underset{\sim}{A}_3$ and the third stage parameters $\underset{\sim}{\theta}_3$, $\underset{\sim}{C}_3$ are known. Interest typically centres on the first and second stage parameters $\underset{\sim}{\theta}_1$ and $\underset{\sim}{\theta}_2$ with the dispersion matrices $\underset{\sim}{C}_1$ and $\underset{\sim}{C}_2$ playing the role of nuisance parameters. Arguing conditionally on $\underset{\sim}{C}_1$ and $\underset{\sim}{C}_2$ it is easy to derive a multivariate normal posterior distribution for $\underset{\sim}{\theta}_1$ or $\underset{\sim}{\theta}_2$ given $\underset{\sim}{y}$. Usually $\underset{\sim}{C}_1$ and $\underset{\sim}{C}_2$ are not completely known: for example a common case is $\underset{\sim}{C}_1 = \sigma^2 \underset{\sim}{I}$ where the scalar σ^2 is unknown and is given a prior distribution. If one puts realistic prior distributions on the unknown parameters, $\underset{\sim}{\phi}$ say, in $\underset{\sim}{C}_1$ and $\underset{\sim}{C}_2$ it is not possible, except perhaps in a few trivial cases, to perform the required integrations analytically to obtain the posterior distributions of $\underset{\sim}{\theta}_1$ and $\underset{\sim}{\theta}_2$.

The obvious solution to this problem is to use numerical integration techniques to tabulate the desired marginal distributions. Except in the simplest cases, one of which is considered in §2, this will be expensive in terms of computer time, sometimes prohibitively so, and we are often forced to settle for answers which are partial, approximate, or both. The computation of such solutions will be discussed in §3.

2. THE ONE-WAY TABLE - AN EXACT SOLUTION

One of the simplest non-trivial hierarchical models is that for a one-way table where the group means are considered exchangeable. Thus we have

$$y_{ij}|\alpha_i \sim N(\alpha_i, \sigma^2) \quad \text{independently for } i=1,\ldots,n \ ; \ j=1,\ldots,n_i \ ,$$

$$\alpha_i|\mu \sim N(\mu, \tau^2) \quad \text{independently for } i=1,\ldots,m \ .$$

We consider only the case when the prior distribution for μ is an improper uniform distribution, i.e. we take a diffuse third stage, and to simplify the mathematics even further we insist that the variance components σ^2 and τ^2 have independent inverse chi-squared prior distributions so that

$$p(\sigma^2, \tau^2) \propto (\sigma^2)^{-\frac{1}{2}(\nu_1+2)}(\tau^2)^{-\frac{1}{2}(\nu_2+2)}\exp(-\tfrac{1}{2}\nu_1\lambda_1/\sigma^2 - \tfrac{1}{2}\nu_2\lambda_2/\tau^2)$$

for $\sigma^2, \tau^2 > 0$. This is a fairly flexible family of distributions and so long as the independence assumption is correct it will usually be possible to approximate prior knowledge about σ^2 and τ^2 by suitable choice of ν_1, λ_1, ν_2 and λ_2 . The author has written an interactive computer program which aids this choice; details of this will be reported elsewhere.

This model has been analysed in print many times, see for

example Lindley (1971), and we will not repeat the details. We merely outline the derivation of the results required, following Lindley (1974) in substance if not in detail.

It turns out to be most convenient to reparametrize the variance components, and we transform from σ^2, τ^2 to σ^2, r where $r = \tau^2/\sigma^2$ is the ratio of between to within variance. Starting from the joint posterior density $p(\underset{\sim}{\alpha}, \mu, \sigma^2, r|\underset{\sim}{y})$ we find that it is possible to integrate analytically with respect to $\underset{\sim}{\alpha}$, μ and σ^2 to arrive at the margin $p(r|\underset{\sim}{y})$, except that we do not know the normalizing constant for this density and cannot find it analytically. Omitting just one of these integrations one arrives at joint densities like $p(\alpha_i, r|\underset{\sim}{y})$ and hence $p(\alpha_i|r, \underset{\sim}{y}) \propto p(\alpha_i, r|\underset{\sim}{y})/p(r|\underset{\sim}{y})$ can be found. This distribution turns out to be Student's-t, that is $\sqrt{h}(\alpha_i - \alpha_i^*) \sim t_\nu$ where the degrees of freedom $\nu = \Sigma n_i + \nu_1 + \nu_2 - 1$ and h, α_i^* are functions of r. The posterior mean $\alpha_i^* = w_i\bar{y}_{i.} + (1 - w_i)\bar{y}_w$ where $w_i = n_i r/(1 + n_i r)$, $\bar{y}_{i.} = (\Sigma_j y_{ij})/n_i$, $\bar{y}_w = (\Sigma w_i \bar{y}_i)/(\Sigma w_i)$, illustrates the type of dependence on r. Similar results hold for any linear combination $\Sigma \ell_i \alpha_i$ and μ, and for predictive distributions for further observations from a new or an existing group.

Given these analytical results one way to find the marginal posterior density of, say, α_i is to evaluate numerically the integral $\int_0^\infty p(\alpha_i|r, \underset{\sim}{y})\, p(r|\underset{\sim}{y})dr$ for a range of values of α_i. The integration variable used in the program we have produced is not r but $\theta = r/(\rho + r)$ which has a finite range $0 \leqslant \theta \leqslant 1$. The constant $\rho > 0$ is chosen by the program as described below.

The program is organised in the following way. After reading in the data and the prior parameters the program investigates $p(\theta|\underset{\sim}{y})$, iteratively choosing a value of ρ which brings the mode of $p(\theta|\underset{\sim}{y})$ close to $\theta = \frac{1}{2}$. In some examples there is more than one mode, and then the central turning point is brought to the middle of the range. With this value of ρ the normalizing constant for $p(\theta|\underset{\sim}{y})$ is evaluated using the compound trapezoidal rule on equally spaced points to integrate over the interval $[0, 1]$. The accuracy of this interval is assessed by comparison of integrals using different numbers of subintervals. Typically 8 or 16 subintervals give sufficient accuracy for our purposes. Suppose n subintervals are used and let θ_i , $i = 1, 2, \ldots, n-1$ be the corresponding points - not including $\theta = 0$ or $\theta = 1$ where $p(\theta|\underset{\sim}{y}) = 0$. The values of $p(\theta|\underset{\sim}{y})$ at these points are stored for later use, as are some of the intermediate quantities involved in the calculation.

The user is now given the choice of a list of posterior and predictive distributions which may be investigated. These include posterior distributions for μ, α_i, and linear combinations $\Sigma\ell_i\alpha_i$, and predictive distributions for new observations. When a particular distribution, that of α say, is chosen, the program first evaluates low order moments by numerical integration of conditional expressions. For example

$$E(\alpha|y) = \int_0^1 E(\alpha|\theta, \underset{\sim}{y})p(\theta|\underset{\sim}{y})d\theta \sim \frac{1}{n}\sum_{i=1}^{n-1} E(\alpha|\theta_i, \underset{\sim}{y})p(\theta_i|\underset{\sim}{y}) \quad .$$

The posterior (or predictive) p.d.f. of α is then tabulated over the range mean $\pm$ 3 s.d. by evaluating the integral

$$p(\alpha|\underset{\sim}{y}) = \int_0^1 p(\alpha|\theta, \underset{\sim}{y})p(\theta|\underset{\sim}{y})d\theta \sim \frac{1}{n}\sum_{i=1}^{n-1} p(\alpha|\theta_i, \underset{\sim}{y})p(\theta_i|\underset{\sim}{y})$$

for values of α at intervals in this range. The c.d.f. is also tabulated by simple quadrature applied to the p.d.f.

The use of the <u>same θ points</u> for all the integrals performed saves a lot of computation, for $p(\theta|\underset{\sim}{y})$ is already tabulated at these points, as are some of the quantities (e.g. Σw_i) needed for the calculation of $p(\alpha|\theta, \underset{\sim}{y})$. Because $p(\theta|\underset{\sim}{y})$ is a much 'sharper' function of θ than $p(\alpha|\theta, \underset{\sim}{y})$ in general it is quite reasonable to use the same points, and the accuracy of the integrals is usually about the same as that of the original integral which produced the normalizing constant for $p(\theta|\underset{\sim}{y})$. We have used the compound trapezoidal rule on equally spaced points because of a cancellation effect which happens with this rule when the function integrated has several derivatives which vanish at the ends of the interval. This effect, which depends on the equal spacing of the points gives the rule more power than one would expect it to have and allows us to use relatively few points. A paper is in preparation discussing these points in more detail.

The distributions are printed out and the user is now given options which include displaying the p.d.f. or c.d.f. on a graphics screen or asking questions like 'what is the probability that $\alpha < 1.6$?'. Answers to these questions are provided by interpolation in the tabulated c.d.f. and are printed to two places of decimals. Our aim in controlling the integration and other errors is to ensure that these two significant figures are correct. Experience is limited as yet, but it appears that this aim is usually achieved.

A similar technique works for the posterior distribution of σ^2, and this may be investigated in the same way. The method breaks down for τ^2 because $p(\tau^2 | \theta, \underset{\sim}{y})$ can be very sharp (as a function of θ) and the program does not, at present, allow one to investigate this distribution. The option offered instead is the posterior distribution of the intraclass correlation, $\tau^2/(\sigma^2 + \tau^2)$, which is obtained by transformation from $p(\theta | \underset{\sim}{y})$.

The program runs on a PDP 11/10 under RT-11 using (optionally) a GT40 display for presentation of distributions. A typical time for tabulating a distribution is half a minute - quite acceptable for interactive use.

Other simple models to which the same techniques might be applied include the "exchangeability within regression" model of Lindley and Smith (1972) which leads to ridge type estimates and would only involve a one-dimensional integration. Since the one-dimensional integral uses few points it seems likely, although we have no experience as yet, that larger problems could be tackled in the same way. Even so, a limit of 3 or 4 dimensions in the integrations possible seems inevitable at the moment, and approximate methods will continue to be necessary in most cases.

3. APPROXIMATE SOLUTIONS

One such solution is provided by Lindley and Smith who suggest using as a point estimate of θ_1 its value at the mode of the joint posterior density of $\underset{\sim}{\theta}_1$ and all the unknown dispersion parameters, $p(\underset{\sim}{\theta}_1, \underset{\sim}{\phi}|\underset{\sim}{y})$. This is equivalent to deriving point estimates of the dispersion parameters in the same way from this joint density, and substituting them in the expression for the conditional mean of $\underset{\sim}{\theta}_1$ given $\underset{\sim}{C}_1$ and $\underset{\sim}{C}_2$, $E(\underset{\sim}{\theta}_1|\underset{\sim}{\phi}, \underset{\sim}{y})$. In a similar way we can approximate the posterior mean of $\underset{\sim}{\theta}_2$.

Clearly one could use alternative estimates of the dispersion parameters to obtain other approximations to these posterior means. It is always possible to find the joint posterior density of the dispersion parameters $p(\underset{\sim}{\phi}|\underset{\sim}{y})$, i.e. to integrate $\underset{\sim}{\theta}_1$ analytically from $p(\underset{\sim}{\theta}_1, \underset{\sim}{\phi}|\underset{\sim}{y})$. It seems reasonable to expect that the mode of $p(\underset{\sim}{\phi}|\underset{\sim}{y})$ will provide a better point estimate, in the sense that it is closer to the posterior mean, of $\underset{\sim}{\phi}$ than will the mode of $p(\underset{\sim}{\theta}_1, \underset{\sim}{\phi}|\underset{\sim}{y})$ which involves many more parameters. It is not so obvious that substitution of this value of $\underset{\sim}{\phi}$ into $E(\underset{\sim}{\theta}_1|\underset{\sim}{\phi}, \underset{\sim}{y})$ provides a better approximation to $E(\underset{\sim}{\theta}_1|\underset{\sim}{y})$ but our experience, which will be reported elsewhere, suggests that it does. Thus as an alternative to the Lindley-Smith modal estimates we recommend the substitution of variance estimates which are based on $p(\underset{\sim}{\phi}|\underset{\sim}{y})$. O'Hagan (1976) discusses this point.

We have produced a program, running on the IBM 360 at UCL, which computes this approximate solution for the 'exchangeability between regressions' model of Lindley and Smith. A standard package routine (NAG) is used to find the minimum of $-\log p(\underset{\sim}{\phi}|\underset{\sim}{y})$, where $\underset{\sim}{\phi}$ has involved up to 14 parameters in successful applications, and the derived variance estimates used to obtain point estimates of the regression parameters as described above.

This technique seems capable of wide generalization. As well as writing specially designed programs for particular models it ought to be possible, at the cost of some efficiency, to produce a package which deals with a fairly large class of models. One problem which remains is the possible existence of several modes of $p(\underset{\sim}{\phi}|\underset{\sim}{y})$, conflicts between prior distributions and data being the most likely source of this. Further work is in progress with a view to providing approximate posterior distributions for parameters instead of just point estimates; this problem is being studied in the context of the one-way table for which we can compute the exact results.

Acknowledgements

Much of the research which led to the production of the programs described was joint work with Mr. D. Walley. Some of this work will be reported jointly elsewhere. The research was supported by the Science Research Council.

References

Lindley, D.V. The estimation of many parameters. Foundations of Statistical Inference. Ed. V.P. Godambe and D.A. Sprott. Holt, Rinehart and Winston of Canada, 435-455, 1971.

Lindley, D.V. Exact analysis for a one-way table. Unpublished report, University College London, 1974.

Lindley, D.V. and Smith, A.F.M. Bayes estimates for the linear model. J. Roy. Statist. Soc. B 34, 1-41, 1972.

O'Hagan, A. On posterior joint and marginal modes. Biometrika 63, 329-323, 1976.

Development of a Path Analysis Program Compatible with the SPSS Conversational Statistical System (SCSS)

J.F. Hall, A.J. Ring and J. Harrison, London

1. Introduction

1.1 Path analysis was first considered as a method for analysing causal models in social systems by the extension of regression analysis to cover recursive systems of structural equations containing "measured" variables (Duncan, 1966; Land, 1969). More recent developments of path analysis have been fragmented and consequently lacking in co-ordination. On the one hand, there has developed an analysis of purely quantitative variables in the form of "linear flow graphs" (Goodman, 1972; Davis, 1974; Davis and Schooler, 1974); on the other hand, consideration has been given to the use of confirmatory factor analysis and the introduction of "unmeasured" variables. (Hauser & Goldberger, 1971; Jöreskog, 1973). Other work has pursued the integration of different methods for the analysis of single equations (Nelder & Wedderburn, 1972) and the extension of causal models to non-recursive systems and two-stage regression (Heise, 1975).

1.2 A number of computer programs already exist which have been developed in parallel with the theoretical aspects of path analysis. Simple interactive programs have been available for some time (Nygreen, 1970) and more specialized programs have also been written, such as CATFIT (Taylor, 1975) LISREL (Jöreskog, 1972) and GLIM (Nelder, 1974). More recently, general packages have been implemented which can provide an interactive environment for a variety of path analysis techniques and form a basis for their integration into a single system, in particular the interactive version of SPSS (Nie et al, 1974).

1.3 The next major development in this area clearly has to be the integration of past theoretical and computational work into a single interactive computer program for the analysis of causal models. Work on such a program "Interactive Path Analysis" started at the Survey Unit of the Social Science Research Council (Ring, 1975) and had reached an advanced stage by the time the Unit closed in September 1976.
The work is being continued at the Polytechnic of North London.

2. Objectives

2.1 The objectives of this project are two-fold. The principal technical objectives are to complete the development of Interactive Path Analysis (IPA) to the design worked out at the Survey Unit, to implement it on several machines, and to provide full documentation for both users and computing installations. A secondary technical objective is to provide an additional procedure to enhance the SPSS Conversational Statistical

System (SCSS) and consequently IPA has been written to language and syntax specifications of SCSS (Franklin et al, 1974; Nie & Hull, 1977).

2.2 The academic objectives involve the provision of a powerful tool for social science teaching and research which will integrate hitherto disparate software work in path analysis, user-oriented interactive packages and general linear models with theoretical and causal modelling work as outlined in paras. 1.1 to 1.3. IPA would thus constitute a means of enabling researchers to develop and test social theories on quantitative data. Its value will lie in its generality, its practicality and its usability in providing instant feedback, conversational language, flexibility of problem definition and a variety of output presentations. It relates to the fundamental process of theory-building, not only through the dialectic between the researcher and his data, but also through the probability that its use will encourage more rigorous thought prior to research design, data collection or analysis.

2.3 There will be direct contributions to methodology in the development of new routines for handling interactive programs, from the integration of existing algorithms and programs into a single program, and from the addition of a comprehensive procedure (IPA) to an existing package (SCSS). Indirect benefits will accrue through education in research and analytical approaches and through encouragement of new research designs to assume a causal scientific approach. Secondary analysis of major surveys from the SSRC Survey Archive at Essex University is an obvious area of application for IPA.

3. Programme of action

3.1 The authors have been in close liaison with the SCSS team since the initial SSRC award was made. A major design conference on Interactive SPSS (held at LSE in April, 1974) was organized by John Hall, who also acted as rapporteur to the working group on user-interface and output options. Exchanges of documents have been frequent and regular. SPSS Inc., (University of Chicago) has no plans to develop a path analysis facility, and are aware of the IPA work in London. Whilst IPA will itself be a stand-alone program, all documentation and coding will be made available to SPSS Inc., so that interfacing can be implemented as quickly as possible.

3.2 Whilst the major focus of liaison will be the SCSS team, the IPA team has a number of contacts in social science computing both in Britain and overseas, and John Hall has been elected Chairman of the newly founded United Kingdom SPSS Users Group (UKSUG). Information on progress will be reported directly to such contacts and indirectly through UKSUG and professional associations (British Sociological Association, Market Research Society, Royal Statistical Society) study groups (BSA Quantitative Sociology Group, BSA Survey Research Group, Study Group on Computers in Survey Analysis, SSRC Sponsored Research Seminars in Quantitative Social Science, Radical Statistics) and publications (Quantitative Sociology Newsletter, SSRC Newsletter, SSRC Survey Archive Bulletin, Edinburgh Program Library Unit, SPSS Newsletter).

3.3 Most of the development work has been done on the CDC6600 at the University of London Computer Centre, and conversion to the ICL 1905E at the London Polytechnics' Computer Unit at the Polytechnic of North London, has followed. If time allows, a conversion will be attempted for the DEC10 at Polytechnic of the South Bank.

3.4 In addition to our own use, it is envisaged that the program will be in constant use by researchers and students in various locations so that feedback from users can be taken into account in the final versions of the program and its associated documentation. The authors would be grateful to hear from potential users who would like access to the program and who could provide the necessary feedback on bugs or user-interface problems.

4. The program

4.1 IPA is a program for performing path analysis interactively on data summaries of two types.

(i) Matrices of measures of association

(ii) Measures of central tendency and dispersion

User-interface is in conversational SPSS type language. The program supplies prompts and generates error messages, and saves all current information and models, thus enabling the user to re-enter at the point he left off in a previous session, even after a system failure. Full naming and labelling facilities are available for files, matrices, variables and models and it will be possible to change any part of the data or its labelling at will. The version to be released will operate in small amounts of core ($<$ 20K) thus widening the range of machines on which it could be implemented. This will benefit institutions and departments with small machines.

4.2 The program presents the user with a series of prompts, each of which defines a context with a specific free-formatted response or set of responses. For example, the program begins with the prompts GET FILE? to which the user must reply with either the file name of an existing IPA file on a local disk-file GTFILE, or with NULL indicating that there is no existing IPA file. The latter elicits the prompt NAME? to which user replies with a file name and an optional file lable. The program then moves into its variable definition context and prompts NAME OF VARIABLE? Variables are defined by name and by matrix row number with optional extended variable labelling. As soon as all variables have been defined the user types a NULL response to the variable name prompt, whereat the program moves into its data input context. Data can be input from some previously defined file INDATA or direct from the keyboard. Three types of data can be defined. These are means, standard deviations and coefficients of association. The prompt DATA? requests the next type of data to be read in, and can be answered by the responses MEANS, DEVIATIONS, or COEFFICIENTS. The response COEFFICIENTS must be used, and elicits the prompt TYPE OF LAYOUT? which can be answered by one of four layout types SQUARE, UPPER, LOWER or SPSS, where UPPER and LOWER refer to triangular matrices of coefficients. When the data matrix has been defined, a NULL response to the prompt DATA? moves the program on to its model-definition context. The prompt LINK? requires the initial path or paths to be specified by a statement of the form variable WITH variable name or variable list in which the first variable specified is the dependent variable. Multiple paths can be specified until the response NULL indicates the completion of path definition. The program then moves into its display context with the prompt DISPLAY? and the user can request any or all of the options CORRELATIONS PATH OR VARS. The latter request will display means, deviations and any current labels for variables in the model. CORRELATIONS will print the matrix of coefficients currently in use and PATH will print out for each model or section of model the standardised regression coefficients (beta-weights) and the unstandardised coefficients — for the independent variables and the regression coefficient (multiple correlation coefficient :R^2).

4.3 A conversational prompting system is ideal for the beginner or the diffident researcher, but experienced researchers with some knowledge of computing will find full prompting both tedious and repetitive. Consequently the system has been designed to allow such users shorthand responses and preemptive specifications, so that only the first three characters of system keywords need to be entered and the entry of a slash ('/') will preempt the next prompt to enable entire sequences to be entered without intervening prompts.

4.4 Even the most sophisticated users make keypunching errors and the program is equipped with a full system for error reporting.

The final version will be designed for the user who has lost track of his analysis to enter the keyword/HELP at which point appropriate messages will appear.

4.5 A preemptive response of/STOP will end the run.

4.6 An additional response to the LINK? prompt has been provided to enable previously specified paths to be deleted. The user types /CUT ALL or var. name FROM var. name or var. list or ALL.

4.7 It needs to be stressed that IPA is not just another example of proliferation of programs for social scientists and survey analysis at a time when existing programs are more than adequate. On the contrary IPA has been designed from the start to avoid duplication of other work and this has been achieved through extensive consultation with others working in the field. As stated above, it has also been designed to the syntac and language specifications of SCSS. It is quite clear that, for social scientists, SPSS is now the de facto package in Britain for most of their requirements because of its availability, documentation and ease of use. This is the case not only in universities, but increasingly in polytechnics, local authorities, and government agencies. In addition to the advantages of SPSS-style English language and conversational operation, IPA offers instant feedback, a variety of output options and great flexibility in enabling the user to vary his assumptions quickly in accordance with the results obtained

4.8 For various reasons the project started seven months behind schedule, but with hard work and good will all round, we hope to provide, at relatively low cost and in a comparatively short time, a powerful, but easy-to-use facility for causal analysis and model-building in the social sciences.

APPENDIX A: SYNTAX OF INTERACTIVE PATH ANALYSIS PROGRAM 31.03.78.

PROMPT (FROM PROGRAM)	RESPONSE (FROM USER)	EXPLANATORY REMARKS
1.0 INTERACTIVE PATH ANALYSIS...		Informative message
1.1 GET FILE?	file name	File GTFILE contains the IPA system-file
	NULL	No system-file has been defined: file definition sequence follows
2.0 FILE DEFINITIONS ...		Informative message
2.1 NAME?	file name	A new file must be given a name: label
2.2 LABEL?	" file label "	is optional, but must be in double quotes, otherwise NULL.
3.0 VARIABLE DEFINITIONS ...		Informative message
3.1 NAME OF VARIABLE?	var. name	Each variable must be entered by name,
3.2 ROW NUMBER?	matrix tow no.	followed by the row number of the matrix
3.3 LABEL?	" var. label "	or table in which it occurs: label is optional. Program will detect and report errors in names, numbers, duplicates etc.
..3.1 NAME OF VARIABLE?	NULL	No more variables to be defined: matrix definitions sequence follows
4.0 MATRIX DEFINITIONS ...		Informative message
4.1 DATA?	MEANS	Optional. Program will expect next row of data to be means of variables.
	DEVIATIONS	Optional. Program will expect next row of data to be standard deviations of variables.
	COEFFICIENTS	Compulsory. Program expects matrix of coefficients of association, but will ask for format of matrix first.
4.2 TYPE OF LAYOUT?	UPPER	Program will expect upper triangle without diagonal:
	LOWER	Program will expect lower triangle without diagonal.
	SQUARE	Program will expect square matrix:
	SPSS	Program will expect square matrix of standard SPSS format. (eg. nF10.7) N.B. LAYOUT? prompt occurs only when COEFFICIENTS has been defined in response to the prompt DATA?
5.0 INPUT DEFINITIONS ...		Informative message
5.1 INPUT MEDIUM "INPUT" OR "INDATA" ?	INDATA	Matrix or table is stored on file INDATA. (N.B. This file name conforms to LSE conventions) Goes to 6.0
	INPUT	Default option. Program expects matrix or table to be entered direct via keyboard of terminal.
5.2 COEFFICIENTS =	free format list of real numbers	Does not occur if data input is from INDATA.
(This section to be substantially modified)	NULL	No more data to be input. Program moves to model-building context.
6.0 PATH DEFINITIONS ...		Informative message
6.1 LINK?	var. name WITH var. name or var. list	Variable specified to left of WITH is dependent variable. ALL vars. to right of WITH are independent. A var. list may include keyword TO or commas as list separators.
	CUT ALL or var. name FROM var. name or var. list	Pre-emptive response to delete paths from existing model.
	NULL	No more paths to be defined: program enters display mode.
6.2 DISPLAY?	CORRELATIONS	Matrix is displayed in F5.4 format
	PATH	For each model or sub-model displays standardised and unstandardised regression coefficients and R^2
	VARIABLES	For each variable defined, displays mean, deviation and label (if any)
	NULL	Program returns to mast recent context?
	/STOP	Pre-emptive entry allows user to finish at any time. Current model and information automatically saved

APPENDIX B.

Specifications for current and final versions of IPA.

IPA is currently implemented as version 1.1 (i.e. the first update of the first generation program). The version to be developed is the second generation program IPA 2.0

IPA 1.1:

1. Data and definitions are stored on disk in a system file identified by name and described by a label.

2. Variables must be defined separately, by name, together with the corresponding input correlation matrix row number and an optional label. Limit of number of variables is 50.

3. All variables are assumed to be continuous or dummy variables.

4. Data must be read in the form of a correlation matrix and optionally means and standard deviations.

5. The data must be read in a specific order: means followed by deviations followed by coefficients. (This can be changed to the order in which data elements are defined in this version if required).

6. Data can be read either through the terminal or from a disk file.

7. The matrix may be defined in a number of formats: square, upper triangle, lower triangle or standard SPSS.

8. There are no facilities for reading totals and hence no significance tests.

9. Once the matrix is read, it is stored in the system file. It cannot be altered, neither can a new matrix be stored in its place, but additional rows can be defined and stored later.

10. Causal models are defined by links between each dependent variable and its predictors. Limit of number of predictors is 25.

11. The model is stored in the system file, together with the resulting path coefficients.

12. The model can be changed at any time, either by introducing new links or by cutting old ones.

13. Three display options are available, each producing information on all variables defined:
    a) A variable list of all the variables in the file, including labels, row numbers, means and standard deviations.
    b) A correlation matrix of all variables.
    c) The path coefficients for each dependent variable specified, together with the unstandardised coefficients and the multiple regression.

14. Processing may be stopped at any time.

IPA 2.0 has following specifications over and above IPA 1.1

1. Variables can be defined in the form of a list, or series of lists.
2. Variables can be of five types as in SCSS (Alpha, zone, discrete, continuous or set).
3. Set variables can be used to define a list of variables.
4. Values can be assigned to each category-scale variable (i.e. 1st 3 types), together with missing definition and value label.
5. Up to 100 variables may be defined, including set variables.
6. Up to 20 different matrices may be defined, each with identifying name and a label.
7. A variable list defines the rows of a matrix: category scale variables have one row for each category scale variable in the list.
8. Missing treatment may be defined (i.e. likewise, pairwise or included).
9. Totals for significance can be defined (either as a matrix of totals or as a single total).
10. The input matrix is in the form of correlations, frequencies and breakdown means.
11. Up to 20 models may be defined at the same time, identified by name and label.
12. Display procedure defines variables to be presented, together with statistics and results for each variable.
13. Any information in the file may be modified or deleted at any time.
14. Program restarts at next context after stopped.
15. Significance testing; comparison of models.
16. Loop detection and looping facilities for non-recursive models.

REFERENCES

BLALOCK, N.M. "Causal Models in the Social Sciences" Macmillan Press Ltd. London 1972

BLAU, P. & DUNCAN, O.D. "The American Occupational Structure" Wiley, N.Y. 1967

DAVIS, J.A. "Linear Flow Graphs as a Mathematical Model for Analysing Contingency Tables" NORC, Chicago. 1974

DAVIS, J.A. & SCHOOLER S.R. "Nonparametric Path Analysis - The Multivariate Structure of Dichotomous Data When Using the Odds Ratio or Yule's Q. NORC, Chicago. 1974

DUNCAN, O.D. "Path Analysis, Sociological Examples," American Journal of Sociology 72, 245-263. 1966

FEATHERMAN, D.L. "A Research Note: A Social Structural Model for the Socioeconomic Career" in American Journal of Sociology. 77, p.293-303 1972

FRANKLIN, M.N. et al "Interactive SPSS Project-Language Specifications 1-17" Program Library Unit, Edinburgh Reg. Comp. Centre. 1974

GOODMAN, L.A. "A General Model for the Analysis of Surveys" In American Journal of Sociology, 77, 1035-1068. 1972

HALL, J.F. "The relationship between objective & subjective indicators of individual well-being; a linear modelling approach", SSRC Survey Unit, UK/USA "Subjective Indicators of Quality of Life" Fitzwilliam College, Cambridge, September 1975.

HAUSER, R.L. & GOLDBERGER, A.S. "The Treatment of Unobservable Variables in Path Analysis" In Sociological Methodology (H.L. Costner, Ed) Jossey-Bass, San Francisco. 1971

HEISE, D.R. "Causal Analysis" Wiley-Interscience, New York. 1975

JÖRESKOG, K.G. "LISREL: A general computer program for estimating a linear structural equation system involving multiple indicators of unmeasured variables" Princeton, New Jersey. 1972

JÖRESKOG, K.G. "A General Model for Estimating a Linear Structural Equation System" In Structural Equation Models in the Social Sciences (A.S. Goldberger and O.D. Duncan, Eds) Seminar Press New York. 1975

KELLEY, J. "Causal Chain Models for the Socioeconomic Career". American Sociological Review 1973, Vol 38 p.481-493. 1973

LAND, K.C. "Principles of Path Analysis" In Sociological Methodology (E.F. Burgatta, Ed.) Jossey-Bass, San Francisco. 1969

MARSH, C. "Job satisfaction - the search goes on" SSRC Survey Unit, UK/USA Seminar, "Subjective Indicators of Quality of Life" Fitzwilliam College, Canbridge, September, 1975.

NELDER, J.A. "GLIM User's Manual" N.A.G. Oxford. 1974

NELDER, J.A. & WEDDERBURN R.M.W "Generalised Linear Models" In Journal of the Royal Statistical Society (series A), 135, 3, 370-384). 1972

NIE, N.H. HULL, C.H. & FRANKLIN, M.N. "Interactive SPSS Project - General Introduction" Program Library Unit - Edinburgh. 1974

NIE, M.H. & HULL, C.H. "SCSS, Preliminary Users Manual Chicago University, (Mimeo). 1977

NYGREEN, G.T. "IPA Interactive Path Analyser", Princeton, New Jersey. 1970

O'MUIRCHEARTAIGH, C.A. & PAYNE, C. "Analysis of Survey Data" Vol II Model Fitting. Wiley, London 1977

RING, A.J. "Interactive Path Analysis" BSA Quantitative Sociology Group, Essex University. 1975

TAYLOR, G. "User's Instructions for the DTSS Program *E85000: CATFITII" N.O.R.C., Chicago. 1975

Users' Regression System for Desk Top Calculators

J. Militký, M. Hoffmann and J. Čáp, Dvur Králové N.L.

SUMMARY

The system for regression treatment of experimental data on Hewlett-Packard desk top calculator with magnetic tape unit and plotter is presented. Particular programs are described and the application of the whole system in mathematical modelling is discussed.

Keywords: Parameter estimation, regression system, mathematical modelling on desk top calculator.

INTRODUCTION

Programmable calculators are recently being used mainly for collection and pretreatment of experimental data. Treatment of experiments is mostly accomplished on computers. However, in these cases the calculators are applicable, too. To find a convenient mathematical model describing experimentally determined dependences it is advantageous to use programmable calculators. Heuristic method of seeking the adequate mathematical models makes it impossible to solve this problem by single execution of the convenient algorithm. It is necessary to use a complex of partial programs which are executed according to instantaneous requirements of the user. Consequently, it is profitable to be given a possibility of interactive decision as to further system activity regarding the results obtained. In this paper a system for regression treatment of physical experimental dependences (mathematical modelling) elaborated for HP 9810 A calculator with magnetic tape unit and plotter as peripheral is described.

Note:

The Hewlett-Packard Model 9810 A Calculator is one of the simp-

lest fully programmable calculators. Programming is carried out in special instruction code. Standard programming features include separate data and program memories. (The program memory can store up to 2036 program steps, and the data memory up to 110 data numbers - in data registers).
The system works in off-line mode being recorded on one magnetic tape where experimental points are stored.

PROBLEM FORMULATION

Suppose we are observing the physical system where output quantity η is functionally dependent on the vector of input $\bar{x}$. The unknown "true" function is defined as $\eta = \eta(\bar{x})$. Physical system possess several diferences in comparison with those, for example, economical ones. This fact effects the regression criterion choice - see Militký (1978a). After all experiments have been finished, subsequent values are at disposal -
a) $n\ (i=1,\dots n)$ vectors of independent variables (exogenous, input) $\bar{x}_i$ (the components x_{ij}, $j=1,\dots m$) correspond to observable (endogenous, output) dependent values y_i. Consequently, the system on the space E^{n+1} having the coordinates $\{(x_{ij})\, j=1\dots m;\ y_i\}\, i=1\dots n$ is proposed.
Note:
Cases where the response (output variable) is a vector are not considered.
b) Assuming p_i measurements $(y_{1i}\cdots y_{pi})$ were made in the point $\bar{x}_i$, it is possible to determine average values $y_{\emptyset i}$ and corresponding variances σ_i^2.
The model relation $f(\bar{x};\bar{a})$ based on physical or other assumptions (Militký (1978a)) is proposed. The result of i-th measurement can be expressed as follows

$$y_i = f(\bar{x}_i\,;\bar{a}) + \varepsilon_i \qquad /1/$$

where $\bar{a}$ is a vector with components $a_r\ (r=1,\dots\dots s)$ denoting the model parameters. Total error ε_i is composed of measuring error and of that due to true function $\eta(\bar{x})$ approximation by model relation $f(\bar{x};\bar{a})$. To facilitate further treatment it is assumed, that $E(\varepsilon_i)=0$ and $E(\varepsilon_i\cdot\varepsilon_j)=0$, respectively, for $i\neq j=1,\dots n$.

The object of regression is to find such estimations $\hat{\bar{a}}$ of parameters $\bar{a}$ in model function $f(\bar{x},\bar{a})$ which are optimal in sense of chosen regression criterion G.All of the regression criterions are based on certain assumptions as for errors $\mathcal{E}_i$.(Their probability density).Provided G is known,the regression problem can usually be expressed as

$$\hat{\bar{a}} = \min_{\bar{a}} \sum_{(i)} G(\mathcal{E}_i) \qquad /2/$$

There are two principal approaches to regression criterion in mathematical modelling: Numerical mathematics (theory of approximation) or mathematical statistics (theory of point estimations).Militký (1978a) brings detailed description of particular methods based upon these approaches which lead from computational point of view to relation /2/.In special cases the solution of /2/ may be converted to that of an equation system.

STRUCTURE OF REGRESSION SYSTEM

Since there is a number of possibilities as for operating the whole system the off-line mode was used.Then,user can decide himself which program to choose.

Regression system includes -

1. Data entry.
2. Non-parametric smoothing for one independent variable.
3. Linear regression for one independent variable.
4. Linearized regression for max. ten regression parameters.
5. Non-linear regression.
6. Computation of values describing goodness of fit.
7. Plotting the regression dependences.

Each block contains several denoted programs selected by simple numerical key.

DATA ENTRY

The program operates with dynamic memory,i.e.automatically splits magnetic tape into files according to the number of independent variables.Optimal size of individual files is computed from the requirement of maximal number of points ($m+1$

coordinates and one weight coefficient w_i) stored in a memory section with 75 registers. In case the measurement has been repeated, computation of average value $y_{\emptyset i}$ and of corresponding variance σ_i^2 is carried out. One special file contains the control data concerning the number of independent variables, number of all data files and that of points in last file.

Note:

Provided the weights are not known, w_i is equal to unity.

NON-PARAMETRIC SMOOTHING FOR ONE INDEPENDENT VARIABLE

Local C^1-piecewise approximation by cubic polynomials described by Militký and Jansa (1977) is used. Resulting dependence is given by a polynomial of max. degree three within each interval with boundary values x_k and x_{k+1} ($k = 1, \ldots n-1$). These polynomials are continuous in the function values and first derivatives on the edges of individual intervals. Smoothed values y_k^* as well as derivatives $y_k'^*$ are computed from cubic polynomial approximating in the interval $x_{k-2} \leq x \leq x_{k+2}$ experimental points in sense of least squares. Militký and Kovářová (1977) give detailed description of the algorithm. This program is used to determine initial estimates $\hat{a}_0$ of regression parameter vector $\hat{a}$ (for example from derivatives or function values in chosen points). It can also be used to plot the smoothed course of experimental dependences.

LINEAR REGRESSION FOR ONE INDEPENDENT VARIABLE

Three programs are include in this block. The first one assessing the regression line coefficients by weighted least squares method. Furthermore, standard method is used to evaluate the correlation coefficient, correlation index and confidence intervals in all the points (see e.g. Draper and Smith (1966)). The linearity and confidence tests of individual estimates $\hat{a}_1$ (or $\hat{a}_2$) are carried out, too.

Second program includes seven possibilities as for regression criterion choice (using the numerical key). Inserting the weights $w_i = y_i^{-2}$ into the relation for computation the regression parameters by weighted least squares method provides the estimates corresponding the least squares of relative deviations criterion. By substituing $w_i = y_i^{-1}$ resulting estimates $\hat{a}_1, \hat{a}_2$ eliminate partially the sensitivity of least squares against large absolute values y_i (refer to Militký (1976)).

In certain sense, the both criterions represent the robust variants of least squares criterion. Späth (1973) proposed the method of computing estimates $\hat{a}_1$ and $\hat{a}_2$ minimizing L_1 and L_∞, respectively. Provided minimization of L_p-norm is required (for given $\infty > p > 1$) an iterative procedure is used. In j-th step the estimates $\hat{a}_{1(j)}$, $\hat{a}_{2(j)}$ by weighted least squares method are determined. Weights being defined as $w_i = [abs(y_i - \hat{a}_{1(j-1)} x_i - \hat{a}_{2(j-1)})]^{p-2}$ (Militký (1978)).

In cases independent variable is subjected to random errors with variances τ_i^2, the generalized least squares method to estimate $\hat{a}_1, \hat{a}_2$ is used. For given variance ratio $K = \sigma_i^2 / \tau_i^2 = const.$ the estimate of regression line parameters is made directly by substituing into corresponding relations. When σ_i^2 and τ_i^2 are not constant for all $i = 1, \ldots n$ an iterative procedure based upon weighted least squares method is applied. In j-th iteration the $w_i = [\tau_i^2 + \hat{a}_{1(j-1)} \cdot \sigma_i^2]^{-1}$ is defined (see Militký (1978b)).

Third program computes robust estimates $\hat{a}_1$ and $\hat{a}_2$ (treating values y_i) on the basis of residual magnitude (Winsorized estimation). Yale and Forsythe (1976) describe in details possible variants of Winsorized regression. Here, iterative procedure with increasing level is used (Militký (1978b)).

LINEARIZED REGRESSION FOR TEN REGRESSION CONSTANTS

There are two programs included in this block. The first one estimates the parameters of the polynomial of a given degree for one independent variable. A generation of polynomials which are orthogonal on sequence $x_1 < x_2 < \ldots < x_n$ is made. The resulting recurrent formula is described e.g. by Militký (1978a). Then, the coefficients of individual orthogonal polynomials are computed and a confidence test is carried out.

The second program is being used to estimate the parameters of models $y = f(\bar{x}; \bar{a})$ which may be transformed, using the function

$g(y,\bar{x})$ into the form $g(y_i,\bar{x}_i)=\sum_{j=1}^{r} b_j \cdot f_j(x_i)$; b_j representing the transformed parameters a_j.Determining the estimates $b_j\ (j=1,\dots r)$ by least squares method leads to solving a linear equation system.A standard Gaussian elimination with pivotting subroutine is applied to compute $\hat{b}_j\ (j=1,\dots r)$.To eliminate the effect of transformation it is possible to use the weights $w_i=[\partial g(y,\bar{x})/\partial y]^{-2}_{y=y_i}$.

NON-LINEAR REGRESSION

The first of two programs included here is constructed specially for the least squares criterion.To solve this problem a method of Taylor linearization described for exemple by Draper and Smith (1966) is used.Initial estimates of model parameters $\hat{\hat{a}}_0$ are determined using programs for linearized regression or non-parametric smoothing.

Second program executes direct minimization of the given criterion.That is why it is possible to choose not only the model function $f(\bar{x},\bar{a})$ but even the regression criterion G.A non-derivative procedure based upon pattern search method (Wilde (1964)) is used.

A convenient strategy of step-length changes in each cycle enables to obtain adaptation of the algorithm according to the form of criterion function in neighbouring stationary points (Militký (1977)).This algorithm has minimal requirements as to active memory range.

COMPUTATION OF THE VALUES CHARACTERIZING GOODNESS OF FIT

The program computes the values $\bar{x}_i, y_i, f(\bar{x}_i;\hat{a})$,residual absolute and relative deviation for each point.Further,the average residual relative and absolute deviation and a residual sum of squares as well as maximal absolute or relative deviation is determined.Modifications for plotting the residual deviations on y_i values or $x_{ij}\ (i=1,\dots m)$,respectively,is easy possible.

PLOTTING THE REGRESSION DEPENDENCES

This blocks includes two programs. The former plots the dependences $y=f(x_1;\hat{a})$ together with experimental points, the latter enables plotting of dependences $y=f(x_1;x_2;\hat{a})$ in rectangular axonometry. Separate part of the both programs is formed by subroutine plotting and lettering the coordinate system.

CONCLUSION

The above described system of mathematical modelling of experimental data on programmable calculator has been compiled on the basis of well-known algorithm. Regarding a small range of active memory it has been necessary to simplify and to modify most of the methods. The whole regression system is very easy to operate.

REFERENCES

Draper N.R., Smith H., Applied Regression Analysis, J.Wiley, New York, 1966

Militký J., Contribution to Regression Criterions, Reprint of Lecture Presented at 23-rd National Conference CHISA'76, Mariánské Lázně, 1976, (in Czech)

Militký J., A Simple Direct Search Method with Adaptive Step for Non-linear Regression, Reprint of Lecture Presented at 24-th National Conference CHISA'77, Bratislava, 1977, (in Czech)

Militký J., Jansa J., Simple Methods of Experimental Data Fitting, Proc. 5-th Symp. Computers in Chemical Engineering 1, 101 - 104, 1977, High Tatras

Militký J., Kovářová A., A Simple Method for Data Smoothing, Proc. 7-th National Conference - Users of Desk Top Calculators, 53 - 68, 1977, Ostrava, (in Czech)

Militký J., The Mathematical Modelling and Optimization of Technological Processes, Script for Postgraduate Course, Isntitute of Chemical Technology, in Press, Pardubice (1978a), (in Czech)

Militký J., A Set of Methods for Parameter Estimation in Linear Models, Proc. 8-th National Conference - Users of Desk Top Calculators, 10 - 22, 1978b, Gottwaldov, (in Czech)

Späth H., Algorithmen für elementare Ausgleichsmodelle, R. Oldenbourgh Verlag, München, 1973, (in German)

Wilde D.J., Optimum Seeking Methods, Prentice Hall, Englewood Cliffs, New Jersey, 1964

Yale C., Forsythe A.B., Winsorized Regression, Technometrics 18, 291 - 300, 1976

Clusters: a Package Program for Computation of Sampling Errors for Clustered Samples

L. Rehlin, London

Summary

CLUSTERS (Computation and Listing of Useful STatistics on ERrors of Sampling) is a FORTRAN IV based package program for the computation of sampling errors for clustered samples; it is written for the IBM 360/370 series computers, and at present no other versions are available. Standard errors, and certain statistics derived from standard errors, can be computed from estimates such as proportions, means and ratios over a given sample, as well as over specified sub-classes of the sample. The package includes flexible facilities for specification of parameters of the sample design relevant to the computations, and also provides a useful set of recoding facilities for defining statistics for which sampling errors are to be computed.

1. Introduction

The principal aim of a descriptive sample survey is to derive estimates of the characteristics of a population (or sub-population such as regions of a country) from a probability sample drawn from the population. In many instances this process involves estimating an average quantity in the population by a (weighted) average from the sample. The difference between the estimate and the true value can be called the total error. This in turn is a combination of two types of errors: sampling errors and non-sampling errors.

Sampling errors are deviations caused by limiting the enquiry to a sample of the population. Non-sampling errors are deviations that would be present even if the entire population was covered. These include reporting errors, mistakes in coding and punching, coverage errors or other errors in implementing the survey design.

The relative importance of sampling errors over non-sampling errors increase as the sample size is reduced or, if for a given sample, attention is focused on smaller sub-groups (or sub-classes) of the sample. For that reason it becomes necessary to compute sampling errors for surveys based on moderate sample sizes, particularly if separate estimates are required for many sub-populations.

A typical survey involves a large number of variables for which separate estimates are made over a large number of sub-classes in the sample. Very wide ranges in values of sampling errors between different variables within the same survey have been found, and it is normally not enough to single out, arbitrarily, just a few variables as "critical" survey variables for sampling error calculations. Similarly, it is not enough to confine the computations to the entire sample when substantive survey results are involved for many different sub-classes.

One of the main obstacles in computing and presenting sampling errors along with substantive survey results has been the non-availability (to many organisations) of an adequate, efficient and (relatively) easy to use computer software package for sampling error calculations. In order to rectify this situation, the World Fertility Survey has developed and is distributing a fairly modest, simple and fast sampling errors program called CLUSTERS (Computation and Listing of Useful STatistics on ERrors of Sampling).

It has been an objective of the World Fertility Survey to ensure that sampling errors are calculated for important variables and sample sub-classes and included in the reports describing substantive survey findings in the participating countries. Furthermore, the usefulness of CLUSTERS is by no means limited to WFS surveys; it is hoped that agencies engaged in sample surveys, both in developing and developed countries, will benefit from this work.

2. Basic Requirements for a Software Package

With CLUSTERS, an attempt has been made to meet the basic requirements for a general and widely usable software package for calculation of sampling errors for descriptive sample surveys. These requirements can be outlined as follows:

(i) The program should be able to handle, simply and cheaply, a large number of variables over different sample sub-classes. It should not require the use of large computers or other very specialised facilities.

(ii) In relation to the study of differentials between sub-populations, sampling errors for differences between sub-classes pairs should also be computed.

(iii) It should be possible to repeat, in a simple way, the entire set of calculations for different geographical or administrative regions; such breakdowns are often required of substantive survey results.

(iv) The computational procedure must take into account the actual sample design, in particular the effects of clustering and stratification which influence the extent of sampling errors. However, the program should not be limited to a particular sample design; it should not assume particular models like "paired selection of primary sampling units" in order to estimate variances.

(v) It should be able to handle weighted data.

(vi) As far as possible, the program should not require any particular arrangement or form of input data. Where recoding of the "raw" input data is required, it is desirable that the software package itself can handle this, without the need to write special programs for that purpose alone.

(vii) In addition to calculating standard errors, it is also desirable to compute certain other derived statistics. These computed values can then be extrapolated to other variables and sub-classes for a given sample and possibly also to future surveys. One of the objectives of calculating sampling errors is to provide information for the sampling statisticians attempting to design other studies under similar survey conditions.

3. Main Features of CLUSTERS

CLUSTERS is a FORTRAN IV based software package (it also requires a standard Sort Program). It can be run on 64K bytes on an IBM 360/370, though if more core storage is available for work areas, more calculations can be done in one run of the program. However, 64K bytes is enough for an average number of variables and sub-classes.

Below the main features of CLUSTERS are summarised in relation to the basic requirements discussed above.

(i) <u>Handling of Different Variables and Sample Sub-classes</u>

We note that sub-classes for sampling error calculations usually are defined in terms of the characteristics used in the cross-classification of the substantive results from the surveys. Often the same system of cross-classification is relevant to all (or most) survey variables. Variables like family size or prevalence of contraceptive use may all be presented after classification of the sample by characteristics such as age or socio-economic background of the units of analysis.

Making use of these common features, the calculations to be performed are specified in CLUSTERS in terms of a rectangular "variable by sub-class" matrix. Sampling errors are then computed for all variables over each sub-class (and automatically over the whole sample) in the specified set. In addition, CLUSTERS automatically computes sampling errors for each sub-class, treating it is a characteristic distributed over the entire sample. As an example, if sampling errors for 20 variables over 15 sample sub-classes are to be computed (a typical WFS survey requirement), it is not necessary to specify 20 x 15 = 300 "problems" separately, but only 20 + 15 = 35 variables and sub-classes.

(ii) <u>Sub-class Differences</u>

The sample sub-classes for which sampling errors are to be computed can be specified in pairs. In that case CLUSTERS automatically calculates the difference and its standard error for each sub-class pair. It is not necessary for any particular sample sub-class to be specified in only one pair, nor that sub-classes in a pair be non-overlapping.

(iii) <u>Separate Results for Geographical Regions</u>

The entire set of calculations for variables over sample sub-classes and for differences between sub-class pairs can be repeated for the separate geographic regions into which the survey universe may have been divided. This repetition is extremely straightforward from the users point of view and does not involve much additional computer time. One restriction regarding this facility in CLUSTERS is that the geographical regions be non-overlapping and the sample selected independently within each region.

(iv) Sample Structure

CLUSTERS computes sampling errors taking into account the actual sample design, in particular the clustering and stratification of the sample. The basic units involved in the computational formulae are the primary sampling units (PSUs), i.e. the first or highest stage units selected into the sample. The procedure is roughly as follows: For any variable under study, a summation (weighted if applicable) is made over the values of the variable for all individual cases (belonging to a particular sample sub-class) in each PSU. The PSU totals are then "differenced" from a mean of all sample PSUs within each stratum according to formulae described in the CLUSTERS Users Manual, Verma, Pearce (1978). These differences are then squared and pooled over the whole sample (or over each geographical region, if applicable) and divided by an appropriate constant to produce estimates of sampling variance.

For a multistage sample, the procedure does not split the overall variance into separate components associated with the individual stages. Hence all that is required regarding specification of the sample structure is an identification of the PSU, stratum and geographical region (if applicable) for each individual case (i.e. each ultimate sampling unit). One of the noteworthy features of CLUSTERS is the fair degree of flexibility regarding the form of this identification; restructuring or recoding of the input data is not normally required. The only restriction required by CLUSTERS is that some arbitrary sampling units higher than the ultimate units (i.e. individual cases) be identifiable from a field in each ultimate unit and that the data file be sorted by these higher stage units. For a multistage area sample, these "higher stage" units may be any units from the lowest to the highest stage area sampling units.

(v) Weighted Data

CLUSTERS handles non-selfweighting samples, i.e. samples in which the ultimate units have been weighted to compensate for differences in probabilities of selection or for defects in sample implementation, e.g. non-response. These sample weights may be scaled arbitrarily and specified either as a data field on each individual record or simply in terms of the identification code for each of the "higher stage" units mentioned in the previous paragraph.

(vi) Recoding of Input Data

It is often necessary to recode "raw" input data before the required statistics like proportions, means or ratios and their standard errors can be calculated. For this purpose CLUSTERS includes a limited set of recoding facilities. These can define new variables on the basis of one or more input data fields. Though using these facilities is not always the most economical means of recoding variables, they are simple to use and have been found quite versatile.

(vii) Derived Statistics

In addition to standard errors, CLUSTERS outputs two derived statistics, namely the Design Effect (DEFT) and the Rate of Homogeneity (ROH). They provide the basis for generalising the computed results to other variables and sub-classes of the particular sample, and possibly also to other sample designs.

DEFT compares the standard error for a particular variable within the given clustered sample to what the standard error would have been had the sample been selected entirely at random. For a particular sample design, cluster size and variable, DEFT is a measure of the loss of sampling precision due to the clustering of the sample. The two main factors on which DEFT depends are the average cluster size and homogeneity (corresponding to a particular variable) within these clusters.

ROH is a measure of average intra-class correlation, and is intended to reflect the characteristics of the variables; it is less dependent on the particular sample design or cluster size than the DEFT values. More specifically, a high value of ROH indicates that the values of a variable within each cluster are more similar than the values for the population at large.

The DEFT and ROH values provide valuable information about the effect of clustering for the design of future surveys. They also perform a useful function in relation to sampling errors for a given survey: They allow sampling errors to be estimated for sample sub-classes other than those for which results were actually computed.

4. Concluding Remarks

Finally, two limitations in the approach followed in CLUSTERS should be noted:

(i) As was said earlier, analysis of variance into components attributable to different stages of a multistage sample design is not included, or at least cannot be done in a straightforward way.

(ii) CLUSTERS is confined to "descriptive statistics" like proportions, percentages, means, ratios and differences in these. It does not handle "double ratios" or linear combinations of ratios (except for difference of two ratios), nor of course more complex analytical statistics.

REFERENCES

This document is largely based on a paper prepared by Dr. V.K. Verma and presented at the Conference of European Statisticians, UN Economic Commission for Europe, during a meeting on Problems Relating to Household Surveys, February 1978.

Verma V.K., Pearce M.C. - CLUSTERS Users Manual, ISI/WFS 1978

Application of the Statistical Program Package P-STAT in an Industrial Environment

S.H.J. Veling, Arnhem

Summary: P-STAT was chosen by AKZO from a number of other packages mainly because this package offered the possibility of being extended to include user-written programs, and because it permits the analysis of intermediate results. At AKZO many other features of the package have proved useful, such as time sharing use, data modification, file manipulation and macros. The inclusion of user programs in the package has improved by the use of the interface designed by AKZO. Finally documentation and maintenance are briefly discussed.
KEYWORDS: STATISTICAL PROGRAM PACKAGE EVACUATION,
EXTENSION OF PROGRAM PACKAGES

1. Introduction

The features of the statistical program package P-STAT were introduced into COMPSTAT by its author Roald Buhler (1974, 1976, 1978). At AKZO, a big company in the chemical field, P-STAT was chosen from a number of other packages to satisfy the need of a powerful system for solving a wide variety of problems occurring in chemical research and in other departments of the company. P-STAT is run at AKZO on an IBM 370/158 (MVS) installation and can be used in batch processing mode or interactively using Time Sharing Option (TSO). There are six versions of P-STAT (differing only with respect to the size of the data files which can be handled). Two of these versions are available to the AKZO users, namely MEDIUM (260K, 500 variables) and JUMBO (680K, 3000 variables).

2. Evaluation

Up to 1975 AKZO designed a certain number of statistical programs to handle the specific needs of chemical research. Special programs relating, for instance, to the analysis of variance of orthogonal designs, multiple linear regression and paired comparisons, were written and frequently used. The disadvantages of handling a set of separate programs became clear after the use increased and the data files became more complex:

- modifications of the raw input data are hardly possible;
- each program asks for its own input organisation and the input has to be specified in a way which is difficult for users with little or no computer experience;
- no facilities to display the results in an adequate way (scatter diagrams, plots, histograms, etc.);
- no uniform documentation.

To solve these problems, the purchase of an integrated statistical program package was considered. Therefore the COMPSTAT symposium held in Vienna in 1977 was visited, and the following packages were evaluated: GENSTAT, SPSS and P-STAT.
Beforehand, two demands were stated:
- The integration of user-written special programs in the package must be possible. No package can obviously contain all the analysis programs that are needed in chemical research. If existing and new programs cannot be integrated, the package will not be used at all in many cases.
- Intermediate results must be available to the user. In statistics one often wants to perform additional analysis on the results of previous calculations as for instance the analysis of the residuals in a regression problem.

Inclusion of user programs in SPSS, though formally described in the manual, turned out to be impossible and the extension of GENSTAT was only feasible in terms of its command language, which was insufficient with respect to the needs of AKZO.
Extension of P-STAT, however, proved possible and relatively easy, using the five pre-programmed user exits.
As P-STAT also makes intermediate results available to the user in the form of a file the choice was not difficult. Other points of evaluation, like reliability, ease of use and efficiency did not give rise to abandon P-STAT.
A report of the evaluation by van Houwelingen (1975), containing a proposal to implement P-STAT, was accepted and effectuated.

3. Use of P-STAT at AKZO

P-STAT was introduced at AKZO by means of an introductory course and workshops. Though much attention was given to the design and preparation of the introduction, it was found that the complex package, as P-STAT is, caused problems to many mostly inexperienced users. An elementary course in the use of computers prior to P-STAT introduction would therefore have been appropriate. The package is now regularly used in various departments (chemical research, medical, psychological, personnel administration).

Fruitful use has been made of the following features:

- Inclusion of user programs, the latter being special purpose programs of the pharmaceutical division of AKZO and a special analysis of variance program.
  Extension will be discussed in more detail in the next paragraph
- Interactive use. A TSO command procedure has been designed which enables the user, just by typing PSTAT followed by the name of a file system, to run the package interactively. There are special P-STAT commands for the time sharing user (to specify the line size of the screen or paper, to send output to a remote line printer, to fix mistyped commands, and so on). In cases where no big files have to be processed the time-sharing use of P-STAT turns out to be very effective.
- Data modification. There are numerous and well-chosen possibilities of creating new variables or changing existing ones. The way "missing values" are treated is very elegant. In each situation it is clearly defined what happens when an involved parameter or operand in an arithmetic expression has a "missing value" (in most cases the result will be a "missing value" too). There are even three logical values: TRUE, FALSE and MISSING. The main advantages of this approach are the reliability of the results, and the little work which is involved in specifying a considerable amount of recodings.
- File manipulation. A very useful feature is the concept of a file system. A file system, which is a physical data file on tape or disc, can contain many P-STAT data files each of which is available during the execution of a P-STAT job. More file systems can be processed simultaneously.

New files can be created in many different ways such as
- after reading raw input data
- after sorting an existing file
- after collating several existing files together
- after recoding or adding variables
- after updating an existing file with new input

Moreover a statistical analysisprogram can create files containing for instance a correlation matrix, residuals, predictions, eigenvectors and factorloadings.

- Macros. Complex composite commands can be joined to a macro. A macro may have input and output parameters (such as files and names of variables). Macros have been used to perform complicated regression analysis (in conjunction with the matrix operation commands like TRANSPOSE, INVERT and MULTIPLY) and also to perform certain distribution free statistical tests like Wilcoxon's test and Kruskall Wallis' test.

4. Extension by user-written programs

There are five P-STAT commands, USER1 through USER5, which can effectuate a user-written FORTRAN subroutine. In this subroutine the programmer can obtain, by appropriate calls to available subroutines, every information on the parameters specified by the user of one of those commands. The five user exits were designed for the purpose of temporary linking the user subroutines only when they are needed.
This has the disadvantage that for runs in which a user command is to be performed the appropriate subroutines have to be linked to the about 700 P-STAT subroutines, which is expensive and inefficient because it has to be done very frequently. The advantage, however, is that far more than five user commands can be designed provided that no more than five of them are needed during one run. At AKZO this problem is solved by using one exit, USER5, as an interface to an indefinite number of user subroutines. The interface program checks the parameters and calls the required subroutines. The advantages of this approach are:
- more than five user subroutines can be permanently linked;
- new user subroutines can now be added more simply as part of the errorchecking work is done by the interface program;

- four user exits, USER1 through USER4, are still avaliable for temporary linking, which for instance is needed when testing new user subroutines.

The extension procedure as well as the facilities of P-STAT, which can be used by the programmer (SUBROUTINES, COMMON BLOCKS), have been documented by Veling (1977), and are available to all AKZO users.

5. Documentation and Maintenance

An introductory as well as a reference manual are available on magnetic tape. The introductory manual will be published shortly in the form of a book. For AKZO purposes the reference manual, though complete, was judged to be somewhat too difficult for many of the intended users. As the introductory manual was incomplete a Dutch reference manual was written by Veling et al. (1977), for use in the introduction course and workshops. This loose-leaf manual now contains a systematic description of almost all commands excluding those for multivariate analysis but including the generally available extensions and installation-dependent subjects like time sharing use and job control language.
New releases of the package are issued regularly (about twice a year). The communication with the author of the package about errors or imperfections is stimulating. Usually errors are corrected in the next release and suggestions on improvement are taken seriously.

References

Buhler R., Supporting P-STAT on 7 types of Computers, COMPSTAT 1974 Proceedings in Computational Statistics, 1974.

Buhler R., Designing Statistical Software for Use in both Batch and Interactive Environments, COMPSTAT 1976 Proceedings in Computational Statistics, 1976.

Buhler R., S. Buhler, Improvements in Data Display in P-STAT 78, COMPSTAT 1978 Proceedings in Computational Statistics, 1978.

van Houwelingen H., Proposal for Purchasing the Statistical Package P-STAT, Internal AKZO Report, Arnhem, 1975 (in Dutch).

Veling S.H.J., Guide lines for adding User Written Programs to P-STAT, Internal AKZO Report, Arnhem, 1977.

Veling S.H.J. (editor), H. van Houwelingen, E.R. Roelofsen, Handleiding bij het Statistische Programmapakket P-STAT, Internal AKZO Report, Arnhem, 1977 (in Dutch).

11. Miscellaneous

On Image Modelling and Restoration

J. Biemond, L.H. Links and D.E. Boekee, Delft

Summary.

In recursive (Kalman) filtering an image disturbed by additive noise the filter is derived from a dynamic model based on the second order statistics of the original image or the imaged object and the noise. For given image statistics it is possible to create different models. The choice of a model may influence the quality of the filter results. To compare different models representing the same image three quality criteria, among which the Cramér-Rao bound, are introduced. Results of this comparison are discussed.

Keywords: Random fields, image models, recursive filters, Cramér-Rao bound

1. Introduction

In recent years digital processing of images has become a very active field of computer applications and research, particularly the digital restoration of images. Image restoration is the problem of reconstructing an image from a distorted version. Techniques used in image restoration may be either recursive or non-recursive.

Because of computational simplicity and low demand on computer memory recursive techniques deserve preference. In this approach stochastic models are required for both the original image and the noise. Given certain image statistics it is possible to design different models. The choice of a model may influence the quality of the filter results. This means that it is very important to know what model should be chosen in order to obtain an optimal design for the restoration filter.

In the following contribution several models are chosen and compared by using three quality criteria.

2. Image modelling

By assuming an image to be a discrete random field of pixel intensities denoted by u(i,j) as the brightness of the image in the (i,j)th coordinate, a manner to represent the image is commonly found in its autocorrelation function. If the image is assumed to be wide-sense stationary the autocorrelation function is defined as

$$R(k,l) = E\,[u(i,j)\;u(i+k,j+l)]\,. \qquad (1)$$

In analogy to the description of a one-dimensional stationary sequence by e.g. autoregressive processes, a two-dimensional stationary random field can be described as

$$u(i,j) = \sum_{S(p,q)} a(p,q)\;u(i+p,j+q) + v(i,j) \qquad (2)$$

where $S(p,q)$ is a set of image points not including the point $(p,q) = (0,0)$. A particular set $S(p,q)$ defines the model which is used to describe the image.

In case $a(p,q)$ are minimum-mean-square (MMSE) coefficients, which means that

$$E\,[v(i,j)\;u(i+p,j+q)] = 0\;, \quad \forall (p,q) \in S(p,q) \qquad (3)$$

the variance of the error $v(i,j)$ will be

$$E\,[v^2(i,j)] = R(0,0) - \sum_{S(p,q)} a(p,q)\;R(p,q). \qquad (4)$$

Examples of this representation can be found in Habibi (1972), Jain (1977) and Woods (1972).

Once a proper representation has been chosen to describe an image, the model must be converted into a recursive relation in order to derive a recursive filter for restoring the additively disturbed signal. A property demanded for recursive relations to be useful is stability, which means that a bounded input does not result in an unbounded output. In other words that the transfer function of (2),

$$H(j\omega_1,j\omega_2) = [\,1 - \sum_{S(p,q)} a(p,q)\;\exp\,(-j(p\omega_1 + q\omega_2))]\,, \qquad (5)$$

will be bounded for all ω_1, ω_2.

Thus the denominator of (5) may never be zero. Often it is sufficient to investigate the real part of the denominator, i.e.

$$1 - \sum_{S(p,q)} a(p,q)\;\cos\,(p\omega_1 + q\omega_2) \neq 0\;, \quad \forall\, \omega_1, \omega_2 \qquad (6)$$

which is satisfied if

$$\sum_{S(p,q)} |a(p,q)| < 1 \qquad (7)$$

However if condition (7) is violated then (5) has to be used to investigate its boundedness.

Note that the brightness of an image is real valued and thus a(p,q) must be real valued.

3. Quality of models

In using recursive techniques for restoring additively disturbed images the result will always be tested by a quality criterion. Whatever this criterion may be, one can say that in general the choice of the model will influence the filter results according to the chosen criterion.

To compare different models representing the same image two criteria of quality will be obvious. The first one calculates by (4) the variance of the model error for each chosen MMSE model. The model with the smallest mean square error is preferred. The second criterion calculates the squared error between the autocorrelation function of the original image and the autocorrelation function of the chosen models, and is defined as

$$\varepsilon_R^{\;2} = \sum_{k,l}[(R_{image}(k,l) - R_{model}(k,l)]^2. \qquad (8)$$

Besides those two tests for model quality a third one will be introduced, namely the Cramér-Rao bound for estimators, which is a lower bound for the mean-square-error in estimating a parameter (signalvalue) from a disturbed observation; Nahi(1975). In the following this lower bound will be derived for estimators based on regressive image models.

Consider the two-dimensional field $\{u(i,j)\}$ given in (2), which for conveniance is written as

$$u(i,j) = \sum_{S(p,q)} a(p,q)\, u(i+p,j+q) + b\, e(i,j). \qquad (9)$$

Note that this implies that

$$E\,[e^2(i,j)] = E\,[u^2(i,j)]\,.$$

Suppose that the observation is of the form

$$\begin{aligned} & w(i,j) = u(i,j) + n(i,j) \\ \text{in which}\quad & E\,[u(i,j)\,n(i,j)] = 0\,, \quad \forall\,(i,j)\,, \\ & E\,[n(i,j)\,n(i+k,j+l)] = 0\,, \ \forall\,(k,l) \neq (0,0), \end{aligned} \qquad (10)$$

and n(i,j) is zero-mean Gaussian noise with variance $\sigma_n^{\;2}$.

Then the Cramér-Rao bound in estimating $\hat{u}(i,j)$ from observation $w(i,j)$, given $u(i,j)$ and the probability density function $p(n(i,j))$ will be for unbiased estimators

$$E\left[(u(i,j)-\hat{u}(i,j))^2 \mid u(i,j)\right] \geqslant \frac{1}{E\left[\left(\frac{\delta \log p(w(i,j)\mid u(i,j))}{\delta u(i,j)}\right)^2\right]} \tag{11}$$

where the right hand term is the inverse of the Fisher information I. From (10) the conditional density function $p(w(i,j)\mid u(i,j))$ is

$$p(w(i,j)\mid u(i,j)) = \frac{1}{\sigma_n\sqrt{2\pi}} \exp\left\{-\frac{1}{2\sigma_n^2}(w(i,j)-u(i,j))^2\right\} \tag{12}$$

and

$$\log p(w(i,j)\mid u(i,j)) = C - \frac{1}{2\sigma_n^2}\{w(i,j)-u(i,j)\}^2, \tag{13}$$

where $\quad C = -\log \sigma_n\sqrt{2\pi}.$

It follows from (9), that

$$u(i,j) = f(u(i+p,j+q),\ \forall\ (p,q)\in S(p,q);\ e(i,j)). \tag{14}$$

Thus (13) can be written as

$$\log p(w(i,j)\mid u(i+p,j+q),\ \forall\ (p,q)\in S(p,q);\ e(i,j)) = C +$$

$$-\frac{1}{2\sigma_n^2}\{w(i,j) - \sum_{S(p,q)} a(p,q)\, u(i+p,j+q) - b\, e(i,j)\}^2. \tag{15}$$

Note, that if the field $\{u(i,j)\}$ is known, $e(i,j)$ will be known for a given set $a(p,q)$. Differentiating (15) with respect to its conditions $u(i+p,j+q)$, $\forall$ $(p,q)\in S(p,q)$ and $e(i,j)$, leads to the vector

$$F = \frac{1}{\sigma_n^2}\{w(i,j) - \sum_{S(p,q)} a(p,q)\, u(i+p,j+q) - b\, e(i,j)\}\begin{bmatrix} a(p_1,q_1) \\ \vdots \\ a(p_n,q_n) \\ b \end{bmatrix}, \tag{16}$$

$$(p_i,q_i)\in S(p,q)\ ,\quad i = 1, \ldots, n.$$

From (16) we obtain

$$E\left[\left(\frac{\delta \log p(w(i,j)|u(i,j))}{\delta u(i,j)}\right)^2\right] = E\left[F^t F\right]$$
$$= \frac{1}{\sigma_n^2}\left(\sum_{S(p,q)} a^2(p,q) + b^2\right). \tag{17}$$

Then the Cramér-Rao lower bound for unbiased estimators will be

$$E\left[(u(i,j) - \hat{u}(i,j))^2 | u(i,j)\right] \geq \sigma_n^2 / \left(\sum_{S(p,q)} a(p,q) + b^2\right). \tag{18}$$

4. Some image models

From (2) it can be seen that a large number of different models can be chosen with respect to S(p,q). As a first approach in chosing image models and testing their quality let us consider the rectangular field in figure 1 and the subset S'(p,q) around u(i,j), denoted as X, in figure 2.

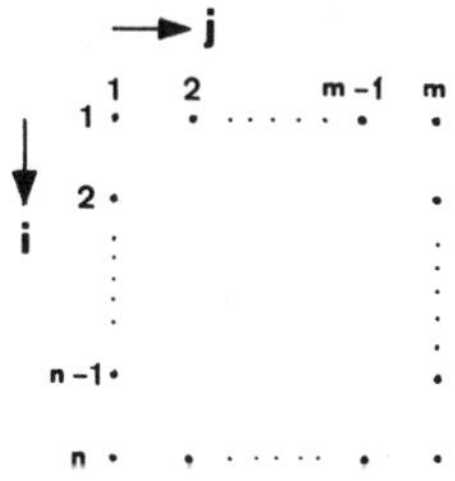

Fig.1

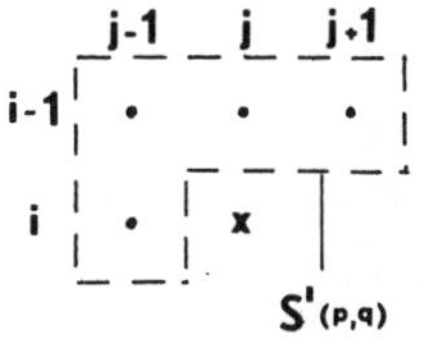

Fig.2

Starting from the left-top corner in fig.1 and scanning the field row after row with the operator S'(p,q) in fig.2 each point of the field can be generated with the models $S(p,q) \subset S'(p,q)$, given the initial values u(i,1), u(j,1) and u(i,m). The possible sets $S(p,q) \subset S'(p,q)$ are tabulated in table 1.

The models in table 1 are causal since only initial values are required. Other subsets S'(p,q) lead to partial difference equations, e.g. Jain(1977) which are semicausal or noncausal, depending on their well-posed conditions.

5. Experimental results.

The models B_1 up to D in table 1 have been tested on the criteria of quality mentioned in Section 3 for images which can be described by the seperable autocorrelation function (Habibi(1972),Jain(1977))

$$R_{image}(k,l) = \rho_x^{|k|}\rho_y^{|l|} \tag{19}$$

where ρ_x and ρ_y are the horizontal and vertical correlation coefficients respectively, and the isotropic autocorrelation function

$$R_{image}(k,l) = \rho^{\sqrt{k^2+s^2l^2}} . \tag{20}$$

The autocorrelation function given in (20) appears e.g. in Jain(1977) with the shape parameter s=1.

In our tests we have preferred to consider a more general autocorrelation function with an isotropic character.

The MMSE coefficients a(p,q) for B_1 up to D have been obtained from (3) for both types of images. It can be shown that cerain models coincide, since one or more coefficients a(p,q) vanish. For example the models C_3 and B_2 and the models C_4 and A_3 coincide for the autocorrelation function as given in (19).

$S_{A1}(p,q)$:	$u(i,j)=a(0,-1)u(i,j-1)+v(i,j)$
$S_{A2}(p,q)$:	$u(i,j)=a(-1,-1)u(i-1,j-1)+v(i,j)$
$S_{A3}(p,q)$:	$u(i,j)=a(-1,0)u(i-1,j)+v(i,j)$
$S_{A4}(p,q)$:	$u(i,j)=a(-1,1)u(i-1,j+1)+v(i,j)$
$S_{B1}(p,q)$:	$u(i,j)=a(0,-1)u(i,j-1)+a(-1,-1)u(i-1,j-1)+v(i,j)$
$S_{B2}(p,q)$:	$u(i,j)=a(0,-1)u(i,j-1)+a(-1,0)u(i-1,j)+v(i,j)$
$S_{B3}(p,q)$:	$u(i,j)=a(0,-1)u(i,j-1)+a(-1,1)u(i-1,j+1)+v(i,j)$
$S_{B4}(p,q)$:	$u(i,j)=a(-1,-1)u(i-1,j-1)+a(-1,0)u(i-1,j)+v(i,j)$
$S_{B5}(p,q)$:	$u(i,j)=a(-1,-1)u(i-1,j-1)+a(-1,1)u(i-1,j+1)+v(i,j)$
$S_{B6}(p,q)$:	$u(i,j)=a(-1,0)u(i-1,j)+a(-1,1)u(i-1,j+1)+v(i,j)$
$S_{C1}(p,q)$:	$u(i,j)=a(0,-1)u(i,j-1)+a(-1,-1)u(i-1,j-1)+a(-1,0)u(i-1,j)+v(i,j)$
$S_{C2}(p,q)$:	$u(i,j)=a(0,-1)u(i,j-1)+a(-1,-1)u(i-1,j-1)+a(-1,1)u(i-1,j+1)+v(i,j)$
$S_{C3}(p,q)$:	$u(i,j)=a(0,-1)u(i,j-1)+a(-1,0)u(i-1,j)+a(-1,1)u(i-1,j+1)+v(i,j)$
$S_{C4}(p,q)$:	$u(i,j)=a(-1,-1)u(i-1,j-1)+a(-1,0)u(i-1,j)+a(-1,1)u(i-1,j+1)+v(i,j)$
$S_D(p,q)$:	$u(i,j)=a(0,-1)u(i,j-1)+a(-1,-1)u(i-1,j-1)+a(-1,0)u(i-1,j)+a(-1,1)u(i-1,j+1)+v(i,j)$

Table 1. Image models.

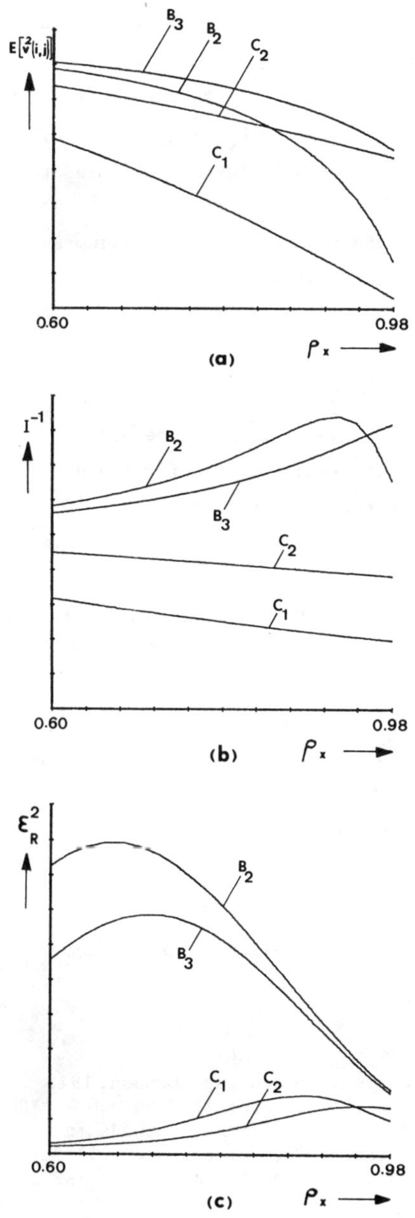

Fig. 3a, b, c. Model errors for three criteria; separable case, $\rho_y = 0.9$.

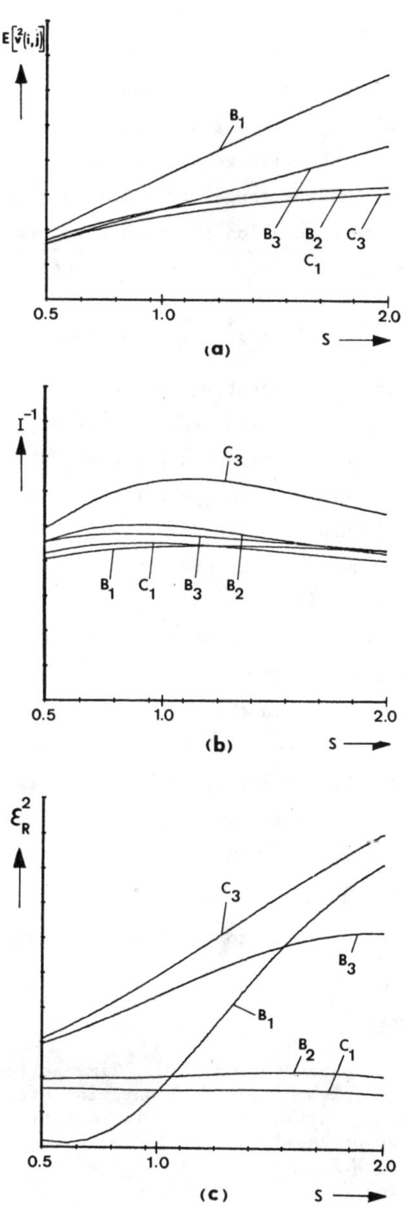

Fig. 4a, b, c. Model errors for three criteria; isotropic case, $\rho = 0.9$.

Some of the most typical results of testing the remaining models for separable images are given in figures 3a, 3b and 3c and for images with isotropic character in figures 4a, 4b and 4c. In the figures 3a, 3b and 3c the vertical correlation ρ_y is equal 0.9 and the horizontal correlation ρ_x ranges from 0.6 to 0.98. In the figures 4a, 4b and 4c the correlation ρ is taken as 0.9 and the shape parameter s ranges from 0.5 to 2.0.

The autocorrelation function $R_{model}(k,l)$ in (8) is obtained by applying an inverse fast fourier transform to the output spectrum (Larimore(1977))

$$G_u(\omega_1,\omega_2) = |H(j\omega_1,j\omega_2)|^2 \; G_v(\omega_1,\omega_2) \tag{21}$$

for uncorrelated input v(i,j) and k,l = 1, . . . , 5.

As can be conducted from figures 3a, 3b and 3c, model C_1 is to be preferred, as can be expected because it is a direct extension of a first order Markov process both in the horizontal and the vertical direction.

Experimental results for ρ_y = 0.8, 0.7, 0.6, which are not depicted here, show the same order of preference.

In figures 4a, 4b and 4c it is shown that the models B_2 and C_1 are quite insensitive to variations in the shape parameter s, as can be expected from their spatial configuration.

We have shown in this paper that there exists a certain sensitivity in the choice of the model with respect to the actual autocorrelation function of the image and the quality criterion which is used.

Presently other models are subject to these criteria.

Acknowledgement.

The authors wish to thank prof. Y. Boxma for helpful discussions and comments.

References.

Box, G.E.P. and Jenkins, G.M., Time series analyses. Holden-day, London, 1971
Habibi, A., Two-dimensional Bayesian estimate of images. Proc.IEEE,vol 60,7,'72
Jain, A.K., Partial differential equations and finite-difference methods in image processing, Part 1: Image representation. JOTA, vol 23, no.1, 1977
Larimore, W.E., Statistical inference on stationary random fields. Proc. IEEE, vol.65, no.6, june 1977.
Nahi, N.E., Estimation Theory and Applications. John Wiley, New York, 1976.
Woods, J.W., Two-dimensional discrete Markovian fields. IEEE Trans. on Information Theory, vol.IT-18, no 2., March 1972

Analysis of Grain Contacts in Rocks Using Graph Statistics

G. Karlsson, Lund

Summary. Neighborhood relations among different kinds of mineral grains, of great interest in the analysis of compositional variations in rocks, can be described by stochastic graph models. The testing of such models is here based on graph statistics which yield the frequencies of pairs and triples of mineral grains having different kinds of neighborhood properties. Such frequencies, called dyad and triad count statistics, are studied for a simple model and for some empirical data obtained from geological maps. The technique can also be applied to maps in general. The results illustrate that dyad and triad counts can be used as summary statistics for the purpose of evaluating and fitting of structural models.

Key words. Graph, map, neighborhood relation, subgraph counts, structural models.

1 Introduction

A thin section cut through a rock will appear under a microscope as a map with each type of mineral grains having different colors. This map, like maps in general, can be represented by an undirected graph having vertices representing the regions and edges connecting those vertices which correspond to regions with a common border line.

Graphs consisting of a great number of vertices and edges are usually described by subgraph counts. We will limit ourselves to subgraph counts of order one, two and three; these are called vertex, dyad and triad counts. The vertex count will give the distribution of the different kinds of mineral grains present in the rock, i.e. its composition, while the dyad and triad counts will describe how these mineral grains are distributed in relation to each other, i.e. the texture of the rock.

In an undirected graph there are dyads with and without an edge for each combination of vertex colors i and j. The dyads will be denoted (i-j) and (i j) with dyads counts f(i-j) and f(i j). A triad having vertices of colors i,j and k can be brought into one of four groups depending on the number of its edges

$$(i\ j\ k),\ (i\text{-}j\ k),\ (i\text{-}j\text{-}k),\ (i\underline{\text{-}j\text{-}}k)$$

where e.g. (i-j-k) means that j is adjacent to i and k but i and k are not adjacent. The corresponding triad counts are denoted

$$f(i\ j\ k),\ldots,f(i\underline{\text{-}j\text{-}}k)$$

Three regions described by a triad of type $(i\underline{\text{-}j\text{-}}k)$ can have the two different kinds of neighborhood relationships illustrated in Figure 1 and 2. In Figure 1 the regions have one point in common but in Figure 2 they have no point in common.

Figure 1

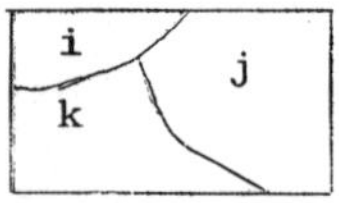

Figure 2

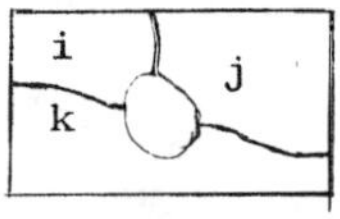

The aim of this paper is to show how a simple stochastic model based on dyad and triad counts can be used in analysing grain contacts in a rock. The empirical data are presented in section 2 and the model in section 3. In section 4 we make some comparisons and the final section is devoted to concluding remarks.

2 Empirical data

We are going to compare three geological maps containing four types of mineral grains labelled 0: plagioclase, 1: quartz, 2: microcline and 3:other types of mineral grains. Maps 1 and 3 are very similar in both the number of grains and their composition, while map 2 is quite different in these respects.

There are $2K + 2\binom{K}{2}$ undirected dyads and $4K + 12\binom{K}{2} + 8\binom{K}{3}$ undirected triads with at most K vertex colors; see e.g. Frank (1978).

With K = 4 we thus have 20 dyads: 10 with an edge and 10 without. We have further 120 triads: 20 with three edges, 40 with two edges, 40 with one edge and 20 with no edge.

Let N be the number of vertices and let D_s be the number of dyads with s edges. Let further T_t be the number of triads with t edges. Table 1 shows N, D_1, T_1, T_2 and T_3 for maps 1, 2 and 3.

The empirical data in tables 2-7 are shown in form of relative counts

$$100\ f(i)/N,\ 100\ f(i\ j)/D_0,\ldots,100\ f(i\underline{-j-}k)/T_3$$

where we note that triads of type (i-j k) have the same distribution as dyads of type (i-j) as far as relative counts are concerned.

By using tables 1-7 many comparisons between special types of triads can be made. We note, for instance, that the triad counts f(1-0-2) and f(1-0-3) are always greater than f(0-1-2), f(0-2-1) and f(0-1-3), f(0-3-1) respectively. In order to make inferences, however, a greater number of maps is needed.

Table 1 Total number of vertices, dyads and triads

Map	1	2	3
N	197	301	194
D_1	453	786	421
T_1	81782	225518	75111
T_2	2840	3899	2457
T_3	291	566	269

Table 2 Vertices of type i: counts in per cent

Map \ i	0	1	2	3
1	12	67	12	10
2	12	33	42	13
3	11	61	20	8

Table 3 Dyads of type (i j): counts in per cent

Map \ ij	00	01	02	03	11	12	13	22	23	33
1	1	15	3	2	45	16	13	1	2	1
2	1	8	10	3	11	28	10	17	11	2
3	1	14	4	2	37	24	10	4	3	1

Table 4 Dyads of type (i-j): counts in per cent

Map \ ij	00	01	02	03	11	12	13	22	23	33
1	4	28	4	3	19	21	11	4	4	3
2	3	10	13	5	6	31	3	22	3	4
3	1	18	11	2	16	35	1	9	5	0

Table 5 Triads of type (i-j-k): counts in per cent

	Map				Map				Map				Map		
ijk	1	2	3	ijk	1	2	3	ijk	1	2	3	ijk	1	2	3
000	0	1	0	102	7	5	8	033	1	0	0	213	0	0	0
001	6	3	3	021	2	4	6	303	0	7	0	132	1	1	0
010	1	1	1	013	1	0	0	111	3	1	4	133	2	0	0
002	1	3	1	103	3	3	1	112	3	6	4	313	0	0	0
020	0	1	1	031	2	0	0	121	10	6	21	222	1	9	3
003	0	2	0	022	1	4	3	113	2	0	0	223	1	2	3
030	0	0	0	202	0	4	2	131	6	1	0	232	0	0	0
011	3	1	2	023	0	0	0	122	5	14	13	233	0	0	0
101	32	2	9	203	0	1	1	212	0	9	2	323	0	0	1
012	1	4	2	032	0	0	0	123	3	2	8	333	1	1	0

Table 6 Triads of type (i j k): counts in per cent

	Map				Map				Map				Map		
ijk	1	2	3	ijk	1	2	3	ijk	1	2	3	ijk	1	2	3
000	0	0	0	012	5	10	9	111	31	4	23	133	2	2	1
001	2	1	2	013	5	3	4	112	16	14	22	222	0	7	1
002	0	2	1	022	0	6	1	113	13	5	10	223	0	7	1
003	0	1	0	023	1	4	1	122	2	17	7	233	0	2	0
011	16	4	13	033	0	1	0	123	5	11	6	333	0	0	0

Table 7 Triads of type (i-j-k): counts in per cent

	Map				Map				Map				Map		
ijk	1	2	3	ijk	1	2	3	ijk	1	2	3	ijk	1	2	3
000	1	1	0	012	12	15	20	111	3	1	3	133	2	1	0
001	8	4	3	013	8	2	1	112	12	10	21	222	2	10	3
002	1	4	2	022	0	9	8	113	9	1	0	223	1	3	3
003	0	1	0	023	0	1	3	122	8	26	16	233	1	0	1
011	22	3	14	033	0	5	0	123	6	2	1	333	2	2	0

3 A stochastic graph model

Consider a graph with N vertices and $R = D_1$ edges, where each vertex can have one of K colors occuring with frequencies $N_1, \ldots, N_K$.

Suppose that the edges are randomly distributed over the $\binom{N}{2}$ pairs of vertices. The probability that we will get a triad with r edges is then

$$P_r = \binom{3}{r}\binom{\binom{N}{2} - 3}{R - r}\Big/\binom{\binom{N}{2}}{R} \qquad r = 0,1,2,3$$

and the expected number of triads with r edges and vertex colors i,j and k is given by

$$N_{ijk}\, P_r$$

where

$$N_{ijk} = \begin{cases} N_i N_j N_k & \text{if } i \neq j \quad i \neq k \quad j \neq k \\ \binom{N_i}{2} N_k & \text{if } i = j \neq k \\ \binom{N_i}{3} & \text{if } i = j = k \end{cases}$$

If $\binom{N}{2}$ is large and $p = R/\binom{N}{2}$ then P_r can be approximated by $\binom{3}{r}p^r(1 - p)^{3-r}$ and we thus get the expectation

$$N_{ijk}\binom{3}{r}p^r(1 - p)^{3-r}$$

for triads with r edges and vertex colors i,j and **k.**

In the above model we have not considered the possibility of differences occuring when the propensity to be adjacent varies depending on the colors of the vertices. This possibility can be taken into account e.g. according to the following stochastic model.

Let $R_{ii} = f(i-i)$ and suppose that R_{ii} edges are randomly distributed over $\binom{N_i}{2}$ pairs of vertices with color i. The expected number of triads with r edges and all their vertices of color i is then approximately

$$\binom{N_i}{3}\binom{3}{r}p^r(1 - p)^{3-r} \qquad r = 0,1,2,3$$

where $p = R_{ii}/\binom{N_i}{2}$. The expected number of other types of triads is derived in a similar manner.

4 Some comparisons

A triad can be classified according to the number of its edges and the coloring of its vertices. A K-color map can thus be characterized by a table consisting of $4\binom{K+2}{3}$ cells. For each cell the expected number of triads is computed according to the first model in the preceding section. In this model the expected counts in per cent for (i j k), (i-j k), (i-j-k) and (i-j-k) will be the same; these counts are given for maps 1,2 and 3 in the following table.

Table 8 Triads with no, one two or three edges: counts in per cent

	Map				Map				Map				Map		
ijk	1	2	3	ijk	1	2	3	ijk	1	2	3	ijk	1	2	3
000	0	0	0	012	6	10	8	111	30	4	22	133	2	2	1
001	3	1	1	013	5	3	3	112	16	14	22	222	0	7	1
002	0	2	2	022	0	6	1	113	13	4	9	223	0	7	1
003	0	1	0	023	1	4	1	122	3	17	7	233	0	2	0
011	16	4	13	033	0	1	0	123	5	11	6	333	0	0	0

The expected counts in per cent in table 8 are to be compared with the observed counts in per cent in tables 5-7. We note, for instance, that there seems to be a difference between triads which have two vertices of color 0 and triads which have two vertices of color 1.

By using the second model it is possible, for example, to distinguish between triads of types (i-j-k) and (i-k-j) for distinct i, j and k. Some comparisons are made in table 9 for maps 1 and 2.

Table 9 Observed and expected number of triads: counts in per mille

	Map 1		Map 2	
Triad	observed	expected	observed	expected
0 2-3	4	4	4	3
0-2 3	4	4	18	18
0_2_3	3	3	24	23

0-2-3	4	4	5	5
0 2-3	4	4	2	6
0-2 3	5	3	7	32

There will usually be good agreement between observed and expected values for triads of the types (i j k) and (i-j k). For other types of triads, however, the goodness of fit of the model varies considerably.

5 Concluding remarks

The study of neighborhood relationships in rocks can be of great interest. Flinn (1969) shows, for instance, that different kinds of neighborhood relationships can occur in two rocks with the same composition and grain size.

Dyads of type (i-j) for K-color maps have been studied for a long time; see e.g. Krishna Iyer (1950).

We have limited ourselves to subgraph counts of at most order 3. The next step would be tetrad counts. However, the number of different tetrads, 996 with K = 4, as well as the amount of computation will increase substantially.

By developing more sophisticated models where e.g. grain size and the number of neighbors are taken into account the number of triads with two or three edges may be estimated with greater accuracy.

References

Flinn D., Grain contacts in crystalline rocks, Lithos, 3, 361-370, 1969

Frank O., Moment properties of subgraph counts in stochastic graphs, To appear in Ann. New York Acad. Sci., 1978

Krishna Iyer P.V.A., The theory of probability distributions of points on a lattice, Ann. Math. Stat., 21, 198-217, 1950

On the Variable Kernel Model for Multivariate Nonparametric Density Estimation

J.W. Raatgever and R.P.W. Duin, Delft

Summary

The variable kernel estimation is a method of nonparametric multidimensional density estimation. The estimator is written, like the Parzen one, as a average of kernels. The smoothness or window-sizes of the kernels, however, depend on the distances to the nearest neighbours. With simulations from normal and lognormal distributions the Parzen estimator and the variable kernel estimator have been compared. For a lognormal density the variable kernel method appeared to be superior to the Parzen estimator. For a normal distribution, however, both methods gave similar results in particular for small sample sizes.

Moreover, a criterion for the estimation of the parameters of the variable kernels, different from the criteria of Breiman et al., is proposed and investigated. The results of both criteria are compared.

KEYWORDS

nonparametric multidimensional density estimation; variable kernel estimation; Parzen estimators.

I. Introduction

Many ways are known for the estimation of a probability density function in a multidimensional continuous space. Cover (1972) gave a survey of these methods. Parzen (1962) introduced the estimation using kernel functions in the training elements. A disadvantage of this method may be that the kernel width is constant over the entire space. Loftsgaarden and Quesenberry (1965) gave a method using windows in which the number of training elements is fixed. So the width of these windows is variable. The variable kernel model, introduced by Breiman et. al. (1977) can be considered as an intermediate form between both methods. Breiman et al. investigated the case of a two-dimensional normal distribution estimated by 400 training elements. It seems to be of interest for practice to test the variable kernel method using smaller sample sizes and different dimensions. Besides it is interesting to test other distributions e.g. having sharp peaks and long tails. Just for these distributions one would expect an improvement with respect to the Parzen estimation, because by the variable kernel method the kernels may be adapted individually to the local density.

The density estimation of the variable kernel method is given by:

$$\hat{f}(x) = \frac{1}{n} \sum_{i=1}^{n} \left(\frac{1}{\alpha_k d_{i,k}} \right)^m K \left(\frac{||\underline{x}-\underline{x}_i||}{\alpha_k d_{i,k}} \right) \tag{1}$$

in which:

$\hat{f}(.)$	= estimated density
$\underline{x}_i$ (i; 1,...,n)	= m dimensional training elements
n	= number of training elements
α_k	= multiplier factor, for a given value of k
$d_{i,k}$	= distance to the k'th nearest neighbour in a point $\underline{x}_i$
K	= kernel function
m	= dimension
$\|\|.\|\|$	= the Euclidian norm.

Different choices can be made for the kernel function. We use the normal kernel, so:

$$\hat{f}(x) = \frac{1}{n} \sum_{i=1}^{n} \left(\frac{1}{\alpha_k d_{i,k} \sqrt{2\pi}} \right)^m \exp \left(-\tfrac{1}{2} \frac{||\underline{x}-\underline{x}_i||^2}{(\alpha_k d_{i,k})^2} \right) \tag{2}$$

Breiman et al. give a goodness-of-fit criterion and a strategy that selects an optimal k and α. This criterium is defined as

$$\min_{k,\alpha} \hat{S} = \sum_{j=1}^{n} (\hat{w}(j) - j/n)^2 \tag{3}$$

in which:

$$\hat{w}(j) = e^{-n \hat{f}(\underline{x}_j) V(d_{j,1})} \tag{4}$$

The values of $\hat{w}(j)$ are ranked so that $\hat{w}(1) < \dots < \hat{w}(n)$ and V(r) is the volume of an m-dimensional sphere of radius r. A drawback of this criterion is that the ranking of the $\{\hat{w}(j);\ j=1,n\}$ makes $\hat{S}$ a non-analytical expression of k and α. So, given a k, different values of α should be tried until an optimal α is found.

Another criterion, suggested by Hermans and Habbema (1974) and Duin (1976) for the Parzen estimation does give a analytic expression in α and k. Modified for variable kernels this criterion is written as:

$$\max_{k,\alpha} L(k,\alpha) = \prod_{j=1}^{n} \hat{f}_j(\underline{x}_j) \tag{5}$$

in which:

$$\hat{f}_j(\underline{x}) = \frac{1}{n} \sum_{\substack{i=1 \\ i\neq j}}^{n} \left(\frac{1}{\alpha_k d_{i,k} \sqrt{2\pi}} \right)^m \exp\left(-\frac{1}{2} \frac{||\underline{x}-\underline{x}_i||^2}{(\alpha_k d_{i,k})^2} \right) \tag{6}$$

Using this criterion it is possible, for given k, to find an optimal value of α from

$$\frac{dL(k,\alpha)}{d\,\alpha} = 0 \tag{7}$$

by which (5) can be optimized fast.

For judging the obtained estimate $\hat{f}(x)$ Breiman et al. used three error measures:

1. Percent of Variance Not Explained (PVNE)

$$\text{PVNE} = \frac{1}{\hat{\sigma}_f^2} \cdot \frac{1}{n} \sum_{j=1}^{n} \left(f(\underline{x}_j) - \hat{f}(\underline{x}_j) \right)^2 \times 100 \tag{8}$$

2. Mean Absolute Error, Percent (MAE)

$$\text{MAE} = \frac{1}{n\hat{\mu}_f} \sum_{j=1}^{n} |f(\underline{x}_j) - \hat{f}(\underline{x}_j)| \times 100 \tag{9}$$

3. Mean Percent Error (MPE)

$$\text{MPE} = \frac{1}{n} \sum_{j=1}^{n} \frac{|f(\underline{x}_j) - \hat{f}(\underline{x}_j)|}{f(\underline{x}_j)} \times 100 \tag{10}$$

in which $\hat{\mu}_f$ and $\hat{\sigma}_f^2$ are given by:

$$\hat{\mu}_f = \frac{1}{n} \sum_{j=1}^{n} f(\underline{x}_j) \tag{11}$$

$$\hat{\sigma}_f^2 = \frac{1}{n} \sum_{j=1}^{n} (f(\underline{x}_j) - \hat{\mu}_f)^2 \tag{12}$$

These error measures take only into account the error in $\hat{f}(x)$ for the training elements $\underline{x}_i$ (i=1,n). For that reason the Kolmogorov variational distance, D, is added as an error measure. This distance computes the integral of the estimation error over the entire space, which may be considered as a more objective measure.
The D is given by:

$$D = 1 - \int_{\forall x} \min\,(f(x), \hat{f}(x))dx \qquad (13)$$

In all our experiments D has been computed by a Monte Carlo procedure based on 100 random points generated according to f(x) and 100 random points generated according to $\hat{f}(x)$.

The following three points are investigated for normal and lognormal distributions and sample sizes varying from 10 to 100.

1. The two criteria $\hat{S}$ (3) and L (5) are compared by the resulting optimal values of k and α, and the error measures D, PVNE, MAE and MPE.
2. The variable kernel estimation is compared with the Parzen estimation. This is done in order to test whether the improvement found by Breiman et al. is also found in the case of normal distributions with small training sample sizes and in the case of lognormal distributions.
3. For each training set the criterion L is optimized for the variable kernel method as well as for the Parzen estimation. For the two distributions used, an investigation is made into the correspondence between the highest L value (Parzen or variable kernel) and the best estimation, measured by D.

II. Selecting an optimal α and k

In order to investigate the behaviour of $L(\alpha,k)$ grids have been made, in which the value of $L(\alpha,k)$ is plotted for different values of k and α. The α-values are varied from 0.1 to 1.5 in steps of 0.1. The values of k are varied from 1 to n-1 because n-1 is the maximum number of neighbours possible for a sample size n. In general the grids looked as follows:
From the point k=1 and $\alpha \approx 1.5$, a mountain-ridge of high values of L, leads to the point k = (n-1) and small α, e.g. α = 0.1. Essential is, that for each k usually just one optimal value of α, α_k is found. Along the mountain-ridge generally more tops are found. These tops may differ in height.

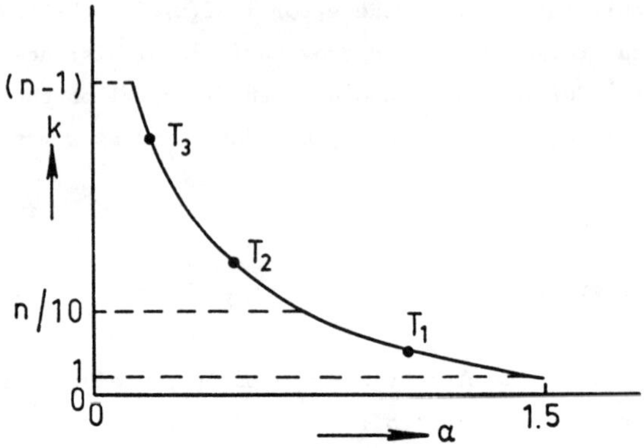

Fig. 1. Example of a mountain-ridge of $L(\alpha,k)$

The same kind of grids were made for the $\hat{S}$ criterion. These grids look similar, the mountain-ridge, however, is often somewhat shifted to the right, what implies more smoothing. Also in this case more tops were found. The number and location of these tops usually differed from those in the $L(\alpha,k)$-grids.

The following strategy for optimizing α and k was proposed by Breiman et al. For k, a fraction of n is taken, e.g. 10%. For this particular k, α is optimized. The optimal value, α_k, is used for finding a λ defined by:

$$\lambda = \frac{\alpha_k\left(\bar{d}_k\right)^2}{\sigma(d_k)} \qquad (14)$$

in which: $\bar{d}_k$ = mean of the distances to the k'th nearest neighbour over the training sample; $\bar{d}_k = \frac{1}{n}\sum_{i=1}^{n} d_{i,k}$

$\sigma(d_k)$ = standard deviation of d_k

After that k is varied in two directions, while for each k the corresponding values of α are calculated by (14). This is an approximation of a search along the mountain-ridge. In the example of fig. 1, by this T_1 or T_2 is found, and not T_3, which may be the highest top (the lowest value of $\hat{S}$).

In order to avoid such difficulties, we scanned the whole mountain-ridge, looking for the highest value of L. Summarizing our strategy for optimizing L is:

1. Scan the mountain-ridge in steps of e.g. $k = n/7$. The corrresponding α_k is found by (7). Suppose the k, belonging to the highest value of L, is k_1.
2. k is varied from k_1 to both sides until a maximum L is found. For each k α_k is found by (7) like in step 1.

The α_k is computed from $dL/d\alpha = 0$ by a iterative method in both steps. It is possible to make the programs faster by computing α_k from a simular relation between α_k and k as (14). If the smoothing parameter h of the Parzen estimation is selected with the same criterion L, the following relations may be used:

$$h = \alpha_k \bar{d}_k \tag{15}$$

or

$$h = \alpha_k \left(\overline{d_k^{\,2}}\right)^{\frac{1}{2}} \tag{16}$$

It appeared from the simulations that these relations hold better than (14). Applying (15) or (16) will give a little inaccuracy in α_k, while a saving in computing time is reached. The criterion L will be very feasable in that case. In the following simulations, however, the relations (15) or (16) were not yet used.

III. Simulation results

The figures 2, 3 and 4 give the estimates of the Kolmogorov variational distance, $\hat{D}$, for a normal distribution with m = 1,2 and 5. The distributions have been estimated using the Parzen method and the variable kernel method. The Parzen method was optimized by the criterion L. For the variable kernel method both L and $\hat{S}$ are used. So three curves are found. The simulations have been repeated over 10 runs. The curves show the mean of these runs.

It appears that the variable kernel method using L behaves slightly better than the one using $\hat{S}$. The variable kernel estimation is not significantly better than the Parzen estimation. Only for small m and n = 100 a small improvement may exist. This corresponds with the results of Breiman et al. who found an improvement, in the case of m=2 and n=400. A tentative conclusion is that for normal distributions the variable kernel method gives a better performance only for large sample sizes with respect to the dimension.

The simulations of a lognormal density give quite different results

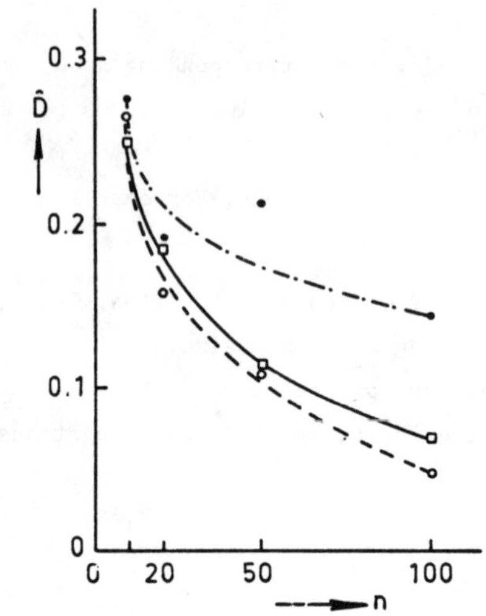

Fig. 2. $\hat{D}$ as a function of the number of training elements for a one-dimensional normal distribution

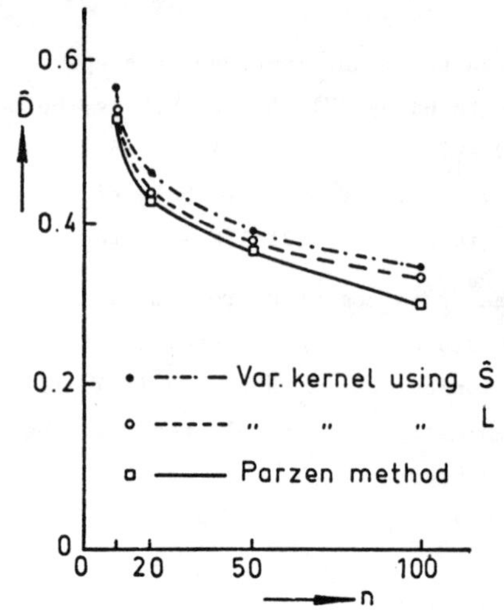

Fig. 4. $\hat{D}$ as a function of the number of training elements for a five-dimensional normal distribution

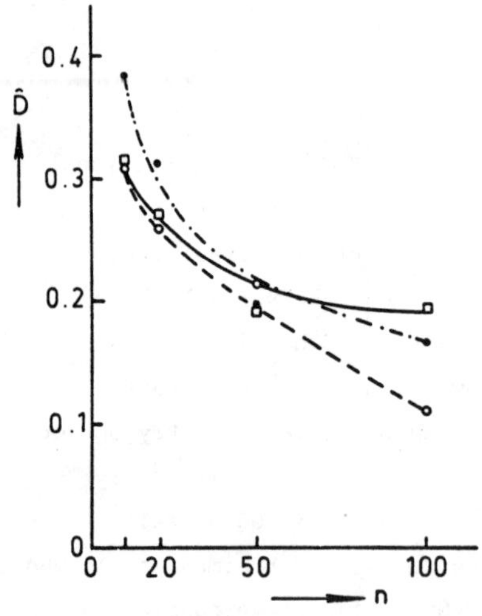

Fig. 3. $\hat{D}$ as a function of the number of training elements for a two-dimensional normal distribution

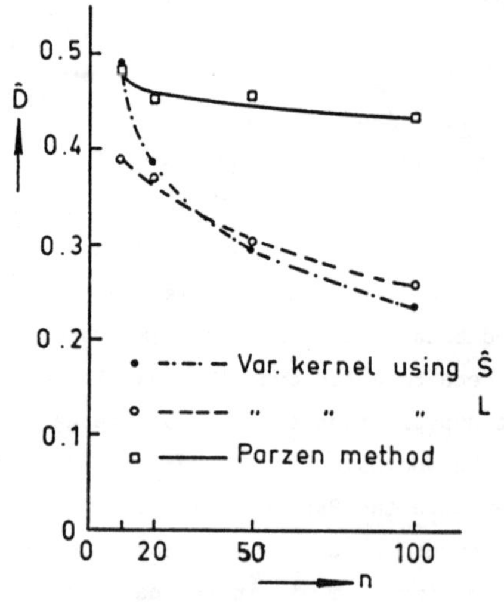

Fig. 5. $\hat{D}$ as a function of the number of training elements for a two-dimensional lognormal distribution

(fig. 5). $\hat{D}$ is much smaller for both variable kernel methods, than for the Parzen estimation. For this distribution the variable kernel method shows its real strength. The difference between the methods using $\hat{S}$ and L is rather small again. For judging this one better uses all error measures: D, PVNE, MAE and MPE.

Conclusions of D, PVNE, MAE and MPE:
For all simulation runs the number of times L respectively $\hat{S}$ gave the best variable kernel estimate, measured by D, PVNE, MAE or MPE, has been counted. The results are shown in table 1. The total number of runs is 155 for normal as well as lognormal distributions.

criterion	D	PVNE	MAE	MPE
L	96	109	101	51
$\hat{S}$	59	46	54	104

Table 1. Comparison of L and $\hat{S}$.

It appears that D, and even stronger PVNE and MAE prefer the method with criterion L. The measure MPE, however, prefers $\hat{S}$. Table 2 gives an impression of the correspondence between the four measures. Here the number of times that each two of the measures correspond, has been scored. The total number of runs is again 155.

	D	PVNE	MAE	MPE
D		109	106	87
PVNE	109		147	88
MAE	106	147		94
MPE	87	88	94	

Table 2. Correspondence of measures

The correlation between PVNE and MAE appears remarkable high. The measure MPE is rather apart from the other three measures.

The parameter k
Figure 6 shows the relation between n and $\bar{k}$, i.e. the optimal k, found by

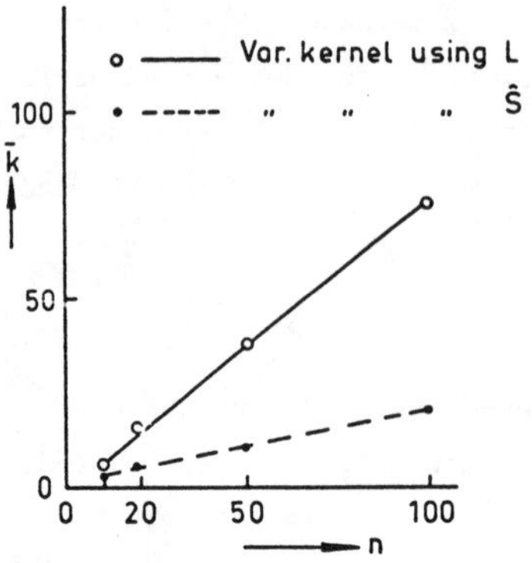

Fig. 6. $\bar{k}$ as a function of the number of training elements for a two-dimensional normal distribution, using criteria $\hat{S}$ and L.

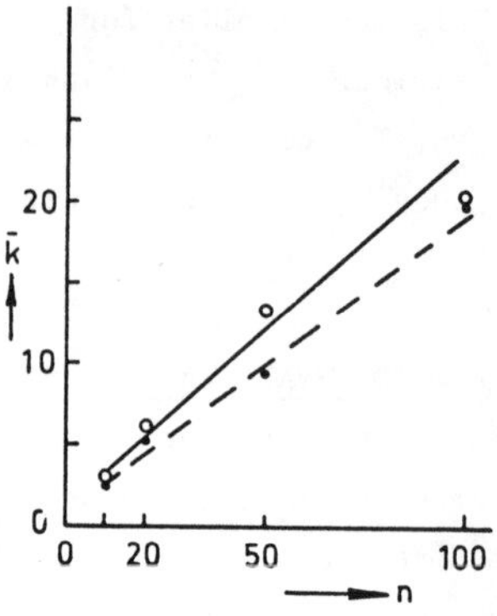

Fig. 7. $\bar{k}$ as a function of the number of training elements for a two-dimensional lognormal distribution using criteria $\hat{S}$ and L.

L and $\hat{S}$, averaged over 10 runs, in the case of a two-dimensional normal distribution. The fact that the criterion L finds much higher values of k, was already discussed in chapter II. This is not a result of a real difference between the two methods, but only of the way the first estimate of k is made in the method of Breiman et al. In our experiments we took k 20% of n for this estimate. (Breiman et al. suggested a choice of e.g. 10%).

Considering the fact that the results of estimation using $\hat{S}$ or L do not differ very much, it appears that k can vary over a wide range. However, we have to remember that all k's are not arbitrary chosen, but are values of k that give a maximum in the mountain-ridge, either from $\hat{S}$ or from L. So arbitrary choosing of k may be dangerous.

It should be noted that $\bar{k}$ depends linearly on n. So taking k as a fixed part of n seems to be attractive. If e.g. $k = (4/5)n$ is chosen, a functional relation between k and n is obtained like proposed by Cover (1972) who suggested $k = \sqrt{n}$ for the method of Loftsgaarden and Quesenberry. But first we have to realize that $\bar{k}$ is the mean over 10 runs and the variation in k is very high. Moreover, the results of the simulations of a lognormal density (fig. 7) show that the $\bar{k}$-values found by the criterion L are much smaller than $(4/5)n$. So the relation $k = (4/5)n$ does not hold for every distribution and selection of k using a criterion remains necessary.

Selection of the estimation method by L

The criterion L was used to select the smoothing parameter h for the Parzen estimation as well as the k and α for the variable kernel estimation. So for each run two values of L were obtained. An examination has been made into the probability of choosing the better of the two methods, using these values. From the simulations it appears that in the case of the normal distribution, the values of L for the Parzen estimation and for the variable kernel method show no significant difference. In the case of the lognormal density the L values of the variable kernel method are significantly larger. So indeed choosing between the two methods can be done by comparing the values of L.

Conclusions

The conclusion of Breiman et al. that, estimating a normal distribution, the variable kernel estimator has to be preferred to the Parzen estimator, is confirmed. This conclusion, however, is restricted to the case of large sample sizes. In the case of few training elements the variable kernels give no improvement compared to fixed kernels. The variable kernel method seems to need more training elements for a good estimate.

When a lognormal distribution is estimated, the variable kernel method is superior indeed.

Comparing the two criteria $\hat{S}$ and L it can be concluded that the method using $\hat{S}$, with a somewhat changed strategy, and the proposed method, using L, give very similar results. However, $\hat{S}$ appears to use somewhat more computing time. Both criteria lead to a good estimation. If calculated for different estimaters (e.g. Parzen or variable kernel) criterion L can be used to select the best estimator. The possibility of using $\hat{S}$ for this purpose has not been investigated.

References

Breiman L., Meisel W. and Purcell E., *Variable Kernel Estimates of Multivariate Densities*, Technometrics,vol.19,no.2,1977

Cover T.M., *A Hierarchy of Probability Density Function Estimates*, in Frontiers of Pattern Recognition (ed. S. Watanabe), Academic Press,1972

Duin R.P.W., *On the Choice of Smoothing Parameters for Parzen Estimators of Probability Density Functions*, IEEE trans. on computers,nov. 1976

Habbema J.D.F., Hermans J. and van den Broek K., *A Stepwise Discriminant Analysis Program Using Density Estimation*, COMPSTAT 1974, Proceedings in Computational Statistics, Wien, Physica Verlag

Loftsgaarden P.O. and Quesenberry C.P., *A Nonparametric Estimate of a Multivariate Probability Density Function*, Ann. Math. Statist.,28, 1049-1051,1965

Parzen E., *On the Estimation of a Probability Density Function and the Mode*, Ann. Math. Statist.,33,1065-1076,1962

Author-Index (Name, Number of Session, Page of Proceedings)

Address-List of First Authors

Aitken, C.G.G., Livingstone Tower, University of Strathclyde, 26 Richmond Street, Glasgow G1 1XH, Great Britain.

Asano, C., Research Institute of Fundamental Information Science, Kyushu University 33, Fukuoka, 812, Japan.

Baker, R.J., Rothamsted Experimental Station, Harpenden, Herts AL5 2JQ, Great Britain.

Banfield, C.F., Rothamsted Experimental Station, Harpenden, Herts AL5 2JQ, Great Britain.

Barhorst, A.J., Akzo Research Laboratories, Velperweg 76, Postbus 209, Arnhem, The Netherlands.

Baron, J.S., Dept. of Business Studies, Aytoun Street, Manchester MI 3GH, United Kingdom.

Bernard, G., Universite de Paris XIII, Institute Universitair de Technologie, 2 Rue de la Liberte, 93200 Saint Denis, France.

Best, D.J., C.S.I.R.O., Division of Mathematics and Statistics, P.O.Box 52, 2113 North Ryde, N.S.W. Australia.

Bianchi, C., IBM Scientific Center-Pisa, Via S. Maria 67, 56100 Pisa, Italy.

de Biase, L., Istituto Matematico, Via L. Cicognara 7, 20129 Milano, Italia.

Biemond, J., Lab. for Information Theory, Dept. of Electrical Engineering, Delft University of Technology, Mekelweg 4, 2208 Delft, The Netherlands.

Birkenfeld, W., Universität Bielefeld, Fakultät für Wirtschaftswissenschaften, Statistik und Datenverarbeitung, Postfach 8640, 4800 Bielefeld 1, W.-Germany

Blohm, D.S., IBM Corporation, Dept. 567/Bldg. 300–425, Hopewell Junction, N.Y. 12533, USA.

Bruynooghe, M., Universite d'Aix-Marseille II, Centre de Recherche d'Economie des Transports, 13 Avenue Gaston Berger, 100 Aix-en-Provence, France.

Bryce, G.R., Brigham Young University, Dept. of Statistics, Provo, Utah 84602, USA.

Buckley, K., 12642 Chapel Road, Clifton, Virginia 22024, USA.

Buhler, R., Princeton University Computer Centre, Prospect Ave. 87, Princeton, N.J. 08540, USA.

Bunday, B.D., University of Bradford, Dept. of Statistics, Bradford West, Yorkshire BD7 1DP, United Kingdom.

Caillot, P., Institute Informatique et Mathematiques en Sciences Sociales, Batiment Sciences Humaines et Mathematiques, 47X–38040 Grenoble Cedex, France.

Chiu, W.W., T.J. Watson Research Center, Yorktown Heights, N.Y. 10598, USA.

Clunies-Ross, C., 49, Norland Square, London W11 4PZ, England.

Collombier, D., Universite Paul Sabatier, Laboratoire de Statistique, 118, Route de Narbonne, 31077 Toulouse Cedex, France.

Conley, W., Coordinator of Quantitative Methods in Managerial Systems Concentration, CC335C, University of Wisconsin at Greenbay, Green Bay, Wisconsin 54302, USA.

Conrad, S.A., Dept. of Management Sciences, Umist, P.O.Box 88, Manchester 1, England.

Critchley, F., University of Glasgow, Dept. of Statistics, University Gardens, Glasgow G12 8QW, United Kingdom.

Darnton, G., Chelmer Inst. of Higher Education, Faculty of Technology, Computer Advisory Unit, Victoria Road South, Chelmsford CMI ILL, United Kingdom.

Degens, P.O., Max Planck Institut für Psychiatrie, Kräpelinstr. 10–12, 8000 München 40, W.-Germany.

Dubois, D.M., Institute of Mathematics, University of Liege, Avenue des Tilleuls 17, 4000 Liege, Belgium.

Dutter, R., Technische Universität Graz, Hamerlinggasse 6, 8010 Graz, Austria.

Ecob, R., Dept. of Mathematics, City University, St.John Street, London EC1V 4PB, England.

Fearn, T., Dept. of Statistics and Computer Science, University College London, Gower Street, London WCIE 6BT, England.

Frank, O., Dept. of Statistics, University of Lund, Fack, 220 05 Lund, Sweden.

Franklin, M.F., A.R.C. Unit of Statistics, University of Edinburgh, The King's Buildings, Mayfield Road, EH9 3JZ Edinburgh, United Kingdom.

Gabriel, K.R., Univ. of Rochester, Medical Center, Box 630, Rochester, N.Y. 14642, USA.

Gorgerat, J.-F., Sandoz AG, Lichstraße 35, 4000 Basel, Switzerland.

Grossmann, W., Institut für Statistik, Rathausstraße 19, 1010 Wien, Austria.

Habbema, J.D.F., Afd. Medische Statistiek, Univ. Leiden, Wassenaarseweg 80, Leiden. The Netherlands.

Hall, J., Dept. of Applied Social Studies, Polytechnic of North London, Ladbroke House, Highbury Grove 62–66, N5 2AD London, England.

Heiberger, R.M., Dept. of Statistics, The Warton School CC, Philadelphia, Pa. 19174, USA.

Karlsson, G., Dept. of Statistics, Univ. of Lund, Fack, 220 05 Lund, Sweden.

Korhonen, P., Computing Centre, University of Helsinki, Toolonkatu 11, 00100 Helsinki 10, Finland.

Lauder, I.J., Dept. of Statistics, University of Hong Kong, Hong Kong.

Lenz, H.-J., Freie Universität Berlin, FB 10, WE 1, Garystraße 21, 1000 Berlin 33, W.-Germany.

Makov, U.E., University College London, Dept. of Statistics and Computer Science, Gower Street, WCIE 6BT London, England.

Militký, J., Research for Textile Finishing, ZD. Nejedleho 770, 544 28 Dvur Kralove N.L., Czechoslovakia.

Mustonen, S., Dept. of Statistics, University of Helsinki, Hallituskatu 11–13, 00100 Helsinki 10, Finland.

Nelder, J.A., Rothamsted Experimental Station, Harpenden, Herts AL5 2JQ, Great Britain.
Niederreiter, H., University of Illinois, at Urbana Champaign, Dept. of Mathematics, Urbana, Ill. 61801, USA.
Pleszczynska, E., Institute of Computer Science, Polish Academy of Science, Palac Kultury I Navki, Box 22, 00–901 Warszawa, Poland.
Pokorny, D., Center of Biomathematics, Budejovicka 1083, 14220 Prague, Czechoslovakia.
Polasek, W., Institut für Höhere Studien, Stumpergasse 56, 1060 Wien, Austria.
van Praag, B.M.S., Economisch Instituut, Hugo de Grootstraat 32, Leiden, The Netherlands.
Pukkila, T., Dept. of Mathematical Sciences, University of Tampere, Box 607, 33101 Tampere 10, Finland.
Raatgever, J.W., Technische Hogeschool Delft, Lab. voor Technische Natuurkunde, Lorentzweg 1, Delft 8, The Netherlands.
*Rechenberg, H.*v., Abt. Biomathematik, im Fachbereich Veterinärmedizin, Universität Giessen, Frankfurter Str. 100, 6300 Giessen, W.-Germany.
Rehlin, L., World Fertility Survey, 35–37 Grosvenor Gardens, London SW1W OBS, United Kingdom.
Ross, G.J.S., Rothamsted Experimental Station, Harpenden, Herts AL5 2 JQ, Great Britain.
Schlee, W., Techn. Universität, Inst. für Statistik und Unternehmensforschung, Arcisstraße 21, 8000 München 2, W.-Germany.
Sint, P.P., Inst. für sozioökonomische Entwicklungsforschung, Fleischmarkt 20, 1010 Wien, Austria.
Skene, A.M., Dept. of Statistics and Computer Science, University College London, Gower Street, WCIE 6BT, London, England.
Tanaka, Y., Statistical Research Section, Takeda Chemical Industries, Ltd., Osaka, Japan.
Tinbergen, J., Haviklaan 31, The Hague, The Netherlands.
Trampisch, H.-J., Abt. Biomathematik, FB 18, Universität Giessen, Frankfurter Str. 100, 6300 Lahn-Giessen 1, W.-Germany.
Trenkler, G., Technische Universität Hannover, Lehrstuhl f. Ökonometrie und Statistik, Wunstorfer Straße 14, 3000 Hannover 91, W.-Germany.
Uchida, Y., Research Institute for Economics and Business Administration, Kobe University, Rokko, Kobe, Japan.
Veling, S.H.J., Akzo Research Laboratories, Velperweg 76, Postbus 209, Arnhem, The Netherlands.
Weber, E., Deutsches Krebsforschungscentrum Heidelberg, Inst. für Dokumentation, Information und Statistik, Im Neuenheimer Feld 280, 6900 Heidelberg, W.-Germany.
Wishart, D., 43 Jeffrey Street, Scottish Education Department, Edinburgh EH1 1DN, United Kingdom.
Yassaee, H., Arya-Mehr University of Technology, P.O.Box 3406, Tehran, Iran.